The Collected Works of James Birch:
Prophet of the Muggletonian Anti-Followers

Edited by Mike Pettit

Visit us online at www.muggletonianpress.com and
view our entire range of Muggletonian Literature

The Collected Works of James Birch

A Muggletonian Press Book

Copyright © Mike Pettit 2009

All rights reserved. No portion of this publication may be reproduced, stored in a retrieval system, or transmitted in any form or by any means, electronic, mechanical, photocopy, recording or otherwise, without prior written permission of the copyright owner. While many of the original texts which form the basis of this publication are to be found in the public domain the texts found herein have been typographically modernised and reformatted at great expense. Please respect the resulting copyright that such work has created.

ISBN 978-1-907466-01-4

Cover Image: Extract from hymn 127 of the 1829 edition of "Divine Songs of the Muggletonians"

Published by:
Muggletonian Press
129 Hebdon Road
London SW17 7NL
England

I would like to make it clear that in editing and publishing this volume I am not seeking to advocate any element of *Muggletonian* theology. I fully subscribe to historic orthodox Christianity as expressed in the Reformed Confessions of Faith and would plead with all the readers of this work to consider the claims of the triune God.

From the Heidelberg Catechism

Question 2. How many things are necessary for thee to know, that thou, enjoying this comfort, mayest live and die happily?

Answer: Three; the first, how great my sins and miseries are; the second, how I may be delivered from all my sins and miseries; the third, how I shall express my gratitude to God for such deliverance.

Mike Pettit

INDEX

INTRODUCTION .... - 1 -
THE DICTIONARY OF NATIONAL BIOGRAPHY .... - 3 -

The Book of Cherubical Reason   5

INTRODUCTION .... - 6 -
CHAP. I .... - 11 -
CHAP. II .... - 16 -
CHAP. III .... - 22 -
CHAP. IV .... - 27 -
CHAP. V .... - 31 -
CHAP. VI .... - 32 -
CHAP. VII .... - 35 -
CHAP. VIII .... - 38 -
CHAP. IX .... - 41 -
CHAP. X .... - 48 -
CHAP. XI .... - 52 -
CHAP. XII .... - 60 -
CHAP. XIII .... - 69 -
CHAP. XIV .... - 76 -
CHAP. XV .... - 85 -
CHAP. XVI .... - 90 -
CHAP. XVII .... - 98 -
CHAP. XVIII .... - 108 -
CHAP. XIX .... - 117 -

The Book Upon The Gospel And Regeneration   125

Chap. I .... - 126 -
Chap. II .... - 133 -
Chap. III .... - 137 -
Chap. IV .... - 142 -
Chap. V .... - 147 -

Chap. VI	- 151 -
Chap. VII	- 157 -
Chap. VIII	- 161 -
Chap. IX	- 167 -
Chap. X	- 175 -
Chap. XI	- 178 -
Chap. XII	- 184 -
Chap. XIII	- 190 -
Chap. XIV	- 194 -
Chap. XV	- 199 -
Chap. XVI	- 207 -
Chap. XVII	- 213 -
Chap. XVIII	- 221 -
Chap. XIX	- 225 -
Chap. XX	- 228 -
Chap. XXI	- 235 -
Chap. XXII	- 239 -
Chap. XXIII	- 244 -
Chap. XXIV	- 250 -
Chap. XXV	- 256 -
Chap. XXVI	- 263 -
Chap. XXVII	- 273 -
Chap. XXVIII	- 279 -
Chap. XXIX	- 286 -
Chap. XXX	- 292 -
Chap. XXXI	- 301 -

A Collection of Letters in the Inspiration of Faith — 311

PREFACE	- 312 -
LETTER I	- 314 -
LETTER II	- 316 -
LETTER III	- 320 -
LETTER IV	- 324 -

LETTER V	- 329 -
LETTER VI	- 335 -
LETTER VII	- 340 -
LETTER VIII	- 344 -
LETTER IX	- 349 -
LETTER X	- 352 -
LETTER XI	- 356 -
LETTER XII	- 361 -
LETTER XIII	- 365 -
LETTER XIV	- 368 -
LETTER XV	- 372 -
LETTER XVI	- 375 -
LETTER XVII	- 378 -
LETTER XVIII	- 383 -
LETTER XIX	- 386 -
LETTER XX	- 389 -
LETTER XXI	- 392 -
LETTER XXII	- 395 -
LETTER XXIII	- 396 -
LETTER XXIV	- 398 -
LETTER XXV	- 399 -
LETTER XXVI	- 400 -
LETTER XXVII	- 403 -
LETTER XXVIII	- 407 -
LETTER XXIX	- 410 -
LETTER XXX	- 413 -
LETTER XXXI	- 415 -
LETTER XXXII	- 424 -
LETTER XXXIII	- 425 -
LETTER XXXIV	- 428 -
LETTER XXXV	- 433 -
LETTER XXXVI	- 434 -
LETTER XXXVII	- 442 -

LETTER XXXVIII	- 444 -
LETTER XXXIX	- 445 -
LETTER XL	- 446 -
LETTER XLI	- 447 -
LETTER XLII	- 453 -
LETTER XLIII	- 457 -
LETTER XLIV	- 460 -
LETTER XLV	- 462 -
LETTER XLVI	- 463 -
LETTER XLVII	- 465 -
LETTER XLVIII	- 472 -
LETTER XLIX	- 475 -
LETTER L	- 477 -
LETTER LI	- 483 -
LETTER LII	- 484 -
LETTER LIII	- 486 -
LETTER LIV	- 487 -
LETTER LV	- 488 -
LETTER LVI	- 490 -
LETTER LVII	- 491 -
LETTER LVIII	- 493 -
LETTER LIX	- 497 -
LETTER LX	- 498 -
LETTER LXI	- 499 -
LETTER LXII	- 501 -
LETTER LXIII	- 505 -
LETTER LXIV	- 510 -
LETTER LXV	- 513 -
LETTER LXVI	- 517 -
LETTER LXVII	- 520 -
LETTER LXVIII	- 522 -
LETTER LXIX	- 524 -
LETTER LXX	- 527 -

LETTER LXXI	- 530 -
LETTER LXXII	- 533 -
LETTER LXXIII	- 535 -
LETTER LXXIV	- 536 -
LETTER LXXV	- 537 -
LETTER LXXVI	- 540 -
LETTER LXXVII	- 541 -
LETTER LXXVIII	- 544 -
LETTER LXXIX	- 547 -
LETTER LXXX	- 550 -
LETTER LXXXI	- 552 -
LETTER LXXXII	- 555 -
LETTER LXXXIII	- 558 -
LETTER LXXXIV	- 561 -
LETTER LXXXV	- 562 -
LETTER LXXXVI	- 565 -
LETTER LXXXVII	- 567 -
LETTER LXXXVIII	- 570 -
LETTER LXXXIX	- 573 -
LETTER XC	- 575 -
LETTER XCI	- 578 -
LETTER XCII	- 581 -
LETTER XCIII	- 583 -
LETTER XCIV	- 584 -
LETTER XCV	- 586 -
LETTER XCVI	- 588 -
LETTER XCVII	- 591 -
LETTER XCVIII	- 593 -
LETTER XCIX	- 595 -
LETTER C	- 596 -
LETTER CI	- 596 -
LETTER CII	- 597 -
LETTER CIII	- 606 -

LETTER CIV	- 607 -
LETTER CV	- 609 -
LETTER CVI	- 611 -
LETTER CVII	- 612 -
LETTER CVIII	- 613 -
LETTER CIX	- 614 -
INDEX	- 617 -

INTRODUCTION

James Birch is an historical enigma, to all intents and purposes he is forgotten to history yet in his time he tore the Muggletonian Church apart, raised substantial followings in both London and Pembroke and left a vibrant sect behind when he died.

What few details concerning James Birch that can be gleaned from history are often vague and incomplete. The normally reliable historian Alexander Gordon leaves us with tantalising details in his D.N.B. entry (reproduced in this volume) but he appears not to have been aware of the "Collection of Letters" (which is also reproduced in this volume) and did not even know when Birch died (October 1800). The British Library incorrectly dates both "The Book of Cherubical Reason" and "The Book Upon the Gospel and Regeneration" and poor James Birch does not even currently have an entry in Wikipedia.

It is unfortunate that Birch's collection of letters has been largely unread for well over a century as the flow of the letters reveals a warm and caring man. We move through the farcical (yet tragic) appearance of young Parry whose enthusiasm masked mental instability through the death of two of his children, his wife and finally his own declining health and material fortunes. However his final years were cheered by the revival of his spiritual fortunes and the publication of his works.

Muggletonian historians largely appear to have seen Birch as a Reevonian, seeking to assert the superiority of Reeve over Muggleton. However the works contained in this volume suggests that this understanding is at best deeply flawed. While Birch does reveal his distaste for Muggleton's influence (especially with regard to "immediate notice") he accepts both Reeve and Muggleton as prophets, yet asserts his own living message over the "dead letter" of both "dead prophets".

Birch's theology was strongly rooted in predestination, the proof of whether someone was elect or not was whether they accepted Birch as a prophet. He did not have to prove his claims; as if truly elect the person would respond to his call. Therefore while Birch accepted that Reeve and Muggleton were true prophets, if their followers (i.e. muggletonians) did not acknowledge his own claims this just proved that that the follower was not truly elect.

Birch seems to have had two main theological disagreements with historic muggletonianism. Firstly he believed that God did take (immediate) notice of his creation and the prayers of his elect and secondly that it is impossible to have assurance of salvation in this life. He also seems to have had a very strong view that those who die in infancy are of the elect and to have had a constant battle persuading his (Welsh) followers that singing was sinful.

While there has been some modernisation of the typography of the three works reproduced in this volume I have not corrected archaic spellings. The editor of the "Collection of Letters" states that he instructed the printer to "comply with my order, omitting grammatical correction, lest it cloud the truth" which may explain some of the anomalies in Birch's writings.

This volume contains the following works:

The Dictionary of National Biography

The entry in respect of James Birch that can be found in Volume 5, page 62 of "The Dictionary of National Biography" (published in 1886), written by The Rev. Alexander Gordon, the Muggletonian biographer and great confidant of the Muggletonian Church. It is this link between Gordon and the Church that makes his insights so valuable and unique; he had access to the oral history and traditions of the Church, a history that has now been lost or obscured.

The Book of Cherubical Reason

This book upon the law was published on July 1st, 1798.

The Book Upon The Gospel And Regeneration

This book upon the gospel was published on July 4th, 1799.

A Collection of Letters in the Inspiration of Faith

This collection was published posthumously in 1813.

THE DICTIONARY OF NATIONAL BIOGRAPHY

BIRCH, JAMES (ft. 1759-1795), heresiarch, was born in Wales, but the date is unknown. He became a watch-motion maker in London, living in Brewer's Yard, Golden Lane, Old Street Road, afterwards in Little Moorfields. He was converted to the Muggletonians, his name first appearing in their records 1 July 1759; that of Mrs. Birch is mentioned 22 July 1759. He wrote in 1771 a rhythmical account of his conversion ('Travels from the sixth to the ninth hour'), fifteen stanzas of eight lines each, dated 5 Dec. (unprinted). In 1772 he rejected two points of Muggletonian orthodoxy: viz. the doctrine that believers have present assurance of salvation (this, Birch thought, was often withheld till death); and the doctrine that God exercises no immediate oversight in human affairs, and affords no present inspiration (on these points Birch reverted to the original views of John Reeve, the founder, along with Lodowicke Muggleton, of the sect). So far he only led a party within the Muggletonian body, which has always been liable to eruptions of Reevite heresy. But in 1778 Birch began to claim personal inspiration; this lost him ten followers, headed by Martha, wife of Henry Collier. The Collierites were regarded by Muggletonians as mistaken friends; the Birchites were known as the Anti-church. Birch was maintained in independence by his followers, his right-hand man being William Matthews, of Bristol. In 1786 there were some thirty Birchites in London, and a larger number in Pembrokeshire. In 1809 they are alluded to in a 'divine song' by James Frost as 'anti-followers;' at this time and subsequently they had a place of meeting in the Barbican. Whether Birch himself was living in 1809 is not known; the last occurrence of his name in the Muggletonian archives is in 1795; two of his London followers were surviving in 1871 in old age. Birch published, about the end of last century, 'The Book of Cherubical Reason, with its Law and Nature; or of the Law and Priesthood of Reason,' &c.; and 'The Book upon the Gospel and Regeneration,' &c. They bear no date, but were sold by T. Herald, 60 Portpool Lane, Gray's Inn Lane. Very incoherent, they are scarcely intelligible even to the initiated in the small controversies from which they sprang. One of Birch's opinions is curious: 'Not one of the seed of Faith dies in childhood' (Cher. Reas. p. 46).

[MS. Records of the Muggletonian Church; Birch's Works (Brit. Mus. 1114 i. 3, 1 and 2); paper Ancient and Mod. Muggletonians, Trans. Liverpool Lit. and Phil. Soc. 1870.] A.G.

THE BOOK

OF

CHERUBICAL REASON,

WITH ITS

LAW AND NATURE;

OR,

OF THE LAW AND PRIESTHOOD OF

REASON:

WITH SOME DESCRIPTION OF THE
LAW, NATURE, AND KINGDOM OF
FAITH;
AND OF THE SERAPHIMS.

BY JAMES BIRCH.

"WHOSO READETH LET HIM UNDERSTAND."

LONDON:
PRINTED FOR THE AUTHOR.
SOLD by T. HERALD, No. 60, Portpool Lane, near
GRAY'S INN LANE.
(PRICE 2s. 6d.)

INTRODUCTION

THE nature of FAITH, as it stood created, flowed forth in life, like unto *crystal Light*, burning with divine satisfaction in itself, and at the sight of different creatures caused its life to flow forth with new joys and praises unto his God, for HIS marvellous works of creation; and this created Faith flowed forth with all divine satisfaction and dove-like heavenly divine virtues from its own nature; why? because it is its own nature, neither will it produce any thing else; but through the *Innocence* of its nature was subject to be tempted into *death*.

Thus stood our first parents in human nature animated with divine Faith, which is a *Creation; a Life; a Kingdom*, distinct to itself, and directly opposite to that of Reason. But Faith being created under a *Law*, which Law is, "not to hearken to the voice of Reason," the grand enemy to God and his created son Adam; for if once you listen to Reason, he will be sure to work on you, and take you into *Captivity and Death*.

And the nature of REASON is strong desire to evil, and from that he will go out to pry after secrets in God's creation. Then he will not find it to his liking, and from that arises his conceited pride, to fancy he can make alterations to add amendments; and his emulative spirit will aspire so high as to condemn the works of God as foolishness. Further, his restless soul delighteth to destroy the whole creation of God; and not only so, but God himself also; therefore the LAW written in the nature of Reason to keep him from those acts, *i.e.* "You shall love God above all, and your neighbour as yourself." And if once this is left undone the life is forfeited, and can no longer live but by *merciful* permission.

But this is to be observed, that neither man or angel was created to be disposed of according to their own will, but were at the will of the divine Majesty their creator. Therefore the most wise Creator, according to his eternal decree, suffered the serpent angel that was cast down from heaven for rebellion, and was seeking to devour or destroy the wisdom of God's creation, to tempt the *innocent dove-like virgin Eve*. And when she once listened to him, the Law of Faith was broke, and the work done was sufficient for him to infuse his diabolical witchcraft, to make her soul consent to, and in, the act;

which was no sooner done, but into themselves was transmuted the fallen, troublesome, and woeful angelic nature, with its Law, whereby the sons of Adam have been so much plagued—Why? Because this act was in *Life* and on *Life*; and this angelic nature became so closely united to the soul as to make but one living and dying man without *regeneration*.

Further, Although the nature of Faith and Reason are so closely united in an elect being, yet in their effects and fruits, there is as much difference as between *light and darkness, Life and Death*, &c.

For the nature of Reason is temptation, pride, covetousness, defraud, theft, whoredom, murder and blasphemy; and in all his ways seeking ruination to, and bring in death, on the works of God; and his wisdom in those things is called serpentine subtility, because in all those things he has a selfish view.

Therefore the law is, "to love God above all, and your neighbour as yourself," as aforesaid. And the nature of Faith is obedience, meekness, long-suffering, love, and innocence, &c. and its law is, "not to hearken to the voice of "Reason," as aforesaid. Again, when the serpent angel came to tempt Eve, Reason did not come to tempt Reason, but Reason came to tempt Faith; why? because her whole life was faith; neither would Faith ever have been brought under the power of death had it not hearkened to Reason. As for Reason to infuse his reason into a faithful vessel, and then Reason tempt Reason, and so bring Faith under the full power of death, which had no concern in the act, is a strange doctrine to me (which has been the doctrine of some *Muggletonians*,) Again, although the souls of Adam and Eve was divine Faith, they being joined to earthen vessels, whereby there was somewhat of a capacity for the serpent's language to rest on; yet this was not done, nor possible could be done, until she had hearkened unto him: therefore the serpent full of evil subtilty, tempted an innocent harmless virgin, who hearkened to his voice; then the law of Faith was broke, and all done sufficient for him to work her overthrow. And whoever you are that say, "Faith did not hearken to the voice of Reason, and thereby *disobeyed God's command,* and for *that* transgression fell under the power of death," I say you are ignorant of the *fall of Man*. Also the law of Faith was not broke by, or through any evil intent, but it was innocence overcome by *subtility*.

Again, the *spirit of Faith* never was charged with telling a lie, or with theft, or murder or any sin that Reason ever committed: Why? Because it is contrary to its nature, and incapable of the act. Therefore no man need much to fear that Faith will break Reason's law, or that Reason will break Faith's law: why? because the natures are quite contrary to each other; and has its own law written in each natures. Again it is the nature of Faith not to *hurt*, much more to *destroy*, any thing; nay, it will suffer itself first to be led into captivity and death, as it were by the serpent angel, *or tree of knowledge of good and evil* (*i.e.* the serpent's nature was all evil; but in that nature was written the holy law, which was good, therefore called the *tree of knowledge of good and evil*.)

Thus fell Faith under the power of Reason, which became the chief actor in the soul of man, because man became subject to its passions, its law, and the angel of the law. And although Faith fell so low, yet it did not fall from, out of the power of God, who never did forsake his *Elect*, but always preserved them by the sacred acts of his divine providence, according to his heavenly wisdom although the soul may not always know it. Again, when God was graciously pleased to make known to elect man what state he was in, and promised him he would redeem him from it, Faith never had any desire after this world's riches, to make an outside appearance, build cities, &c. but its desire was to get as near God, from whence it came, as possible it could.

Again, the LAW of Angels was given forth by roses, who was the *external Angel* of the Covenant of that *Law*, and the law was branched forth into many fine commands, to do many good acts; yet it extended no further than this, "You shall love God above all, and your neighbour as yourself;" and to bring in your *oblations* for the priest to offer, to *stay* God's justice, which was a plague in Israel.

Moreover there is an *internal Angel* of this Law standing before God's divine justice *in the soul of man, strictly watching his way*, that whenever he doeth evil, this angel seals him down unto death. Again created Faith being of that innocent nature as aforesaid, that there was no one to be found in heaven or in earth but the Fountain of Faith only (*i.e.* God himself) could ever keep its *Law*; therefore the most wise Creator saw it good to transmute himself into flesh and take on himself his own created nature of Adam, which was human nature animated with Faith in a fallen state, and so brought himself under the law of Faith, *i.e. not to hearken to the voice of Reason*: and this is the *Law* he put himself under; for HE *took no on himself the nature of angels*, therefore not its law—for whoever keeps the *Law of Faith*, by him the *Law of Reason* is trod underfoot.

Thus God became man, and uttered and established his holy covenant of grace on this foundation of *Faith*; and waded through the temptation and scourge of Reason, and never listened to it. Again, the most wise God created in that he well knew the creation, as God the Father. But his divine wisdom moved him to transmute himself into his own creation of Adam, to take his part, his travail, and experience, *in his own creation* aforesaid, to redeem and regenerate his Elect, and give them *spiritual Birth* to his holy covenant of grace, and seal them with his own spiritual seal, to enter his glorious kingdom.

Again, at this day, when a Messenger comes from heaven, in the *upper waters*, or *covenant of Grace*, in the COMMISSION *of the* SPIRIT, and by his declaration, with divine assistance from heaven, quickens the spirit of Faith from its womb or seed, in an elect vessel, there is standing in the soul (even at this day) FAITH, which is of the TREE *of* LIFE, as well as *Reason*, which is the *Tree of knowledge of good and evil*; and the command, or law is, "not to hearken to the voice of Reason;" for if you do, you will be captivated by him, and scattered abroad from the *Messenger*, and not gather knowledge in the Way of God; yet grow wonderful wise in your own conceit. Therefore Jesus said, "*whosoever* putteth away his wife and marrieth another committeth adultery and whosoever marrieth her that is put away from her husband, committeth adultery," *i.e.* the womb or seed of Faith was given as life to man in the beginning; and although captivated by Reason, yet when a *Messenger* comes, his voice is directed to this womb, or seed and quickens the *Spirit* into act, and this is the true *spiritual Wife* the soul must cleave unto, and commune with, to follow the *Messenger* godward; for if you hearken to the voice of Reason in you, then you will *put away your wife and marry another* which being done, then you *commit adultery* with, or adulterate the true intent of declaration made by the *Messenger*, laying *stumbling blocks* in the road to Heaven. And *whosoever marries her that is put away committeth adultery, i.e.* some of the seed of Reason will come even in the life-time of the *Messenger*, and by their own will, and in their *own Way marry* themselves to the *Declaration*; and the spirit of emulation will tell them they have true faith in it, and it doth belong to them; neither will they live any where else; and by this spirit and power go and preach: then such *commit adultery* with, or adulterate the *truth* of the declaration, and block up the true road to heaven. Therefore this spirit of *emulated Reason* is the *Wife* that the elect do, or should *put away* from their soul, so as not to hearken to it; and it will be acceptable in the sight of God; why? because it is for *spiritual fornication.*

Again, on these acts of the soul come forth the literal and spiritual *Jew* and *Gentile*, or *Rich Man* and *Beggar*—for the *seed of Faith* when they come to *true* knowledge, they are poor in spirit, and in the state of *beggary and prayer* unto God; but the seed of Reason is mighty *Rich* in the letter, and knows every thing in his own conceit.

Moreover, the *Seed of Reason* receive a mighty, wound in the Days of a *Messenger*, why? because their traditions and gathered knowledge from the letter is cut asunder, and their little peace turned to wrath against the Messenger and the *Elect*. Yet Reason cannot get this *wound healed* no other way, but after a while, to transform themselves into this *Messenger's* declaration, and there again to reign kings of the dark spirit, at the time of *silence* in the nether *heaven* of FAITH.

OF THE

LAW, NATURE, *and* PRIESTHOOD

OF

REASON, &c.

CHAP. I

AS concerning the angels in their creation, there were two orders the cherubim and seraphims. The seraphims are the holy, or the angels elected; to remain in their created purity, to live in the kingdom of heaven in the presence of God in all eternity; and are spiritual bodies and their souls Reason, which is from the earth or chaos: and its nature is entirely opposite to Faith, which is the divine nature of God. But as they were created by the LORD GOD of HEAVEN, his very act of creation makes the being or beings so created to come forth pure; and in this nature is written this pure law, "You shall love God above all for creating you such marvellous beings, and each other as himself:" Because the Lord God of heaven created you all, this by the help of God's divine incomes according to his blessing in creation, *is* done by the seraphims in the kingdom of glory; which makes them pure rational souls with bodies spiritual, fit to ascend or descend at their own will, or rather to obey the will of the divine majesty their creator. Furthermore, even this *pure* Reason is capable of desire, and was it left to itself, Reason would spring forth with desire after the secrets of God in his creation; for Reason is very fond of his own judgment on the works of God, but all in the wrong let him be ever so well pleased with his wisdom. That wisdom will take him down to chaos, from whence he was taken by the creating power of the divine majesty.

Therefore the most wise God by his divine power created this seraphic host or order of holy angels; and also has power to preserve them in their created purity for his own glory in all eternity.

Again, concerning the order of cherubims, there was but one created, which was the serpent angel, and this angel was endowed with more piercing rational wisdom and brightness of person than any of his angelical companions. Then there was none equal with him in his rational wisdom, or godlike glory; neither was there any appointed to fall into generation but himself, and of consequence none other of his order; if there had, they would have been as wise and glorious as himself. And further, this cherubical angel was created a body spiritual, and soul rational, as was the other angels, and laid the same law written in him, but more quick in his wisdom and brighter in his glory, he being a cherubim as aforesaid.

Moreover, what is a law to any created Being? without a manifestation of that law, through the wisdom of the Divine Majesty the Creator, to the Being created. Therefore the divine wisdom of God moved him to with-hold the flow of his blessing according to creation from this cherubim, and he being left to his created strength and own nature, which soon mounted up to rebellious pride against the LORD GOD his creator, and dislike to his fellow-creatures. Then he had broke that holy law written in his nature, for which he was cast clown from heaven. Thus, by the divine wisdom of God, this holy law was manifest to the holy order of seraphims, that they might admire his power, and praise him for his free elective love to them: and also, to shew forth his infinite godhead power to elect men and angels by his mighty wisdom and glorious works, to recover his own again when time should come. Thus fell this cherubim from heaven when he had broke the law in eternity, and never could see the face of God any more.

Then here stood God's own children, Adam and Eve in paradise who also was created under a law, which was the law of Faith, and that law is *you shall not hearken to the* voice of Reason, for if you do you shall surely die, *i.e.* Reason will transmute himself into you and take you down to death, and there be kept; (though notwithstanding Adam and Eve's life was forfeited for breaking their own law) and when this cherubim or serpent had overpowered the innocent virgin

Eve, he was lost in the act, by being transmuted into flesh; so by this means they brought on themselves the curse. Then the Lord God of heaven came and communed with Adam in the *cool of the day*; and he also cursed the serpent in the womb, because he was to live to be a man and father of a large generation.

Again, although Adam's soul was of the divine nature of God, yet it being joined to an earthen vessel, there was somewhat of a capacity for the serpent angel's language to rest on. And when the serpent angel was transmuted, his nature became so closely united to man as to make but one living and dying being or beings, without regeneration: Therefore Adam took in himself the serpent's nature and of consequence its law, and the justice of that law: and the serpent angel also had somewhat of the woman's nature by transmutation.

Furthermore, although Adam which was of Faith took into himself or tabernacle where Faith dwelled, the angel's nature; yet God did not so create him: and also the angel who was born, Cain, had somewhat of the woman's nature in him, yet God did not create him so; but God suffered it so to be that he may shew forth his infinite wisdom against this serpent's subtilty, and his being intombed in the womb to be born of Eve, God's own child with somewhat of her own nature; yet him and all his posterity that live to manhood should go their way according to the attribute of God's divine justice; and also to manifest his infinite power of his becoming a son, which is the God of mercy to the elect, to redeem and regenerate the harmless seed of Faith, who hearkened to the voice of Reason.

Again, the LORD GOD said, "Behold the man is become *as* one of us to know good and evil: now least he put forth his hand and take also of the tree of life and eat and live for ever: so he drove out the man and placed at the east of the garden of Eden, cherubims, and a flaming sword which turns every way, to keep the way of the tree of life" (Gen. 3.) Thus Adam and Eve was drove out or fell from paradise under the power of Reason and its law, and the internal angel of that law, to get his bread by the sweat of his face: *i.e.* he must get his natural bread as he could, and to get his spiritual bread, to undergo great troubles and temptations, &c. by the spirit Reason, as well as death for disobeying of God's command: and this internal angel stood in his soul, to keep him from the communion with God concerning his mercy; but when God was graciously pleased to reveal it to him above the power of this angel. Thus in briers and thorns he waded through this life by stedfast Faith and true prayer, to get back from whence he was fallen, by regeneration, *i.e.* to die under the mercy of the son.

Furthermore, this place of holy writ concerning the cherubim and flaming sword to guard the tree of life, lest the man that was drove out of Eden put forth *his* hand and take *also* of the tree of life, eat, and live for ever, did not wholly attend to Adam, but on the contrary, chiefly to the serpent; afterward born Cain, why? Because Cain was appointed to live to manhood, therefore this internal angel will keep him and all his posterity that live to manhood, out from the tree of life, according to God's divine justice to all eternity; but it was not so with Adam, for he Communed with God; also God promised Adam the seed of the woman should bruise the serpents head: and further, at times Adam received God's divine assistance; and also Adam was the *son of God*.

Therefore this internal angel which is of the cherubim, did not keep Adam from eating of the tree of life and to live for ever; but *as* he took the dark *earthy* spirit of Reason into himself with it's law and the angel of that law, he must be subject to it; and which internal angel would keep him from communing with God relative to his mercy, only when God was graciously pleased to reveal it to him.

Again, God said to Adam (Gen. 3) "Cursed is the ground for thy sake, in sorrow shalt thou eat of it all the days of thy life." *i.e.* the spirit of Reason, which is of the earth or chaos, that Adam took from the cherubim into himself, to him became a curse, for he must bear the wilds, temptations and heavy threats of Reason, in the sorrowful vale of death, which is eating the bitter herb of the internal and spiritual field of Reason, as well as its external oppression and persecution, which is a hell here in this life to the seed of Faith; besides their own fallen nature, and the justice of God who was father to that nature. Notwithstanding all this, Adam and his posterity *has* and *will* by the merciful of God, eat of the tree of life and live for ever.

Furthermore, although Adam was under the power of death, yet his soul was created of the divine nature of God; and when God was graciously pleased, he could, and can find the nature of Faith in Adam, and all his children the elect: and further, God has and doth call elect men into his own council concerning his divine mysteries of salvation, why? Because in elect men can be found FAITH: and when arose from death to life, *that* by divine assistance is able to commune with God: also, Adam being of the divine nature of God he was his own son, and of consequence the nearest to God of all his creation. Further, God had decreed that he himself would become a man, and that Adam, and all elect men, his sons, should be glorified in heaven with God himself; with the glory of Faith, at the end of time: this being so near to God, that he said at the creating of man, "Let *us* make man in *our* own image, and after *our* likeness."

Again, concerning the serpent angel or cherubim when he was cast down from heaven, the internal angel of justice in his soul told him, he was cast from the presence of God for rebellion against him; then the greatest subtilty he was master of, was how to invade heaven again; therefore his wisdom led him to tempt the innocent virgin Eve, who was a child of God: and further, this cherubim understood somewhat of the act of generation, otherwise by his insinuating lustful desire, why did he tempt the innocent virgin to that act? Furthermore, he, by his subtilty very well knew, that by his acting with the virgin would infuse his nature into her, and also would draw her nature into himself, then he thought he would be one with *the children of God*, and all alike to know both *good and evil*, as by that means he thought he could invade the favour of God; but here again he was mistaken, for he went further into death by his being lost in the act, which I believe he did not expect, for he said to the woman, "Ye shall not surely die."

Again, although this cherubim now was incarnate, with his pernicious diabolical nature, that would grievously plague Adam and all his posterity unto their death; and *also this* angel *who* was born from the womb of Eve with somewhat of her nature; yet, God to shew forth his infinite wisdom and prerogative power, *would* take Adam and his children to himself into his *mercy*: and Cain and *his* seed that grew to manhood, should go their way into death under their own justice, according to his eternal decree, before he created man, or angel

Moreover, the LORD GOD said, "the man is become *as* one of us, to know good and evil," here God spoke in the plural, which related to himself and his son Adam, and all their children the elect, for God had decreed to become man in the loins of Adam, so was the *second* man *Adam*, then he would not only *know*, but also receive *evil* enough at the hands of the sons of Cain.

And also when Cain was born, he had somewhat of the woman's nature in him, and was appointed to live to manhood, and did know he was born of woman, and had somewhat of her nature; which is being *as* one of us; but not one *of* us; which in itself the woman's is *good*, but Cain's own nature is *evil*, and so far he would *know* good and evil on that head. But as the cherubim was created with a life and soul of reason, and Adam was created with a life and soul of Faith; and God suffered them so to act in or for generation, Adam did not take such a quantity of the angel's nature, by the mercy of God, as would disinherit him of his life of Faith; neither did the angel take such a quantity of the woman's nature for himself, or any of his posterity, that live to manhood, ever to be brought back to the presence of God.

Again, I would not have you think that Adam fell under the power of death, altogether by the power of Reason, although justice would keep him there; but he fell under death for breaking his own law, which is *not to hearken to the voice of Reason*; for when God took on himself the created nature of Adam, *i.e.* Human nature, animated with divine Faith, and become man, and kept law of Faith, *i.e. not to hearken to the voice of Reason*; yet this created nature of Adam fell so much under death, as to bring a death on the soul of the eternal God that created heaven and earth, *who took not on him the nature of angels*, which is Reason, and never hearkened to it in the least.

CHAP. II

THIS great wisdom that the cherubim had in the creation extended no further than to rebel against God, and when he was cast down, his subtilty in his temptation, to become like as unto God's children, was the cause of his being transmuted into flesh; then he was under the power or death; but all the cherubical wisdom, with somewhat of the seraphic nature, and wisdom, (he being created an angel) and the law of Reason, and the internal angel of that law, with the mighty acts through God's justice, and the rule and law of nations, was brought into this world by this cherubim; and this power has a priesthood, and it must be obeyed according to God's justice.

Now as before, God said, "Behold the man is become as one of us, to know good and evil; now lest he put forth his hand and take also of the tree of life, and eat, and live for ever:" signifies that some was; but the *man* that *was* become as one of us to know good and evil, and was drove out of Eden; it signifies that *he* never was to eat of the *tree of life, and live for ever.* And although God spoke this before Cain was born, yet (as aforesaid, God had appointed that Cain should live to manhood) then was he drove out of Eden, *i.e.* from the mercy to a cherub; and the *cherubims and flaming sword* was placed to *keep the way of the tree of life, i.e.* the internal angel of justice was *placed* in his soul, to watch over his own law, which is the law of Reason; and as he to be the father of nations and kings, they would set up a law; then there would be an external angel to punish, or acquit, according to that law which also is a cherubim.

And further, as touching this internal angel. This cherubim or serpent-angel was created in reference to God's divine justice, there is somewhat of God's divine justice in him, that was given through and in creation under that attribute, which was but as a part or quality from God of his divine justice through the act of creation. But in the cherubim become a quantity sufficient, that when he had offended against God, in breaking the holy law written in him, to cast him from heaven, and keep him from ever seeing the face of God any more.

Therefore, he who was created under justice, hath a sufficient condemnation in himself of God's justice, to keep him from the tree of life; for although the cherubim had broke the law, he could not break the justice of that law, why? because it is of the attribute of God, and stands in the soul of man so strong, before the attribute of divine justice, that no man of himself can get clear of it; for this justice being given of God to the cherubim in the creation, that let him do what he will, or go where he will, this justice goeth with him and watch him; so when he doth evil it seals him down, and with its flaming sword *will* keep him from the tree of life; why? because it is in itself, as pure as the attribute of God's divine justice.

Therefore this justice was given to the cherubim and is of the cherubim from eternity: the spirit calls it a cherubim, according to the purity of God's creation; and its being transmuted into flesh, it is here ire the soul of man, to keep him from the tree of life, with a flaming sword, which is an act of justice; the which call the internal angel in justice, or the internal angel of the law, or the angel of the Lord, to keep the way of the tree of life. Also, this internal angel, God has and can commune with; so that the angel shall know the way, and do the will of God, according to the attribute of his divine justice, which was placed in Cain and all his posterity that live to manhood, therefore called cherubims and a flaming sword. Also, this angel was created in reference to infinite justice, and fell from heaven under justice, and was born here in time under justice, and so brought that justice into this and when the seed of the serpent grew to manhood, this justice takes place, and to them becomes *infinite*, because it was so eternally decreed.

Again, as aforesaid, Adam being of the divine nature of God, was under MERCY, and the nature of *mercy* is to pray for mercy, and to shew mercy; this is of the sons of Adam the children of God. And although Adam hearkened to the voice of Reason, and so tell under the power of death, yet God would not so lose his children; but the unbounded mercy of God filled him with glorious wisdom, to become a son in his own linage, to keep the law of Faith, and give up his soul unto death, for the transgressions of this seed of Faith, to redeem them *from* death, and regenerate *them* unto the mercy of the son: so God's *mercy* to them is *infinite*.

Further, as Adam took into himself Reason and its Law, and the angel of the law, for where Reason is, there that also is; and from this comes the priesthood of the nether waters, or priesthood in cherubical justice. And Adam was obliged to pay his souls obedience to this justice of God in this Priesthood. And the internal angel would keep him out from God, until God was graciously pleased to CALL above the power of the angel, and *commune* with Adam, as GOD the FATHER (only with his glory veiled and promised Adam he should enter his glorious kingdom, by the mercy of the son: also, he enjoyed at times the divine incomes of God, that come to his own spirit of Faith, to help him in this fallen state, and died with his spirit of Faith, united with the spirit of God for Christ, to be raised by the mercy of the son. This eating of the tree of life, and no other way can man eat of the tree of life. Now this is the very state of the elect; but no man can come here to do this, until called unto by God himself, which is in effect, saying, "Adam, where art thou," and "come up hither." But he *that* was drove out of Eden, with the cherubims and flaming sword, placed to keep the way of the tree of life, will not as aforesaid, eat of the tree of life, and live for ever.

Thus stood the two attributes of God, over his creatures in the beginning, his attribute of divine MERCY, to the sons of ADAM, the elect, and his attribute of divine JUSTICE, to the sons of Cain, who grow to manhood: and as *Faith*, by divine assistance, can commune with God relative to his mercy, so *justice* can commune relative to the attribute of divine justice; Why? Because God gave justice through the creation of the cherubim which was pure; and when the cherubim broke the law, the purity of God's justice acted upon him, and cast him down, and so he brought that *justice* into this world with him, and stands pure in the soul of man to this day.

Now, although Adam disobeyed God's command, and fell under the power of death, yet God was, and is graciously pleased to CALL *Faith* into his merciful communion: so, from those two heads, came forth the two *priesthoods, viz.* of justice and mercy; the priesthood, in or under justice, *i.e.* of the cherubim, is invested on the tribe of Levi, and that of Melchizedec is of God, of which, Christ, the KING of *Faith*, is high priest, this is the priesthood of mercy.

Again, when Cain grew to manhood, and made an offering, as also did his brother Abel, who was Adam's own son, Abel's offering was the first-fruits of generated Faith, that offered for the mercy of God, and there it was accepted: And Cain's offering was of Reason, which was under justice, and that incense could not be accepted into mercy as Abel's was; then "Cain was wroth, and his countenance fell;" and the Lord said to Cain, "why art thou wrath? and why is thy countenance fallen? if thou doest well, shalt thou not be accepted? and if thou doest not well sin layeth at the door," (Gen 4) which is the true voice of justice speaking in the soul. But Cain would not hearken to this but slew Abel, then was spoke condemnation in his soul by the angel, which also is the voice of true justice, and spoke by the internal angel in justice, in Cain's soul, that stands before the attribute of God's divine justice to do the will of God, and which is as a God to the spirit of Reason. And when the spirit of Reason is questioned by internal angel of the law then sometimes it will speak motional voices of condemnation in the soul, and let loose the soul again, that he shall go into his old waters, and preach up his great experience he had from this angel in justice, under the powder of death, as did old Cain in the beginning to his posterity.

Further, God has and can present vision or dream through this angel, that shall foretell of things to come, as he did by king Pharoah's butler and baker, and Pharoah himself, which greatly troubled his soul; and also to Nebuchadnezzar, when he was troubled by a dream; also Belshazar, when he saw the hand-writing on the wall which made his soul tremble at God's power.

Moreover, God revealed to Joseph and Daniel, a far superior knowledge of vision and dream, they being his own servants, that they could tell the will of God by those dreams, in what he, by his unbounded wisdom, would bring to pass, in or upon those kings and nations, &c. according to his divine justice, they being under that attribute: and Joseph and Daniel received gifts, which was also according to justice, because they did that which no other man could do.

Again, God can bind men up by this angel, in justice in the soul, that they have not power to act in this unjust world; and also can let men loose to the spirit of Reason, that he shall go forth and do wicked acts against God; accordingly God will bring his justice upon those men even upon nations and kings, for to manifest his prerogative power in justice, as he did to Pharaoh and the Egyptian host, when they would not let the Israelites go with Moses.

Further, this angel can veil himself in the soul of man, that he should be bound up by the spirit of Reason, so as to enslave the souls of men, to gather great riches, and say within themselves, they do great charity but this charity is not to let a man have his fill of bread, to be his or their slaves, and excuse themselves by the covetous hard dealings of other men with them; and as so, this internal angel in justice in the souls of the poor, will cry for a deliverance according to God's justice which will surely come anon. And also they will be bound in the slavish spirit of fearful Reason, so as not to do one charitable act without a selfish view, saying, they have a right to do as they will with their own. But, alas! when they have gone their length, to fill their cup in justice to God's wrath, this internal angel will seize the soul at the hour of death, and let them know, God has also a right to do as he please with *his* own.

Furthermore, this Angel will direct the spirit in some men, that they will do great charitable acts, both in public and private; and as the law quick in them, *i.e.* "You shall love your neighbour as yourself," which those men endeavour at as well as they can, and have peace with this angel in the soul; so that a covetous man can hardly look him in the face—why? because his own angel condemns him of his guilt.

Again, Reason in man will conceive evil against another, and will work his evil conceptions up to the resolution of an act to overthrow the object in view; and just as his plot is ripe for executions with all his expected benefits, the internal angel will catch the soul as the man is going to act, and so prevent his committing of murder, or treason, or other act that would work another's overthrow or hurt; this also the angel doth in justice; for it is against the law for one to do evil to another, and happy is the soul so prevented. For many are suffered to commit those wicked acts, then the internal angel has them under the condemnation of justice, and will seal the soul under death, though he may let him go with this curse to wander here till death comes.

Moreover, as aforesaid the cherubim brought this into the world with him; and this justice being of the cherubim, is placed in the soul of every man, *to keep the way of the Tree of Life*; and is called a *cherubim*, because of the purity of God's creation; and is now cherubims, because it is in the soul of every man to act justice, which is a *flaming sword*; and no man can commune with God for his mercy, until God is graciously pleased to reveal it to him above the power of this angel. For this is the angel of the nether waters, which are the waters of Reason, and strictly watcheth the ways of Reason according to its law; and can let the waters of Reason run free, and stop those waters and plague the earthy soul of man according to the will and power of divine justice.

Now, as the law and justice thereof came by the fallen cherubim, and this justice is so closely united to that divine attribute of God, as to be one and the same thing; and it is, as it were, a God to Reason, or *the God of the earth*, that this law of Reason *standeth before*; and all men who are not regenerated to mercy, will find justice enough in them to weigh them into the second death. Also in this life one man is raised up to punish another, or nations and kingdoms punish each other with war and bloodshed, and all in justice; and many other troubles that attend the soul relative to justice, that to the seed of

Faith, this is a life in death, and no man can get from justice without being translated to mercy.

CHAP. III

AGAIN, concerning the law of Reason brought into this world by the cherubim, which now constitutes kings, rulers, and laws of people; and the mighty ruling power of nations and kingdoms, with all their magnificent grandeur; and those gentlemen of the law that are in themselves Levites, which make the best of lawyers. The more they do true justice the more they imitate the way of God; but it must be a justice with a *merciful* eye to the offenders, as God hath and has had to people, nations, and kings, that would obey his reproof, so his justice has been stayed for years, or until the next generation; therefore the power of this justice invested on man extends no farther than this life; for all men at their death or resurrection hear a voice saying, "Justice is mine, and I will repay it;" or translate you from it to my everlasting *mercy.*

Further, "and the ANGEL of the LORD appeared unto Moses, in a flame of fire, out of the midst of the bush," (Exo. 3) *this angel of the Lord*, was the LORD himself, at the head of the attribute of *that* divine justice; and whosoever sees him eire, must see him in a flame of fire, either external, or internal, or both; for HE was the highest angel of that attribute, when he did appear as God the father, and creator, which is the God of justice. And not only so, but he would make the man Moses, the great external angel of the covenant of that law, that should stand before people, nations and kings. Thus the man Moses, was inspired by, or under the attribute of God's divine justice, with the knowledge of that pure law, that was written in the cherubims nature before his fall and also, with the justice of that law answerable to the internal angel in justice, placed in the soul of every man, to *keep the way of the tree of life.*

And as Moses was the first man inspired of God by the attribute of his divine justice to give forth this law of angels or cherubims, under the attribute of this *justice* of God, he is called the angel of that covenant; and also may be called the anointed cherubim, because he was of God, anointed with the wisdom of that pure law and justice that was placed in this cherubim, by the purity of God's creation. And when Moses uttered or gave forth this law to the Israelites, there was in the spirit of Reason, not only this law, but also the justice of the law, for the words of Moses to rest upon, and quicken this law of Reason and justice into true action on the bodies and souls of men; for Moses was truly Gods witness in justice external, as was the internal angel in justice that is placed in the soul of man. Those two angels being in union; because the internal angel is of God's justice, and the external angel declares *from* God's justice, and witness one to the other; and even unto this day, when the external angel passes judgment on a man for evil doing, nothing pleases the external angel better, than when the internal angel makes the man confess the justice of his judgment: but as aforesaid, as Moses was the external angel, and this internal angel in the soul are both *standing* before the attribute of God's divine justice, what man can escape? for if you pass the notice of the external angel, the internal angel will take you, and seal you under justice for your punishment, either to be brought to pass in time or in eternity.

Furthermore, Moses, after the manner of God's inspiration, was a cherubim; and the external angel of the law, or in justice, and the internal angel of the law, or in justice, placed in the soul of man, is also a cherubim; because it is of the cherubim, and given to him in the purity that God created angels; and although this cherubim broke the holy law and fell, he never could break the justice of that law as aforesaid; but brought it into this world as pure as the attribute of God's divine justice, which was the cause of Moses being inspired by God himself, with the law and justice that was brought into this world by the cherubims; therefore it is the law of angels, or of Reason.

And God commanded Moses, to make an ark of Shittim wood, and over-lay it with pure gold, within and without; and also he should make upon it a crown of gold round and about, which was to shew forth the righteousness of that man who could obey the commands of Moses: And further, God commanded Moses to make a mercy seat of pure gold, and two cherubims of beaten gold-work, and place them upon the ark. Those *two cherubims* represents the internal and external angels of the law, *i.e.* Moses and the internal angel of the soul, who were *cherubims*; for God inspired Moses through the cherubim his bringing this *law* and *justice* into this world; therefore see Exo. xxv. 22, "And there I will meet with thee, and commune with thee from above the mercy seat, from between the two cherubims which are upon the ark of the testimony, of all things which I will give thee in commandment unto the children of Israel"—therefore this law and commandments was given by God, under his attribute of divine justice, through the cherubical power that fell from heaven to earth. And Moses became the anointed cherubim, by his inspiration, with the wisdom of that law: And when the voice of God came to him in Justice, it also came between him as a commissionated man, and the internal angel in the soul of man; Why? because it is all in cherubical justice: and also this internal angel would witness to Moses's declaration. And as God communed with Moses by the way of the cherubim, was because this law was brought into this world by the cherubim. And it also signifies, that God would commune with him, from between the cherubims who had life, according to his great inspiration as aforesaid.

Again, In the ark was put the testimony that God gave to Moses of his merciful and powerful acts under that attribute, such as the Pot of Manna, &c. and all their evil doings and murmurings which was a written record against them as a witness between them and the LORD GOD their creator: and further, this ark signifies the body of man, wherein dwells the internal angel of the law of Reason. This angel *truly* will witness not only to the justice, but also to the MERCY of God offered to man; and to the truth of all declarations, that comes from heaven, in the souls of *despisers* at the day of judgment; and in all secret evils that Reason shall do. It is put into this ark as a memorial against man, *i.e.* this internal angel when a man has done evil, let it be ever so secret, seals the soul unto judgment, or unto the second death, according as they are of the seed of Faith, or the seed of Reason; therefore this great outward appearance made by Moses, by God's command, signified the justice and judgment to the soul of man. And this internal angel is the stronger witness before God's divine justice; for although the ceremonies and worship under this law is over, nor any *Messenger* of the law come from heaven, since the days of Jesus, according to the external commission of Moses, yet this angel stands now in full power, and will to the end of time, witnessing to what Moses hath written, and to God's justice in every respect; but punishment will come anon: and also helps to uphold the law and justice of nations, which is now the external angel, it being of the attribute of justice in the souls of men. And this mighty *internal* angel of the law is, what I call the arch angel in justice, because it dwells in the soul, by which men will become their own witness to their own condemnation.

Again, as aforesaid, this internal angel is the stronger witness; for the external angel may err before the Lord, as did Moses at the rock when he smote with his rod for the waters: But this angel never will err before the Lord; for God communed with this internal angel of Moses and Aaron relative to their error, by which they did not enter the land: See Numb. xx. 13, saying, "This is the water of Meribah, because the children of Israel strove with the Lord, and he was sanctified in them." Here the children of Israel was glad and thankful when they received the water by the power of the Lord, for their present relief; and he was more sanctified in them, then lie was by Moses and Aaron's fetching it out of the rock. Here it is plain God communed with Moses from between the *two cherubims, i.e.* between him, a cherubim by inspiration, and the internal angel in the souls of men, which also is a cherubim: therefore the spirit calls it a cherubim; for if a man make a declaration from God, or *profess* a declaration *made,* and *act contrary* to it, he is *condemned* by that declaration; and the angel in the soul also *condemns* him. Then between those two comes the voice of justice, which is the voice of God under that attribute.

Also Joshua vii, where Achan took and concealed a Babylonish garment, shekels of silver, and wedge of gold, which brought great trouble on all Israel; and Joshua, as the external angel of the law, by the law did not find him out; but the internal angel of that law in the soul of Achan communed with God, and God revealed the evil unto Joshua, and how he should take the man. A further proof even at that time, the internal angel was the stronger witness before God; and how God communes from between the two *cherubims.*

As the ark was overlaid with pure gold, and the crown, and the mercy seat, and the cherubims of gold, and the golden candlestick, and seven lamps thereof with the lights, ALL was to shew forth the light and purity God created the cherubim under; under this pure law. And also the fine twined linen, curtains that was blue, and purple, and scarlet, with cherubims of cunning work for the inside of the tabernacle. And the veil was made of fine linen of cunning work, with the cherubims that was hung up in the tabernacle, to divide between the holy place and the most holy: and the ark was put in the most holy place, where Moses went to commune with God from between the *two cherubims*, (Numb. vii. 89,) where *Moses went into the tabernacle to speak with him, and he heard the voice of one speaking unto him from off the mercy seat, that was upon the ark of the testimony from between* the TWO CHERUBIMS, AND HE *speak unto him*. But all those riches and external show doth not equal the angels glory, who had not broke the law; much less the glory of God in his creating the cherubim. And Moses was inspired with such great wisdom of this cherubical law that he could go within the veil and speak with God. And the veil signifies the wisdom of the people was not like the wisdom of Moses, so they must obey the voice of the *Messenger*.

Moreover, all the garments Aaron the priest wore signifies the righteousness and blessing to the sons of Reason that did obey Moses's commands: The breast-plate and precious stones, with the names of the children of Israel, according to their tribes, signifies the mercy, purity, and glory of the stay of God's justice on the soul and spirit of Reason. And as Aaron bore the breast-plate before his heart, and Moses put into the breast-plate of judgment, the *Urim* and the *Thummin*, which judgment was to know the transgressions, and to offer the offering that would atone before the Lord; in this he bore the judgment of the children of Israel, when he went in before the Lord. This wisdom was given of God through the man Moses, because the priesthood of Levi was invested on Aaron and his sons; but all those offerings and holiness extended no further than to stay God's justice to the soul and spirit of Reason, as aforesaid; otherwise they would have been cut off by plagues, &c.

The *altar of incense*, whereon Aaron burned sweet incense every morning and evening, it was to offer up the obedience and prayers of the people Israel in the worship of the law of Moses, according to God's command: But he must offer no strange incense thereon, which is the vain excuses in the wild priesthood. And when he made an atonement upon it once in a year with the blood of the sin-offerings, it was to atone for such neglects of the people Israel, to stay God's justice, and reconcile them together, it being pleasing in the sight of God: but all this doth not extend to eternal life; for the law being written in Reason it was given to *Reason external*, that they should *love God*, above all, as their creator, and who also created this earth for their inheritance and *each other* as himself, that they may enjoy this inheritance; and whosoever did obey this law and priesthood, would have peace of mind, a good inheritance, riches, &c. But it did not extend to eternal life, for the sons of Reason must go their way according to God's infinite justice. And the sons of Adam was among the sons of Reason, and with them, at times, they would be greatly perplexed; but at times God did commune in spirit with them, relative to this mercy of the son. For even then every man must offer his *own* offering of Faith to be accepted, as he must now; and at the hour of death they were translated to the merciful power and glory of the son; which translation was equal as great as was Enoch's, Moses, and Elijah's translation ; but they never came back to tell this *Tale*.

CHAP. IV

CONCERNING the *fathers* of old that see God and *communed* with him. Adam, he communed with him relative to his justice, before he did for his mercy. Enoch also saw and communed with him in his justice, before he did for mercy; for he prophesied that "God would come with ten thousands of his saints, to execute *judgment* upon all ungodly sinners for their ungodly deeds." And Noah, who was of Adam, he *communed* with God, in and for the justice of God; and Noah was spared according to God's justice, for Noah was not guilty of that abomination before the Lord, as was the world; for it would be contrary to the Justice of God, that them who was found righteous in his sight should be destroyed with the wicked, (Gen. vii. 1.) "For thee have I seen righteous in this generation before me:" as then there could hardly be found one born in this world for the eternal mercy of God: So God in his justice destroyed this world, and preserved Noah and his family to have a better generation for the sons of God, to be born into this world for his divine mercy. And in all Noah's communion with God in his justice, and to prophecy of the destruction of the world, and live to see his prophecy come to pass;

yet when he communed in spirit with God concerning his *eternal mercy,* and to prophecy of his *salvation,* that prophecy as far transcended the other, as from death to life.

Abraham; he obeyed the voice of God to leave his father's house and country, and go to a land that God should shew him; and God met, and blessed, and established his covenant with him, as he was to be *Father* of many nations, *viz.* the Jews, Arabs, &c. But this was all under *justice:* And *Melchizedec king of Salem,* (*i.e.* peace) *priest* to the most HIGH GOD, which Melchizedec was GOD, promised in CHRIST, *and he blessed him,* and *Abraham gave him a tenth of all* the goods, this was also under *justice,* because God delivered the enemies of Lot and Abraham into his hand. Also it was to shew to Abraham, God would establish a priesthood under the attribute of his divine justice, according to the covenant be made with him concerning the natural kingdoms of the Jews, that he would take the *tenth*: And this priesthood was invested on the tribe of Levi; but the PRIESTHOOD of MELCHIZEDEC is his own spiritual, royal, and merciful ever living priesthood ; which is his merciful *communion,* by his holy spirit, that flows from his blessed person to the spirit of Faith in the souls of the elect, to seal and sanctify them to enter his glorious kingdom, and as far transcends the priesthood of Levi, as from earth to heaven.

Thus God in his glory *communes* with, and receives the harmless, innocent, and trembling PRAYER of Faith, from the elect, it being of his own divine nature. But at this day he receives nothing from Reason, or, *i.e.* natural; this duty must be done before the internal angel of the soul; and that incense will ascend to them who sit in the glory of justice: So what was formerly offered, now give to your poor needy brethren, and it will be an acceptable offering, and you will have peace. So from henceforth, without excuse, give to the poor that which is for the poor, and to God that which is for God.

And to *Abraham* appeared three men in the plains of *Mamre,* this was God himself and two angels, to shew forth the power of God by his internal and external angel in justice, the kingdom being not yet come where the external law was to be given. And Abraham being a great man of God, and a merciful man, he *communed* with God, and said, "wilt thou also destroy the righteous with the wicked?" and God heard Abraham, and would have saved Sodom through Abraham, if *ten righteous* could be found; this was also under *justice*; and the Lord went his *way,* and Abraham to his place, and the two angels in *justice* went to Sodom, to take Lot and his family away, and destroy the place, according to God's divine *justice*. Further, *Abraham* was a man greatly beloved of God: That God's name is enrolled in Abraham's, and Abraham's in God; and Isaac did tipe Christ, though at a distance, for through him came the nation of the Jews, whereunto the law was given: These great men of old were obliged to see and experimentally know the power of God in his *justice*, and by his merciful and spiritual *divine assistance* to wade through it, before they was translated to, under the MERCY of the SON, which was mostly at the hour of death.

Also *Sarah*, being of the lineage of Faith from Adam, was promised she should bear a son in *old age* unto Abraham, to whom the covenant was made. This covenant was the covenant of the law, unto which the priesthood of Reason or the nether waters was given and signifies also the spiritual covenant of grace, because Christ the KING of Heaven is here enrolled the son of Abraham, according to the spiritual genealogy of Faith; and even when the gospel was declared, and people believed, yet there remained a spiritual birth to sanctification. And *Sarah* truly signifies the internal daughter of Faith, that will bear the son of inspiration unto God, under his holy and spiritual gospel at this day, but it will be in *old age* that is the *Messenger* by the power of God, from the womb, or seed of Faith in the soul, quickens the spirit into act, which is the *virgin*, daughter of Faith, BORN to the spiritual and internal covenant of the law, so as the soul must be obedient to it, to be brought through it. But this new *life*, or *virgin*, is only under the justice to Faith, yet promised she shall bear a son unto God; but it will be an *old age*. For when this spiritual *virgin*, daughter of Faith, has waded through the power of Reason, and made her true offering before the God of Faith, and obedience to the internal angel, and come through as *refined gold*, then at the hour of death her prayer strongly ascends to God, whereby he is graciously pleased, by influence, to unite his *holy spirit* with this *virgin*, daughter of Israel, which is the spiritual *marriage*, then he begets to himself a *son*; this son is the INSPIRATION of the soul for the kingdom of heaven, then having a sight and seal thereof. But very few come back to tell this *Tale*, which is truly bearing a *son in old age*.

Further, it is said, GOD *tempted* Abraham, which was to make trial of his Faith, to offer up his *only son* whom he loved. Now *Isaac* was more to Abraham than all his earthly possessions, yet he did it without any excuse; for excuses are of Reason, on any demand of God:

And whosoever thinks to save themselves by excusing themselves will lose themselves in their excuses; and whosoever obeys the will of God to the loss of their own lives, will find their own lives again, in the love and blessing of God, as Abraham did in his son.

Again, The spiritual *son* of *Faith* is truly the Lord's as Isaac typified; but as a man must be born natural before he can spiritual, the power of the law or Levites is took instead, according to his being born into this world by natural birth the seed of Faith—therefore Moses, by God's command, numbered all the first-born of the children of Israel, and took the number of their names. (Numb. iii. 41.) "And thou shalt take the Levites for me. *I am* the LORD instead of all the first-born among the children of Israel; and the cattle of the Levites instead of all the firstlings among the cattle of the children of Israel." (And viii. 17.) "For all the first-born of the children of Israel are mine both man and beast. On the day that I smote every first-born in the land of Egypt, I sanctified them to myself;" so all the first-born of Israel is the Lord's, and an offering as such was made, when the days of purification of the mother were fulfilled, *i.e.* as man being born here under cherubical justice, that law, and priesthood of that water takes him, and he must go through it, before he is regenerated or translated to grace. As *Abraham* went to offer up Isaac, which truly shews forth these things, the ANGEL of the Lord, which was God himself, called to Abraham that he might not slay the lad. Here Abraham, by the power of Faith, would give up his son to the Lord; and the Lord gave him to Abraham again with a great blessing, because he was of Faith, and could not be offered up to die a cherubim: Also from him was to come the nation of the Jews, to whom the law and Levitical priesthood would be given. *And Abraham lifted up his eyes, and saw a ram caught in a thicket by his horns*, which he offered instead or his son. Here *Isaac* tipified the son in Faith, being *born* and *offered* to God according to his justice, and he is graciously pleased to transfer him to his ROYAL covenant of MERCY; but as Abraham. did it externally, it is now to be done internally, and to this very day God *tempts* Faith, which is his own nature, *to do his will, i.e.* to come to him. And the ram that offered instead of Isaac, was to signify the priesthood that would be given to his posterity under the law; for the ram not only became a burnt offering for the priest, but the man Moses, by God's command, used a Ram to consecrate the priest; (Exo. xxix. 26.) "And thou shalt take the breast of the Ram of Aaron's consecrations, and wave it for a wave offering before the Lord, and it shall be thy part."

Therefore all the great men of old was obliged to *offer* according to God the father's justice, before they were translated to, under the *mercy* of the SON.

CHAP. V

THE *fathers* of old, Adam, Enoch, Noah, Abraham, Isaac, Jacob, Moses, and Joshua saw the face of God, as God the *father*, but with his glory veiled; for he is so exceeding fiery glorious in his *justice*, that no man can see his face and live, therefore it was under a veil: also his *justice* is so exceeding pure, and of such unlimited power, that was he not to veil it, and stay it in the souls of men, even at this day, it would consume them from off the earth. Hence all written records or declaration of a messenger when living will not deliver a man from justice; it must be the work of the infinite Majesty. CHRIST, the *king* of FAITH, giving birth to the spirit of Faith that is born to the first covenant; (*i.e.* of water, and the nether water of Faith). I say *Christ only* can give BIRTH in *spirit* to his holy covenant of grace (*i.e.* the upper waters of Faith), and *seal* the soul for his glorious kingdom, or translate them to the mercy of the SON, as he did the seed of Faith in days of old, ere he became man. Now as God sent messengers under the law at times, until he *himself* came to bring in the *gospel*, so God sends messengers under the gospel at times until he *himself* comes to bring in *eternity*; and every messenger must deliver his message that God is graciously pleased to send: and men who live in a messenger's day, will be judged according to the days of that messenger, because he lived in no other's time; and the internal angel in *justice* will seal them as such.

There is another appearance of God, *i.e.* by way of *vision* and *dream*; as when Aaron and Miriam speak against Moses, for marrying the Ethiopian woman *"The Lord came down in a pillar of a cloud; and called unto Aaron and Miriam, and they both came forth* (Numb. xii. 5, 6;) *and he said,* "Hear now my words, if there be a prophet among you, I the Lord will make myself known unto him in a *vision*, and will speak unto him in a *dream*," which afterward he did unto *Samuel* and others; but when God doth appear to any man in vision, at the same time there is given to man knowledge to know the *similitude* of God from that of an angel, and the *voice* of God from that of an angel, and that man will truly know a spiritual vision from a natural vision: But all this was *under* and *for* God's justice, to go forth and prophecy of evil to come, upon brethren, people, and nations according to God's justice, which is no pleasing thing to a meek and merciful spirited man. Further, all natural wisdom, earthly possessions, riches, and power, which are blessings, are given under justice; therefore the possessors of those things must have a true and strict eye in the soul, how they manage and dispose of them; otherwise in the end they, to them, will become a curse. But those great men of old, who was inspired *by* or *under* the attribute of God's divine *justice*, to go forth and do mighty acts, such as to command the earth to swallow men up, or call fire from heaven to consume men in justice. When they came to die, they were translated to the merciful spirit of God, and there sealed, to be raised by the mercy and glory of the SON; so died in the *bed* of *mercy*, *i.e.* in effect hearing the voice of God saying, "Come up hither;" which far surpasses *that* of "Go forth in justice." And they all lay here in this earth, except Enoch, Moses, and Elijah, who were translated into heaven, but to no higher GLORY than that of the FATHER.

CHAP. VI

AGAIN, of the *cherubims and flaming sword*, the *internal* angel placed in the soul of every man; and he who is inspired under the attribute of God's divine justice, is truly the *external* angel, who those two angels represented who came with God to Abraham, then sent to Sodom: but they represented more of the *internal* than the *external*, they being two SERAPHIMS from HEAVEN who always will be preserved in the created purity; (*i.e.* they never *fell*, so are true and just on any errand whom God is graciously pleased to send them of). And as aforesaid, though the cherubim broke the law, he never could break the justice of that law, but brought it here into this world as pure as the attribute of God's divine justice, and is *now* witnessing in the soul of man, unto God's divine justice, and will to the end of time. Also this *internal* angel in the soul can speak *motional voices* in the soul of man, and can *loose* man, for man to go forth and do the will of God according to his divine justice; and the voice of this angel has been taken to be the voice of God; as has a *Seraphim* from heaven, on an errand, been taken to be God; as did Lot when he lingered to come out of Sodom, *the (two) men laid hold of his hand* to hasten him away; and when they had brought him forth, said, "Look not behind thee, but escape to the mountain lest thou be consumed;" (Gen. xix.) *and Lot said unto them*, "Oh! not so *my Lord*: behold thy servant now hath found grace in *thy* sight, and *thou* has magnified *thy* mercy which *thou* has shewed unto me, in saving my life," &c. Here it is plain Lot took one of those angels to be God, as no one but those angels came to destroy Sodom, and save Lot; and thus he talked to those angels, and addressed them concerning his escape.

Also, (Judg. xiii.) where the angel of the Lord came to Manoah's wife who was barren, and promised she should conceive and bear a son, and when she told Manoah, he intreated the Lord, and the angel came again and communed with Manoah, and he detained him until he had made an offering, and when he offered, the angel *ascended* in the flame that went from off the altar: *then Manoah knew he was an angel* from heaven which he took to be God, (ver. 22.) And Manoah said unto his wife, "we shall surely die," because we have seen God: therefore there is a great distinction between a man seeing and communing with God, by or from his Royal PERSON, than communing with an angel of God, let it be the internal or external: but him who never saw God, nor heard his voice immediately from his ROYAL PERSON, may say he hath seen or heard God; but it is by the *way* of the angel which is the *will* of God, according *to*, and *in* his justice: and every one must *see* and *hear* God himself either external or internal, or both, from or by his Royal PERSON, for his MERCY to enter his glorious kingdom.

This internal angel in justice in the soul of man, pure as the attribute of God's divine justice (as aforesaid) can commune with God relative to the wickedness, or relief of men: So when people or nation *oppress* people by their wickedness, the internal angel in justice is ready to commune with God of their wickedness; and also touching the oppressed, the internal angel is ready to commune with God for their relief (and all in justice) as he did in the days of old, when the Israelites were oppressed in Egypt; yea GOD communes with the internal angel in the soul of man, and when this is done, every man will be his own witness to his own condemnation, or relief, before the Lord, as was the Israelites and Egyptians. Also, when God spoke to Moses (Exo. iii. 7.) *and the Lord said,* "I have surely seen the affliction of my people which are in Egypt, and have heard their *cry* by Reason (of) their task-masters, I know their sorrows;" which he did by the internal angel in justice, as aforesaid.

Also God communed with the internal angel in the soul of man in the days of Noah, when *he saw the wickedness of man was great in the earth; and it repented the Lord that he made man on the earth, and it grieved him to the heart*, (Gen. vi. 6.) And which as plainly shews the most merciful God has no pleasure in the destruction of man, let whatever external angel in justice come forth and say to the contrary: this I know by the information of the divine Majesty from heaven; yet, notwithstanding, this must be done according to the attribute of divine justice, which became of an infinite consequence through the fall. Also God communed with this internal angel when men sought to build the Tower of *Babel*, and *he scattered them abroad upon the face of the earth.* (Gen. xi.) Moreover God communed with this angel in the days of Lot; (Gen. xviii. 20.) *and the Lord said,* "because the cry of Sodom and Gomorrah is great, and because their sin is very grievous:" for the days of Noah and Lot are somewhat alike, and are so mentioned by JESUS when he prophesied of the end of the world. Again, when Hagar and Ishmael was in distress, *and the angel of God called to Hagar out of heaven.* (Gen. xxi.) This voice came by the *way* of the internal angel in the soul, and it was as if this internal angel had spoke, and her eyes were opened, *and she saw the well of water.*

CHAP. VII

FURTHERMORE, there is three ways or sorts of vision and communion in the soul. The *first* is with the very PERSON and spirit of God when he raiseth the spirit of Faith from death to life; then it communes with God in the royal Priesthood, concerning the great works and mysteries of Faith in Creation, Redemption, Regeneration, and Salvation. This not only produces vision and dream, but also brings you to see the glory of the Father, *i.e.* of *justice*; and of the Son, *i.e. mercy*. The *second* is according to the cherubical inspiration, *i.e.* by the *way* of the internal angel in justice, as Moses and others communed and received instruction, to watch and rule Reason, and to make an offering to stay that justice in the Priesthood of Reason, &c. &c. as afore written: also to bind or loose men to do the will of God in this his justice, will produce vision and dream, and also is of God in that covenant. The *third* is to commune with your own spirit of Reason, *i.e.* the devil, the which they (false teachers, &c.) call God, or the instruction of God, by which men seek to do their own will, and have their own way, which is nothing but evil; and then bring their own excuses, and transform themselves into a declaration from heaven, and imitate its language and practice; this is the *Wild* Priesthood of Reason: this also will produce vision and dream, and the consultation of the devil, as when Balaam was intreated to go and curse the children of Israel; for Balaam was a wise man of *Midian*, and a sort of a *priest* who practised divination, and had some knowledge of Moses, his laws, manners, and practices which he gathered from the camp of Israel, being in the wilderness so long. And he did bless and curse in imitation of those blessings and cursings declared by Moses the man of God: and when the elders of *Moab* and *Midian* came to him for to go and curse the Israelites, he said lodge here, and I will bring you word again, as the Lord shall speak unto me; so Balaam used to go and enquire of God, in this he also imitated Moses; but Balaam's god was his own spirit of Reason that he used to commune with calling it God, *it* being loosed by the internal angel, that even in *this* the name of the God of Israel is magnified.

Also when Balaam made an offering, he offered a bullock and a ram which was the priest-offering in the camp of Israel; all this, with somewhat of the law he gathered from Israel, and constructed it, and set it forth by his own *wild* spirit of Reason which he called God, so by this he became a great man, and might fancy his self as wise, if not wiser, than the man Moses. However *Balak*, king of *Moab*, had great confidence in him, (Num. 22.) saying, "I wot that he whom thou blessest is blessed, and he whom thou cursest is cursed;" for when Balak saw such a number of people that had come out of Egypt overcoming other nations, he was afraid; and as was his Faith sent to Balaam to come and curse them, and when Balaam went to inquire all Israel, was brought there by the power of God, worshipping that God who brought them there; their Law and practice being good: But Balaam by all his gathered knowledge, shifts, and turns of Reason could not equal Moses; but in his own soul must say, Moses had a power above him, and so could not prove them vagabonds, because God was on their side; nor could be make any amendment to their law or practice, he himself falling short of either; so could not make any oration to curse them as vagabonds, much more to overcome them by enchantments: then he found it his best way to let them alone, and dismiss the messengers, saying, "the Lord refuseth to give me leave to go with you." After that, there came messengers more honourable to offer him a great reward; then Balaam's honour was at stake, because Balak's Faith was in him; then went he to enquire again, and his god said "he may go:" *i.e.* Balaam by his sober Reason wherein the law was written, found he could not curse them neither could he bear to lose the honour of men: then from the womb or seed of Reason came forth a son, which I call *aspiring pride* that will not hearken to the law, for in Reason is written the law, but what is thus born, I call *lawless*, therefore fit to go forth to curse any thing of God, was it in his power: - Thus Balaam mounted his *ass*, which is the emblem of Reason, and himself the son *aspiring pride, i.e.* born of Reason, and rides thereon: Now the ass saw the angel and fell, *i.e.* Balaam could go no further, and knew not of the angel, but was angry with the *ass* for the law being written in Reason, Reason will *see*, and *fall* by the power of the internal angel, with this son aspiring pride; and he will not know for what, until the soul is made sensible too late.

This angel that met Balaam in the way, was a *Seraphim* from *heaven* representing the internal angel, or rather the voice of God in his justice to the internal angel: Then the internal angel bound Balaam to speak the truth, which was good things of Israel in blessing them; as this internal angel, will do as directed, by any angel or voice from heaven: - For when Balaam said "he would get back." *The angel of the Lord said,* "Go with the men, but *only* the word that I *shall* speak, unto thee, that thou shalt speak;" *i.e.* the internal angel did bind him to speak well of Israel, and in all their burnt offerings, and in his enquiry, when he came back, he was obliged to speak well of them to Balak, being bound so to do by the internal angel; so Balak dismissed him in anger. Even so if any come forth as an external angel, in or under the covenant of justice, and bless or curse men, for time or to eternity, if the internal angel in the soul, will not bear witness to it, it is of no value at all, also, in other *Messenger's* time, there has been found such men, and is at this day (when the seed of Reason transform themselves into the declaration of a *Messenger*), who would be glad to seek *kingdoms*, as Balaam did in Moab; and may fancy themselves more wise than the *Messenger*, and on occasion will imitate to curse. Also, the *Messenger* being dead, there is silence in the nether heaven till another comes, and when come, he finds Reason has usurped the rule of the letter, and teaches the way of God all in the wrong; and the church full of traditions, which he declares against, setting Reason on fire with anger. Then the most dark atheistical man in spirit, who hath diverted them with his prattle (their Faith being in him), seeks to curse the living *Messenger*, and by the spirit of Reason, overlooks the Letter, to find a way to do it, and can find none; then if he does as Balaam did, he will let the man alone, as he may find a voice say, in *himself,* "if you are sure of your *own* salvation, that man cannot hurt you;" but his dislike to this *Messenger,* to maintain his former power, will become full of *fiery zeal,* which is the daughter of Reason born; and she being eager for the former doctrine and traditions, to maintain that *Wild* priesthood, and the desires of the people together, gives *birth* to the spiritual born *son of perdition,* born of zeal (*i.e.* the daughter of Reason), and this son, *i.e. lawless* can attempt to go forth, and curse this *Messenger* of God. But he also (as Balaam) will find his adversary in the *way*, for when he comes forth full of his cursing wrath, thinking to curse the *Messenger* and the elect, the *internal angel* seals him under his own cursing and wrath which is his *adversary* in the *way*, for in all frothy thoughts of power and safe proceedings, he will ride into that *narrow place* well secured by the power of sin and death, and there cannot turn aside, then there stands the *angel* and *flaming-sword*.

CHAP. VIII

AGAIN, Saul was made choice of to be king of Israel, and as such, was anointed by the prophet Samuel, then he met the prophets according to Samuel's word, and the spirit of the Lord came upon him, and he did prophecy among the prophets according to Samuel's word, and the Spirit of the Lord came upon him, and he did prophecy among the prophets, this prophecy of Saul was under justice, for then he obeyed Samuel, who was a *messenger* of God, under his attribute of divine justice. Further as GOD in his *wrath*, gave the kingdom unto Saul, God also communed with the internal angel in justice that was in Saul, to fill him with wisdom to rule the people, and also to war with other nations, but this wisdom and his prophecy was in *justice* and *wrath*. For when the people of Jabesh Gilead would make a covenant with Nahash, the Ammonite, who said, "it should be on that condition, that he may thrust out all their right eyes, for a reproach upon all Israel," *and the elders required seven days respite, to send messengers, and they came to Gibeah of Saul*, (1 Sam. xi. 6.) "and the Spirit of God came upon Saul, when he heard those tidings, and his anger was kindled greatly." Now if the Spirit of God kindles a man to *anger*, it must be in justice, as was Saul together the people Israel. Then they went and slew the Ammonites, and Samuel approved of the act, and made Saul king before the Lord. Also Saul had *dreams*, and God answered him by prophet and dream; but all Saul's answers were *through* and to the internal angel in justice, *i.e.* the Cherubim; but Balaam's was with his own *wild* spirit of Reason calling it God. Also God has communed with man by this internal angel in justice, that he shall go forth, and destroy, according to the *execution* of God's justice, and after that, God can withhold his communion, and leave the man naked and bare, and take from him his kingdom, and give it to another, and all in justice; and the former man shall become equal with him or them, whom he hath cursed or destroyed. Moreover, there is *two* kingdoms God doth give man, *i.e.* the kingdom *in* or *under justice*, and his *own* kingdom of *mercy*, notwithstanding all men must travail through justice, before they are translated to mercy: but there is more kept in justice by the internal angel, than there is translated to mercy by the LORD GOD of Heaven: And many have transformed themselves to the bare Letter, or outward declaration of the Gospel, and go forth, and preach by permission, and do the will of God, in and according to his divine justice, and men do believe according to their liking, and make to themselves the great assurance of salvation, by reading the letter, and understanding it their own dark way. But when they are arraigned before justice, the internal angel will keep them under it, as they were born into this world: Because they could not be born the true SPIRITUAL BIRTH; so are unnoticed to God in respect of translation to his divine mercy, thus they will become one with those, whom they have cursed to eternity.

Again, when David was near his death, he gave charge to Solomon his son, to walk in the way, statutes, judgments and commandments of God, written by Moses, so flourish in his kingdom, and when he was established, he went to sacrifice at Gibeon, where it is *said*, the Lord appeared unto him, (1 Kings iii. 5.) "In Gibeon the Lord appeared to Solomon in a *dream* by night, and God said, ask what I shall give thee," but he asked for no more than cherubical wisdom, to rule *the people*, and give just *judgment* to parties (v. 9.) and is the greatest thing to be desired by any king ruler or judge in this world, who is a cherubim, and it was granted as written, "I have given thee a wise and understanding heart," also *riches* and *honour* were added, which he asked not for, yea if any man in justice, is desirous to act according to God like justice; riches and honour will be added. And it was said to Solomon, "If thou wilt walk in my ways to keep my statutes and commandments, as thy father David did walk, I will lengthen thy days," (14. v.) but nothing *asked* for, or *promised* but natural wisdom, riches, honour, long life, &c. For all *divine* wisdom of God's eternal *mercy* was not mentioned; and he awoke, and behold it was a dream. Now he whom Solomon saw in his dream, was not God, but the similitude of an angel, (a visionary *Messenger* of God in his justice unto Solomon); for it is the nature of Reason to call such an appearance God; and indeed, they are not much mistaken for the internal angel in justice, is as it were a God to Reason, that will keep the seed of Reason under justice in all eternity. The seed of Faith, when an angel hath come to tell of things to come, or deliver men from destruction, have by mistake said, it is God, but theirs was a personal appearance and *communion, i.e.* far greater than any angelic visional appearance, it being only a dream, and as the vapours of this life without *regeneration.* For as the seed of Reason was cast out from *communion* with the tree of life, it must be by the way of the angel, whether in or out of vision or dream, that *they* go forth to do the will of God according to his divine justice. And Solomon was brought up by or under his father David, and knew the letter of the law of Moses, and was instructed by him how to reign in Israel; also Solomon was appointed of God to build the temple, with all its magnificial ornamental beauties, which was a great piece of cherubical wisdom. But all his fine building, cherubical wisdom and splendid glory, came far short of that glory God created the cherubim to, which was the cause of his seeing somewhat of the glory of the cherubim before his fall. By this angel Solomon saw a similitude in his dream, that came by God's order to instruct him in cherubical wisdom, and was filled at times with this wisdom, to instruct and judge of the cunning work of man, to build the temple.

Also he was blessed with peace and plenty, that he might build the temple according to the will of God, in that beautiful appearance, that would delight the spirit of Reason, to use their ceremonies and worship, according to the law of Moses. Therefore this temple was called the house of the Lord, and at its dedication "the priest could not stand to minister, because of the cloud," for the glory of the Lord, had filled the house of the Lord," (1. Kings viii. 11.) Neither was there any temple in the whole world of magnificence, beauty, riches and grandeur, &c. like that at Jerusalem which bear the name of the "house of the Lord". And Solomon was filled with more cherubical wisdom than any of the sons of Reason that reigned in Israel, and had ALL that Reason need to desire. And when he had *ended* his prayer, in which he asked for no more than natural prosperity, even *that* was promised by the man Moses, if they worshipped God according to his law. Also, when he had offered offerings, "That the Lord appear to Solomon the *second* time *as* he did at Gibeon (xi. 2.) and said I have heard thy prayer, and if thou will walk before me in integrity of heart, as did thy father David, there shall not fail thee a man upon the throne of Israel;" but he loved strange women, which is the *emblem* of Reason, and they turned his heart aside after other gods; and then his kingdom was divided, which is done *in* the House which bears the name of Israel unto *this day.*

Moreover, this *second appearance* of God unto Solomon was as before, an *angelical visional appearance,* from God, with power to instruct Solomon; for whoever doth see the royal person of God, and commune with him either personal or visional, it is sure to fill the soul with such knowledge of him, that he will cling fast to him, indeed he may err before him, but he never will turn from him. Yea there never was such a cherubim that was *only* a cherubim, as was Solomon,- that was filled with wisdom and just judgments; and had such riches, peace and grand appearance, and did commune with heaven, but all under God's justice; - for all his wisdom ended in *death*, and all the magnificent buildings and grandeur ended with *destruction*, according to God's divine justice. Also God by his divine wisdom in his justice, by virtue of his creation, can raise up any cherubim, and fill him with wisdom, that he shall do according to God's will, yet by this, man cannot claim eternal life, for therein, man doth no more than his duty, he being God's creature, and God the author of his being, and of all the good he doth possess. So God is not indebted to man, but man to God. Therefore God can according to his justice, leave man as he was born into this world under justice, and not translate him to his divine mercy.

CHAP. IX

AGAIN, as aforesaid, the host of seraphims, which are in heaven, was created under the pure law of angels, or of Reason (*i.e.* to love God above all, and your neighbour as yourself), and are preserved in their created purity, by the overflowing of the holy spirit of the divine Majesty (*i.e.* the spiritual power by which he created them); for while man or angel remain pure as God created them, they can commune with God either in person or spirit; and this seraphic host, or holy order of angels are spiritual bodies, whose likeness is this, *Peradventure*, the divine Majesty was pleased to create the body of a man out of fine crystal water, and set that water on fire, by a fire more glorious; Thus appear an angel crystal and glorious, and like water can pass through a narrow passage, and reassume its own form again. Thus the cherubim was transmuted into earth, through whom came the *law* of Moses or *Commission of Water*, wherein Reason might live and flourish (*i.e.* or may be likened unto the *moon*). But the Body of GOD, before he became flesh, was spiritual Fire, and the *life* of that fire, was the spiritual and glorious fire of FAITH; so when God transmuted himself into human nature, that he created in Adam; then from him came forth the *commission* of the Gospel (*i.e.* likened to the *sun*).

Further relative to the cherubims, of which order but one was created, who was more piercing in his wisdom, and glorious in his person, than any of the holy seraphims, and fell from heaven with that wisdom and glory, and was transmuted into flesh, and became man, and the internal angel in justice, which he brought into this world with him, placed in his soul to keep him from the tree of life (*i.e.* the mercy of the Son), as neither him nor his posterity that live to manhood will be kept from justice under the Father's power: Also the internal angel can commune with God relative to that justice, but will keep them out from the mercy of the son (*i.e.* the tree of life, in and for regeneration). Yet notwithstanding all this, God will not lose the Glory of his *creating* the angel, nor the glory *of* the angel, for in the day of resurrection, there will be cherubims raised to great glory; as the wisdom, power and glory of God in creating the cherubim is exceeding great, and there will be such a great glory resound to God by his divine wisdom therein, that no man or angel can comprehend; therefore knowledge in those things is an heavenly gift to the divine Majesty.

And as this angel or cherubim as aforesaid, fell with his created glory and wisdom, and was transmuted into flesh or earth, becoming man in generation, and all his seed that live to manhood; the angel in justice taking place in their soul, keeps them from taking of the tree of life, to eat and live for ever; so they must go their way according to God's infinite Justice. But all his seed, who die in their childhood or minority will be raised at the last day, to a greater knowledge and glory than the cherubim fell from; and this will be the *heavenly* HOST or glorious *order* of CHERUBIMS, that will live in the kingdom of God to all eternity. Therefore by the unbounded wisdom of God, in his creating this cherubim, and suffer him to fall, and transmuted himself into flesh, there will be millions go their way, according to God's divine justice, and millions more raised glorious cherubims, to compose that angelic glorious order in heaven, and *all* from this *cherubim*, who fell from heaven. Also this cherubical fallen nature being borne here in time, enjoying life, in flesh, blood and bone, and then as it enters into death, it will be a great refining to the understanding of Reason: Why? because Reason will be experimentally wise of the power of God, in the change and conditions it has gone through; and will be raised to the glory of heaven with a body of flesh and bone, much refined, by passing through death *to* and *at* the glorious resurrection: Yea, they will be raised with the aforesaid refined knowledge of Reason, so will have perfect understanding; they have borne the *image*, and enjoyed life in a body of flesh below; therefore, will be an order of angels higher in knowledge and more glorious than the seraphims (they remaining as they were created.) Further, they will have bodies from this earth, a fine framework of flesh and bone, like a transparent crystal stone; or earth refined by the power of God, and also, will know that this life in glory, is the *second* life they enjoy by the almighty power of God; and will be glorified in full *statue* like unto GOD, and his *royal* ELECT; only this, God and his elect will be glorified with the glorious fire of FAITH, as no one is capable of the glory of Faith, but them, whose *life* is of Faith, as will be the elect in the morning of the resurrection, for they will come forth with the glorious life of Faith, as the brethren or SONS of GOD by *regeneration*, and will intirely commune with him, *with or by* his own nature, (*i.e.* divine Faith).

And the *glory* of Reason is a glory God is graciously pleased to give, when he calls it into life, for the nature of Reason is from chaos, and although it came forth pure by the creating power of God, yet it being not of God's divine nature, it is incapable of both, that *in* and *outshining* glory of Faith, but is a glorious fire inferior, being more of the moon-like glory, than that of Faith. Yet this heavenly HOST, or glorious order of cherubims, will be raised up to greater glory than the cherubim their father fell from, and appear in heaven next to the most glorious ORDER, the seed of Faith. Thus the glorious wisdom of the divine Majesty moved him to create the cherubim, more wise and more glorious than any of the seraphims, and suffer him to fall: That through him by generation, God would have those millions to praise him for his merciful power in recovering them to himself such glorious beings.

As the *children* or cherubims die here, and go to earth or dust, they needs must be recovered to God in the *resurrection;* which would not have been, had not God became man to redeem, so *died* and *rose* again, gaining to himself the power of a *resurrection.* Therefore, those cherubims will be benefited by the REDEMPTION, as by that means they will be raised to glory; and for ought I know, with somewhat of the woman's nature, which the angel took at his incarnation, which will be somewhat of a capacity in them to hear the *Echo* of the divine VOICE, for God to raise them to glory; but their souls will be of Reason, therefore incapable of the glory of *Faith*, as also to commune with God by a soul of Faith, as the elect or sons of God will.

So I declare those cherubims are benefited by the redemption, but no part *in* the redemption, in respect to the glorious mysteries of *Faith;* yet they may say Christ died for them, which is the language of the cherubical nature. As if a *Messenger* is inspired and sent forth by God in his holy gospel, or covenant of grace, so as to prophecy Christ will come, which is the *upper* waters or waters of Faith, and there is given him *one* to be his *Mouth*, and he will be a *priest*, in the nether or cherubical *Waters*: When that *Messenger* is gone, the doctrine of that priest hardly extends higher than the resurrection and glorification of the glorious order of CHERUBIMS, Why? because his knowledge is in the *nether Waters*; Yet from the *Messenger's* declaration, he will trace the *Person* of God, from eternity through time, to eternity again; and greatly talk of his death and resurrection, saying, Christ died for *me* and you, &c. and that God taketh no *immediate notice*, but by his law, and the blood of God, is sufficient for salvation, if you can *believe* and do as the *priest* shall order; also that it is your Faith *within you*, that will conduct you into heaven, which is truth in itself (if so much *Faith* can be found in man as to be capable of the *first* resurrection, but the other is the language of the aforesaid cherubims, that will be glorified; and did the infant cherubim or child know his own state, he or they would speak the same words, and sing or rejoice in their conditions, as doth the *priest* and people.

If any man comes forth in the first covenant, *i.e.* at this day, the spiritual covenant of the law or *nether waters* in the *commission* of the *spirit*, and in that covenant be instructed by that revelation to declare many things; yet in his declaration falls short to direct any one to the spiritual birth, and *holy* spiritual marriage with JESUS in *glory*, to seal the *Seed* of Faith here in time, to enter his glorious kingdom (mostly done at the hour of death), and that every *man must* be spiritually born (*i.e.* translated to the holy seal of Jesus); for *he* cannot die a cherubim to enter the kingdom of heaven: As such I can hardly draw a line of difference of such a man's declaration in effect to amount any higher than the resurrection and glorification of cherubims.

Many people have transformed themselves into the letter of the *Third Record*, and greatly rejoice therein, making cherubical songs, singing great praises to God for the *Literal Record*, as by it they may read of the *Person* of God: But this is no other than cherubical wisdom and mirth; yea, they will greatly rejoice and sing, and say Christ died for them: yea, so he did for the child or cherubim: Also, will say, the blood of God is sufficient for them; so also, it is for the child or cherubim, further they will say, they have assurance of eternal life; yea, it is *truly* so of the cherubim, did he but know it; and that they need not use prayer, neither need the cherubim; also they will say, Christ did the work for them, so he did for the cherubims. But when *those* come to be arraigned before the internal angel in justice, they will be found *liars*, but the children or cherubims will truly possess those things. But those *Literalists* being grown up to manhood, and the internal angel took place in the soul, they cannot die cherubims, to be raised to that glorious order in heaven.

As the *law* given by *Moses* came through the cherubim, under the attribute of God's divine justice, so *by the* Law *no man can be saved*, therefore all the mercy that extends to salvation under this covenant of justice, is to the child or cherubim, and natural Ideot, as the internal angel in justice doth not take place in the soul of either; further, the *ark* of this covenant of justice, signifies the *body* of man, and the *outward* ornaments shew forth the natural blessing men would have, if they would obey Moses in the law and worship; also in the ark was put the testimony of the law, and the *pot* of *manna* and Aaron's *rod* that *budded* as a *token* against the rebels, and also the *tables* of the covenant. All this was *witness* for, or against *man*; and is to shew forth the power of the internal angel in justice IN the body and soul of man; which I call the arch-angel, and is called a *cherubim*, and has a *flaming sword*, and standeth before the attribute of God's divine justice, strickly *watching* the *law* and the *ways* of man; so when he doth well, this angel excuseth him, but when he doeth evil, his own evil goes into his own *ark*, as a *witness* against him, the angel sealing him under justice; therefore, let men say what they will, or do as they please, if they pass this internal angel, all will be well.

The *Mercy-seat* upon the ark signifies the glorious mercy of God in that covenant unto children that die in minority, and natural ideots, who will be raised glorious cherubims, therefore, those *cherubims* will cover the *mercy-seat*: Also God communed with Moses from *above* the mercy-seat, *i.e.* God communed in justice with Moses, relative to Moses and the Children of Israel, who was in manhood, which is *above* the state of childhood, therefore from *above* the mercy-seat; also God communed with Moses from *between* him, as an anointed *cherubim* and the *internal angel* in the souls of the Israelites; for if Moses erred the *angel* would commune with God, relative to that error; and when the Israelites rebelled, or murmured against Moses, and against God, God in his justice brought judgment among them, through the communion of this angel, and this is communing *from between the two cherubims*. And those cherubims of *gold*, or glory, that *covered* the mercy-seat upon the ark, was far short of the glory God created the cherubim in, so much less, the glory of God will raise the *holy* order of cherubims *to*. Now, if any man of Reason can keep this law of angels, *i.e.* "to love God above all, and your neighbour as yourself," then he may be raised a cherubim: But I would not have any one think to put the question, Did Christ raise a cherubim? for the answer is no, because *God took not on him the nature of angels*, and of consequence, not its law; but God took on him the created nature of Adam, which was human, animated with divine Faith, which fell for hearkening to the voice of Reason, *i.e.* breaking the law of Faith. But Jesus, when he was here, kept the law of Faith, *i.e. not to hearken to the voice of Reason*, and this *no one* but Jesus could *do*, so he died, and rose again the very ETERNAL GOD.

My desire is for the Elect to know the difference between the glory of the cherubims, which is of Reason, and the glory of Faith, that the elect will be glorified with, which is the divine nature of God: Also to know, that when men and women come to maturity, the internal angel takes place in the soul and they cannot die cherubims to be raised to glory; and that *many* at this day, who profess the letter, preach, sing, and are merry, is no other than imitating the cherubims, and is in the *dark-waters of Reason, i.e.* the *great river Euphrates, in the land of Nod*: For professing the letter only will not do; you must be spiritually born to the first covenant, and in sorrow wade through that, to get as near to Jesus in spirit as possible you can, and then to be given birth in spirit by the LORD JESUS in *Glory*, to his holy spiritual covenant of grace, with his royal spiritual seal, to enter his glorious kingdom; and this is the *mercy-seat* to the elect, and is *covered* not by cherubims, but by angels of the royal lineage of Faith.

Here it may be said, do any of the seed of Faith die in their childhood? if so, to what knowledge and glory will they be raised; for they cannot have the knowledge and soul, feeling experience in the new spiritual birth, or translation to Christ the king of Faith, as can one that is in *manhood?* I answer, it is my Faith that not one of the seed of Faith die in childhood: If there ever was, they have been raised again to this life by some godlike-power given from heaven, to further manifest the glory of God: Likewise Adam was created here a man, so all his children live to manhood, that *they* may be truly made sensible, that Faith fell in Adam, and that *they* have hearkened to the voice of Reason, as Adam did; and *so* to be called to in manhood, by the voice of God, as Adam *was* for *spiritual* generation, or translation: but the child is not out of natural generation being *then* in spirit, as it was born; and also, as Faith fell in Adam, in manhood it will be raised alive in Christ in manhood: For there is no such thing throughout the scripture as regeneration in spirit for *children*, indeed a man must become as a child, *i.e.* a preparative to his regeneration to enter the kingdom of heaven. Therefore regeneration, or translation to the throne or covenant of grace truly to receive the seal of the living God, in or from his throne of glory, done is in manhood.

But some may say, God inspire Samuel in childhood; yes, but that was the cherubical inspiration, under the attribute of divine justice, and was to live to manhood. Also the angel said, "John should be filled with the Holy Ghost from his mother's womb, *because* he was to prepare the way of the Lord;" and to have the Holy Ghost from the mother's womb, is little more than to be born the elect of God; as it *is* said, "the *word* of God came unto him in the *Wilderness*, and he came *Out,* and preached and baptized:" But both Samuel and John was under the law, and in *manhood*, was translated to the throne of grace; but they never came back to tell this *Tale.*

As *Adam* was created in this world, and came forth in full *manhood*, with a life of Faith (*i.e.* the divine nature of God); therefore, when a child is born with the *seed* or *spirit* of Faith, predominate in the soul (*i.e.* for regeneration), that Child will live to *manhood* as Adam was created; - For the *divine nature* of God is not sown into this earth, and in generation become the essential *life* for regeneration, but that being will live to *manhood*: Yea, the divine nature of God *never* will come short of manhood; and so to be able to offer the true prayer of Faith. But the created cherubim being transmuted into earth or flesh, as aforesaid, was *born* a child growing to manhood; therefore many of his children *die* and not grow to manhood, and because their father was born into this world a child. So as Adam, "who was the son of God," was created, and came forth into this world a *man*; therefore *all* the *sons* of *Adam* will live to *manhood* as CHILDREN of GOD.

Query. May there not be some living in *childhood* of the *seed* of Faith, when Christ comes to put an end to time, and judge the world? To this I answer, the man who asks the question cannot tell whether there will or will not: But Jesus said, "as it was in the days of Noah, and of Lot, *so* shall it be in the days of the son of man;" therefore, there was no *children* went into the Ark to be saved, nor any children called out of Sodom to be saved, but *men* and *women* only: But, however, if there is any in childhood of the *seed* of Faith, at the *coming* of *Christ*, they will immediately, by his *mighty power*, become *men*, to be born the spiritual birth before they are translated into *glory*.

CHAP. X

THE law of angels or of Reason as aforesaid, being brought into this world by the created cherubim, according to the pure law and glory God created him to: therefore Moses and others were inspired under the attribute of God's divine justice, through this cherubim with the wisdom of that *law*, the worship God required under it, to stay his justice; and also did know the plague of that fallen *cherubical* troublesome nature. And *so* of all the prophets, under the law, except *Isaiah*, who was inspired by God, under the attribute of his divine justice, by the *way* of the *seraphims*, who are glorified in heaven above (and whose nature is Reason with the law written therein, as had the cherubim in the purity of his creation). But the cherubim became *impure* (as before written), and fell, whilst the *seraphims* remain *pure* as they were created, so their nature is *pure* Reason.

And Isaiah in his *vision*, "saw the Lord sitting upon a throne, high and lifted up, and his train filled the temple, and above it stood the *seraphims*, each one had six wings, with twain *he covered his face*, and with twain he *covered his feet*, and with twain *he did flee*." (Isa. vi. 1, 2.) Those wings are spoken of in respect to God's *glorious creation*; free *electing* love and *preservation* of them. For God created them glorious spiritual bodies, fit to ascend or descend at their own pleasure, or rather to obey the will of the divine Majesty, their Creator, which (glories) are the *wings* or power that they *flee* with: Also God preserved them in their created purity by his electing love, when he suffered the cherubim to fall, which is the *wings* or power that *cover their feet*, and on which they *stood*, also God filled them with glorious revelation that they should never fall into or *face* evil, but remain in their created purity in his royal presence to all eternity; which is the *wings* or power that preserves them, and as such *cover their face*: Therefore, for those great and glorious acts of the divine Majesty, *viz.* his creation, preservation and divine revelation to them, they return unto God, their great creator and preserver, thankful praises, for those *Three* glorious acts, and the *cry* of the *seraphims* is, "*Holy, Holy, Holy* is the *Lord* of *Hosts*," and this is the true language of the seraphims, because they rest under, or in his created purity.

Further, when Isaiah *saw* in *vision*, the glory of God and of the seraphims, he said, "woe is me! I am undone, I am a man of unclean lips, - for mine eyes have seen the KING, the *Lord* of *Hosts*:" Here Isaiah not only saw God, but the difference between *pure* and *impure* Reason; for the cherubical nature, with somewhat of the seraphic that Isaiah had in himself was fallen, as the serpent-angel, brought it into this world. "Then *flew* one of the *seraphims* with a live coal in his hand, that he taken from off the altar with tongs, and laid it upon Isaiah's mouth, saying, lo! this toucheth thy lips, and thine iniquity is taken away, and thy sin is purged," *i.e.* to fill him with wisdom, and open his *mouth* through that pure seraphic nature of Reason, that never fell in the *seraphims,* and also to inspire Isaiah's seraphic nature, as well as his cherubical, according to the inspiration of *Moses's* declaring the covenant and worship of the law. The *altar* from which the *seraphim took a live coal*, signifies the obedience, honour, praises, glory and thanksgivings of the seraphims unto God, which is offered at his royal feet for his creating and preserving them such glorious beings, to live in his royal presence, which is the *incense* of *pure* Reason for those great and glorious acts.

And the *altar erected* by Moses, according to God's command to burn *incense*, according to the worship of the law, to *stay* God's divine *justice* (that Reason may *here* enjoy their inheritance, as the Lord promised) is, the incense of *fallen* Reason, in that given *priesthood*.

Therefore, *Isaiah* in his *vision*, saw God, and the heavenly host of seraphims, and was inspired by God himself, under the attribute of his divine justice through the seraphims which made him very *sharp* in his reproof to the children of Israel, for their idolatrous worship and rebellion against God. Also as those seraphims are preserved in their pure created nature by the *power of God*; they are *eager* to keep *close* to *obey* the will of God; therefore, *Isaiah* writes "the ox knoweth his owner, and the ass his master's crib, but Israel doth not, my people do not consider," (Isa. i. 3.). Also declares from God, (by or through his seraphic nature,) "to what purpose are your sacrifices, saith the LORD: I am full of burnt offerings of rams, fat of fed beasts, I delight not in the blood of bullocks, or lambs or he-goats:" for they did not act according to the law given by Moses; but Reason went *Wild* into *pride, covetousness, oppression,* &c. to seek their own *will*, to have their own *way*; and in *this spirit* brought in their oblations to atone, which is an abomination in the sight of God.

Also, *Isaiah* by his inspiration, well knew the difference between pure and impure Reason, and of *sober* Reason, that would hear and obey Moses, and *Wild* Reason that would skulk from Moses to do their own will, the which *Isaiah* reproves, adding, "their vain oblations, incense, new moons, &c. is an abomination;" because not done as was ordered of the Lord by the man Moses: Now this pure Reason of the seraphim is not so ceremonious, but as aforesaid, will keep *close* to the will of God; but the cherubim will lose himself in his ceremonies.

Further, if those ceremonies were done as Moses commanded, yet when Isaiah came forth, they would not obey this prophet; then when they come to be arraigned before divine justice, no one required it at their hands, they should have obeyed the *Messenger* of God; for obedience to the word of God is better than all the sacrifice Reason can bring: Also, if any man should hear the *Messenger*, and yet think to go to God, and neglect the *Messenger*, he will find himself utterly mistaken, for he will make his own idol, and in time hide himself in a rock or den, if possible he can be hidden from the internal angel in justice; yet he will think himself a wise man to carry both heaven and earth: And thus Isaiah writes (chap. v. 20, 21.) "Woe unto them that are wise in their *own* eyes, and prudent in their *own* sight; woe unto them that call *evil* good and *good* evil; and put the *darkness* for light and *light* for darkness, *bitter* for sweet and *sweet* for bitter." This judgment is very positive but an infallible truth, as let it be remembered, he received his power in vision, and the *heavens* were opened to him, and inspired by GOD himself in visional *glory* under the attribute of his divine justice, in or under the *law* of Moses, by the *way* of the *seraphims* (*i.e. pure* Reason,) which gave him great knowledge and judgment of *fallen* Reason here below, both of the cherubic and seraphic nature; by which cause he brought forth such positive judgment, gentle and kind invitations, and great prophecies, for he not only spoke of the natural captivity of the Jews, but also of their spiritual captivity under the GOSPEL, and when he prophecies of CHRIST and the *Holy Gospel*, the spirit hardly admits of any time (in some places) for he writes as if the things was then in act.

Yea, Isaiah keeps close to righteous judgment, "To relieve the oppressed, judge the fatherless, and plead for the widow." And writes (chap. iii. 12.) "As for my people, children are their oppressors, and women rule over them," saying from the Lord, "they do beat *my* people, and grind the face of the *poor*." And complains of great pride, and wantonness, *minching as they go*, and of all their jewels and ornaments, and *fine changes of apparel*: All these things, Isaiah prophecies greatly against, for all pride is displeasing in the sight of God: Yea, the seraphic nature dislikes the pride of cherubical nature, in all their external grand appearance: So when Judgment for this is given, it comes more powerful through the seraphim, than it doth through the cherubim; as the cherubim hath the same pride in himself. Also there is the same judgment and woes under the letter of the GOSPEL: "And in *that* DAY, seven women shall take hold of one man, saying, we will eat our own bread, and wear our own apparel, only let us be called by thy name, to take away our reproach." (Isa. iv. 1.) *i.e.* the spirits of Reason, as the *women* did transform themselves into the letter of the gospel, and be *called Christians*, but would have and understand Christ according to their own spirit of Reason; and would declare themselves ministers, and set *it* forth (*i.e.* the gospel or Christ as *food* and *clothing* their *own* way) by their *own* imagination: And this thing is done even to this day; but pride and excuses are left to the internal angel; and judgment will come anon: and, as I said before, men have nothing more to do then to pass this internal angel and all will be well.

CHAP. XI

AS the divine Majesty was graciously pleased to create the cherubim to such high glory, wisdom, and power, and suffer him to fall with his glory, wisdom and power, and become man in generation, then from or through him came the *Law*, and all ruling *earthly* powers, desire of earthly *glory*, the wisdom of Reason, with all the high *imaginary* spiritual power, and *self* promise of glory; and are *here* on this earth, and this earth is given them to *wander* on, and *rule* in; and they *will* do it, if not in person, yet in spirit; but all under God's divine justice. And *Ezekiel* the priest being translated to a prophet by the word and power of God, was inspired under the attribute of God's divine justice, in or under the law of Moses; by the way of or through the cherubims; *i.e.* according to the glory God created the cherubim to, and the pure law he created him under, before his fall. "And when Ezekiel was among the captives by the river Chebar, the heavens were opened and he saw the visions of God," (chap. 1.) *i.e.* God by his glorious inspiration *opened the heaven* of Ezekiel's understanding, and also *opened* to him Reason's *heaven* here below; therefore the *visions* which he saw, was the powerful acts, nature and manner of the cherubims under God's justice, for no where are they yet to be found but on this earth, in active life, or *in* this earth, in the sleep of death.

Therefore Ezekiel in his vision, "beheld a whirlwind come out of the north, a great cloud and a fire infolding, and out of the midst thereof, as the colour of amber, - out of the midst of the fire, came the likeness of four living creatures, - and they had the likeness of a man:" - Now the *north* signifies *darkness*, for when the seed of Reason come to judge, and put in execution their judgment of spiritual doctrine from heaven, they do it by their own *dark spirit* which is called the *north*. But when Jesus was born, there came wise men from the *east* to Jerusalem, saying, "where is he that is born KING of the JEWS, for we have seen his Star in the *east*, and are come to worship him." (Mat. ii. 2.). Now the *east* signifies the *seed* and *spirit* of Faith, of which are the children of God; also the natural sun rises in the *east*, to the great delight and comfort of man; this also is the emblem of the *spiritual sun, i.e.* from Jesus comes the heavenly enlightening, and heavenly graces to sanctify and seal the soul as a preparation for the elect, to meet him in his royal personal glory at the last day; this also cometh out of the *east*: therefore Jesus said, "For as the lightening cometh out the *east*, and shineth even to the west, so shall also the coming of the SON of MAN be" (Mat. xxiv. 27.).

But of the *vision* of *Ezekiel*, he saw the *acts* of the cherubims (here in generation), in their power and glory under God's divine justice; and the cherubical nature is contrary to Faith, Faith being the divine nature of God; and those *four living creatures* that *come out* of the *cloud*, may well be said to have the *likeness of a man*, because they are *men* and *women* on this earth, actuated by the cherubical nature, *i.e.* fallen Reason, which is the devil: Therefore they bear the form of the *man* Adam, but not actuated by the pure nature of Faith, which was the *life* of Adam according to God's creation; and as the cherubim is transmuted into earth or flesh, and has somewhat of the woman's nature; therefore the cherubim hath *forced* himself, and became in nature *such* a creature as God did *not* create according to the *purity* of his creation, and as *so* the cherubim is become a monster or *beast* in creation, and has *four* (heads or) *faces*.

Also those *four* heads or *faces* are spoken of in respect to the *capacity* and *acts* of the cherubim; also there was *four living creatures*, and every one had *four* faces; the face of a *man*; the face of an *ox*; the face of a *lion*; and the face of an *eagle*; those are the four particular heads or *faces* that appear by the cherubims being *in generation*, by the power of God's creation: First he who has the face of a *man*, is the *child* who dieth in minority, and will be raised a cherubim to *glory*, and in a body of flesh and bone will *see* God, and as so have or will have the *face of a man*: Further *Moses* was an ANOINTED cherubim, as he was inspired under the attribute of God's divine justice with the wisdom of that pure law, and worship accordingly, as was all the prophets under the law, that were inspired by God himself under his divine justice; all going forth, acted by the power of God, and as so they all had the *face of a man*; (but they must be translated to, under the mercy of the Son); and this is the cherubim that also hath *the face of a man* (but on this earth *only*, for when they are glorified in heaven, they see God with a face of Faith:) *Secondly*, when there was no inspired prophet of God in the nations or world, *then* the *false* prophet and priest takes this power, and imitates the *true* prophet in his *god-*

like power of teaching the worship God required, and prophecies of things to come, but *all* in the *wrong*; this is of the cherubim, therefore *likened* to the head or *face of an ox*. Thirdly, the *lion's* had or *face* signifies the ruling power of nations which are princes and kings, for an earthly king is a cherubim, and the power and wisdom by which he rules is cherubical, given under the attribute of God's divine justice and so likened to the *face of a lion*. The *fourth* is the *eagle's* head or *face* signifying him or them, whose judgment is good, and his genius quick in the cherubical law (*i.e.* the law of Reason) so that when he sits to judge, his understanding is quick, like to the *eagle's* eye, to discern truth from error, and give good judgment: Those are the *four living creatures, that had the likeness of a man, i.e.* the *child that dies*, or HE that is *inspired of God* hath the face of a MAN; and the *ruling power* in the king's majesty, hath the face of a LION; and the *false prophet* and *priest* hath the face of an OX: and the *Levites or Lawyers*, who have knowledge in the law hath the face of an EAGLE.

Further, *every one* had those *four faces*, which is spoken to declare the *desire* or *capacity* of this cherubical nature, which is Reason: And as I said before, the created cherubim was born into this world a child, and appointed to live to manhood, yet many of his children afterward die in childhood, therefore when a child of Reason is born, it hath in itself the *capacity* of death, and many has and do die in their childhood, so will be raised glorious cherubims able to see the face of God in all eternity; and so as aforesaid, have the face of a *man*. Moreover, the child of Reason has life and may live to manhood, which many has and do; then the spirit of Reason become *active* in manhood, and this cherubical nature lusteth to be great, and to have an outshining earthly glorious appearance and ruling power; this desirous spirit of Reason is in most men, although many would seem to hide it; but they like and try to be great in what degree they can; and the spirit is the same if not worse, than that in the high cherubims, had they power to act: But the height of this cherubical power and glory is to manage and rule nations which is done by those *three* heads or cherubical faces, aforesaid: Now the ruling power of a king is very *great* and *wise*, and the law with the given priesthood is very great and *good*, and thus is JUDAH and LEVI in *ruling power*, therefore the *emblem* is the *lion* with great power, and the *eagle* with his quick eye in the *law*: and if the priest teaches that *worship* or *doctrine* that God will not *own* he is likened to the head of an *Ox*; for Aaron received the gold of the children of Israel and *fashioned* it with a *graving* tool after he had made it a molten *calf* (Exo. xxxii. 4.) so as to the *capacity* of this *cherubical Reason* it is such even in one man, by tuition, as to be mounted up to *either* of those cherubical heads or faces, *i.e.* a man may be made *king* or a great *lawyer*, or he may be made an high *priest*, or he may die a *child* and never live to manhood; and so *every one had four faces*: But when Reason lives to manhood, if the "*wheel within the wheel*," moves the man to justice and truth, that man may be said to do right according to *justice*: Therefore these are the great and powerful *acts* of the seed and nature of Reason that *Ezekiel* saw in his *vision*, which is the cherubims on this earth in generation, and this whole earth is given them to *act* on, and *rule* in, under the attribute of God's divine justice, and the whole cherubical wisdom and power is comprehended under those *four heads*, and judged according to the wisdom of the divine Majesty.

Here I would not have any one think, that I mean that none but the *seed* of *Reason* are kings, lawyers, or priests, for the *seed* of *Reason* are cherubims only; and, as I said before, the *seed* of *Faith* has the nature of Reason in them, and must be subject to the *law* of *Reason* and its given *Priesthood*; therefore *Moses* was inspired under the attribute of God's divine justice by the *way* or *through* the cherubims with the wisdom or that *pure law* God created the cherubim under, and also how to *rule* the rebellious cherubical nature on this earth; so *Moses* was an *anointed* cherubim, and *Moses* was a *king* and a *lawyer*, (Deut. xxxiii. 4, 5.) "Moses commanded us a *law* even the *inheritance* of the Congregation of *Jacob*, and *he* was a *king* in *Jeshuran*, when the heads of the people and the tribes of *Israel* were gathered together." *David*, who was also "a man after God's own heart," was also a king; but the law and wisdom to rule the people is all cherubical and under the attribute of God's divine justice; because the cherubim brought the law into this world. Also *Aaron* was a *priest*; and *Ezekiel* and others administered the *worship and offerings* under the law, that God required to *stay* his justice, that kings and people may enjoy the good things of this earth in peace and plenty as the Lord promised by the man *Moses*; but *by the law no man can be saved*, therefore all good *kings* of the *seed of Faith*, and *lawyers* and *priests* was translated to, under the *mercy of the Son*.

Again, (Ezek. i. 7,) "And their feet were straight feet, and the sole of their feet was like the sole of a calf's foot," *i.e.* the *calves* or cloven *foot*, signifies the cherubim had *broke* the pure law he was created under, for which cause he was *cast down* from heaven, and could no longer stand there on the *feet* of created purity; for by his breaking the law he broke his *footing* in heaven on which he *stood*, as thereby his *feet* were split asunder, *i.e.* he could no longer *stand in heaven*, but was cast down from the presence of God, and became *Man* here, in generation, to wander in the *state* of *forgetfulness* like unto a *beast* with a *split hoof-foot*; and is a true *token* that the cherubical nature of *Reason*, did eternally break the law in heaven, as well as the *mark* set on *old Cain* for his wicked acts. Further, the *split hoof* on which they *stand* on this earth, signifies that God, by his almighty power, will raise those that die in childhood to *glory*, and suffer those that live to manhood, to go their way according to his infinite *justice*, yet all from this cherubical nature; therefore the *footing*, on which they *stand* on this earth, is *split* in the *eye* of the divine MAJESTY; for as the cherubim was created *out* from chaos by the LORD GOD of HEAVEN, and he broke the law he was created under, then his dark nature was *cast down* from heaven as a *whirlwind*, and himself *infolding* in it with the *fiery cloud* of justice, and was dissolved into generation under justice; and from thence *came out* the cherubical *appearance as the colour of amber*, because it was fell from its created purity and glory, and *was* under justice: "and they sparkled like the colour of burnished brass;" this is relative to the cherubical outward appearance and power.

"And every one had *four wings*." Those *wings* is the *power* of *action* of the cherubical nature: "*Two wings* of every one were *joined* one to another, and two *covered* their bodies." Those *wings* that were *joined together* are, in the *first* place, *joined* by the law (*i.e.* the *law* of Reason;) "You shall love God above all, and your neighbour as yourself;" and if men would but observe this, they may see how we are bound or *joined* in love and duty to each other by, and according to, the law of Reason: also they are *joined* together by the *power* of generation, therefore the child is included, as all are children before they come to manhood; and without the child, this cherubical power must cease. And when the sovereign ruling power of a *king*, and the *law*, and the *priesthood* all *join* together in the good rule of the people; and the people *love* and *help* each other and their sovereign also, that nation will FLOURISH and make a glorious appearance.

Also those *two wings* that *cover* their bodies is *self-cunning*, and *private acts* on self-serving *subtil* occasions, and may think they can do *private* evil, and no one know it but themselves; and the *use* of those *wings* is, that no one should know it but themselves; for they would seem to act *so*, as to have a good name among men in the run of the world; yet their will is to *rise* from one degree of cherubical greatness to another; and *justice*, humanity, and religious virtues are trodden under foot. The outward *word* and *shew* is retained; as if those go, the cherubim will lose part of his *glory* and *covering*; and from this people of one mind enter into the *act* of rebellion, and so form a new government, law, and priesthood; and those *wings* greatly work in excuses, to *cover* their body, *i.e.* the *appearance* of their actions. But *under* those *wings* was *the hands of a man, i.e.* the *Hand* of *justice* on every one that live to manhood; and the *internal angel* in justice will condemn them in their excuses: Also a child being of Reason has those acts in childhood, but dying a child, the *internal angel* in justice doth not take place in the soul, so is not charged with the law; therefore the *Hand* of God is on *him*, to raise him a glorious cherubim even under that covenant.

"And the *appearance* of the living creatures was like the *burning coals of fire*," *i.e.* the *law* is written in this cherubical nature, and the internal angel in justice *is* in the soul to *watch* over the law, that when a man is wicked, and delights in his wickedness, this angel in justice will be as *a coal of fire* to burn him up in his own wrath. But if a man hearken to the voice of *truth* and justice that will become *as a coal of fire* to instruct him in the truth of the law; and that man's *ways* and *judgment* will be as *burning lamps* in the light of the law, and comes forth *like lightening* which is the light of that law. And if a set of people regard not God or man, yet when there is a *command* or *judgment* by God's permission, it comes *like lightening*, and must be obeyed, otherwise, in some degree, they will be *consumed.* Such great power is given to the cherubims under *divine justice.*

"And the living creatures *ran and returned as a flash of lightening,*" *i.e.* when Reason is mistaken in his intent and obliged to make a quick return.

"And the wheels and their work was *like the colour of a beryl.*" This is spoken according to the *pure* act of God's creation, for the wheel is the *life* of the creature, and in that *life* is the law, *pure* as God created it. And "the *wheel* within the wheel," is what moves the *soul* to act, as when any desire is greatly conceived *within*, that desire will move the soul to accomplish any conceived art or thing so desired. Also on any spiritual message, rule, doctrine, or judgment that *was* under the law external, or is *now* under the law internal, if God *moves* this internal and spiritual *wheel* for the man to go forth and act *thus*, that man is right, and God will own the *act*; but if this *wheel* is *moved* by the proud emulative spirit of Reason for the man to go forth and attempt to act those things, then God will never own the act, but to the condemnation of the man.

Again, "As for their *rings* they were so *high* they were *dreadful*, and their rings were full of *eyes round about* them four," (v. 18.) *Now*, as I said before, the whole cherubical powers are included under those *four* heads according to their *capacity* or desire; and those *Rings* are *justice*, therefore let the *cherubim* mount *up* ever so *high* in his imagination, worldly greatness, *high* power of life, or great wisdom of Reason, which is *dreadful* to some other men, the *wheel of Reason, i.e.* his *life* is mounted up against him. And in that life is the *law* which is over against *them*, and they have their *rings* or spheres to move or act in: and their *rings* are *full of eyes* round and about them, *i.e.* the *internal angel* in justice that strictly *watches* them, therefore Reason with all his art and *cunning* never can get out of the ring or scope of justice, and anon will find himself intirely surrounded with justice.

Further, "Whithersoever the spirit was to *go* they *went*, thither was the spirit to *go*, and the wheels was lifted up over against them, for the spirit of the living creature was in the *wheels*." (v. 20.) *i.e.* when the cherubical spirit has its *own* will, it will desire and make choice of its *own* evil, so with pleasure *go* or ride hastily into it, let him flatter himself in what he will to the contrary: Also when one mighty nation is loosed by the angel in justice to *go* forth and war against another nation and overpower it, because it is a wicked people; and thus the cherubims do the will of God according to his divine justice. Further, this *victorious* cherubim may exercise his authority too far in *cruelty* over the vanquished, and so incur God's displeasure; then he himself will be visited in, and according to God's justice, in his turn. This the scripture is full to prove, for *Babylon* was destroyed for their *cruelties* to *Juda* and *Jerusalem*, (Jer. xxv. 12, &c.) so the cherubical spirit, which is Reason, is sure to *go* to its own condemnation, for *thither is the spirit to go*, and the cherubim will have pleasure in *acting* to his *own* condemnation, for all his great wisdom in his shifts, turns, and excuses; as by his excuses he will be condemned, by the internal angel in justice, for the *spirit*, which is the life, is in the *wheel, i.e.* Reason, and in that life is the law; and the *wheel* within the wheel is that which moves the soul to go forth and act.

Also it is written, "when those went, those went; and when those stood, those stood," *i.e.* when the great cherubical powers go forth to war, make new decrees, or put any judgment in execution that they have conceived, then this power moves and *goes* their way; and when they are sick of their actions, or stopt by the *internal angel* in justice, then they *stand*. This is not only done in public but in the private *chambers* in the soul of *man*; for often-times *man* will be *lifted up* in the spirit of imagination above the earth in what he intends to do; but the power of the law, justice, &c. is *lifted up* over against him, for where one *is* there the other also *is*, to *watch*, as this is all of one man.

Also, "The firmament was as the colour of the terrible crystal stretched forth over their heads above," *i.e.* GOD in his THRONE in reference to his divine justice, can instantly know all the acts of Reason; (which is the cherubim) by his *internal angel* in justice in the soul of man: Further, when God is graciously pleased he can look through his whole creation, *i.e.* through heaven, earth, angels, and men, and know their thoughts and desires, therefore it is a *crystal* to God; also when the eye of justice comes to the soul of men, then *they* will find it a *terrible crystal* indeed; but men must be arraigned by the attribute of divine *justice* before they can be *born* or translated to divine MERCY.

Therefore when those cherubims went, "Ezekiel heard the noise of their wings, as the noise of great waters, as the voice of the Almighty, the voice of speech as the noise of an *Host*," *i.e.* when the mighty cherubical powers go forth to conquer, captivate, and rule over, their motion is as the *noise of great water*; and the command of the grand cherubim must be obeyed as the voice of the ALMIGHTY. Also in their going forth to conquer, they do the will of God relative to his divine justice, therefore it may well be called the voice *of speech like the noise of an Host*.

"And there was *a voice from the firmament* that was over their heads, when they had stood and let down their wings," *i.e.* the *voice* of justice in secret speaking from heaven to the cherubims: *First*, to stop their proceedings. *Secondly*, after the heat and power of action, justice will speak condemnation to the soul for *unjust* and *wild* acts; and this very thing is to be found in all men. And after Ezekiel did see the power and acts of the cherubims, with all their desire and glory here in this world, "he saw above the firmament the likeness of the

THRONE of GOD, and he saw the appearance of a *man* above upon it," which was GOD himself. "And he saw the appearance and likeness of the glory of the LORD, and fell upon his face, and heard the voice of one that speak," which was God himself to give him inspiration under the attribute of his divine justice by the way, or through the cherubims, with the wisdom of the cherubical law, and the obedience and worship God required under that law as aforesaid.

CHAP. XII

AGAIN, *Ezekiel* saw this vision when Israel was in captivity, and the cherubical power *loosed* to act according to its own *Wild* nature; for when he was told of the iniquity of the house of Israel, and Juda, saying, "the Lord hath *forsaken the earth,* and *the Lord seeeth not,*" (ix. 9.) and this captivity was for their disobedience to the commands of God, then was he sent to call to, and prophecy against them, (see ii. 9.) "And when I looked behold an hand was sent unto me, and lo, a *role* of a book was therein." This role of a book was his inspiration, with the law of Moses, *i.e.* the cherubical *law* and worship God required in that Priesthood under the law. Also his prophecy against *Israel* and *Juda* for their idolatry and abomination; and other nations for their wickedness; therefore the *roll* was spread, and there was written therein, *lamentations, mourning, and woe, i.e.* what would come to pass according to *Ezekiel's prophecy*; and he was commanded to "eat this roll and go and speak to the house of Israel; then he eat it, and it was in his mouth as honey for sweetness," *i.e.* he was inspired with the *way* and will of God under the covenant of the *law*, and so was removed from wandering in the letter, unto the *light* and *love* of God, which is very *sweet*; but being under the attribute of divine *justice*, and there to go forth and prophecy for evil to come upon men, nations, &c. that is *bitter*.

And Ezekiel again, "heard the *noise of the wings* of the living creatures that touched one another, and the noise of the wheels over against them, and the noise of a great rushing," *i.e.* the acts of the cherubims as aforesaid; for in all the hurrying emulated acts of life that the cherubims delight in, there doth go with them their own witness to their utter condemnation. Again, he said, "so the spirit lifted me up and took me away, and I went in bitterness, in the heat of my spirit; but the hand of the Lord was strong upon me," (iii. 13, 14.) Hence it is clear that those cherubims was the seed and spirit of Reason in *act* here upon this earth. Also *Ezekiel* was sent, under GOD's divine justice, to speak and prophecy to those people in *bitterness*, that God's wrath should come upon them, except they obey the *word* of God by his mouth. This is *bitterness* to a meek spirited man.

Further, "*Ezekiel saw six men* that came from the way of the higher gate – and every man a slaughter weapon in his hand, and one man among them clothed in linen, with a writer's ink horn by his side." (ix. 2.) Those men that *Ezekiel* saw in similitude, was *men* that was inspired by or under the attribute of God's divine justice, and sent unto *Israel* before *Ezekiel's* time. And *the man with the writer's ink-horn*, was the *man Moses* who gave forth and did *write* the law and the worship God required according to the law under his divine justice;) the same, in consequence, as if God had gave it forth in his ROYAL PERSON: Also "those men went in and stood beside the *brazen altar*, and the GLORY of the GOD of *Israel* was gone up from the *cherub*," *i.e.* when those men was living, some of the house of *Israel* did offer the *true* burnt offering according to *Moses*, who was the *anointed cherubim* by inspiration, with the wisdom of the cherubical law to its *truth*: And the *internal angel* in justice in the soul of man (that turns every way to keep the way of the tree of life) is a *cherubim* also, and as pure as the attribute of God's divine *justice*, and can commune with God relative thereto, (as oft before written); therefore the GLORY of the LORD is sure to *go up* from this *cherub* either to *excuse* or *accuse* Men according to the law.

"And the *man* was called to, with the *writer's ink-horn*; and the Lord said unto him, go through the midst of the city, through the midst of Jerusalem, and set a mark upon them that *sigh* and *cry* for all the abominations." This was done by Moses when he wrote the law, &c. as aforesaid; and them who was obedient to the *law* and *worship* of *Moses* was spared, according to God's *justice*, which was the *mark set* on them who *mourned* for the abominations of Israel. Hence the *man* clothed with linen, with a *writer's ink-horn,* was *Moses* who declared and *wrote* the law, worship, burnt-offerings, and incense God required, thereby setting a *mark* upon all people who would be obedient when there came a *Messenger* of God; and *this man* who first went through the *city* or people, was *Moses* as a *law-giver.*

"And to the others he said, in mine hearing, go ye after him through the CITY and smite; let not your eye spare, neither have ye pity," (ix. 5.) Those *men* as Ezekiel saw in vision, was the *Messengers* of GOD in the covenant of the law, under the attribute of divine justice, before *Ezekiel's time*; and those *slaughter weapons* they had, was the *power* of God in their *declaration* and *prophecy* of *evil to come* upon all rebellious and disobedient people; like as *Moses* in his time, by his god-like power and declaration caused many men to die. *Elijah* also did the same by his godlike power and declaration, which was but *little* in comparison to what would come to pass, by the prophecy of those *six men with slaughter weapons* in, and according to God's divine justice on all *wicked, disobedient, and idolatrous people.*

"And those six men was to *begin at the sanctuary* and slay all, both old and young, who had not the *mark* set on them," (ix. 6.) "And while they were slaying them, and I was left, that I fell on my face and cried, *Ah!* LORD GOD, *wilt thou destroy all the residue of Israel."* (ix. 8.) This *Ezekiel* saw in his vision, and according to his INSPIRATION under the attribute of divine justice; and by the prophecy of those before him, those things had come to pass by sword, famine, and captivity, so that Israel and Juda was almost desolate. And further, they *out* of captivity, as well as those *in*, had lost the *true knowledge* of the law and worship of God, except a *few* who patiently waited the Lord's *will*, to send his *Messengers* for their spiritual and natural relief; and for those *few*, Israel was always preserved from being intirely *scattered*, until the coming of CHRIST; *also* the children of Israel was *then* in that degenerate state to be cut off according to God's justice, and the prophecy of those before; and also what Ezekiel *must* declare and prophecy, only, as above, *some* would *believe* and obey him according to the *mark set.*

Therefore Ezekiel cried unto the Lord, in his pouring out his fury upon *Jerusalem*, not to have the residue of Israel destroyed; and he was told, "the iniquity of the house of *Israel* and *Juda* was very great, and the *land full of blood*, but I will recompence their *way* upon their *head*," (ix. 10.) So he must declare and prophecy against the people, nations, &c. he being under the law. "And the man *clothed with linen*, with the ink-horn by his side, reported the matter saying, I have done as thou has commanded me," (ix. 11.) This man was *Moses* as aforesaid, inspired by God himself, and to *write, act,* and *prophecy* as I have already written, and he declared the just JUDGMENTS of GOD, and prophecied of the blessings that would follow them that obeyed his commandments from God; and also of the curses that should come upon all disobedient people: And *Moses greatly communed with God* relative to the law and the people; and God owned the *acts* of Moses, and said, "He is faithful in all mine house;" and as so Moses *reported the matter unto God.* And further, Moses is buried *in* the soul of man, and *report the matter* at this day; then *Ezekiel* being inspired in the covenant of the law under the attribute of God's divine justice, he saw the power of God in that covenant from the man Moses even unto his day, and himself in the true line of that prophecy.

"And *Ezekiel* again saw the *likeness of the throne* of God above the head of the cherubims." Here he saw the cherubims according to God's inspiration of that law and Priesthood. And here *the man clothed with linen* was said to, "Go, in between the wheels even under the *cherub*, and fill they hand with coals of fire from between the cherubims, and scatter them over the CITY." *i.e. Moses* was inspired with the wisdom of that pure law God gave the cherubim in his glorious creation; for the cherubim was created in reference to divine justice, and there went such a *quality* from God of his justice, through the act of his creation, that when the cherubim came forth into life, in him became a quantity sufficient as when he break the law to *cast him down*, and there for ever keep him under *justice*, let him go where he will, and do what he will; for although he broke the *pure law*, he never could break the *justice* of that law, as that remains entirely *pure as created*, in the *soul of man* to this day, (*i.e.* the *internal angel*, or *Moses buried*.) And as Moses was inspired by GOD under the attribute of his *divine justice*, by the *way* or *through the cherubim, he* bringing this law into this world, this was *his filling his hand with coals of fire, and scattering it over the city,* or people.

Also God *communed* with *Moses* from between the *two cherubims*, in what he gave him in commandment unto the children of *Israel*. And when *Moses uttered the law*, there was in the spirit of Reason the law *internal*, and the *justice* of that law, (there it is that Reason is *compelled* to take *Moses*, not only as by God's creation but by God's command); and this law *acted* on the bodies and souls of men, that when Man acted contrary to the commands of *Moses*, he caused the earth to open and *swallow them up*; also *fire came and consumed them*, (Num. xvi. 35.) "There came out fire from the LORD and *consumed* the two hundred and fifty men that offered *incense*:" This is the *fire* and *wrath* of God's justice *without Man*; and there is the same *fire* and *wrath* of God's justice *within Man;* and it will, in like manner, *swallow* and *burn* him up. This *internal angel* in justice, always *would* and *will* bear witness to the acts of *Moses* according to God's command, and every man will be his *own witness* to his *own condemnation*; for the declaration of Moses worked on the souls of men, and *searched the reins and hearts*, and doth to this day; and brought fiery wrath and judgment out of the soul, that many men has murmured and died in *wrath*; and the *seed* of Reason would have got clear of Moses if possible they could, but they never *was* nor *will* be able to do that; therefore Moses's *hand was full of fire, i.e.* the *justice* of the law; and this justice is *in* the soul of man; *i.e.* between the *wheels* under the *cherub* where *Moses went in* by his declaration, for the *wheels* is the *life* of the cherubims; and as the *law* rules the life, so *justice* rules the law: So when Moses executed justice by God's power in Israel's camp, the internal angel, in justice in the soul of man, bore witness to the just judgments of God, which is bringing *coals of fire* out of the soul of man. This is the true meaning of *Ezekiel* seeing, in vision, *the man clothed with linen, going between the wheels under the* CHERUB, *and filling his hands with coals of fire.*

"Now the cherubims stood on the right side of the house when the man went in, and the cloud filled the inner court," (x. 3.) *i.e.* when *Moses* went into the *mount* to receive his instructions of God in the law (by the *way* or through the cherubim) and bringing it into this world; so any man when he communes with God, he is in the *inner court*; and also Moses went into the tabernacle to commune with God, from off the mercy-seat from between the *two cherubims*, and the cloud descended, (see Exo. xxxiii. 9.) "And it came to pass when Moses entered into the tabernacle, the LORD talked with Moses." Also it is written, "And the glory of the Lord went up from the *cherub.*" *Note,* The *Lord* was (then) there himself; and *Moses* was the *angel* of the covenant of the law, and the *anointed cherubim*; and the *internal angel* in justice is a *cherub*; for he is *of* the law, therefore the *truth* and *glory* of the Lord will go up from those *cherubims*: But all those great and glorious things were to shew forth the glory of God's creating the angel or cherubim, and the *pure law* he created him under; yet all the *ceremonial* worship, *offerings*, and *incense* of the *law* was but cherubical, *i.e.* the incense of Reason, for by it only, *no one could be saved*; yet it then must be done to *stay* God's divine justice, and glorify the *name* and *power* of the God of Israel. And if they had obeyed Moses's commands, there would not have been such another *kingdom* in the *world* for wisdom, power, and glory; and it would have been more pleasing in the sight of GOD for Reason to obey Moses, to enjoy the good things of this world than to have their peace taken away, as must be to all disobedient people according to God's justice – so great *was* the law external, and *is now* the law internal.

And it is written, "The sound of the cherubims wings was heard even to the utter court, as the voice of the ALMIGHTY when he speaketh," (Ezek. x. 5.). This was when Moses gave forth the pure law to the cherubical nature, which was soon heard throughout the camp of Israel, and acted on the spirit and life of the people, as if the *Almighty* speak; for the law is, "You shall love God above all and your neighbour as yourself." This binds their wings (*i.e.* their action) together; and if Moses's commands is disobeyed, the act of justice takes place which caused great outcries in Israel: also from Israel this *pure law* and *worship* accordingly was heard of by other nations, and wherever it was heard the internal angel in justice would witness to it; so that people never could get away – for *Moses* who was the anointed CHERUBIM, and *others* who acted according to his command, the sound of their wings may be said to be heard in great part of the world; but the *internal angel* in justice will witness to the divine justice of God *all over the world*.

Moreover *Moses* was inspired with such great wisdom in the law under justice, that he could give just judgment between the cherubims, which often-times come like *fire*, and had power to *call vengeance from heaven* to come and destroy the disobedient; and had the *power of prayer* to stay God's justice on those who would turn to their *obedience*. And the internal angel in justice in the soul of man, will be to the man his own witness to his own condemnation, which is as *coals of fire* in the soul; and against the voice of the living *Messenger* that man will utter cursing expressions, full of *fiery wrath*, which is taking *coals of fire* from out of the soul of man, even under the cherub. This cherub is the *internal angel* in justice, that seals the soul under justice, unto wrath, from whence those fiery acts and expressions proceed; this thing was done in the days of Moses, as well as now.

Again, under the wings of the cherubims was the form of a man's hand, *i.e.* the internal angel in justice when the cherubim comes to manhood, as I said before: "And one *cherub* stretched forth his hand and took fire from between the two cherubims, and put it into the hands of him clothed with linen." This was the *internal angel* in justice in the soul of man, witnessing to Moses's declaration, therefore Moses took fire from the spirit in man, and *scattered it over the city,* which was judgment on their *own heads*: - *Ezekiel,* in this *second* visional sight, saw the cherubims in *act,* according to the law and days of Moses, which was commanded of God, and if they were disobedient to the offerings, rules, and worship according to the law, they were visited with present justice. *Note* – (as aforesaid) there is no cherubims to be found but in this world, either in active life or in the sleep of death; and those cherubims are the seed and spirit of Reason unto whom the law of Reason, or cherubical law, was given, and all under divine justice.

"And their whole bodies, and their backs, and their hands, and their wings, and the wheels, were full of eyes round about, even the wheels that they four had," *i.e.* the life and acts of men and women under the attribute of divine justice; and those eyes is the watchful eye of justice that strictly doth watch this cherubical law and nature: So *Ezekiel* being inspired after the manner as was *Moses, saw* and *knew* the will of God in the *law,* and the worship God required in the law, and the *all powerful justice* of God that was over mortal man, ready to be executed; and he must go forth and *declare* and *prophecy* to the people according to his inspiration, which was his message: Yea, as aforesaid, the *life* of the cherubim is in the *wheel,* and in that life is the *law,* and *justice rules* the law.

Yea, *Ezekiel* saith, "As for the wheels, it was cried to them in my hearing, O WHEEL!" (x. 13.) *i.e.* Wo! to the life of man that would not be obedient to the law and worship God required. But more so, when no life can be translated from under *justice* to, under the *mercy* of the SON: Also (ver. 14.) "Every one had *four faces,* the *first* face was the face of a CHERUB, the *second* face was the face of a MAN; and the *third* the face of a LION; and the *fourth* the face of an EAGLE." This was a visional sight of the cherubims in and according to the law and ordinances of God, though notwithstanding the cherubical nature is *capable* to become either of those four *heads or faces*; but there is a great difference between a *man* becoming one of those faces by *self-wisdom* than being placed there by the *inspiration and power of God*.

Note. The *first face* was the face of a *cherub, i.e.* the CHILD that dies in minority, so will be raised a cherubim to glory, and be able to see the *face* of GOD when he is a glorious cherubim.

The *second* was the *face of a man, i.e.* him who hath the PROPHETICAL power to order and rule the Priesthood and worship according to the law, as *Moses did*, being inspired by God himself under the attribute of divine justice.

Further, as *Moses saw* the face of God, and *communed* with God, and acted in the power of GOD, so Moses had *the face of a man.* Likewise all others who came after him, that *communed* with God (either in person or spirit) and acted in the power of God, had this *face of a man*; but this was under *justice* as then *he* was the God of justice. But when God *communed* with any of those *great men* relative to the *mercy* of the SON, by which they prophecied of God's becoming *a Son to redeem*, it was far above the power of the *internal angel* in the soul of man, so of consequence above the cherubical inspiration; therefore all the *elect* (at the hour of death) were translated, to under the *mercy* of the SON, to be raised to glory *in* and according to the covenant of GRACE: But the *eye of God* is on the cherub to raise him to glory *in* and according to the *first* covenant (*i.e.* of the law or of angels) as when the cherubim dies in childhood, the internal angel in justice takes not place in the soul, so is not charged with the law, therefore *he* will be raised a glorious cherubim by the merciful power of God, even under that covenant; and not be translated to, under the *mercy of the Son*, or *second* covenant, as that belongs *only* to the *seed of Faith, i.e.* the SONS of GOD.

The *third* that *Ezekiel* saw was *the face of a Lion,* this is the Kingly ruling power of the *tribe* of JUDA.

And the *fourth* face was *the face of an eagle, i.e.* the LEVITICAL power and judgment in the law: Now this is a true sight of the cherubims, according to the will and ordination of God; but when *he* saw the cherubims according to their own *wild* nature, (as in chap. first,) then there is the *false prophet and priest* there likened to the face of an *ox.*

Therefore, According to the *true act* of the cherubims under the law and Priesthood it is written (x. 20.) "This is the living creature that I saw *under* the God of *Israel* by the *river Chebar*, and I *know* they were the *Cherubims*," this was men and women in *act under the law, according to the days of Moses*: But *Israel and Judah* had "forsaken the statutes of the Lord, and *done* after the *manner* of the Heathen round about;" and said "the Lord *seeeth us not*, the Lord hath *forsaken* the earth; and had seen *vain* vision and spoken lying divination, whereas ye say *the Lord saith it*, albeit I have not spoken." (xiii. 7.) This is too much done at *this day*; therefore the wicked imagination of some men is *cloaked* with the scriptures and dedicated to God as a sanction to their wickedness: And as aforesaid *Ezekiel* saw the great abominations of Israel *and the streets of the city filled with the slain;* now the *city* is the people, and the *streets* the goings on of the people, and Ezekiel *saw* all was *slain* according to God's justice: Then he was told "a remnant should be saved," adding, "I will give *them one heart*, and I will put a *new spirit in you*, and I will take the stony heart out of *their* flesh, and will give *them* an heart of flesh; that *they* may walk in my statutes, and keep mine ordinances, and do them, and *they* shall be my people and I will be *their* GOD." (xi. 19, 20.) But *them* that would do their own will and follow their abomination, was left out and prophecied against.

"Then did the *cherubims* lift up their wings and the wheels beside them, and the glory of the GOD of ISRAEL was over them above," (v. 22.) *i.e.* those people of *Israel* that did obey the word of God by *Ezekiel*, and *returned* to their worship, as commanded by Moses; and *offer the true burnt offering and incense,* (which signifies no more than the *prayer* or *incense* of Reason) *i.e.* its obedience; and that they may know God was the author of their Inheritance, and the good they posses; having power to drive them out, and take away their *peace* for their abominations; so here the cherubims was in *true act, then* the glory of the God of Israel was *over* and *above* them for their preservation: Hence earthly ruling powers, wisdom, and arts, is cherubical (*i.e.* the wisdom of Reason) and men must be *translated* or *born* to the *powers* of *divine Faith* to enter the *glorious kingdom of Heaven.*

CHAP. XIII

DANIEL the prophet, of the captivity of Judah, after he had interpreted the dreams of the kings of Babylon, was visit himself by the power of God, with VISION and *Dream* that he might prophecy of more troubles yet to come in the time of the law, and not only so, but also of great troubles to come at the beginning or bringing in of the GOSPEL.

So *Daniel* spake, "I saw a *vision* by *night*, and behold the four winds of the heaven strove upon the Sea." (chap. vii.) This *heaven* is the heaven of Reason, and those *winds* that strive, if of man for that heaven: As, *first* when there is a *desire* conceived in the soul to attain such kingdoms and rule of people: *Secondly*, the *art* how to put this into execution: *Thirdly*, to *gather* or *rule* the power by which it is done; and *fourthly*, their *self-satisfaction* in those acts; as in those things there is a *priestly* ruling power which they *will have* to their own liking, therefore the *priest* justifies their acts, otherwise they would be divided amongst themselves: And this *sea* that *Daniel* saw in his vision, is the *waters of* Reason, *i.e.* in the soul of man; scripture also calls it *the great river Euphrates* (and is in the land of Nod, *i.e.* forgetfulness) wherein dwells the *wisdom* and all the *vain glory* of Reason, with all their *spiritual hope* of future happiness.

"And four great beasts came up from the sea diverse one from the other." Those beasts are kings or *monarchies*, which are cherubims; "the *first* like a LION and had *Eagles* wings, and he stood on his feet as a *man*, and a man's heart was given to it."

"The *second* like to a BEAR, and it had ribs in the mouth, between the teeth of it, and they said thus "unto it, *arise* and devour much flesh."

"The *third* like a LEOPARD, and had on his back *four* wings of a fowl, also four heads, and dominion was given to it."

"The *fourth* was diverse from all the beasts before it." (Those four monarchies was in the time of the *law*, and was cherubims).

Now the *first beast* or cherubim was like a *Lion, i.e.* relative to the kingly properties he was possessed with, whereby he did, with wisdom, rule the people; and his *Eagles wings* signifies that he understood something of the law, and observed it to the best of his power in the rule of the people, (for whether of *Israel* or another country, the law is written in the cherubical nature through the whole world) therefore it is written *he stood like a man*, and a *man's heart* was given to it: And the *second* like to a *Bear, i.e.* one that was given up to his own wild cherubical nature, that will cut off and destroy before him, to make good his *conceived* intent like a powerful Bear; the *ribs in his mouth* signify he was a *great* destroyer of men, by his *war* and *actions*, therefore it was said, *arise, devour much flesh*: And the *third* like a *Leopard, i.e.* for his artful insinuations, to gain the people by his great promise of liberty they should enjoy under him; and the *four wings of a fowl on his back*, is his quick and ingenious acts of self wisdom, for their intent is to grant people their desire, in order to strengthen government, or a kind expostulation why it could not be done, while at the same time wishing it could; this appears as white spots in his *Rule*; and he also had *four heads, i.e.* four kingdoms to rule over; therefore it is written *dominion was given to it.*

Moreover, those great powers was raised up *under* God's divine justice to do the will of God *according* to his justice, *i.e.* to drive, destroy, and take peace from each other for wicked and abominable acts in the sight of God. But I would not have men think that those *strivings on the sea* or waters of Reason is in kings alone, for in almost every individual is found the *strivings* of Reason for its kingdom; as when Reason is desirous of any *thing, that* is its Heaven, and the Reason *in* man will strive for *this*, as a king doth to get or maintain a THRONE; and when the spirit of fear doth possess the soul, they will greatly murmur, and when they lose, or are likely to lose, what they enjoy, they murmur as much as doth a king to lose his throne; also Reason in man finds in himself a *Priest* to justify him; and this lying *Priest* is the spirit of Reason, whereby men excuse themselves either to get, or maintain, their heaven of Reason; and which lying *Priest* is more hearkened to, than is the voice of God by his *Messenger*, but, as I said before and do now (let men get from it if they can) the *internal angel* in justice will condemn them in their excuses.

"After this *Daniel* saw in the night *visions*, and behold a *fourth Beast* dreadful and terrible, with iron teeth it devoured and brake to pieces, and stamped the residue with his feet, and it was diverse from all the beasts before it, and it had *ten* HORNS." This *fourth Beast* was the Roman powers or emperor, for they not only conquered and subdued *Israel* and *Judea*, but other countries round about: And *this beast was diverse from all the beasts before it*, i.e. this beast made war with JESUS and his *Saints*, but none of the others did; indeed others made war with Israel and Judah who professed the name of the LORD; but this fourth beast warred against them who profess the name of JESUS, because the *seat* or principle of persecution was under the Roman power.

And it had ten horns. Now the scripture speaking of beasts with a number of heads, signifies an emperor who rules over as many kingdoms; also those *ten horns* are *ten kings*; and as I have said, there is kings of the earth, and kings of the dark spirit, and those *ten horns* are kings of the dark spirit, *i.e. priests* or *people* who might think themselves wise enough to conduct people to heaven by their doctrine; and two ways men go forth to *write* or *teach, i.e.,* by *immediate inspiration* by God himself from his glorious THRONE; and by the dark emulative *spirit of Reason* in the soul of man, by which man sends himself: Now those two spirits never can agree, as one is of *light* and *life*, and the other of *death* and *darkness*; and this spirit of darkness in the *soul* will speak motional voices in *man*, and persuade himself he is of God, and that he is doing God service; yea, those are in the sight of God *dark* spiritual kings, and all are seeking a kingdom, *i.e.* a congregation of people to teach and rule over.

Also those *ten horns* was *ten* such men that had power in the *Roman empire* (and was over many people) that would persecute the saints, but this could not be done without the consent of the emperor or his governor, whom he placed as his representative in a distant kingdom; so when the people got the *grant* to persecute the Saints, they acted as *kings* in that persecution; but when they had put the SAINTS to death their power ended, for they had no kingdoms or people of their own, but what was subject to the *Roman power*, therefore John's Revelation saith, "the *ten horns* which thou sawest are *ten Kings* which have received no kingdom as yet, but receive power, *as kings, one hour* with the beast." (xvii. 12.) So the *Jews* was under the *Roman power*, and their will was to crucify JESUS, but they could not until the Roman Governor gave him up to them, then they crucified him, acting according to their own dark and wicked spirit, and this is receiving power *with* or of the *beast* as kings *one hour*.

Yea, those *ten horns* are kings of the *dark spirit*, and was spoken (as ten) relative to the *ten* persecutions, and those kings did greatly lust for natural kingdoms of their own, that they might pour out their wrath on the saints *as* dark spiritual kings: Further (Rev. xvii. 13.) "those have all one mind, and shall give their strength and power unto the beast," *i.e.* they had *one mind* to persecute the saints, and the beast gave them power so to do, so they gave all *honour, praise, and power* unto the beast for giving them power to make war, and persecute the LAMB and his SAINTS: As when *Pilate* sought to release Jesus he said unto the *Jews*, "Shall I crucify your king?" the chief *priest* answered, "We have no king but Caesar," so gave all honor and *power to Caesar*, to receive power as kings for *one hour* to put to death on a religious account; and in this they worshipped the beast, or his image, *i.e.* his power. And sometimes great kings have been perswaded to give, promise, or sign a decree, that artful people taking advantage to satisfy their wrathful desire, that kings have repented, as did *Herod* and *Darius the Mede*, the one caused Daniel to be put in the lion's den, and the other John the Baptist to be beheaded.

And "*Daniel* considered the *horns*, and behold there came up among them another *little horn*, before whom there were *three* of the *first horns* plucked up by the root, and behold in this *horn* were eyes like the eyes of a man, and a mouth speaking great things;" this *little horn* was a man of eloquence and power in the Roman empire, that could expostulate to the emperor that the saints were an innocent people, and patiently bore their trouble, even to the wounding of sober men, and they preached repentance and forgiveness of sins: This being applied *cooly* to the soul of a man, in God's time, man must confess the necessity thereof; this is the *little horn* wherein were eyes like a man, so prevailed with the *emperor* to stop persecution, and in time to transform themselves into the *apostolical* letter or declaration, then all the kingly power or horns of persecution to those professing the name of JESUS, were *plucked up by the Root*.

Again, Having transformed themselves into the apostolical letter; they sometime after began to usurp the power and rule thereof, and *form* according to their own imagination (on the *dead* or *bare letter*) what must be done to have salvation; and they took the *seat* and *power* of the *Apostles*, and would practice the act to pardon, purge, and absolve sin; and this is the *mouth in the little horn that spake great things*: But even this is no less in the eyes of the divine Majesty then to murder and take possession; (though some men may not *intend* any such thing; but to stop persecution and search into it, that people may be benefited by it if possible). But after this *spirit*, in persecution of saints, was stopt, it then transforming itself into the apostles letter, persecuted *people* that would not believe according to the rules their persecuting power prescribed; thus they killed the apostles and righteous men, took possession of the letter, and claimed all the *promises* made to the *seed of Faith* only.

"Daniel beheld till the *thrones were cast down*, and the ANCIENT of DAYS did *sit*," (this is relative to God's coming to judgment) "A fiery stream issued and came forth from before him, a thousand thousands ministered to him, and ten thousand time ten thousand stood before him, the judgment was set and the books were opened." (vii. 10.) I would have men observe this, there is and has been particular judgments came from God at times, as under the law by *Moses, Elijah*, and others, who prophecied of great Troubles to come upon nations, &c. then was *judgment set* against them, and a *fiery stream* (of God's wrath) *issued from before him.* JESUS also judged the *world* when he was here, and left the world under *judgment:* Others also by the *inspiration* of *Jesus* have *judged* the world according to their time and being: Also when *Jesus* is graciously pleased to make his glorious appearance, either personal or in spirit, unto the *soul* of man, giving him birth in spirit to his *holy* and spiritual covenant of *grace*, then CHRIST is come in judgment to that man, and the *books are opened*, and a fiery stream of mercy issues from before him, to seal and sanctify that man for the kingdom of heaven, and the man enters into death in the bed of *mercy:* But very few comes back to *tell this Tale.*

But Daniel in vision (v. 10.) saw the *judgment* at the GREAT DAY, and then *time* would end; then *the books will* be opened; *i.e.* the book of *life*, and the book of the *law*; now the *Lord Jesus* the KING of FAITH in glory opens the book of LIFE; and the *internal angel* in *justice* in the soul of man, opens the book of the LAW; and those in the time of law, who could not be *translated* to under the mercy of the SON; and them in the time of the gospel who could not be *born the spiritual birth* to the holy covenant of grace, for the mercy of the SON, will not be found *written in the book of life*; and the internal angel in justice *in* the soul will prove them to be as they were born into this world, (*i.e.* touching justice) then every man will be his *own witness* to his *own condemnation*, because they are not translated nor regenerated to the *mercy of* JESUS: And this internal angel keeps all those under justice to, and in eternity: But *they* whose names are found in the *book of life*, will enter the *kingdom* of heaven with CHRIST the glorious KING of Faith, and be glorified with the glorious FIRE of FAITH, living and *communing* with *their* glorious king in all eternity.

Further, those *beasts and kings* under the *gospel* are more the spiritual power than the temporal, and the *Great Whore*, or the *Dragon*, is the *Will* and false conceptions of *Reason* whom they worship: Though, notwithstanding in the *Apostles* time, those *dark kings* had power to persecute the saints, (of the temporal power) yet is was of, the spirit of Reason, who is called in scripture, *a dragon, a serpent, a beast,* &c. And John "saw one of his heads, as it were, wounded to death, and his deadly wound was healed, and the whole world wondered after the beast." (Rev. xiii. 3.) *i.e.* when the ten (first) persecutions was nearly ended, then some as aforesaid got the letter of the saints and declaration of Jesus, and found there was more spiritual wisdom there than any where else, as that overpowered all others: Then they found their *forefathers* had erred, and those living was in error who blasphemed the name of God and Christ, persecuting the saints, &c. This *wounded one of the heads of the beast, as it were, to death,* and this *head* that was wounded, was the power in spiritual rule, by which they did persecute the name of Jesus: *And this deadly wound was healed, i.e.* he or they who had the power, or those who succeeded to the power, transforming themselves into the apostolical letter, claiming the promises made to the *seed* of Faith, also might confess their fathers was wrong, or they had been wrong but have repented, and as so could read the forgiveness of sins: Thus was the *Beast* healed of his deadly wound; and no other way can the *spirit of Reason* be healed (when he has spoken evil of, or persecuted a declaration from HEAVEN, and wounded thereby) but to transform himself, if he can, into that declaration; yea, this is in private individuals even as in kings, &c. "*And the whole world wondered after the beast,*" *i.e.* those great powers who *had* uttered blasphemy against God, and persecuted the saints, have *now* owned their declaration, and transformed themselves into it; yea, professors of the name of Jesus, instead of being persecuted, are not protected by this ruling power; this caused a great wonder through the empire and many a wrathful spirit to blaspheme anew against GOD, but their time was up, and their power ended: Thus *the whole world wondered after the beast* that was wounded; and was healed by transforming himself, or themselves into the apostolical letter.

Again, "*John* beheld another beast coming up out of the earth, and he had two horns like a lamb, and he spake as a dragon," *i.e.* when the spirit of Reason had transformed itself into the apostles letter, then the beast appeared with *two* HORNS like a LAMB, *One horn* was to *preach* from the letter, repentance and forgiveness of *sins*, expostulating with the people the necessity of redemption, thus making converts in the name of *Jesus*: The *other horn* was the *Power* to compel, or persecute, under the sanction of the letter, cloaking their actions by saying they did it for the good of the souls of men, to bring them to Christ which is salvation. "And he spake as a dragon," *i.e.* he spake and acted from the *spirit of Reason*, the grand enemy to God and his tender hearted *elect*. "And he exerciseth all the power of the first beast before him, and causeth the earth and them that dwell therein to worship the *first beast* whose deadly wound was healed," (12.) which was to worship under the letter, according to the imagination of the *spirit of Reason*, which is the *beast*: The beast thinking his form of worship would please God, because it pleased himself; therefore people worshipped according to the will of the beast, which is called in spirit, worshipping the beast who was wounded and healed as aforesaid. The idolatrous spirit of Reason transformed from its former refuge to, under the refuge of the *apostolical letter*, coloured their *acts* with the name of, and prayers to JESUS, which was greater *abominations than before*; and the principle *miracles the beast did* in the spiritual was by his cunning art of Reason, coloured with the *letter* to *Deceive men*; and when any was in doubt of salvation, or had acted according to their cherubical *Wild* nature, and come to talk sober, the *internal angel* will tell him he is a sinner and cannot redeem himself, so must be redeemed by a power from HEAVEN; then they say CHRIST came from heaven to REDEEM *Men*, which is their doctrine, and as so, they *make fire to come from heaven unto the earth in the sight of men.*

This *little horn* that DANIEL "*saw come up on the beast, wherein were eyes like the eyes of a man, and a mouth speaking great things,*" is the same in spirit as *John* saw, *viz.* "*the beast coming up out of the earth, who had two horns like a lamb, and he spake as a dragon.*" So the *three horns that were plucked up by the root*, was as aforesaid, *viz.* transforming himself into the *letter* of the gospel, and there rule and persecute in the name of the DISCIPLES of JESUS: Also, as I said before when there is a prophecy of beast or kings to come under the *gospel*, it is more the spiritual or *priestly* power than the temporal: But under the *law* it is more the *kingly* power to govern temporal kingdoms; for kings were set up by God's *order* to rule the people, but

God never *commanded* false worship to be set up, as that is of the *spirit of Reason*, which wars against the true worship of God.

And this *war* under the *gospel*, is a spiritual war with the *saints* or the *elect*, and even with themselves, for the *kingdom of heaven*; for when *Daniel* would know the truth of what he saw, he was told, "These great beasts which are four, are four kings, which shall rise out of the earth; but the *Saints* of the *Most High* Shall take the kingdom, and possess the kingdom for ever, even for ever and ever." (vii. 17, 18.) This kingdom that the *saints* shall possess, is the *kingdom of heaven* after a troublesome *war* with the *spirit of Reason*: But I would not have people think that spiritual war ended when the Roman power became desolate, in respect to its arbitrary general rule in the apostolical letter; for there is a spiritual *war* at this day among sects of religion, and the spirit of dislike, which is the seed of persecution; but let men look into their own soul, and there they will find the *seat of war* and persecution; and for the *kingdom* of heaven, between the *spirit of Reason* and the *spirit of Faith*.

Further, *Daniel* saw and was told, "This *fourth beast*, shall be the *fourth kingdom* upon earth, and shall be *diverse* from all kingdoms, and shall subdue *three kings*, and spake great *words* against the MOST HIGH, and wear out his *saints*, and think to change *times*; and LAW, and they shall be given into his hand until *time* and *times*, and the dividing of *time*;" which is God's time to *put down* and appear himself in spirit; but this fourth kingdom was (outwardly originated in) the Roman power as aforesaid.

CHAP. XIV

DANIEL "saw a *ram* which had two horns, - and the highest came up last, - so that no beast might stand before him, nor any could deliver out of his hand; but he did according to his will and became great." After this, he saw "an *he-goat* come from the west, - and touched not the ground, and had a *notable horn* between his eyes,

- and smote the *ram*, - and there was no power in the ram to stand before him; - and he waxed great even to the *host of heaven*, and cast down some of the host and stars, – and an host was given him against the daily sacrifice." (ch. viii.)

This part of the *host* and *stars* that was *cast down*, was relative to the captivity of the jews, and *power against their daily sacrifice was given*; and the *priest* and *levites* who appeared as *stars* in their *sacrifice* and offerings, was then *desolate* of power to sacrifice, being captives in a strange land, which grieved every one who had any knowledge of God at heart; and the *Jews* followed the devices and desires of their own hearts in the *wild priesthood*, and worked abomination in their worship before God, breaking the commands of *Moses*; so God, according to his divine justice, brought *desolation* on them.

And *Daniel* heard one *saint* speak to another, saying, "How long shall be the *vision* concerning the *daily sacrifice* and transgression of desolation, to give both the sanctuary and the host to be trodden underfoot? And he said unto me, unto two thousand and three hundred days, then shall the sanctuary be cleansed," (v. 13, 14.) *i.e.* during the time of the captivity of *Israel* and *Juda*; then they would be brought back to *Jerusalem*, according to the word of prophecy, and as JESUS was to be born of the *tribe* of *Juda*.

And when *Daniel* sought to know the meaning, *then there stood the appearance of a man, and he heard a man's voice between the banks of Ulai*, which called and said, "Gabriel make this man to understand the *vision*," (v. 16.) so was made to understand that the *ram* which he saw, having two horns, were the kings of *Media* and *Persia*, and the *rough Goat*, the king of *Grecia*, and was informed of their actions; and also of the king of a *fierce countenance*, and understanding *dark sentences*, that should stand up, *prosper*, and *practice*, and *destroy the holy people; i.e.* the *Roman* power, who *destroyed the saints; understanding dark sentences, i.e.* his worshipping the apostles letter, sending forth their *dark* judgment of it as a perfect rule for people to walk in.

Further, it is said, "And through his policy, he shall cause craft to prosper in his hand; he shall magnify himself in his heart, and by peace shall destroy many; he shall also stand up against the PRINCE of *princes*; but he shall be broken without hands," (25 v.) *i.e.* the

Roman *spiritual power,* proceeding from the wisdom of Reason, who went forth and worked *abomination, (i.e.* they persecuted and put to death them who was *inspired* by JESUS to preach his name and doctrine;) and this abomination maketh *desolate,* as they did not fully stop until they had put to death every one that was *inspired* by Jesus, so as to stand before him in spirit: and as so the *spirit* of Jesus was *silent,* in the *heaven of grace,* in the souls of men, which is spiritually called desolation, and this was as before, "The abomination that maketh desolate." Thus *stood up against the prince of princes,* for there was many living who professed the name of Jesus (but had not the spirit and power) when the Roman power transformed themselves into the *apostolical letter,* which by their *politic* wisdom they exercised as a *craft,* and *magnified* their *spiritual power,* (the beast) above emperors and kings, and subjected them, becoming a spiritual *ruling power.* And through the name of *Jesus,* which is *peace,* they have *destroyed many,* both in their lives and natural inheritance; *but he shall be broken without hand, i.e.* many priests, &c. who was *dark* spiritual kings, in, or under that Roman *spiritual power,* went forth to seek kingdoms of their own, and denied that power, (thus *break* off,) and would be no more obedient to it; thus in time *it* became desolate to what it formerly hath been, thus it was *broken without hand;* but this was Daniel's prophecy of the desolation and abomination that would come to pass in the time of the gospel: but the *transgressions of desolation, and the sanctuary and host to be trodden underfoot,* was relative to the Jews *then* in captivity, and more *yet* to come, for their great transgressions and abominations in the sight of the Lord.

In the first year of Darius, DANIEL understood by books, whereof the *word* of the LORD came to *Jeremiah* the prophet, that he would accomplish seventy years in the desolation of Jerusalem," (ix. 2.) then Daniel did seek *by prayer and supplications, and fasting, unto God, and confesses the transgressions of Juda, and includes himself among the brethren, and he prays for Jerusalem, and the sanctuary that was made desolate for the Lord's sake.*

Then GABRIEL appeared again to *Daniel* in his *vision,* and said to him, "understand the matter and consider the vision; seventy weeks are determined upon thy people, and upon the holy city, to finish the transgression and to make an end of sin, and to make reconciliation for iniquity, and to bring in everlasting righteousness, and to seal up the vision, and prophecy, and to *anoint* the most holy," (v. 24.) This *Gabriel,* who appeared unto *Daniel,* was *one* of the *three* who was *translated* into heaven; for the extent of *Daniel's visions* was so great that it not only includes the captivity and deliverance under the *law*, but also desolations and war under the *gospel;* and the deliverance from that spiritual captivity; for he is given to understand, the Jews return from the Babylonish captivity to build the walls and temple at Jerusalem, and also that MESSIAH who is CHRIST should be born of the *tribe of Juda*, &c. "And after threescore and two weeks shall MESSIAH be *cut off*, but not for himself; and the Prince of the people shall destroy the city and sanctuary, and the end thereof shall be with a flood; and to the end of the war desolations are determined," (v. 26.) This relates to the persecutions under the gospel, and the very passage that Jesus speak to his disciples; for the *Roman power* not only destroyed the *Temple at Jerusalem* and *sanctuary* under the law, but also persecuted and put to death Jesus and his saints under the gospel (but could not destroy that sanctuary) then was *desolations determined* to that time.

Relative to this captivity of the *Jews*, Shalmaneser king of Assyria (in the *sixth* year of Hezekiah king of Juda, and *ninth* of Hoshea king of Israel,) did carry Israel captive to Assyria (after he had besieged Samaria (*three* years) and put them in Hala and in Habor by the river of Gozan, and in the cities of the Medes. The Jehoahaz king of Juda, went captive into Egypt, and Jehoiakim they made king of Juda, and *taxed* the land. Then Nebuchadnezzar king of Babylon came and bound king Jehoiakim, and carried him to Babylon, (and with this king, Daniel went captive also), and Jehoiachim reigned in his stead; then he also was carried captive to Babylon, and with these two Kings they took vessels of the house of the LORD. Then Zedekiah reigned, but he would not be obedient to Jeremiah the PROPHET nor yet to Nebuchadnezzar, so he was wrath and sent and break down the walls of Jerusalem, and burnt the HOUSE of the LORD, and carried the holy vessels to their temple at Babylon, taking the people away captives: These are the different captivities of Juda to Babylon, and the captivity of Israel to Assyria, for their great idolatry and disobedience to the *Messengers* of GOD.

The *Time* of *Israel's captivity*, and *desolations* to Jerusalem, was *seventy* years, as was the *word of the Lord by Jeremiah.* And at the *Time* of deliverance but *few* returned to build the temple and walls at Jerusalem (and to observe the law and worship as was commanded by *Moses*) that JESUS might be born of the *Tribe* and *in the land of Juda*, the spiritual king of the *Jews, i.e.* the KING of FAITH; for the greater part of the children of Israel, did not return from that captivity, but wandered, and in their own *Wild* cherubical Nature *Lost*; yea became so degenerate as not to observe the *statutes* which Moses commanded, wherein was the *Seat of Learning* for the whole world. Thus time came, that *Time* should be *divided* even in the Time of the Law, *i.e.* when the time of captivity was accomplished, some returned to Jerusalem unto their duty, according to the will of God; while the others went *Wild* in their own nature, never more to be called together as a nation, with full authority to act according to the literal light of Moses's law; and the *seed of Faith*, who were scattered among them through the power of Reason, will be called to, under the *mercy* of the SON, to the heavenly *inheritance*, but not as by Moses aforesaid. Thus was *Time divided in Israel* in the time of the law.

Further, when Jesus was born to bring in the gospel, and to become the SPIRITUAL KING of the *Jews*, the Jews would not receive him, put persecuted him for his good works, and got *power* from the *beast* to *act* as dark spiritual kings for *one hour, i.e.* to *crucify Jesus*; and they also *acted* in persecuting and killing his saints, so Jesus left the Jews, and their city, and sanctuary *desolate*, and the Roman power came and destroyed the city, with the temple and sanctuary. Thus they were *desolate* indeed, according to the prophecy of Jesus; so they became *literal wandering Jews* in spiritual *desolation*, also to *wander* in the *letter* of Moses to the world's end. Also when persecution of saints was ended, and the spirit of Christ killed on this earth *in* those saints, and with-held by Christ in heaven, this was *shortening those days* of persecution, (Matt. xxiv. 22.) Now persecution hath been stopped, for a time, by a tyrant's being cut off; but the *shortening* of it was because the *holy spirit* was not on this earth to be persecuted. Then the Romans transformed themselves into the apostolical letter because the spirit of Jesus was *desolate* on this earth, and many would wander in the *apostles* letter, destitute of the spirit of Jesus to the world's end: Then the two desolations of Jew and Gentile was *determined* (indeed). Moreover the spirit of Christ being *desolate* on this earth, every elect soul must patiently wait for the *coming of Christ*, either by a *Messenger* or a *call* to sanctification at the hour of death; and blessed is he that *knows the voice of Christ* by his *Messenger*, for that will lead the soul to sanctification; and then *Time* becomes *divided* under the gospel, *i.e. some* would in their life-time have every thing bow to their dark understanding of the bare Letter; and *some* would patiently *wait* and leave the issue to God –

thus *time* goeth, and thus is *time* spiritually divided.

After this, *Daniel* saw in *vision,* by the river Hiddekel, and said, "Then I lift up mine eyes and beheld a certain man clothed in linen whose loins were girded with fine gold of Uphaz." (Dan. x. 5.) This *man in linen,* was the similitude of the *man Moses,* who was translated into heaven to the glory of the father, so sent to commune with Daniel; for Daniel was inspired under the attribute of God's divine justice, (by the *way* or through the cherubim's bringing the law into this world, with the wisdom of that law after the manner of the inspiration of the *man* Moses; so *Daniel* was greatly visited by *vision,* but it was in *dream*; for he says, "as *Gabriel* was speaking with him, he as in a *deep sleep*;" and he was let to know the *power* of God under the attribute of his divine justice; and that God would raise up one kingdom to punish and pull down another (in the time of the law) according to his justice, for their abominable wicked actions. And he also saw, and was let to know by vision, of the vial of God's wrath being poured out on the SON, and his *saints*; and that the *abomination* of Reason in man would make the man *desolate*; and that the *kingdoms of this world* are given into the hands of CHRIST, *i.e.* the *elect* Jew or Gentile, let them be ever so much *scattered* on this earth, it is in no one's power but the LORD JESUS only, to give them *Birth* to his spiritual covenant of grace, and sanctify them to enter the kingdom of heaven, which is truly CHRIST'S KINGDOM on earth, and this way *only* doth he restore his *lost kingdom Israel,* let whosoever look for, or say to the contrary. Again, Enoch, Moses, and Elijah being translated into heaven to the glory of the Father, they had power, by God's command, to commune with and inform *man in vision,* of the great works and sufferings of God here in time: Also when God was here a child, they answered the *prayer of Faith,* and did help Faith, and guide it, and receive its lively *record* when it was translated, to under the MERCY of the SON. Further, when Jesus uttered his gospel, they directed the Spirit of Faith to Jesus, also sent Jesus assistance from heaven according to his prayer, therefore they were translated to have this power; but all quickening power as to creation and redemption belong to God.

And when the *man clothed in linen* "came to let *Daniel* understand what should befall his people in the latter day, for as yet the vision was for many days, then Daniel set his face toward the ground and became dumb; then one like the similitude of the *sons* of men touched his lips, and he opened his *mouth* and speak." (v. 16.) This was the similitude of God's becoming a *Son,* and that he would open the *mouths* of the *elect* in *prayer*, and their *hearts* to *understanding* in his holy covenant of Grace – Daniel also writes, (xii. 1), "At that time shall Michael, the great prince, stand for the children of thy people, (*i.e.* Christ) and shall deliver every one that shall be written in the book; (*i.e.* the book of life) then of the *resurrection*, to everlasting life, and to everlasting shame" – and (v. 4.) "but thou, oh *Daniel*! shut up the words and seal the book even to the *time* of the *end*. Many shall run to and fro, and knowledge shall be increased." Now I would have the elect to *understand* that when the spirit of Christ is *active* on this earth, there is a resurrection in the soul of man from the *death* of sin, and he is brought on in the true *knowledge* and *path* of God, towards the holy covenant of grace, which is for Christ's *kingdom*; and when Christ is graciously pleased to give any one spiritual *Birth* thereto, *then* Christ reigns in that man on this earth, let him live one minute or forty years, as it is the same for his entrance into the kingdom of heaven.

Further, the spirit of Jesus *acts* in bringing *life* out of *death, i.e.* He takes the man from the bare letter wherein he was *bound* by the spirit of Reason, to follow his *Messenger up* to the covenant of grace: also *acts* where the *messenger* is not; or when there is *silence in* (the nether) *heaven* giving spiritual *birth* so seals the man for himself at the hour of death; but the *acts* of Reason is dwelling on the bare letter, by their own dark judgment (because he is left *desolate* of the spirit of CHRIST) and moved with dislike, when such distinguishing power of Christ doth appear, working himself down into death and hell, and if possible *deceive the elect*, thus take the *seed of Faith* with them; therefore Reason runs *to and fro* in imagination of the *bare letter*: as when Christ is graciously pleased to send a *Messenger*, he comes with wisdom higher up nearer ETERNITY, and thus is *wisdom* increased, and Reason continually being left desolate; and thus *Daniel* saw in visional glimpse somewhat of the *acts* under the gospel, and how *Men* would be prepared to be raised to *Glory*; also how *Men* would fall and lay under justice, to be raised to *shame*, and this resurrection he writes of, is the resurrection at the *last Day*.

Daniel also *beheld two others standing, one on this side of the bank of the river, and one on the other side of the river; and one said to the man cloathed with linen, who was upon the waters of the river*, "How long shall it be to the end of those wonders?" (xii. 6.) This *man cloathed in linen* was *Moses*, and the *river of waters* he stood upon was the spirit of Reason, he being the law-giver to that seed, and as so, *stood* on all their *waters,*(though translated by the power of Faith to the glory of the Father); and *him* who speak to *Moses,* was the similitude of enquiring *Faith* (*i.e.* Faith in the *time* of the *law,* before translation to, under the mercy of the *son,* as then the *time* of the *gospel* was not come in) which Faith also *enquired* of *Moses and Elias,* when they sat in the power of the Father and Christ upon this earth.

Then the *man clothed in linen,* lift up his *right and left hand to heaven,* "and *swear* by him who liveth for ever, that it shall be for a *time,* and *times* and a *half.*" (*i.e.* as aforesaid, God's *time*; but this is found in the life of one man) "and when he shall have accomplished to scatter the power of the *holy people,*" these "*holy people*" was the Jews, and when the gospel was brought in, their *power was scattered*; but spiritually, the *holy people* are the *elect,* whose *power* is *scattered* all over the world, under the power of Reason, and when that is *accomplished,* (or finished) by their being gathered to Christ, *time* will end in their resurrection to glory; this Daniel heard, but *understood not,* and desired to know what *shall be the end of those things?* and he said, "Go thy way *Daniel,* for the words are closed up and sealed till the *time* of the end." (ix. ver.) Now there was the *time of the end* to the captivity of *Juda*; also to the persecutions in the *apostles days,* and there will be a *time* when Faith is clear of the power of Reason.

Again, touching *the abominations that maketh desolate*; as Faith hearkened to the voice of Reason, and fell in *Adam,* under the power of death, so *Jesus* took that nature of Faith on him, to make it alive by his death; so those *dark* spiritual kings (by their *abomination*) put Christ to death that he may rise again, which was doing the *will of God*; also they persecuted the *saints,* but by the power of Faith they held out to the *end,* whereby Faith was *refined,* this also is doing the *will of God,* even by wicked men, which made the spirit of Christ *desolate* to the literalist: And when those dark spiritual kings hated the Roman spiritual power, and sought kingdoms of their own, (as *broken* therefrom) so left the Roman *desolate,* this also was doing the *will of God*: Yea, at this day the spirit of Christ appears on this earth by his *Messenger,* who calls to the elect, and when the soul can see that the *abomination* of Reason had made the *act* of Faith *desolate* in his soul, and his *daily sacrifice* has been *taken away, i.e.* his *prayer of obedience* in *true Faith* unto God, has been stopped by the power of Reason, then there comes on an internal and spiritual war and persecution, from the spirit of Reason to the spirit of Faith; that Faith, by holding out to the *end,* may be *refined* as pure gold; thus, even here, the spirit of Reason doth the *will of God*; but such a man may daily look for the internal coming of Christ, while he who cannot follow the voice of God, by his *Messenger*, is left desolate on the bare *letter* of the former Messenger, let him flatter himself in what he can to the contrary.

Again, I have given a hint of *Time* and of *Times* and the *dividing of Time*; but this was before our *Time*, and those who lived in that Time, will be *judged* according to that Time; and them who live in my *Time* will be judged according to my Time; as at *this day*, when the *spirit of Faith* is quickened by the voice of GOD, by his *Messenger*, that soul will find he has lived in the *Time of darkness*: and when he is *born of water*, he will find *Time to offer his daily sacrifice, i.e. the true prayer*, and will also find the *Time of war* with the spirit of Reason in his own soul, which is the *Times*: And when a man is *born in spirit* to the HOLY covenant of GRACE, his Time is *divided*, if he live but one minute, but if he live to come *back* to tell his *Tale*, he will find his *Time divided* by God himself: and as aforesaid, this is all in God's Time. And as *Moses* said to *Daniel* in his *vision*, "Blessed is he that *waiteth* and *cometh* to the thousand three hundred and five and thirty days." (xii. ver.) *i.e. Blessed is he that cometh* at the *call* of God's *Messenger*, to go through *his travail* in the *priesthood* of Faith, which is called in spirit, *a thousand three hundred and five and thirty days*; for NOW is THE BOOK of the scriptures *opened*, and the *whole* is here, *i.e.* the LORD JESUS CHRIST, the KING of FAITH, *He only* hath the seal of the *living God*, and that all men must be sealed by Christ *himself*, with his own *spiritual seal*, to enter the *Kingdom* of HEAVEN: And the *internal angel* in justice, in the soul of man, has the *seal of justice*, whereby men are their own *witnesses* to their own *condemnation*, and as so, are *sealed* by this *angel* to *eternal* DEATH.

CHAP. XV

ZECHARIAH, the prophet of the Lord, was sent to the Jews at Jerusalem, after their return from captivity, to speak and prophecy with the prophet *Haggai*, that they should not stop their work because they were overpowered by their enemies, but should proceed to build the House of God again at Jerusalem, it being his divine will: Then *Zerubbabel* the governor of Juda, and *Joshua* the high priest, and people, went to build the House of God, and with them were the prophets of God helping them, and they prospered: now *Zerubbabel* was of the lineage of the kings of Juda, and grandson to Jeconias, the second king of Juda, who was carried captive to Babylon; and at their return to Jerusalem he was made governor of Juda, and greatly assisted to rebuild this Temple; and at this time lived *Zechariah* the prophet, who *saw* and *prophecied* of great things, saying, "I saw by night, and behold a man riding upon a red horse, and he stood among the myrtle trees that were in the bottom, and behind him were three red horses speckled with white." (1. viii.) This *red horse* and his *rider* that *Zechariah* saw in *vision*, was the similitude of the *internal angel* in justice, in the souls of men, (*i.e.* "the cherubims and flaming sword that turns every way, to keep the way of the tree of life,") which *internal angel* was brought into this world by the cherubim, and is as pure as the attribute of God's divine justice; for although the cherubim break the law, he never could break the justice of that law, so it is pure as God created it in the souls of men to this day, yea, is in the souls of every man through the act of generation; but *all* is comprised under one head, *viz.* under the attribute of *divine justice*, which was the cause *Zechariah* saw the similitude of this *angel* on a *red horse*; this may be well called a *red horse*, because it is the sinful soul of man, for the soul of man doth become as *red* as *scarlet*; by the wicked and abominable acts of Reason: also, in all the outgoings of Reason, such as oppression, adultery, idolatry, bloodshed and persecution, and other sinful acts, whereby the soul becomes dyed in or with his own blood; this *internal angel* in justice in the soul, has full power to watch over the man, and to seal the soul under justice, and keep him wallowing in his own blood unto death eternal, (and no one can open this seal but the KING of FAITH, *i.e.* the LORD JESUS CHRIST in Glory) and thus doth the *internal angel* ride on the sinful *soul* of *man.*

And he stood among the myrtle trees that were in the bottom; these *myrtle trees* are the conceived delights or pleasures, by the spirit of Reason in the soul of man, which is a garden to that spirit, and this spirit goes forth and acts according to its conceived delights, which is the *flower* of its life, for take the delights of Reason away, and it goes into madness or death; and the myrtle trees being *in the bottom*, is because it is the bottom or *root* of Reason's delight, by which the spirit in man goeth out, and acts to its own condemnation, as there is nothing so sweet to the spirit of Reason as to make choice of its own evil and *ride hastily into it.*

And behind him in the myrtle tree, were three red horses speckled with white; those *three horses* is the *going* out of Reason to act from the soul of Man, *i.e.* when a man is moved by the *internal angel* in justice by God's order, to go forth and punish people, nations, &c. according to *God's divine justice* for their wickedness; then this MAN *rides* one of those *horses, i.e.* Reason riding on Reason to execute justice; for he goeth forth in the power of Reason, and hath power over the spirit of Reason in others: Also when man has conceived any desire by the spirit of Reason, and goes forth in act to accomplish that conceived desire, this Man also *rides* one of those *horses*; for the nature of Reason will destroy all before it, was it not for the law written in that nature (which law is, "You shall love God above all, and your neighbour as yourself.") And in all the goings *out* of Reason, to act in any thing he *shall* delight in, or *for* any thing that he shall desire to *have*, which is called, in spirit, to *walk to and fro the earth*, this law goeth with him, and the *internal angel* in justice, in the soul of man, watches over the law; therefore when Reason breaks the law, this *internal angel* in justice seals the *soul* under the attribute of divine justice unto *death*, though may let a man wander on this earth during his natural life.

Again, in the travail through this life we are in death, why? because men are under the seal of this angel in justice; as in *all* the goings out of Reason this angel strictly watches man's ways, binding him up to some good acts; yea, a *tyrant* has but his limited power; for he is bound up by the law with this *internal angel* to some good acts, and that he shall not cut off or destroy, nor amass to himself no more than by permission; yea, this *internal angel* has power over man to bind him, or loose him according to the will of God; and let the spirit of

Reason transform itself to what colour or act he can, the law goes with it, and this *angel* in justice accuses or excuses according to the law, thereby some good acts are forced out of the spirit of Reason, by the *internal angel* in justice according to the law written in Reason (*i.e.* let a man be ever so *bad* in some things, there is *good* to be found in him at times; also they will *contribute* to uphold this world, as well as to *oppress* and *cut off*, that the world shall stand until God is graciously pleased to *accomplish and call his elect*.) And these *good acts* come by power of the *internal angel* in justice in the soul of man, and good it is for a man to hearken to the voice of this angel, for then will follow the blessing of God. Now those *good acts* are the *white specks* or spots on the *red horse, i.e.* the spirit of Reason, which carries the Man *to and fro* this earth, and the law is in Reason, and he must return to his house or *ark* again (*i.e.* the body of man); then this *internal angel* of the law, or *angel of the Lord*, records the *evil* of man, and stand as a witness *for or against* him before the attribute of GOD'S divine justice, and thus do they answer the angel that *stands among the myrtle-trees*, which I call the *ark-angel*, because he dwells in the soul of man.

Note: This *internal angel* in justice, or *cherubim with a FLAMING sword, turning every way to keep the way of the tree of life*, is a faithful and true servant unto God, standing before the attribute of his divine justice in the soul of man, *watching* and recording the evils of man, *ready* to commune with God relative to his divine justice. The *cherubim* bringing this law into this world, from whence proceeded the *first covenant, i.e.* the covenant of the law, and Moses being inspired under the attribute of God's divine justice, with the wisdom of this pure law that was written in the cherubim's nature before his fall; therefore Moses was the *anointed* cherubim by God himself, with the wisdom of this pure cherubical law and worship God required under it.

Also *Zechariah* was inspired by God himself by the way or through the cherubim, after the manner of Moses's inspiration. And *Zechariah* had great communion with God relative to his will in the time of the law, by the way, or through this internal angel in the soul, (which I call a cherubim, and is the *internal angel* of the law:) Also he saw in similitude the *external angel* of the law, who was the man *Moses* translated into heaven; but the chief of *Zechariah's* communion, was with the *internal angel* in justice that he saw in similitude in his vision.

So when *Zachariah* desired to know what those *red horses speckled with white* were, the *angel*, that talked with him, said, "I will shew thee what those be; and the man that stood among the myrtle-trees answered and said, those are them that the LORD hath sent to walk to and fro through the earth," (v. 10.) *i.e.* as before, the will of man that *rides* on the *spirit of Reason*, or *red horse* speckled with white, that goes out *to and fro* to cut off some people, and Captivate to rule over and oppress others: Thus God has raised up one Nation to punish another for their great wickedness: as he did *Assyria* and *Babylon* to punish *Israel* and *Juda*, and this is doing the *will of God* according to his divine justice; and *Reason* in the mean time does his *own* will, for he greatly delights to gather treasure, and have Nations, people, &c. to rule over; but when the heat of action is over, and the *spirit* of Reason become cool, then the man is questioned by the *internal angel* in his soul, and is found wanting in the balance of *justice*, which is *truth*; then the angel records him to be visited in God's time according to his *divine justice*.

Again, (v. 11.) *And they answered the angel of the LORD that stood among the myrtle-trees and said, we have walked to and fro through the earth, and behold all the whole earth sitteth still, and is at rest, i.e.* after the heat of action, when the *cool of the day* comes on, the *spirit* of Reason must return to its own tabernacle, and the law written in Reason; thus it answers the *angel of the Lord* that stands among the myrtle-trees (*i.e.* the *internal angel* in justice in the soul of man:) Also when Reason is stopped by the power of God, through this internal angel, then the earth *sitteth still*; and if he is not immediately brought up to condemnation by the Angel, then he may *rest* till that time come.

Zechariah, in his *vision*, saw those things which at that time attended to the *captivity* and *deliverance* of the Jews; also the *earthy* hearts of the Babylonians *rested*, so as to let the Jews return to Jerusalem: Yet I would not have any one think that this mighty *internal* power ended there, but altogether the contrary; for *Zechariah* being one of the latter Prophets under the law, it was made known to him by vision, the power that was committed to this *internal angel*: yea, I say this internal angel of the law, or *angel of the Lord*, has power in or over the soul of man to this day, and will to the *end of time*, as had Moses in his time being the external Angel of the law. So I would not have men lose themselves by thinking those *desires* and *acts* of Reason are in kings and great men only; no: Let all men but look into their own soul, and they will there find those very *acts* and *desires* of Reason, and the *power* of the internal Angel.

As all the Prophets under the *Law* were inspired under the attribute of God's divine justice, by the way or through the *cherubims*, except *Isaiah* who was inspired by the way of the *seraphims*. However they all greatly communed with God, by the way or through this *internal angel* in justice in the soul of man, (*i.e.* a cherubim, and spiritually, I call him so;) and was the angel, *Zechariah* saw in similitude and communed with in vision; also this angel communed with God; and *Zechariah* was informed of the will of God thereby, relative to the law and attribute of God's divine justice, (see verse 12.) "And the angel of the Lord answered and said, O Lord of *Host!* How long wilt thou not have mercy on Jerusalem and the cities of Juda, against which thou has had indignation these three-score and ten years," (v. 13.) "And the *Lord* answered the angel that *talked with me*, with good words and comfortable words," (v. 14.) "So the angel that *communed with me*, said unto me, cry thou, saying, thus saith the *Lord of host*, I am jealous for Jerusalem, and for Zion, with great jealousy." Thus Zechariah's literal declaration confirms the power of this angel, and that God communes with, and instructs men by way of, or through this *internal angel*, according to the *first* covenant, (*i.e.* the covenant of the *law*, and that *priesthood, i.e.* of Reason). This sober unprejudiced men may perceive.

And the *angel* said to *Zechariah*, "I am very sore displeased with the heathen that are at ease; for I was but a little displeased, and they helped forward the affliction," (v. 15.) *i.e.* as I said before, after the *Assyrians, Babylonians,* and others had *scattered* the power, and *captivated* Israel and Juda according to the will of God, for their wickedness and idolatry, which brought great affliction on the Jews. But when they return to Jerusalem again, then the work of the Babylonians, &c. was done, touching that captivity, then *the earth sat still and was at rest,* as was answered the *angel of the Lord* that stood among the myrtle trees, (*i.e.* the *internal angel* of the law in the soul of man.) And *he was displeased with the heathen that were at ease, i.e.* they were recorded for justice to be executed on them for their cruelty to Juda and Jerusalem; but it was to come in God's time; for the power of this angel in justice, in the souls of men, is so great, that were not the divine Majesty to *stay* it, when men had offended by breaking the law, they would immediately be cast into death (as was the cherubim cast from heaven, by the same angel in justice,) let men say or think what they will to the contrary; so Zechariah saith, the Lord answered the angel with *good and comfortable words.*

Zechariah was to cry yet again, "Thus saith the *Lord of hosts*, my cities through prosperity shall yet be spread abroad," which then was to build the temple at Jerusalem and the city; and cities in Juda should for a time, be inhabited by Jews, and should have the glory to exercise their worship at Jerusalem: Then *Zechariah saw and beheld four horns*; these *horns* are the goings out of Reason to act; and Reason will delight in his own evil actions; yet he shall do the will of God, as is his divine justice, (as ver. 19.) "And I said unto the angel that talked with me, what be these? And he answered me, those are the *horns* which have scattered Juda, Israel, and Jerusalem;" and those *powers* was under the seal of justice, to be visited with affliction; and his vision of the *four carpenters* was, that the Temple of Jerusalem should be rebuilt.

CHAP. XVI

AFTER this, "*Zechariah beheld a man with a measuring line in his hand,* and said to him, whither goest thou?" And he said, "to measure Jerusalem, to see what is the breadth thereof, and what is the length thereof." I would have Men to *understand, i.e.* there was the city of *Jerusalem* where the temple was to be built, the *breadth thereof,* to the amount of as many Jews as God was graciously pleased to call there, to observe the law and worship commanded by Moses, And the *length* of it was, till Christ come to bring in the gospel. And there is another *Jerusalem,* relative to the law of Reason *in the soul of man;* this I call an *internal* and *spiritual Jerusalem;* for as there was an *external city* of Jerusalem, and temple built by the hands of man, wherein the *law* and *worship* was observed, *justice* administered, and the true *records* kept, and was the *great City* in the time of Moses's law; so there is a *Jerusalem* and *temple* built by the hand of God, which Temple is the body of *Man;* and in the life of Reason, is this spiritual *law* written, with the internal angel strictly watching over the law, accusing or excusing according to the act, and seals the soul unto divine justice according to the law. *Thus* as Moses had power, as the *external angel* of the law, over the natural lives of men, so has this *internal angel* in justice, power over the spiritual life of men; and it is the souls of men that compose this great *spiritual* JERUSALEM. For Jerusalem is of the law which *genders to strife,* justice and death.

Now it is the internal angel, in justice that has the *measuring line or reed,* to measure this *Jerusalem;* "and he measured it according to the measure of a man, that is of the angel," *i.e.* the *internal angel* in justice in the soul of men, whereby men will be their own witness to their own condemnation before the attribute of God's justice. "And the length and breadth of this city is equal," *i.e.* the *breadth* of it is God's infinite justice and the *length* of it is endless eternity; and the *height* thereof is, that man cannot get above it, except he is *born* or translated to the *mercy* of the SON. So this City is *equal* in length, breadth, and height.

Further, there is another *Jerusalem, i.e.* the HOLY CITY, or *seal and sanctification of God:* The foundation of this Jerusalem, is the Lord Jesus, the KING of FAITH in glory; this is the *City of Faith,* and for Faith, and no one can enter this City but by the power of Faith and help of the LAMB, *i.e.* Christ in glory; and the *Wall of this City* is Justice, and has been ever since "the cherubim and flaming sword, has kept the way of the Tree *of Life."* - And "the foundation of the wall being garnished with *precious stones,"* is the *promise* of God to his Elect, that *they* shall enter this *Holy City* Jerusalem: this Promise was first made to Adam and Eve, for God communed with the spirit of Faith in them after the fall, above the power of the internal angel in justice; *i.e.* when God called to Faith which he created in Adam, he raised it from death to life; which he communed with for regeneration, and by this communion with God, by the spirit of Faith, they prophesied of their own salvation, and at the hour of Death they were translated to, under the *mercy of the Son, i.e.* the *holy City.* Also it is written, "the wall had twelve Gates, and at the Gates twelve Angels, and names written thereon, which are the names of the twelve tribes of the Children of Israel." (Rev. xxi.) This is in reference to the external law being given to the Children of Israel, to shew forth the power of the internal law, and that men must wade through the law under justice, before they can enter the Gate of this City; (not altogether outward or ceremonial, but the law and justice in the internal soul of man, for by the law and worship according to the law no one can be saved, being only the incense of Reason.) Also there was many of the *royal seed* translated to, under the *mercy of the Son, i.e.* this *holy City,* before the external law was given, hence it is the *Prayer* of Faith, which is the true *incense* that ascends up to God for his divine assistance, to help the soul through this vale of tears, and of temptation, under the law and justice.

Also it is written, "and the wall had twelve foundations, and in them the Names of the twelve *apostles* of the lamb," *i.e.* relative to the apostles preaching the death and resurrection of Christ, for them the ceremonial part of the worship of the law ended; and as the *apostles* preached the gospel they further *garnished the wall,* by the glorious promises Christ made to his *Elect,* and who must all enter the *holy city* according to the doctrine the *apostles* preached, *i.e.* by the *power* of Christ; for by the hearing and believing the bare word and ceremonies only, will not admit any one into the Kingdom of Heaven; therefore *justice* is a *Wall* to keep the souls of men from *mercy,* as the firmament is a wall to divide heaven and earth; and all men must be taken through the *gate* of justice, to enter the *Kingdom* of Mercy.

Also, "the twelve gates were of twelve pearls, every several gate was of one pearl," *i.e.* the *inspiration of* JESUS to the twelve *apostles,* for they all preached the gospel, and invited to the mercy of Jesus: Further, a true *Messenger* in the covenant of grace quickens the *law in the soul, i.e.* the first covenant; and by assistance from heaven gives birth to the *virgin daughter* of faith, from its womb, or seed; and she will gather from the same spirit as the *living Messenger* doth, and follow him through the internal law, and bear the wiles and temptations of Reason, offering its *own prayer,* which is the true *incense* that ascends up to God, for his divine assistance to help on, in its travail: and when the soul is arraigned before the attribute of divine justice, by the internal *angel;* then there, God appears as a *consuming fire,* at which time the eager prayer of Faith ascends from the *virgin daughter,* for God's divine assistance, then CHRIST the Redeemer, and King of FAITH, is graciously pleased to descend in spirit, and unite with this *virgin daughter* in the soul of man, *i.e.* the bride prepared as *pure gold,* by standing against, and coming through the powers of Reason, *meet for Marriage* with the LAMB: Now this is the *Marriage with the Lamb,* or *the heavenly Jerusalem descending from the THRONE of GOD* to that soul; and the *spirit* of the Lord Christ, being united to this *virgin* of Faith, begets to himself a *son,* called *Inspiration,* who, when born ascends into an high *Mountain* of Faith, and is *sealed* by Christ himself for his glorious Kingdom. This is the true spiritual *Birth,* to see the Kingdom of Heaven; and this *way* doth the soul pass from the internal Angel in justice, (who is Angel of the *nether waters)* to the Angel of the covenant of grace, (who is Angel of the *upper waters),* which Angel is Christ the King of Faith in *glory;* - HE is the gate, or *door,* to this HOLY CITY; for he *only* can give spiritual Birth, or translate the soul from under the power of the internal Angel in justice, to his holy covenant of grace, where is found the seal of the living God: - Now this is the holy City Jerusalem, where Christ is king, but very few live to come back to tell this *Tale,* but die in the bed of mercy to be raised to the kingdom of glory: and the angel that has this *measuring line, or golden reed,* is the angel of the covenant of grace; *and be measured according to the measure of a man, that is of the angel, i.e.* the angel of the covenant of grace is graciously pleased to *seal* and *sanctify* the soul to enter his glorious kingdom, and the *breadth* of this HOLY CITY is Christ's infinite Mercy, and the *length* of it is all eternity, and the *height* is the Love of Christ: - but more of this holy city anon.

Also *Zechariah* said, "And behold the angel that talked with me went forth, and another angel went out to meet him, and said unto him, Run - Speak to this young man, saying, Jerusalem shall be inhabited, as Towns without walls for the great multitude of men and cattle therein," (chap.2.) This was the similitude of the internal *angel* in justice that *Zechariah* saw, and did commune with; and the other angel that went out to meet him was the similitude of GOD; for whether Moses or Elijah, they (being translated into *heaven,* to the glory of the *Father)* was very capable, by the will of God, to commune with *Zechariah* of certain things that would come to pass, even when Jesus brought in the gospel, much more to commune with him in what things God would yet bring to pass in the time of the law: Hence the angel, who was the similitude of God, said unto the internal angel in justice, "Run, speak to this young man [*Zechariah*] concerning Jerusalem."

Now Zerubbabel laid the foundation, and had the plummet in his hand, to build the temple at Jerusalem, and the Jews should worship there till Christ came to bring in the gospel; *then* that ceremonial worship of the law, and temple of Jerusalem should end, as was the will of God. Further, the External, or law of Moses, was given to shew forth the power of the Internal, and Angel in the soul of man; and this external law was given to the children of *Israel,* to manifest the name and power of God on this earth, according to his divine justice, (*he being then* in the condition of God the *Father* and *creator*), but none of them could keep that law: - also there was a worship and *priesthood given,* which was of Reason, whereby men should observe that worship and offering according to the law, to stay God's divine justice in the Camp or *Kingdom of Israel,* and this law attended to the law of Reason written in man; and had the Jews but observed the law and the worship accordingly, they would have been the *most wise* people in this world: why? because by the law they would have been a *Light,* and able to instruct all other nations; and by offering the *true offerings and incense,* would have *stayed* God's justice.

This *External Law* and Worship was not given to the Gentiles, which caused a partition Wall between Jew and Gentile, and the Jews looked on the Gentiles as a vile, base people, not worthy of notice, as they were not in the external Covenant of the law and worship (that should be) observed by them, who bore the name of God's people, (but under *his* divine justice). But the Gentiles *were* in the covenant touching the law *internal,* and that Jerusalem built by the hand of God. Further, when Christ came he called to, and prayed for, *his Elect,* both Jew and Gentile, throughout the whole world; breaking down the *partition Wall,* it being the *worship* according to the law of Moses; which worship was but the incense of Reason, for by it *no man can be saved,* therefore no more to be used by the *Elect,* CHRIST coming to redeem *them* by the power of Faith, *i.e.* his own nature, establishing his holy gospel, Covenant of grace, and Holy City Jerusalem, which is the sanctification of the soul: - Therefore the Elect must gather by the spirit of Faith as *he* did, and offer the true *prayer of Faith,* which is the true *incense* that ascends up to God.

Also if Christ had not come, Moses's commission would have ended in *death,* therefore God the *Father* as the *Creator,* (according to his creation, was a God of *justice,* because both man and angel broke the law they was created under, and *fell*; and this very God the *Father,* or of *justice,* was graciously pleased to think it good to transmute himself into flesh, and take his own created nature of Adam, (*i.e.* human nature animated with *divine Faith* in a fallen state); thus God became a *Son* to his own power of the Father, and waded through the power of Reason, and kept his own law of Faith, (*i.e.* "not to hearken to the voice of Reason"); yea this human nature, animated with divine Faith, was fell so low as to bring death on the soul of the eternal MAJESTY! Who gave that nature pure in the creation of man, so he went through the powers of Sin, Death, Hell, and Justice, conquering all by his own power, *i.e.* the power of Faith, it being the divine life and nature of God, and is the quickening power: Thus God by his own *inherent power,* in compact with Moses and Elias, translated into heaven to the glory of the *Father,* worked the great work of *Redemption,* established his *holy covenant* of grace, and *crowned* the Faith of those who were translated to under the mercy of the Son at the hour of death! *Then* God the *Father,* or the God of *justice,* was become God the *Son,* or the God of *mercy:* and the power of justice is given to the internal *Angel* in justice in the soul of man, so as to seal him under justice and keep him down to, and in *death eternal;* which internal *Angel* is sure to do the will of God, according to his creating the cherubim which was under the attribute of his divine justice.

Again when Jesus had declared the *Gospel,* and worked the *Redemption,* the ceremonial worship and temple at Jerusalem was thrown down, never more to flourish, though the Jews set a great value on themselves, as they was in the covenant of the law and bore the name of the Lords people, whereby his name may be known on this earth, in reference to his divine justice. Further, the power of God's divine justice was manifest on the nation of the Jews, for their disobedience to the commands of Moses, equally as much, or rather more than it was on the Gentiles or Heathen, from the giving forth the law till the coming of Christ; so they valued themselves for having the law given them, and by this law they was condemned.

Moreover, the *external law* given by Moses was to shew forth the *internal law;* and the mighty judgments Moses brought on the children of Israel, as the *external Angel* of the law, was to shew forth the power and judgment that was and would be given to this *internal Angel* of law; for Moses truly gave forth the law external, according to what was written internal; therefore this internal *angel* in justice will witness to Moses's declaration, and act as Moses on the souls and spirits of men, to the end of time and in ETERNITY. So this is the great CITY and *spiritual Jerusalem,* relative to the *internal law* and *angel* in justice in the soul of man, where true *record* is kept, and true *judgment is and will be given:* And this great CITY of the *law,* or of *justice,* began to *act* when Cain slew his brother Abel; then Cain was arraigned before this *internal Angel* in justice to his condemnation; for it was this internal Angel only that Cain communed with, calling him *Lord,* for this is the angel of and lord to Reason, in respect to giving true judgment against it, before the attribute of divine justice; and as Christ is the *angel of Faith,* this is the *angel of Reason:* Now Faith can face its own angel, and offer at his PREROGATIVE royal feet to be accepted or rejected, according to his *prerogative Will;* but Reason cannot bear to face its angel, for then it will cry, "his punishment is greater that he can bear." Thus, this *great city Jerusalem* began to act, and has continued to this day, for the law of Moses was given many years after this, and ended in respect to ceremonial worship when CHRIST came; only this, the letter of the law of Moses is a great help to the cherubim to rule people, nations &c. but the *power* of justice *is* given to this internal Angel touching *eternal Misery,* and this judgment is given *in this spiritual Jerusalem;* and as judgment was given against CHRIST by the spirit of Reason in the *temporal city* Jerusalem, so there is and will be judgment given against the spirit of Reason in the *spiritual city* Jerusalem, which is of the law, by the internal angel in justice; and this is the Jerusalem that the angel was to tell *Zechariah, should be inhabited as towns without walls, for the great multitude of men and cattle therein,* which comprehends the whole world, *i.e.* God's justice is over the souls and spirits of men throughout the world; for the external Jerusalem and Temple would pass away, but this will for ever stand; neither can anyone get from this Jerusalem to the *heavenly Jerusalem* but by the true *prayer of Faith* and God's *divine assistance.*

Again, *Zechariah* (ii. 5.) "I, saith the Lord, will be unto her a wall of fire round about, and will be the glory in the midst of her." This has relation to the HEAVENLY JERUSALEM, kingdom of mercy, or kingdom of grace and sanctification *i.e.* the kingdom of CHRIST: And the *wall* of this city is divine justice, as I have written, *i.e.* the *fire of God,* and God's justice which is a *consuming fire,* is as a *Wall,* and divides the Kingdom of Justice from the Kingdom of Mercy, as the firmament divides heaven and earth - why? because Kingdom, or the *City of Justice,* is surrounded with justice, and the Kingdom, or *City of Mercy,* is above justice; and the divine MAJESTY was, and is, in the midst of this Kingdom, or City of Mercy, and is the *Light* and glory thereof.

Moreover, this *heavenly Jerusalem is the kingdom of Christ,* and this kingdom has been building or gathering together ever since the death of Abel; for Abel was the first man that was translated from justice, and died under the mercy of the SON: also the elect of old was subject to the *wiles and temptations* of Reason and the law internal; and the angel of the law did keep them from communion with God touching his mercy, until God was graciously pleased to commune with the spirit of Faith in them, above the power of the internal angel in justice; and every man then, as well as now, must stand distinct to and for himself, before the divine MAJESTY, and offer the *prayer of Faith,* which is the *true incense* that ascends up to God. Thus God has been, and is now graciously pleased to help the spirit of Faith on, in this sore journey of flesh, and at the hour of death, to translate them to under the Mercy of the Son: and they died in this faith, *viz.* that God the *Father,* who was the *God of Justice,* would become God the *Son,* and the *God of Mercy,* for to establish his covenant of redemption and grace to his elect; and by the ALMIGHTY GOD working of this great work, they would be raised to everlasting glory by the mercy of the *Son.*

Again, as God's Elect was *scattered* in different parts of the world, they were and are thus called together for and to the *Kingdom of Christ,* whether bearing the name of Jew or Gentile, &c. This was done before the external law was given by the man Moses; for the law is not the Kingdom of Christ, but the *kingdom* or *incense* of Reason, and under justice: and in the *time* of the law God communed with his Elect, above the power of the internal *angel* in justice, by his merciful spirit, by which they prophecy of their own salvation, and God *would* become a *Son,* and they *were* translated at the hour of death, as aforesaid. Thus the LORD of glory, by the power of Faith, became a *Son* to redeem, in the midst of this *Great City* or *kingdom of Faith, i.e.* the Kingdom of CHRIST; and He is the Light, Life, and Glory of this *Holy City* or Kingdom, *i.e.* the NEW JERUSALEM.

CHAP. XVII

ZECHARIAH, communed with the similitude of the internal angel in justice, as aforesaid. "And he shewed him Joshua the high-priest standing before the angel of the Lord, and satan standing at his right hand to resist him," (iii. 1.) This *angel of the Lord* that Joshua stood before, was the angel that *Zechariah* communed with; for the inspiration according to the law, came from God through this internal angel in justice, and the *priest*, priesthood and worship, in the time of the law, stood before this angel, because it was according to his divine justice; and if they obeyed Moses's commands, and offered the true offering and incense, (which was of Reason) it is ascended before the attribute of God's divine justice, by the way of this Angel, to excuse men: and when men were disobedient, acting according to their *Wild* Reason, their evil went before God's divine justice, through this Angel in justice to man's condemnation; for this Angel is truly in justice before God, relative to acts of Reason in man.

Further, *Satan stood at Joshua's right-hand to resist him.* This *Joshua* (when the Jews returned from the captivity) was of the priesthood, and the *high-priest*, and they did build the Temple against the *resistance* of their enemy, that the worship, according to the law, should be done again at *Jerusalem*, as many would have hindered the building, if possibly they could; thus the spirit of Reason in man, which is *Satan,* stood before the angel *at the right hand of Joshua to resist him*: also the spirit of Reason stood on the right hand of the *Priest* and *People,* to allure them from the *Truth* of the declaration, into false worship, *i.e.* the *Wild Priesthood* of Reason, both internal and external, and has brought God's displeasure upon them, and he suffered them to go into great captivity, &c.

Again (Zechariah iii.) And the Lord said unto satan "The Lord rebuke thee, O satan, even the Lord that hath chosen Jerusalem rebuke thee, is not this a brand plucked out of the fire?" This *Lord* that spake to satan was the internal Angel in justice, for he is Lord to Reason in this world, therefore he said "the *Lord that hath chosen Jerusalem rebuke thee,"* which is the LORD of HEAVEN, *i.e.* the internal angel in justice, (Lord to Reason) would have the GOD of HEAVEN to overthrow *Wild Reason* in its intent, according to his divine justice, that the Jews should enjoy their worship again at Jerusalem, because they were as *a brand plucked out of the fire*, being then taken from their captivity.

Also "Joshua was clothed with filthy garments, and stood before the angel." Those *filthy garments* were those he wore in his captivity, and not those fine garments according to the priesthood in the time of the law; but those *filthy garments* were taken from him: and it was said, "Behold I have caused thy iniquity to pass from thee," *i.e.* the time of the captivity according to the transgression of the Jews was up, and God was graciously pleased to bring them back to Jerusalem. "And they set a fair mitre upon his head, and clothed him with change of garments, and the angel of the Lord stood by," *i.e.* the angel that communed with *Zechariah*. "And the angel of the Lord protested unto Joshua, saying, Thus saith the LORD of HOSTS. If thou wilt walk in my ways, and if thou wilt keep my charge, then thou shalt also judge my house." This *house* was the Temple at Jerusalem, for Joshua was the high-priest, and in this obedience he should have wisdom to judge people according to the worship of the law of Moses, which is but the incense of Reason, as aforesaid; and all this was done before the angel of the LORD, *i.e.* the internal angel in justice, that *Zechariah* saw in similitude and communed with.

Moreover, I would have the elect to *Understand*, that all the fine priestly garments Joshua wore under the law, and all the ceremonies and ordinances, were but cherubical, or an outward shew of Reason, and in the eye of Faith but as *fading garments*: also all the invented worship from the *Letter* of the scripture, by the spirit of Reason, with their outward shew of self righteousness, quick turns in argument, to justify themselves in their conceited gathered knowledge, own choice of religion, and feigned holiness therein, now reigning at this day, appearing as *fine garments* to cover the acts of filthy Reason in the soul of man, is but *filthy garments, of old rags,* in the sight of the ETERNAL MAJESTY, whose nature is divine Faith; neither can it pass the internal Angel, to the Divine Majesty; so it must be all put away.

"HEAR NOW, O Joshua the high-priest, and thy fellows that sit before thee, for they are men wondered at; for behold I will bring forth my servant the BRANCH," (8 v.) Now the high-priest and Jews were *wondered* at, because they were gathered to Jerusalem, and did build the Temple in the midst of enemies; and was promised the continuation of that priesthood to abide in Juda and Jerusalem, till

CHRIST came, who was to be born of the Tribe, and in the land of Juda, the *spiritual* king of the jews, and the Royal *Branch of Mercy,* to CROWN the Faith of the Elect of old; also opened the kingdom of heaven for all his Elect to come in under the gospel: and as Zerubbabel was of the lineage of the Kings of Juda, and Joshua of the Levitical priesthood, so Zerubbabel laid the foundation of the *second* Temple at Jerusalem, "and brought forth the head stone thereof with shoutings, crying, Grace! Grace! Unto *it,*" This *head stone* typified the coming of Christ in the flesh, to work the Redemption; but touching *his* coming in spirit in our days, Note, When a *Message* or *Declaration* comes from heaven, and Man comes to acknowledge or believe it, by hearing from *word* of mouth, or written *record*; and in this *Message* is contained justice, as well as invitation to mercy, and man from the letter should preach CHRIST and his gracious Promises, thereby forming a righteousness, or holiness, according to his *own Imagination,* and greatly talk of the coming of Christ; yet if such a man cannot be brought further than the outward word or bare letter, he must die as he was born, *i.e.* under the attribute of divine justice, and this is similar to the *first Temple* at Jerusalem: But when a man hears or reads those glorious promises, and looks into his own *dark evil soul and spirit,* and truly asks himself, whether he is worthy of those gracious promises, *yea,* or *nay?* Then if the answer comes from the spirit of Truth, it is this; - "I am a sinner, and unworthy to inherit those things." Then by this answer, the spirits of man sink into the fear of death, and works the soul into a *spiritual death*; now this is a death to Reason and disobedience, or the putting off of *filthy garments,* or rags; then by this *Death,* from the womb of Faith, is *quickened* a new *Life,* and this life that quickens is the spirit of Faith, from its womb or seed: This is the *virgin daughter* of Faith, *born of water* or the first covenant, and she will follow the *Messenger* through the temptations of Reason, briars and thorns, this dark spiritual earth is productive of; and *offer* her own prayer, *i.e.* the true *Incense,* and at times will receive heavenly *Gifts,* by the divine incomes of the HOLY SPIRIT of JESUS, to help on in her travail; and by or from those divine incomes, she prophecies of *Christ* to come in spirit to *sanctification*; and this is similar to the building of the *second Temple* at Jerusalem.

After this, when the virgin daughter has travailed the above sore journey, and come to the *Baptism of water* in and to the soul of man, *i.e.* this, the soul is truly sensible that this declaration is from heaven, and they have truly followed the *Messenger,* having had at times a secret *light* of the holy spirit shining in their soul, to help them on, and confirm to them the truth of the *Messenger's* declaration; and they are united to him by the power of Faith, and shall enjoy by him the promise of CHRIST, and having forgiven all, and in love and friendship with the whole world; this is the height of health, or the *Baptism of the nether waters,* a state very desireable to be in, yet under the internal angel in justice. After this CHRIST makes his *spiritual appearance* to the soul; then you are arraigned before the Prerogative of God, and there kept by the internal angel in justice; then asked the question, *What* have you done, whereby you are worthy to enter the *Kingdom of Heaven?* Or, *Are* you united to *Christ in God* by spiritual REGENERATED FAITH? - Here the soul is in great distress, for the answer is, No! And he would fain go back into those *fine waters* where he came from; but no! they are all turned into blood! Nor more *Life* there! The angel will not let you go back; but forward to Christ and his *glorious waters* you *must* go, or into *life eternal!* Then the eager *prayer* of the *Virgin* ascends for divine assistance, and HE is graciously pleased to unite in spirit with this *Virgin Daughter* of Faith, and begets to himself a *spiritual Son* for the KINGDOM OF HEAVEN! Then the spiritual *travail* and building of Jerusalem is over to such a man, as then *Christ is come* in spirit, and he dies in the *bed of mercy,* to be raised to *eternal glory!* And if he comes back with this *Tale,* his life is preserved by the almighty power; for this (spiritual birth) is *death* to this *life.*

Again Zechariah (iii. 9.) "For behold the stone that I laid before Joshua, upon one stone shall be seven eyes, behold I will engrave the engraving thereof, saith the Lord of HOSTS, and I will remove the iniquity of that land in one day." In these words is also contained a prophecy of Christ's coming to *redeem,* and the *time* of Christ is counted *Day;* thus he desired them to *work while it was Day:* and the *stone* that was *laid before Joshua* signifies the *priesthood* according to the law should then end, as *Christ,* who is the very God, would bring in his own *royal priesthood, i.e.* the priesthood of MELHIZEDEC, which is of Faith, Grace, and Mercy: and the *stone* that upon it should be *seven eyes,* was and is the *seed of Faith, i.e. the good ground* in the soul of man, for JESUS to work upon, as there is the seed and spirit of Reason for the man MOSES to work upon: Therefore when Jesus came he called to and quickened Faith, and brought it to the *knowledge* of its own lost condition, and of consequence, the necessity of a Redeemer then came. Also Jesus brought forth the *fruits of Faith,* not only in himself, but in the souls of his Elect by his all-quickening power, whereby to him *the tree was known by its fruit,* and this *Fruit* of Faith is the *seven eyes* or *engraving* done by God himself; thus Faith in scripture, according to redemption and sanctification, is likened to a "white *stone,* and a new name written in the stone, which no man knoweth, saving he that receiveth it;" and this *new name* is the sanctification and seal of Christ the living God, as those *seven eyes or engravings* is the *fruits* of Faith brought forth in the soul of man, viz. PATIENCE, MEEKNESS, OBEDIENCE, LONG-SUFFERING, LOVE, MERCY, CHARITY, &c. &c. and those *Eyes* of the spirit of Faith in the soul of man, the *Eyes* of the angel of the covenant of grace, are to and fro this earth, beholding by the mystical union of Faith, between him the *Fountain* of all Faith, and *his* children the *Sons* of Faith, upon this earth, *scourged* by the power of Reason.

Also Zechariah saith, "And the angel that talked with me came again, and waked me, as a man is wakened out of his sleep," (chap. 4.) This was the internal *Angel* in justice, and *he* doth the same thing even to this day; as when many of the Elect are *lulled to sleep* by the alluring spirit of Reason, this angel will *awaken* them out of that sleep, unto instruction; and good it is for them that he doth.

And "Zechariah looked, and did behold a candlestick all of gold, with a bowl upon the top of it, and seven lamps thereon, and seven pipes to the seven lamps, which are upon the top thereof, and two olive trees by it, one upon the right side of the bowl, and the other upon the left side thereof." And the angel that talked with Zechariah said, "Knowest thou not what those be?" And he said, "No my lord." And the angel said, "this is the word of the LORD unto Zerubbabel; Not by might, nor by power, *but by my spirit, saith the LORD of HOSTS."* Now, as Zerubbabel was appointed by God to build the second Temple at Jerusalem, he also was instructed by the *prophets* Zechariah and Haggai; the former receiving instruction from God by the way of this internal Angel in justice, whom he saw by vision in similitude, who also saw the *candlestick of gold* that Moses *received the pattern of in the Mount,* (which was made for the Tabernacle in the wilderness) by which he ordered and instructed one to be for the *second* or new *Temple* at Jerusalem, which was *the word of the Lord unto Zerubbabel,* by Zechariah, as he was told by the angel: and the *candlestick* (with a bowl on the top, and seven pipes to the seven lamps) typified the *candlestick of Faith* (but at a distance), as in the building of this *second Temple* is contained a prophecy of CHRIST, of which I speak anon: But this *candlestick* was in the time of the Law; and to burn oil in *the lamps upon it,* relates to the ceremonies and worships of the law, which then signified no more than that Reason should be enlightened in the law, and that priesthood; and all the ordinances, lights, offerings, and incense, according to the worship of the law, was but the *incense* of Reason; for by it only eternal life could not be had, yet it must be done that Reason may enjoy its Kingdom: Also it was "pure olive oil for those *lamps,"* i.e. relative to the *purity* of God's creating the Cherubim, and the *pure Law* he created him under, and the *Stay* of God's *pure Justice* to Reason; and as Moses was inspired under the attribute of divine justice, by the way or through the Cherubims bringing that Law into this world, he was the ANOINTED *Cherubim* by God himself, with the wisdom of the cherubical law, as were all prophets *under* the law, (by the way, or through the cherubim) inspired by God himself; only Isaiah was inspired by the way of the *Seraphims,* but all after the *inspiration* of the Man Moses, under the attribute of *Justice,* with the wisdom of the *pure* cherubical Law, and worship of God required under it to *stay* his justice.

Note, This *inspiration* of the first covenant, (*i.e.* of the law and worship accordingly) that *only* will not admit a man to eternal life? Why? Because the man, so inspired, could not keep the law, nor any created Being, as being partaker of the *fall;* so the law genders to bondage, strife, justice, and death; and if such a thing could be for a man to keep the Law, and offer the true *incense* of Reason, he being in a *fallen* state, must die or be changed, then he would be raised to the glory of the cherubims, after the manner of a *Child,* to whom the law is not charged; but his life in the Kingdom of Heaven will not be of Faith, neither can he commune with God in the glorious *union of Faith,* as can the *Elect the children of God,* nor be glorified with the glorious fire of *Faith.*

But of the *candlestick of Faith,* as I have said, God was graciously pleased to *commune* with his *Royal Seed,* above the power of the *internal Angel* in justice, in the soul of *Man,* (*i.e.* the cherubim and flaming sword that turns every way to keep the way of the tree of life), and this *Revelation and communion* was from the DIVINE MAJESTY to the spirit of Faith in the souls of his *Elect,* by which *they offered* the prayer of Faith, which is the true *incense* that ascends up to God for his mercy, and prophecied that the God of *justice* would become the

God of *mercy* to redeem them, and at the hour of death were translated from under the power of this *angel* in justice, to under the mercy of the *Son;* and this was done long before Moses's commission gave forth the external law; and even so, from the days of Moses till the coming of CHRIST, God *communed* with the prophets and his other Elect by the *merciful spirit* of Faith, of his becoming a *Son,* the GOD OF MERCY, to redeem them from under the *Law* and power of the angel: thus they prophecied of their own salvation, and God becoming a *Son,* and left it on *record,* with some of the *Acts* and sufferings of Jesus, his death and resurrection; which revelation and *communion* with God far transcends the cherubical inspiration (that being under the attribute of divine justice, with the wisdom of that pure law and worship God required according to the law) which is but the *incense* of Reason; for though many great acts, according to justice, by that inspiration was done, yet it *only* ends in death, under justice; but the *communion* with GOD in the *merciful* spirit of Faith; leads to *Life and Mercy;* consequently the Elect, at the hour of death, were translated to under the *mercy of the Son.*

Thus of king David, who was not inspired after the manner of Moses's inspiration, so was no prophet *in* and according to the *Law* as was Moses and Samuel, yet GOD revealed himself to him, and *communed* with him relative to the attribute of his *divine mercy,* by which David prophecied God would become a *Son,* and of his own salvation, leaving it on record, so that Jesus when on earth quotes his words, and as *so,* David was a great prophet concerning the coming of CHRIST, and this is the prophecy that Christ did and doth regard, saying, "*all things* must be fulfilled which were written in the *law of Moses,* and in the *prophets,* and in the *psalms* concerning *Me,*" (Luke xxiv. 44.) And this is the *Revelation and Communion with God,* and *Prophecy* that God would become a *Son,* with the *prayer of Faith,* which is the true *incense* that ascended up to God in or from the *Elect* in the days of old, when God was in the state of *God the Father,* from the days of Adam till Christ came; and *this is one* of the great *Prophets, prophecies,* or WITNESSES, to and with the *spirits of Faith,* which is God's own divine nature; therefore *his own WITNESS, of the Spirit* that he himself would become a *Son,* and this is the *Candlestick of Faith,* whereby Faith communes with, and prays to God; and the true *Olive Tree* or *Branch,* that stands before the *LORD of the Earth;* but this Candlestick, or Olive Tree, stood when God was in the state of God the Father, and now stands recorded in the BOOK OF LIFE.

Therefore see *Zechariah* (iv. 12.) "And I answered again, and said unto him, What be those *two* OLIVE BRANCHES which through the two golden pipes empty the golden oil out of themselves?" This *olive branch* is the *seed of Faith*, as I said before, and their *emptying* the golden oil *through* the golden pipes, *out* of themselves, is this; the *golden oil* is the *prayer of Faith*, which is the true *incense* that ascends up acceptable to GOD, therefore called the *golden oil;* and the *golden pipes* mean this – the incense of Faith ascends *intirely pure,* and *distinct* to itself, so that the incense of Reason cannot *mix* with it, nor go that *way:* Thus, when He is graciously pleased to enlighten the souls of his *Elect,* the heavenly *enlightenings* of the HOLY SPIRIT comes from God to the *spirit* of Faith *in* the soul of man, which is the Golden Oil *through* the *golden pipe* to the hungry soul of man, by which he prophecies of his own salvation, but in great humbleness, and ofttimes after great trouble of soul, which is *Sackcloth;* and this is the *true incense* or *golden oil,* that burned, and yet *burns* in the *soul of man,* which is the *Lamp* or CANDLESTICK of FAITH, or royal OLIVE TREE, and WITNESS of the SPIRIT, that stood before GOD, when he was *God the Father* only.

The other *Olive Tree, Branch,* or *Witness of the Spirit,* is the *Seed* of Faith, that *stand before GOD,* now he is become a SON, and the *GOD of Mercy;* and the prayer of Faith is *offered* for his *Mercy* as a Son and a Redeemer; and by his glorious inshining *Light* from heaven, the soul truly witnesseth that he is become a *Son,* and prophecies that he will *come to him in* spirit, to seal and sanctify him for the kingdom of heaven, and that Christ will raise him to glory at the last day: Thus this is the other great PROPHET that prophecies, and great WITNESS of the *holy Spirit,* CANDLESTICK, or OLIVE TREE, that stands before God, now he is become a *Son:* and when Jesus was here a *true Son* to the *Power* of the Father, *He* offered the prayer of Faith, which is the true *incense* that ascended before the *Throne.* Jesus was also in the midst of this *great city of Faith,* and is the KING, the LIGHT, and GLORY of *Faith,* and those two great *Witnesses* witness to each other's Faith, and prophecy of each other's glory: thus it is Faith in Faith, and Faith upon Faith, and all *centers* to CHRIST the KING of Faith and Glory.

And those *Olive Trees* being one on the *right* side of the candlestick, and the other on the *left,* is this; - One great *Prophet* stood before God the *Father*, and the other now he is God the *Son.* Also *Zechariah* saith, (verse 13.) "And he answered and said, Knowest thou not what those be? And I said, No my Lord: then said he, Those are the two ANOINTED ONES that stand before the LORD of the whole earth," *i.e.* his royal Elect, as aforesaid, one great *Prophet,* or *Witness of the Spirit* standing in the BOOK of LIFE before him, as when he was *God the Father,* and the other now he is *God the Son,* and are ANOINTED by the HOLY SPIRIT.

Again, concerning the *light* or *incense* of Reason, it is from or by the law being written in that nature, which law is. *You shall love God above all, and your neighbour as yourself,* and there is the internal angel, or cherubim that strictly watches over the Law: therefore if a man hearken to and watch this law, and in all his acts and dealings seek to do good to his neighbour, and to hurt no one living, but have a charitable disposition to do good to all, that man will have peace: also if a man is injured by another, so that he will seek redress by the hand of justice, let it be done with a tender merciful eye, always be careful to remember that God was the author of his being, and all the good he possesseth; and further, that God according to his justice is not only able to dispossess him of all the good he enjoys, but also to cut him off from the land of the living; And if a man hath hurt another, let that man go and ask forgiveness, and, if possible, make that man amends, and be content in the situation that God by his providence has placed him also to know all the good he enjoys above a perishing condition, God is the author of; therefore be thankful to God for his goodness.

Moreover, the *outward* Word, or bare *Letter* of the Gospel, is given to Reason, and he may read therein, and that will enlighten him in his duty according to the law; for in that letter is contained *justice* as well as invitation to *mercy*; and if this be done with, and in the *fear of God,* and the true prayer and offering to atone before him, the internal angel in justice in the soul of man will not accuse him of that evil; then there flows peace and thanksgiving in the soul: and this is the *oil* that is conveyed or let *burn* by the internal angel in justice in the spirit of Reason, from those good acts, by the *light* of the Law, which is the *oil* or *incense* of Reason burning in its LAMPS, and is the internal *Jewel* to that soul or spirit of Reason; but this Jewel far surpasses any external Jewel to the eye of the world; this is the true *Lamp,* or *incense* of Reason, but is quite different from, and distinct to, the *Golden Oil* of Faith; for when CHRIST comes in spirit, the *Golden Oil* of Faith cannot be found in the lamps of Reason.

Again, as aforesaid, the building of the *second Temple at Jerusalem, greatly typified* (but at a distance) *the coming of Christ:* And *Zechariah* saw great things by *vision,* and had great *communion* with GOD by way of the internal angel, whom he saw in similitude: and when the foundation of the *second Temple* was laid, many of the *priests* and *Levites,* and chief of the *Fathers,* who were *ancient men,* that had seen the *first house,* wept when the foundation of the *second* was laid, while others rejoiced, and shouted for joy. Those that shouted for joy, did signify the *seed of Faith;* and those who wept, did signify the *Seed of Reason*; for the spirit of Reason is very fond of magnificent external glory: therefore the prophet *Haggai* said, (chap. ii.) "Who is left among you that saw this house in her first glory, and how do ye see it now? – is it not in your eyes, in comparison of it, as nothing?" This is the true nature and acts of Reason; for when reason has transformed themselves into a declaration that comes from heaven, they take to themselves *a priesthood* from that declaration, which gives them a *Wild power* over the spirits of men, and that they glory in; but when the *second CALL* or *Order* comes, this Reason cannot endure, because it is against their *Acts and Wild priesthood,* then, of consequence, *less* glorious to the seed of Reason; but it is *more* glorious to the seed of Faith, as there is a further prophecy of the coming of CHRIST, (Haggai ii. 9.) "The glory of the latter house shall be greater than the former, saith the LORD of HOST; and in this place will I give *peace,* saith the *Lord* of *Host."*

And in this manner do I speak relative to the COMMISSION of the SPIRIT; which of you lived in the days of the *first Messenger,* or saw the glory of it when it was first declared? You have conceived a glory you never saw, and assumed a power that to you was never given: for the glory of the *second CALL* is greater than that of the *Declaration;* for one *calls to stedfast belief,* and the other to the *spiritual BIRTH and sanctification;* and this is *more* glorious to the seed of Faith but *less* glorious to the seed of Reason; because of *this* they never can know, viz. the *glory of Sanctification!* But may wander on, or in, the bare *Letter.*

CHAP. XVIII

AFTER this, "*Zechariah* looked and beheld a flying Roll; the length thereof is twenty cubits, and the breadth thereof ten cubits. Then said he unto me, This is the curse that goeth forth over the face of the whole earth, and every one that *stealeth* shall be cut off as on this side, according to it; and every one that *sweareth,* shall be cut off as on that side according to it," (chap. v.) This *flying Roll* is the *justice* of GOD, which *goeth forth over the whole earth;* for the *Law* being written in the nature of Reason, it rules that *Life* and *justice* rules that *Law;* and many has been and are *cut off* by the *external Angel* according to this *Law,* and many has been and will be *cut off* by the *internal* Angel according to this *Law:* also many *false prophets* have sworn and prophecied in the name of God, in the time of the Law and have been found liars: And the same has been done in the time of the Gospel; therefore many will be found recorded on *that side of the Roll* that contains the time of the *Law.* And many on the *other side* that contains the time of the *Gospel;* for the *internal Angel* in justice is in the soul of every man through generation, therefore every man is sure to bear his own condemnation before the attribute of divine justice, for this internal *Angel* has great power over the soul of man.

Again many of the seed of Reason has usurped the *outward Word* or bare *Letter,* and gone forth *false teachers,* or Wolves in *Sheep's clothing, - i.e.* this lying and deceiving spirit of Reason took the letter of the scripture and preached the name of JESUS, and the worship God required unto salvation, according to their *own dark* judgment on the bare letter, and *clothe* themselves with the scripture and the name of JESUS, and as so will be found *thieves and robbers;* and this is spiritual *Stealing,* because they take to themselves that which doth not belong to them; and also they publish themselves *Ministers of the Gospel,* which is preaching, prophecying, and *swearing falsely* in the *name of Jesus;* and this is spiritual *swearing,* because *their* doctrine is not from heaven *by inspiration,* but by their own imagination on the bare *Letter,* written long ago by other men: Therefore (verse 4) "I will bring it forth, saith the LORD of HOST, and it shall enter into the house of the *Thief,* and into the house of him that *sweareth falsely by my name* and it shall remain in the midst of his house, and it shall consume it, with the *timber* thereof and the *stones* thereof," *i.e.* the seed of Reason, with all their excuses for the evil they do, and their *prayer* and *self-righteousness,* which is as *timber* or *stone* (as they may think) against this *Roll* of justice; yet this internal *Angel* in justice, in the soul of man, will *seal* him under *death,* according to *justice:* and it is called a *flying* Roll, because it is in the soul of *every* man; therefore when CHRIST doth come, *every* man will be his *own* witness to his *own* condemnation.

Then the *Angel* that talked with *Zechariah* said, "Lift up thine eyes, and see this that goeth forth: *and I said, What is it? and he said,* This is an *Epha* that goeth forth: *he said moreover,* This is their resemblance through all the earth; and behold there was lift up a *talent of lead,* and this is a *Woman* that sitteth in the midst of the *Epha;* and he said, This is wickedness, and he cast it into the midst of the *Epha,* and cast the weight of lead upon the mouth thereof." This *woman* mentioned here is the *spirit of Reason,* and the *Epha that goeth forth,* is the *imagination of Reason,* and the *talent of lead* is the *seal of death* to Reason; and all this is *recorded* in the flying *Roll* by the internal *Angel* in justice in the soul of man; for all the *Acts* of man, from the imagination of Reason, is *continually* evil in the sight of God, and it leads to and centers in death. Also in the *wisdom* of Reason in the scriptures, their preaching and expostulating concerning them, it doth not lead *to life,* but unto *death*; and if they promise you *life* in that *promise* is contained death; and although they make use of many fine expressions and glorious promises to dress up *their* language and cover *their* dark spirit, yet this *Language and Promise* was never made nor directed to *them,* but to the *seed* and *spirit* of Faith, which is the divine NATURE OF GOD, quite contrary to the nature of Reason - why? because the *nature of Faith* came from God, who is all *Light, Life,* and *Glory;* and the *nature of Reason* proceeded, or came forth from *Chaos,* which is *death* and *darkness,* only it was called forth from thence by the creating power of the DIVINE MAJESTY. – Those natures are here on this earth, and when a *Messenger* comes from God and tells his *Tale,* those natures will shew themselves to the *Messenger, i.e.* the INNOCENT seed of Faith will come as near the *Messenger* in Faith as possible they can, to follow up to God: And the seed of Reason will think themselves as wise, or more so, than the Messenger, and so go their own way. Thus the two natures are very eager to get back from whence they came, and each will venture their salvation on the road they go: But, think you, is it possible for any man to teach the way to *Light* and *Life,* and he himself under the power and seal of *death* and *darkness!* So by this *weight of lead being cast upon the mouth thereof,* comes forth the language of death and darkness, let them dress it up as they can, or think as they will.

Again *Reason* is called a *Woman,* because of this; - there is the *womb* or *seed* of Reason in the soul of man, as well as there is the *womb* or *seed* of Faith; only this -Faith is called the *good Ground,* but the womb or seed of Reason the bad Ground, which produces thistles, thorns, tares, &c. Now Reason is capable of spiritual generation, and this is its process: he will conceive God according to his *own* liking, and worship his own way, and divide into different *Sects,* according to their understanding of ceremonial parts, as will please God, or rather themselves best, and those are *spiritual Kingdoms,* and Agents of the *dark* spirits are *teachers;* and although they may differ somewhat in form of worship, yet their essential points of *Faith* is one and the same: And when God sends a *Message* on this earth, and the voice of *Truth* is uttered, then those *dark agents* are soon full of *fiery Zeal* to maintain their notional worship against the *Messenger's* true declaration, because their dark *spiritual Kingdom* is then in danger, and this *fiery Zeal* is a *daughter* that is conceived in false worship, and born of the womb of Reason, which I call a *daughter of Babylon,* or a daughter against the *secret divine Truth of GOD.* And this daughter is very eager to take the erroneous *traditions of men,* and to uphold the *dark* spiritual Kingdom *as* a spiritual inheritance. Then of this *daughter Zeal* is born a spiritual son, called *aspiring Pride,* who in itself is lawless - Why? Because the *Law* is written in Reason; but what is thus born of Reason is *lawless,* and it will ride on Reason when it doth curse, or spiritually crucify the *sacred teachings* of CHRIST, the King of Faith; until the internal *Angel* in justice appear to Reason with the *flaming sword* then Reason fall under this spiritual-born *son of perdition:* this is the great WHORE of BABYLON, *with whom many has been made drunk with the wine of her fornication,* and this is the fruit and effect of the Whore.

But I would not have any one think that *spiritual whoredom* was committed in Babylon *only* touching *former times,* but in Israel, and Juda also; for thus the word of the Lord came to Ezekiel, (chap. xxiii.) saying, "There were two *Women,* daughters of one *Mother,* and they committed whoredoms in Egypt in their youth, and the names of them were *Abola* the elder, and *Aboliba* her sister, and they were mine, and they bear sons and daughters; thus were their names, *Samaria is Abola,* and *Jerusalem is Aboliba.* And *Abola* played the harlot when she was mine, and she doated on her lovers, on the Assyrians her neighbours, And *Aboliba* increased in her whoredoms, when she saw men pourtrayed upon the wall (the images of the Chaldeans) - And she doated upon the Assyrians, and committed whoredoms with the Babylonians *i.e.* thus the spirit of Reason is very eager to leave that worship ordinated by God, to worship idols ordinated by Reason, which is their *Wild priesthood.*

This *Zechariah* was shewn, when in communion with the Angel, (chap. v. 6.) "And behold there came *two Women*, and the wind was in their wings, for they had wings like the wings of a stork, and they lift up the *Epha* between the EARTH and HEAVEN," *i.e.* this *woman* or *women*, being the spirit of Reason, in going on their *way*, which is contrary to the *way* of God, bears its *Epha* of imagination between *heaven and earth*, and with its *stork's wings* (*i.e.* false worship) flies hastily into death: thus, verse 10 and 11. "Then said I to the angel that talked with me, Whither do those bear the *Epha?* And he said unto me, To build an house in the land of *Shinar*, and it shall be established and set on her own base:" And this base is death; for as I said before, this nature came from *death* and *darkness*, which was always contrary to God, who is *light* and *life*, and even before creation where the DIVINE MAJESTY was, *there* it was all *light;* but if he did absent himself from that place, *darkness* would hover, and, If possible, take place; like to the sun, when in our horizon it is light, but when it is gone darkness ensues; for I would have all men to know, that *darkness, sin* and *death*, has its center, as well as *life, faith* and *glory;* and now this darkness is called into active life, and this life is Reason, and the cherubim has fell from the purity of his creation, therefore Reason will act contrary to Faith, and with eagerness work its way into *Death* and *Chaos*, from whence it came.

Also I would have the Elect to know, that the *Messenger* is an enemy to the spirit of Reason, for his *Message* is an enemy to his own Reason; therefore in your acts and conceivings it is good to watch this great spiritual *Whore* in your own soul, for she is not only ready to destroy *Truth* within you, but the *Messenger* without you. And if there is any act in the *Messenger* whereby any evil may be questioned, then in the souls of one or more by this great *Whore, is filled a vial with wine of her fornication,* then with the *wings of a stork* they are about to invite others to *drink* with them, which is soon done, for it is a delicious cordial to the spirit of Reason; but this cordial leads to death and hell, therefore watch and keep from it.

Again - "*Zechariah* lift up his eyes and looked, and behold there came four chariots out from between two *Mountains,* and the mountains were mountains of *Brass.* In the first chariot were *red Horses,* and in the second chariot *black Horses,* and in the third chariot *white Horses,* and in the fourth chariot *grisled* and *bay Horses,"* (chap. vi.) Those *four chariots* is the power of Reason, with the law written in that nature; and those *Mountains of Brass* they *came out from between,* is the LAW and JUSTICE, which amounts, by the acts of Reason to *Sin* and *Death;* therefore when the seed of Reason comes to manhood, and the internal angel taken place in the soul, then they are charged with the law, and by their actions they break the law, which is Sin, then justice takes place in the soul which is Death: - and those *Mountains* of *Sin* and *Death* are called *Mountains of Brass* because no one can remove them saving the LORD JESUS, the KING of FAITH in GLORY.

This Vision *Zechariah* saw was concerning Israel and Juda, and the Babylonians and Assyrians; but it extended to the whole world, as you may see by what the Angel said that communed with *Zechariah:* therefore those *red Horses* and *chariots* is according to the temporal ruling power, that delights to go forth to shed blood and rule over men; and to him, or them that do this, there is no wisdom like unto it.

The *black horses* and *chariot* is the going forth of the *dark* superstitious spirit of Reason, that seeks to rule over and convert men to think as *they* do, and act like *them;* then to such people this is the greatest wisdom on earth.

The *white Horse* is the law, that is written in the nature of Reason, and goeth forth with Reason; and according to this law, there was the External Law, and worship God required according thereto, which doth demand obedience from Reason, because the law is good, and the righteousness of the law must be observed: thus such that obeyed the law to the best of their power, as Moses gave it forth, and offered the true offerings and incense according to that worship, to stay God's justice so far as this life; *those* had natural prosperity, and enjoyed a peace above other men who obeyed not; also such men could give forth charitable and good judgment, and those things is a crown of cherubical righteousness in this life, therefore the wisest thing that Reason can do.

The *grisled* and *bay Horses* is the going forth of *Death,* to and fro through the earth on the life of man; and as *bay* Horses signifies those who have died tyrants either in power or spirit, and have been the cause of much bloodshed, or maliciously shed man's blood themselves, or seek to devour men in any respect; and the *grisled* Horse is them that has gone forth by the *dark spirit* in false worship, and made or make a great outward show of righteousness, yet die under the power of the *dark spirit*; and is to shew how men fall into death under the power of their different *acts of evil;* and under those two heads do most of the seed of Reason die, *i.e.* under the *bay* or *grisled* Horses, and some under both.

And, "*Zechariah* said unto the angel that talked with him, What are those, my Lord? And the angel answered and said unto me, Those are the four spirits of the *Heavens,* which goeth forth from *standing before the Lord* of all the earth," *i.e.* the spirit of Reason, with the law and the effects of the law; for Reason has gone forth from standing before the *Lord* of all the earth, to walk to and fro through the earth, seeking and gathering what they can: but Reason stands before *the cherubim and flaming sword that turns every way, to keep the way of the TREE of LIFE,*" *i.e.* the *internal angel* in justice in the soul of man: But Faith being so much inveloped in the waters of Reason, that it lays inactive, and has no concern with Reason in walking to and fro through the earth, neither can it be quickened into act but by the power of GOD from HEAVEN, then it will not go with Reason, but quite contrary, for it will get as near God the divine Majesty as possible, from whence it came, and stand before him in *Prayer.*

Moreover, "The *black Horses* which are therein, go forth into the *North* country, and the *white* go forth after them and the *grisled* go forth toward the *South* country: and the bay went forth, and sought to go, that they might walk to and fro through the earth: And he said, Get ye hence, walk to and fro through the earth: so they walked to and fro through the earth," *i.e.* the seed of Reason when they come to manhood are cast out from God, and never more can or will stand before him, but must wander *to and fro through the earth,* and the law goes with them, and the internal angel in justice seals the soul under the power of DEATH, followed with *Hell* at his heels: therefore it was said unto the *bay Horse (i.e. Death) Get you hence, walk to and fro through the earth.*

Further, those that went forth into the *North Country,* according to public acts in former time, chiefly mean the Israelites when they went out of Egypt, and the external law went after them, so as to be given them in the *Wilderness;* and while they obeyed Moses in the Law, and Worship accordingly, *Justice* was quieted; and after they was disobedient, they was taken captives into a strange land, and brought back according to *Prophecy,* then *Justice* was also *quiet,* because their time was up according to the will of God; therefore it is said, (v. 8) "Behold those that go toward the north country, have *quieted* my spirit in the north country." But, as I said this *vision* extends to the whole world.

Further, these things are acted in man's *internal* soul, for the *Soul of Man is dyed* in his own blood, with his own evil, and is become as *Red as scarlet;* and the internal angel in justice *rides on this Horse,* because he *seals* and keeps the soul in *Death.* except CHRIST takes off the seal: therefore this is the great RED HORSE, because it is in the soul of every man; and if any should say, this is a *red Horse,* or that is a *red Horse,* let him look at this, his own *red Horse.*

The *black Horse* is also in the soul of man *i.e.* the *dark* spirit of Reason, whereby men commit their evil acts and *self excuses:* And also this *black Horse* will carry the soul, so that men will act as *Ministers of Jesus,* and declare they have the assurance of eternal life, yet at the same time live or *ride* in their own blood, or filth over the *horse's back.*

Moreover, the BAY and GRISLED Horses, they take the spirit of Reason into *Death,* and this is found working in the soul of man: for when a *Message* comes from HEAVEN in the covenant of grace, this Message quickens Faith in the soul, and it grows strong to work its way by prayer, against the power of Reason, to get as near God as possible, from whence it came. Further, I would have men to *understand,* that most of the outgoings and acts of Reason, is comprehended under those two Horses, *viz.* the *red* and *black;* therefore when Faith is *quickened* from its *womb* or *seed* into act, it has the whole power of Reason to *War* against the soul and every one will find his own enemy.

Now the *Passions* of Reason in some is this - Everything must give way to their desire, and can hardly bear a sharp word or hasty answer, nor like to go back from a greater power, but are very arbitrary in their rule and positive in their arguments and proceedings, and soon moved to shew the spirit of tyranny; and this spirit is very able to go forth *to and fro this earth,* and act in bloodshed subject to its rule, &c. was it in such a place and power; and this is the *red Horse,* although in an *Elect* being: - But the *Spirit,* or *virgin Daughter* of Faith, grows strong; and by prayer, in time, with GOD'S divine assistance, will get above this tyrannical spirit of Reason, so very unwilling to give way, and will cause great troubles and agitations in the soul of man; because this spirit, if possible, will have the ruling power therein; and although this turbulent spirit may appear invincible, yet the spirit of Faith will be brought above it, by *divine assistance* as aforesaid. Also when the *virgin Daughter* of Faith is in her *travail,* the law becomes quick, and the internal angel acts with more power to curb the spirit of Reason in *Elect* men; and as *Faith* grows strong, *Reason* gets weak; then the *bay Horse* begins to act; for as this *red Dragon*-like spirit of Reason *dies* from its power, the soul *changes* in its disposition, *i.e.* in *colour,* in the eye of the Spirit; therefore as this *red* Horse dies, (which is losing its power) it becomes *bay;* and the soul of man can submit to, and *patiently* bear things in this life, leaving the folly and cruelty of this world behind.

Again: - The *Passions* of Reason in others is this; - they are very superstitious, and bound up *to* their own *judgment* in Religion and understanding of the scripture; and though many convincing *proofs* are brought to shew them their error, yet they will fly back to their own *judgment,* (like to a bow when bent) apt to remember their former tuition, or childish education, which is, in effect, a desire to die as they were born, without being *born again to Regeneration.* So powerful is this *dark spirit* in man, that it will keep the soul in bondage to it, against convincing proofs of error; and the man will go forth and preach, and declare from this *dark spirit,* as if it was the *Heavenly divine Light.* This is the *BLACK Horse in the soul* of man, and is to be found in the souls of Elect men: But, as aforesaid, when the *virgin Daughter* of Faith is born by the power of God, it has this *black* Horse to war against, which will cause great trouble of soul; but by *prayer* and *divine assistance* of God, Faith will get above it; then the *GRISLED Horse* begins to act. Further, this *dark spirit* is very *obstinate,* and will shift any way to allure the soul; but the internal angel in justice will *bridle* the power of this *black Horse* so that Faith by *prayer* shall go

Godward, and get above *this Passion* of Reason; then it will weaken in power, which is a death - so become a *grisled Horse:* So by degrees, this BLACK Horse *dies and becomes GRISLED;* then the man can bear or do any thing for the sake of *divine Truth:* therefore those *Horses* the *Elect* are to observe and strictly watch, is the RED and BLACK, because they are *within* themselves; But by the power of Faith, and God's divine assistance, death is brought on Reason's *Passions, i.e.* the *red* and *black Horse,* and by the power of this death they become the *BAY* and *GRISLED.*

Now those *two Horses* only, go forth in the *passions* of Reason, *i.e.* the *Kingship* and *priesthood* of Reason - not that priesthood which was given to Reason, to *stay* God's justice, (for that is of the *white Horse);* but that which Reason is productive of which is *Wild*; and as the law goes forth to condemn Reason, and death is the consequence of Reason's acts; so happy are they in whom this *red Horse (i.e.* the kingship of Reason) dies in this life and becomes *BAY;* and the *black Horse (i.e.* the priesthood of Reason) dies and becomes *GRISLED;* - for under those two heads are comprehended the acts of Reason; and when those Horses become *bay* and *grisled* in the soul, Faith becomes strong, to be *regenerated* unto CHRIST, and the essential Soul for the Resurrection, and enters into death in the *Bed of Mercy,* under the power of the *PALE HORSE,* like unto CHRIST their KING, and by him will be raised to eternal GLORY.

Again, *Zechariah* (chap. vi.) saying, "Behold the man whose name is the BRANCH, and he shall grow up out of this place, and he shall build the Temple of the LORD," This was a prophecy of Christ to come; for our glorious God was graciously pleased to leave the glory of the Father, *(i.e.* of justice) and transmute himself into flesh, which was *building the Temple of God,* because the very God was *become a Son* to the *Power of the Father,* and in a body of flesh worked the works of redemption, and ASCENDED into HEAVEN, God the SON, and the glorious GOD of Mercy. This he did by the power of Faith, *i.e.* the *white Horse* of Faith, that he went forth upon, *conquering and to conquer;* and he kept the law of Faith, which is *not to hearken to the voice of Reason:* This no one beside himself ever could do; therefore that righteousness is *his own.* So it was his own power of Faith, and his own righteousness of Faith, which is the *WHITE HORSE.* That HE went forth upon conquering and to conquer, and not the righteousness of Faith in the Elect; for they all have, and will break the law of Faith, which was the cause of GOD'S coming to REDEEM:

Therefore no one can wear the *Grand CROWN* of the righteousness of Faith but God himself, and he is now crowned the God of RIGHEOUSNESS, and God the SON which is of MERCY; and the God of all power to give *Crowns of Glory to his Elect.*

And further. HE is in his heavenly THRONE of Glory, and is graciously pleased to enlighten the souls of his Elect, and give *Gifts* of his holy Spirit to help *them* on in this sore journey of flesh; therefore all the fruits, prayer, or incense of Faith ascends to him, and he accounts it righteousness *in* and *from* the souls of his *Elect,* and *He* rules over them, or *rides* upon that righteousness; because HE is the giver of all divine Gifts, and receiver of their prayer, which is the INCENSE of FAITH.

CHAP. XIX

BY way of conclusion, I shall write more of the *Law internal,* and that *given Priesthood, and Glory* of the cherubims in HEAVEN above: - Now I have already declared, when the seed of Reason came to manhood, how they are cast out, and the cherubims and flaming sword placed to keep the way of the tree of life; Also when Moses was inspired, it was to give forth the law to Reason, and the worship of God required to stay his justice; and that this inspiration was cherubical, because it was given forth to Reason, after he had brought Israel out of Egypt.

Moreover, *God said to Moses,* "I am the God of thy father, the God of Abraham the God of Isaac, and the God of Jacob;" and Moses was to tell the elders, and children of Israel. He was sent by *the God of your fathers, the God of Abraham, the God of Isaac, and the God of Jacob, who had seen what was done in Egypt, and have surely visited you:* - yet this Inspiration and Message wholly was to Reason, for they was lineally descended from Abraham by natural generation; yet Moses might know by this, which God said, that HE was not the God of Reason (no further than creation, and of the law HE created them under, and of that justice which took place through Reason breaking his law) and with which Jesus answered the Sadducees concerning the resurrection, (Mark xii.) "Have ye not read in the book of Moses, how God spoke unto him in the bush, saying, I AM the GOD of Abraham, the GOD of Isaac, and the GOD of Jacob: He is not GOD of the *dead,* but GOD of the LIVING: therefore ye do greatly err."

Here the Elect may see. Although Moses was inspired with the cherubical inspiration, yet in time he was let to know God was not the GOD of Reason, no more than I have just before said; for Reason is incapable of regeneration, therefore is dead in the sight of God, under cherubical Justice, which is its *outcast* condition: But Faith is capable of the *first* resurrection to Regeneration, and of the *second* resurrection to *Life Eternal;* therefore Faith is capable of *Life* and *Will,* and can and doth *Live* in the sight of God, and before God; therefore this is the *Living* that *God is God of,* because Faith is of the divine nature of God. Now the Elect may see the difference between the *kingdom of Faith* and the *kingdom of Reason,* although men has much endeavoured to make them as one, by their not knowing the Scripture nor the power of God, and this is the general error among men.

Again, God said to Moses, "Cast thy rod on the ground, and he did, which became a serpent." This *rod* signifies the law; that when Moses the external angel gave it forth, it should rule the life of man, and a *rod* or staff in his hand to walk with: also his *casting it on the ground,* signifies that man would break the law; *then it became a serpent,* which is the Emblem of cherubical justice; and as soon as the law is broke, this justice begins to act to devour man; for as the law rules the life, so justice rules the law, and the nature of man is to *fly from before justice,* as Moses *fled from before the serpent:* Then God said to Moses, "Take it by the tail," which he did, *then it became a rod in his hand;* - which shews forth, God would *give a Priesthood,* that when man breaks the law, he should bring in his oblation, and offer before that justice of God, that it may be stayed from *devouring* of men, which is *taking by its hind part or tail,* then it is stayed and *become a rod in the hand.*

Moreover, (Exodus vii. 1.) "And the LORD said unto Moses, See I have made the a god to *Pharaoh,*" *i.e.* a God to Reason; for in Egypt, where *Pharaoh* was king, Reason mounted up to great riches, grandeur, pride, arts, and emulations, and to enslave the souls of men, to maintain them in their theme of greatness under their own Law and *wild Priesthood;* but when Moses came to take away the Israelites, the Egyptians resisted the will and power of God, and was *overthrown* in the justice of God, in the midst of their arts, emulations, &c. Also the spirit of reason in the Israelites, was mistaken in their promised land, and inheritance; for they thought to possess a land according to their own *will* and *way,* and become great as did the Egyptians; which may be seen by their *murmurs in the Wilderness,* but the *land* and *inheritance* they was to possess, was the *Law and Priesthood* given forth by Moses; for the *Law* of Moses; is the *Kingdoms* of this world; and the *given Priesthood,* to stay God's justice, is the *Glory* of the Kingdoms; for what would any kingdom be, was it not for the law to guide and rule Reason, that every one may enjoy his lot or inheritance in this life, and a priesthood to atone before God, to stay his justice, that man may not be *overthrown.* This is to stand before the power and justice of God in *fear,* then floweth all the blessings of this life, and this is the Kingdom of Reason, if he will take it: and, *mind* - Man is not able to give God a law and priesthood, neither will he *own* what man pleases to prescribe for himself.

Further - When *Moses* died, his *Body* was buried in the *Soul of Man, i.e.* as Moses gave forth the *law and Priesthood,* and executed justice in a body of flesh and person of man on this earth, (inspired so to do by the LORD GOD OF HEAVEN); and this *law,* justice, &c. centered to the *soul and spirit* of reason, and there abode; because the *internal Angel* in justice, and the *law* in the *soul of man,* truly bears witness to what he declared; therefore when *Moses* died, he left this behind *in the soul of man:* and in this manner was he *buried,* and this is his *burial place.* And this *Angel* is the *internal Moses;* and when CHRIST came, and brought in eternity, then this *Angel* had full power to take the soul of man into eternity.

Also this *internal Law* and *justice* stands thus: when the seed and spirit of Reason come to *manhood,* this angel takes place in the soul; then man is charged with the *Law* and *Justice* of God; and as the God of Heaven made Moses a God to *Pharaoh* the King, where Reason was in high emulated act, even so is this internal angel made a God to Reason; and, as aforesaid, they come into manhood, so charged with the law, it is given forth into lively act by the *internal Angel* to rule the life of man, and is a *Rod or Staff* in his hand to walk with; and when he breaks the law, the *Rod* falls and *becomes a serpent* to devour man; and man would *fly from it,* as did Moses; but he must *take it up by the tail,* as Moses did, to have justice stayed in the soul. Now this is to all and every one.

Moreover, Reason from the child springs up in pride, and lusting to be great and grand, and to rule over others; and its life flows forth in a desire after riches, arts, and emulations; all endeavouring to shine with, if not surpass each other, in this their kingdom; and their self cunning to gather up and to enslave the souls of men, to support their theme of greatness, that they may live and flourish in this arrogant Kingdom: and the spirit of Reason will act the *priest,* and counterfeit the way of God to excuse them in evil, in this *wild* Kingdom vanity and arrogance, where men are seeking to have their own will and way. Now this is the kingdom of *Egypt,* even *in* the soul of man; and when the call is for men to come out, and have the law given them, if the spirit of Reason (who is *King of that land)* will not let you come to take and observe the law of God, you may depend on being overthrown in this *kingdom,* as was *Pharaoh* and *Egypt,* in the midst of self wisdom, grandeur, arts, emulations, &c.

Again, - The Law is to *love God above all,* because God created all, *and your neighbour as yourself,* because we are all God's people according to creation, and in the goings out of Reason your neighbour must be minded as yourself; and in all the *Blessing* in this life, be careful of its use, lest you incur judgment, and are overthrown in his justice: And what was offered on the *Altar* now give your brother who hath need, always remembering it was given to you of God, and *you* are under his *justice:* and if a man has hurt another and implore forgiveness, and man cannot readily forgive, then let *him* ask of God for power to forgive, because forgiveness is a great crown of happiness in this life: and in all the outgoings in this world, seek righteousness, and to stand before the law with fear, and thanksgiving to God for his *blessing* you enjoy; and be careful not to return to Egypt, for man's life doth not consist of his *own will,* nor in *abundance,* but to stand before God for his blessing.

Now when man is charged with the law, in all the goings out of Reason the *Law* goes with it, and *Truth* rides on the law; so when man is tempted to break the Law, the voice of *Truth* says he must not do it, for it is wrong; then if he will not hearken to this voice, but breaks the Law, then this internal angel seals him under justice, and the *rod* doth *fall and become a serpent,* which, as I said before, *man would fly from,* and that is the way to be *devoured* by it; for he must with true relentance offer himself up to the will of God according to his justice, before this *internal Angel,* (who is in communion with them who sit in the *glory* of justice); then justice will be stayed; and this *is taking the serpent by the tail, to become a rod again.* Also, when any go with this offering to the angel, which is the *Altar* of Reason, he must in himself be in friendship and forgiveness with all and every one; for it will not do for man to desire God to *stay his justice* on him, and he will not *stay his wrath* on his brother; yea, every sin requires its *Oblation* to atone before justice. Now this is the *Law and given Priesthood* of Reason, to stand before God, and receive his *blessing of this life,* which is the *kingdom of Reason,* if he will take it.

And, as I have said, the communion of God with Moses, *from between the two Cherubims upon the Ark,* did signify God would commune with him from between the Cherubims that had life, *i.e.* between Moses the ANOINTED *Cherubim,* and the *Cherubim and flaming Sword,* who is the angel in justice in the souls of men, as may be seen between the acts of *Moses,* and of *Korah, Danthan* and *Abiram,* and how God's justice swallowed up those three. And further, God in his justice communes from between the Cherubims to this day; for as the Cherubim and flaming Sword is in the soul of every one, there God walks by his justice, and communes from between every one: and *mind* – it is a dangerous thing for any one to slight or question the *Messenger,* for the sake of the Egyptian kingdom; and if any one has *offended or hurt his brother,* let him go and ask forgiveness, and if possible, make amends; for in all the private acts of evil that man may think to conceal in himself, there will *Serpents* come from where he thought not of, and severely *bite* him; and as *Moses set up the Brazen Serpent in the Wilderness,(i.e.* the emblem of cherubical justice) and them that could behold, or face this serpent, was healed, and did live: and it is even so at this day – for every one that can behold the *internal Angel* in justice, and face that to atone for sin, *Justice will be stayed* :- And I would not have any one think to run into sin, through the tempter saying you may escape Justice, for every one must face his own evil before Justice; - therefore it is good to *stand in fear,* and *WATCH.*

As aforesaid, the *created Life* of Adam was *Faith,* and the divine virtues that flowed forth from that *Life,* has been set forth in a beautiful manner; yet I would have you understand, when Adam *hearkened* to the voice of Reason and *fell,* those properties became *inactive and dead* in his soul, and Reason, with its *Law,* and *Justice* took possession and ruled the *Man* until God was pleased to raise Faith from that *Death* to a *new Life* for REGENERATION: therefore, as the *Elect* have Reason in them, they must be subject to Reason's *Law and Justice;* and *they,* when enlightened, will give up to the *justice of God,* as did the *Nobel-Man* of old, who said, "Although thou kill me, yet will I trust in *thee."*

Also as I said before, GOD is not the God of Reason but the GOD OF FAITH: And Moses was obedient *to,* and incumbered *with* the *Law* and *Priesthood,* so must all the *Elect: -* And when Faith is *rose* from the *Dead* to Regeneration, they are let to know that GOD is the God of that *Living Nature,* which by regeneration becomes the essential soul, and is capable of the resurrection to *Eternal Glory;* and all filthy matter with Reason, which is deemed as the body of *Elect Man,* will be left here, and buried in *Chaos* where *Justice* will for ever live in the souls of them who was not capable of Regeneration, even as the body of Moses *was, is,* and *will* be buried. Thus you may see how the soul and body of *Elect Men* are separated by REGENERATION.

Further - In CHAP. XVIII, I have wrote concerning the *Horses and Chariots* that came out from between the two *Mountains,* (viz.) the *Black, Red, Bay, and Grisled Horse,* and of the *White Horse,* which, as aforesaid, relates to the coming out and acts of Reason; yet I think it necessary to write something more of that *White Horse;* which WHITE HORSE had its being by or through the *purity* of God's creating the *Cherubim,* and the *pure Law* he created him under. Then, when the *Cherubim* broke the *Law* and fell, *Justice* took place, and God became the God of Justice to that order of his angelic creation; and although the *Cherubim* broke the *Law,* he never could break the *Justice* of that Law, nor the *pure Act* of God: And when the *Cherubim* transmuted himself in flesh, he took *Justice* with him intirely *pure;* and when the seed of Reason came to manhood, and this *Justice* takes place in the soul, they are charged with the Law, which goeth with them; and this *Law* and *Justice,* and *given Priesthood* and *Obedience,* which Reason should shew to God, to receive his *Blessing* on this earth, and his *Mercy to the Child,* are the *White Horses* and *Chariot,* that came out from between the two *Mountains,* to walk to and fro thro' this *earth.*

So, although the Cherubim broke the Law and fell into generation, yet the *Purity and Glory* of God's creating the Cherubim remained *intirely pure* to himself, as I said before; then, of consequence, he had all power to execute his Justice, or send his Blessing on Reason, according to its obedience or disobedience; and to be above the Law of Reason, is the grand *White Horse* relative to Reason.

Again - *Enoch, Moses,* and *Elijah,* had fallen Reason in them, and was subject to its Passions, Law, Priesthood, &c. yet by *Regeneration,* Faith became the essential Life, and was *translated into Heaven,* but to no higher glory than that of the Father, *i.e.* of Justice; then they rode this *White Horse,* relative to Reason - why? because they were *under the Law;* but by regeneration and translation, they are glorified *above the Law* and nature of Reason. Also, where *Enoch, Moses,* and *Elijah,* was translated to, GOD himself came from, to *seek his own kingdom* of regenerated Faith, which he gained by the *Works of Redemption,* and ascended into his *own Kingdom, i.e.* the *Glory of Mercy:* and *Enoch, Moses,* and *Elijah,* sit in the *Glory of Justice* to this day.

Moreover - By the works of Redemption CHRIST gained to himself the *Power* of the Resurrection; and the *Child* that dies, and the *Ideot* to whom *Justice* doth not take place in the soul, (then they are not charged with the Law) so they fall under mercy according to the glory God created the Cherubim in; yet the glory of this mercy could not be attained without the *Resurrection:* therefore when CHRIST calls his *Elect* to glory, the Cherubims will hear the *Echo* of that voice and follow, and will be glorified in bodies of this earth; and with that refined knowledge and experience, as I have declared, (CHAP. IX.) – and the *Crown* they wear is the *purity and Glory* God created their father the Cherubim to, with a more transcendant Jewel added to it, which is, they enjoy it through the Merit of CHRIST; and may say *Christ* died for them, and in this they will ride the *White Horse* in all eternity, which relates to Reason that fell: for although this Horse is *rode* by them who sit in the *Glory of the Father,* yet at the Resurrection *they* will be translated to the *Kingdom and Glory* of the *Mercy of the Son:* then the *seventh Seal* will be opened, for the kingdoms of this world will be no more, and the Justice of the Father will be no more; and this Crown, or *White Horse,* is reserved to be worn or *rode* in *Mercy* by the glorious order of Cherubims, who have been in fallen Reason *under* the power of *Death,* but by the power of God then recovered far *above* that, to glory; yet they are not capable of the *Glory of Faith,* and to *commune in Faith,* but by refined Reason, as I have before said.

FINIS

PREDICATE

Is it not well for man to know
The wisdom that from God doth flow?
Then great it is, however odd,
To know man's *self* as touching God:
For this, *the Book*, to all must come,
But the Elect shall pass the doom.
Christ he will come above the strife,
Shewing their name i'th *Book of Life*.

Note, of externals, we've no shew,
But see the *Man*, as *born* anew
Thus to ourselves, become so odd,
As all we are, is all in God.

T. H

THE
BOOK
UPON
THE GOSPEL
AND
REGENERATION

By JAMES BIRCH
AUTHOR OF THE BOOK OF THE LAW AND
CHERUBICAL REASON

Christ said, "These things have I spoken to you in
proverbs:
"The time cometh when I shall no more speak unto YOU
in
"proverbs, but I shall shew you P L A I N L Y of the
Father"

LONDON:

PRINTED FOR THE AUTHOR
And sold by T Herald, No 60 Portpool Lane, Near Gray's
Inn Lane

(Price 4s.)

OF THE
GOSPEL,
AND
REGENERATION

Chap. I

NOW, concerning the beginning, or bringing in of the Gospel. It was done by the *Most Merciful* GOD the CREATOR, according to the attribute of his DIVINE MERCY; for, as I have before written the cherubim was created in reference to God's divine *Justice;* and there was such a quantity of *Justice* given in and to his soul, when he was created, or through his creation, that when he had broke the *pure Law* he was created under, to cast him down from heaven, from the presence of GOD: And when he was transmuted into flesh, and grown to manhood, this *Justice* charged him with breaking the *Law* when he slew his brother Abel. And this *Angel* in *Justice* in the soul of Man is, "the cherubim and flaming sword that turns every way, to keep the *Way* of the *Tree of Life;*" therefore all the seed of Cain that live to maturity, this angel takes place in the soul; and then they are charged with the *Law,* for this law is the law of angels, or of Reason: and further, this internal *Angel* in justice has full power to seal the soul under the power of *Death* and *Hell,* and there keep it. And thus dwells the attribute of GOD's *Justice* on the souls of the seed of *Cain* that live to manhood, and charged with the law, which is, to *Love God above all, and your neighbour as yourself.*

Again, the creation and life of *Adam* was human nature, animated with *Divine Faith,* which is the *Divine Nature* of GOD; therefore Adam was the Son of God, because his life was of the *Divine Nature;* and he was created under the LAW of *Faith,* which is, "*not to hearken to the voice of Reason,* for the day you do it, you shall fall under the power of death," which Adam and Eve did through temptation; but this death is only temporal. Thus GOD, according to his creation, became a GOD of *Justice,* through the acts of Man and Angel; only *He* is distinguished in this, *He* is God the creator, and of *Justice,* to the seed of Cain, but although *He* was God the *creator* and of *justice,* to the seed of Adam, yet to that seed *He* was GOD the FATHER.

Then the glorious Creator thought it good to leave his glorious *Throne of Justice*, and his *Fatherly condition* to the *Elect*, and transmute himself into his own created nature in Adam, which was human Nature, animated with divine faith, that fell in Adam his own son; and took *His own* part, in *His own* creation; and kept the *Law of Faith*, which no one but the *Fountain* of Faith could do, it being of that harmless innocent nature, and *He* had his portion of temptation and persecution, which ended in death, by or from the hands of the sons of Reason.

Again, I would not have any one think the glorious Divine Majesty came to walk through the moral law, which is cherubical, or of angels; because that is the law of Reason, for "God took not on him the nature of angels," which is the nature of Reason, and of consequence not its law; neither had he any thing to do with that *law* and *priesthood*, for that was given forth by *Moses* who was the *anointed cherubim* according to his inspiration, and that only ends in *death under Justice*: For the LORD GOD *of Heaven* was incapable to take the nature of Reason on him; for if *He* had took that nature on him, which is of the devil, then God and devil would have been one; and God would have been lost in his own works, by their being swallowed up in confusion; therefore them that look for Regeneration and salvation, learn to know what nature God was capable to take on him, that he could redeem. But God took on him his own nature of Faith, which fell in Adam under the power of Death, for hearkening to the voice of Reason, and went through this sore journey of flesh, and never hearkened to Reason, so as to be tempted to evil by it; and in that he kept the law of Faith.

Moreover, the *Merciful Priesthood of GOD* was his *sacred communion*, in the days of old, with the *spirit of Faith* in the souls of his *Elect*, that he himself would become a Son, the *God of Mercy*, and restore them to his *Heavenly Kingdom* by this his divine and powerful act of *Mercy*; and this holy communion, by the spirit of Faith in the souls of the *Elect*, with God the FOUNTAIN of *Faith* and *Mercy*, far transcends the cherubical inspiration; why? because one ends in *Death under Justice*, and the other leads to *Mercy and Life* eternal: and in this *faithful communion* were the elect of old, at the hour of death, translated from *justice*, to under the MERCY of the SON, to a glorious *Marriage* and resurrection to eternal *Life*. But Enoch, Moses, and Elijah were translated into *Heaven* ,but to no higher Glory than that of the *Father*; therefore the Divine Majesty made a spiritual and heavenly compact with Moses and Elias, that they should sit in the *Glory of the Father*, while God himself become a SON; therefore in Psalm cx. and Luke xx. "The Lord said unto my Lord, sit thou on my right hand, till I make thine enemies thy footstool." This is relative to the mystical union between God and his Elect, and of Moses and Elias sitting in the glory of the Father and of justice, while GOD himself become a SON, and they was the *Angels* who had *charge concerning him*. This being accomplished, according to the merciful will of the divine Majesty, then he left the glory of *Justice*, and that of the *Father* to the *Elect;* and transmuted himself into earth or flesh, and was born of Mary a virgin, of the House of Israel; the which I call the *Virgin Daughter of Israel*, who personally bore the Son of God. And this mighty work was done, because the GOD *of Justice* would become the GOD *of Mercy;* and was found a child; and grew to manhood on this earth, to redeem his *Elect*.

Again, He calls himself the SON of MAN, why? because he took the created nature of Adam (on himself) that fell in manhood, and also the *Law* of Faith that Adam was created under; then, according to the spirit and genealogy of Faith, *He* was enrolled among the seed of Faith, and recorded in holy writ the SON of DAVID and ABRAHAM, yet the very GOD that created *Heaven* and *Earth*. Also it is written "He came by water and blood." *i.e.* he became a true SON to the *Power* of the Father, and was subject to circumcision, prayer, baptism, &c. And when *He was brought to Jerusalem, to be presented before the Lord, they offered a pair of turtle doves, and two young pigeons, according to the law of Moses;* but He being the *Son of God*, he was SANCTIFIED to God; neither need he be redeemed unto God, for He was *born of God*. Also he was not born of sin, or of any desire of Reason, but by the pure desire and Act of Faith; but this was suffered to be done, because *He* was the *first-born Son of Israel*, to bring in the holy *Gospel*; therefore *turtle doves* was offered for Him. And in this he *came by water*, because he took the fallen nature of Adam on him, and was subject to the *Power of the Father, i.e.* of *Justice*; but this justice extends no further than persecution and troubles in this life, and a temporal death; but he never took the nature of Reason on him, neither had he any thing to do with that *Law* and *Priesthood*, or *Justice* of that law; but to leave it behind him, to the *internal Angel* in *Justice* in the soul of man.

Further, "When Jesus came from Galilee to Jordan, to be baptized of John, then John forbid him, saying, *I have need to be baptized of thee,"* (for John's baptism was of water.) But Jesus said, "suffer it so to be now, for it becometh us to fulfil all righteousness." Then Jesus was baptized of John's baptism, which was the *baptism of water*, therefore *Jesus came by water, i.e.* He came out on the prophecies of the Elect of old, and in the time of the *Law*, when they stood and prophecied before the *Throne*, when GOD was in the condition of the *Father*, which is but as *Water* or *Moon-like glory*, to Faith; for then the *virgin Daughter* of Faith could not bring forth a *son* in Regeneration, until God became a *Son* to his own *Power*, and was baptized with this *Baptism of Water*, (which was equal to the elect being translated from under the *Law*, and united to GOD for CHRIST.) "And when he came out of the water (of Jordan) then the *spirit of God* descended like a dove and lighting upon Jesus – and a *Voice* came from heaven." This *spirit of God*, which he received, sent him forth and enabled him to declare his holy Gospel. Further, the *Holy Ghost* and *Voice* from heaven saying, "This is my beloved son in whom I am well pleased," was from *Moses* and *Elias*, who then sat in the glory of the Father; and when Jesus went forth to declare his *holy Gospel*, then to him those *Waters* were turned into *Blood*.

As concerning *John the Baptist*, he was the last and greatest *Prophet* in the time of the *Law*; not that he was a prophet according to the cherubical inspiration, neither did he regard that *Worship* (for, as I have said, it was but the *incense* of Reason) but he was a great prophet in the *spirit and lineage of Faith*, whereby men communed by the *spirit of Faith* with God, and prophesied of the coming of Christ: And, as I have said, this *sacred communion* with God is entirely distinct from the *inspiration of the Law*, therefore all the Elect of old, and in the time of the Law, and all the *Prophets* of the Law, was called to this *holy communion* with God at times, and so prophesied of the coming of Christ. And *Enoch, Moses, and Elias* was taken from the law; nay, far above the law in spirit, and was in the humble state of *friendship and forgiveness* to the whole world, and in strong *Union* with Faith in the Elect, and also with God relative to his becoming a SON, so that by the power of Faith they could say, "here is CHRIST come," then they were *translated* into heaven, and never came back to tell this *Tale*. And they was called to this state, and *brought forth the fruits worthy of repentance,* and forgiveness of sin to *prepare the way of the Lord's coming*; for in this condition of soul, *the ax is laid to the root of the tree,* which brought forth the *true prayer* of Faith, and they received *the grace of God*; then they were translated, to under the mercy of the SON, and could in spirit truly say, Christ is come, then entered into death, in the *Bed of mercy*, therefore this is the true *Baptism of Water*, which is the end of the *Law*; for when the soul received this, the law was ended with him, and Christ appeared in spirit even at the door, for the soul was prepared for his coming.

Again, There was no prophet to preach this righteousness or preparation until *John, that the way of the Lord might be prepared*; for John came forth in that very condition of soul, or spiritual inspiration, that the *Prophets* and the *Elect of old* was brought to in spirit, before they was translated into heaven, or died in the *Bed of mercy*, translated to under the mercy of the *Son*; therefore Jesus said, (Mat. xi. 9.) "But what went ye out to see, a *prophet*? yea, I say unto you, *more than a prophet,*" i.e. after the prophets of old had prophesied of the coming of *Christ*, yet there is a *preparation* of soul to meet him in *spirit* as well as in *person*; and IN this condition of soul fit to meet him, is greater than the prophecy OF him, therefore IN this spirit and inspiration from heaven, John came forth GOD's *Messenger to prepare his way*, which no one ever did till John, therefore John's baptism of water is the end of the law, and the next is CHRIST! And that is the *translation!* He that hath eyes to see let him see this INTERNAL MYSTERY! For the external act is past. And Jesus said, "Among them that are born of women, there hath not risen a greater than John, notwithstanding he that is least in the kingdom of Heaven is greater than he," (Mat. xi. 11.) because the *spiritual sanctification* of CHRIST is the *kingdom of heaven*, and John required a translation to that himself.

Again, John the *Baptist* is said to come "in the spirit and power of Elias," (Luke i. 17.) *i.e.* Elias, in his day, prophesied according to the law, which is the *law prophecy*, and that ends in death, *under Justice.* Also he prophesied of the coming of Christ which leads to, and centers in, mercy and life, even through death; and Elias was brought to that condition of soul fit to be *translated* to see GOD, whereby *the way of the Lord was prepared,* and in this very inspiration or portion of spirit, John the Baptist came forth in, to declare or *prepare the way* of the LORD CHRIST, therefore he *came in* this very *spirit of Elias.* Further, Elias was translated into heaven, and sits in the glory of the *Father,* for then CHRIST was on this earth *born a son*; and Elias, who sat in the glory of the *Father,* inspired John the Baptist, whereby the went forth to prepare the way for the Lord Christ, and for this very cause John came forth in the spirit and *power of Elias*; for when Jesus was here, the Jews questioned him by the prophecy Malichi (ch. iv.) saying, "Elias must first come." Jesus said, "*that* Elias is indeed come, and they have done unto him whatsoever they listed, as it is written of him;" and *this* Elias was *John the Baptist*, therefore (Mat. xi. 13, Jesus said,) "for all the prophets and the law prophesied until John; and if ye will receive it, this is the Elias that was to come;" therefore John came forth not only in the spirit of prophecy, they prophesied of the coming of Christ; but also in that very condition of soul, as they was prepared to see GOD, and in that he was a *great Prophet.*

Further, John the *Baptist* "preached in the wilderness of Judea," (Mat iii.) *i.e.* he *preached* to people whose understanding was *Wild*, they being in the *Wild priesthood* of Reason; neither could any know the power of his preaching until true understanding was given. And John's *preaching* was "Repentance for the remission of sins," and this was his *Cry*, to prepare the *Way* of the LORD, that the soul may be prepared to follow the GOD of *Heaven*, who then was become man, and ready to go forth, and utter the fruits and power of Faith, declare his holy covenant of grace, and redeem his Elect. Also John's heavenly inspiration gave him wisdom to know them, that there was no possibility of *fruits unto repentance* to be brought out of their souls, therefore when the Pharisees and Sadducees come to his baptism, he called them *a generation of Vipers*, and said, "who hath warned *you* to flee from the wrath to come;" for those men had usurped the *Letter* of the *Prophets*, and by their imagination on that, sat to judge and determine all spiritual causes, and dedicated their *judgment* for God to own as *Truth*; because they said they had *Abraham* to their father, and was *in covenant* with God: For all those great *Men in conceit* on the bare *Letter*, either in the first, second, or *third Dispensation* has more opinion of themselves, than God has of them; and when *Christ* come either in person, or in spirit, they will find themselves to be most in general cast out; therefore John said unto them, "bring forth therefore the fruits worthy of repentance; and begin not to say within yourselves, we have *Abraham* to our *father*, for I say unto you, that God is able of those stones to raise up children to *Abraham*," (Luke iii. 8.) *i.e.* from common fishermen, whom the rulers thought ignorant, and was as a *stone* in respect to the knowledge of the *faith of Christ;* yet when Jesus uttered his *Voice*, it centered to the womb, or seed of Faith, in the soul of elect man, and quickened the spirit into act, so that they *followed him*, and truly believed him the SON OF GOD; and this is *raising up children unto Abraham* of those *stones*. Thus Jesus said to Peter, "Thou art Simon the son of Jona; thou shall be called Cephas, *i.e.* by interpretation, *a stone.*"

Moreover, John *baptised publicans, soldiers, &c.* and said "The axe is laid to the root of the tree; and every tree therefore which bringeth forth not good fruit is hewn down, and cast into the fire," *i.e.* every soul that Faith cannot be brought out of, sufficient to *follow* Jesus unto Regeneration, is *cast* from the *covenant of Grace*, and left under the *internal angel* in justice; therefore when the people asked him, *what they should do*? (Luke iii. 11.) he answered, and said unto them "he that hath two coats, let him impart to him that hath none; and he that hath meat let him do likewise." And unto the Publicans he said, "exact no more than is appointed you" And unto the soldiers he said, "do violence to no man, neither accuse any falfely, and be content with your wages." Now this was to bring the proud, selfish and lying spirit of Reason down, whereby the soul may be in love and friendship to all; and receive the *warning* of the *coming of the Lord*, that they may leave the whole world behind, to *follow* CHRIST, the KING of FAITH, and this was John's preaching *the baptism of repentance for the remission of sins.*

Again, John the *Baptist's* inspiration was so great, that he had strong communion by the spirit of Faith with him, or them, that sit as God in the *Glory of the Father* in heaven: that he bear witness of Christ who *was* God the Father, *then* become a Son to be the GOD *of* MERCY, that all who come into this world the *Seed of Faith* may, by this great Light of Christ, be enlightened into the holy covenant of grace, prepared as a *Bride* to meet the *Bridegroom* for the *kingdom of Heaven*: Also for Christ's *unbounded mercy*, and his *incomparable love and innocence*, John calls him, "the *Lamb of God* that taketh away the sins of the world:" Also saith, "he that cometh after me, is preferred before me;" and (John i. 16) saith, "and of his fullness have we all received, and grace for grace," *i.e.* from the man *Adam* until

John, the royal *Lineage* of Faith, prophesied of Christ to *come*, and at the hour of death received the fullness of grace from heaven, to prepare the soul to meet Christ, and entered into death with soul and spirit translated, to under the *Mercy of the Son*; then, in this spirit, or inspiration, John came forth and preached repentance to prepare his *way*.

Further, I would have the Elect to understand, that from *Adam* until *Christ*, Faith that was born from its womb, or seed, in the soul of man, or brought forth into act by the power of God, it was but the *birth of water*; neither was it any more than the *Daughter* of Faith, or the *Virgin Daughter* of Israel according to the internal and spiritual generation or regeneration; for Christ was the *first-born Son of Israel*, who was the SON of FAITH, MERCY, GRACE, and TRUTH, and the BRIDEGROOM for *Marriage* with this pure *Virgin* DAUGHTER OF FAITH: And this holy communion, by the spirit of Faith, with God its fountain, is distinct to, and far transcends the cherubical inspiration; therefore John the *Baptist* saith, "The *law* was given by Moses, "but *Grace* and *Truth* came by Jesus Christ," (John i. 17.) Also John by the power of Faith, "saw the spirit descend from heaven like a dove and abode upon Jesus, and I knew him not; but he that sent me to baptize with water, the same said unto me, upon whom thou shalt see the spirit descending and remaining, the same is he which baptizeth with the Holy Ghost. (v. 33.) And when John was speaking concerning his bearing *Witness* of Jesus, John answered and said, "a man can receive nothing, except it be given him from heaven." Neither *can* any man declare divine truth at this day, except it be given *him* from heaven; and whenever you see the *Dove of Faith* rest in the soul, that is your brother in the true Faith of Christ.

And although *John* had this great *Peace* and *Joy* of soul, and great *Communion* with heaven, yet his *Baptism* was of *Water*; neither was the internal and spiritual state of *John* himself, but at the *Baptism* of *Water*, for his great communion with heaven was with that of the *Father*, which is *Justice*, therefore *John* must be translated, to under the mercy of the SON; for when the soul, by the *prayer of Faith*, has waded through the Law internal, and suffered the Wilds and temptations of Reason, and come to this state of soul, the *Baptism of Water*, which is the highest state he ever was at, yet he will and did find those *waters turned into blood*, before he can, or could enter the spiritual waters of the holy *covenant of grace, i.e.* the WATERS of CHRIST. But this *Baptism of Water* is at the end of the *Law*, nay, above the Law, because, by the power of Faith, the soul is brought through that covenant; and this was the state that the elect of old was brought to *by* the power of Faith, which is the *baptism of water*. And *Christ*, the son of *Man*, according to the royal lineage of Faith, received this baptism of John, and went forth to declare his *holy gospel*, then those *waters were turned into blood* to himself.

Again, John the *Baptist* (Mark i. 7.) preached, saying "there cometh one mightier than I, after me, the latchet of whose shoes I am not worthy to stoop down to unloose," *i.e.* he was unworthy to *unloose* or declare the holy Gospel of peace and salvation unto the Elect; for Jesus walked through the whole power of Reason, and *never* hearkened to it, to be tempted by it; and by that he kept the LAW of FAITH, which is the true path of righteousness and peace; and redeemed his Elect, and left the power of Reason behind unto judgment; therefore no one could utter and perform the covenant of Faith and grace, but HE who created Adam, whose life was of Faith; and that was the work of the very God of heaven. Again, John said (Mat. iii. 11.) "Whose shoes I am not worthy to bear, he shall baptize you with the Holy Ghost and fire," *i.e.* when Faith by *prayer* and *divine assistance* from heaven, is brought through the first covenant, to the baptism of water, which is required of Faith to follow the voice of God *there*; then CHRIST, the *King* of FAITH, takes the soul into his spiritual covenant of grace, and baptizes it with his *holy spirit*; and that is the glorious *Fire* of Faith; then the soul is redeemed and sealed unto LIFE ETERNAL. This John the Baptist saw, but never entered into it, in this life, to *come back*; for John came out *in the spirit and power of Elias,* to prepare *His Way* for those *Waters to be turned into blood*; but he could not *unloose* the footsteps of his holy Gospel, nor *declare his* (spiritual) *generation,* which is *regeneration*; for there must one come out *in the spirit and power of* CHRIST to do that.

Chap. II

NOW, when Jesus was baptized of John's baptism, and the spirit of God descended in form like a dove (which is the emblem of innocence) and this, that was given Jesus, was to the spirit above measure, in *Lamb-like Innocence, Love, and Mercy*; for as Jesus was born of woman into this world a *Spotless* BABE and grew to manhood, he was compelled to receive the spirit of GOD from HEAVEN, to give him spiritual Birth, to go forth and declare his *holy gospel*; and also to be in the obedience of a *true Son* to the *Power* of the Father. Also it is written (Mat. iv. 1.) "Then was Jesus led up of the spirit into the wilderness to be tempted of the devil," *i.e.* to be *tempted* of man; for when any comes forth by the *inspiration* of Faith from *heaven*, he has his friends or brethren to seek, which are the elect of God; and until he meets with one or more of his brethren, he is *tempted of the devil*. And further, when any *declaration* comes from heaven, and the *Messenger* utters forth *some things*, there will be men found, that can listen to it, and like it, because they do perceive it will over-top the whole world; and they will *tempt* the Messenger to *fall down and worship him* or *them, i.e.* the *tempter* will desire the Message or doctrine may be rendered according to his liking; then he will direct it to the people that he may rule over them, and turn the doctrine contrary to the intent of the *Message*, then the Messenger will become a servant to Reason, which is the *devil and tempter*. Also Reason will ask questions from the scripture, or from their imagination, saying, If thou art from God thou can do, or answer this? and here they also *tempt*; but they will not find it to their liking in the end – then they will say he is a false witness or Messenger, and leave him in wrath – then some seek to destroy him, and in time take possession; and others will, at a distance, transform themselves into his language; and in this Reason is a *murderer* and *thief*.

And this was the very thing with JESUS, who met with a wise man or men, that were Rulers in the *Law of Moses*, and *tempted him* to act according to their liking; *and the devil taking him up and setting him on a pinacle of the Temple*, it was to shew to him the excellence of the *worship* according to the Law of *Moses*, for this worship was greater than any in the world that was public. And further, this worship was ordinated of God, and he being the *Son of God*, why should he not bow to it? For if you be the *Son of God*, it becometh you to own and obey the commands of your *Father*, by the *man Moses* – but by *Him* this could not be done; because that worship is but the *incense* of Reason, which to him was a great temptation; but Jesus answered him from the writings of Moses, "thou shalt not tempt the Lord thy God," (Deut. vi. 16.) And when "*Jesus was taken into an exceeding high mountain*, and shewed the kingdoms of the world, and the glory of them." This *high Mountain* was the *inspiration* of the Law of Moses, that ruled over the souls and spirits of men throughout the whole world; and if men did but obey that law and worship accordingly, they should have prosperity, as Moses had promised, and that is the *kingdom's glory of this world*; but CHRIST's *Kingdom was not of this world*. Also the *worship* of the *Law of Moses* ended in death, under *Justice*; but Christ came in *Mercy*, to bring *Life* out of *Death*, therefore could not hearken to Reason the *tempter*, but said it is written, "thou shalt worship the Lord thy God, and him only shalt thou serve." (Deut. vi. 13).

Further, "When Jesus had fasted forty days and forty nights, he was afterward an hungry," (Matt. iv. 2.) Now the *fasting* of Jesus was his being tempted to be a servant to Reason, *i.e.* to bow down and worship and deliver his holy doctrine, as Reason should think right and proper; and this is the great *Wilderness that Jesus was led into by the spirit*, where he was *tempted of Satan* – "and was with the *Wild Beast*," *i.e.* by the spirit of Reason, he was tempted in some individuals, for he was among his enemies. Now Jesus did not come to call *Reason*, and be a servant to them; but he came to call his *Royal Elect*, which was, *his lost sheep of the house of Israel*, and be a *servant* to them; therefore during the time he was *tempted* of Reason, which was *forty days*, that was the *Wilderness* he was in; for the Language, and *temptation* of the spirit of Reason, is a *Wilderness* to the spirit of Faith; and until he had called some of the Elect to himself by his own Voice, which is the utterance of Faith, *he was an hungry in spirit*, for this is the *wilderness* and *hunger* that CHRIST, the KING of FAITH, suffered in spirit. Also the *tempter* seeing him have no one to commune with, in his own spirit of Faith, which was *hunger to Jesus*, he said, "If thou be the Son of God, command that those stones be made bread," *i.e.* to *command* any man's spirit to be converted to Jesus's liking; for John the Baptist had said, "God is able to raise up children unto Abraham of *those stones*;" but the *tempter* could not prevail, for Jesus said, " It is written, man shall not live by *bread alone*, but by every *word* that proceedeth out of the *Mouth of God*," (Deut. viii. 3.) Here Jesus answered Reason from the Book that was given to Reason, and that was to its own condemnation for all those things Moses had given in commandment to the *Children of Israel*.

Note. Of the Devil tempting of Christ, it was a man, or men, that underftood the *Law of Moses*, and had a ruling power in that law and priesthood; for this, *understand*, when *the hour of temptation is come*, there always appears him, or them, or that, which is very able to *tempt*.

Also, it is written, "Then the devil taketh him up into the Holy City." This *Holy City* was the *given Priesthood* of Reason; and he shewed him the excellence of that worship commanded of God, and there men *must* bring in their oblations, and *flee* for refuge; so of consequence all must bow down there, or receive the plagues for disobedience *again* – "and setteth him on a pinnacle of the Temple." This *pinnacle of the Temple* was to shew him the *stay of God's Justice on man*, which is the *height* of that Priesthood; for when man had sinned, and brought in the true offering, that incense or prayer ascends to God, and God *would stay* his *Justice* on the soul of man. Now the *Devil* would give Christ that *place*, where he would offer the true incense, or prayer, that would ascend to heaven, for God to stay his justice on the soul of man, that man may have forgiveness, and enjoy the blessings of this life; and in this he would have communion with God. Now this is the *height* of the *given Priesthood* of Reason; and for that, it is called a *Pinnacle of the Temple*, "and as Christ was the *Son of God* he may *cast himself down* and take it, seeing it was of God, for he could do no wrong nor come to any *harm*, seeing his *angels had charge concerning him."*

Again, "The devil taketh him into an exceeding high mountain, and sheweth him all the kingdoms of the world and the glory of them." This *high Mountain* is the *cherubical inspiration*; and the *Kingdoms of the* World is the *Law of Moses;* and the *Glory* of the kingdoms is the *Stay* of God's Justice; for the *law and priesthood* that Moses gave to the Israelites, was that *land or kingdom* that would flow in plenty; for if men do but observe and obey the *Law of Moses*, and when they have sinned, to offer the true oblation or prayer to have God's justice stayed, then the beauty of God's creation, his blessing, and preservation, shine sweetly to and in the soul; but if disobedient, then *Justice* frowns, and will come into act; this all people, nations, &c. are subject to. Then the *Devil* would have made Christ a king or head ruler over the *Law and Priesthood* if he would but *hearken* to him, which made him say, "All those things will I give thee, if thou wilt fall down and worship me;" but Christ could not, because this *Kingdom was of Faith*. Now this, *understand*, the *wild priesthood* of Reason is a *Desart* to Faith; and the *given priesthood* of Reason, is a *Wilderness* to Faith.

Again: When Jesus was tempted of the Devil *forty days*, during the time of that temptation, he called no disciple, neither did he any external *miracle*, as you read of, for when the spirit of God descended and rested on Jesus, he was given up to his *own* strength to be *tempted of the devil*; for no man doth *truly* know the temptation of Reason unto Faith, without the *spirit* of God from heaven; - therefore as Adam was created with a life of undefiled faith, but, under this law, "you shall not *hearken* to the voice of Reason," but when he was left to his created strength, he broke this law, through *temptation*, and fell under the power of death; and *Jesus* took the fallen nature of Adam on him, and when he received the *spirit from heaven* he was given up to his *own* strength to be *tempted of the Devil* (as aforesaid;) and although (Jesus was) under the power of death through Adam, yet he bore the *forty days* temptation of Reason the devil, and never *hearkened to it* in the least; for during this time of temptation he called no disciple, nor did any external miracle. Yet his bearing this temptation of Reason, the devil, by his own strength, and never hearkened to it but left it behind him. Now to the spirit of Faith he never did a greater *Miracle* from his going forth until his death, for on this MIRACLE depends the whole power of *Redemption!* For the *first* man Adam, when he was left to his *created strength,* hearkened to the voice of Reason and fell under the power of death, and lost *his Paradise*: But the *second* man Adam, in *fallen* human nature, was left to his *own strength*, and given up to be tempted of the devil, and *never break* the *Law of Faith*, so went through the power of Reason, death, and hell, and gained the *Heaven of Mercy*.

Again it is written (Matt. iv. 11.) "Then the devil leaveth him, and behold angels came and ministered unto him," *i.e.* the devil could not prevail with Jesus to bow down to Reason's worship, and be a Ruler in Reason's kingdom, so he *left him* for a season; and the *Angels* that *ministered unto him* were *Moses and Elias,* who sit in the *glory of the Father.* After this, Jesus went forth and declared his *holy Gospel,* and called his disciples, worked miracles, &c. Then Reason sought to entangle him by questions, and overthrow him in persecution, therefore this is the *great Wilderness* that CHRIST the KING of FAITH went through, at that beginning, or bringing in, of the holy Gospel, which is a royal pattern or example to his Elect, who also will be tempted of the devil.

Moreover, any *Messenger* in the covenant of grace, must be very careful not to hearken to the tempter, nor give way to the temptation on any thing concerning his *Message* - also any elect Being after he has heard the voice of God by his *Messenger*, and the spirit quickened into act, whereby the soul *gathers Truth* from the declaration, and well knows it leads to *Light* and *Life*; then the *spirit of Reason* in Man (which is the grand enemy to man) will *tempt* the *spirit of Faith to bow down and worship him, i.e.* Reason would take the *Messenger's* language and render it his own way, which is *contrary* to Faith and the *intent* of the Declaration. Thus the *Spirit of Reason* in man will *tempt* the *spirit of Faith* in man, and, if possible, keep it from the *Communion with God*; for Reason will allure the soul to preach his own way, only to rule over people, and shew forth greatness. But the spirit of Faith seeks to get as near GOD as possible for sanctification, and leave the whole world behind, therefore BLESSED IS THAT SOUL that is not overcome by this *temptation*, for Reason greatly delights to rule over the soul; but Reason *without* man, as well as the spirit of Reason *in* man, will *tempt* the soul to sin. Now that is no more than Reason *tempt* Reason, and that sin, which is the sin of Reason, falls under the moral Law, which is the law of Reason, and the *internal angel* in justice seals and keeps that nature down in death. But the transgression of Faith for *hearkening* to the voice of Reason, is of more high consequence, because that must come before the *Justice of the Father*, and pass through that to the prerogative of the *Angel of Faith*, which is *Christ the King of Glory*.

Chap. III

NOW, after Jesus, by the *power* of FAITH, had *overcome* the *temptation* of the devil, did, by his mighty work or MIRACLE declare himself worthy in the great *compact of Faith* to go forth and work the *work of redemption*, and after that to open the BOOK OF LIFE unto his royal elect; therefore, as aforesaid, Jesus was *God the Father*, or the *God of Justice*, then become *God the Son,* the *God of mercy* to his elect; and his life and nature is divine faith, by which he was, and is able to accomplish his almighty works. And he took his own created nature on himself that fell in Adam, which was human nature animated with divine Faith, that he may redeem or recover his own children with great advantage again to himself; for they will experimentally know the power of sin, death, and hell in their own souls, and also the *merciful glorious redemption* from it.

Moreover, there is but *two covenants* either literal or *spiritual, i.e.* the Covenant of the *Law*, and the Covenant of *Grace*; and, as I have said, Moses was the *Anointed Cherubim*, according to his inspiration, and when he uttered and gave forth the law, there was the spirit of Reason in man for Moses to work upon by his declaration, and that very law written in the nature of Reason that Moses gave forth; and the *internal angel* in justice that would, and truly doth, close with Moses's declaration; therefore Moses was the *External Angel* of the covenant of the law, and had the spirit of Reason to work upon, according to the cherubim's fall and becoming flesh.

But JESUS being the true *Son of Faith* and Mercy, uttered and gave forth his *Gospel of Mercy*, and his holy *covenant of grace*; for the voice of Jesus is one utterance, and that was Faith and Mercy to his elect: and Jesus directed his voice to the womb of Faith in the soul of man, Faith being the created life of Adam; and this is the *good seed sown into the good ground;* for as Moses had Reason to work upon, when he gave forth the Covenant of the *Law* – so Jesus had Faith to work upon, when he gave forth the Covenant of *Grace*. Now, on these principles, went forth the declarations of the two covenants; but in themselves they are as distinct to each other, as life is from death; and each nature will hear their own *Call*.

Again, JESUS came to call and gather his *lost kingdom, Israel*; and his kingdom Israel is the sons of Adam, who are the elect, that are scattered throughout the world: and when he had called some of his disciples, and a multitude of people followed, he taught his disciples by his *holy Utterance*, from the essential spirit of Faith, which was in himself, *that* centered to the *womb* of Faith in the souls of his elect, and quickened *it* into act, to bring forth such fruit of Faith, as would follow him up to the *Regeneration*; and pronounced his own blessing upon it, as in Matthew, fifth chapter – ver. 3. "BLESSED are the poor in spirit for theirs is the kingdom of heaven," *i.e.* when Faith is quickened into act in the soul, it greatly dislikes the conceited spiritual riches of proud Reason. And further, it finds itself in a fallen state, and in the midst of death and hell; neither can it get back from whence it came, without Christ's *divine assistance* and influence to help the soul in Regeneration; therefore in this *poor spiritual state of soul* will come the *prayer of Faith*, which ascends to heaven.

Ver. 4. "BLESSED are they that mourn, for they shall be comforted." *i.e.* in the aforesaid *mourning* condition of soul, the prayer of Faith *will be offered*, which is the true *incense* that ascends up to God, and the soul *will receive comfort* from heaven.

Ver. 5. "BLESSED are the meek for they shall inherit the earth," *i.e.* the spirit of Faith is *meekness*, and in *meek and humbleness* of soul will leave the whole world behind to follow Christ in spirit, when He appears on this earth; also in true prayer will give itself up for

Christ's spiritual protection, and all thoughts of a natural living here is left out, for that is of Reason. But *Note* this – that soul whom CHRIST spiritually protects, He also naturally protects, for by his doing the *great* that commands the *less*; and, according to God's will, that soul shall enjoy things in this life; for as he has given up his essential efforts of Reason, he will find his support by divine *providence*; therefore the *meek soul* will enjoy even this *natural Life,* beside *eternal Life* hereafter, because the *Meek spirit* will that Christ shall rule over him.

But, if a Man shall make ever such pretences of his faith and love in the *Gospel* that was declared by Jesus; or any divine light, or message that Jesus shall be graciously pleased to send from his *Heavenly Throne*, in, or under his spiritual and holy gospel, to invite the soul up to his holy *sanctification*; and man cannot leave the whole world, with all its folly behind, to follow the voice and divine light of Jesus. Let men judge within themselves are they worthy of his salvation? The spirit saith, *No!* and CHRIST, when on earth, said *No!* for the active spirit of Reason will fill the soul full of fears on the one part, and say, except he use his efforts, the being will be reduced to poverty and shame; - and on the other part, will allure the soul after vain things of this world, whereby they may have honour of men; and this *Ruler* of the soul will keep the being fully employed, and from every *Act of Faith.* *Thus* Reason will do evil to keep himself from evil, and by this evil he is condemned; and let men think what they will to the contrary, Christ doth not *Rule* over such a being as this.

But more concerning, *Blessed are the meek, for they shall inherit the earth.* Now the grand *inheritance of this earth*, is in a *Glorified* body in all *Eternity*; neither can Faith be compleatly Glorified without a body of this *earth;* for as the GOD of *Faith* and *Mercy* thought it good to leave his Throne of Glory, and transmute himself into *Earth* or flesh, and by the *meek spirit* of Faith, wade through the powers of Sin, Death, Hell, and Justice, and ascended into *Heaven* with a body of *Earth* or flesh, and is Glorified in it, and will *inherit* it in all eternity; So in like manner, by his *Divine Assistance,* will the *meek spirit* of Faith follow Him, and by Him will be raised to glory, and will be glorified in a body of flesh, and like unto God himself will *inherit this earth* spiritualized and glorified in all eternity; therefore this is the grand desirable *inheritance of the earth*, to the seed and spirit of Faith.

Ver. 6. "BLESSED are they which do hunger and thirst after righteousness, for they shall be filled," *i.e.* when Faith is rose from death to life, and the spirit of Faith has received a *Call* from Reason's captivity, and it finds itself in a strange Land, and greatly surrounded with enemies; and will offer its prayer for God's *Divine Assistance*, to help it on in this sore journey of flesh; and when it receives the *heavenly help*, which is the *divine incomes* of the HOLY SPIRIT of CHRIST, to confirm the soul he is in the *Truth* and *Way* for Heaven.

Then this fills the soul with such satisfaction, peace, and joy for a short space, that in remembrance of this, the *soul is Hungering and Thirsting after this Righteousness*, and seeking, by prayer, to get as near Christ, the KING of Faith, in spirit, as possible; and the soul, by the power of Faith, and the divine help of Jesus, *will* be brought up to the *spiritual Birth*, and holy *Sanctification* – then *the soul is filled with the righteousness* of *Christ*; and that *righteousness fulfils all righteousness*, then enters into death, in the *Bed of Mercy*, to be raised to *Eternal Glory*.

Ver. 7. "BLESSED are the merciful, for they shall obtain mercy." Now that faith, which is of the divine nature of GOD, is *Mercy*, and will act merciful, and that is the Faith of CHRIST; and the faith for Christ even in the soul of man; because Christ is the King of Faith and *Mercy*. But if a man is sent forth in the *nether waters, i.e.* the priesthood of Aaron, or of Reason, even in the *Commission of the spirit*, that man comes forth under *Justice*, and acts in the *Justice* of that priesthood; and that man's faith is more in that power he is invested with, than it is of Christ; neither is it properly the Faith of Christ, because HE is the God of *Mercy*. Now such a man must be *spiritually born,* or translated to the merciful Faith of Jesus at his death; or left behind under *Justice*. But, as aforesaid, the Faith of Christ is meekness and *mercy*, and has no joy in the death of a sinner; and its nature is to act merciful to all men in what it can: Also its *prayer* which is the *Incense* that ascends before God, is to be forgiven, as that forgives them that trespass against it. And I know nothing that has trespassed against Faith, but Reason; neither is it possible for Faith to live or die in any anger or dislike to any one, therefore this is the true and merciful Faith of CHRIST, which is his own divine nature; and HE takes it into his divine *Mercy*, and seals it with his own royal spiritual seal for his glorious kingdom.

Ver. 8. "BLESSED are the pure in heart, for they shall see God," which is this, when CHRIST came to work the Redemption, and declare his holy gospel, he directed his voice to the womb of Faith, in the soul of man, and quickened it into act, whereby the virgin daughter of Faith is born, and she is very eager to follow the BRIDEGROOM, which is CHRIST, up to the holy and spiritual marriage with him; and her travel is not only through the external wilderness of his world, but the internal wilderness, which is the temptation of reason within, and offers the prayer of Faith; for this is the spiritual travail through Justice to Mercy. And as the declaration of the *Holy Gospel* is the fruits of Faith, and Faith is vey desirous to be master of the soul to follow Jesus *in* the fruits of Faith, which will be done according to its ability by *Prayer*, and *divine assistance* from HEAVEN; then that man's heart becomes *pure* by Faith, and will be born in spirit to the *Seal* of the LIVING GOD, and *see the face of God* in his glory, under the attribute of his divine *mercy,* and live. But no man can *see the face of God* in his glory and live, under the attribute of *justice*; therefore it is by the fruits of Faith, that the heart is made *pure to see God*, in his glory and live, and not the righteousness of the law; but however let the soul be productive of the fruits of Faith, which is the *great* and the *least*, will follow.

Ver. 9. "BLESSED are the peace-makers, for they shall be called the children of God." Faith is *Peace*; but as it *hearkened* to Reason, and fell under its power, it is much perplexed with it here in this life, at times; but by its *Prayer* and *divine assistance* from *Heaven*, it will become the *Essential Life, or Soul of Man*, for the resurrection unto Life Eternal: And even for all the efforts of Reason, Faith will act in the soul, when it is risen from death to life, and grow strong; then it flows forth with *peace*, meekness, love, mercy, charity, &c. and will seek to make the *peace* of Christ, and for Christ, among his brethren, to the utmost of its power, for Faith is so harmonious in itself, and flows with such love, that were it possible, he would convert the souls of his brethren to his own likeness, whereby it may enjoy the sweet innocent *peace* of Faith.

Again, CHRIST is the grand *Peace-maker* of all to his Elect; because the very God who created left his *Glorious Throne,* and became a Son, to be the King of PEACE and Mercy to his Elect; and called them from the bonds and contentions of Reason, to his own *Peace*, which is the *Peace* of Faith; and also by his death and resurrection, will bring them through death to everlasting life, to enjoy the glorious *peace* of Faith, in his glorious kingdom, in all eternity; therefore Faith, when enlightened from heaven, will seek the *Peace* of Faith for his brethren, and to make it among them; then in that he *follows Christ*, and is a *Child of God*.

Ver. 10. "BLESSED are they which are persecuted for righteousness sake, for theirs is the kingdom of heaven," *i.e.* Faith is of that innocent lamb-like nature, that it will leave the whole world behind to follow its God. Also the nature and voice of Faith, is so contrary to Reason, that it cannot understand it; yet Reason will find it superior to itself, and cannot tell how, for by the innocent language of Faith, Reason will find itself condemned. Then Reason will tempt Faith to worship him, and be in his kingdom; but when Reason cannot prevail, he will conceive anger, and call Faith a liar, but the lie is in himself. And when he asks his cunning questions, the answer of Faith is to Reason's condemnation; then Reason will see there is a spiritual kingdom coming distinct to his own, and will condemn it for the kingdom of darkness, as his own is; then Reason will *persecute Faith for his righteousness*; for the *righteous* fruits of Faith is acceptable to CHRIST, and not the pretended *righteousness* of the law; but let the soul produce the fruits of Faith, and he will be more *righteous* in the law. But it is the spirit of Faith, which is of the divine nature of Christ, can bear the persecution from the spirit and power of Reason, why? because when it is rose from the dead, and receives a

Call from heaven, it will follow that Call through all the powers of Reason, without murmur, to get to its fountain from whence it came, which is done by the dint of *prayer and patience,* then they are found worthy of the KING of FAITH, and by him are given *spiritual Birth* into his holy covenant of grace, and sealed for the kingdom of heaven. For mind this, the promise of eternal life is only to them that hold out to the *End;* and holding out to the end, is to be approved of by the divine MAJESTY.

Ver. 11. "BLESSED are ye when men shall revile you, and persecute you, and say all manner of evil against you, falsely for my sake." Now Reason will soon be angry with Faith; for when any *Message* comes from heaven, the nearer the *Messenger* is in spirit to Christ, the more angry is Reason; for the sacred divine Truth of Jesus, appears blasphemy to the spirit of Reason; and the *Messenger* is condemned for blasphemy by the spirit of Reason; and all the Elect that follow witnessing to the truth of the declaration, and bringing forth the fruits of Faith unto God, they also will have the mock and jeers of Reason, and be spoke evil of; for the lying envious spirit of Reason cannot speak the truth concerning Faith; but this always was when the voice of God was on earth, and always will be; therefore blessed is he that hath Faith and patience to overcome those things, it being the works of Faith to follow CHRIST, and his reward is the KINGDOM OF HEAVEN.

Chap. IV

AGAIN, Those fruits of Faith is what Christ came to seek, and bring out of the souls of his Elect, whereby Faith may grow strong and become the essential life or soul of man in regeneration to the holy covenant of grace and mercy: And this is the *light* of Faith that *shines in good works even before men,* that God the *Father,* or the God of justice, is *glorified* in becoming the God of mercy, to the soul that is productive of the righteous fruits of Faith.

Moreover Jesus said (Matt. v. 17.) "Think not that I am come to destroy the law and the prophets, I am come not to destroy but to fulfil;" *i.e.* this, Christ took on himself the law of Faith, which is, *not to hearken to the voice of Reason,* and he fulfilled that law, and in that he fulfilled all, to redeem his Elect; for *God took not on him the nature of angels,* which is Reason; and of consequence not that law: Therefore whosoever thinks Christ took on him the moral law to keep that, are greatly mistaken, for he had nothing to do with it, but to leave Reason behind, under it, unto judgment.

Further, If CHRIST had not come, Moses's law would have ended in death; but Christ went through the power of death into a merciful and glorious life, and gained to himself the power of a resurrection, to raise his Elect from death to a new and glorious life, and be glorified with the glorious *fire of Faith* to live in HIS *royal presence in all eternity:* Thus the coming of Christ will take men from time to eternity; which also brings punishment on the souls and bodies of the reprobate in all eternity, for the internal angel in justice has full power to seal the soul under death, and there for ever keep it in the second death.

Also when CHRIST was on earth he owned the law to be given of GOD to *Moses* and *God spake to Moses in the Bush*; then by his death, and Resurrection, he caused justice (according to the law of Moses) to take place in eternity: And in this *Christ fulfilled that Law*, Because through him the justice of that law takes place in eternity. Therefore Jesus said, "Till heaven and earth pass, one jot, or one tittle, shall in no wise pass from the law till all be fulfilled," *i.e.* them that are left behind, by the holy spirit of Jesus, the *Law is fulfilled* in them in *eternity*; and them that follow Jesus in spirit, the *law is fulfilled* in them in *Time*; because they must come through it in all obedience to that *Law and priesthood*: Henceforth the *Elect* may know the way to *Mercy* is through *Justice*; neither can any one be truly convinced of the declaration of mercy, but must know the power of justice within themselves, therefore it is from the righteous *fruits of Faith*, that proceeds all true obedience to God (according to his divine justice) and the true *Prayer* of Faith, for his divine Mercy, by which he is graciously pleased by his *divine assistance* from HEAVEN, to bring the soul through *Justice*, and give him *spiritual Birth*, and regenerate him to his holy covenant of grace and *mercy,* and seal him for his GLORIOUS KINGDOM; then the law is *fulfilled* in that soul, because he is passed from death to life; and the first *heaven and earth is passed away*, and the soul is entered into the *new heaven* of grace, even in this earthly body, and dies in the *bed of mercy* to be raised to glory, and this is the *righteousness that exceeds the righteousness of the scribes and pharisees*; for CHRIST said, "Except your righteousness exceed the righteousness of the scribes and pharisees, ye shall in no case enter the kingdom of heaven."

Again, The *Fruits of Faith* is mercy and love; but the *Fruits of Reason* is anger and hatred, and according to his own evil spirit, will give judgment, therefore Christ forbids any *anger* to be amongst brethren: and also says, that "Whosoever shall say thou fool, shall be in danger of hell-fire," *i.e.* to condemn the *prayer* of obedience, and the *divine truth* of Christ as *foolishness*, and the man a *fool* for following it.

Further, If a man shall profess any letter or declaration, and *Anger* dwells in his soul, that man never has offered the *true incense* of Reason, to have God's justice stayed on himself; than much less to have offered the *prayer of Faith*; for where *Anger* dwells that soul has not been accepted of GOD; nay, never will, without he can put anger away free of excuse, and truly repent of that evil: Also Reason will conceive evil against his brother, and this evil will grow strong, until it comes forth in judgment, unto condemnation against his brother: for Reason ignorantly thinks the evil is in his brother, but all the while the evil is in himself, for Reason is sealed under death unto wrath, by the internal angel in justice, and from this spirit comes out his wrathful condemnation: Therefore the same degree of judgment he metes to his brother, is measured to him again; for Reason can bring forth nothing but spiritual lies which declares his own condemnation before the holy spirit; therefore Jesus said (Matt. xii.) "O generation of vipers, how can ye, being evil, speak good things, for out of the abundance of the heart the mouth speaketh."

Again, Jesus in his lamb-like innocent, merciful and faithful utterance of his holy *Gospel*, teaches his disciples the pure innocent acts, or *fruits of Faith* by which the soul is to enter the *Kingdom of Heaven*: Therefore He said to his disciples, "Swear not at all, neither by heaven for it is God's throne, nor by the earth for it is his footstool; neither by Jerusalem, for it is the city of the great King," *i.e.* men should make no private resolutions, or public declarations of what they would do in time to come, seeing they have it not in their power to perform any thing but evil; also Reason by his *imagination* on the *bare Letter* of the Scripture, will declare or *swear* his is the true Faith that leads to God, and *teach and preach* the salvation of God and of Christ, by or according to this *Imagination*, and say it is of God; and some has said from this spirit they had or have the *Assurance* of eternal life, which is *swearing falsely in the name of God*; Further Reason will *Vow* certain things which tends to evil, and bring themselves under the law, and if he perform them he will reap the evil, and if he do not, he is found a liar by the angel of his own law before whom he *sware*: (This man will do, yet may scruple to declare what he knows to be truth, before a magistrate) Or in any thing that man shall say to himself, or of himself, what he will do on the morrow, is evil; for he has no power to perform, and even if permitted, it will attend to some evil to himself; therefore, it is best for Reason not to *swear*, nor make *Vows*, but leave the current of life to the will and power of God; for in the sight of God, this is *swearing by yourself*, which is equal with or worse than *prophane swearing*, which must be discommended; for "man cannot make one hair of his head white or black." Therefore Jesus said (Matt. v. 37.) "But let your communication be yea, yea, and nay, nay; for whatsoever is more than those cometh of evil:" *i.e. elect men* must hearken to Jesus, and that will bring the soul to an innocent *Child-like* condition, for Faith to be *born* from its womb, to produce its righteous fruits to follow Him;

then they must be taught by him, and not by emulation; for if they put themselves forward, it is by the spirit of Reason, and that act and communion is of evil.

Further, (as aforesaid) God left his glorious throne of justice, and became flesh to become the *God of mercy*; and his holy covenant is grace and *mercy,* and the *fruits* of Faith is *mercy*: Therefore HE said unto his disciples "They should not resist evil," for if Reason would, let him *smite both cheeks*; and "If man would *sue at law* and take thy coat, let him have cloak also, and give to him that ask, and him that would borrow turn not away, and love your enemy, for if we love one another only, the world do the same;" therefore (Luke vi.) Jesus said "But I say unto you *which hear,* love your enemies, do good for them which hate you: *Bless them* that *curse you,* and *pray* for them that *despitefully* use you," for the mighty *merciful* Act of Jesus was to call his Elect, and redeem them to himself, then by those *fruits* they much follow him; and Reason which cannot follow, is left behind under *Justice*; therefore would not hurt *them* in this *Life,* which is their *kingdom*; and this is according to his divine nature which is *Faith and Mercy.*

Moreover, Jesus said to his disciples, "When thou dost thy alms, let it be in *secret*," for God knoweth the *secret* charitable heart through Faith, and he will *reward* them: Therefore, *Blessed* is that man that is charitable for Faith's sake, for he will be *rewarded from Heaven*: Now, when the fruits of Faith is active in the soul it ascends to God in *secret,* therefore Christ said, "Your Father knoweth what things ye need before ye ask him:" And HE also taught the true *Prayer of Faith,* which is this, "OUR FATHER which art in heaven, hallowed by thy name," *i.e.* Faith directs its prayer to *Heaven* for God's *divine assistance* to help the spirit of Faith through the powers of Reason, Sin, Death, and Hell, that his holy name may be glorified by the fruits of obedience, and the righteous fruits of Faith in the Elect, and that the kingdom of Christ may shine in the *glory of mercy*: "Thy kingdom come," *i.e. God's kingdom*; for Christ is *mercy,* which Faith prays in spirit it may *come to*: "Thy will be done in earth, as it is in heaven," which is, Faith truly submits in *prayer* to the *prerogative will* of GOD, to be disposed of as HE is graciously pleased: "Give us this day our daily bread," *i.e.* he will be graciously pleased to send his inshining light from *heaven,* which is spiritual *bread* to Faith; and also to give natural *bread,* or if he please the *bread* of affliction: "And forgive us our debts, as we forgive our debtors," *i.e.* Faith is of that meek innocent nature, that it *prays* for its own *forgiveness,* as that *forgives,* then of consequence it is in *Love, Mercy,* and *Charity* with the whole world: "And lead us not into temptation, but deliver us from evil," *i.e.* let us not be carried away by the *temptation* of Reason into his kingdom, *for* his kingdom, and there perish *with* his kingdom, now this *evil* Faith prays to be *delivered from*: "For the kingdom of God is the kingdom of mercy, power, and glory, for ever, *Amen.*" This is the true *prayer* of Faith; and if it is but *newly born* from its womb, the motion or desire of the spirit is this, "Lord, *I pray* thee, help me to *Pray.*" Now the spirit of Reason may repeat this Prayer from the *Letter*, but that *Incense* never can ascend to the divine Majesty, Why? because it is contrary to its nature: But from the motions or the desires of the spirit in the *secret Closet* of the soul is the *prayer of Faith*, which is the *golden incense* that ascends up to heaven before God.

Again, By these *fruits of Faith* the soul follows Christ, who came to quicken Faith, and gather his Elect for his glorious kingdom; and he went through the powers of Reason and never hearkened to it, but *left* it behind in its vain glory unto judgment: So a man must *leave* the whole world to *follow Jesus, as one given to HIM out of the world*; and his prayer of Faith ascends before the DIVINE MAJESTY; and his *treasure is laid up in* HEAVEN, where no *thieves can break through and steal;* for he is *a wise man* in Faith, who has *built his House on a Rock*: but the world must be *left behind* for this; therefore Jesus said (Luke xiv.) "If a man come unto me, and hate not his father and mother, and his wife and children, and brethren and sisters, yea, and his own life also, he cannot be my disciple."

Again, When the *spirit of Reason* rules over the soul of man, he will keep the man in his own kingdom let him profess either first, second, or *third Declaration*, and Reason will fill the soul so full of employ after the folly of *this World*, and with covetousness to uphold *this Kingdom*, to live after the manner of Reason's fashion, that the man is an intire slave if he did but know it: - Also this spirit will *allure* the man in this *busy World*, that scripture and religion is become hardly worthy the name of a servant, and the *lying spirit* of Reason is become his *Priest*, and will fill the soul with so many excuses, that there is little else to be found in him.

Further, *Reason* will keep the soul in spiritual drunkenness, so that he shall wallow in the sottish mire of this world, that when the soul is invited to worship God, or to the kingdom of heaven, Reason, he is so full of business in this world that he has not time to come, therefore will *excuse* himself, and seek his peace in that *Excuse*; and if he is shewed the *Letter*, or told the *Word*, he will say it is right and true, but instead of "striving to enter in at the gate," he will fly back to his own Center, like unto a bended spring when let go, and say "he has great incumbrance in the world, and must do it because it is his duty," and I say let him; therefore let Reason do his duty in and for his *Kingdom*, and Faith do his duty for his *Kingdom*: Now this is the *right Eye*, which is the *Eye of Reason* in the soul, and Man is born with this *Eye* open, and tutored in and with the sight of this *Eye*, therefore it is called the *right Eye*; but when the *Voice of God* is active on this earth, it call to *Faith*, and quickens that into *act*, which is another *Eye*, and this *Eye* by divine assistance from HEAVEN, is to *light* the soul into the Kingdom of *Grace and Glory*: And this *Eye* is to become the essential *light, life, and soul*, to him that is regenerated, because this *light, life, and soul*, is to be raised to Eternal Glory; therefore "if the *right Eye* (which is Reason) is offensive it must be plucked out and cast away, and the right hand also (which is the same meaning) for it is more profitable for that to perish, than body and soul, to be cast into hell:" Therefore Jesus said (Matt. vi.) "For where your treasure is, there will your heart be also: the *Light* of the body is the *Eye*, if therefore thine *Eye be single*, thy whole body is full of *Light;* but if thine *Eye* be evil, thy whole body shall be full of *darkness*; if therefore that *Light* in thee be Darkness, how great is that darkness." *Thus* you may see the difference between the *Eye* of Reason, and the *Eye* of Faith, and what each *Eye* looks after.

Chap. V

NOW when Jesus declared his *holy Gospel*, his fame spread abroad, so that multitudes of people came, and many followed him, for HE declared the *Peace of Salvation* unto his *Elect*; and also *called* them out of *captivity*, "heal the sick, make the lame walk, the dumb speak, the blind see, raise the dead, &c." *This* he did by the power of Faith: And the Elect of Old was very desirous to live in those days; and I do confess it was a release to the seed of Reason that followed, for this is to be understood, that many followed, for the outward *Word* or *Declaration*, for Jesus called them from the outward *ceremonial Worship*, according to the *Law* which was a burthen, for they was obliged to bring in their offerings, oblations, and tythes, according to the *Law of Moses*, and attend to, and obey the *Ceremonies*, but by following of Jesus they was eased of that burthen, and left to their own will.

And Reason when it had transformed itself to follow Jesus it was suffered to preach the word, nay, even do *Miracles* in the *Name* of JESUS, as Judas did; for Reason is very fond of subjecting the devil, by the *power of the Word* in another; and at the same time knows not the *Actions* of his own: Also Reason is very fond of external miracles, and more so when he bear the name of a Disciple of him that works them; yet Reason would oftimes shew himself to Jesus by coveting and murmur: But as *Jesus* came in *Mercy*, his most *merciful spirit* suffered them to follow the *outward Word*, for when John said "Master we saw one casting out devils in thy Name, and he followed not us, and we forbad him," (Mark ix. 39.) But Jesus said "Forbid him not, for there is no man which shall do a miracle in my Name, that can lightly speak evil of me; for he that is not against us is on our part." *This,* is according to the *outward Word* which was to be declared abroad; and the seed of Reason that followed Jesus for the *outward word and Miracle* would not be against him, so as to persecute him, nor betray him, until his time was come, and so far they were on *his part.*

Further, Jesus being in *Mercy,* had compassion on the *seed of Reason,* whenever any of them found they were wanting his help, and in obedience to him, come and asked him to do it, for his fame spread abroad by the *glorious miracles* he did, that many who were infirm were desirous to be healed; and as he had healed so many, it did in great measure take off doubt; therefore (Mark ix.) when "the man brought unto Jesus his son, which had a dumb spirit, and Jesus asked the father how long since it came upon him? And he said from a child, (ver. 22.) but if thou canst do any thing, have compassion on us, and help us: Jesus said unto him, *if thou canst believe,* all things are possible to him that believeth: And the father of the child said, with tears, Lord, I believe, help thou mine unbelief;" which was a prayer of obedience; and JESUS had compassion on the father and child, and he was healed by the *merciful power* of CHRIST: Also (Luke xvii.) where *ten men met Jesus who were Lepers, and they lift up their voices and said* "Jesus, Master, have mercy on us;" *and he said unto them* "Go shew yourselves to the priest," *and as they went they were cleansed, and one of them when he saw that he was healed, turned back, and with a loud voice* Glorified God, *and he fell down on his face at his feet giving him thanks; and he was a Samaritan!* and Jesus said "were there not *ten* cleansed, but where are the *nine*? there are not found that returned to give glory to God, save this stranger." Now him that returned to give thanks and glory to God was an *Elect* being, but the other *nine* you may judge who they was by what is written.

Again, JESUS became a true son to the power of the father, and had spiritual communion in the mystical union with *Moses* and *Elias* (who sit in the glory of the Father) unto which he directed his prayer for heavenly assistance, to wade through the powers of Reason, Hell, and Death, and also at times to do his powerful miracles, wherein God was glorified in his *Son,* as may be seen when he raised Lazarus from death to life; and also when his disciples asked him *why they could not cast out the dumb spirit in the child?* (Mark ix. 29.) and HE said unto them, "this kind can come forth by nothing but by prayer and fasting," *i.e.* by the true *prayer of Faith* to heaven for *divine Assistance,* and patiently waiting until it comes.

Further, the miracles of Jesus was done by the power of Faith; and as men was external healed by the power of Jesus, it was to shew forth the internal soul and spirit of Faith by him would be healed, and raised to glory for the *Kingdom of Heaven*; therefore *Christ's* Declaration and Miracles had a two-fold operation, *i.e.* the *outward* declaration and miracle is taken by the seed and spirit of Reason, and with it they will go their own way; but the *internal* miracle and declaration takes the seed of Faith into the royal Priesthood of CHRIST, and then to his glorious kingdom; (see Luke viii. 2.) where you may find it written, "Mary, called Magdalen, out of whom went seven devils;" this woman was not only externally healed to the sight of men, but became internally healed to the sight of God also, because she followed him in person and in spirit, for she did believe to his liking; this is one instance to the seed of Faith; and the *nine* lepers who was externally healed, and went their *way*, not returning thanks to him that healed them, is one instance to the seed of Reason.

Yea, The miracles of JESUS was very great and glorious, and done by the power of *Faith* and *Prayer*, for many of the seed of Faith was healed by the power of those miracles; yet the *external* miracles in themselves was more to convince, or rather condemn, the seed of Reason, than it was to redeem the Elect; for if the Elect had been externally healed only, they never had been redeemed; for in the miracles they was but made whole according to creation, which plainly shews HE was God the Creator: And raising the dead was bringing the Being back to this life, and must die again; But this also shews he had power to raise Faith from death to life in his royal priesthood, and would have power to raise the dead for eternity; therefore in all those miracles GOD is greatly *glorified* in his SON, because Christ came in *Mercy*, and all that came to him, and would be healed, he healed by his declaration and miracles; and the seed of Faith followed in spirit to be internally healed, by the power of his internal miracle, for the sake of the Kingdom of HEAVEN – but the seed of Reason would be no more than external healed, and went their own *Way in Spirit*, for if they followed in person, it was for the sake of the *outward Word* and miracle.

Moreover, I shall mention a miracle of JESUS, (Matt. xiv.) Where *great multitudes followed him out of the cities on foot*, "And Jesus went forth and saw a great multitude, and was moved with *compassion* towards them, and healed their sick; and it was evening and in a desart place, and his disciples said send the multitude away that they may go and buy victuals, but Jesus said, they need not depart: Then JESUS commanded the multitude to sit down, and he took the two fishes and five loaves, and looking up to heaven, he blessed, and brake, and gave the loaves to his disciples, and his disciples to the multitude, and they did eat and were filled, and them that eat were five thousand men, beside women and children, and the fragments that remained was took up and filled twelve baskets." This great miracle was to shew forth the power of the acts, and declaration of Jesus, to his Elect; for although Faith fell under the power of death, and the soul actuated by the spirit of Reason, and was under that law; yet Christ would raise Faith from death to life, and bring it through those powers, and regenerate it to his own likeness: For JESUS came and directed his voice to the womb of Faith, and called his *Elect* to himself, and quickened the spirit of Faith into act, and offered up his prayer before the THRONE for *them*, and redeemed *them*, and regenerated THEM to his holy covenant of grace, and sanctified *them* to enter his *Glorious Kingdom*; for when Jesus declared his *Holy Gospel*, and made his gracious promise to his Elect, and worked his glorious miracles, and uttered his holy parables, to display the likeness of the *Kingdom of Heaven*, this declaration is made with words and *outward* shew, but the *internal* and spiritual help of Christ, according to the word, by the mystical union of Faith comes to the *Elect*, and this divine assistance of Christ comes from heaven, and is that which taketh the soul to his spiritual and holy covenant of grace; then the soul by the *lively union* of Faith, with the *spirit of Christ* eats of the TREE OF LIFE, and is filled with the righteousness of Christ, for the Kingdom of Heaven; but the *Letter or outward Word* is left behind as a *fragment,* and given to the *Seed of Reason,* and that will keep them fully employed on a spiritual account.

Also the *twelve Apostles* went in the spirit and power of Christ, to preach the glorious acts and redemption of Christ, and called the Elect to his Faith, whereby he was graciously pleased by his holy spirit to confirm the soul according to their preaching, and not only so, but also to lead the soul through the wiles and temptations of Reason, and take the soul into the glory of his *divine Mercy*; but the *outward Word* or letter is left behind as a *fragment*: - CHRIST said, "his words are *spirit and Life*," but any one to know the *spirit* by the word spoke must be in the mystical union, and spiritual compact, and priesthood of Faith with Jesus, to be taught by Jesus; for the *outward Word* or bare letter is but a *fragment,* what the spirit hath left behind: therefore the heavenly doctrine that Jesus gave to the *twelve Apostles* was to call the *Elect* to Jesus in *Spirit*, and through *Him they did eat*, and by *Him they were filled*, (for the Kingdom of Heaven) with his glorious *internal* Miracle of redemption and sanctification; and the *outward Word* or letter is *the fragment that filled twelve baskets*, answerable to the *twelve Apostles*, and was given to the seed of Reason that they might hand about to each other, and make what merchandize they can of it, for let there be *seven* baskets or *one* basket, it is same thing in consequence.

Again, The *Letter of the Apostles* declaration of Jesus was given unto the *Gentiles*, for the *Jews* could not enjoy it without transforming themselves from one letter to the other; and when done they was eased of the laborious ceremonies and oblations according to law; and all others that was transformed into the *Apostolical Letter* they may read of CHRIST, and he forgive sin, and many men has gone forth as *teachers of this Letter* by their own imagination, and has subjected men, and got great gain; also many men has dissented from the first established opinion, which was the *Church of Rome*, and others has dissented from them, so that it is branched forth, or taught according to the different opinions of men, for there is a *seeming* scope in the *Letter*, and every man will ground his judgment on different parts or sayings, but all in the wrong; for no one can tell the mind of God in the *Scriptures* without he is *inspired by* JESUS CHRIST *from HEAVEN*, for it is not his reading them over, and the spirit of Reason rising into emulation, and then call that spirit, the spirit of God, *for* there he is found a liar before the *internal angel* in justice, for that is the spirit of the devil: Now the spirit of God guides to *Light and Life*, and the spirit of man guides to *death and darkness*; therefore all offerings which is prayer, that is made to Christ by the spirit of Reason, is an *abomination* to him; but, as I said, the *Letter is but a fragment or Garment* which the spirit left, and those men whose judgment is grounded on different sayings in the *Letter,* they all hold forth and *Cry, here* is salvation, which is casting lots upon the *Letter*, as they did at Christ's crucifixion (Mark xv. 24.) "And when they had crucified him, the parted his *Garments casting Lots* upon them, what every man should take;" and this thing the seed of Reason do by the *Letter* at this day.

Further, When Jesus was on earth, as I said, he came in *Mercy*, and his spirit is *Merciful* for many followed him, and they brought them that were diseased (Matt. xiv.) "and besought him that they might only touch the hem of his garment; and as many as touched were made perfectly whole," for they drawed *compassion* from Jesus, and *Virtue* went with compassion to heal the *diseased*: Now when any one come to Jesus that was *diseased* and desired to be healed by *touching the hem of his garment*, it is no more than being made whole according to creation and Generation; but to be *healed or made whole according to Redemption,* you must *eat his* FLESH*, and drink his* BLOOD; therefore in the day of accompt, there will be found a great difference between touching the hem of his *Garment*, and eating his *Flesh* and drinking his *Blood*; for I would have men *understand* that all who were called by the declaration of Jesus, did not work the *Works of Faith*, neither will they all enter into the *Marriage Feast.* (Matt. ix. 37.) "Then saith he unto his disciples, the harvest is truly plenteous, but the labourers are few;" and (xxii. 14) "For many are called, but *few* chosen."

Chap. VI

AGAIN, Those of the *seed of Reason that followed Jesus was on his part,* so far as not to persecute him for his declaration; and there was others that was taken with *Anger against him*, and sought to entangle him in his words, persecute him, and take his life; *thus* the declaration of JESUS had a two-fold effect on the *seed of Reason;* some was taken with *Emulation* and others with *Anger;* for when Jesus called his Elect, by the voice of Faith and Mercy, it being so contrary to the dark superstitious conceived notions of Reason on the scripture, that it set it on fire in envy and wrath, &c. that Reason became greatly troubled in the soul, for all their ruling power, and joy they had in the worship of the *Law,* received such a wound, that it never could be healed for man to have common peace again, but to transform himself into the *Letter of Jesus.*

Now when *Jesus constrained his disciples to get into a ship to go before him,* "and the ship was tossed in the sea for the wind was contrary; and about the fourth watch of the night, they saw Jesus walking on the sea, and they were troubled, but Jesus answered, it is I, be not afraid." This *Miracle* of JESUS, his *walking on the Sea,* is to shew to the spiritual man, that Jesus by his miracles and declaration which he made by the power of Faith, was *above* or *walked upon all the waters* or powers of Reason, which is a *Sea,* but not the *crystal Sea,* or *Waters* of Faith; and sometimes this *Sea* or waters of Reason, was in a *Calm,* and sometimes in great *Trouble; i.e.* this, the seed of Reason, that transformed themselves to follow Jesus for the *outward Word and Miracle,* in their souls the *Waters* of Reason was in a *Calm;* but Christ must not be led aside by the *temptation* of Reason in that condition, not even in the *Elect,* as may be seen (Matt. xvi.) where Jesus said, "He must go to Jerusalem and suffer many things of the elders, and chief priest, and be killed, and be raised again the *third* day; then Peter rebuked him, saying, be it far from thee, Lord;" here Peter, with love to his master, not willing any harm should come to him, spoke this, but it was from the spirit of Reason (for see verse 23.) "But he turned and said to Peter, "get thee behind me *Satan,* for thou art an offence to me; for thou savourest not the things that be of God, but those that be of man;" therefore would not hearken to Reason, so as to be *tempted* by it: And those of the spirit of Reason that their *Waters was troubled,* sought to bring all manner of evil against him, and devour him, like the relentless *Waves of a troubled Sea;* yet HE walked on those *spiritual Waters* by the power of Faith; for he never was tempted by the *insinuating* spirit of Reason, nor drove out of his *Way* by the *wrathful* spirit of Reason; and this is the *straight and narrow path* he had to go, to gather the Kingdom of Heaven to himself.

Again, A *declaration* made by the *sacred inspiration of Jesus,* is a Message in the spiritual *Covenant of Grace, i.e.* Faith and *Mercy;* and them that would follow the *Messenger,* if they keep the *Word of Faith and Patience* according to the declaration, they never will *sink into the Waters* of Reason, so as to be drowned; for the *Voice of God in the Messenger,* may be likened to a ship that sails on the natural sea, which is directed by God's providence to come *safe to Land,* through the midst of tempestuous waves, and whosoever abides in that ship, *will also*, come safe to Land; *so*, in like manner whosoever doth abide in the aforesaid *spiritual ship* will be brought through the *tempestuous sea* of Reason, to the holy spiritual *Birth and sanctification of* CHRIST THE KING OF FAITH, to enter his glorious kingdom: But if a man through emulation should think himself more wise than the *Messenger* in some things, and be tempted aside from the *Messenger*, or if a man through his distress of mind, on any occasion, should think he may go *a little* aside, now in either of those things they *tempt* the spirit of God, and are out of the *Ship* in the *Waters of Wild Reason*, and let them take care they are not drowned; they think to the contrary, true it is! Otherwise they would not do it; but this I say, the more they think to the contrary, the deeper they are in the waters of Reason!

Moreover, In this Miracle *Peter desired to come to Jesus on the Waters,* and Jesus bid him come, which he did by the *Power of Jesus*, for no mans Faith can keep him up on those waters, in a *convinced state* only, as Peter then was in: Therefore "when the sea was troubled he was afraid, and beginning to *sink,* he cried. *Lord, save me,* and Jesus caught him and said, O thou, of little Faith." This was to shew that all power and inspiration of Faith, belong to Christ the KING of GLORY; for this miracle was done by the power of Faith in Jesus, and Peter was let to know that he must *sink* without the help of Jesus, for although Peter was in no more than a *convinced state*, yet Jesus was here at hand to help him; but *now*, Jesus is ascended into *heaven*, and it must be the true *Prayer of Faith*, to reach him for his *divine assistance*; also when a man is inspired by Jesus and *sent forth* in the holy covenant of *Grace and Mercy*, and those men that follow the *Messenger* in spirit will find his assistance is wanted at times, for the *Messenger* must walk on the waters, according to *his Message* he is sent on; but he stands before the *Throne*, so as to offer the prayer of Faith, for Christ's *divine assistance*, to help him through the *tempestuous Storms* of Reason.

Further, at this day this Miracle is to the *internal* spirit of Faith in the Elect, for Faith has the power of Reason to wade through, to get master of the soul, and sometimes Reason will be *Calm* in order to tempt the soul, and sometimes it will be in such a violent *Storm* in the soul, as if it would *drown*, or devour the man: *Anon* the inshining light of CHRIST appears in the soul to the assistance of Faith, then the soul is affrighted at his own darkness; but the divine light of JESUS is *understood* by the spirit of Faith in the soul, as if it was to say, "*It is I, be not afraid!*" therefore this is the *straight and narrow path* that Faith has to travel, which is between the *temptations* and *Storms* of Reason to gather *knowledge* of the *Messenger,* and *divine assistance* from Heaven.

Again, The *Parables* of JESUS tends to *spirit and life*, nay, are spirit and life, but no man can *know* the true meaning of Jesus in his parable, without his *divine assistance* from heaven; therefore (Matt. xiii.) "A sower went forth to sow, and when he sowed some seeds fell by the way-side, and the fowls came and devoured them up, and some fell upon stoney places – and some fell among thorns." Those that *fell by the way-side* is this, the seed of Reason that hear the word, and the *power* of the word cannot find Faith in the soul to quicken into *understanding*, then it will be in the way of Reason, for Reason takes it by his *own* understanding, which is contrary to that of Faith; then Reason condemns the spirit and utterance of Faith, to be of the devil, and treats it with contempt and scorn, for he has no understanding in this condition but that of *wild Reason*; and the teachings and understanding of wild Reason is the common or *broad way that leadeth to destruction;* therefore the Reason of man, which is in man, is the devil, or *wicked one*, for to the seed and spirit of Reason, that only guides the soul, and is that which *devours the Word* of Faith, therefore called *Fowls* which is of the *airy* imaginary *devouring* spirit, and goeth hastily into destruction.

And *that seed* which was received into *stony places,* is them that *hear the Word* and are pleased with it, so transform themselves into emulated joy, because they have the word, and may flourish for a *season*; but there will be difficulties attend, such as time, and expence and the mock of Reason, &c. then Reason will take the mind aside, in order to save himself by his own cunning, because the *Word* cannot take *much root* in a heart of *Stone;* also *they* will not bear the internal wilds, and temptations, and persecutions of Reason, which must be done to bring forth the fruits of Faith, for the Son of Righteousness to save them, but *they* will turn from it, therefore *wither away*, and *lose* themselves by their *own wisdom.*

And *them that received seed among thorns,* is also some that *hear the Word* and are pleased with it, then *they* transform themselves to the *word or letter,* but the spirit of Reason takes the soul after the *deceitfulness of riches, which incumber the soul, and lead it after cherubical grandeur, which is the vanity of this world, and the* word is choaked; *also in* other some, the spirit of Reason will fill the soul with the fear of poverty, and keep the soul fully employed in the cares of this world, so that the word *dies away,* and the soul is *unfruitful*; for although poverty may speak against riches, yet if the soul is overcome by the spirit of Reason in the inthralment of either, it is the same thing in consequence: - *Now* in the *three* foregoing states or conditions of soul, there is very little hope of the *Kingdom of Heaven,* for in the parable is contained *Life* to the *Elect*; but the *outward word* is but a *fragment*, and it puts Reason into agitation, then let them go which way they will with the word, or do as they will with it, there is always a priest to be found, internal or external, that will excuse them; but let them be ever so wise in themselves, the mysteries of the kingdom of heaven is hid from them; for when his disciples asked why he spake to them in parables, (ver. 11) he answered and said unto them, "Because it is given unto you to know the mysteries of the kingdom of heaven, but to them it is not:" so Reason take the *outward word or fragment*, but the *spirit and life* from God take Faith through death to *Life*.

Ver. 8. "But other fell into good ground, and brought forth fruit, some an hundred fold, some sixty fold, and some thirty fold. (ver. 9.) who hath ears to hear let him hear." I would have the seed of Faith to observe, whenever Jesus saith, *whoever hath ears to hear, let him hear*, there is mentioned the *fruits of Faith* required unto salvation; or that all *quickening power* to bring forth Faith into act and redeem it, is in HIMSELF: Now the *good ground* is the Womb of Faith in the sons of Adam who are the Elect; therefore when the *Voice* or Echo of Faith is uttered, it centers into this womb of Faith, and there rests, then that quickens Faith into the knowledge of its own *Call*, and it will follow the Messenger who is the angel of the declaration; also the *Voice* of Faith will work strong in the Womb, and will discover to the soul its own inherent darkness, and the man will be filled with fear and trembling, and say within himself, "It is impossible for such a dark soul as he is to be saved," then this reduces the soul into *Death*, which is a death to Reason, but in this death there is a *resignation* in the soul, so as to express itself in spirit, "the will of God be done," which is the *motion,* or the effect of Faith: Like unto the toss or throb of a *Child* that presses to be born from the womb of its mother; then by the *death* of Reason, Faith quickens from its womb or seed, and comes forth into act, and this is the *Virgin Daughter of Israel*, or of Faith, being internally and spiritually *born* to the first spiritual covenant in the *soul of man*, which is the *birth of water.* Now Faith being *born* or brought forth into act, by the power of the *Word, or seed sown, and God's divine assistance from heaven*, it has given to it *a censor with incense, i.e.* Faith is the *Censor* and its prayer the *Incense* that ascends up to heaven, to God for his divine assistance for its own increase, and patiently wait the Lord's leisure, and with meekness bear the insults of Reason: Now this is the *fruits or Works* of Faith that the soul is productive of, and is called by the spirit, *thirty fold.*

Again, Faith being *born of Water*, and finds itself in a fallen state, and under the power of justice and death, and surrounded with the wiles and temptations of Reason, who is seeking always to devour the soul, like unto the cormorant or a ravenous serpent: And this is what the spirit of Faith has to wade through, to get back to God from whence it came, which can be done no way but by *patience and prayer* for God's divine assistance in *regeneration:* Now the law and the angel is quick in the soul, and the spirit of Reason will tempt the soul to sin, then the man will be arraigned before the law, and threatened by the angel with eternal death! Which put Reason into great agitation, and worry itself as it were to death in the soul of man, for it cannot bear to face its own angel; then Faith is the strongest in the soul, and will in prayer submit to the justice of God before the law and the angel; but at the same time very eager to get forward to be rejected by GOD himself; then the inshining light of JESUS in secret shines in the soul, and help, and let the soul go forward and it has fine conceptions which the messenger will confirm; thus the spirit of Faith grows strong, and offer its own offering: Anon the spirit of Reason is arrested by the *internal angel in Justice*, which is its own *Angel*, and that Reason cannot bear to face, therefore must die before him, then Faith offers itself to the will of God through *Justice,* and the secret voice comes from heaven to the angel, "Let the soul live," then the soul is taken forward unto greater communion with God in spirit, and see itself in the *true path* of God, which is the clear *road for heaven*; and also prophecies that Christ will come in spirit and give him *spiritual Birth*, and regenerate him to himself, in his *holy covenant of grace to seal and raise him to his glorious kingdom*: Now in this state of soul, is the *time or glorious days of prophecy*, wherein a man prophecies of his own SALVATION! Which is the greatest prophecy for himself, and this degree of Faith the spirit calls *Sixty fold*. Also I would have the seed of Faith mind this – the *spirit or Daughter* of Faith is very desirous to go up in spirit to its own Angel, who is Christ the king of Faith in glory and offer at his royal feet; but the spirit of Reason cannot face his *own Angel* and live, which is the internal *angel in justice,* or in plain terms, your *own conscience* who will condemn you; therefore the *travail* is hard up to *Sixty fold* portion of Faith.

Yea, After this the soul is still in *travail*, and has its sorrow in the *clouds of darkness!* And its joy with the divine *light from heaven!* Anon, he is called before God's divine justice which is the power of the father; then the voice of JESUS comes through the justice of the Father, and asks what fruit you have brought forth to be *born and regenerated* to his holy covenant of grace? Or what fruit have you brought forth to touch his *Mercy* in his holy covenant of grace? Then (this voice of spiritual *Mercy* speaking through spiritual *Justice* into the *virgin Daughter* of Faith) HE begets to himself the spiritual son of Faith for his holy covenant of grace; and this *Son* of Faith will press hard to be *born*, to ascend to Jesus in spirit, which when born it doth, and is sealed and sanctified for the kingdom of heaven; this is the holy *Marriage* with the pure virgin daughter of Faith, and the spiritual birth; and the BOOK OF LIFE being opened to the soul! and the man that comes back with this message, is a *Messenger* in the holy covenant of grace; and he comes under *Mercy!* and his Faith is an Hundred fold. Now I would have the Elect to understand, that the *hundred fold* portion of Faith will be theirs also; for they will be called forward to the spiritual birth and regeneration; "But many that are first will be last, and the last will be first," because this is mostly done at the hour of death, and it is according to the will of God, and the life of man; and when God is graciously pleased to send a *Messenger* with this *hundred fold* portion of Faith, happy is that soul that is found without murmur against that *Messenger!*

Chap. VII

AGAIN, (Matt. xiii. 24.) Jesus put forth another parable, saying, "The kingdom of heaven is likened unto a man which sowed good seed in his field, but while men slept his enemy came and sowed tares among the wheat, and went his way:" Now this was first done when Adam and Eve hearkened to the voice of the serpent angel, which was, and is, the devil, because many of his posterity are yet living; therefore when Adam and Eve was left to their created strength, the *Law of Faith slept* in them, which they should have *watched*, then innocence was overcome by subtilty; and this serpent angel *sowed* his spiritual body into the womb of Eve, and her soul was incumbered with his evil spirit, which she could not get intirely clear from until her death, when she was translated to, under the *mercy of the Son*, and now layeth in the bed of mercy!

Moreover, it was by this *evil spirit* she tempted and overcome Adam, then his soul was also incumbered with this *evil spirit*, and he could not get clear from it, until his death, when he was translated to under the *mercy of the Son!* Thus Eve bare Cain by or from the serpent angel's transmuting himself into her womb, and this was the *enemy* (or devil) *that sowed the tares and went his way; i.e.* after he *sowed* himself into the womb of Eve, *he went his way*, so as to be brought forth a man-child in this world, which is *the field* for generation under the attributes of justice and mercy.

Further, After Cain was born, there was left as aforesaid, the *evil spirit* of Reason, an inhabitant in the souls of Adam and Eve, which was not only a grand enemy to the spirit of Faith in them, but also to their sons and daughters to this day; thus the *evil spirit* was *sown* in the Elect; which is *their* grand internal *enemy* to the spirit of Faith, for it produces *briers, thorns, tares, &c.*

Also when Can grew to manhood he slew his brother Abel, and so became a *Murderer*: and when he was arraigned before the internal angel in justice, whom he called lord, there he told a lie to excuse himself, then he was found both *a liar and murderer*; but God's justice was stayed so far, that he should be loosed by the angel for a time and go into *the Land of Nod, i.e.* to *forget* the power of the *Angel* so far, that hopes for forgiveness may rise from the spirit of Reason; because from him was to come a large generation, which are called *serpents and vipers,* because they are of his spirit; then he preached to his children his great experience he had before the angel, because he was loosed for a time; and then according to the imagination of Reason, he formed his own *forgiveness* and friendship with God: Now this is the *Water* of Reason, because it waters the souls and spirits of the seed of Reason, relative to the *Hope* of their eternal happiness; and is called *the great river Euphrates in the Land of Nod,* which now runs in the souls of men.

Moreover, concerning this Worship imagined and formed by the spirit of Reason (and by it is dedicated for God to own) it is become so powerful, that when the *Voice and spirit* of God appears on this earth, to declare his divine will and pleasure to his Elect, it is so contrary to the will and worship of Reason, that it cannot bear the *spirit of God,* or the *spirit of Faith,* which is of the divine nature, should live, therefore will seek all they can to *murder* it; for to the spirit of Reason the voice of God appears as great blasphemy, and as such they *condemn* it, which is spiritual *Murder;* if not, murder the man that brings it, as a blasphemer: This the seed of Reason will do, that cannot transform themselves into the *outward word* or bare letter, and so follow the man (but in their *own way*) to exalt themselves higher up in emulation by the language.

Again, Those of the spirit of Reason that endeavoured to *kill* Faith; After the Messenger is dead, will in time transform themselves into *his Letter,* for that is but *killing the man, and taking possession,* and claim all the *Inheritance of the promises* made to the Elect, and the *prophecies of the coming of* CHRIST, and say that belongs to them; but when Christ *comes* either in person or spirit then they know him not, but will contend with him, as may be seen in John's gospel, (chap. viii.) where the Jews contended with Jesus, for that they read in the *Letter of Moses,* and claim it as their own; Now according to the cherubical inspiration of Moses, (which is the law) is their own, and the internal Angel in justice, who is in the soul of man, has power from Heaven to condemn them, according to the law; but the *mystical union and spiritual communion* in Faith between God and his Elect, wherein the promise of salvation was made to them, and the *prophecy of the coming of* CHRIST, that belongs to the Elect only; therefore when Christ came in person to redeem, the Elect was made known to him, but the seed of Reason knew him not, so contended with him, saying, "they had *Abraham* to their father;" JESUS answered and said unto them, "If ye were Abraham's children, ye would do the works of *Abraham:*" *i.e.* to believe in him and bring forth the fruits of Faith, as *Abraham* did: And he also said, "But now ye seek to kill me, a man that hath told you the *Truth;*" then the *Jews* said to Jesus, "We are not born of fornication, we have one Father, even God;" and (ver. 44.) Jesus said, "Ye are of your father the devil, and the lust of your father ye will do; he was a murderer from the beginning, and abode not in the *Truth*, because there is no *truth* in him, when he speaketh a lie he speaketh of his own, for he is a liar, and the father of it:" Now their father was Cain, who was the first born son of the devil into this world; and is called the *wicked one* because he is of *the wicked one*, for he killed Abel, who was born the *seed of Faith, and HIS offering* was accepted; therefore Cain murdered Abel, and afterward told a lie to excuse himself, and as so was *a murderer and liar from the beginning*, and his children *do the deeds of their father*, as Christ told the *Jews*; because they are the *tares that was sown by the enemy*, and are enemies to God and his Elect, who are the *wheat or good seed*.

Again (Matt. xiii. 26.) "But when the blade was sprung up and brought forth fruit, then appeared the *tares* also," *i.e.* when the *Spirit* of Faith is active in the Elect, it well knows there is manifest a contrary nature to that of Faith, for this contrary nature will mock, belie, and persecute Faith, because it cannot agree or unite with it; so has killed many of the servants of God, for their Faith and prophecy. Now when God was, or is, graciously pleased to commune with the spirit of Faith, above the power of the internal angel in justice, which is the mystical union and spiritual communion between God and his Elect; then the spirit of *enquiring Faith* by prayer is this, *O Lord God, thou did'st create man in thy own image, and after thy own likeness* – which is this, the soul or life of man was created of the divine nature of God, whereby man is called the *Son of God*, by the holy spirit, thus God *sowed* Faith in man, which is the *wheat or good seed* brought forth by generation in this world, which is the *field*: Then the spirit saith, *from whence came those tares* that are such great enemies to the fruits of Faith and divine truth? and the answer is, *an enemy hath done this*: then the spirit or *servants* in justice say, *wilt thou that we go and gather them up*? But God said, "No, least ye root up the Wheat also," *i.e.* because they are so closely connected by generation, therefore must grow together, and them that are the seed of Faith will by God's divine assistance, bring forth the fruits of Faith for SALVATION, and are taken into the holy and spiritual covenant of Grace, or mercy of the SON; and the other are left behind under the power of the internal angel in justice, whereby men will be their own witness to their own condemnation.

Further of this *Parable* – When the God of justice transmuted himself into his created nature of Adam, which was human nature animated with divine Faith, and become flesh, to become the God of mercy; thus God become man and called himself the *Son of Man*, and his voice was of one utterance, which was Faith, to call his Elect to his divine mercy, and directed his voice to the womb or *seed* of Faith in the souls of his Elect, to quicken it into act, and bring it up and regenerate it to his holy covenant of grace and mercy: therefore God *sowed the good seed* of Faith into Adam and Eve when he created them, and was in the condition of God the Father: And when he became a true son to the power of the father he again *sowed the good seed* of Faith into Faith, which was for his redemption and mercy, and that Faith should bring forth fruits in *Regeneration*, acceptable to him for his grace and mercy.

Again, When JESUS uttered his declaration, there was some of the *seed* of Reason transformed themselves so as to *follow him* for his outward word and *Miracle*; but as the fruits of Faith could not be brought out of them, they must judge of him according to the spirit of Reason: therefore will *sow* their Reason which is the *Tares*, in and among the true declaration, which is the *Wheat*, even in the name of Jesus: as (in Mark xiii.) where Jesus himself said "For many shall come in my name, saying, I am Christ, and shall deceive many;" and this spirit of Reason will cause contentions, and bring in temptations to allure the soul from divine *Truth*, to follow the spirit of Reason, and also bring in vain excuses, to excuse themselves in evil, and seeking after this world, which is *making their belly their god*; and those *tares that sow* themselves into any declaration that come from *Heaven*, under the attribute of divine mercy, the *Elect are to WATCH*.

Moreover, There is this evil spirit of Reason in the Elect, that was sown by the *enemy*, as I said before; this also the *Elect must WATCH*, for this is the great *Enemy* of all, because this will keep your own spirit of Faith back from *following* CHRIST, if possible: Now this is a *Plant that God the heavenly Father* (to the Elect) *did not plant* in the souls of his Elect; therefore Jesus said to *his* disciples (Matt. xv.) "Every plant which my heavenly Father hath not planted, shall be rooted up," *i.e.* the voice of Jesus centers to the womb or seed of Faith in the souls of his Elect, and gives *birth to a virgin daughter*, which I call the spiritual daughter of Faith or of *Israel*, and she has to wade through the *wilds and temptations* of Reason, both external and internal, which she will do by her *prayer and God's divine assistance from heaven*; then Faith becomes the strongest inhabitant of the soul; and this *virgin becomes a Bride meet for marriage with* JESUS! then HE unites his holy spirit with this virgin daughter, and begets to himself A *Son* called inspiration, which is spiritually *born* for the Kingdom of Heaven! And *sealed* for the Kingdom of Glory, with his royal spiritual SEAL! And dies in the bed of mercy! So Faith becomes the essential life of man for the resurrection, and Reason is *withered away, or rooted up*; and Faith will get clear of it. Also the spirit of Reason in the Elect, signifies the *Fig-tree that Christ found no fruit thereon*, then he said, "Let no fruit grow on thee henceforward for ever," *and presently it withered away*; therefore when the VOICE of GOD even in the *Messenger* calls to Faith, Reason is also touched, and will, by degrees, *wither way as a useless plant* (to bear fruit for the kingdom of heaven) like unto the *fig-tree.*

Again, I would have the seed of Faith to know the power of Reason is a *three-fold* enemy to them; *i.e.* there is of the seed of Reason that will thunder out *blasphemy and persecution,* seeking all they can by force to drive you from CHRIST: Also there is of the seed of Reason that will *transform themselves* into your own declaration, and declare themselves your brother in Christ, and at the same time *tempt* you from him: and there is your *own spirit of Reason* in yourselves, which will *tempt* the soul, and is very eager to hear *temptation* without, to allure the soul from Jesus, therefore WATCH *and sleep not,* if possible, lest Reason, *the enemy, sow tares among you,* and take you into captivity; for this is the *Way,* the world is, in generation and darkness, and Faith has hard *travail* out of it; therefore when the disciples of Jesus said unto him, "Declare unto us the parable of the *tares* of the field," and he said unto them, (as Matt. xiii.) "He that soweth the good *seed* is the son of man; the field is the world, the good *seed* are the children of the kingdom, but the *tares* are the children of the wicked one, the enemy that soweth them is the devil, the harvest is the end of the world, and the reapers are the angels." I would have the Elect to know, that *Christ is the Angel* of the covenant of *Grace,* and them that are *born* in spirit, are angels *in* the covenant of grace, and the Elect are the angels *for* the covenant of grace; therefore in the days of a Messenger, the spirit being *active* on this earth, they gather the Elect to the *seal* of the living God; and when there is no Messenger on earth, CHRIST gathers his *Elect* at the hour of death, by his holy spirit; And the *children of the wicked one* are manifest, and under the seal of the internal angel in *justice*; and as every man hath his own angel, they are gathered out of the kingdom under *justice*; thus the two *Seeds* or generations are gathered to *Mercy* and *Justice,* then fall in death, and there lay till the Resurrection.

Chap. VIII

AGAIN, *Jesus* said (Luke xiii.) "Unto what is the kingdom of heaven like, and whereunto shall I resemble it; it is like a grain of mustard seed, which a man took, and cast into his garden, and it grew and waxed a great tree, and the fowls of the air lodged in the branches of it." Now I would have the *seed of Faith to understand,* that Christ who is the eternal God, has the essential spirit of Faith, which is by himself likened to *a grain of mustard seed,* and this spirit of Faith is all-powerful, to work, or bring things to pass, according to his divine will and pleasure; and not only so, but also, if his divine wisdom should suffer his works to be invaded, then by his *holy spirit, or grain* of Faith, he has power to recover it again, with great advantage to himself and his Elect: Thus the divine Majesty was graciously pleased to create Adam and Eve with a life of Faith, which was and is of his divine nature: So the Grain of Faith was *sown* into this earth, and became a *Garden* in the souls of his Elect, or *good ground*, to bring forth the *fruits* of Faith, unto translation or *regeneration for the kingdom of Heaven.*

Then the serpent angel, or devil, came and *sowed* himself both in person and spirit into Eve; then she tempted and overcame *Adam*, as I said (Chap. vii.) so Reason came and *lodged* itself in the tabernacles of Faith, who was the *Branches* of God; and by its lying imagination, on vain *airy* things, will *tempt* and captivate the soul, because it thinks it is become one with, or *above* the spirit of Faith, even in the elect, when rose from the dead: And the children of Cain, who are *the fowls of the air*, they, according to their imagination, think and say they are one with the seed of Faith, or children of God, who are of and for the *kingdom of heaven*: Thus the kingdom of heaven was invaded in the beginning, *and the fowls of the air came and lodged*, according to God's creation of Faith, and his promises made to that *Seed;* so the Elect are much troubled with those *fowls of the air*, both external and internal.

Again, when the very eternal God (who was become the God of justice through the acts of man and angel) transmuted himself into flesh, to become the God of Mercy; he took his own created nature of Adam on himself, which was human nature animated with divine Faith; and left Reason to itself, to die and wither away in the Elect; for he took only the nature of Faith, which was under the power of death, to keep its law, and make it alive by his death and resurrection: - Thus the *uncreated grain of Faith sowed himself* into his *own created grain of Faith,* and was born a child, and *grew* to manhood, and redeemed the Elect world.

Further as I have said, When JESUS uttered his holy gospel of peace and mercy, he had the womb, or *seed of Faith* in the souls of his Elect to work upon, which is the *garden or good ground that HE sowed* in creation: then there was the *Voice of* GOD, which is the utterance of pure divine Faith; *sowed* in Faith, which was in a fallen state, yet capable of hearing the voice of God; which was *sowed as a grain of mustard seed*, to raise Faith from death of life, for the redemption and salvation of his Elect, and to recover his lost kingdom again in mercy, to himself: Thus JESUS *sowed* his holy covenant of grace and mercy in the garden of Faith, which is in the souls of his Elect, even out of the world, and gathered them together out of the world; because the works and fruits of Faith is contrary to the works of Reason, for that is of the world; and HE *offered* up his prayer for his Elect, before the throne of the Father; therefore Jesus said, (in John's gospel xvii.) "I pray for them, I pray not for the world, but for *them* which thou has given me, for *they* are thine." Because Jesus created them his *own children* when he was in the glory of the Father.

Yea, by the power of this holy *grain* of Faith JESUS went through the power of Reason, sin, death, and hell, and ascended into the glory of mercy, and has power of justice: Thus the spirit of Faith which is *likened to a grain of mustard seed that was sown* into its own garden, *which is but a small seed, yet it grew up* through the power of Reason, sin, death, hell, and justice, *and his top reaches the high heaven* of mercy. – Also Jesus when he was ascended into his glory of mercy, he gave his holy spirit to his Apostles, who then become *branches of this tree,* and by their preaching, *this tree branched forth* into many glorious promises made to the Elect, and CHRIST *came, and doth come,* in spirit to the Elect, according to the promises made; and gathers them into his heaven of grace.

Again, The power and acts of Jesus in gathering his glorious kingdom of Faith together, is *likened unto a grain of mustard seed,* in this – When JESUS went forth to utter his holy gospel, he declared himself the SON of GOD; and came to redeem his lost kingdom, *Israel,* and salvation could not be had but through HIM; this being done by a MAN who was in *weakness and shame,* in the eye of Reason, and his *language* contrary to their imagination; this *seed being sown* in and among the world, it appeared very *small* in the eye of Reason, nay impossible to be, therefore treated him with contempt and scorn; but this *small seed* fell into his own garden of Faith, and they came and followed him both in person and spirit, and brought forth the fruits of Faith, and by him was healed for the *kingdom of heaven*: Also Jesus went forth declaring his holy gospel and working miracles, so his fame spread abroad, that multitudes of people came to him and was healed, that some of the *seed* of Reason transformed themselves to him, for his outward word and Miracle; neither could the persecuting spirit of Reason stop him in his declaration until he had finished his testimony, and after he was ascended he sent his *Apostles* by his holy spirit, which are the *branches,* so that Witnesses to, (and the declaration of) his holy Gospel *spread abroad, and waxed great.*

Moreover as I have said, no man can make any declaration or promise, without words, on this earth, therefore when the word is spoken by the Messenger of GOD, the *spirit* of that word centers to Faith in the Elect, but the *bare word* is but a fragment, what the spirit has left *behind*: Also the spirit comes from JESUS in glory, according to promise to his Elect, and heals them, but the bare word or *Letter* is a fragment, what the spirit has left behind to others: Also man must be *born in spirit* to the mystical union and spiritual communion with Christ, to *know* the mystery of the kingdom of heaven, by the *word spoke,* for the bare word of *Letter* is but a fragment, what the spirit hath left behind as aforesaid. Now when the declaration of the *holy Gospel spread* abroad, there came many of the seed of Reason, and transformed themselves into the outward word or letter, and laid their claim to Jesus, but *sowed sedition,* and brought in heresies, contention, &c. thus the kingdom of heaven was invaded, and *the fowls of the air, came and lodged in the declaration,* almost from the beginning of the gospel.

Again, When the persecuting spirit of Reason had put Christ and his servants to death, then they or their children, transformed themselves into the letter of the gospel, and claimed all the promises that was made to the Elect; for when there is no Messenger on earth the seed of Reason can put what constructions (on the letter) they please: Now I would have the Elect *understand* this, when any man (or men) is inspired by God himself from heaven, that man can, by the power of Faith, *enquire of God,* because the spirit of God is *active* in the soul of such a man, but when this man dies the spirit is withheld, and the letter is but a fragment without the spirit; now it remains in the will of the DIVINE MAJESTY, when he will be graciously pleased to send again, *i.e.* to inspire a man, with his holy spirit in his holy covenant of grace, *and send him back into this world to tell his Tale,* thus God can, thus God can *send* which of his Elect he please, without consulting any created, or generated being in heaven or earth: Then CHRIST *is come again in spirit,* and the power of the *Letter* is known by his holy inspiration from heaven.

Moreover from the death of one *Messenger* to the inspiration of another, there is *silence in the nether heaven* of Faith in the souls of his Elect, in respect to public act and declaration, for they know not what to do, they being so *captivated* by both internal and external Reason, until the hour of death, when CHRIST is graciously pleased to raise Faith from death to life, and *Call* by his holy spirit, and take it into his holy spiritual covenant of grace, and then it dies in the bed of mercy: this was known to God and themselves *only,* for they never came back to tell their brethren; so at this time of *silence* in heaven, *the fowls of the air came and lodged in the* declaration of the gospel, which are the out *branches*; thus, *the kingdom of heaven has suffered violence, and the violent take it by force,* not only in person but in spirit, by their imagination, from the days of JESUS until this day, and is also done in, or by the declaration of the *Third Record.*

Further, as no other *Name* was ever given from heaven, that salvation was, or is, to be had, but that of JESUS *ONLY,* therefore as through the *Merits of Jesus,* the Elect world are saved, his acts and declaration being left behind on *literal Record,* that multitudes, nations, &c. has transformed themselves into this *Letter* and claim all the promises made to the Elect; Also the declaration of, and concerning JESUS, is very scopious as man may think, because of different sayings written therein; yet I would have men *understand* that these sayings center in *two Heads, i.e.* in *promises* to the Elect, and *Threats* to the children of the wicked One, generation of Vipers, wicked generation, &c.

Again, Many men who has *lodged* themselves in the declaration, has gone forth and preached in the name of Jesus, and according as they find different sayings they differ in judgment for want of *heavenly knowledge,* thus on the off-set their imagination is divided concerning *Christ,* for some will have him all *influence,* and no person, - others will have him all *person,* and no influence, but the outward word or bare letter, - others will have him the *second* person in the trinity, - others will have their *own* imagination on the letter, to be the influence or spirit of Christ: Also in the *salvation* of Christ they equally differ; some will have the light of Christ within to guide them, but will own no glorified personal Christ without them (therefore whereunto is this light to guide *them*): others say their *belief* in the letter is sufficient for them, without prayer or the influence of Christ from heaven, and by that say they have the assurance of eternal life, - others will have *free-will* – and others *free-grace*; but if men will ask for grace they may have it, which is the same thing as a man to be saved by his *own free-will*: Also there is others who say, Christ died to save the whole world, and all *may* or *will* be saved! Thus men by their evil imagination will divide Christ according to their *own* will; and invoke him by his holy Name to own their goings out of the spirit of Reason on the *Letter,* which is to invoke him to be a servant to the imagination of man's heart, which is evil, and this is making things according to the *Will of man.*

Moreover the *seed* or spirit of Reason never did, or possibly could make any declaration, prophecy, or promise of the coming of Christ, or the salvation of the Elect; this was done by the *seed* of Faith; they being inspired from heaven so to do: then the seed of Reason would transform themselves into that declaration, and claim the promises and preach it up; but in this they can bring forth no more fruit by the declaration, than they did in bringing of the declaration, *i.e.* they brought forth no fruit in bringing of a declaration, nor no fruit in the declaration brought by another, because the seed and spirit of Reason is *barren* of fruit for the *kingdom of heaven;* for as *it is not given them to understand the mysteries of the kingdom of heaven* by Faith , which no one can without, then they must preach it by the spirit of Reason; therefore as CHRIST by his holy spirit likens the kingdom of heaven unto *Light and Life,* they, by the letter, liken the kingdom of heaven according to their *imagination* which is death and darkness; *i.e.* men read the *Letter,* and by their spirit of Reason make to themselves their own redemption, and invoke his holy name to *cloak* their evil spirits and acts, and at the same time call him a liar, not only before the spirit, but in the *Letter* also.

Now I would have men *understand* that whoever goeth forth to preach the name of CHRIST by any spirit contrary to the holy spirit of Christ, and render him, or his glorious acts contrary to what he is, or his holy intent by his almighty acts, that man or men are *false Christs*, and preach falsely in his name, and they *cry, Lo, here is Christ, and, Lo, there is Christ*, as HE prophecied would come; and thus heaven was invaded by the seed and spirit of Reason, who are *the fowls of the air, that came and lodged in the* declaration.

Further, the kingdom of heaven is given to the seed of Faith, who can bring forth the fruits thereof, and become the children of God; now the *Gospel* centers to that head, but in it there is also *Threats* to the seed of Reason, that transform themselves into the letter of Jesus, and claim and *take the kingdom of heaven by force,* that it *will* become one with the children of God, and *preach and pray* in his name; therefore this is to be minded, when the spirit speaks to Faith, and when it speaks to Reason, as (Matt. vii.) Jesus said, "for every one that asketh, receiveth; and he that seeketh, findeth; and to him that knocketh, it shall be opened." Here Jesus speak to the seed of Faith, to whom the kingdom of heaven will be given: again, Jesus said, (ver. 22.) "Many will say to me in that day, Lord, Lord, have we not prophecied in thy name, and in thy name have cast out devils, and in thy name done many wonderful works? And then will I profess unto them, I never knew you, *depart* from me ye that work iniquity." Here Jesus speak to the seed of Reason, and particularly to them that are *Preachers*.

Again, When any man is *inspired* by the holy spirit of Jesus, *and sent back to tell his Tale*, then CHRIST is *come* in spirit, that the soul may be warned and prepared to meet him, to receive his seal, which is the *Seal of the Living God*: After this the man is fit to meet him, in his personal glory, in the resurrection to eternal life: therefore the voice of Jesus Christ, through the Messenger, centers to Faith in the souls of his Elect, and calls it into act, then there is Faith united with Faith, in communion with each other, in the true worship of God, and the mystery of its own prayer; now this is the *nether heaven* of Faith, for the *heaven* in Faith, on this earth, and the seed of Faith being *called*, will come into *this heaven*, and are the *fowls that fly in the midst of (this) heaven*, because they are united by Faith, and *gather* their way (by the prayer of Faith and divine assistance from heaven) to *Mercy*, as Christ himself did, to his most high glorious THRONE *of Mercy*.

Moreover, (Rev. xix.) "And I saw an angel standing in the sun, and he cried with a loud voice, saying to the fowls that fly in the midst of heaven, come gather yourselves together unto the supper of the great God." This *Angel in the sun* is Christ, who was the God of *Justice*, and is now become the God of *Mercy*, by his becoming a *Son or Servant* to his own power: - And by his holy spirit, which is Faith and Mercy, he now *calls* his Elect to his mercy, and they must *sup with God!* Now this *Supper of the GREAT GOD!* "is to eat the flesh of kings, and the flesh of captains, and the flesh of mighty men, and flesh of horses, and of them that sit on them, and the flesh of all men, both free and bond, both small and great;" this is the seed and spirit of Reason that *persecuted and tempted* CHRIST, *and do persecute and tempt his elect*; for when Jesus was here they persecuted and tempted him, and blasphemed against his holy spirit and power, this He *bore in sorrow* of soul, which is *eating the flesh of kings, and of captains, and of mighty men*: for Reason, both *great and small*, with all their power combined to persecute him, by their own *dark spirit* (which came from *Chaos*) and poured out their wrath upon him, which he was compelled to take and *bear in sorrow!* Now this is *in spirit to eat the flesh of (Reason) both great and small, and of all sorts, i.e.* to *bear* whatever Reason should say of him, and do to him; and whoever comes into *this heaven* of Faith, must in this manner *sup with the Great GOD of Mercy!* as HE did, when HE was here.

Chap. IX

FURTHER, (Rev. xix. 19.) "John saw the beast and the kings of the earth and their armies, gather together, to make war against *Him* that sat on the horse and against *his* army;" he who *sat on the horse* was CHRIST, for HE went forth and *conquered* by the power of Faith, which is righteousness, and this is the *white horse Christ sat upon*: Also the Elect will *conquer* by the power of Faith and divine assistance of Christ from heaven; and their souls will be made *white* by the power of God in regeneration, then the soul will sit on the *horse* of Faith also. Now the *fowls that fly in the midst of this heaven* of Faith, go forth to conquer by the power of Faith, and *follow Christ* who is their *King*; and those *who gather together against him and his army*, are the seed and spirit of Reason, *They* ride the black horse, and persecute Faith, which is giving them their *flesh to eat*, because it is all their strength and power (in a body of *flesh and blood*) in persecution: This is the warfare between Reason and Faith, when CHRIST was on this earth in person; and when HE *is in spirit*, then the spirit of Reason go out against the *holy spirit*, with blasphemy, murder, &c. and *fill* themselves on the destruction of the *Saints*, and are made *drunk* with their own *wrath*, and curses against the seed of Faith; but by *Mercy, Meekness, Long-suffering, and Prayer,* Faith will overcome; then the internal angel in *justice* has sealed them unto wrath, and will *double unto them double,* of their own *flesh* or wrath to feed upon for ever, what they in their life, gave the saints to eat.

Again, When the voice of God is uttered on this earth, the seed of Faith will come; why? Because Faith knows its own *Call,* to follow God in spirit, *and the fowls of the air, which lodge* in the declaration or bare *Letter,* will belie and persecute the seed of Faith, who are the *fowls that fly in the heaven of Faith, i.e.* to follow God and be under his teachings, instead of wandering in the bare Letter. Also the voice of God is a *sharp sword* to the spirit of Reason, and *then,* in this war, they will *fill the fowls that fly in the heaven of Faith* with their *flesh, i.e.* with persecution; but Faith by its meekness and long-suffering will overcome: And them that persecute and prophecy against them, are taken by the internal angel in *justice,* in their own *wrath,* which will burn for ever and ever.

Moreover, When JESUS was here in a body of flesh, and declared his holy gospel, there was some of the seed of Reason transformed themselves to his outward declaration, as I have said, and was on his part, as not to persecute and disturb him therein; but as they could not *understand* him by his heavenly *Mystery* of Faith, they must understand by the spirit of Reason, so would *scatter from him* in spirit. – Note, *i.e. Except the Spirit in the word centers into the womb of Faith, and there rest, and quickens the spirit into act, and by this spirit of Faith gather their Way to his glorious mercy, as HE himself gathered HIS Way, to HIS glorious throne of mercy, they scatter abroad by the spirit of Reason!* Therefore Jesus said (Matt. xii.) "He that is not with me, is against me, and he that *gathereth not* with me, *scattereth abroad.*" Here Jesus speak intirely against Reason, for them *that did not follow HIM, was against him,* and those of Reason *who did follow, scattered abroad,* because they *gathered not* by his holy spirit, for them *who follow* CHRIST, *will sup with* CHRIST *the* GREAT GOD! so must *taste and eat* of persecution, in this bewildered and dark kingdom of Reason.

Again, JESUS when he eat the Passover or supper with his disciples: they *eat bread and drank wine,* but it was in *Sorrow,* because it was unto his *death;* for after this *He went out to pray in great sorrow and agony! So that sweat dropt from him, as it were drops of blood!* Then the powers of Reason *took and crucified him;* in this HE *eat the flesh of kings, captains, &c.* in persecution unto his death: Also JESUS *break bread* and gave them, and said, take, eat, this is my body," and gave them *wine,* and said, "drink ye all of it, this is my blood of the new testament, which is shed for many, for the remission of sins." Also John's gospel (vi. 53.) Jesus said, "except ye eat the flesh of the son of man, and drink his blood, ye have no *Life* in you;" now if eating *bread* and drinking *wine,* under any ordination, or consecration appointed by men, will gain *Heaven,* I say it is easy gained; also to *believe* that Christ crucified without the gates of Jerusalem, was the *eternal God,* and shed his blood for the sins of his Elect, if bare *belief* of this, or rather repeating the declaration of *another man,* will gain *heaven,* it is easy done; for this, *the fowls of the air that come and lodge* in the declaration, can, and will do; yet *gather their way* and understanding of Christ, by their *dark spirit* of Reason, and persecute the spirit of Christ when it appears.

Further, of *eating the flesh, and drinking the blood of Jesus,* who was the GOD *of Justice,* and transmuted himself into his own created nature of Adam, to become the GOD *of Mercy!* thus God became perfect man, and a true *Son* to the power of the *Father;* therefore HE took the *fallen* nature of Faith, or *human* nature on HIM, and found himself in Reason's kingdom, in the midst of persecution and temptation, so he eat the flesh of Reason in this sorrowful vale of death! – this HE bore by the spirit of Faith and *Mercy,* for he was *merciful* to all, so far as it would extend according to his eternal decree: Also in this *vale of death,* he refused this world, and with meekness left it behind, under the *Justice of the Angel;* also in this sorrowful vale, he kept the *Law of Faith,* and in the mystical union of Faith with them who sat in the glory of the *Father,* to whom he offered his prayer for divine assistance, and by this power of Faith he *gathered his Way* to his glorious kingdom of Mercy; therefore in CHRIST was found the *Fruits of Faith,* which is PATIENCE, MEEKNESS, OBEDIENCE, LONG-SUFFERING, LOVE, MERCY, CHARITY, &c. These *He bore,* and this *He produced* in a body of flesh, in this sorrowful vale of death. Further, in obedience to the *power* of the Father, HE *gave* himself up to death, and lost himself in his own blood in death, *under* the *Justice of the Father,* to quicken in spirit to the glory and *Mercy of the Son:* Now whoever doth this according to the portion of the creature, I do confess he *follows Christ,* and eats his *flesh* and drinks his *blood;* because he finds himself in that condition, as Christ was in when he was here, and must *suffer in flesh* as Christ did.

Again, When the disciples of JESUS *eat bread and drank wine* with him in his life time, it was no more than an *outward Sign* or confession, for there must be the *internal* and powerful works of Faith come after, otherwise he is in danger of this saying (John xiii.) "He that eateth *bread* with me, hath lifted up his heel against me." Therefore when the apostles received the Holy Ghost to preach Christ crucified, they found they was obliged to *eat the flesh* of Reason, in persecution, and also found themselves in fallen Faith, and human nature, and well knew they were but *pilgrims* in Reason's kingdom! Therefore in this *vale of Sorrow*, or death, by the fruits and prayer of Faith for the assistance of Christ from heaven; and in obedience to the mystical union of Faith between Christ, which was the *spiritual wine* he promised when he entered his kingdom, they gave up their lives, and was lost in death in their own blood; but then they received the *Seal* of Christ their king, and died in the bed of *Mercy* to be quickened into an intire *pure life* of Faith: And in this they *eat the flesh and drank the blood of JESUS*, by working the works of Faith, and drinking the *Cup* of sorrow in a *body of flesh* as he did.

Further, When Jesus eat the *Passover* with his disciples, it was in obedience to the commands of Moses who ordained it to be kept as a *memorial*; but to the spiritual *Wise* man was to shew forth Jesus in the travail of this life has *passed over the Angel*: Also when Moses instituted the *passover*, it was by taking "a male lamb without blemish, out from the sheep or goats, and to strike the door posts with the blood, and in the night eat the flesh roast with fire, his head, legs, and with the Purtenance thereof," and this was the *token, to the destroying Angel, to pass over Israel,* and save them alive, when he struck dead the *first born* of all Egypt: Now this was because Israel obeyed Moses, and they was to worship God according to the cherubical inspiration: Also this *Lamb* was to shew the power of God concerning his creation, and the cherubical *Law*, and of that justice, and that he was master of all the creation, therefore if Reason worship God in that *Law* and priesthood given forth by Moses, the *destroying angel* would *pass over* them.

Again, this *Lamb* was to shew Reason if he obeyed the commands of God he would bring them out of *bondage,* and that they should stand under his protection, and enjoy the blessing of God's creation, but they must be obedient to his will, and worship him in all trouble, sorrow, distress, &c. in the travail of this life, without murmur; which is *eating the flesh of the Lamb, with the purtenance, and with bitter herbs*; and then God will bring them out of *bondage* to his blessing, then the Angel will *pass over*, or justice will be *stayed* on them.

Also, *Egypt* is wild arrogant Reason, that seek to do their *own* will and have their *own* way, seeking *vain* glory, *fading* greatness, and to rule over the *souls* of men, and will not be obedient to the commands of God, but pursue, according to their *own will*; and in this they act against God, let them pretend or say what they will to the contrary:

further, in *Egypt* their grand hope, or eager desire, and great care is their *first born*, that the destroying *Angel*, who is now the internal angel in justice will cut off, for in the end they will not find it to their liking, but to their sorrow of soul; also if man possess riches. &c. let him look where they are given him, because he worships God according to the cherubical inspiration, and that given priesthood; if not, it is given as a trial, and lays liable to be cut off through the internal angel in justice; but if a man worship God, then what is *given* is his own, and the angel will *pass over* him, and all will end well so far as that relates.

Moreover as aforesaid, When the *Passover* was eaten by Jesus and his disciples, it was to shew Jesus had *passed over* the justice of the *Angel*, which is justice to Reason, for he took not the nature of Reason on him, nor had any thing to do with that nature, law, or covenant, but to leave it behind under the power of the *internal Angel* in justice, which is now the *destroying Angel* to Reason, and in this he *passed over* that angel: but JESUS had took the created nature of Adam on him, and *passed under* the justice of the *Father*, and then was going to *pass* into death *under* the justice of the *Father*, and *through* death, and the justice of the Father, to his royal kingdom of divine *Mercy*: Also when JESUS *brake and blessed bread*, and gave them, saying "eat, this is my body," and gave them the cup, saying, "drink, this is my blood of the new testament, which is shed for many, for the remission of sins;" which was to shew forth, the very God of Heaven became man to redeem his Elect, and eat and drink as man, and with man, and lost himself in death in his own blood, and rose again for the redemption; for until that was done the *new Testament* could not take place; and that he would unite Elect man to himself, and make them flesh of his flesh, bone of his bone, and spirit of his spirit, by the power of his *regeneration*, and holy MARRIAGE! – He that hath *wisdom, let him understand this!*

Again, When this *Passover* was eat, the Angel had *passed over* eleven disciples (because Judas fell) for then *they* would be taken into the compact and *priesthood* of Faith, and the *prophecy* of JESUS, and to *sup with him in spirit*; therefore blessed is he whom the Angel has *passed over*, for him to be taken into the royal *priesthood of Christ*, and then he will *pass by* the *Angel* (in Justice of and to Reason) because of regeneration; for he cannot pass *over* it as Christ did, but he must *pass under* the justice, and through the justice, of the Father, which is justice to Faith, as Christ himself did.

Moreover, (Matt. xxvi. 29.) JESUS said, "but I say unto you, I will not drink henceforth of this fruit of the vine, until that day when I drink it new with you in my father's kingdom;" *i.e.* CHRIST had taken the *cup* of sorrow unto his death, and lost himself in his own blood in death, and rose again, and is ascended into his high Heaven of Mercy, *to prepare a place for his Elect*, and from thence he *gave gifts* of his holy spirit, and rose Faith from death to life, and it is taken into the royal priesthood of Christ under the justice of the Father; then in a body of flesh and blood, they must *eat and drink* as HE did, and work the *works of Faith* as HE did, and *overcome* the world as HE did, and *lose themselves* in death in their own blood, under the justice of the Father, as HE did; for the *justice of the Father is justice to Faith*, and those works of Faith being done there, it is done in the *Father's kingdom*; and as Christ did those things before them, and is now ascended into his throne of mercy, he now assists his Elect by his holy spirit, to do those things under the justice of the Father; and in this *he drinks of the vine, new with his Elect*, who are *in his Father's kingdom*; because he assists them to work the works of Faith, and receive their incense of Faith, which is fruit of the vine of Faith in regeneration, *in his Father's kingdom*, which is his drinking *of the vine anew*, because it is in, and to his eternal joy, to see the increase of his kingdom of regenerated Faith; but when on earth it was in *Sorrow*: therefore in this manner the Elect must *eat HIS flesh, and drink HIS blood*, to have *part in him*.

Again, observe, when JESUS bore the scoffs, scorns, malice, and persecution of Reason, then HE *eat the flesh of kings, captains, mighty men, &c*. which is the flesh of Reason, and in this he *overcome* the world; for as Faith fell for hearkening to Reason, Reason has power to persecute it; and when GOD took fallen Faith on him, and became CHRIST to redeem it, Reason had power to persecute *Him*: - but in *His* keeping the law of Faith; *His* true obedience to the power of the Father! *His* prayer! *His* travail through this life, in a sorrowful vale of death! *His* standing and working against, and overcoming the powers of sin, death, hell, and justice! And HIS losing himself in death in his own blood, under the justice of the Father! Now in this he eat his *own flesh* and drank his *own* blood; because he did it in fallen human nature, in a body of flesh and blood: and when Faith is rose from death to life, and taken into the royal priesthood of Christ, the Elect must do the same in a body of flesh and blood, by his divine assistance, which is *eating his flesh and drinking his blood*; and in the sorrowful heavy trouble, and travail of soul, they may, and will remember CHRIST HIMSELF was there! which is doing of it *in remembrance of HIM*. And (John's gospel vi. 56.) Jesus said, "he that eateth my flesh, and drinketh my blood, dwelleth in me and I in him;" *i.e.* as CHRIST took the *Cup* of sorrow unto his death, so must his Elect by his divine assistance; and as CHRIST lost himself in death in his own blood, under the justice of the Father, so must his Elect by his divine assistance, and this is *eating his flesh, and drinking his blood*, in the grand union and works of Faith, which is *the Elect in him, and he in them*; and no other way can his flesh be eaten and his blood drank, for salvation; for the Elect cannot *Pass over the justice of the Father*, nor the justice of the Father *pass over* them; for they must pass *under* it, and go *through* it.

Now, I would have Elect men observe what it is to *eat the Passover of the paschal Lamb*, which is the *Lamb* of, or according to Reason, or rather to shew forth the power of God all *over* this creation, and his blessing and preservation to them that obey his word, and worship him according to the cherubical inspiration, that man may not be cut off from *His Blessing*, nor *His Blessing* from man: And mind, *not a bone of the Lamb was to be broken! i.e.* the *Power and Justice* of God will not be *broken!* although it may be *stayed* for a time: And to mind what it is to *eat the Passover*, according the Christ and his disciples, for then the *destroying Angel* has *passed over* the man, and his life is preserved, and Christ has *prayed* for him, and is found worthy to enter the royal priesthood of Faith and Mercy! and to sup in spirit with the GREAT GOD OF MERCY! for although this *destroying Angel* may *pass over* man in this life; *i.e.* God's justice may be *stayed* on man, yet if he cannot enter the priesthood of Christ, he must die under the power of the *destroying Angel*; therefore blessed are those that come and *eat this passover*, for then they will pass from the yoke and bondage of Reason, to under the power and teachings of CHRIST.

Again, And to mind what it is to *pass under* the justice of the Father, in obedience, prayer, patience, &c. and to bear the evil report of Reason, his scoffs, his scorns, malice, oppression, persecution, &c. (for this is eating the flesh of kings, captains, and mighty men, or the flesh of Reason) for as Faith hearkened to Reason and fell, Reason has power to oppress and persecute Faith. And also to eat the flesh and drink the blood of Christ, for Christ is the LAMB OF GOD, and lost himself in death in his own blood, yet *not a bone of him was broken! i.e.* the power of God in Christ, would not be *broken* in his *Redemption, Regeneration, Mercy, and Salvation* to his Elect! therefore I would have the Elect *understand*, they must *eat the paschal Lamb*, which is *the flesh of beasts, &c.* (according to the will and power of God) and the *flesh* of men of Reason and *eat the flesh, and drink the blood of Christ*, then you will *sup* with him in spirit.

Moreover, I would not have any one think when the Apostles received the holy spirit to preach; that, that only was the *Seal* of the living God; no, for John the beloved received with the others, and went forth and did preach; therefore (Rev. v.) when "John saw the book sealed with seven seals, and no one to open it, he wept much:" here John was lost in himself, or his own blood, 'till CHRIST *opened the Book of Life, i.e.* to be found worthy of Christ and receive his *Seal* for his spiritual grace and Mercy, therefore man may *know*, there is a great *Work* to be done!

Further, at this time the COMMISSION OF THE SPIRIT *is in act*, and the mighty works of Faith are done *internal*; - and for men to wade through the power of death and hell (in their own soul) is heavier to the soul than any external punishment, or temporal death! also now of days, the holy spirit is *active,* and when the VIRGIN DAUGHTER of Faith is born, she has to wade through the power of death and hell in the soul, which is very hard to be done, for in this travail the soul will find he must *eat the flesh of kings, captains ,mighty men, &c.* and all *in itself, i.e.* by the power of Faith man must bear the wilds, temptations, and heavy threats of *his own* Reason, which is *eating his own flesh*; for the *Reason of man* will threaten the soul with destruction various ways to come: Also *it* will transform *itself* and tempt the soul, and *it* will promise great things if the soul will be guided by *him*: This the Elect may expect to have, and must bear from their *own Reason* in themselves.

Again, The spirit of Faith that is quickened from its womb, has a *Censer with incense, i.e.* Faith is the *Censer,* and its prayer the *incense,* that ascends to heaven for Christ's divine assistance; Also she finds herself in a fallen condition, therefore stands trembling before the power of God! because she is surrounded with the power of Reason, and in a fallen state, and under justice, and has the mountain of death and hell, to wade and travail against, which is done in great *sorrow,* and by dint of *prayer* for the assistance of Jesus from heaven; now this is human nature animated with divine Faith, that Christ took on him, and gathered his *way* to his glorious kingdom; - and this nature when called into the covenant of Faith, will follow its *Guide,* and work the *works of Faith,* and also truly find, that CHRIST the king of glory was in that very condition!

Then will man give up the kingdom of Reason to follow HIM; - for the soul being called into the covenant of Faith, hearkens to this *Virgin Daughter* of Faith; then when Faith is in distress, it offers its prayer, which ascends to JESUS, and He (by his divine incomes in secret) helps the soul through its trouble because the soul is *called by the Messenger,* to come into the spiritual covenant of Faith; to *follow* CHRIST! therefore this human nature animated with Faith, *gathers its Way* as Christ did, in a body of flesh and blood; and this is to *eat the flesh and drink the blood of* CHRIST! John's Gospel, (vi. 57.) "As the living Father hath sent ME, and I live by the Father, so he that eateth *me, even He* shall live by ME," *i.e.* when Christ was here *He* was in the covenant or compact of Faith with them who sit in the power of the Father; - and in the mystical union of Faith with them, in a body of flesh *He* worked the works of Faith, and gather HIS *Way in Sorrow!*

Through sin, death, hell, and justice, to his *own* glory of mercy! *SO*, in like manner must the Elect, when they are called into the covenant of Faith to *Him*, then with *Him*, or by his divine assistance from heaven, must work the works of Faith, and gather *their Way*, according to the portion of the creature, in *Sorrow* as HE did, then they will *eat his flesh, and drink his blood.*

Chap. X

WHEN Reason hath transformed itself or themselves into a *Declaration from Heaven*, it gives them a new language, and from that raise a further emulation by preaching the word, which will overpower others; then men should submit to it; for if men strive against it, and come to declare it a lie, blasphemy, &c. with a desire to extirpate it out of the world, then the *internal Angel in justice* will charge them with spiritual *murder*, because it is *preaching* from the declaration of the messenger who came from God in the covenant of mercy: And this Messenger's declaration is *recorded in heaven!* for *I* would have men to *understand*, that the mystical union of Faith between the *Elect* and GOD their FOUNTAIN is recorded in *Heaven!* and all the *holy fire, or incense of Faith* that ascends to heaven in *Prayer* for God's divine assistance, by which man prophecies of his own salvation, is *recorded* in the ever-living *Breast* of the GLORIOUS KING OF FAITH: Therefore when a Messenger is sent in the holy covenant of grace and mercy, to declare the will of God to his brethren, and prophecy of his glorious *Coming* in spirit, to seal and sanctify them for his glorious kingdom; that *Prophecy is recorded* in heaven, and in the souls of the Elect on this earth, beside being left on *literal record*.

Yea, this Messenger's *Declaration* is contrary to all the powers and efforts of Reason, that would *invade Heaven;* - nay, it is an enemy to his own Reason, for he must *deny himself* of it. - And *Man* will find the *fruits and incense* of Faith that ascends to heaven and is acceptable to God, to be quite contrary to the *dark incense* of Reason, for that cannot ascend to be accepted in the holy covenant of Mercy; therefore when Reason transforms into the *Declaration*, it is much delighted to preach the word, and his *own Way* if he can, but while the Messenger lives *He is the Adversary*. - Also after while, you may see the spirit of Reason restless, for he wants something and cannot get at it, and this restlessness of soul declares the man is not accepted: Further, he will transform himself in spirit, and dwell at times, on different parts of the records or *Declaration*; for the spirit of Reason will say, *Lo! here is* peace, and, *Lo! there is* peace; and *lead the soul through dry places to seek rest, but can find none*; Neither can he flourish in his *own* kingdom while the Messenger lives; because *He is the Adversary*, for then *Satan is bound*; now in this condition there is great trouble and agitation of soul, and grievous to bear; but it is no more than Reason eat Reason, because disappointed in his *own desire*; therefore doth not amount to the *Supper of the great GOD* which is *to eat the flesh of kings, captains &c. i.e.* to bear the wilds, temptations, and persecutions of Reason *within* and *without*, by the power and prayer of Faith; also in this lively compact, and priesthood of Faith, gather their way through justice to *Mercy!* Thus the Elect when called by the *Messenger*, are taken into the spiritual *Covenant* and compact of Faith, and fed on the divine incomes of God which is *Life!* but Reason is left with the bare letter, and to feed on itself, which is *Death.*

Further, This GLORIOUS COVENANT, or compact *of Faith*, is this; GOD created Adam of human nature animated with divine Faith, which is the nature of God, so they was the *Children of God,* but they broke the law of Faith, when they *hearkened* to Reason, and by that fell under the power of death, and was wholly under the justice of the Father; and also subject to the angel of the law of Reason: - thus the *Children of God* was tempted by Reason into the *Priesthood* of Reason, *i.e.* the *Priesthood of the law, or of Aaron*; and Reason was, and is very desirous the *Elect* should inherit his wisdom, which is the *knowledge of good and evil* in that Priesthood, for this wisdom, Reason will worship as God: - but GOD was graciously pleased to promise he would come and redeem his *own Children*: Further, when GOD was graciously pleased, *He communed* from his GLORIOUS THRONE with the spirit of Faith in the Elect (when it was rose from death to *Life* above the power of the *Angel* of the law of Reason) by which men grew strong in Faith, and come to prophecy of their own salvation: - Now, this is the *mystical union* or *spiritual compact* of Faith between God and his *Children, in* HIS ROYAL PRIESTHOOD.

Moreover, when God was graciously pleased to *make all things New, i.e.* to turn HIS glorious kingdom into *Mercy*, which is the *Kingdom of Heaven* for himself and his Elect, *He* left the glory of the *Father, and of justice*, and transmuted himself into his *own* created nature of Adam, which was human animated with Faith, and took the SONSHIP on himself, which was subject to the power and justice of the *Father,* - thus God the *Father* became God the *Son*; or the God of *Justice*, the God of MERCY! – and became KING *of the holy Gospel! KING of Faith and Mercy!* elder BROTHER *of the Elect, in the holy*

Gospel, who serve the younger! LORD of all-quickening power to Faith! Royal BRIDEGROOM to the Virgin Daughter of Faith! FATHER of Regenerated Faith! And the GREAT GOD and KING of the New Heaven and Earth! &c. Because he came to seek *his Elect!* and *redeem them*, and *gather them* to his glorious Kingdom, which is the kingdom of Faith! glory! and mercy!

Hence, (Matt. xiii. 44.) JESUS saith, "Again the *Kingdom of Heaven* is like to treasure hid in a field; the which when a man hath found, he hideth, and for joy thereof, goeth and selleth all that he hath, and buyeth the field." This parable declares the *Union and Compact* of Faith and mercy between God and his Elect; for when God was in the glory of the Father, and of justice, HE received the *prayer or Incense* of Faith for his divine mercy from the *Elect of old*, which ascended up to God in his glory, and God was graciously pleased to *commune* with them in spirit, that he would become the God of *Mercy!* then they prophecied of CHRIST which was *Salvation!* and by this mystical *Union and Compact* of Faith, between God and his *Elect*, God well knew, and repeatedly found, the increase of his *own Children*, which was *hid* from Reason, (from the beginning) in this world, which is the *Field*; yea this *mystical Union* of Faith, God always *hideth* from Reason, why? because the internal Angel in justice will keep them out: Also in this sacred *Union* of Faith, God hath great *Joy* in his children, as they are his great and only *treasure!* whereby he will compleat the *kingdom of heaven*, in the full glory of Faith!

Therefore, for his unbounded *Love and Mercy* to his children! and for the great *Joy* and glory to come, as GOD will have with them, and they with him, HE left the glory of the Father, and of *Justice*, (which was all he then enjoyed) and invested it on *Moses* and *Elias*, then transmuted himself into his own created nature of Adam, and became a true Son to the *Power* of the *Father*, to *seek* his own brethren the Elect, who are of and for the *kingdom of Heaven!* Further, when he was here declaring his holy Gospel, the *kingdom of heaven was hid* from Reason; indeed they might take the outward word or letter, but could not enter the spiritual compact and priesthood of Faith, therefore, "It is not given to them to know the mysteries of the kingdom of heaven." – Yes, JESUS went through the powers of Reason, and gave up his godhead life, which was what he enjoyed here, for the redemption of his Elect! which purchased them; and is ascended into the high heaven of mercy! thus IS and WILL BE, the glory of the *Father* completed, in the high and mighty glory of the SON, in the *Compact* of Faith with the Elect.

"*Again* (Jesus said) the kingdom of heaven is like unto a merchant man seeking goodly pearls: who, when he found one pearl of great price; he went and sold all he had, and bought it," (Matt. xiii. 45.) This is to the *Seed* of Faith, *likened unto a merchant seeking* a good purchase of exchange; for the *Seed* of Faith has the kingdom and priesthood of Reason to exchange; for the priesthood and kingdom of Faith, which is death for life; and they must *seek* him, who can and will give that exchange, *i.e.* when they are called by the voice of God in the Messenger, and Faith is risen from death to life, and enters into the lively compact of Faith, then in this *mystical union*, will know they are in the true way for heaven, and will follow their *Guide*, and offer the true incense which ascends to heaven; - and in love and union with their brethren, will *gather their Way*, by prayer and God's divine assistance, to the spiritual birth, seal, and sanctification of the KING OF FAITH, which is the *pearl of great price*, and the Elect must part with all *to buy this pearl, i.e.* to part with *all* their gathered knowledge of Reason from the Letter, and become a *Child!* yea, their whole possession, which is the Kingdom and Priesthood of Reason! so that *nothing* remain to hinder the soul from working the *WORKS OF FAITH*, - then he will *Sell* the kingdom of hell, for to *Buy the kingdom of heaven*.

For, As GOD who sat in the glory of the Father, and of justice, left that glory and become man, and worked the *works of Faith*, to redeem his Elect, and became the God of mercy to them; *Man* must leave his *own* conceited knowledge, and the glory of this world, to work the *works of Faith*, as is the portion given him, to *follow God*, then in the *lively Union* of Faith, God becomes united in Spirit to his Elect, and the Elect to God, to bring forth the fruits of Faith for glory: for in this Compact or *Union* of Faith, the *Prayer* ascends to God, by which man is made to prophecy of his own salvation! therefore *Blessed* is he that will *lose all*, even his *Life*, for the sake of *regenerated* Faith; for in this heavenly compact of Faith, man will *find his Life* again in CHRIST, for he is king of Faith. Hence all the fruits and prayer of Faith, ascends to him in his glory, as a *sweet incense*; and CHRIST will give him his life anew, with a CROWN of everlasting glory!

Chap. XI

AGAIN, (Matt. xvii.) Jesus said, "If ye have Faith as a grain of mustard seed, ye shall say unto this mountain, remove to yonder place, and it shall remove; and nothing shall be impossible to you."

This *Mountain* to be removed, is the *power* of sin, death, hell and justice, from the souls of the Elect, and by the *power* of Faith as a *grain of mustard seed:* Now as I have said, CHRIST who is the king of Faith, he only has the essential spirit of Faith, and in him it is a *full seed*, by which he is able to compleat his almighty works, both in heaven and earth, as in the beginning he created Adam of his own divine nature, then there was Faith sown into *Earth*, and by generation has come forth many of that royal seed, who are the *Sons of God*; also as aforesaid he became Man, and a brother with or to his own Elect, and is recorded among them as the son of Abraham, according to the genealogy of Faith; so now he has worked the works of redemption, and ascended into the high heaven of mercy.

I would have the Elect to *understand* that *Faith in them* may be likened to *a grain of mustard seed*, why? because the Faith in them assisted by the divine incomes of JESUS from heaven, they will brought up before God according to regeneration, to be regenerated: therefore BLESSED is he that can enter into priesthood and follow up to the *spiritual Birth*; for if man enter the kingdom of heaven, he must work the works of Faith, to be called upon by the DIVINE MAJESTY, distinct to, and for himself; and of God, to be found worthy of his spiritual birth, and holy sanctification; for by *Regeneration*, Faith is made the *Essential Life* of man to be raised for glory, for the kingdom of heaven: for in Elect man is found Faith to offer its prayer, and by God's divine assistance, to grow up to the kingdom of heaven, and then the soul will be in great union with his brethren, because this is the Faith and LOVE OF CHRIST! In his united church, in his KINGDOM of REGENERATED FAITH! so woe to them by whom offences come!

Therefore when the Elect are called, and die from their gathered knowledge of Reason, and quickened into the knowledge of Faith, which is their OWN by the voice of God in the Messenger and quickening power from heaven; then when the spiritual daughter is *born*, that man will enter into the spiritual compact and royal priesthood of Faith, which is the mystical union and spiritual communion, by the spirit of Faith in them, with God their *Fountain*; and by this heavenly light, man will find himself to be full of darkness and death, and in the midst of the *Wilds*, temptations, oppressions and persecutions of Reason, not only without, but in their own soul, which is the worst of all, for it must be removed to inherit the SEAL of the king of Faith.

Further, those *Powers* of death and hell being in the soul of man, and oft-times acting forth with great power are those *Mountains to be removed*, which is impossible to be done according to Reason: but Faith being in the compact and priesthood of JESUS, and oppressed by those powers, it will *offer its Prayer*, which ascends to heaven for *divine assistance, i.e.* the influence of the holy spirit of JESUS, which HE will be graciously pleased to send for the dint of true prayer: then the soul by influence of this holy and essential *grain* of Faith, receive power to *remove* (internal) *mountains*; for I would have the Elect *understand*, as Faith came from God in the creation for *generation*, so do Faith come from God, to raise and help created Faith on its way to spiritual *Regeneration*.

Again, The Elect, when in the *Compact of Faith,* will at time have great fear, darkness, oppression, temptation, persecution, &c. which proceeds from the consequence of Reason, death, hell, and justice in the soul of man, endeavouring to devour Faith if possible; for those are *mountains* in the soul of man and in Faith's way; now it is on the part of the Elect to seek the removal of those *mountains*, which is *impossible* to be done by or according to Reason, but to Faith it is *possible*; for when the Elect are in their own compact, and oppressed by the power of Reason then! if the soul can motion forth with prayer in love and union with his brethren, and can and will do, or suffer any thing for the sake of the kingdom of heaven, in this *royal priesthood* of Faith, having given up the kingdom and priesthood of Reason, love his enemies, &c. (not *doubting* the priesthood of Faith, nor God's help from heaven) he will have the divine assistance from heaven, and this *mountain* will be *removed* by the power of Faith.

Yea, it is the nature of Faith to *Pray and not to faint,* why? because it is very eager to work its way in spirit, as near its own Angel as possible, which is CHRIST in *Glory*, and while under justice offer at his royal feet, which is done by *Prayer*, to remove internal *mountains* out of the way: for as every Elect may be likened unto a *grain* of Faith, and for the kingdom of heaven; therefore they must work the works of Faith, that those internal *Mountains may be removed* through their *prayer and fasting; i.e. praying* for God's divine assistance, and *patiently* waiting till it comes; for when Jesus is graciously pleased to make his royal priesthood known from his glorious throne to mortal man, to invite the Elect, his brethren, to enter in, that God should rule over Faith in them, by his divine incomes; the overflowing of his holy spirit, or the essential *grain* of Faith, is so transcendently powerful and glorious, that one glimpse will make impure Reason dissolve to chaos, if his divine will should move him; and also convert fallen Faith to his own will and pleasure: Therefore JESUS is KING and only ruler of Faith in his royal priesthood, for HIS holy spirit flows forth so infinite pure, glorious, and all powerful in himself, that he can by his glorious wisdom send his divine assistance to Faith in man according to its need, or as it *ask in prayer*, by which Faith is helped; and Faith will return grateful thanks, which ascends to heaven; for Faith came from God in creation, and by his ALMIGHTY POWER he redeemed that Faith; and Faith comes from God to help Faith through this sore journey of flesh; - and Faith comes from God to give spiritual

Birth to his holy covenant of grace, and seal the soul for his glorious kingdom; and returns to him again from the soul of man, in spirit; which is the *sweet incense* that ascends to God: Thus it is Faith on Faith; and Faith united to Faith, in *Prayer, divine assistance, and thanksgiving;* - *i.e.* the incense of Faith ascends in *prayer* and thanksgiving to God, from Elect man; and divine assistance descends from God to Elect man; and this friendly mystical union is the priesthood of Faith, which leads to life eternal!

Further, when elect man is entered into this royal priesthood by being born to it, and offering the *true Prayer* of Faith, which is the works of Faith; and when answered from heaven by the overflowing of the holy spirit of JESUS, which comes so *sweet* and infinite *pure*, to the spirit of Faith in man, as if it would convert the soul to *ALL divine purity*; and when the soul has tasted of this divine blessing, it is in a longing condition for, and mourning after more, and will seek to get as near Jesus in spirit as possible, because it will make the soul speak the language of Faith, and prophecy of his own salvation, which no one can do but by entering into this ROYAL PRIESTHOOD: So the children of God must leave the whole world for this, that when they are oppressed by the powers of death and hell in themselves, and offer the *prayer* of Faith and *doubt not* in this royal priesthood (for the union of Faith is so great between God and his children that *nothing will be impossible to them*, for whatsoever they ASK in pure Faith *they will receive*, and those *Mountains* will be removed.

Also, when the Elect are thus united in the royal priesthood, to work the works of Faith, to *follow Christ*, then what love will flow forth among brethren! For every one is seeking forgiveness! And ready to forgive: *Nay*, even lay down their lives for each other! (if occasion requires) why? because this is the CHURCH of CHRIST, and he rules over them! therefore they must *not be separated!* "For (Jesus said) where two or three are gathered together in my name, there am I in the midst of them." *i.e.* when HIS divine assistance is asked in Faith's *Prayer*, HE will answer by his holy spirit from heaven; that the soul *shall* be assisted to work the works of Faith, in HIS *united* CHURCH, to the great joy of the brethren: for as I said, it is on the part of the Elect to seek by *prayer* to remove the fumes of death and hell, which is as *Mountains* in the soul, that stand in Faith's *Way*; which is done by PATIENCE, MEEKNESS, LONG-SUFFERING, &c. and by working the works of Faith to *follow Christ*, the *King* of Faith and mercy; then HE removes the grand *Mountain of Justice*, by giving the soul spiritual *Birth* to his holy covenant of mercy: - and of *Death*, by raising the soul to life eternal in his glorious kingdom.

Again, As in the beginning Faith came from God, HE being the full *Seed* for essential *Grain*, from whence all other *grains or seeds* of

Faith proceed; and HE *sowed* himself in person into this created Faith; then call the Elect his brethren, and worked the works of Faith; therefore of consequence, the Elect must work the *Works* of Faith to *follow* JESUS: "For (he saith) whosoever shall do the *Will* of my Father which is in heaven, the same is my brother, and sister, and mother," (Matt. xii. 50) Now the *Will* of the Father is what he himself became a SON to do, *i.e.* to work the *Works of Faith* under the *Justice of the Father*, against all the *Powers* of Reason, sin, death, and hell, and by the *Power* of Faith, in mystical union with them who sit in the *Glory of the Father*, HE gathered his *Way* through those Powers and the *Justice* of the Father, to his own glorious Kingdom of *Mercy*, and the Elect when *Called* must do in like manner, according to their *Portion* given: - For as Faith fell wholly under the *Justice of the Father*, and was subject to the angel of the law of Reason, it must, in obedience to the power of God, gather its Way *through* the powers of Reason, Hell, &c. in *Prayer, Meekness, Love, Mercy, and Charity*, and MOUNTAINS *will be removed*; then the soul will be called upon, through the Justice of the Father, and there must give himself up to that *Justice* in his own blood, - and their lose himself in his own blood! before he can be born in spirit, or translated to the mercy of the *Son*: Now if the soul do this, he will do the will of the Father and be *saved*; therefore Jesus saith (Matt. vii. 21.) "Not every one that saith unto me, Lord, Lord, shall enter into the kingdom of heaven; but he that doeth the *Will* of my Father which is in heaven." From hence men may in some measure see what it is to enter into the *Priesthood* of Faith.

Again, When JESUS *found no fruit on the fig-tree*, He said, "Let no fruit grow on thee, hence forward, for ever," *and it withered away: then his disciples saw it, and marvelled, saying,* "how soon is the fig-tree withered away." This fig-tree signifies the spirit of Reason *in* the Elect, that will be *withered away* by the *Power* of Faith, and it is the same thing in consequence as to remove (internal) mountains, that Faith become the essential life to be raised to glory! also the *fig-leaves* are acts and excuses of Reason, and not only so, but also the *wild priesthood* of Reason, wherein man will feign the knowledge of the *Will* of God, priesthood of Faith, and kingdom of heaven, at the same time know nothing of it, and if possible possess less; yet he will preach the knowledge he has gathered from the outward word or letter, and render it according to his own judgment, which is as *leaves on the fig tree, i.e.* the judgment of Reason on the doctrine of Christ, and excuses they will make to cover their own evil: for in Reason and its priesthood is found no fruit for the kingdom of heaven; but these conceited-knowledge, self righteousness, and plenty of excuses, which are all death to the soul, and must be removed in the Elect, that Faith may *follow Christ* in his royal priesthood; for when Faith is quickened from its womb or seed, *as a grain of mustard seed,* and it grows up and work the works of Faith, in and for regeneration, and become the essential soul for the resurrection, the *fig tree* will be *withered away* or rooted up.

Therefore (Matt. xxi. 21.) JESUS said, "If ye have Faith and doubt not, ye shall not only do this which is done to the fig tree, but also, if ye shall say unto this mountain, be thou removed, and be thou cast into the sea, it shall be done," which is not to *doubt* the power of Faith in the *royal priesthood,* for in this compact and priesthood of Faith, the union is so great between Christ in glory, and the *incense* of Faith in prayer, produced by the Elect, that they *will* receive *Power* from heaven, to remove internal *Mountains,* or over power Reason, by the power of Faith: and (Jesus saith) "all things whatsoever ye shall ask in prayer, believing, ye shall receive." So I would have the Elect mind, as JESUS worked against and *conquered* the powers of death, hell, and justice, by the powers of Faith, the Elect must *follow* HIM according to their *Portion* of Faith, for Christ is the great and *first fruits*.

Moreover, when Faith is sown by the power of the holy spirit of God, in to the womb or seed of Faith in the Elect, which is but as a *small grain of mustard seed,* yet by that power it will quicken and motion forth in prayer for divine assistance and be taken into the priesthood of Faith, and by divine assistance, work the works and grow up through justice in Regeneration, to the seal of the King of Heaven: thus Faith for Regeneration, is likened by the holy spirit unto a *grain of mustard seed,* which is but a small seed, yet by its prayer and divine assistance from heaven, it will grow up through justice and wrath, to the holy covenant of grace and Mercy, (then it will be the essential life of man) and so it is *grown* to, or become a *Tree* for the kingdom of heaven.

Again, in his holy compact and priesthood of Faith, should be, nay IS – incomparable brotherly love! why? because it is the love of Faith! then such a CHURCH IS in the strong union of Faith with each other, and with Christ their King: Also it is the nature of Faith to get as near in spirit to JESUS as possible, for his divine assistance unto *Salvation*; and as *the love and union of Faith* brings us to Christ for salvation; the same *Love* will unite his Church: - also if a man want salvation, he must go to CHRIST for it, and he may say, "he can and doth," yet at the time cannot come to the *Union* of the united church of Christ in his *royal Priesthood*: now if he cannot do the *less,* he cannot do the *great*; and if he cannot love his brother in *this* Faith, he cannot love God' for it is the nature of Faith to *forgive,* and rejoice in forgiveness. Therefore JESUS said (Luke xvii.) "If thy brother trespass against thee seven times in a day, and seven times in a day turn again to thee, saying, I repent, thou shalt forgive him," *and the apostles said unto the Lord, increase our Faith, and the Lord said,* "if ye had Faith as a grain of mustard seed, ye might say unto this sycamine-tree, be thou plucked up by the root, and be thou planted in the sea, and it should obey you." This *sycamine-tree* (or sycamore) is the same in effect as the *fig-tree,* or the removal of internal *Mountains* from the

Elect; for this *sycamine-tree* is the seed and spirit of Reason and its wild priesthood; for when Reason transforms itself into any declaration from heaven, it will take it into its own wild priesthood, and preach it according to their imagination, and flourish forth before men with great expression, to tempt the Elect into the wild priesthood of Reason.

Now, the *Wild Priesthood* of Reason is to excuse Reason for a time, and they will not fail to plead excuses; for the best produce of this *sycamine-tree* is conceited knowledge, self-righteousness, pretended forgiveness, and plenty of excuses to *cover* their own evil, and thus flourish like green leaves on this *Tree*: also from this *sycamine-tree* proceed spiritual darkness, temptation, self-conceited preservation, vain excuses, anger, dislike, unforgiveness, deceit and self-cunning, spiritual thieving, &c. which is the seed of further evil; and this is a *plant* that God did not plant in the Elect, therefore it must be *rooted up*, and must be done by the power and prayer of Faith: NOW when an external tempter comes, he will be disappointed by the *Power* of Faith, as if his self-cunning was *struck dead* in his soul! and the internal powers of Reason *are* overcome by the dint of Faith's prayer and divine assistance from heaven in the *royal Priesthood* of Faith; then the evil *Plant* will *be rooted up and wither away*, or perish as the waters of Reason that are cast off from *Faith*.

Chap. XII

AGAIN, The *priesthood of Faith* (as aforesaid) is the mystical union and heavenly communion, by the power and prayer of Faith, with and to Christ in glory; but men must be *born* to it, before they can enjoy it, even as men are born into this world to enjoy the things of this world; for as Moses had Reason to work upon in the souls of men; JESUS had Faith to work upon in his Elect: For on the *fig-tee*, i.e. Reason, was found no fruit for Jesus, and it *withered away*: Therefore when Jesus is graciously pleased to give any one *spiritual Birth* to his holy Covenant of grace and *Mercy*, and send him back to tell his brethren, that Messenger calls to Faith in the Elect; and when the *Call* takes root in the soul, it truly makes the soul sensible of its own *nakedness and lost condition*; and can bring forth nothing but vain excuses for what he has done, which are the *fig-leaves* of Reason, to *hide his nakedness* if possible; and when he forsakes his gathered knowledge of Reason and vain excuses, he will lose himself in this hard water of death! and by true prayer, Faith will be quickened out of its death, then the *Virgin* daughter of Faith is *born* to the promise of Christ! NOW, this the *first Birth* to Faith for *regeneration*, and is called the *birth of water*, because the soul works under the justice of the internal Angel or *Cherubim and flaming sword*: But then the spirit of Faith is *quickened* for to do its work and go its *Way* for *regeneration*.

Also, Faith being so *Born* from its womb or seed, can offer its *own Prayer*, which is *incense* that ascends to God above the power of the internal Angel, because it is the will of the DIVINE MAJESTY, being only under the justice of the Father, and at times has divine assistance from heaven, and will grow strong, and come to prophecy of its own Salvation! – This was the very state of *Adam* (or condition) and Elect of old, and in the time of the Law; for when born the first birth for regeneration, they worked the Works of Faith, against the powers of Reason, death, hell and justice, and were obedient to the *cherubical Law, i.e.* the Law of Reason; and at the hour of death *they* were translated to under the Mercy of the Son! Now this is the *Priesthood of Faith*, wherein is found the spirit of prophecy for salvation; and on, or in this priesthood of Faith, CHRIST came and established his holy covenant of Grace and Mercy.

Again, I would have the Elect *understand,* the works of Faith for regeneration was the same in the days of old, as now, for they prophecied the God of justice would become the God of mercy, and redeem and raise them to glory at the last day; then at the hour of death they were translated to under the mercy of the SON, and died in the *Bed of mercy; i.e.* the spirit of Faith in them, was called up and united to the spirit of God as a *Son and Redeemer* to them; then they could truly say, "here is Christ come;" then entered into death, and are recorded in the *book of life! i.e.* in the memory of the *ever-living* God of Mercy, to be raised to his *Glorious Kingdom!*

Even so, Now, under the declaration of the Gospel; for when Faith is born of its womb or seed, it has the internal powers to work against, and must be brought up to the *prophecy of its own salvation,* as the Elect of old did; for although Christ has *Come* in person, yet he must *Come* in spirit, to seal the soul for his glorious kingdom: *otherwise,* Moses is the prophet to that soul, which Christ doth not come to in spirit; therefore the Elect must *seek* to enter into this royal *Priesthood* of Faith; for it is not to read the Letter only, and thereby think you have the promise of Christ, for that is the priesthood of Reason; for Reason has and will take the *Promises* to the Elect, and *prophecies* of the Elect, into his own priesthood, setting them forth according to the spirit of Reason, which make them say, "they shall inherit them;" But *Faith* must be born the first birth to *regeneration,* for to spiritually know what the *Promise* of Christ is; then will work the *works of Faith,* to inherit that promise.

Therefore JESUS said, (Matt. xxv.) "Then shall the *kingdom of heaven* be likened unto *ten virgins,* which took their lamps and went forth to meet the bridegroom; and five were *wise,* and five were *foolish."* This *kingdom of heaven* was, and is, the declaration of the holy Gospel or promise of JESUS to his Elect: For the glorious *Declaration* of Salvation in the holy Gospel, far transcend any other, because men in soberness of mind, must confess themselves under the power of sin and cannot save themselves; hence when Jesus declared his holy Gospel, it *shined* forth in its glorious purity like to a *Lamp* of sweet saving *Incense burning* before the power and glory of the Father, and Elect men unto salvation; yea, the *Call* in the declaration of the holy Gospel, was so great to his Elect, that many of the seed of Reason transformed themselves, and took the outward word: NOW the words of JESUS are as *Lamps*, being the greatest utterance in the whole world, that when men take his word and preach it up, it *shines* before other men as a *Lamp*, thus both Faith and Reason took the word of Jesus and followed: - But as *Adam* was the first man of Faith for *generation*; CHRIST was the second man of Faith (and came) for *regeneration*: therefore Faith must be born from its womb or seed for *regeneration* to the promise of Christ, before it can follow HIM in his royal priesthood of Faith; for this is to be *understood* by the Elect, that Christ came to work life out of death, as he saith, (John xii.) "Verily, verily I say unto you, except a corn of wheat fall into the ground and die, it abideth alone, but if it die, it bringeth forth much fruit," *i.e.* except the spirit in the word centers in the womb of Faith in the soul and there rest, and reduce the soul down to *death* in spirit, there to know and fear the *second* death; then out of this *death* by prayer, to quicken into a new *life*, which life is Faith, *quickened or born*, its first birth for regeneration; and if this is not done, the word *abideth alone*, as it has not effected the soul, so as to bring those things to pass according to Faith for regeneration; but if done, which will be in the Elect, then the soul will enter into the royal priesthood, and bring forth fruit for the kingdom of heaven. - NOW when JESUS uttered his holy Gospel, there was some of the seed of Reason came and took his words, as well as the Elect; and being first declared, it took the souls of men in their *virgin-state*, relative to the holy Gospel, *i.e.* in what the seed of Faith would bring forth, and what the seed of Reason would bring forth by declaration: For as they took the declaration and promise of Jesus, which are as *Lamps* to them, *and went forth to meet the Bridegroom, i.e.* to *meet Jesus* in spirit after he ascended into his high GLORY *of MERCY*, in spiritual and holy marriage with them. (ver. 2.) "But five were wise, and five were foolish." - Those *wise Virgins* are the Elect, that the *spirit* in the word centered in the womb of Faith, *and died*, then quickened Faith into active *Life* from its womb or seed, and this is the spiritual *Virgin daughter* of Faith, born from its womb, and enters into the royal priesthood, and will work the works of Faith against all the powers of Reason, death, hell, &c. for to this spiritual *virgin Daughter, is given a Censer with incense, i.e.* Faith is the censer, and its prayer the incense, which ascends to JESUS in his high *Glory of Mercy*, and is found worthy of Jesus to enter into the royal spiritual *Marriage* with him! THUS, *the wise Virgins took oil in their Vessels with their Lamps; i.e.* The spirit in the word, quickened Faith in the womb, and it come forth into act, to bring forth the fruits of Faith, according to the word, meet for Marriage with the BRIDEGROOM of heaven or KING of Faith; therefore the Elect can declare the *Word* of Jesus, which is the *Lamp*; and not only so, but bring forth the fruit of Faith according to the *Word*, which is *Oil in their vessels with their Lamps.*

The *foolish virgins* were the seed of Reason, that transformed themselves into the Declaration, and *took the words of JESUS* which are the *Lamps*: - But as the spirit in the word, *did not die,* to quicken Faith in them, *it abode alone,* why? because their souls was *barren of the good ground,* which is the womb of Faith for regeneration, therefore they could bring forth no fruits, by or according to the word, for the spiritual and holy marriage with the bridegroom: NOW as aforesaid, when Jesus declared his holy gospel, it *took the soul in a virgin state,* why? because it was a *New* language, and as so, are called *Virgins* in the declaration, which took Faith by the power of God, into the *Priesthood of Faith;* but Reason took the outward word, and went into its own *Wild priesthood or water, i.e.* the great river Euphrates that runs in the Land of *Nod,* in the souls of men: - Thus Faith and Reason *took their lamps, and went forth to meet the Bridegroom, i.e.* Christ in spirit. And Reason by the *Lamp,* which are the words, he *took and went his Way,* was and is, in himself, very sure he should *meet Christ,* and greatly preach and contend for the same thing, as is his imagination on the *Words of Christ*; but as the Word *abode alone,* and did not *die to quicken* Faith in them, they judged of it according to their imaginary wisdom, and think themselves wonderful wise; but as there is no *fruits of Faith* brought forth in all this; therefore they are called "*foolish virgins*" in the holy gospel.

Further, "While the bridegroom tarried they all slumbered and slept," yea, JESUS, the *Bridegroom* always did and will *tarry to come* in spirit to assist the spirit of Reason, because it is of a contrary nature to the spirit of Faith, and gathers a contrary *Way;* for Reason will take the words of Jesus, which are their *Lamps,* into their wild priesthood of Reason, and there judge and suggest them, by and according to their imagination; and if they can will tempt Faith into their priesthood, which will give liberty to the soul, to seek the *Kingdom* of Reason; for the *outward word* is sufficient for them because it is all they can have: - Thus, Reason is *bound up* in himself and his kingdom, and his priesthood, which is full of excuses to cover their acts, *i.e.* contrary to the words of Christ, turning his words so as to serve their present purpose; now in this, *they slumber and sleep,* in respect to the words of CHRIST, and dead to the works of Faith, – and it is *midnight with them,* in the sight of God, let them think what they will to the contrary, as the life of reason shines at present.

Again, "Then all those virgins arose and trimmed their lamps." *Those* are the *wise virgins* who entered, and will enter, into the *Royal Priesthood* of Faith, and work the *works of Faith*; for when a Messenger comes in the Priesthood of Faith, he finds Faith *sleeping, and midnight* with them also, as it has been silence in the nether heaven of Faith, and Faith captivated by the power of Reason; then there is a *CRY or prophecy* by the living Messenger, that CHRIST will come, and call this spiritual *Virgin* daughter of Faith, to his holy *Marriage*; therefore "*go you out to meet him*," which is done by the power and prayer of Faith, which ascends up to God, and they receive HIS *divine assistance*, to wade through the powers of Reason; and in MERCY, MEEKNESS, OBEDIENCE, LOVE, CHARITY, &c. *patiently waiting* and expecting his coming; and to keep the soul in a condition to *meet him*, according to the warning given! and to leave behind them as *filth*, that which Reason embrace as great *treasure!* Now this is *trimming their Lamps* in the priesthood of Faith, under the holy gospel when the CRY comes from heaven; for by working the *works of Faith*, they are brought up to prophecy of their own *Salvation, i.e.* of his coming in spirit to seal them for his glorious kingdom; thus, *those wise virgins* have not only the *promise* by the declaration, of the coming of Christ, but by working the works of Faith, they receive the sacred incomes of CHRIST, which confirms the *Promise* in the declaration and are brought up to prophecy as aforesaid, which is *Oil in their vessels with their lamps!* Thus, *the wise virgins* (who are of Faith) *took their lamps*, and gather their *Way* to Life; and the *foolish virgins* (who are of Reason *take their lamps*, and gather their *Way* to death, and all from the same declaration.

Yea, *Those foolish virgins*, in the time of life and health, never will enter the priesthood of Faith to go up to the holy *Marriage*, because their *own cunning* keep them from the works; also they will slight and condemn the messenger, that comes to invite to the holy Marriage: But when death comes, the internal *Angel* in justice, who is as *Moses, opens his book*, wherein is written justice and death to the soul, then instead of being called to by *Jesus*, are called to by *Moses*, who is buried in the soul, and is such a man's prophet; then they say, "*give us of your oil for our lamps are gone out*," *i.e.* the letter or promise of Jesus was no use to them, for want of the works and fruits of Faith; but would willingly *die the death of the righteous*, therefore they cry, "*give us of your oil?*" *i.e.* of your fruits of Faith, but the answer is, *No! you must go and buy for yourselves, i.e.* you must deny yourself to Reason, and *work the works of Faith, and follow Jesus* (if you inherit his divine mercy) *while it is day*; then they would fain go back, and try at a new life, but no, they are shut in and must die under the seal of the internal Angel in *justice!* Then, *what would not man give in exchange for his soul?*

Again, Those wise virgins being in the *Priesthood*, (and worked the works) of Faith, *then* when death comes, Faith is called to by JESUS through the justice of the *Father*, which is justice to Faith, and far above the justice of the angel, Why? because the justice of the *Father* is justice to Faith, and the justice of the *Angel* is justice to Reason: - But Faith being called above the Angel, and the Angel will not let you go back, because this *Call* to Faith is as in the days of old; only this, GOD is become a SON, therefore the *Call* is high up in regeneration, and is "*Adam* (or Faith) where art thou?" Here Faith is called upon for breaking its *own Law, i.e.* Faith has hearkened to the voice of Reason, and fell under the power of Reason and its Angel, because in the beginning Faith was tempted into the priesthood of Reason and died, and must come back by regeneration; therefore when Faith is born its *first birth* for regeneration, it is born to the *promise of Christ* and is the *birth of water,* then it will work its works and receive *divine assistance from Heaven*, to go through the powers of Reason, and is found worthy to be *called* upon by JESUS through the justice of the Father; and there it will find, although it has worked in the *nether waters*, and received sweet incomes at times, yet its works cannot save itself, for the question is, - you have hearkened to Reason, and what have you done to save yourself, or be united to Christ in holy *marriage*, for *He* only has kept the *Law of Faith*, from his birth to his death? Now here the soul confesseth his guilt and unworthiness without excuse, for this very state is at the PREROGATIVE *of God!* therefore no *fig-leaves* can appear! – You may look back from whence you came, but – the angel will not let you go back: - beside *those waters are turned into blood*, and no more life there! Now forward to the holy *Marriage with* JESUS you must go, or no *Life Eternal!* - then the eager prayer of Faith, from the pure virgin daughter, (born from the womb or seed of Faith for regeneration) then in distress, ascends to CHRIST for help, and he is graciously pleased to unite himself in spirit with this *Virgin daughter of Faith*, and there begets to himself the *spiritual Son* of Faith, who is born of this pure Virgin daughter to Christ, and by him sealed for his *kingdom of mercy and glory*! then the soul dies in the bed of mercy to be raised for glory; - for if after this your natural life is given you, to be sent back to tell your brethren, then you are a Messenger of Christ, and your *Declaration* will tell from whence you came; this IS the HOLY and SPIRITUAL MARRIAGE with JESUS, - and the spiritual birth to enter the *kingdom of heaven*: - therefore, blessed are *those wise virgins* who will *enter into this holy marriage*; - for the promise to the Elect IS, they shall bear a spiritual son of Faith to God, but in *old age*, for it is mostly done at the hour of death, as aforesaid.

Further, I would have the Elect *understand*; when Faith fell, the man Adam and Eve not only fell under the justice of the *Father*, but also into the *Priesthood* of Reason through temptation, to become *as gods, to know good and evil* in that Priesthood; - and when Faith is quickened by the voice of God in the Messenger, it will come into its *own Priesthood,* and grow strong, to be called *under* the justice of the Father; then it has *passed* the angel of Reason, and must *also go through* the Justice of *Father* to the Mercy of the SON: for as Faith fell it must go back by *regeneration,* which cannot be done in sleep, or by dream, but will be truly sensible of its passage: - for the letter only will not translate any one into HEAVEN, because men must be approved of by CHRIST: - thus the Priesthood of Faith leads to life, and the priesthood of Reason leads to death.

Chap. XIII

THOSE wise and foolish virgins, tend similar to the *rich Man and Beggar* (Luke xvi.) this *rich Man* is the Literalist, who has took the letter into the priesthood of Reason, and there can press into the *kingdom of God* according to his *imagination:* and also seek the *kingdom of Reason* for *Riches,* and so *fare sumptuously every day,* both natural and spiritual: - But he that work the *works of Faith is full of Sores,* seeking to get to CHRIST to *be healed,* internal unto salvation: - Also when Faith is quickened to the knowledge of JESUS *and his Promise,* then, when *in Act,* it will *pray* for his divine assistance, why? because it is *sore afflicted,* and them who profess the same letter will hold him at scorn, if the cannot *tempt* him into the wild priesthood of Reason, to do as they: - IF there is no Messenger living, and Faith is secretly influenced by the holy spirit of God, so as to know something of its *sore condition* (but no man on earth to guide him) he will be apt to go to them who profess the same letter, thinking to find some relief; but behold they be all *Rich* in the letter, having got it into the wild priesthood of Reason, and feed upon it by the spirit of Reason, and make to themselves the promise of Jesus, so are sure of salvation without further trouble: - *Then,* Faith cannot find *one crumb fall from this table* of Reason to feed upon, and if he tell his condition, they will say he doth not believe as they do, and has not true Faith, if he had he would have the *Assurance* and peace like them, which further wounds the soul, and tempt him to be like them: - but if he tell strangers of his condition, they will pity him, and if able will help him, and in this manner are *external sores* pitied: - Thus Elect man must be a *Beggar,* not only to pass through this life, but also for the *Kingdom of Heaven* (ver. 22.) "And it came to pass that the beggar died, and was carried by the angels into Abraham's bosom." Now

Abraham's bosom is the second paradise to Faith or bed of Mercy; for God communed with *Abraham* in the royal priesthood of Faith, the same as he did with the Elect of old; only *Abraham* is mentioned because of the promise, and to shew forth the difference between the literal and spiritual *Jew*, and those wise and foolish virgins do between the literal and spiritual *Christian*, but all terminate in one head. NOW in Regeneration there is *three Steps to the Seal of Christ,* which is in HEAVEN, *i.e.* Faith is quickened and taken into the royal priesthood, and work the works of Faith; then by divine assistance it grows strong, and power is given to prophecy of its own salvation; after this it is called up before the justice of the *Father*, and from thence given birth to the *Mercy of the Son*; (as Mark iv.) Jesus likens the kingdom of God, 'For the earth bringeth forth fruit of herself, *first* the Blade, *then* the Ear, *after* that the full Corn in the Ear." - Now, in this Priesthood or road for heaven, *Angels ascend and descend, i.e.* Faith's prayer *ascends* to God for his divine assistance, and the influence of this holy spirit *descends* from heaven, to assist Faith in its journey; - this is Angels of Faith! or, *the Angels of God!* thus is *the beggar carried by angels into Abraham's bosom*; for Abraham is translated to under the mercy of the SON, which is second and great paradise to Faith, as Faith never will fall from this paradise, for the next state is glory.

"The rich man also died and was buried," *i.e.* when death seizes the literalist who is *rich* in his own wisdom; or he that has given himself up to Reason's liberty, to seek after *riches*, that he may enjoy the good things of this world, or do as he like, yet profess the *Scripture*, but instead of being obedient to it, they will turn and construct the scripture, so as to be obedient to their *Acts*, and as so justify or rather forgive themselves: then as aforesaid, when *Death* comes, the soul is called by the *internal angel* who is as *Moses*, and there bound under the seal of justice; then *he is dead and buried* from all his former glory, for he cannot *go back* to it, neither can he *pass* the Angel in justice, to the *Mercy of Christ*.

Ver. 23. "And in hell he lifted up his eyes being in torment, and seeth Abraham afar off, and Lazarus in his bosom." Now in this *hell or torment* of soul he could *see* he had gathered by the spirit of Reason concerning the scripture, all in the wrong; for instead of being in the *royal Priesthood* to work the works of Faith, he took the Letter, Call or invitation, into the *wild priesthood* of Reason, and sought that Kingdom, and justified himself in, and by, that priesthood, which was *then* all ended with *him*, and the promise in the letter of no use to him.

Ver. 24. Ánd he cried and said, father Abraham, have mercy on me." Now, the literal Jews thought much of themselves because they were *Abraham's seed by Generation*, and because of that, said "they never was in bondage to any man." But according to *Faith and Regeneration* they were not *Abraham's Children*; therefore Jesus said, "If ye were Abraham's children, ye would do the *Works* of Abraham," (John viii. 39.) *i.e.* the *Works* of Faith in the *royal Priesthood* for regeneration, and then they could be born or translated, to under the mercy of the SON, as *Abraham* was: - Now, *Abraham who was afar off, and Lazarus in his bosom*, was *cried unto for mercy* by the literal *Jews* who claimed him as their *Father*, and thought themselves safe in, and through him; and his being *afar off* is this, Abraham, by the power of Faith, gathered his way in the royal priesthood to be translated to under the mercy of the SON, and died in the *bed for mercy, i.e.* under the *Seal* of the living God, for the kingdom of mercy and glory, and in this very condition the Elect dies in, which is *Abraham's bosom*, or second paradise to Faith: But as aforesaid, the seed of Reason took the word or letter, into the priesthood of Reason, and did as they pleased with it, and so *fared sumptuously every day* in the waters of Reason: but when death comes, then the soul is bound by the internal angel in justice, and those waters are dried up, and the soul sealed for the *second death*; which is *afar off from the bosom* of Abraham, who is sealed for Life ETERNAL: Then *the rich man desired Lazarus to be sent to him, i.e.* he would fain partake of the fruits brought forth by the Elect in the royal Priesthood, to *cool his tongue*, which was burnt up from the true prayer of Faith, and hope of salvation, but his answer was, he had his liberty in the priesthood of Reason to gather *the good things of this life*, and went his *Way* to the seal of the angel in justice; which *Lazarus* had not, *but receive evil things* from Reason, when he gathered his *Way* in the royal priesthood of Faith, to the seal of the *Angel* of Faith and Mercy: - And this *great Gulf which is fixed between them*, is the two priesthoods, *i.e.* the priesthood of Faith, and that of Reason, as one leads to life, and the other to death; for when Reason is taken to under the seal of his *Angel*, his heaven is ended; and when Faith is taken to under the seal of his *Angel* his hell is ended; as then Reason can no more tempt and persecute that soul, for Faith dies under his *Seal*, and Reason dies under his *Seal*, therefore cannot *pass* from one to the other, because *the gulf* is then become so mighty and so *great*.

Moreover, when *the rich man* could not get from the seal of justice, he would have *sent to his brethren*: as, (ver. 27.) then he said "I pray thee therefore father, that thou would send him to my father's house." Here you may see, he then understood the Name, *Father-Abraham*, unto the *literal Jew* was but titular, for now he calls him *Father*, and prays he would *send Lazarus*, saying, "to my *Father's house*, for I have five brethren, that he may testify unto them, lest they also come into this place of torment." Now his *Father's house*, is the house or *lineage* of Reason, wherein dwelleth the *Law* of Moses, and the *true* Priesthood of Reason, because given to them by Moses; but the *Wild* or Libertine priesthood, that is produced by Reason; therefore his answer was, "They have Moses and the prophets, let them hear them, if not, they will not be persuaded, through one rose from the dead." For *Moses* is the Prophet to the seed of Reason, and JESUS is the prophet that WAS *to Come*, and IS *to Come* to the seed of Faith; ALSO when any one is spiritually born, or translated to the mercy of the SON, and his natural life given him, to be sent back to tell the Elect his brethren, he is never sent into the priesthood of Reason, but into the priesthood of Faith; and if Reason was loosed by his angel, so as to come back, he would go into his own waters, *i.e.* as old *Cain* did, when *he* was loosed by the *Angel,* and *went into the land of Nod*, and there produced a wild priesthood to himself, which has continued to this day.

I would have the Elect, now told of the *Priesthood of Faith*, to seek that, and be mindful of temptation, not to be tempted into the priesthood of Reason, and there lulled asleep, in the follies of this life: For there is *many* that profess Jesus and expect to be saved by him, and will talk of great things, yet are born into this world to go no higher than the priesthood of Reason, and aim to inherit the good things of this world: now this is the greatest things to them, because they were born to inherit no other; and they will tempt the Elect to come into this sottish mire with them: BUT Faith is to *seek the kingdom of Heaven*, as (Matt. vi.) Jesus taught, to *avoid worldly care*, in what they should *eat or drink, or be clothed, or thought for the morrow*; "But seek ye first the kingdom of God, and his righteousness, and all those things shall be added unto you." Now, in *those* (worldly) *things*, Reason is very fond of possession, and to reign himself in it; the same as he is, in making choice of his own salvation by the letter, that he has taken into the wild priesthood of Reason, and so become an enemy to Christ's kingdom of regenerated Faith, for they cannot bear the priesthood of Faith, that Christ should *reign over them;* therefore (Luke xix.) Jesus said, "but those mine enemies, which would not that I should *reign* over them, bring them hither, and slay them before me," *i.e.* they will be called and *slain* by the internal angel in justice, under the feet of mercy; therefore every man is sure to be called upon by JESUS to be *sealed* for life eternal; or by the *Angel, as Moses*, who has already sealed him for death; and no one knows when the *Call* will come – then, *Blessed* are the Elect, that are prepared for the *Call of Jesus!* but the *literal Christian* may call on Jesus, as his *Saviour*, but he will find no more benefit than the *literal Jew* did, in calling on Abraham as his *Father*.

Chap. XIV

JESUS speaks another parable (Matt. xxii.) saying, "The kingdom of heaven is like unto a certain king, which made a marriage for his *Son.*" This *certain king* WAS and IS the *King of heaven*; for as I said, the LORD GOD of HEAVEN, and of Faith, created heaven and earth, and all things therein; but the greatest of all his creation was his *own children* Adam and Eve; why? because they were created with a life or soul of Faith, which is the divine nature of God, and as so his own children; and Faith being joined to an earthen vessel, and of this earth by creation, which, made pure human nature; - thus, appeared *Adam and Eve*, beautiful and perfect by creation, in human nature animated with divine Faith; now this is the true creation of *Faith*; which was created under a Law distinct to *itself*, and that is, *You shall not hearken to the voice of Reason*, for when you do, you will surely be brought under *captivity* and *Death*: Therefore Adam and Eve, whose life was of Faith, was suffered to be tempted by the *serpent angel*, who *hearkened* to him, and by him was tempted, not only to *fall* under the *justice of the Father* which is death, but also into the *Priesthood of Reason*, because they took Reason into themselves; for his temptation was as such, *for them to become as gods* (like unto himself) *to know both good and evil*; for as they fell under the power of Reason, they were subject to that *law and priesthood*, and also the *Angel* of that *law*; hence knew both *good and evil*, and the law and priesthood of Reason: Neither can Faith, or the Elect, be tempted any; lower than into the priesthood of Reason; and him or them that tempts Faith or the Elect, into the *priesthood of Reason,* is as, and acts as, the *serpent* angel did in the beginning.

Yea, *God the creator* and *Father to Faith*, became the *God of justice* through the acts of his own children, why? because they broke the *Law of Faith* they were created under and fell under the power of death: Further, when God created *Man* and *Angel*, it became of an *infinite* consequence; as thus, the seraphic host, ever to stand in their created purity, by the preserving power of the Lord God their creator: Also to suffer the *Cherubim* to break his own law, and fall for, and into *generation*; and after that suffer him to *tempt Faith* to break its law: - Now those laws being broke, is of an *infinite* consequence; that when the seed of Reason, which is the cherubical nature, live to manhood, and the *internal Angel* took place in the soul, they are charged with the law, then must go their way under *infinite* Justice according to the *Law*: - And for Faith breaking its *Law,* was a consequence of its *losing its life*, and for ever to lay in *silent death*, disunited from its creator and *Father*, then it remained a work for the DIVINE MAJESTY to recover his *own children* from *death* to life, again to himself, without acting against the glory of his creation, or the *Law of Faith* he created them under; therefore this could not be done but by *Regeneration*, which is working *Life* back again out of *Death*; and not only so, but also to *pay the grand debt* to the *Law of Faith*, and the infinite *justice of the Father*, which took place when that *Law* was broke: - And this could not be done, but by the very *eternal God*, that created, and gave a *Law* to Faith, that when it was broke, there followed an infinite effect or consequence, according to the power and glory of God's creation; - therefore; *The very eternal God, or seed-spring of Faith that created, with his creating power transmuted himself into his own created nature of Adam, which was human animated with Faith* (that was fell under the justice of the Father, by breaking the *law of Faith*) and this was all he *took on himself, i.e.* his own created *Nature* of Faith, and the *Law* of Faith, to go through the *justice of the Father*, relative to Faith; - for he *took* nothing of Reason on him, neither its Law, nor Nature.

Thus, the great *king of heaven*, or God the *Father* to the Elect, transmuted himself into flesh, and took *the fallen* nature of Faith; then he was become a true *Son* to the *great power of the Father!* and although he had on himself the *fallen nature* of Faith, yet he went through the power of Reason in LAMB-LIKE innocence, and never hearkened to it, and in this he kept the *Law* of Faith! Yea further than this, *He* having the *fallen nature* of Faith, - and because of that, he was compelled to go through the *justice of the Father* which is death: Therefore when the *Law of Faith* was broke, and the *justice of the Father* took place, it was of an *infinite* consequence, and an *infinite* Effect must be worked to keep that *Law!* and satisfy that *Justice!* - Then for this cause, God the creator was graciously pleased to become man and keep this law, and in obedience to that justice, gave his Godhead life up to death; - THUS the *justice of the Father* was of that consequence, as not to be satisfied; without taking the very *Eternal God* who created, into death; therefore the very God both in person and spirit, that created Faith under a *Law*, (which was broke by man from whence the justice of *Father* took place was taken into *Death* to satisfy that *justice*, it being of an *infinite force!* and that *justice* was satisfied! why? because it took the *Almighty God*, with his creating power, under it, in death! (which was the cause of its *being*, through his creation) and no other way than this, could that *Law and justice* be satisfied, and the creation not acted against, but to remain pure, according to its decreed order, and shine forth in its glorious purity.

Thus is the Elect world redeemed, by the very GOD becoming *Man*, and giving his *Godhead life* up to *death* in his own *justice*, and quickened out of that *death* into a new and glorious life of Mercy! -

thus *God the Father become God the Son*, or the *God of justice* went through his own justice to become the *God of infinite Mercy* to his Elect; and in this manner was the Elect world redeemed, and *Life* worked out of *Death* by regeneration, for the kingdom of heaven: For I would have the Elect *understand,* that after the Fall, Faith was not only *dead* in the sight of God, but also *dead* in itself from the *Communion* with God, and was in itself *Lost,* till God was graciously pleased to *Call to Adam* and promise he himself would become a *Son* to his own *Power,* and redeem them; then Faith was quickened from death to *Life* or born from its womb or seed, into *Act,* and to the promise of Christ, and be brought on in regeneration to the mercy of the *Son*.

Again, Adam, in his *spiritual travail* in the *Regeneration,* found to his *sorrow* the great incumbrance of Reason, and its law and priesthood (that he fell into through temptation) to *know good and evil in* the priesthood of Reason; for Reason in his own priesthood is *as a god,* for he does as he please, and will give judgment against man: Therefore, when this *virgin Daughter* was born, which is life quickened out of death for regeneration, Adam found his soul incumbered with spiritual *briars, thorns, thistles, &c.* that was and is produced by this dark *earthly* spirit of Reason: - FOR as Faith fell so low, as to be wholly under the power of death, and disunited from the spiritual *Communion* with God; it must be quickened from that death to life, to *commune* with God, for that must be done with this quickened spirit; and this is the royal priesthood of Faith, wherein is found the *Promise of* CHRIST, and the *prophecy* of your own *Salvation*; therefore Adam by the prayer of Faith, in the mystical union, or spiritual communion receive the divine incomes of the holy spirit from God, which helped him through this sore journey, and to prophecy of Christ, which was of his own salvation; and at death was called up to under the justice of the *Father,* and from thence translated to under the mercy of the SON, and then was united to the *God of mercy, i.e.* Christ; and died in the bed of mercy, to be raised unto the *glorious kingdom* of CHRIST; and in this he put forth his hand, and took of the *tree of Life,* and eat to *live for ever.* This IS the *royal priesthood* of Faith, *i.e.* the *priesthood of Christ,* in which he gathers his united kingdom of Faith to his *glorious Mercy*; for I would men *understood* this, - as Faith fell under the power of death, and the justice of the Father, it needs must have a *priesthood* to offer its prayer, which is the golden and acceptable incense that ascends to *heaven* for the glorious mercy of the SON: And also Reason has a priesthood, but the true priesthood of Reason was given forth by *Moses,* and that priesthood was to stay God's justice, that Reason should enjoy his kingdom here, in peace; but Reason was more fond of his own *wild* priesthood, than its *given* Priesthood; which was the cause of the great troubles brought upon Israel in the time of the *Law:* therefore as Faith and Reason each broke their own *Law,* they require each their own priesthood; but the priesthood of Faith is of *Mercy*, and leadeth to *mercy*; and that of Reason is of *Justice*, and is bound under the *justice* of the *internal angel*.

And thus were the Elect of old, in *secret* taught by the holy spirit; but they must be quickened from death to life by the power of God as Adam was; for this is to be *understood* – when children are born into this world, they are born to, or under the *Law* and priesthood of Reason; for when they come to manhood the *internal Angel* in justice takes place in the soul, and are charged with breaking the *Law*, then the *priesthood* took place to excuse Reason for a time: Also Reason in man may be inspired without any *new Birth*, only a little agitation of soul, and they will talk of great things, yet die as they were born into this world, relative to the true knowledge or works of Faith: - But it is not so with Faith; for as I said, - as *Faith* was quickened out of death into a new life, or born from its womb or seed in the man *Adam*, to the promise of Christ, and royal priesthood of Faith, so it must in all his children the Elect; for one man to hear of, or read of another man's promise, or prophecy, that is all dead to him, until Faith is quickened from death to life, to the royal priesthood, works of Faith, and promise of Christ, as it was in him or them, who before prophecied; for every one must work the works of Faith, for to stand before the justice of the Father, distinct to, and for himself.

In this *royal priesthood* WAS and IS the *Kingdom of Christ* gathered; for in days of old, Faith in Elect men was quickened from death to life, and in *Secret* taught, and guided by the holy spirit of God: and in mystical *union*, and holy *communion* the prayer of Faith ascended, and divine assistance descended, to help the soul through this sore journey, and to prophecy of his own salvation! then at the hour of death they were united or translated to under the mercy of the SON; and in this, took of the *tree of life*, and *eat to live for ever*; thus, from the man *Adam*, till the coming of *Christ*: For in the royal Elect, Faith being quickened from death to life, and taken into the royal priesthood of Faith, and offered the true prayer of Faith, which is the sweet saving incense that ascends to God, and God was graciously pleased to assist them to *prophecy* of their own salvation; *i.e.* God the Father who was the God of justice, would become God the Son, and the God of mercy, and redeem them; and in this royal priesthood of Faith, they were united to God for Christ in spirit, and were a WITNESS, OLIVE-TREE, or CANDLESTICK, in whom the candle of Faith burned, that *stood and prophecied in sackcloth before God; i.e.* they, against all the powers of Reason, and in sorrow of soul, which is *Sackcloth*, did work the works of Faith, and *prophecy* of salvation *before God*: - this is one of the *Witnesses of his spirit, Olive-tree*, or *Candlestick*, and was that *who stood before him*, when he was in the condition of God the Father, or of justice; - BUT in the days of *old*, and in the time of the *Law*, this holy communion between *God,* and the spiritual *virgin Daughter* of

Faith, quickened in the souls of his Elect, was in secret, and intirely distinct to the cherubical inspiration, and priesthood that was given to Reason; for the *Law* of Reason rules the *Life* of Reason, and justice rules that *Law*; and the *priesthood* is but the *incense* of Reason, to *stay* God's justice for a time; therefore no witness to the *spirit of Faith*, which is the divine nature of God, nor the *new Life* out of death, nor his *royal priesthood*, nor his mighty *works of Redemption*, nor his holy *Seal* of salvation; for as I said, when Elect men are born, they are born to the law and priesthood of Reason; - then Faith must be quickened from death to life, to come into its own *priesthood* to the spiritual knowledge of Christ.

Yea, GOD who became the God of *Justice* through the acts of man and angel, became a Son to his own power, to become the God of *Mercy* to his Elect: For as Faith fell under the justice of the Father, nothing but the godhead *Life* going into *death*, or being taken into death under that justice, could satisfy that justice, why? because it became of an *infinite* consequence both to God and the Elect, when it took place: Therefore Jesus came in; or upon the prophecies of his Elect, who prophecied in the royal priesthood of Faith, of his coming to redeem them: And in Jesus *was*, and *is*, the essential spirit and power of Faith, by which he created, and worked the mighty works of Redemption: ALSO Jesus coming in, or upon the *prophecies* of his Elect, he came in his *royal priesthood*; now, *understand* this, - all the Elect are born into this world, to the law and priesthood of Reason, but JESUS *was born into this world to the Law of Faith* and that *royal priesthood!* which, is the cause that Faith must be *quickened* from death to life, or *born* from its womb or seed, to the grand Union, and lively mystery of Faith, and Christ; for Jesus came forth in his own royal *Priesthood*, and he declared his holy gospel, covenant of grace, works of Faith, and salvation for his Elect, *in* his own royal and *merciful* priesthood which he uttered; - and redeemed the Elect world. NOW this is the "*marriage feast* that a certain king made for his son," because God himself become a *Son*, to be the God of mercy to his Elect; and when Faith is quickened from death to life, and taken into the royal priesthood to work the works of Faith, and in the spiritual communion with Christ, who is the God of heaven, become a *Son* for salvation, IS in the sonship of God, by which means the spirit of Faith in man becomes the essential Life in *Regeneration*, and is united to CHRIST to receive the divine incomes of his heavenly grace and mercy, which is the *Marriage feast!* or taking of the tree of life to eat and live for ever!

Chap. XV

YEA, Jesus uttered his holy gospel, and worked those mighty works of Redemption, and united himself to his Elect through his divine mercy (for JESUS is the *Elder Brother* of the Elect in his holy gospel, who has served and doth serve *the younger*) also HE is the *first* who quickens Faith, for to bring it on in regeneration; and the *last* that is to sanctify and seal it for the resurrection to his glorious kingdom; therefore all quickening power to Faith for regeneration, which leadeth to salvation, is in, and of the Sonship of God, why? because he made all things new to himself for his own glory; and also had and will make all things new to, and *in* the souls of Elect man for their salvation; and when man has worked the works of Faith in the royal priesthood, to be called upon under the justice of the Father, then – Christ takes the man into his mercy, through HIS mighty works of redemption, FOR *understand* this, when Faith is quickened in Elect man, and he has worked the works of Faith aforesaid, according to his portion; then upon this (man's works of Faith, and prophecy) Christ comes and finishes the mighty works of Faith for the salvation of such a man!

Further, as JESUS came in, or on, the Prophecies of the Elect of old, which was a *Witness* of, or to, his holy spirit (when he was in the condition of God the Father, or of justice) HE uttered *his* holy gospel, holy covenant of grace, and the works of Faith in *his* royal priesthood; then the Elect was, and would be invited, into the *royal priesthood*, and *they* will come and work the works of Faith, for to stand before him in spirit, and *will that HE should rule over them, and drink of the cup that he himself did drink of*; and by the divine incomes from heaven, *prophecy* of their own salvation, *i.e.* as Christ has come to redeem, he also will come in spirit, and unite himself to this *Virgin daughter* of Faith, in spiritual and holy *Marriage*, and give them *spiritual Birth* to his holy and spiritual covenant of grace, and seal this spiritual born *son of Faith* for the kingdom of glory.

This IS the *Church of Christ*, and the WITNESS *of his holy spirit that stand before him and prophecy*, as he is now in the condition of God the SON: - For as the Elect of old, and in the time of the Law, when *Faith* was quickened from death to life, and taken into the royal priesthood, *It stood and prophecied before God*, when He was in the condition of the FATHER, and is the *Olive-tree, golden Candlestick,* or *Witness* of his spirit (for "testimony of Jesus, is the spirit of prophecy") and at the hour of death were in spirit united to God for Christ, or *translated* to under the mercy of the *son*; and as so, *stand* recorded in the *Book of Life*; and *have the name of the Father written in their foreheads,* so when CHRIST had worked the works of redemption, he ascended the high HEAVEN of MERCY, and took possession of this his kingdom of regenerated Faith, or *Olive-tree, Witness of His spirit,* or *Candlestick* in whom the royal *incense of Faith burned*: - And the other *Olive-tree, golden Candlestick,* or *Witness of his spirit,* are the Elect when Faith is *quickened, and taken to the royal priesthood,* and *stand before him* and *prophecy,* now HE is in the condition of a SON, and are gathered and united to him by the power of *Regeneration,* and as so, *stand* recorded in the BOOK OF LIFE: Therefore as JESUS has worked the works of redemption, and ascended into the high heaven of *mercy,* HE has *made the marriage feast to the son*; "and his servants was sent to call them that were bidden, and they would not come," *i.e.* when men profess any prophetical letter, or letter of the gospel, and thereby say or expect Christ to come to save them which is the *bidden notice,* - then when Christ *came* in person, or doth *come* in spirit, and the *marriage door is opened,* they *would,* nor *will enter in*; because Christ doth not *come,* according to their expectation and liking.

Again, (Matt. xxii.) HE *sent forth other servants,* saying, "Tell them which are bidden, behold, I have prepared my dinner, my oxen and fatlings are killed, and all things are ready, come unto the marriage;" *i.e.* Christ has worked the works of Redemption, so in that, *made ready* for the *marriage feast*; and when any man or men are sent forth by Jesus, inspired with his holy spirit, they come in the covenant of *Grace,* and the *marriage door is opened,* and *all things ready,* then they *invite men to come* into the priesthood of Faith, and work the works, that they may go up, and enter into the spiritual and holy *marriage with Jesus,* to have his royal SEAL for the resurrection to eternal life: - "But they made light of it, and went their *Way,* one to his farm, and another to his merchandize." Now when this *Call* comes, it tells them, they must leave all their efforts of Reason, *i.e.* the whole world behind, for the holy marriage and kingdom of heaven, which is hard to the spirit of Reason: For Reason has gathered from the letter according to his own wisdom, which is contrary to the *wisdom* of Faith, which is the *wisdom* of Christ: Then they cannot *understand* it, and so *make light of it, and go their Way, one to his farm, and another to his merchandize; i.e.* one has his *House* to mind, another his *Land,* another his *Trade,* another his *Wife,* another his *peaceable Living,* another his *Children,* another the manners, follies, and fashions of the *World,* and another his *honour* among men: For as the seed of Reason is born into this world, for the wisdom and *vain pleasures* thereof; therefore if they gain them, which is their *desired World,* that is their *Heaven*; for although they *read and profess* the letter of Jesus, yet their *Will* is to *seek* the world, and then let the *kingdom of God be added,* which is contrary to the command of Christ; (Matt. vi.) "But seek ye first the kingdom of God and his righteousness, and all *those things* shall be added unto you," *i.e. necessaries* for this life; but it is a hard thing for Reason to trust God even in this. Also, I would have the Elect, that have obeyed this *Call,* and *waiting* for the holy

Marriage, to mind the *temptation*, for Reason will *tempt* you if possible from the Messenger after those vain alluring things; for it is no easy thing to be *in*, and keep *in*, the Priesthood of Faith; indeed the spirit of Faith is *willing*, and will pray, but when that is inactive, the soul of man is *weak* unto temptation Further, there is some of seed of Reason will conceive anger against the Messenger, and in a godlike manner judge, and condemn him (who *calls* to the holy *marriage*) for blasphemy; so the Messenger is slighted, and condemned, which is spiritual *Murder*; and they will dwell on a *dead Letter*, that they may construct to their liking, to justify themselves in evil doing.

Again, When the Messenger doth invite, and has invited men, to come into this holy *Marriage*, and they *will not come*, then it causes a mourning in the soul of the Messenger, because he comes in the covenant of *Grace and Mercy*, where there is *no joy in the death of a sinner*, - also the Messenger being in spiritual communion with God, which is the *priesthood of Faith*, therefore this spiritual *Mourning* with the cruelties of Reason ascends to heaven, and centers to him or them, who sit in the justice of the Father, as well, as it is recorded by the internal angel in justice in the soul of man, who has power given him over the spirit of Reason; for as the Messenger came out from *Heaven*, the *Acts* of the Messenger ascend to *Heaven*, and is also recorded in the soul of man, which, tend to the mercy of justice to man.

Ver. 7. "But when the king heard thereof he was wroth, and sent his armies forth, and destroyed those *murderers*, and burnt up their city," *i.e.* them who will not come to the holy *marriage feast, i.e.* to the divine mercy of Jesus, are left behind *desolate* under the seal of justice (which is *wrath to come*) in all their self-cunning, slights, and evil utterance, full of wrath against the Messenger, that if possible they could they would extirpate the *spirit*; and they being sealed under their own evils, they take them wherever they go: - For the *internal Angel* who seals every man under his own evil, has spiritual union with *him*, or *them*, who sit in justice in heaven above, so that every one will be his own witness to his own condemnation; thus all their care and wisdom to enrich themselves and families, *i.e. building cities* to enrol their *names*, will come to nought; and all their gathered knowledge by their own dark spirit, is but conceited wisdom, from the letter of the gospel, become their spiritual refuge or *city* wherein dwells their spiritual hope, which will be *burnt up by this king's armies, i.e.* every man has this internal *Angel in justice* in himself, witness to the acts of man, and is the seal to his conscience, bearing true record before the attribute of justice, so that every one will be his *own* witness of his own condemnation: - THIS is the great *army, or armies*, that *the king has sent forth*; for when death comes, some are called and taken by this *Angel*, whose *book is opened*, then they would fain go back to their former pleasures, but they cannot, then *their city is burned up*, and all their hopes of salvation is *burnt up, i.e.* their spiritual city; for under the seal of this *Angel* they must die: Also there is others that may enter into death more composed, *i.e.* because the angel has stayed justice in the soul; and *the book will be opened* in the resurrection, for if they cannot come into the holy marriage with Jesus, they must die under the seal of the internal angel in justice: Further, if wickedness and cruelties extend too far, justice may overtake and overthrow a man, even to misery in this life, for the *Angel* being in *act*, and them who sit in justice commune in secret with the *Angel*, then if from heaven he is suffered he will do his work, and overthrow man in his evil.

Ver. 8. "Then saith he unto his servants, the wedding is ready, but they which were bidden were not worthy." Now under the gospel there has been invitations come from God, for them who come in the royal priesthood of Faith, - not only *invites*, but also *prophecies*; and them who came and worked the works of Faith in the *days* of a Messenger, *entered* into the *holy Marriage*; but after the decease of the Messenger and of them who worked in his *Day*, then others who professed (but could not, or would not come into the priesthood of Faith) took full possession of the letter, and invited others to come, and went their *Way* with the letter into the *Wild priesthood* of Reason, and there flourish like green *leaves* on the *Sycamore-tree*, and make to themselves the *promise*, according to the dark spirit of Reason, and as so they have too great opinion of themselves (like unto the Jews in the days of Christ) because that *Light* in them is *darkness*: For if man come into the priesthood of Faith JESUS is his prophet, but if man do remain in the priesthood of Reason, then Moses is his prophet, let him profess who he will, or say what he will; therefore when a Messenger comes to call to the holy marriage with JESUS, them that will not come, are found *unworthy*, and left *desolate* on the bare letter, and will go their way under justice, where they will find Moses.

Ver. 9. "Go ye therefore into the highways, and as many as ye shall find, bid to the marriage;" *i.e.* when the Messenger has *invited* them, where he is sent, that only, is not the extent of his *Call*, because the Elect are *hid in many churches and places*; and it is the will of God they should come into HIS priesthood and HE *to rule over them*; then that is the TRUE CHURCH of CHRIST, because this message is to the Elect, be where they will, and they will be gathered in according to this message, it being of God: - Also there is *many*, by their conceited wisdom on the letter, are become *teachers* and *spiritual guides*, &c. to the people; and are become so self conceited in it, as to abide by it, for to have salvation, and would gather the whole world to their *wisdom* if they could; - but the Elect who are but *fools* in the eyes of those men, will come in before them and be *healed*, so that *the marriage will be furnished with guests*; for JESUS said, bring in hither the poor, and the maimed, and the halt, and the blind." And those *will come in*, to be internally *healed* of those spiritual *infirmities*, while those of conceited wisdom will be kept out: - Further, I would have the Elect *understand*, that all who profess the Letter of JESUS as said to be *bidden to the marriage*, but none will come but the royal Elect: - Also in the days of a Messenger; if any come and take the word, and do not work the works of Faith, he will go into the priesthood of Reason, and not be chosen to go unto the *marriage*, so he is *cast out*, and must die under the justice of the *Angel*, and this is him or them, *who has not the wedding garment, for the fruits of Faith* is the *wedding garment*, and they only are chosen, as ver. 14, "for many are called, but few are chosen."

Again, of the *priesthood of Reason*; there is the *given priesthood* that was given forth by Moses, when he gave forth the *law*, and *officiated by Aaron*, he being the *high Priest* in that *priesthood*, which was, and is to *stay* God's justice for a time: Also there is a *Priesthood* that the spirit of Reason is productive of, to excuse itself, *i.e.* the *Wild* priesthood of Reason; and the Jews in the time of the *Law* was too apt to slide back to this priesthood, they being more fond of that, then they were of the given priesthood, for which cause great troubles were brought on that kingdom, Israel. – YEA this *Wild Priesthood* produced by Reason, was first found in *Cain*; from whence it took place, for Reason to fly to, for when Cain was loosed by the *Cherubim and flaming sword*, or internal Angel in justice, whom he called Lord, he *went into the land of Nod, i.e.* the *State* of forgetfulness so far as this, - when Justice is *stayed* in the soul for a time, the spirit of Reason *forms* to himself his *own* forgiveness, or that he will be forgiven of God, from whence springs the *hope* of Reason, under the justice of the angel, and this *hope* is the waters that Reason live in, which I call the great *river Euphrates in the land of Nod*, that runs in the soul of man to this day: For on this *river* depends the rivers and fountains of water, from whence flow the delights to Reason: And when justice was *stayed* in Cain, and this *hope* took place *he formed* to himself his own forgiveness, and what would please God by his *Acts, Offerings,* &c. which is the *Wild priesthood* of Reason, and as so become an *experimental preacher* and *teacher*, by, or from what he had gone through, before he was loosed by the angel (in his own family when born to him, by Lamech, the fifth from Cain, Gen. iv.) when he called his two wives, saying, I have slain a man to my wounding, and a young man to my hurt;" also said, "If *Cain* shall be avenged seven fold, truly *Lamech* seventy and seven fold." Here it is plain *Cain* taught his own children, and that himself should be *avenged seven fold, i.e.* in effect to say, *His* punishment should be in this life.

Further, (Gen ii.) "And a river went out of Eden to water the garden, from thence it was parted and became into four heads." This great river is the waters of Reason, and *came out* by permission from the *tree of knowledge of good and evil*, which is Reason with its law written in it, and go forth to delight Reason, which is a *garden* to that spirit; and to do this *it parted, and become into four heads*: Now the first three *heads* are to be understood by expression according to the rise and fluctuation of the world; for those *waters* is the desire of Reason to shine in his kingdom, therefore terminate the same, though not always expressed alike: But now in general it runs thus, - as *first*, the spirit of Reason desire to get Gold, &c. to become rich. – *Secondly*, then it thirsts after lands, mansions, delicious fare, grand appearance, *Rule* over Souls, honour, &c. *Thirdly*, after Arts and Emulations; that the *two* first must come to the *third*, to have their desires compleated. And the *fourth* is Euphrates, *i.e.* the spiritual hope to Reason for salvation (as aforesaid) and if this *river* stop the others are no more. *Also*, in the time of *Lamech* this river began to divide in his sons; as thus, "*Jabal* the father of such as dwell in tents, and of such as have Cattle: *Jubal*, the father of such as handle the Harp and Organ: *Tubal-Cain*, an instructor of every artificer in brass and iron;" thus Reason divided into branches to raise his kingdom, and formed a *worship* and *Priesthood* to excuse itself, which went on with increase, and continue to this day.

Reason being so fond of this *Priesthood*, and *delight in those Waters*, that in the time of the *Law*, when the *given Priesthood* was in act, the Jews would slide back to the *wild priesthood*, which was called whoredoms and abominations in, and among them, for all *they* owned and followed Moses. *Also* under the gospel, if a Messenger comes from JESUS, in his holy covenant of mercy to call to the holy marriage with Jesus, he is sure to find men in the *strong-hold* of the wild priesthood and waters of Reason, let them profess what letter they will; therefore Jesus speak this parable of the *great supper*, which is the same in consequence as the *marriage with the Son*, and he sent his servant at *supper time* to call them that were bidden, saying, "ALL THINGS ARE NOW READY," (Luke xiv.) *and they all with one consent began to make excuses; the first said unto him,* 'I have bought a piece of ground, and I needs must go and see it, I pray thee have me excused'; *another said* 'I have bought five yoke of oxen, and I go to prove them, I pray thee have me excused' *and another said* 'I have married a wife, and therefore I cannot come': Thus you may see the *three* head of the *waters* of Reason, wherein that soul and spirit is watered with delights, to rise, support, and shine in his kingdom, but all in his own way, and in the great *Euphrates* in this spiritual land of Nod, *i.e.* the *waters of hope* to Reason, where he will find excuse from his own spirit, which is his priest, if not, there is plenty of external priests in this great river that will find excuses for him or them; for Reason likes to be king in himself and do as he please in his own priesthood, and to make choice of his own *Way* to heaven, which is acting as a God: therefore BLESSED are they that can come out of this *priesthood* and waters (when the *Call* comes) into the priesthood and waters of Faith, for Christ to rule over them; for when Jesus was or is graciously pleased to send a Messenger to call to the holy marriage, there is those found that will refuse the kingdom of heaven for the kingdom and priesthood of Reason; And also them who will leave the glory of Reason, for the priesthood of Faith and kingdom of heaven; which must be done, let the suffering be as it will in this life; as Jesus said, "and whosoever doth not bear his cross, and come after me, he cannot be my disciple."

Further, concerning the *priesthood of Faith* and the holy *Marriage* with Jesus, who is the LAMB OF GOD, for all *Rule* and power over Faith is in him, and the fruits of Faith centers to him, who has worked redemption for his Elect, and become the God of mercy to them, because he has waded through the power of Reason, which is temptation to evil, and through the power of death and hell, and the justice of the Father; for the all-powerful works and righteousness of Faith in CHRIST, is the glorious *Incense* that ascended, and *ascends with the prayer of the saints*, which is for their salvation: Thus CHRIST is the golden altar, *i.e.* the GRAND ALTAR OF FAITH, that has the *four horns*, which are four powers, *i.e.* power over the *Justice* of the Father (which is justice to Faith) and power over *Sin,* and over *Death* and *Hell*: And all the prayer of Faith in the Elect, which is the true incense ascends to this *Altar*, that the soul may be taken through *Justice* to the glorious mercy of the SON: - *Also* when Faith is quickened from *death* to *life*, or *born its first birth* then it will know the *Promise* of Christ, and is taken into the royal priesthood; then the *Temple* of the tabernacle of the testimony of Faith, between Christ and his Elect, will in God's time be *opened* to Faith: for the priesthood and works of Faith is the *Church* of Christ, who is the LAMB as was slain, having *seven horns and seven eyes*, which are the SEVEN *spirits of God, sent forth into all the earth, i.e.* to his Elect wherever they are found!

Now those *Seven spirits of God,* or powers of Faith, are in CHRIST, and are made known to Elect man in the *Regeneration*; for in the royal priesthood of Faith, which is the mystical union, and spiritual communion with CHRIST, Elect men will find they must receive those heavenly *Gifts* from Christ, through his divine mercy, to enter his glorious kingdom: Also let the Elect *understand*, the horns and eyes of this *Lamb* is his *Power and spirit,* which in the kingdom of Faith is inseparable, because CHRIST IS GOD; yet notwithstanding, in this I shall mention here, differ something from the *Voice* of the seven Angels, as that is in regeneration from the *fall* of man unto the *resurrection*, and include neither; but this includes Creation and Resurrection, and is all to shew forth his power and glory; but in this – the spirit rather incline to that *Witness* of his spirit that *stood before him and prophecied,* when he was in the condition of the Father: As *First*, In CHRIST is found that spirit and power of Faith, by which he created Adam and Eve of his own divine nature, which is Faith, and as so, were his own children when he was in the condition of God the Father! – *Second*, When created Faith fell under the power of justice, death, &c. through temptation; in CHRIST is found the spirit and power, to quicken Faith from this death to life for regeneration: and promise, himself would become a Son to his own power, and redeem his Elect! – *Third*, When Faith is quickened and taken into the royal priesthood; in CHRIST is found the spirit and power to assist, and help it through this sore journey of flesh, also give it power to prophecy of his coming, *i.e.* of its own salvation! – *Fourth*, in CHRIST is found the spirit and power to redeem Faith! – *Fifth*, in CHRIST and power is found the spirit and power to unite in spiritual and holy marriage with this pure *virgin* of Faith, that has *come through great tribulation,* and give spiritual *Birth* to his holy and spiritual covenant of grace! – *Sixth,* in CHRIST is found the spirit and power to seal and sanctify this spiritual *born* Son of Faith, for the kingdom of glory! – *Seventh,* in CHRIST is and will be found the spirit and power to raise Faith, which lay *sleeping in the bed of mercy,* to his glorious kingdom, and crown it with an everlasting crown of glory!!! – Therefore when Faith is quickened from death to life, and taken into the royal priesthood, those things will be *opened* and *given* to them by JESUS; and by the works of Faith, and divine assistance from heaven, be made able to receive the *testimony* of Jesus, *i.e.* the spirit of prophecy of your own salvation.

Those are the seven *spirits of God,* or the seven glorious *Stars* to the Elect, that are *held in the right hand* of Him that sits in the glory of *Mercy;* because by his mighty works of Redemption he gained to himself the high kingdom and glory of mercy, and with it all power; and took possession of his kingdom of regenerated Faith, which is the fruits of that *Witness of his spirit that stood and prophecied before him* when he was in the condition of the Father; and was the first fruits by regeneration unto God for Christ; and now walk in the midst of the *Church of Christ*, according to his heavenly *Gifts* of the holy spirit – For *understand* this, - if a Messenger is sent in the covenant of mercy, to *call* and tell them the will of Jesus, he may be called the Angel *of* the declaration, because he brings the message; but the Elect are also Angels for the covenant of grace, as well as the Messenger; for all must have the seal of the living God, being the last thing to enter the kingdom of heaven (except the resurrection). And when the Elect have received those gracious *Gifts* of the holy spirit, from Jesus, the *Ark of the testimony* of the covenant of Faith, and the BOOK *of* LIFE is *opened* to them by JESUS to sleep in the bed of mercy to inherit eternal glory!

Again, when Faith fell under the justice of the Father and the power of death, it was then dead in itself from all knowledge of its ever, again, being in united friendship with God, till the quickening power of the sonship of God was given: For *understand* this – all the power of creation and generation is of the *Father*, but all the *quickening* power to Faith for and in regeneration, is of the SON, or the *Father* becoming a *Son* (John v.) "For as the *Father* raiseth the dead, and quickeneth them, even so the *son* quickeneth whom he will. For the Father judgeth no man, but hath committed all judgment unto the Son;" *i.e.* all *judgment* over Faith in regeneration and salvation: Therefore Faith when created hearkened to the voice of Reason, and fell under the power of death, then when quickened from this death, or born from its womb or seed, it came forth in a *new* life, which is done by the spirit and power of CHRIST, who brings a *new life* out of this death throughout his whole kingdom of Faith: And this *Spirit* or *Virgin daughter of Faith* comes forth pure, and will not hearken to the voice of Reason; for as created Faith hearkened to the voice of Reason, but when *quickened* from that death for *regeneration*, it will not hearken to Reason: True it is, when this Virgin is *inactive*, man may, nay, will be tempted to evil by Reason, but this Virgin daughter of Faith, will not hearken to it; as when she is *active* it burns with *prayer* and *patience* as a Lamp of *sweet incense* that ascends up to heaven before GOD; and will go through *tribulation*, and come up to the *Marriage* with the LAMB righteous and pure! So John saw (Rev. xix.) thus, "Let us be glad and rejoice, and give honour to HIM, for the *Marriage* of the *Lamb* is come, and his wife hath made herself ready, and to her was granted, the she should be arrayed in fine linen clean and white, for fine linen is the righteousness of saints, and he saith unto me, write, blessed are they which are called unto the marriage supper of the Lamb, and he saith unto me, those are the true sayings of God." So BLESSED are them that enter the *royal Priesthood* of Faith, and work the works to go up to the holy marriage with the Lamb: *i.e.* to be united in spirit to JESUS, and have his royal Seal for the kingdom of glory!

Chap. XVI

JESUS puts forth another parable (Matt. xx.) "For the kingdom of heaven, is like unto a man that is in an householder, which went out early in the morning, to hire labourers into his vineyard." The *kingdom of heaven*, is the glorious kingdom of CHRIST, and himself the *householder*, and the gospel, which is the declaration of the *kingdom*, is the *vineyard*, and is as thus – There is an outward literal *Declaration*; and an inward and spiritual *Testimony* which come from heaven, *i.e.* the mystical union, and spiritual communion with JESUS, which is his royal Priesthood, or spiritual *Vineyard* of Faith, that he walks in, and assists his royal Elect by the influence of his holy spirit, and rule over them: And the outward or literal *Declaration*, the spirit of Reason (when transformed to it, may walk in it and make use of the name of Jesus, then do the best they can for themselves: Hence when the *Declaration* is made, men may come *and work in the vineyard*, and there is a reward promised, which men are sure to find according to their *works*: Now JESUS was he that uttered and brought in his holy gospel, and as so *went out early in the morning*, because he WAS and IS the glorious SON of *Mercy* that *arose* to heal and redeem his Elect, then *he agreed with the labourers to work in*, or by his declaration, *i.e. his vineyard.*

Moreover, since the holy *Gospel* was declared, and redemption worked by Jesus, and he ascended into heaven, it has proceeded according to the heavenly wisdom, and glorious mercy of CHRIST the KING of FAITH, that he is graciously pleased to *open* and *bestow* on his Elect; for the overflowing of the holy spirit of Jesus flows forth with a glorious increase of salvation mysteries to his Elect, and not *stand* as a dead letter: therefore the internal *seal and sanctification* of Jesus in the holy Gospel, is made known to Elect men let them live in any *hour of the day*; why? because they are sure to be *called* by JESUS, and *He opens the seals* at their death, that they may read in the BOOK of LIFE, and be united to, and recorded in, the ever living memory of Jesus, for eternal glory! But who has come back to tell this in *plain* terms before? So *one Hour* to the Elect in the holy Gospel is as a *Day*, and a *Day* as an *Hour*, or thus, *one day as a Thousand years, and a thousand years as a day*: For the holy Gospel is likened unto a *Day*; and the *coming of* CHRIST in spirit by his Messengers at different times, are *Hours of the Day*; for when Elect Man come in a Messengers *Day or Hour*, the mysteries of the redemption, Seal, and sanctification of Jesus, will be made know to Elect Man for his salvation; and it is the same thing from Christ's ascending into heaven in person, to his coming in person to judgment.

Ver. 3. "And he went out about the *third hour*, and saw others standing idle in the market place. And said unto them, go ye also into the vineyard; and whatsoever is right I will give you; and they went their way." Now this world is the *field* for regeneration, and Christ come in person, and doth come in spirit, to *Call into* his holy gospel, and as so a *marketplace;* because he gathers his Elect out of this world to his divine mercy. "Also he went out about the *sixth* and *ninth hour* and did likewise, and also about the *eleventh hour*." Those different *hours* of the *Day*, are Messengers sent at different times, as aforesaid, only this – the later the hour, the nearer the end of the day; and the *eleventh hour* nearer eternity than the *third*; and as Messengers come out one after the other, every one utters his voice nearer the *Seal* of the LIVING GOD OF FAITH, and every one prophecies in his *Day or hour*, for the mighty workings of Jesus on the spirit of Faith in the Elect, do not stand as a *dead letter*, but will bring the soul up to his royal and spiritual *Seal*.

Hence every one utters as he comes out, as thus, the *Apostles* was inspired and sent forth to preach Christ the *Son of God,* bear witness of his *death and resurrection,* to redeem his Elect, and *prophecied* of his coming again*: - John the Divine* received the holy Ghost with the other Apostles, yet he live 'till Christ come again: And when *John* saw him (in vision) "he fell at his feet as a dead man;" and he saw that JESUS *only, could open the Book of Life*; and saw and prophecied of the holy *Marriage, Seal, and sanctification of GOD,* to enter the kingdom of glory; and that *Christ was GOD,* and prophecied again of his *coming*: But this book of John's visional Prophecy, was for Christ to *open* when he come in spirit at the hour of death to his Elect, bringing his *reward with him, i.e.* to give spiritual *Birth* to his holy covenant of grace, and seal this spiritual born *Son* of the *virgin* daughter of Faith for his glorious kingdom: - And *John Reeve* come out and declared in plain terms, that *Christ* was the very ETERNAL GOD, and no one could redeem the Elect but *Him, that created all things*; and prophecied of Christ to *come*. – ALSO there is *another* come out, in the *spiritual Birth* to the holy Covenant; and in *plain* terms, declares the royal PRIESTHOOD *of Faith, Holy MARRIAGE, Spiritual BIRTH, Seal and Sanctification of CHRIST, the God of Mercy* to enter the kingdom of glory; and *prophecies of his coming* in spirit; to seal his Elect, and *warns* them to *prepare to meet him*: Now he that hath *wisdom,* let him *understand,* the coming of Christ in those *Hours* of the *Day,* and also to mind in what *Hour* of the Day, he himself lives in, by this warning given. Yea, the royal Priesthood, and holy Gospel, is the same in spirit to his Elect: For *Him* that has last come from Christ, doth declare CHRIST *has opened the Book* of John's *prophecy* to his Elect; and will open it again to his Elect. Also this Messenger (last come) from JESUS, is the first man that has declared those things in *plain* terms, why? because he is come from Christ with the VISITATION and *Acts* of Christ, according to *John's* prophecy; and as so, not only a witness to that *prophecy,* but also to the *Acts of Jesus* on that prophecy; for which cause he doth declare the *Priesthood of Faith,* spiritual *Birth, seal,* and *sanctification* of the king of Faith, to die in the bed of mercy, to be raised to everlasting glory, in *plain* terms! ALSO *prophecies* that Christ will *shortly* come again in spirit to *open the Book of Life* and *Seal* the Elect his brethren for the kingdom of glory: - And though this Messenger has come out from JESUS, in the spirit that the Elect were *born* to, and *sealed* for glory, declaring their condition in *plain* terms, and the first from Christ that ever did; yet, all others that has gone before are in the bed of *Mercy,* or second *paradise* before him; for it is the same thing in the priesthood of Faith in the holy gospel, from first to last, relative to the seal of Christ, let them come in, to *work* the works of Faith in any *hour* of the *Day;* for the powerful works of Christ in his redemption, seal, and sanctification which is of the holy gospel, is bestowed, and has its effect in one Elect man, as in every Elect man, from the day of his *ascension* in person, to the day of his coming to *judgment* in person, being sure to be called upon and sealed by Jesus.

Every Messenger that comes from Jesus in his holy covenant of grace, comes higher up, or nearer his Royal *Seal* to enter his glorious kingdom; therefore BLESSED are they that can hear and follow *Him* that hath come out from the ALTAR, *i.e.* him that has been given *birth in spirit*, from under the *Justice* of the *Father*, to the glorious *Mercy* of the *Son!* and called up into the high MOUNTAIN of Faith! and saw the glory of the Son in his royal *Mercy seat!* and his royal spiritual *Seal* and *Sanctification*, and offered the *prayer of Faith*, after the spiritual *Birth* was past, at the *feet* of him that fits in the Glory of *Mercy*, for his royal spiritual Seal and sanctification, which is the *great and grand ALTAR of Faith!* and after this, *send back to declare it!* and *prophecy* to the Elect, his brethren; and this *Declaration from CHRIST is faithful and true.* – And he also saw in this manner the Elect was called, and came up to the seal of the living God of Faith and was sealed, *i.e.* after the spiritual born *son* of the pure *Virgin* daughter of Faith comes forth, it offers its prayer, to be *united* to the king of Faith, in his holy covenant of Mercy, and WAS and IS united to Jesus by the *immortal spirit of regenerated Faith* and there remain in the breast of the everliving KING of Faith and Mercy, which is the records of his royal seal for the resurrection to his glorious kingdom! – *This,* this Messenger was shewed by the *holy ANGEL* OF THE *Covenant of Grace!* and he saw it, and doth declare it: and the *holy* ANGEL of Faith *i.e.* JESUS is his *Witness.* And although he saw it, and is the first that came back to declare it in *plain* terms; yet them that were before, are in the *bed* of mercy, or *second* paradise before this Messenger.

Again, The seed and spirit of Reason may, and do come and *work in the vineyard*, but it is only on the *bare word* or Declaration aforesaid; and when they transform themselves, or are transformed into the declaration of Jesus or his Messenger, they are relieved from their former *captivity, i.e.* from the *burthens* that has been laid upon the souls of men by the *priest* of Reason and *tradition of men.* ALSO they go forth and preach in the name and power of the Messenger, and by the declaration they overpower and subject the spirits of others; for if men are offended with the doctrine, become angry, then to wrath, then to blasphemy, they who preach see those men fall before their face; and if men are patient to hear they must submit, why? because they cannot overthrow it, nor get from it. NOW this power is given to the seed and spirit of Reason, when they take the letter of a Declaration that comes from heaven, and preach it up, and spread it abroad, which is the *workings* of Reason *in the vineyard*; and they have power given them over Reason in other men, and relieved from former burthen, and this is a new flow of life, or emulated joy to the soul of man, which has been called the "ASSURANCE *of* ETERNAL LIFE," because they are above the hope of Reason in other men; yet they themselves act by the spirit of Reason, on the declaration of another Man; yea, Reason doth expect eternal life for this *Work.*

Ver. 8. "So when *Even* was come, the lord of the vineyard saith unto the steward, call the labourers and give them their hire, beginning from the last unto the first." This *Even* is God's time, hour of death, or at the end of all time, and, as I said, every one is sure to be *called.* NOW when any Elect are *called* in old age by the Messenger, *they* will enter the Royal Priesthood and works of Faith, then at death are called by JESUS through the Justice of the Father, and are given *spiritual birth!* and are *Sealed* by Jesus to enter the kingdom of glory! When as another Elect being who *come into the Vineyard* before him, may be called after him, *FOR understand* this, the Elect are *called* to, through the Justice of the Father, and *chosen* by Jesus to enter into the holy *Marriage and spiritual* Birth; but the seed of Reason are never *called* by Jesus, therefore as so, the Elect are called *first,* and take their *part* in the *first resurrection* which is their *Penny* or portion; but the seed of Reason are *called* by the *Angel in justice,* and let to know, they have received their *penny* or portion, then fail in their expectation, and go *murmuring* into death. ALSO when the Elect are in the spiritual *vineyard*, and work the works of Faith, the power of sin and death is made know to them, and they are so much incumbered with it, that oft times they think they are unworthy, and almost impossible they should be saved when looking at the purity of the DIVINE MAJESTY, and the impurity of their own soul, and as so afraid they will be the *last* called if ever called by Christ; but the seed of Reason are filled with high emulation on the outward word or bare letter, and by that think he is already in the favour of Christ; therefore expect to be *first called*, and have a greater portion than the Elect whom he looked on beneath himself; but when Christ come, he that heard to be *last* called, is the *first* and he that expected to be *first* called, is *last, i.e.* the seed of Reason is never *called* by Jesus, as I said, then go their way, *murmuring against the good man of the house,* whereas Reason never entered the royal priesthood of Faith to be *called by Jesus.* Yet when Reason *come to work in the vineyard,* they are taken from their former *bondage and labour,* and in this they are external *healed*; but will go their *own way* again, with another language; for they will soon begin to wander anew, with the declaration, in their own wild priesthood, even in the *Day* of a Messenger; for although Reason has the declaration of *work in,* yet he will set it forth according to his own understanding, and there is no more done for him in the spiritual than to bring him *out of Egypt* to die *murmuring in the wilderness*; yet the seed and spirit of Reason, is very ready, nay the *first* to go forth and preach, according to his dark wisdom on the letter, and thereby expect to be *first* called, and will be the *last* called. – ALSO two men may come in the days of a Messenger, and take the declaration, the *one shall be taken* into the priesthood of Faith, *and the other left* in the priesthood of Reason on the bare letter, and *he that is left* will tempt others into that priesthood if possible, and think he is doing his duty, and God good service.

Again, as I said, there has been Messengers come from CHRIST in his *holy gospel*, and prophecied in the royal priesthood of Faith – Now Reason is very eager to take the letter into his own understanding; and when the Messenger is dead, and they that prophecied in his day, then Reason will take possession of the letter, and teach his *own way*, in his *own* priesthood; at which time there is silence in the *nether heaven* of Faith, touching public declaration and prophecy; and this *silence* in heaven is from the death of one Messenger to the sending forth of another; NOW men in their travail of this life, may come and take the letter if they please, and work in it according to their own will; and when they do, they will construct it to their liking, and excuse themselves as they please, and make to themselves concerning the promise as they like, which is their *own agreement*: Then when the *Messenger* comes who is a *Steward* sent of God, (and utters his voice from God) *He Calls* to them that *work in the vineyard*: NOW this is also reckoning day; but here the *Messenger* also calls to Faith, which is the *first* and it will hear and *come and see*; then in God's time will be quickened and taken into the royal priesthood, when those of Reason will go their *Way murmuring*, in wroth: ALSO, some men may have been working on, or in the letter many years, and some but few; and some scarce know the last declaration; but he that has faith to obey the voice of God when the *Call* comes, will be *taken* (let him have worked in the letter a long time or short) and enter the royal priesthood of Faith; when others will *go their Way murmuring* with the bare Letter, whereas it is all they *agreed* for, because Reason will *agree* for nothing, but his own wisdom on the bare Letter, and at last go off *murmuring*, saying he has done great things, *born the burthen and heat of the day*, yet has all that he *agreed* to have.

Chap. XVII

YEA, the holy gospel is likened unto a *Day*, and that day, as a *thousand years*, or to what time God please; for it is from CHRIST's ascending into heaven in person, to his coming to judgment in person; so when a Messenger is sent from Jesus, to declare his Will unto the Elect his brethren, that is the *Hour, Day, or Time* of open declaration and prophecy, to the Elect that are called into the spiritual *Vineyard, i.e.* the *priesthood* of Faith; - also the life of man is as a *Day*, and when the spirit of Faith is quickened into life, and taken into the mystical *Union*, and spiritual communion with JESUS which is the priesthood of Faith, then is the *Gospel* began to that soul; and when the *Virgin* daughter of Faith offers her prayer, (which is the incense of Faith) that ascends to God for his divine assistance from heaven and *patiently waits* God's time, it is the *Works* of Faith in the holy gospel; and when Jesus is graciously pleased by influence of his holy spirit to help this *Virgin* daughter of Faith, it is *day-light*, or sunshine to that soul, yea, when the spirit of God is thus active to Faith, it is *bright* spiritual day-light to the soul, according to this portion of Faith that is given him.

Understand also, that the power of the holy gospel and redemption, is worked on the souls of Elect men, living in any *hour of the Day, i.e.* in the time of the *Apostles*, or in the time of the other *Three*, who came out one after the other, and as they came uttered their voice nearer the seal of JESUS the *Living GOD* of *Faith*; therefore the Messenger when come, taking the man by his declaration, this man's life is in the Messenger's *Hour* or *Day*; and men come in at different age of life, which is different *hours of the day, i.e.* one man may come in, as soon as in full manhood, as Adam was created to, by the LORD GOD of heaven, which time is the *third hour of the day*, and he will follow the Messenger, and the prayer of obedience is found in his soul that he may be *obedient* to him, and *stand still* and *wait* the salvation of God: *Anon*, the power of the declaration assisted from heaven, becomes great in the soul, and is made sensible that Faith is *fell* in him, and disunited by death from God the Father, (it being created under that power) and is, as it was in the man Adam; then there is a *new life* quickened out of this death, which is the *Virgin* daughter of Faith, *born* to the promise of Christ, and made able to offer her own prayer, *i.e.* the prayer of Faith in the royal priesthood, which is the *Sixth hour of the Day,* and his love will become double to the Messenger and his brethren; then this Virgin daughter work the works of Faith against the powers of death and hell, and patiently *waits* Christ to come, according to promise, also prophecied of by the Messenger, and that soul will be found worthy; – Then CHRIST in his own time come in spirit and give the *spirit of prophecy, i.e.* Christ has come in spirit and will come again, to seal the soul for his GLORIOUS KINGDOM, this is the *ninth hour* of the day, then his love than is treble to the Messenger and brethren.

After *this*, the soul work the *Works of Faith*, greater than before, and keeps stedfast *Watch*, not to be found *overcharged* with the *Folly* of Reason, *Cares* of this life, and *Drunkenness* in Reason's priesthood, but *patiently wait* the Lord's coming; then he is again found worthy by those *Works* of Faith and called to by JESUS through the justice of the Father, and Jesus unites in spirit with this *Virgin* daughter of Faith, and give spiritual birth from under that Justice, to his own spiritual and holy covenant of Mercy, *i.e. Mercy of the SON!* this is the *eleventh hour of the day*. AFTER this, the spiritual born son of Faith is sealed in the holy kingdom and covenant of Mercy to the raised to glory! and falls asleep in Mercies Bed, and will be raised to glory! and this is the *twelfth Hour*, then the *Day* is ended; as the soul has gone through the mighty *Works* of Faith and *tribulation* in the holy gospel, which is of the sonship of God for salvation! – then *the kingdoms of this world are become the kingdoms of CHRIST, and he will reign*, in and over his kingdom of regenerated Faith, *for ever*, and all done in a *Day* or *Hour* which is the life of a man.

Yea, one man may *come in* young which is the *third hour* of his day; another more advance in years, the *sixth hour* of his day; another further in years, *i.e.* the *ninth hour* of his day; and another in old age, which is the *eleventh hour* of his day; and he that come in the *vineyard* in old age Christ will bring through the mighty powers of death and hell, and may be *called first*, and sealed by Jesus for eternal glory; for the glorious King of Faith is very able to make man *perfect* in what time he please. ALSO some men may have *Revelation* before others; and some have the gracious *Gift of* prophecy before others, who have *worked longer in the vineyard*; for it is in the will and power of JESUS, who is the KING of Faith, and HIGH-PRIEST in his royal *Priesthood*; hence all quickening and ruling power to Faith is in, and of Jesus, and he can make a man *perfect* in his working, from the *eleventh hour*, as he can from the *third or sixth*; for ALL THE Works of Faith, and *Prophecy* of Faith, is a Witness to the *Spirit* of Jesus, and *they* also witness and prophecy to each other, and one for another; and this unites *them*, in the LOVE of Faith, and is the CHURCH of CHRIST! for it is the nature of Faith to rejoice in anothers *revelation* and *prophecy* Why? because it WILL BE his own portion; but Reason will question it, and murmur against it, because he is *withering away*: FURTHER *understand*, when the seed of Reason is called by the declaration, it has but the bare letter, and it is the *third* hour with them, let them be at any age in manhood, and there they will stand, at the *third hour*; but when the Elect are called at the *third hour* (as I said some are,) then, in God's time, Faith in them is *quickened* from death to LIFE, which is the *sixth hour*; then they are taken into the Priesthood of Faith, (but the seed of Reason is left with the bare letter, in his own *Wild priesthood*,) and to the Elect this is the *second or last Call* relative to the declaration of the Messenger, for then they must follow him up to the spirit of *prophecy*, holy *Marriage*, and spiritual *Birth*; and when *Even is come* the Elect who are taken into the *priesthood of Faith*, the second or *last Call* to them relative to the declaration, then they are called under the *Justice of the Father*, and it is the *eleventh hour* to them, and are given spiritual *birth* to the *Mercy of the SON*, and those are *they* that are *first called*, and have their *part in the first resurrection*; BUT Reason remain with the letter as he was *first* called touching Works of Faith, as the *third hour,* who is become *withered and cast forth* by his own wisdom, and the last called, *i.e.* not called at all, but under the justice of the angel, then he will *murmur*, whereas he has all he agreed to have; so Jesus said so the *last* shall be first, and the *first* last, for many are called, and few chosen," *i.e.* Reason stand as he was *first called*, but the Elect are *called* again, or taken into the *priesthood* of Faith, which but is the *last Call* of the declaration, and will be *first called* to the spiritual *Birth*; for the whole world is *called* to the outward declaration, but *few chosen* to enter the royal Priesthood, to be sealed by Jesus for eternal life.

Again, JESUS who was God the Father, and the God of Justice is now become God the SON, and the God of Mercy, and it was him that created the Man Adam, from whence the Elect proceeded by generation; therefore HE was the *First*, because the created Faith, and he only could redeem it, and as so the *Last*: Also HE WAS, and IS the *First* that quickens Faith from death to life for regeneration; and the *Last* to give it spiritual *Birth*, or translate it, into his glorious and holy Covenant of mercy, that HE has purchased to himself by going through his own Justice; also Adam was the *first Man* of Faith for *generation*, and HE who created Adam became the *Last Man* of Faith, for to bring in *Regeneration;* for without the divine assistance of Christ in regeneration, man can do *nothing*; further, CHRIST WAS the *First* that uttered and brought in his holy gospel, and that offered the royal and *essential* Prayer of Faith, before the THRONE of the FATHER, (which is of justice) for his Elect, which is his *Kingdom* of Faith, or his *Kingdom Israel*, that IS and WILL BE under the attribute of his divine Mercy! and IS the *Last* to seal *them*, and raise *them*, to his glorious kingdom: So throughout the whole kingdom, covenant, priesthood, and works of Faith CHRIST is the *First*, and is the *Last*.

Moreover a *Messenger* may come out from JESUS and declare HIS Will, yet many that he declares it to, may by and according to that declaration, enter the bed of mercy, before him that declares it; therefore it is the nature of Faith to rejoice at his brother's increase, also to pray for one whose soul *mourns* for the Priesthood of Faith, and mercy from Jesus; for all must be sealed by JESUS to enter his glorious kingdom, and it is of no signification who is sealed first or last, so that he is but sealed by JESUS; for all will be raised by the call of Jesus, and all together be crown'd with the glorious crown of mercy, in the glorious and merciful kingdom of the SON OF GOD: But Reason coming to work in the vineyard, it will agree for no more than his own wisdom on the bare Letter, and there will remain at the *third hour* of the *Day*, and never will or can enter the priesthood of Faith, which is the *sixth hour* of the *Day*, or beginning of regeneration; and Reason being in his own wild priesthood with the letter, it will have *wild* conceivings, and preach a doctrine *in the name of Christ* that will *deceive many*, but he is kept out of the priesthood of Faith by the internal Angel in justice, who is *the cherubim and flaming sword, who turns every way to keep the WAY of the tree of life*; and when Reason is called by this angel he will *murmur* against Jesus who is *the good man of the house* of Faith, whereas Reason has all that ever he *agreed* to have.

Again, "All the Elect are sealed by JESUS to enter his glorious *kingdom*". i.e. the spiritual born son of Faith is united to *Jesus in spirit, in his high covenant, and glorious kingdom of divine mercy! and for his mercy!* and although the person dies, or fall asleep in this bed of mercy, yet this spirit of regenerated Faith is of an *immortal* nature, and is united to CHRIST in GLORY and *lives* in the memory of the *everliving KING OF FAITH*, which is the *lively record* of his royal Seal: And when the *number of his Elect are accomplished*, (which is only known to himself) then the firmament or heaven will open, and the mighty JESUS, the royal KING of Faith, will come in *person*, full *power*, and great *glory*, with his might *angels* Enoch, Moses, and Elias, and his heavenly *Host*, and *stand* between heaven and his earth, and with HIM, bring his royal *Seal* and the *records* of that seal, and cry with a *loud voice* unto his Elect who are all sealed, and the spiritual power, in the *word* centers to the soul (which produced this Regenerated Faith) that is *sleeping* in the bed of mercy, to all the Elect as to one man, and quickens it into a new spiritual and glorious life, and also give it a body of fine flesh and bone that this purified spirit of Faith may shine in, to shew forth the inexpressible glory that God has given it, for *obeying* his voice here in time, and *following* through the powers of death and hell! And in this very manner the Elect will come forth, and ascend to him and with him in glory! Therefore when the Elect are *sealed*, and prophecy of Christ to *raise* them to his heavenly glory, and fall *asleep* in this bed of mercy! then, - When they find themselves again, it will be in a *New* and glorious everlasting *Life*, that CHRIST has called his Elect to, and gave them; and from the time of their *falling asleep* in the bed of mercy, to their finding themselves with Christ in glory, it will appear to them but as a short and sound *Sleep!*

The next appearance in the *Resurrection* is the glorious order or *host of Cherubims, i.e. Children* of Reason that died in minority, and the internal angel in justice did not take place in their soul, so are not charged with the Law of Reason; and this is the *MERCY to Reason*, according to God's suffering the created cherubim to become flesh, that he may gain to himself millions of *Cherubims*, and glorify them in a body of flesh and bone, to live in the royal presence of him and his Elect in all ETERNITY, as well as millions to go their way under the justice of the angel: Then when JESUS *Calls* to Faith to come up to HIM, this ALMIGHTY VOICE is so great that the *Child or Cherubim* will hear the echo and follow, they being appointed of God for glorification – Yea from the mighty effect of those *Resurrections Death and Hell will also give up their Dead, i.e.* the seed of Reason that are *Dead* from mercy and sealed for the wrath of God, the internal angel in justice will *give them up* under his seal to enter on the *second death* which is *Wrath* as a lake of fire burning for ever, FOR think not that Jesus speak into the souls of them that are sealed under the power of death and hell; for if he was, his voice is so infinite, powerful, and pure, that it would give them *new Life* – But the contrary as I said, Jesus speak into the souls of his Elect, who are sealed with his own royal Seal and raise them to his own glory, which is the glory of Faith; - and the *echo* of that voice will raise the *Cherubims* to the height of Reason's glory, who will come forth and appear with bodies spiritualized like unto the Elect) and glorified with great glory, which glory will be given to this *cherubical* Reason that is not charged with the law; - and is refined by twice passing through death; yet *understand* that this glory which is given to Reason, is much inferior to the glory of Faith, which is the glory of GOD: - Then, form the effect of those *Resurrections* the power of *Justice, Sin, Death, and Hell* will be let loose, and never will be stayed any more, and the Angel in *Justice,* will do the will of God according to the attribute of *Justice*, and give up the dead that are under his seal, who will come forth in wrath, both in and under the power of *Death* and *Hell*, and there to remain for ever.

Again, when JESUS was here and declared his holy Gospel, from HIS utterance, this very effect was worked on the souls and spirits of men in this life: Also when any of his Messengers who come out in HIS holy covenant of grace and royal priesthood of Faith, are here, the same effect is also worked on the souls and spirits of men in this life, because the voice of Faith is uttered, and it is to call the Elect to the *Mercy* of Jesus, which is a true Emblem of the great *Resurrection* at the end of all time; for when the VOICE OF GOD is uttered, it is to

Call to Faith, and is directed to the womb or seed of Faith in the Elect which in itself is dead, according to the justice of the Father; and by this *Voice*, and *power* from heaven in God's time, Faith is quickened from this Death into a new life, and taken into the royal priesthood to work the works of Faith; a true *Likeness* of CHRIST's *coming* in person, *calling* to his Elect, and *raising* them to his everlasting GLORY! Then, when the *Voice* is uttered, and centers to the womb of Faith, Faith quickens it, brings it forth into a *new Life* which is of Faith, and is taken into the priesthood of Faith, - this, is the intent of the *Call*, and errand of the Messenger; Yet, there will remain the outward word, bare letter, or a fragment, what the spirit hath left, and *this* is the Echo from the royal and true utterance, which some of Reason's seed can and will transform themselves to, and live in it, or by it, according to their *own wisdom, i.e.* of Reason, and by virtue of this *Echo*, they receive a greater emulated joy, and have power given them over others of Reason, that cannot come to be quickened by this echo, which will give them power to speak the language of the cherubim in a great degree, but they never can come into the priesthood of Faith; - Now this is the true *Likeness* of CHRIST when he raise the cherubims to their glory, by the *Echo* of his divine VOICE calling to his Elect, and raise them to the glory of Faith, which is his own glory.

Also others of the seed of Reason are effected through the *Call* or utterance, who will come forth in anger, and from thence to wrath, persecution, and blasphemy, - then in this, *death and hell give up their dead, i.e.* the internal angel has sealed them for the *second death* under wrath; - and the power of the declaration will bring those wrathful spirits forth that the Messenger and the Elect will see and know *they* are sealed for wrath! For under this seal of death, come forth the spirit and power of wrath, that will *war* against the spirit and power of God; and if possible they could the would not only destroy the spiritual *Virgin daughter* of Faith, but also the spiritual *Son* when born of this pure *Virgin* to the seal of Jesus unto life eternal; for such is the nature of wrath, to judge and condemn the wisdom of God by the wrathful spirit, that is seal under the power of death and hell; and had it power, would destroy the works of God, in and according to his divine mercy, by acting against regeneration, which is *spiritual sodomy*, in that they will *war* against, and blaspheme his divine wisdom and power anew, instead of *repenting of their evils*, and in this, *death and hell give up their dead*, even in the face of the Messenger; but they are under the power of the angel and can go no further than permission, which is a true *Likeness* of death and hell being given up, at the *great day* of judgment when CHRIST comes, to call his Elect to glory; and the cherubim will follow by the *Echo* of his divine *Voice*.

Further do you *understand;* the *third hour* of the *Day* is a dangerous time, Why? because its at the time of the resurrection of the cherubim by the *Echo* from the utterance, which as I said *many* will hear, and come to the outward word or bare letter, then they will speak a new language, go into emulation, and from then go wild, and become tempters even to the Messenger, and too apt to pass judgment; for being incapable of the *first resurrection* to Faith, they must stand at the *third hour*, and will seek to do as they like, and go their *own Way* with the Letter, which is their *penny* or portion in full, thinking there is no wisdom like theirs, for which cause they take liberty, and will attempt to cultivate their wisdom – AND whereas, the *Elect* when called in at the *third hour* (which is as the state of *convincement* to them,) I would have to be very careful, for it is a dangerous *time*, for the *Cherubim* that is rose by the *Echo* of the declaration will *tempt* you, and your own spirit of Reason within will *tempt* you, and it is uncertain how long man may stand at the *third hour*, and how many things may happen; Yet, there is another *Call* to come relative to the declaration; so it is good for the Elect to *watch* the temptations of those days; and it is on every ones part to be careful not to act as the Cherubim, but to have and mind the true Prayer of obedience, meekness, and patience, to *wait the Lord's leisure* for the second *Call* relative to the declaration; - then, you will come to the *sixth hour*, for that is the beginning of regeneration without regard to man being in old age.

FURTHER of the *Kingdom* of *regenerated* Faith, which is the *Kingdom of CHRIST:* Now to gather in and compleat this harmonious, united, and glorious *Kingdom,* the consequence, run as such, the first, is *last*, and the last *first*; for Christ WAS and IS the author and beginner of regenerated Faith; and as so the FIRST, and the last to seal it for, and raise it to, his glorious kingdom, and as so the LAST: Also the *royal Elect*, when Faith was rose from death to *Life*, taken into the royal *Priesthood*, received the *Testimony* of Jesus, *stood before him and prophecied* concerning his merciful redemption when he was in the condition of the Father; and WAS his *Witness* of his spirit, *Olive-tree*, or *Golden-candlestick* in whom the Royal Incense and prophecy of Faith *burned* – and were *gathered in*, and *united* unto God for Christ, and were the *first fruits* of regenerated Faith unto God for Christ: And *have his Father's name written in their forehead,* because they were *Virgins* unto and for Christ: Therefore God the Father left his glorious throne which was of justice, and invested it on *Moses* and *Elias*, become a true son to that power, redeemed his Elect, - become the royal Bridegroom, to the pure *Virgin* of Faith, ascended into the high heaven of mercy, and took possession of this, his kingdom of VIRGINS, or fruits of regenerated Faith, of that *WITNESS of his spirit* or OLIVE TREE, that *stood and prophecied* before him, when he was in the condition of the *Father*!

Moreover, When JESUS had *uttered* his holy Gospel and Regeneration, *Redeemed* his Elect, and *ascended* into his high kingdom of mercy, then, *Regeneration* was worked by *Him* and to him in HIS holy Covenant of *Mercy,* Why? because HE was become the royal *Bridegroom* to the pure *Virgin* daughter of Faith; therefore when Faith is called to, and given birth, or rose from death to life according to the *Voice* of the *First Angel* in regeneration, then they have his divine assistance, and his Testimony, which is *HIS Spirit of prophecy,* given from heaven, then they must work their *Way* to the voice of *seventh Angel,* and this is the other WITNESS of his *Spirit,* OLIVE-TREE, or GOLDEN CANDLESTICK in whom the royal incense burns, which *stand before him* and prophecy now HE is in the condition of the SON, and they are gathered into, and united to him, in his holy covenant of grace, and sealed by him for his high kingdom the GLORY of *Mercy*! And although this is the second, or *Last Witness* of his spirit, yet it is the *First* that bore the spiritual Son in regeneration to be sealed by JESUS; for though the *first* Witness stood before him and prophecied when he was in the condition of the *Father,* and was gathered in, and united to God for Christ and the *first fruits* unto God for Christ, yet this spiritual *Virgin* could not bear a spiritual *Son* in regeneration to be sealed by Christ, until God become Christ, and worked the redemption, &c. NOW this *last* Witness is regenerated to the SON, for HE unites in holy marriage to this pure *Virgin,* and begets to himself a spiritual *Son* of this *virgin Daughter,* and he ascends into the high *Mountain* of Faith, and is united to Jesus, and sealed by him for glory; so the *first* is *Last* and the *last First, i.e.* the *Last* Witness is the *First* that bore a *Son* to Christ; and the *first* is and will be the *last,* for in the morning of the resurrection there will be a translation relative to the *first Witness* and the *seventh Seal* will be *opened* in full, for then, the *Virgin* will bring forth a *Son*; and Moses, Elias and Enoch, will be translated from the glory of Justice, to the glory of *Mercy* which is the glory of CHRIST; and *All* enter into the high and mighty glory of regenerated Faith which is the glory of Christ! – So BLESSED, are them that enter the *Priesthood* of Faith, for the mercy of Christ is their *reward*! – But as this world is the *Field* for Generation, the Elect are gathered out of it, in and for Regeneration; and the consequence of Redemption and Regeneration, to compleat the kingdom of Christ run as such, the *first* is *last* and the *last first!* – But it is all one of the other, *in* the other, *on* the other, and *for* the other, so of no signification who is sealed *first* or *last* for this Kingdom; for Christ is KING HIGH-PRIEST, FIRST and LAST of this kingdom! Now you may see how the kingdom of regenerated Faith is gathered together, and who those *Witnesses of his spirit, Olive-trees* or *golden Candlesticks* are; so I pray for, and recommend the works of Faith, prayer, patience, and the love and assistance of Christ, *Amen.*

Chap. XVIII

AGAIN, of the *First Resurrection and Regeneration*, which IS the works of Christ on the souls and spirits of his Elect, to recover is *lost kingdom* of Faith: Therefore, when the voice or spiritual power of GOD comes from heaven according to the second *Call* touching the declaration, or Voice of the *first angel* in regeneration, (Rev. viii.) "And the *first* angel sounded, and there followed hail and fire mingled with blood and they were cast upon the earth and the *third* part of trees was burnt up, and all green grass was burnt up," *i.e.* When the voice or spiritual power of God calls to Faith, which is *dead* through transgression, and *quicken* it into life and sensation of itself, then the *justice* of God follow and poured out on it as *hail*, and his wrath as *fire*; and it is *mingled with blood, i.e.* in this life you must wade against, and go through the powers of Reason, and the *smoke*, and venomous spit and spue of death, and hell; and at last lose yourself in death in your own *blood* under the *justice* of the *Father. And they were cast upon the earth, i.e.* Adam was created of this *earth*, and God gave him a life or soul of Faith, which hearkened to Reason, and in that broke its own law, then died; then it was become *fallen* human nature; and Reason become the actuator of the man, then upon this *earth* which WAS and IS in active life, those *plagues* was and are *Cast;* - *And the third part of trees was burnt up, and all green grass was burnt up*: Those *trees* that was *burnt up*, are the *Imaginations* of Reason, which *mount* very high, and *spread* wide, whereby man may think to *hide* himself from GOD; and all the excuses that he has or can form to excuse himself, yea, on sayings of scripture, which Reason constructs to his own liking, which is as Standards to them, and become *trees* and spread wide, wherein and amongst, Reason thinks to hide and excuse itself: The *green grass*, is all the *hope* or refreshment of hope, and all delight in expecting the favour of God for salvation according to his former thought which was of Reason; and all excuses for acting as men of the world, (or of Reason did or do, in the common acts of life) is all *burnt up*, and departed as a *smoke* in a mighty wind, when the mighty power of the LORD GOD of Heaven calls to Faith to raise it from death to life for regeneration: - And the *third part* of Trees being burnt up, is this, - that although the life of Elect man, is so agitated and pressed down by the mighty weight of Justice that all his power and hiding places shall depart from him, yet there is a *part* left for God, whereby he brings *Life* out of death, *Light* out of darkness, and make the man anew by regeneration – Now when those things come to pass which is at the SIXTH HOUR of the Day, or beginning of regeneration, Man will find he cannot *hide himself among the trees* from God; but must stand as a dead man *naked* and bare before the LORD GOD of Heaven; and those *plagues* is the *Virgin daughter* of Faith born to, and she must *labour* to be brought out of death, and through death by the power of Christ.

Moreover, when Faith is rose from death to life, or born from its womb or seed, then from this spirit or *virgin Daughter*, Christ makes Elect men anew by regeneration; therefore when CHRIST was here he did many miracles, whereby men were made perfect according to creation in generation, and in this the *Father* is glorified in the SON; For if men had Faith, that *He* could heal them, and asked him, it was to them according to their Faith; hence (Matt. xi.) John sent his disciples to Jesus saying to him, "Art thou he that should come or do we look for another?" *Jesus answered and said unto them,* " Go and shew John again those things which ye do hear and see, the blind receive their sight, the leper's cleansed, the deaf hear, the dead are raised up, and the poor have the gospel preached unto them." Now, *this* was done to the external sight of man, and hearing of the outward ear; but it is the *internal* works of CHRIST on the soul that make men *perfect* unto salvation; therefore when Faith is rose from death to a new life according to the voice of the *first Angel* in regeneration, then the dead is rose internal for regeneration, and then the soul finds itself very *poor* and unable to heal itself, then of consequence in great need of the salvation of CHRIST, and when the promise of Christ is given, then is *the gospel preached to the poor*, but this is all internal and spiritual, in the royal priesthood of Faith.

Again, this spirit of *Virgin daughter of Faith* being a new life in Elect man, and assisted by the divine incomes of Christ, for to it is given a *censer with incense, i.e.* Faith when rose from the dead is the *censer*, and its prayer the *incense* which ascends to HEAVEN for the divine assistance of CHRIST, and makes Elect man *speak* with a new *tongue*, and *see* and *know* the power of God, and of Christ, which before he was *blind* to, and *hear* and *understand* the Will and Power of God which before he was *deaf* to; for as Elect man has Reason in him and when that actuated the soul, man was *dead* to those things But by this new life of Faith which will grow strong, and Reason get more weak, than the man sees his infirmities, leprous spots and the strong dye of sin; for the power of regeneration is so great, that it separates Faith from Reason, life from death, or as it were soul from body: FOR as at the Voice of the *first Angel*, "There followed hail and fire mingled with blood, and were cast upon the earth, and the third part of trees was burnt up." *This* that *was* and *is* to be *burnt up*, cast out, or done way, is the spirit and power of Reason in Elect man; for there is only Faith, which is God's *part* of Elect man, that can stand; and by or from Faith Elect man is and will be made *perfect* by regeneration: For this do you *understand*, Elect man may fitly be compared to the leper;

but as *hail, fire, &c. is cast upon the earth*, and Reason is *burnt up* and done away, and human nature greatly refined; in this the *leper* is internal and spiritually *healed!* and Elect man made *perfect* by regeneration, to stand before the LORD GOD of Faith!

AGAIN, this *fallen* human nature God himself took on him and made it alive in Christ, who became a true SON to the power of the Father, and had on him a body of flesh, blood and bone of this earth, that he created in Adam, and as so was *perfect Man*, and had God's justice and Wrath poured out upon him, and was subject to *hunger, thirst, cold, sorrow, and death*, as he had on him *fallen* human nature; and also to the *mock, scourge*, and persecuting power of Reason, &c. which is the spew of death and hell: But in his keeping the law of Faith, and his wading through those mighty powers, *fallen* human nature become so much refined, that he ascended into *Heaven* in a body of this *Earth*, which he will inherit as a glorious *Trophy* in all eternity: ALSO when here, in *His* standing against, and *overcoming* the temptation of the devil, by his *keeping* the law of Faith? His losing himself in *Death* in his own blood under the justice of the *Father!* And *quickening* out of that death unto a new and glorious life of Mercy! Now in this he shewed himself God. As (Mat. xxiv.) he said "Heaven and earth shall pass away, but my word shall not pass away." (John ii.) Jesus answered and said unto them, "Destroy this temple, and in three days I will raise it up:" Again (chap. xi.) said "I am the resurrection and the life he that believeth in me, though he were dead, yet shall he live." Also (chap.vi.) Jesus said, "I am the bread of life – whoso eateth my flesh and drinketh my blood, hath eternal life, and I will raise him up at the last day – the words that I speak unto you they are spirit, and they are life." In this, HE speak as God, and in the spirit and power of the very eternal God: - But, in HIS true *obedience* to the power of the Father; and *worshipping* the Power of the Father which was God! and in his *declaration* and *prophecy* as a *servant* to the power of God and of heaven in the royal priesthood of Faith! and in his *trouble* of soul! And in his *prayer* to heaven for divine assistance, and that the cup might be taken from him, "But not my WILL, but THINE be done!" His *Thanksgiving* to heaven! and his death commending his Spirit into the hands of the Father, which was of *Justice!* In this HE speak as *Man;* and acted as man, and was of the *prophets*, and of his *brethren*, who have his *testimony* in regeneration, which is the *spirit of prophecy*, and WORSHIP GOD!

Moreover, as man took Reason in him at the *fall*, and it became the *Actuator* of man when Faith *died*, so when Faith is *rose* from death to life, and human nature come into act, then, the nature of Reason gets weak in man, by *devils being cast out, &c.* and the soul of man greatly *changed*, and human nature grow strong, and can *hear, see, walk,* and *speak*, for it can *work* the works of Faith; and *declare* the wonderful works of regeneration; and has given to it the spirit of PROPHECY from heaven! Now this *human* nature *God* himself took on him, and worshipped *God* in the SON, and worked the works of Faith unto, and for his glorious kingdom of *Mercy*, and prophecied; and in this, God became a *fellow-servant* with his Elect, and was *of the prophets*, and kept the GRAND COMMANDMENT, *i.e.* "Worship God." – Thus you may see the great and grand *Union* between God and Elect man, by the power of *regeneration*; for what is regenerated is the very *nature Christ took* on himself, then of consequence *it* is regenerated to him, and without *regeneration* there is no union: - FOR by regeneration the *angelic nature, i.e.* the nature of Reason, is *cast out* of Elect man, and done away, and is *cast on*, or center to them, that are under the power of death and hell, and in this God's wrath is *double unto them double* for lightly esteeming and *dispising* the regeneration of Christ, and persecuting them who bore his *word and testimony*: but *human nature* (aforesaid) is so much *refined*, that Faith become the essential soul for salvation and eternal glory! and Elect man will ascend into *heaven* with a body of this *earth*; which he will *inherit* in all eternity, as a glorious token of the power, and mercy of Christ's *regenerating* Elect men, from under the powers of justice, sin, death, and hell!

Again, when Christ *was*, or any of his Messengers in regeneration *are here*, Reason never can *understand* Regeneration, Why? Because they are *dead* to it; hence when a man declares himself a Messenger of CHRIST, Reason thinks to find something extraordinary, for he looks for *pure* Reason, as it was in the *Angel before his fall*, and as man has *fallen* Reason in him, he is subject to infirmities, and sin, which Reason may soon find, then they say he is no Messenger of GOD, for his declaration is contrary to their imagination, then if they find no evil in the man, they will make evil of the man, as they did of the LORD CHRIST, because the language is a *parable* to Reason, yet he finds himself condemned by it: Thus they look for their own *purity*, and their own nature to be made *pure*, and for external *signs*, by which they are lost, for they never can know how Elect men are made *perfect*, and united to God by *regeneration*, until they find it in, and to their own condemnation.

Chap. XIX

AGAIN, as to *casting out devils*: Now the devil always did and will while he can, act against God according to his creation in generation by driving or binding men, &c. from their appointed and proper stay of senses and disposition, as madness *raving*, madness *melancholy, dumbness, sullenness, despair,* &c. and even *infirmity* of body: For when Reason is given up to eager desire, much disappointed, or to grief, not able to according to its will, and have its own way, then his oftimes *drives* the senses beyond the proper stay, and the life is *turned*, and the mass of blood *drowned* with confusion, like unto the sea or great river by a mighty *wind*, being drove over its banks or bounds, and drown a fertile piece of land which bring forth corn or fruit, so drowned in confusion, that its appointed bounds, stay, shores and springs can be of no use, to bring forth its former fertility; which, will produce uncommon and *unclean spirits* in men, which are *devils;* and will *drive* men to uncommon and unclean actions and expressions; and sometimes it comes through the blood in generation, and in this, is *the iniquity of the father visited on the children.*

Further, see Matt. viii. where, "two men met Jesus possessed with *devils* coming out of the tombs exceeding fierce, so that no man might pass that way;" also, Mark v. and Luke viii. speaks of a man, "and he was bound in fetters, and in chains, which he break in pieces, neither could any man tame him, and he was *driven* of the *devil* into the Wilderness, and he was day and night in the mountains, and in the tombs crying and cutting himself." NOW, let the number of men, be as it will, yet it is the same miracle wrought by JESUS to shew forth the *power of GOD*; for one man by this *unclean spirit*, may be drove *many* ways, and to *many* evil and unclean actions, called *devils*, which is the *Legion*, for Legion means no certain number; "And when JESUS came, he commanded the *unclean spirit* to come out of the man, or men."

Again, when this *unclean spirit* or *devil* has full power over the man, it is very eager to keep his possession; yea, when HE appears who hath power over it, this spirit soon *know it,* and also knows he shall be *tormented,* as (Mat. viii.) "Behold they cried out, saying, what have we to do with thee, *Jesus thou Son of God*? Art thou come hither to *torment* us before our time." Therefore the power of Jesus took hold and bound this *strong Spirit* which *was master of the house*, for it *drove* the man or men, to *many* uncommon, evil and *unclean* actions, which are called *Devils*; and this *Spirit*, or spirits, *knew* Jesus had power over it, and to *cast it out*; and it being eager to live, therefore would agree with Jesus, and *besought him* to have another dwelling place, as ver. 31. "So the *devils besought him*, saying, if thou *cast us out*, suffer us to go away into the herd of swine; and he said unto them, go," *i.e.* granted their request: This *herd of swine* was men and women, who owned Moses and the name of *Israel;* and by the letter of *Moses and the prophets* according to their imagination formed a worship, offered prayer and incense, and dedicated it to the *God of Israel*, and made use of his *Name*; and this overtopped all who did not own the Law of Moses; thus Reason by the letter and its own hope was *mounted* high up in imagination, which is this *Mountain*; and they were a superstitious, possitive, stubborn people in their will and way, which they were called *Swine* and their teachers, priest, &c. the *herdsmen* that *fed the swine on this mountain* of imagination.

Those *Gadarenes* by all their lying imaginary *assurance* and self assumed, high conceited power, by their doctrine, could not cure or help the man, "And he was exceeding fierce so that no man might pass that way." And when Jesus came the evil spirit or devil, *knew* him, and *cried out*, for see Mark i. "He was casting out many devils and suffered not the devils to speak, because they knew him;" but this devil or *legion* was suffered to speak, and *cried to Jesus* not to be *tormented,* or if *cast out*, that they may *enter the herd of swine*, yea, this spirit is eager to live and reign in man, so its theme or desire is, that if it be *drove or cast out* from one dwelling, it may enter into and reign in another; therefore when Jesus commanded this *unclean spirit to come out of man* or men, it *died* or ceased acting, and passed away as if it had never been there; and in this way it came out of the man, and quickened in those people, which is the *herd of swine*; for when they saw that Jesus had *cast out the legion*, the *spirit* of fear, dread, anger, dislike, &c. *quickened* and took place in them.

Yea in all their high self-conceit, in worshipping GOD they never could *cast out the devil, nor cure the man*, but when JESUS came he did; then they knew the power and doctrines of Jesus was far above theirs; and the *Spirit* of anger, dislike, fear, dread, &c. took place; *then*, their conceited imaginary power was struck with confusion, and *fled hastily down this hill or mountain, and was choked* in their own *waters*, which was their hope for the waters of Euphrates in the land of Nod is the *river, sea or lake,* that waters the spirit of Reason, which is their *hope*; and through this hope with reading the scripture they go up this *mountain* of imagination; then when the power of GOD is manifest to them, they *run down this mountain, and are choked in this water,* which is their hope.

Those that *fed the swine* called *herdsmen, i.e.* their priest and teachers, *fled and told in the city and country what was done*: "And they came to Jesus and see him that was possessed with the devil, and had the legion, sitting, and clothed, and in his right mind, and were afraid;" – Further, the devil in the man *cryed out*, "What have I to do with thee Jesus, thou son of the most high God." and desired not to be *tormented*; AND when they saw the *legion was cast out*, then the spirit of fear, *torment,* &c. took place in their souls, and produced the same language as the devil in the man before he was *cast out*, praying, *Jesus to depart their coast*, because they would have nothing to do with him, nor be *tormented* by him! But, *the man prayed to be with JESUS*; and Jesus said, "Go and shew how great things God hath done for thee;" thus, the *devil was cast out*, and entered the *herd of swine*, by the powerful miracle of Jesus in number about *two thousand*, which was not *Hogs*, (for they were *unclean*, and their flesh forbidden to be *eat* by the *law* of Moses, and this was amongst the Jews who regarded not keeping of *Hogs*) but man cannot bear the devil to be in himself, so any where else but at home.

Moreover, "And in the *Synagogue* there was a man which had a spirit of an unclean devil, and cryed with a loud voice, saying, let us alone, what have we to do with thee thou Jesus of Nazareth, art thou come to destroy us? I know thee who thou art, the *holy one of God;*" (Luke iv.) Here also the devil *knew* Jesus, and was suffered to speak and say who Jesus was; "And Jesus rebuked him, saying, hold they peace and come out of him."

Again, (Mat. ix.) "As they went out, behold they brought a dumb man possessed with a devil: and when the devil was cast out, the dumb speak; and the multitudes marvelled, saying, it was never so seen in Israel! But the Pharisees said, he casteth out the devils through the prince of devils." *Also*, ch. xii. "Then was brought unto him one possessed with a devil, blind and dumb, and he healed him, insomuch as the blind and dumb, both speak and saw! And all the people were amazed, and said, is not this the son of David? But when the Pharisees heard it they said, this fellow doth not cast out devils but by Belzeebub the prince of devils;" and Luke, xi. Said the same; NOW you may see and know how the devil was *cast out*, and who it *entered into*; for it produced in the Pharisees, lies, anger, murmur, prejudice, wrath, blasphemy, &c. – Also, (Mark ix.) a man brought to Jesus his son, which had a *dumb spirit*, and of-times it had *cast him into the fire*, and into the *water;* and "when JESUS saw that the people came running together *he* rebuked the foul spirit, saying unto him, thou *deaf and dumb spirit*, I charge thee, *come out* of him, and enter no more into him." And (Mat. xvii.) called a *lunatic*, and the spirit which possessed him a *Devil*, THUS you may see how the *devil* acts against GOD, in his generation according to his creation by driving some into madness *raving*, others into madness *melancholy*, and to be *deaf* and *dumb*, and on a sudden shall *start* and drive the being into many evils, even to *destroy* itself! Anon he will become *sullen,* and deaf and dumb to all you say; others he will drive into *despair,* &c. and also to *infirmity* of body, as Luke xiii. Where a woman was bound by the *spirit of infirmity* eighteen years, whom Jesus healed! And when Jesus did any of those glorious *miracles,* the Jews and Pharisees sought something to accuse him with, as ver. 14. "and the ruler of the synagogue answered with indignation, because Jesus had healed on the Sabbath day." Why was it? because the *devil* when cast out, entered into *them*; and Jesus called him *hypocrite,* and told him *what they would do* on the Sabbath day, saying, "and ought not this woman being a daughter of Abraham, whom *satan hath bound,* lo, those eighteen years, be loosed from this *bond* on the sabbath day:' *Thus,* JESUS CAST OUT DEVILS, and restored men to their *right mind,* and disposition; and by those mighty MIRACLES, men, &c. were made *perfect* according to creation and generation: and in this, the FATHER *is glorified in the* SON; for the *Devil* will act against GOD, not only to destroy the *order* of his works, but his *Works* also if possible, and seeing a miracle done in the *kingdom of God* is angry, for *he,* likes miracles done according to his own will and power, for his own kingdom to *shine.*

Chap. XX

THE foregoing miracle was to make men perfect, according to *creation and generation,* that man may have his natural senses and power, to act his natural and lawful business; But there is *spiritual madness,* being *those* in their natural senses, that will receive instruction and power of men to preach CHRIST unto salvation; and he whose dark understanding of the redemption, springs forth into emulation, to fancy he can preach the *Will and Power* of Christ unto salvation, and knows nothing of HIM, but as he fancies, by imagination on the dead letter; others have said, to be "*Assured* of eternal life," and ready to devour him that questions them! Others will *curse* men to eternity, because one's confidence differ from the other! Thus the spirit of emulated Reason drive them into the wild priesthood of Reason which is the *wilderness,* and there they dwell on the *mountains and among the tombs; i.e.* they *dwell* in the letter of the *Prophets,* and of *Christ* and the *Apostles,* and *John Reeve,* which are dead to them, which is their *Tombs*; and they will *garnish those Tombs* because it is their *dwelling;* and can construct it their own *way,* and go out on those *mountains* of imagination, and there rave and roar *amongst those tombs;* and sacrifice themselves according to their imagination, which is *cutting themselves:* and if they are told their

Act, and condition, and that they should not preach the salvation of CHRIST and not *know* it, nor *sent* by HIM, which is their *chains or fetters*, yet they will *break those fetters and chains*, and be so raving that it is a hard thing for a man to *pass* this spirit, which is *the Devil as a roaring lion, seeking whom he can devour.*

On those *Mountains* of imagination in the *Wilderness*, some will have free will, and some free grace given to all, at least to them joined in society of like confidence, but if you leave them it is in danger: some an universal redemption: and some to be saved without works; some by their works: some will own election; and some will have God to be understood one way, and some another: Some will have Christ the second person in the trinity; and the very God; some have him all person and no influence; and some all influence and no person: and some have their *imagination* on the letter to be, the *spirit* and influence of Christ: So they divide the *Godhead* and make a confusion of *Christ's redemption*; and turn his *Record* to their self-serving purpose, either to a *merchandize,* or for a *Weapon of war* against each other; or to cultivate their dark wisdom and *cloak* their evil – thus, this *evil spirit* drive them into the *Wilderness*, and on those *mountains* to seek congregations which is kingdoms, and hold forth, and cry "*lo here* is Christ, and *lo here is* Christ," that a salvation teachers are become as plenty as *Trees in a Forrest.*

Further, on those *mountains in the Wilderness*, and among those *Tombs, are gathered together, the tribes of the whole earth,* and are *in number as the sands of the sea;* and they act on two gigantic hypothesis; the *One* is their *assuming* to themselves the PROMISE *of* CHRIST, made to his Elect, and their *disobedience* to the GIVEN PRIESTHOOD of Reason: and the *other* is their taking the Letter of JESUS or the Gospel, into the *Wild Priesthood* of Reason, and there *teach and preach* (by the *spirit* of wild Reason,) salvation for them through Christ, yet *war against* HIS holy Spirit, HIS Regeneration, and Salvation; now those gigantic powers the Spirit call *Gog and Magog*, who proclaim against, and *War against* CHRIST the KING of FAITH; and this *wilderness* is so great, that every one is become as it were a *god*, and make choice of his own *Way* to Heaven, or at least a *king* to do as he please and excuse himself; for if he do not like one salvation *teacher*, he may go to another, 'till he meet one agreeable to himself, or that will excuse him in his evil doings, and then cry "*Lo, there* is Christ, and *lo, yonder is Christ*; because the spirits of those *teachers*, agree with *their evil spirits*:" Thus they cover the *Doctrine of devils* with the name of CHRIST, and so gather together, and become kingdoms in, and of the *dark Spirit*, and assume to themselves according to their own will, a power to, both naturally and spiritually to protect themselves, which is also *Gog and Magog: Others*, there is that think themselves more wise that *those teachers*, and by reading the *letter* and adding their own *wisdom* to it, which when blended together, then that stand for the living ORACLES of GOD and CHRIST, then *they* also become *kings* of the dark spirit, *but has receive no kingdom,* yet they will try to cultivate their wisdom, and invoke God to own it, and hold argument who wisdom shall be the rule, although it be *contrary* to each other: thus they *war* against each other, and use the Letter as a *weapon:* and if they cannot prevail to *rule* over others they remain *kings* in and of themselves, and are very zealous and dogmatical in *their Way,* and will endeavour to make as many as they can like themselves, and of themselves and regard not the *Law and given priesthood* of Reason; and as to the salvation of Christ, they will have it according to their own will, and go their own *Way* to it: thus the superstitious and emulated *Spirit* of Reason, which is the *devil, drive men into the wilderness,* and on those *mountains* and among those *tombs.*

Moreover, in the *Wilderness* is found, the devil will drive Men into many more different acts, and to transform himself into many different shapes, and act in or under, different colours; therefore when a man is given *birth and Spirit,* to the high covenant of Grace, and taken into the high Mountain of Faith in *regeneration,* and see CHRIST in the glory of *Mercy,* and his royal *Seal to enter his glory of* Mercy, and sent back by Christ, he is a Messenger in *regeneration,* and *come in the spirit and power of CHRIST*; and when he come he found himself in the midst of this *Wilderness;* then when he begin to utter his voice, there is a devil will soon know him, much admire him, call him by his name, and transform himself into pretended friendship with him, in order to *tempt* him, and promise him great things, for he see another *kingdom* coming beside his own, and greater than his own; then if he can tempt the Messenger to render the declaration and language his *Way,* that it may be brought *down,* and *turned* to the liking of those who will presume to *dispose of themselves,* or *kings* of the dark spirit, he will promise him a great congregation, which is a Kingdom in the *Wilderness*; but this cannot be done, because that is serving and worshiping the *devil* and his kingdom; then when the devil cannot prevail, he will go away in *torment.*

Again, there is others that may hear what the Messenger has to say, and may be on his part to vindicate him in what they can, because the spirit of rank prejudice is struck passive or dead in them, and pass away, and it will quicken in others, who will murmur against him, and say they will have no more *messengers of God*; therefore when a Messenger so *Come!* where shall he find Faith? for in this *wilderness* is found *spiritual madness, blindness, deafness, dumbness, captivity,* &c. Yet notwithstanding this *foul spirit* of Reason, which is the *devil,* knows the power of *Christ* in the Messenger, also knows he shall be *tormented;* therefore when the power of Christ, in, or by his Messenger, take hold and *bind this strong spirit,* (who has been *master of the house,* and has ruled the same.) *He* is now commanded *out,* then he will be tormented, amazed, tremble and in great agitation, but cannot get away; then he would agree with the Messenger to transform himself, or do anything if he may live and *reign* in the house, but *No*, he is *bound* and must come *out*! – Then, he will desire to *enter the herd of swine; FOR when man come to know that the letter cannot save him; and to read of another man's faith, and forgiveness, and blessing in former times, that do not belong to him, but the man to whom it was given, and that he never saw or knew the spiritual power of Christ unto salvation, nor what it is to be BORN of WATER, to enter the royal compact and priesthood of Faith, nor heard the Divine natures VOICE of Christ, nor received none of his DIVINE incomes, nor to KNOW any thing of his kingdom, power, and glory, and that he was not born in Heaven above to the knowledge and glory of that kingdom, and how should he claim his inheritance there! But, was born on this earth, in sin, corruption, death, darkness and ignorance! And that all his gathered knowledge of the scripture, is by this DARK RAVING SPIRIT, and that it has DROVE HIM into the WILDERNESS, and on those Mountains, and among the Tombs of the dead! and that HE is as ignorant as he was born into this world! only condemned for what he has done! because it has been all in the wrong!!!* Then, (as aforesaid,) when a man is made *truly* sensible of this, he is become as a *Child!* And in the *right mind* for Regeneration! for then this *raving devil or Legion is cast out and entered the herd of swine!* Now as I said, *Moses* in the time of the Law, forbid the eating of *Swines flesh* nor to *touch* their dead Carcase, because they were *unclean*; (Deut. xiv.) And all men and women that are incapable of Regeneration are *unclean*, to Christ's PRIESTHOOD and KINGDOM, because this *devil* cannot be *cast out,* nor they be *made clean*, for which they are called *swine*; therefore the *devil* when *cast out* of Elect men for regeneration, it is sure to enter this *herd of swine*.

Moreover, *the* Spirit and Power of JESUS is a torment to this *spirit* of Reason; and when the Messenger utters his voice, it torments the earthly heart of man or men, because this spirit cannot flourish in his kingdom as before; then there is a *dread and anger* take place in their souls, and will desire the Messenger to *depart their coast* or company, and say, "they want no more Messengers of God," therefore will have nothing to do with him, nor want to be *tormented* by him: ALSO, when a man or men believe in the same letter, and of the same principles, which in an inhabitant of the same *country*, and is so powerful in his argument, even against their will; for they have long sought to overthrow him, or *chain* him in his argument, but could not, for what *chain* they could put he would *break asunder:* but when the *Spirit* and power of *Christ* come, and *bind this foul Spirit,* and cast it out, then the man is become as a *Child,* and in his *right mind* for regeneration; and when they see this they are struck with wonder, fear, and dislike, then *quicken* and come forth cavilings, anger, envy, prejudice, lies, wrath, cursings, blasphemy, &c. Why is this? because the *Devil when cast out* of Elect Man for regeneration, it *enters the herd of Swine*, and produce this effect; and thus they are and will be *tormented*, and gather together with their dislike, raving, and cursings, and encourage each other therein.

Again, this found *Spirit* of mad Reason will bind the man that if possible he shall be *Blind, Deaf, and Dumb*, to what is said concerning the *kingdom of Christ*; and *drive the man* into the *World*, to seek refuge among men of the world, or into the *Wilderness*, or any where else for life and delight beside the Messenger; for this spirit dearly like to be *master and ruler of the house*, and knows the Messenger, and that the Message is an enemy to him, and that it will *torment* him, though notwithstanding he would transform himself so as to infuse the *Being* to exert himself to act to the contrary; *this* the Messenger also knows; but when *he* is took and *bound* by the power of CHRIST, he will *cry out*, and must *come out* of the man, and will *enter the herd of Swine*; for its theme and desire is to live, and if it be cast out of one dwelling, it may enter into another which is granted to it, and there it will shew itself, although it will endeavour to transform himself: FOR when any one is incapable of regeneration he is dead in the sight of *CHRIST the King of Faith* and the first resurrection for regeneration, and as so must bear their own witness to their own condemnation, and they will *war against the kingdom* of Christ, because they are *tormented* through it, and this the *Devil* knows, whether he is or is not suffered to speak: Also the Messenger will agree with the devil as, if he is very raving and roaring against the Messenger, and is not or cannot be *cast out*, the Messenger will tell him to join the *herd of Swine*, and there live as well, and as long as he can, because he do not care to torment him; and the *Devil* that *is cast out* of Elect man, is suffered to *enter the herd of swine*; for every *foul spirit* will be gathered under justice, and *herd* together, for it is only capable of its own center, *i.e.* death and darkness; and he whose Devil is not *so cast out* for regeneration, will keep him within, let him think what he will to the contrary.

Further, the *Devil* can hardly bare reproof, or even to be questioned, or to be under restrain, or constrain; and when this comes he would drive the Being any where, for to any thing to get from this, and tempt or drive any where from the Messenger, for he dearly like to have *rule* and be *master*: but alas! alas! where will he go to He is within the *Orb or Ring* of Justice, which is *full of eyes*; and although this *spirit* accuse the Messenger and the Elect continually, yet this *accuser is cast down*, and will be no more heard; but if he can procure himself to live for ever, and this world to last for ever as his habitation, he may be under the first *Moses*, but if he die this declaration take him by the *second* Moses! ALSO when any possess this declaration, and the *Devil is not cast out*, he will feign agree with the Messenger to transform himself, and his highest delight of all is to a *Priest* or *teacher*; also in time he will look on his brethren beneath himself, and exalt his own wisdom above theirs, set a great value on himself, and think he deserve homage. This, was the act of the Serpent *Angel* after he was created, which is fully and truly declared by *John Reeve*, for the serpent did not create himself, neither did the *devil in the man* bring the declaration, also the *devil* will drive the man, first to one place and to another, and to one thing and then another, for he cannot get what he wants, then of consequence no *rest*, and his restlessness is plain to be seen! Now this *devil* the Messenger would have out if possible.

Moreover, this *Devil will take man into the Field of Argument, i.e.* when a man profess the declaration, and own the Messenger, yet the *Devil* will be very strong, and full of murmur, and temptation in him at times: Anon he take him into this *Field, i.e.* "whether the Messenger is truly from God or not, or whether he may not be saved by some other Faith, or for why should the doctrine of the Messenger exceed all others, seeing they have the scripture, or as he is a man under God's power, for what cause should not God save him, if he *is* disobedient to the Messenger; and seeing the Messenger is guilty of natural faults, why is *he* not as good a man, and what has he done, that God should not accept him, as well as the Messenger; therefore why should he abide by the Messenger and be so tormented, whereas he may live at ease in the wilderness" But here the Messenger stand in the way, you must kill him to get there: Now in this very *Field* I have known *two*, one's devil has been *cast out*, and the other's has been left to kill the Messenger, for if you curse the Messenger, or trample down the doctrine, you are guilty of spiritual *murder*, and would destroy a Son in *regeneration,* even as Cain did a son in *Generation*, and you may be suffered to join the *herd of swine in the wilderness*: but *Cain's mark* will be *doubled* unto you *double*; AND this I would have you *understand*, when men act together by, with, or according to their imagination on the salvation of CHRIST, and preach, and teach it, as the true *Way,* they invade HEAVEN and *war against Christ's kingdom* of regenerated Faith; and by their blind zeal and wrath, would cut off and destroy *regeneration* which is spiritual *Sodomy*; for as the men of *Sodom* according to their wild desire and filthy nature acted together, whereby they would stop or destroy *Generation,* which is Sodomy; and them who by their imagination act against, persecute, and would cut off and destroy the *regeneration of* CHRIST is spiritual *Sodomy*, and this is "*The Great City* which spiritually is called *Sodom* and *Egypt,* where also our Lord was *crucified*," Rev. xi. 8.

AGAIN as the *first* man Adam took Reason, which is the *Devil* into him at his *fall,* (and so it go on in generation) it needs must be *cast out* by the *second* Man Adam*, who make men* perfect by his Redemption and Regeneration; for God never *planted Reason* in man at his creation, therefore it will be *cast out or rooted up* by regeneration: also this foul *Spirit* or *Devil*, that is to be *cast out* of Elect man, in itself is *Heterogeneous*, and its *Vision* shew the form of many living creatures, such as God never created, as are in a manner, act in a manner, and move in a manner intirely different, according to the pure creation of God: and as I said, must *come out* of Elect man; therefore BLESSED are them that see this *devil or legion*, and to have prayer for him to be *cast out*, and not adore him, as their friend, God, and guide, and be very careful of *self conceit*, spiritual *pride*, and self assumed *wisdom;* and of an *evil eye* to your neighbour, *Envy, Judgment,* and *Condemnation*; and *rejoice* when you see a *Devil cast out* for I had rather see one *devil* or *legion cast out*, and *enter* the herd of Swine, than to see a thousand *join* the herd of swine: and as I said before, where must the Messenger find Faith? Why, truly it must be *rose* from death to life, before he can find the *lively Faith* in regeneration; and that is brought on, and become the *Life and Soul* for salvation, and the Devil is *cast out* and enter the herd of *Swine*.

Further, in the aforesaid *Wilderness,* I have seen (in *Vision*) the *head* of a man separated from his body, and the head could and did *speak*: which did shew the knowledge of some men lay in the *head* and tongue only: also I have seen a strong looking *gigantic man* with people gathered about him, and he made a *Proclamation*, and declaration, as do one mighty king when he declare *War* against another; and he said in his declaration, that whosoever would put themselves under his power, should be *protected*; and when I saw, he appeared *Low*, I went up to see, and he had no *legs* to stand upon, for they were *withered* away, neither could he move from that *place*; and I wondered he should declare he would protect others, and could not *help* himself, nor *move* from that place; also I looked again, and lo his *genitals* was at his breast, at which I wondered greatly and when I was told what I saw, *it was* – this gigantic man in the spirit and power of Reason who in the *wilderness* proclaim against, and *War against* CHRIST the KING of Faith, and his royal *Priesthood*: and his having of no legs, is, he cannot stand before the LORD *GOD* of HEAVEN, nor against his Power; and is not being able to *move* from that place, is, that he is *under* the Justice and Wrath of GOD, and cannot get away; and his Genitals being at his *breast*, is that he beget and propagate a doctrine by or according to his own imagination.

Also I saw the *head* of a man with only his bare *backbone* to it, and that in a *perishing* condition, but the *head* was whole and could *speak,* but his *body* was burned up, and gone by his own wrathful *spirit*, and his own *Acts* and *blasphemy* against God; and I wondered at the disagreeable sight: then there came an order, in that condition he should be *buried*, and there was no *grave dug* but the *earth* rose up and left a *Grave* of itself, in which him and others was to be *buried*, this also is the spirit of Reason, which is *dead* in the sight of GOD;

and by their acts against God, they become *burnt up*, rotten, or *withered away*; yet notwithstanding there will that of them remain, to bear and *speak* their own witness to their own condemnation, and they will be buried in the *second* death in *Chaos* under Justice *without the hands* of man.

AGAIN, *In this wilderness*, I have seen in *Vision*, Ducks with *serpents* heads, which was very *hurtful*; and *Dogs* of different colours, and all with *wings*; and on occasion could transform themselves; and many more different creatures, but *heterogeneous*; and the skeleton and half skeleton of creatures who had their time and action in the *Wilderness*, which is all according as the Spirit of Reason *drive* or infuse men to different acts:

ALSO I have seen the *Waters* of Reason, and *Fish* in those waters, which appeared very fine; and I looked and behold I saw the *fountain* from whence those waters came, and it was *filthy*, and I marvelled to see such *fish* in the stream; then I was told they were *serpents*. And very pernicious, although they bore the form, and appearance of *fine Fish*: and I also saw the *stream* could be *stopped*, or made *filth* at any time, from its *Fountain*, which is, "the *great river* Euphrates in the land of Nod;" and if Elect men take a fish of those *Waters*, they will be sure to find him a serpent.

Therefore every *foul Spirit* will be gathered to its center; and the *Devil* when *cast out* of Elect man, will *enter the herd of swine*; and in this God's wrath will be *doubled* unto them; and although they gather together, and *war against* the *holy Spirit of CHRIST and his holy Regeneration*, yet "strong is the Lord God of Heaven who judgeth them." And will surely *visit* them with the *plagues* of his Justice; for when the *angel in justice* open to them his BOOK of *Justice and Death*, they will fall hastily from their *Mountain* of Imagination into the *lake* of God's justice and *wrath*, and there they are *choked, and perish!*

Chap. XXI

AGAIN, When the serpent Angel was created, he was an Angel of *light*, and bore the name of CHERUBIM, because he came forth *pure*, by and according to the purity of GOD's creation; but when he rebelled against GOD, and was *cast down* from HEAVEN, then he bore the name of *Devil*, serpent, &c. And in him was the *Root or Essence* of Darkness and *Evil* in active life, that was suffered to go into Generation, and act against *God,* his *Children,* his *Works,* and *Kingdom* of FAITH; and when he was transmuted into Eve and Adam, he became a very tyrannical and troublesome inhabitant in their, and their *Children's* souls, even unto this day, and as aforesaid must be *cast out* for as he was transmuted into *Vessels* of Faith in active life, he needs must be *cast out* of them *Vessels* in active life and go to its own center, *i.e.* the herd of Swine, and in this is every foul Spirit gathered together, and all in active life; then of consequence it is by or from Faith which fell in Adam, which is raised from death to life that Christ gather his kingdom: Therefore as I said, the *Devil* or *Legion*, which is of the *Serpent* Angel is cast out of Elect man, for he to be in his *right mind* for regeneration; he then is *become as a child*; and then the *Virgin daughter* is, or in God's time will, be born of the womb or seed of Faith, to the *Promise* and union of CHRIST*;* and is *a child for the kingdom of Heaven*; and a *Bride* to the royal BRIDGEGROOM of Faith.

Further, when the Disciples asked Jesus *who is GREATEST in the kingdom of Heaven,* Jesus called a *little Child and set him in the midst of them,* as Mat. xviii. And said, "Verily I say unto you, except ye be converted, and become as *little Children* ye shall not enter the kingdom of Heaven: whosoever therefore shall humble himself as this *little Child,* the same is GREATEST in the kingdom of Heaven." Now, here you may see, what state a man must be brought to, and *converted,* to be made anew by regeneration; for he must part with all his former wisdom which is of Reason by Reason being as it were *pounded in a Mortar,* and cast away, and become as a *little Child* at the feet of Jesus, to be taught of him, and born to him, to enter his kingdom of mercy. For as the LORD GOD OF HEAVEN parted with what he enjoyed, which was the glory of justice, and was born of Faith a *Babe* into this world, to redeem and gain his new kingdom, which is the glory of mercy, even so must Elect man part with what he *possess*, and be *humbled,* and born of Faith in *spirit* to *follow* Christ to enter his kingdom; - and this Virgin daughter is a *Child* of Faith, and *born* to the promise and union of Christ: (v. 5.) *Jesus said* "and whoso shall receive one such *little Child* in my name receiveth ME:" *Because* the union is so great between Christ and this *infant* daughter of Faith, that the Messenger of Christ would rather err in offending of him, than err in offending of this *Virgin* daughter of Faith, why? because she is *born* of Faith, and to the works of Faith in regeneration, and IS and WILL BE the *pure Bride* to the royal BRIDGEROOM of FAITH: v. 10. "Take heed that ye despise not one of those little ones, for I say unto you, that in Heaven their Angels do always behold the face of my father which is in Heaven," *i.e.* to this *Child or Children* of Faith is given a *censer with incense, i.e.* Faith so *born* is the Censer, and its *prayer* the incense, which ascend up to Heaven before GOD, for divine wisdom and assistance; and this *new Life* of Faith, which flow forth with *Wisdom, Obedience, Power, and Prayer* is the Angel or *Angels* of Faith (that is in the compact and priesthood of Faith, which is the *nether Heaven* of Faith) and *behold the face of the Father.* NOW, the *face of the Father* is the power and glory of the Father, which is of justice, and the *Will of the Father.* is what *Christ came to do, i.e.* the works of Faith under the justice of the Father; and this *Child* or *Virgin* daughter of Faith by divine assistance will *follow Christ* in those works of Faith, under the justice of the Father; and in this they are so united to CHRIST as to be his *Brother, Sister, and Mother.* (Mat. xii.) So of such *Children or Babes* is found the fruits of Faith, and is the CHURCH and UNION of CHRIST! So woe! woe! unto them that persecute and war against those *Children*; for they are the church of Christ to inherit the *kingdom of Heaven*; It had been better for them that they had never been born, or died a child, than live *to persecute* or *offend* those children, v. 6. "But whoso shall offend one of those *little ones* which believe in me, it were better for him that a millstone were hanged about his neck, and that he were drowned in the depth of the sea," *i.e.* if this had been done when he was a child he would have been raised a *Cherubim to glory*, and have been of that heavenly *Host*; but now he is left *desolate* to be swallowed up by death and hell, let him set what value he please on himself: BUT *offences will come* and woe unto them by whom they come, for Reason will open his *Tombs* of death, or the *Tombs of the dead* against the *living in Christ*, and appear with his dislike, exceptions, demurs, murmurs, complaints, anger, lies, wrath, blasphemy, persecution, &c. And like unto a ravenous serpent, cormorant, or cannibal, would devour the *Child of Faith*, and destroy the kingdom of Christ, was it in his power; therefore you are to *watch* this devil and *tempter*, for he will entangle you in his kingdom if possible; so whatever is offensive to the *Kingdom* of Christ put away, let it be ever so near or dear to you.

AGAIN, *Regeneration* begin by Faith being raised from Death to life, or the *Virgin daughter being born* from its Womb or Seed, and this is a *new Life* which Elect man never before enjoyed; and this *new Life*, by the mighty power of the regeneration of Christ, is to become the essential soul for salvation and its life, nature, sight, desire, and acts, is contrary to that of Reason, and *singular* of itself, because it is of and for the *Kingdom* of Christ; and by this *single eye* of Faith, Elect men must enter the kingdom of Heaven: BUT as Elect man has Reason in him which is an *enemy* to Faith and the kingdom of Christ, and will devour the *Virgin* daughter of Faith, was it in his power, even as a sharp frost will devour a young beautiful tender plant, by his strivings in and for his own kingdom, and setting forth the value and necessity of his acts, his consequence, with his fears and outcries, if he should fall in his kingdom, for he dearly likes to be strong therein, that he may act against the *regeneration of Christ*: NOW, here you may see the *Eye* of Faith, and the eye of Reason, and *two kingdoms* striving in one man; but the *right Eye* is of *Reason,* because man was born into this World with and to that *light* and wisdom, which is of and for this World; but the *eye* of Faith is not of and for this World, but *of and for, CHRIST's* kingdom of Mercy and Glory; therefore this *Eye* or *Light* conveys to, and centers in *Mercy and Light* but *Eye* or *Light* of Reason conveys to and centers in, Justice and Death: therefore Jesus says, and "if they *right* eye offend thee, pluck it out and cast if from thee; and if they *right* hand offend thee cut it off, and cast it from thee, for it is profitable for thee that *one of thy Members* should perish, and not that thy whole body should be cast into hell," *i.e.* this *eye, hand or foot* is the sight, desire and strivings of Reason, in, and for his own kingdom; and of consequence will be *offensive* to Faith in regeneration, because of the opposition of their lives, natures, desires, and kingdoms; and it must be *plucked up, cut off, and cast away,* for it is impossible for Elect man to enter the kingdom of Heaven with the spirit of Reason in him: therefore this fallen Reason, which is the Devil, must be cast out of Elect man by regeneration, and go to its own center, *i.e.* the herd of *Swine*; and where this cannot be done man must be *cast away,* with *two* eyes, hands, and feet, as he was born into this world, which is a desire and power to beget his own likeness in generation, and power of action in this life, which was mostly against God.

Moreover regeneration is so *singular* of itself, that it make man *anew* for Christ! therefore the *old* man must be put *away,* and the *new* man *taken,* and be made by this *new life* (which is the *Virgin* of Faith) and the divine assistance from HEAVEN! For *the Life of this Virgin Daughter is pure! and flow as supernatural, or rather celestial fire, which transcend the finest crystal or diamond! her life is wholly bent on the love, works, union, mercy, and salvation of Christ, and his kingdom! and her sweet flow of joy is one center, which is in her brethren and Christ, and thanksgiving to Heaven! and is always longing for and rejoicing at the divine incomes of Christ! and is of meekness, innocence, and harmless as the lamb or dove! and is of love, mercy, charity, and forgiveness! she has a strong WATCH over Reason, and will not hearken to him, nor have any thing to do with him or his kingdom! She has an eager desire to face her own Angel which is Christ! and bear him a spiritual Son in regeneration! She is born to sorrow under the justice of the Father, and there tremble at the power of God! and will follow Christ in the works of Faith, under the justice of the Father! For finding herself in a fallen state under the power of Justice and Death, her desire is to go through that to mercy and life! She is obedient to God, and will worship God and Christ! She is of long suffering, and can bear oppression, temptation, persecution and the scourges of Reason, for Christ and his kingdom! She has Prayer which ascend to Heaven for divine assistance! and Patience to wait the Lords leisure! And in true obedience submit to the will and power of God! Also prays that she may not be left here in Hell, but by the divine assistance of Christ be brought through great tribulation: now this is the pure lamp of Faith, which burn crystal and fair in the new born Elect, and is the sweet saving incense which ascend to Heaven, for divine assistance and WILL be brought through great tribulation, and come forth a pure BRIDE, meet for marriage with the LAMB.* NOW this *new Life* being in the *new born* Elect, it will grow strong, and greatly change and *refine* the man; for as Faith grows strong, Reason will grow weak by Devils being cast out; for when the soul has tasted of the divine incomes, and assistance of CHRIST, he is in a longing condition, and state of prayer after more, and his affections is wholly set on the *kingdom of Christ,* and will be made able to bear the insults of Reason; also Reason may at times *cloud* the man, and *drive* him concerning his will and consequence, or like the *Raven* after the carrion of the earth; and men shall be in agitation, like unto *a troubled Sea in a great storm*; then this Virgin of Faith go into her *ark* or *Bower,* for she will have nothing to do with Reason, as I said, but when the *Storm* is over, and it become *Calm,* then like the *Dove,* she will come forth into act, and sweetly shine as the *crystal Lamp of Faith;* and it is by this *new Life* and the divine assistance of *Christ,* that man is made anew by regeneration; for this new life become the *essential soul,* for salvation: thus you may see man must become as a *Child* and be *born again* for regeneration, to enter the royal compact and Priesthood of Faith, and *into* the works, love, mercy, union, and church of Christ; and the *Virgin Daughter* of Faith has no other *life,* or joy but in Christ, and her brethren, which is HIS *Church,* and there *she* will center and come!

Chap. XXII

WHEN the Pharisees came and *tempted* Jesus, saying, "is it lawful for a man to put away his wife for every cause" (Mat. xix.) *and he answered and said unto them,* "have ye not read, that he which made them in the beginning, made them male and female;" because the LORD GOD OF HEAVEN created them of this *earth,* and breathed into them the *breath of life* which was his own divine nature, and as so, they were the *Children* of God, faithful and true, and came forth pure, by and according to God's creating the *Man and Woman,* which was joining his own *divine* nature to earthen *vessels,* which animated the Man and Woman; therefore they were *bone* of each others bone, *flesh* of each others flesh, and *life* of each others life; than of consequence they had great union with each other, also with the Lord God their creator; (because their lives was of him;) ALSO they were created *male and female* for generation, that by their great union in generation, that Faith as *a grain of mustard seed,* which was *sown into this earth* (in them) should come forth a generation of Elect men (who are of *Adam*) to raise the kingdom of Faith unto God and Christ: and *said,* "for this cause shall a man leave *Father and Mother,* and shall cleave unto his *Wife,* and they twain shall be one flesh: wherefore they are no more twain but one flesh, what therefore God has joined together, let no man put asunder," for the Lord God created them, and *joined them together* for generation, and blessed them, and said unto them, "Be fruitful, multiply, and replenish the earth," that in and by generation, they should raise up the *fruits* or *children* unto God, v. 7. they say unto him, "Why did Moses then command to give a writing of divorcement and to put her away?" (Deut. xxiv.) "He saith unto them, Moses because of the hardness of your hearts, suffered you to put away your wives, but from the beginning it was not so;" Because in that pure *union,* and blessing God created, united and placed them for generation, as I said, but in steps the *serpent Angel, i.e.* the devil, between the *Man and Woman,* and *sows* his discord, strife, and contention, with his whole diabolical nature, and disturbed, or rather destroyed their united happiness, but he never could destroy their union in generation, for that God would have go on although in trouble and sorrow: AND Reason is very fond of a Law or Precedent, but not for to rule over him, or that he may be punished thereby, but that he may rule over and punish others; and Moses suffered this in his time, but it was for the *hardness of hearts*; than of consequence to their own condemnation: therefore I would have you look at the *pure ACT* of God in the beginning, and from that learn, and also to know and remember, who was the first that stept in between *Man* and his *Wife,* and caused discord, and then you may know who and what nature causes discord, and parts them even to this day: v. 9. "And I SAY unto you, whosoever shall put away his wife, except it be for fornication, and shall marry another, committeth adultery: and whoso marry her which is put away doth commit adultery;" Here Jesus speak to Reason in answer to their tempting him; and if Reason do so, put *away his wife,* he do it in wrath, then at the same time let him be sure he is intirely clear of evil himself, and do so keep himself, otherwise it is to his own condemnation. So I would not have *you* seek justification after the manner of Reason; if you do you must take

Reason's *Lot* and consequence, but learn how it was in the *beginning*, for *Adam* did not put away his *Wife* for *fornication*, but she repented of her evil, and was forgiven.

Further, Jesus did not come to give a *carnal Commandment* but for regeneration, and this verse tends to regeneration; for as I have said, Elect men are born into this world, with the eye of Reason, and to the wisdom of this world, because Reason is the life of man, and spiritually is called the *Wife* of man, because so closely united to man, that all his desires, acts, fruits, effects, &c. brought forth by man is of reason, except some good acts forced out of him by the angel of Reason, for Reason is the *life*, and spiritual *wife* of man, and so closely united to man, as to make but one living and dying Being without regeneration: THEREFORE when the *Voice* of Jesus, in his Messenger come for regeneration, it centers to the womb of faith, give new wisdom, begets the prayer of obedience, in Faith to the declaration, and with an humble and patient soul, wait the Lord's leisure, then in God's time the *Virgin* daughter of Faith will be born which is a new life in the soul, and this new life which is Faith, the man must hearken to and abide by, because this is the *Life* and spiritual *Wife* of Faith, whereby man will truly understand the declaration, and the mysteries of GOD and CHRIST in his redemption and salvation, and will follow Christ in the works of Faith in regeneration, and by his fruits be found worthy of Christ for Salvation! ALSO Faith was the life of man in creation, but they hearkened to the voice of Reason, then it *died* or became *inactive*; and Reason took possession and became their *Life* and actuator, and so it go on in *Generation* until it is rose from that death to a new life for *Regeneration*; and by this *new Life* which is given to man for regeneration, he is taken into the royal *Priesthood* of Faith, and greatly refine him by the *Works* of Faith and regeneration, and unites him to Christ, and he is made *flesh of CHRIST's flesh! Bone of HIS bone! Spirit of HIS Spirit! and Life of HIS Life*; by the strong *Union* and *Marriage* with Christ! Thus you may see how Elect man is made *anew*, and the strong *Union* of Faith with Christ in, and by regeneration; and it is this *Virgin* daughter of Faith that is worked on for it, which man must hearken to, and abide by as a *Wife*, to bring forth the *fruits of Faith* unto Christ in regeneration: BUT Reason cannot *understand* the mystery of God in regeneration, nor *inherit* the kingdom of Christ, therefore would force itself to commit *fornication* with it, commit *adultery* with, and *adulterate* the Declaration of the Messenger, lead the soul astray, poison and corrupt the man; so the Elect must *put away this Wife* of Reason, because it is for *fornication, marry and cleave unto the wife* of Faith, to bring forth the *fruits* of Faith unto God and Christ; for regeneration must come forth entirely *Pure*, faithful and true; so the Elect do not commit *adultery* in putting away the wife of Reason, and marrying the *wife* of Faith: And *whoso marrieth her which is put away, doth commit adultery, i.e.* some of the Seed of Reason will come and transform themselves into the declaration, then the spirit of Reason will rise into emulation, and say it belong to them, and claim their inheritance there; and by the *foul Spirit* of Reason *marry* themselves to the declaration; and with the *Spirit* of Reason preach it up, and set if forth, and excuse themselves according to their *Will* and *Way*, which is of Reason, and by this new wisdom, and *self assumed* authority, this *spirit* of emulation will go forth in judgment over others, and say his understanding is great concerning the *doctrine*, and at the same time all in the wrong! for Reason cannot enter the royal priesthood of Faith: NOW this *Spirit* of Reason is the *Wife* the Elect must *put away*; and the Seed of Reason will take this erroneous *Spirit* of emulation, embrace, and marry it; and with it commit *adultery*, or adulterate the declaration of the Messenger: and this is the true spiritual meaning of Christ in this verse, which tends to regeneration, (as aforesaid) for ver, 10. "His Disciples say unto him; if the case of the man be so with his wife, it is not good to marry, but he said unto them, all men cannot receive this saying, save them to whom it is *given*." Because no man can *understand* the power, works, and mystery of Faith in regeneration, and its mystical union with CHRIST, except it be *given* him from HEAVEN; but they may understand a *carnal commandment*: ver. 12. JESUS said, "For there are some eunuchs, which were so born from their mother's womb; and there are some eunuchs, which were made eunuchs of men; and there be eunuchs which have made themselves eunuchs for the kingdom of Heaven sake, he that is able to receive, let him receive it:" Those *Eunuchs* for the *kingdom of Heaven*, is him or them, that hath no desire, propensity, capacity, or power, to listen to, and unite with, or be concerned with the spirit of Reason, to beget, give birth, propagate, give suck, or maintain, any false declaration, assertion, doctrine, works, or error concerning the kingdom of *Christ*, or false worship to *God*: Now CHRIST was a spiritual *eunuch* and was *so born into the world*, because he was born of Faith, and unto God to keep the *Law of Faith*, work *redemption*, and bring in *regeneration* to himself, that the Elect may be regenerated to *Him:* AND when the *Virgin daughter of Faith* is born of its womb or Seed, or rose to active *Life*, then Elect men will be *refined* by the power of Faith, and the divine assistance of CHRIST; and by devil's being cast out, and *putting away their wife* Reason, then they have a *strong WATCH* over Reason; and in time, will *lose* their spiritual properties, or power of acting with Reason, to beget, bring forth, or maintain any false or erroneous doctrine, or worship concerning the *Kingdom of God or Christ*: Now this is the spiritual *Eunuch*; and thus are *Eunuchs made* for the kingdom of Heaven: But natural *Eunuchs* are made through the pride, desire, and barbarity of men; and them that are so born of their *mother's womb* is by a defect in generation; but regeneration is intirely *perfect, pure, faithful and true*: THUS, you may see what it is *to put away a Wife* according to creation and *Generation*; and what it is to put away a *Wife* according to, and for *regeneration*, and how those *spiritual Eunuchs are made* in, and by regeneration, for *the sake of the kingdom of Heaven; therefore BLESSED* are them that can receive this, and enter into the works of Faith; for those things are done by the mighty power of regeneration, to and for the kingdom of Christ, which is the glory of Mercy.

AGAIN, as I said, *Man* must become as a *child* to enter the kingdom of Heaven; for when they brought unto Jesus *little Children* the he should *put his hand* on them, and *they were rebuked by his disciples*; but JESUS said, "Suffer *little Children* and forbid them not to come unto ME, for of such is the kingdom of Heaven: and he laid his hands on them, and departed thence." This also shew the necessity of regeneration; for Elect men must become as a *Child*, for the *Virgin* daughter of Faith to be spiritually *born*, who is a *Child* of Faith unto Christ; *then* he put his *hand* which is his power *on it*, and raise it up in regeneration for his kingdom of glory: ALSO by the mighty works of redemption, JESUS gained to himself the *Power* of the resurrection: therefore the Child of Reason that dies in minority will be raised to glory; for as this Child of Reason died in *minority*, the angel in justice never took place in the soul, and as so, was never charged with the law, so will be raised a Cherubim to glory: for the children of Reason that die in *minority*, and the *natural Ideot* which is same thing in consequence will be raised *Cherubims* to glory, to compose that *heavenly Host*, or glorious *order* of cherubims in Heaven above in all eternity: THEREFORE *little Children* even of Reason are *suffered to come*, and do *come unto CHRIST,* and he *put his hand on them*, and raise them *Cherubims* to glory: Thus you may see one *Hand* of Jesus is on the *child* of Faith to *raise* it up in regeneration, and make it like unto himself; for his *kingdom of Faith* in mercy and glory! And his other *Hand* is on the *Child* of Reason to *raise* it, a Cherubim to glory: But none of the Seed of Reason but children, or them of that state or condition which is the natural *ideot*, can enter the kingdom of Heaven.

Moreover, the Elect all live to *manhood* for regeneration, therefore they must become as a *Child* for the *Virgin daughter*, or child of Faith to be spiritually born, and taken into the royal priesthood of Faith; and this *Virgin daughter* which is born of the womb or *Seed* of Faith, being in *active* life and espoused to CHRIST in spirit, has prayer to HIM; and can ask divine wisdom and assistance of HIM; but the Seed of Reason is incapable of regeneration, and the life of Faith cannot be brought forth in them; so they are as incapable to ask assistance of Christ in regeneration, as a dead man is to ask assistance of one that is living; but by this *Virgin daughter*, and the divine assistance of

Christ, the Elect are brought on in regeneration under the *Justice of the Father*, and from one *Mansion of the Father* to another; and the higher you go, the more you know, and *tremble* at the *power* of God, and become a *Child* to it, and a *Servant* to Faith in the Elect his *Brethren*: Now such a one is GREAT in the *kingdom of Heaven*, and this union of Faith is the CHURCH of CHRIST, for when *two or three are met* in, and for this *union* of Faith, and ask instruction from Heaven it *will be* granted; but when the seed or spirit of Reason transform themselves into the declaration, and set a value on himself for this great knowledge, and by the *spirit* of emulation question and judge the *Brethren*, such a one is not in the *kingdom of Heaven*, for he never has become as a *Child*.

Chap. XXIII

ACCORDING to my former intention, I shall write a little concerning the *dispute* about the Body of *Moses*, then of consequence must declare Moses's *Body* and its *burial place*: Now as I have ofttimes declared, the Cherubim was created under the Law of Reason, and in reference to God's divine justice; and there was a part, or *quality* of justice given to him, or centered in him through the *pure Act* of creation of the LORD GOD of HEAVEN, that whenever he broke the pure law he was created under, that in him would become a quantity sufficient to act on him and cast him down from Heaven, and from the presence of God: ALSO he was created on purpose to fall into generation, therefore was suffered to break that Law and *fall* from Heaven to this earth; but this *understand*, although he broke the *pure Law* he was created under, he never could break the *pure Justice* of that law, but let him do what he will, or go where he can, he will take it with him intirely *pure*, as it took place through God's creation; and when he was transmuted into flesh, he brought that *Law* and *Justice* into this world, which has continued to act on the soul of man to this day.

Moreover, when he was born into this world, be bore the name of *Cain*; and when he grew to manhood, this *pure Justice* took place in his soul, and he was charged with the *Law*; and this *pure justice* in the soul is the *Cherubim and flaming Sword that turns every way, to keep the Way of the TREE OF LIFE*: Then when he slew his brother *Abel* this *Cherubim and flaming sword* acted in the soul, and the *life* of

Cain was arraigned before *him*, and Cain communed with *him* and called him *Lord*, for he acts as lord to Reason, because he is the *Cherubim and flaming sword*, or the *internal Angel* in justice, Angel of the Law, or *angel of the lord*, for he acts in the power of the *Lord*, and is faithful and true, to do his *Will*: Thus the *Law* of Reason, and that *justice* was brought into this world, by this *Cherubim* that fell from Heaven; and it being *internal* in man, it will instruct man in a *Law*, and *Justice*, although Reason would run wild from it.

Further, *Moses* was inspired by the Lord God of Heaven, at the head of that, his *Attribute*, with the wisdom of this cherubical Law the angel was created under, that he may external and public give it forth to Reason; so Moses was the *anointed Cherubim* by his inspiration and was the *external* Angel of the covenant of the law; and this *Cherubim and flaming sword* is the *internal* Angel of the law; therefore when Moses uttered, and gave forth the Law *external* to Reason, there was the law *internal* in Reason, not only to witness to it, but also close with it; and when he administered justice by God's command, there was also justice in Reason, not only to witness to it but also close with it; and he also gave forth a priesthood that God's Justice should be *stayed* on them, and if they brought in their offerings to attone, according to that given priesthood, justice was stayed on them, and if disobedient to it, *plagues* was sent them; this also centered to, and in the life of Reason: Thus Moses had life to work upon; and his declaration and works, centered to and in the life of Reason, as well as his external written record, that is left to instruct Reason.

AGAIN, when this cherubim or serpent angel, transmuted himself into Eve, and so by nature into Adam, his infusion was so great, as to fill them so full of his own nature which is Reason, as to become their acting life; and they was subject to its law and the justice of that law, and that given priesthood because Faith which was their life, hearkened to Reason, so broke its own law, then for that *died*, and Reason took possession, animated and actuated them; and they was subject to its passions, law, &c. as aforesaid; AND although Reason was so powerful in *Adam* and *Eve*, and *was* and *is* in their children the Elect by generation, yet *understand*, it was and is but temporary or superficial in them, because the LORD GOD did not place it there in his creation; but they took it through and by temptation, and God raise Faith from death to a new life and make Elect men anew by regeneration.

Moreover, Moses was the son of Adam, in the generation of Faith, and was an Elect of God for regeneration; yet he had Reason so powerful in him, that he was very capable of the cherubical inspiration; and the *Lord* made him a *God* to Pharoah, which is a God to Reason, (Exo. vii.) and he gave forth a law and priesthood, and executed God's justice, and judgment, in a body of *flesh* and person of Man inspired and instructed so to do by the LORD GOD of HEAVEN; so Moses acted on the life of Reason, and his declaration and acts centered to and in the life of Reason, and there it abode and was BURIED! for Moses being an Elect man of God for regeneration, Faith was rose from death to life in him, and he was taken into the royal priesthood of Faith, where he greatly communed with God, concerning the *great mystery* and works of Faith, the *kingdom* of Christ, and salvation of the Elect; and he prophecied of Christ, and by this new life which was Faith, he WAS made anew by regeneration, and it became his soul for salvation; for with it he ascended into Heaven to the *Glory of the Father*, and was united to God for Christ: THEREFORE the angelic nature of Moses, *i.e.* Reason, the cherubical inspiration to give forth the law, and that priesthood, the administration of that justice, and the *law* itself is but the BODY of *Moses*; because he gave it forth in public. In a *Body* of flesh and *Person* of man; and it centers to, and is *buried in,* the *Soul* of the Seed of Reason! and when he died, or was translated on *mount Nebo* in the Land of *Moab*, all Reason with its Law, &c. was cast or struck out, and centers to the *Souls* of the Seed of Reason which is the *herd of Swine*, and there he was and is buried, and that is his *burying* PLACE, for he ascended into Heaven with a life or soul of regenerated Faith: HERE you may see how soul and body of Elect men are separated by regeneration; for as I said, *Adam* and *Eve* took Reason into them by or through temptation, and although they, and the Elect their children was, and are so much troubled with it, and must be subject to its law and priesthood, and the angel of that Law; yet it is but *temporary* or superficial in them, and is but the *body* of Elect men, for they are troubled with it, only in this life, and spiritually is called the *Body* of the Elect; for Faith in them is rose from death to life, and brought on in regeneration to Christ, and it become their *Life* and *Soul* for salvation; and by or with it they ascend into Heaven, and there live and reign with Christ in the glory of mercy in all eternity; and Reason with its law, &c. is *cast out*, and go to its own center, or home, as I said before.

NOW, as to the *dispute* concerning the *body* of Moses (as in *Jude*.) "Yet Michael the archangel when contending with the devil, he disputed about the *Body* of Moses, durst not bring against him a railing accusation, but said the Lord rebuke thee." This *Michael the archangel* WAS and IS *Christ*, because he is the *Angel* of Faith, from whence Faith proceeded in creation, and it is gathered to him again by regeneration to make up his grand *Host* and Kingdom of regenerated Faith in his glory of mercy: This *contention* or *dispute*, was when *Christ was tempted of the Devil*, and the *Devil* that tempted him was a *Man* of Reason, who then well understood the *Law of Moses,* and that given priesthood of Reason, and had a ruling power therein, and was very able to *tempt;* for he admitted Jesus to be the *Son* of God, as Jesus said he was, then he tempted him to *bow down and worship* in and according to the law of *Moses,* and *there* do his miracles according to the will and pleasure of the *devil his tempter,* so would have had the SON OF GOD come into Reason's kingdom and rule over it, and crown that by his becoming a Son: And his taking him to the *holy City,* was shewing him the *given Priesthood* of Reason, where men must flee for *refuge*; and the *pinacle of the temple* was the *stay* of God's justice on the soul of man, which is the *height of* that *given Priesthood*; and the *exceeding high mountain* was the cherubical inspiration, which is the *kingdom of this world*; and would have given Jesus great rule and power in it, if he would but hearken to him, for the *power* of the tempter was, that is *Law and Priesthood* came from GOD by the *man Moses,* and Jesus being the *Son of God,* why should he not bow down to it, seeing it was of God? and could come to no harm, seeing *his angels had charge concerning him*? Here, in this *the devil rebuked* Jesus, but *brought no railing accusation against him*; but Jesus answered him from the book of *Moses,* which was given to Reason, (as I wrote Ch II.) and brought no railing accusation against the *devil*: NOW the law and that priesthood, with all its forms and ceremonies was given to Reason as their *inheritance* and Reason will contend for it, but it is only the *body* of Moses, and it may well be called the *Body* of Moses, for Moses is afcended into Heaven, with a life and soul of regenerated Faith, and left the law, &c. in and with Reason here below.

Moreover, the Kingdom of JESUS *was* and *is* of Faith, therefore he came on the *prophecy* of Faith in regeneration, (that stood before him and prophesied, when he was in the condition of the *Father,*) and he kept the *Law of* Faith, redeemed his Elect, and regenerated them to himself; for the nature of regeneration is to divide Faith from Reason, and the *Soul* from the *Body* of the Elect; for by regenerated Faith, Elect men are made *anew,* and it become their life and soul for salvation, and for CHRIST; *therefore* the Reason in *Moses,* and the *Law,* with all its consequence that he gave forth to Reason is but the BODY *of Moses,* and it belong to Reason which is the *Devil*: But his *Soul* which is regenerated Faith, with which he ascended into Heaven, that belong to JESUS, and it is even so with all the Elect! but do you *understand*, while you have Reason in you, you must be subject to its *Law,* &c. although but the *Body* of Moses: THEREFORE this was the *dispute or contention*; the Devil for the *Body of Moses,* which is the *Kingdom of Reason,* and CHRIST for his own *Kingdom,* which is Faith in redemption and regeneration; neither must he hearken to the *Devil* or take his kingdom; and when the devil came again after he first tempted him, then he brought *railing accusations, persecutions,* &c. even unto death; but CHRIST *overcome,* and the VICTORY is his own! and he is *faithful and true!* Yea, he brought in eternity! and he has left the *Body* of Moses *buried* in the Seed of Reason: and this is the *Cherubim and flaming sword*, or the *internal Angel* in justice, is the *internal Moses* to whom the Seed of Reason, *i.e.* the *devil* is left, and as so they bear their own witness to their own condemnation.

Further, (Rev. xii.) "and there was war in Heaven, Michael and his angels, fought against the dragon, and the dragon fought and his angels." This *Michael* is Christ, who is the royal *Angel*, and KING of Faith; and his *angels* are the Elect, who work the works of Faith, and *follow him*; and this *Heaven* is the nether *Heaven* of Faith, which is the royal priesthood and compact of Faith, where *Christ stood* to work the works of redemption; and when Faith is rose from death to life, in the Elect, *there*, they are *taken*, and did and do work the works of Faith in and for regeneration, and *follow Christ*; AND the *Dragon* is the is the spirit of Reason which fell from Heaven in the serpent Angel, and was afterward born Cain in generation, from whence has proceeded a great and mighty Generation, and *many* has become kings of the dark spirit to *war against* God and Christ; and when Christ was here one or more that had power began to persecute Christ and his saints; and those of the same spirit which are his *Angels* assisted in the *War* and *persecution,* and continue to this day to the utmost of their power; nay the spirit of Reason in the Elect will *war against* the spirit of Faith in them: But CHRIST *has overcome the dragon and his angels*, and the Elect by his divine assistance has and will *overcome* them; and *no place* in Heaven can be *found* for the *dragon and his angels*; and they are also *cast* from the nether *Heaven* of Faith, which is the priesthood of Christ, because incapable of regeneration, for which they are angry, and will *war and blaspheme* against Christ and his kingdom; ver. 9 " and the great dragon was cast out, that old serpent called the devil; and Satan which deceiveth the whole world, he was cast out into the earth, and his angels were cast out with him." HERE, you may see who and what was *cast out of Heaven*, and the same tempted Christ and his brethren the Elect, and the same *war against them*, and it may well be said he *deceiveth* the whole world, for the *whole world* is gone after him, and worship him, *i.e.* they worship the *Spirit* of Reason and its *Imagination*, which is the *beast and its image*, and set a great value on themselves, and are of great consequence to themselves, and enter into contract with each other, and eager to fulfil that contract, to have each others commendation: *Therefore* when a Messenger of Christ come and offer regeneration and salvation, Him, they cannot take or endure, and so full of business, contracts, and engagement, that the Messenger is put off with excuses, and they are well content, and seek refuge one of another, so had rather not be *tormented*: BUT, at the voice of the Messenger, some will be *tormented*, and come forth in wrath, anger, lies, &c. Against him, and violently accuse him with blasphemy against God, call him a devil, and curse him and the Elect his brethren, as devils to eternity; now this *Spirit* which is the *Dragon and old serpent*, is the *Accuser* of the Elect that *follow* Christ; but Christ and his Elect, has, and will *overcome the dragon and his angels*; "For the accuser of our brethren is cast down, which accuseth them before our God day and night." *Because* the Dragon is so very earnest to keep his own kingdom and power, that they bring violent accusations, lies, persecutions, &c. against the kingdom of Christ, it being in their judgment against God, and would tempt God to own their acts and think they do God service! Thus they *accuse* the Elect of God who work the works of Faith and worship God; and at the same time, themselves, worship *the image of the beast* which is the *Devil*, under the name of *god*; and in this they are bound up, in such eager emulation as to *sacrifice themselves*; for they are cast out from the nether Heaven of Faith, and must enter the first death both body and soul, and the internal Angel in justice, opens his book of justice and death; then, they find this *Dragon and old serpent* called the devil has *deceived* them: Thus fall their great anxiety, labour, and consequence, that in *one hour* it all come to *desolation* with themselves.

AGAIN (Jude) "and the angels which kept not their first estate, but left their own habitation, he hath reserved in everlasting chains under darkness, unto the judgment of the great day." *This*, is the Cherubim or *serpent* Angel, which fell from Heaven to this earth, and into generation; and in, and by generation, has come forth *many*; and the *Apostle* declared their acts, and manner of acting: Now of those that *Jude* write *many* had transformed themselves into the *apostolical letter* or declaration, and there cultivate their own lasciviousness, and brought in railing, exceptions, sporting on people, and give themselves up to wild libertinism, excuse, &c. which is all of the *Devil*; so did, and do, transform themselves to the letter of declaration of JESUS, and think to get clear from *Moses*: NOW the bare letter of Jesus, is but a fragment or garment, what the spirit has left behind; and by its seeming scope, one will have it one way, and one another, &c. so they *divide his garments, and cast lots for his Vesture, i.e.* who shall be made *whole* by the Letter, which is but a *Garment*; so there will be a great difference found between *touching his garment,* and *eating his flesh and drinking his blood*: Therefore *Moses* is the great Prophet to the Seed of Reason, and is *buried* in their souls; and JESUS is the great Prophet to his Elect, and they are regenerated to him.

Chap. XXIV

OF *Immortality and Life*, and *Mortality and Death*: Now as I have abundantly declared, the created life of Adam and Eve was Faith, which is the divine nature of God; and God said to Faith, which he had created, "The very day thou eatest of the fruit that I forbid thee, thou shalt surely die," therefore when they hearkened to the serpent Angel, which is the Devil and tempter, and *eat* of his diabolical wisdom and nature, Faith broke its own law and *died*: For although their created life was *Faith; which flowed forth as a crystal light burning with ease and divine satisfaction, as love, concord, union, joy, innocence, patience, meekness, harmless, righteousness, wisdom, and truth, that at the first sight of different creatures, immediately gave them names according to their form and nature; and at the sight of different creatures and things, caused its life to flow forth with new wisdom, joy, communion with, and praises unto his LORD GOD, for his marvellous works of creation; and was of divine satisfaction, qualification, heavenly harmony, virtue, &c. like unto God, but as a Son which was joined to this earth, in and by creation*: Then, when they hearkened to the devil, and *eat of his fruit*, they broke the Law of Faith; *then* all those created virtues, *properties, qualification,* &c. which was of Faith, become inactive and dead in the soul; and Reason with its law, justice, &c. took possession and ruled them; and they were filled with horrid fear, shame, and excuses to get away if possible; for then the justice of the *Father*, (which is justice to Faith,) took place, and created Faith became disunited from its living creator and Father, in, and by death through his justice; and never more could flow, or act in the soul of any created or *generated* being, in the manner or condition it was created, to this day; then all things was made and became *anew in the Kingdom of Faith* for the salvation of Elect man.

Hence, as Faith fell in *Adam* and Reason in the cherubical *Angel*; and fallen Reason was the devil or *serpent* that tempted Adam; then Faith *died* according to the word of the LORD God for breaking its law: Thus God became the God of *Justice* through Man and Angel each breaking their own law; but *Faith* became so involved in justice in death, that *Reason* took possession and ruled the Man; because Reason was suffered to take this world by *violence*, and permitted to enjoy it as his kingdom for a *season*, yet under the power of justice and *death* for breaking his own law; thus are the *two* natures or kingdoms brought on by generation: NOW *Light, Life, and immortality* is of, and to that *nature*, that God was capable to take on HIM that he might redeem, and that was his own *nature* which was Faith he created in Adam: For God was *incapable* to take the nature of Reason, which was the Devil's nature, on him; if so, God and Devil would have been one, nay, HE would have been lost in his own works, by their being swallowed up in confusion; *this* is what the Devil would have, and contends for, but he never can take the *Kingdom of CHRIST* by *violence* as he was *suffered* to take this world.

Moreover, "when God walked in the Garden in the *cool* of the day," and *called to Adam*, He raised Faith to a new life for regeneration, and promised himself would become a son to his own *power* of justice, and redeem him: Also let him know the *Curse* and condition of the serpent; and the enmity put between the *serpent's seed*, and the *seed of the woman*, which was and is the seed of Faith; for although she bore *Cain* through the incarnation of the *Devil*, and by that she was the *Mother of all living*, yet she was created with a life of Faith, and the Elect are called the *Seed of the Woman, Sons of Adam, Children of God,* &c.

AGAIN, this *garden of Eden that God walked in,* is the GARDEN of FAITH for regeneration: There is also a *garden of Eden*, which relate to the purity of God's creation, by which man may enjoy this life, for in this garden grow, and is gathered, all the corn, fruits, herbs, plants, cattle, beast, fowl, fish, water, &c. to nourish and support the life of man; and fine shrubs, trees, ivory, wood, and bone; fine spices, gums, &c. and fine colours, silks, cottons, linens, and wools; gold, silver, and other metals; diamonds, and all other fine stones; fine pearls, earth, springs, minerals, &c. And the *Life* of Man will go out with delight on those things, and is given for the use of Man; and may convert it to want form or condition he can, for his own nourishment, use, and delight; and all the different verdure, seeds, and roots, with their various use and beauty; and all different Flowers, for their respective use, and various beauties to refresh and delight the *Life* of Man: Yea, this *Garden* flow with bounty and plenty by the pure *Act* of God's creation, and given man, to nourish and delight his life: Now men walk in this *Garden*, because it is the garden or *Field* for generation, in which men have their delight and care; into this *Garden* went the great *River which parted and became into four heads*, which was and is to water the soul of man.

Also, there is another *Eden*, which relate to the purity of God's creating the cherubim; and this *Garden* on the one part relate to *justice*; for although the *Cherubim* broke the Law, he was created under, and became the *tree of knowledge* of good and evil, after he was created pure, yet never could break that pure *justice*, so when Reason came to manhood, then this pure *justice* take place in the soul, which is the internal *angel*, or *Cherubims and flaming sword*: Now in the soul or on the *Life* of Reason, is the *Garden* where this Angel walk in the power of God: Also in this *Garden WAS* and *IS* the cherubical inspiration, and that given priesthood of Reason; so Moses also walked in this *Garden* on the life of Reason; and the other *Garden* prospered according to their obedience or disobedience to the man Moses; but the *cherubims and flaming sword* walk there at this day: Also there is one that ride the *black horse*, which is *Truth* in or of the law of Reason, that ride on the *dark spirit* of Reason, and on its *black acts,* which is the *black horse,* that when Reason is about to do evil, this rider will tell him that it is wrong, and he must not, then if he do it, this rider report him, unto him that ride the red horse, which is the *Angel* in justice, and he seal him under justice for calamities and death: so I would have men be careful, and hearken to this rider, lest they fall into trouble under judgment; for *he carry a pair of balances in his hand, and it is a measure of wheat for a penny, and three measures of barley for a penny, and see you hurt not the wine and oil* (Rev. 6.) *i.e.* love your neighbour, and not keep back from the poor; for it is the fruit of the other *Eden's Garden,* which God appointed to support man, and peculiar those who WORSHIP HIM.

Further, the other part of this *Garden* is, that God raise and gather his kingdom of cherubims; for the Child of Reason that die in minority, the angel in justice do not take place in the soul, and as so, are not charged with the law; so the footing on which Reason stand is *split* asunder; for them that live to manhood, the *Angel* take place in the soul, and must go their way according to infinite justice, and them that die in childhood, are taken according to the purity and glory, GOD created the cherubim, to compose the glorious order of cherubims in Heaven above; for which the Child of Reason dying in minority, and natural ideot, which is the same thing in consequence, will be raised to glory! Thus you may see who, and what, walk or ride, in those two *Eden Gardens*: But as the paradise of created Faith was lost, through created Faith breaking its own Law, and all things is made anew for the salvation of Elect man, then as I said, the *Garden of Eden* that God walk in, is the GARDEN *of* FAITH in and for regeneration, because his holy spirit goeth out on his Elect in MERCY, REDEMPTION and REGENERATION, and in the *midst of this Garden* stand Christ in *Mercy,* and regeneration for glory, who is the TREE OF LIFE, and *immortality*; and from out of this *garden was drove the man, i.e.* the man of Reason, and "cherubims and a flaming sword placed, which turns every way to keep the *Way of the tree of life,* lest he take also and eat, and live for ever;" thus in the beginning was fixed *immortality and life* and *mortality and death.*

Yea, the *Garden that GOD walk* or ride in, is the GARDEN *of* FAITH in and for regeneration; therefore when Faith was rose from death to life, and taken into the royal compact and priesthood of *lively* Faith, in and for regeneration, and this new life WAS and IS the *Virgin daughter* of Faith, and to her was and is given the promise of *Christ to come,* and power to work the works of Faith under the *justice* of the Father, and the spirit of prophecy of her own salvation; in this *they walked with God*, in the royal compact and GARDEN OF FAITH in regeneration, see (Rev. 6.) when *the first seal was opened*, "and I saw and behold a white horse, and he that sat on him had a Bow, and a Crown was given unto him, and he went forth conquering and to conquer," this was Christ, or God promised in Christ, and the *white horse* is his own power and righteousness of Faith, for he never broke that Law; and is *faithful and true*, and wear the righteous *Crown* of Faith; and HE has *conquered* sin, death, hell, and justice! And HE goeth out on the *Virgin* daughter of Faith in and for regeneration, for whom he has *conquered*, and also assists to *conquer*, and by the grand Union with God and Christ in regeneration, come through *great tribulation faithful and true*, and is united to GOD for CHRIST: Also Enoch *walked with God* in the royal compact of Faith, which is the *Garden* for regeneration, *and he was not for God took him*; for Faith being *risen* from death to life, and by divine assistance can work the works, pass through *death*, and quicken or be quickened again, because it is of an *immortal* nature, and can be worked through *mortality and death; to immortality* and *life*: So by this spirit of regenerated Faith, man may be *translated* into Heaven; so Enoch *was not* left here, but by virtue of the spirit of regenerated Faith *God took him* into the kingdom of *immortality and life*, and was united to God for Christ in the royal compact of regeneration: ALSO Moses and Elias *walked* with God, and was in the same manner *taken* or translated into Heaven; for when Faith is risen from death to life, by regeneration, it become the soul of Elect man for salvation, and with this *life* Enoch, Moses, and Elias, was taken into Heaven, and Reason was *cast out*, and went to its own center and home, by *Death*, &c. being conquered; thus you may see this spirit is of an *immortal* nature, as by it men are brought through the mighty power of *death*, hell, &c. to *Life* and *immortality*, and then it is at its own center or home; and this spirit is of so powerful ascending nature, that it will take the *person* also, if God please to assist, as it did Enoch, Moses, and Elias, who were united to God for Christ in the holy, and immortal compact of Faith, in and for Regeneration.

Again, as Enoch, Moses, and Elias was translated into Heaven by virtue of regeneration, and then united to God for Christ by this *immortal* Spirit of regenerated Faith, and there sit in the glory of the Father, in *life and immortality*, that the royal, merciful, and glorious united compact of Faith, may be compleated, by redemption and regeneration; therefore as they bore a body of flesh, and had the *first resurrection*, and was regenerated, and ascended into *Heaven*, with a life of regenerated Faith; *they* was very capable to sit in the glory of the *Father*, while He became a SON to his own Power, redeem and gain, a new kingdom, which is the glory of Mercy! Therefore all the Elect of *old*, and time of the law, Faith in them was risen from *death to life*, and taken into the ROYAL PRIESTHOOD where they *walked with God*, and had the promise of Christ, and spirit of prophecy, and did prophecy of Christ to come; and in this way were they brought through the powers of Reason, &c. by regeneration, till the hour of death; then this incense, prayer, prophecy, or spirit of regenerated Faith, went through death, and was called into Heaven, and united to God for Christ, even as Enoch, Moses and Elias were, only they was *person* and *Spirit*, but the other Elect by this *immortal Spirit* of regenerated Faith, and then died or fell asleep in the bed of mercy; but it is all in the lively compact of regenerated Faith, which centers to, and is recorded in *immortality and Life*, and not in *mortality and death*: Thus, in and with the Elect of old, and in the time of the law, was the *Way of CHRIST prepared*, and the fruits for his kingdom, centers to his kingdom, which is *Life and immortality*.

Further on this first resurrection, prophecy, prayer, and incense of the Elect of old, His witness of His spirit that stood before the *Throne* and prophecied when he WAS in the condition of the *Father*, which ascended into Heaven and is recorded in the *immortal* compact of regeneration, which is the BOOK OF LIFE! *GOD became CHRIST* to complete this *immortal* compact! declared his holy gospel, and regeneration; redeemed his Elect, and brought *life and immortality* to Light! And when he ascended into his own royal kingdom of *divine Mercy*, HE had gained, he took possession of his kingdom of regenerated Faith in *life and immortality*; See Rev. xiv. "and I looked, and lo, a lamb stood on Mount Sion and with him an hundred and forty-four thousand, having his Father's name written on their forehead." *This*, was the spirits of Faith, of them that we regenerated from the earth, and united to God for Christ, and were in the *immortal* Records of regenerated Faith, in *Life and Immortality*, - John saw them in *vision*, and so have I on this high Mountain of regenerated Faith, which spiritually is *Mount Sion*; and Christ took possession of this his Kingdom, for they *stood before him and prophecied* when he was in the condition of the *Father*, and as so *have his Father's name written in their forehead*: Ver. 2. "And I heard a voice from Heaven as the voice of many waters, and as the voice of a great thunder; and I heard the voice of harpers, harping with their harps!" This was the utterance of rejoicings so Faith, because Christ had overcome the devil, and the powers of sin, death, hell, and justice, and took possession of his kingdom of *Virgins* of Faith in and by regeneration, which filled the *Heaven* of Faith, with great utterance, joy, and rejoicing in the concord of regenerated Faith, in *life and immortality*: "And they sang as it were a new song before the throne, and before the four beasts, and the elders; and no man could learn that song but the hundred and forty and four thousand which were redeemed from the Earth."

This *new song*, was, that Christ had *overcome* and took *possession* of his Kingdom the glory of mercy, and regenerated Faith in *immortality and life*: The other *song* was of prophecy, and union to God for Christ, which is the song of *Moses*; but now Christ has took possession of his kingdom of *Virgins* and united himself to them in *immortality and life*, which is the song of the LAMB: For this, *understand*, the *Union* of regenerated Faith is so great, that when Christ gained his kingdom, the natures *Voice* of regenerated Faith, of each individual in the *Book of LIFE* have joy, and rejoice, in the true concord and harmony of united Faith, like unto a well tuned harpsichord, in the joyful utterance of the thanksgiving in praise of the divine wisdom, power, honour, glory, &c. unto the LORD GOD of Faith and mercy, their king, and redeemer, who will live and reign in the merciful and glorious united *immortal* kingdom of regenerated Faith for ever! Yea the natures voice of every *individual* have its utterance, which make the glorious Heaven of regenerated Faith, sound aloud in rejoicing and thanksgiving.

AGAIN, you may see, *no man could learn that song* but those that were *redeemed from the earth*; and it was *sung before the THRONE, and before the four BEASTS* and the ELDERS; as to the four Beasts, *Enoch* is one, *Moses* one, *Elias* one; the other JESUS, who that the *face* of a man, because he hath passed through ALL and from ALL to his high kingdom the *Glory of Mercy*; the other *three* sit in the glory of justice, but more of this anon: AS to the *Elders*, the LORD GOD OF HEAVEN is an *Elder*, because he created all things, and is the *foundation* of Faith, *Adam* also and Enoch, Abraham, Isaac and Jacob, Moses and Elias, and others are *Elders*, because this is his first *witness* of his spirit, and that which *stood before him and prophecied* when HE was in the condition of the *Father:* They are called *Elders*, because God's *communion* with, and *promise* of eternal life to *them, is left on* RECORD; also Christ is *recorded*, the Son of David, of Abraham, and of Adam, in the *genealogy* of Faith, because the union is so great; for this *understand* HE came by way of the *Elder* or the *Father* to inherit the *Son and Brother*; so, you may see "they were not defiled with women for they were *Virgins*;" *i.e.* as I said, this *Virgin* will not hearken to, or have to do with Reason; so men in regeneration must put away their wife Reason; ALSO, this *Virgin* did not bear a *son* in regeneration to Christ, until *God become Christ*; also you may see "they were redeemed from among men, being the first fruits unto God and to the Lamb," therefore this song of Faith in regeneration was *sung in immortality* because Christ had worked the redemption, overcome, took possession of, and united himself to those *Virgins*, who was regenerated and *redeemed from the earth*; and crowned their Faith, *Prophecy, and Union*; and HIM *only* was found able and worthy to do that; for which they *offered* at, and cast their

Crowns before HIS *Throne;* and this caused great utterance and rejoicings in the *immortal* Kingdom of regenerated *Faith.*

Chap. XXV

BY what is written, you may see how the WAY of Christ was *prepared* in the *days of old,* when *He* was in the condition of the *Father;* How his Kingdom was *gathered;* How he *united* himself to them; and how they stand *recorded* in the Book of *Life and immortality,* therefore *CHRIST came, to crown their Faith and prophecy,* and work *Life* out of *Death;* for as Faith fell in Adam and became inactive and dead, and Reason took possession and ruled the *man and woman,* and so it go on in *generation;* then CHRIST raise Faith from death to a *new life* (in Elect man), and then HE has got the *victory over the Beast,* which is the *Spirit* of Reason; because this *Life* of Faith is far above, and contrary to that of Reason, for it is taken into the royal Compact and Priesthood of Faith, to be regenerated to CHRIST, and *it* is only subject to God and Christ; *i.e.* to work the works of Faith, under the justice of the Father, and to *follow Christ* through death and hell, to his royal Kingdom of *divine Mercy;* for Christ rule over it, and him it will *follow,* it being regenerated to him, that by regeneration it become the soul of the Elect for salvation, and is of an *immortal nature:* THEREFORE (Mat. x.) Christ said to *his disciples* 'and fear not them which kill the body, but are not able to kill the soul; but rather fear him that is able to destroy both soul and body in hell;" Now, here you may see the difference between *generation* and *regeneration,* and of *immortality and Life* and *mortality and death;* for if a man is incapable of regeneration he is *dead* in the sight of God, and his soul is *mortal* and must *die;* as in this case the soul and body is inseparable, and both together must enter the *first death,* and then to go into the *second death,* then both *soul and body is destroyed in hell;* so mighty, and so great is the power of the LORD GOD OF HEAVEN: But by this *new life* which Christ raiseth from death of Faith which fell in Adam, Christ worketh on it, for regeneration and salvation; and by divine assistance, it is brought through the powers of Reason; and the justice of the Father, and it grow strong, and become the soul of Elect man for salvation; it ascends to Christ, is united to him, and recorded by him, in his *immortal* record of divine Mercy, which is the BOOK OF LIFE; then is *Life and immortality brought to Light,* to the Elect! So no one can *kill that soul* because it belong to Christ, nor *pluck it out of his hand,* because it is united to him in *immortality:* Now, this is, and will be the condition of the Elect, for Christ came to *redeem*, and *work life* out of death, and by regeneration *gather* Faith to his Kingdom, and bring *life and immortality* to his Elect.

Moreover, the *first resurrection*, that he who hath *part therein, the second death hath no power over,* Why? because he is and will be passed from death to *Life* by regeneration, as John v. 24. "Verily, verily, I say unto you, he that heareth my word, and believeth on him that sent me, hath everlasting *Life*, and shall not come into condemnation, but is passed from death to *Life*," Why? because he is raised from death to *Life* in the *first resurrection*; and by regeneration he is passed through the powers of Reason, and of Sin, Death, and Hell; and from those powers to Christ in *Immortality*: AGAIN (John's Gospel 11th.) *Jesus said unto her*, "I am the resurrection and the *Life*, he that believeth in me though he were dead, yet shall he *live*," *i.e.* He that *knows* the Voice of Jesus when he hear it, and come to believe in HIM by the true spirit and prayer of obedience, though he was dead in Faith, yet Jesus will *raise* that Faith into active *Life*, and it shall *live* and work in regeneration: "And whosoever liveth and believeth in me shall never die;" *i.e.* Faith when *risen* from death to *Life*, it *live* in and for regeneration, and *believe* and work the works of Faith in that royal priesthood, and its fruits, incense, prayer, or *breath,* and spirit ascend to Christ, and is united to him in *immortality*, and do not *Die*, because it *live in* , and with him; ALSO Luke xii. "And I say unto you *my friends*, be not afraid of them that kill the body, and after that have no more that they can do," Why? because this spirit of regenerated Faith become the soul of Elect man for salvation, and it belong to Christ and by HIM *is* and *will be* brought through all the powers of Reason, and of sin, death, and hell; and from all those, for no one can stop it by *death*, nor *pluck it out of HIS Hand*, because it is united to him in *immortality*, as an *earnest* of eternal glory.

AGAIN, as Adam was created out of the dust of the earth, and the nature that animated him was *immortal*, while it stood in obedience to its *Father and Creator;* but when it broke its own law it died, and Reason took *possession, ruled* and *drove* them; then they must lose that *life* also, and become putrefaction, and go to earth from whence they were taken; and this is its *lost* condition, without regeneration; then, in steps the LORD GOD *of Heaven*, who is CHRIST *the Redeemer*, and raise Faith to *active Life*: Now as Faith was of an *immortal* nature before it broke its own law, and for that became *mortal* and died; then when it rose from that *death* to a new *LIFE*, that new *Life* is also of an *immortal* nature; having passed through the first death to a *new Life* for regeneration, to Christ in *Immortality*: For *mortality and death* cannot pass through mortality and death, neither can *corruption and death*, pass through death and corruption, nor can *Justice and death* pass through Justice and death; therefore its that which is of an *immortal* nature, that *Death* cannot keep under his power, to pass through those great and mighty powers.

JESUS said, (John's Gospel 6.) "It is the spirit that *quickeneth* the flesh profiteth nothing: the words that I speak unto you they are *spirit,* and they are *Life,"* i.e. Jesus whose words are *spirit and Life,* raise Faith to *active Life*; for the power of his word, or his *natures Voice* and divine assistance center into the womb of Faith, in the Elect, which is the *good ground,* and quicken Faith, or give birth to the *Virgin,* from its womb or seed; and this *quickened* spirit is of an *immortal* nature; and is what *quicken* and actuate the Elect in regeneration, and with divine assistance will come through the powers of *Justice and Death*; but, *the flesh profiteth nothing*; for at the voice of the *third angel* in regeneration (Rev. viii.) "and the *third Angel* sounded, and there fell a great *Star* from Heaven burning as it were a lamp, and it fell upon the *third* part of the rivers, and fountains of waters," this *great Star* is God's Justice that *fell from Heaven,* through the fall of Man and Angel; and it *burn* like a clear *lamp* to enlighten the earthy heart of man; and rule over him bright and clear; the *rivers it fell upon,* is the Life and acts of man; and the *fountains of waters,* in that man enjoy the waters of (this) *Life,* under the powers of *Justice and Death:* "And the name of the Star is called Wormwood, and the *third part* of the waters become wormwood, and many men died of those waters, because they were made bitter." This *Star* may well be called *wormwood,* and that it made the *waters wormwood,* and that *many men died of those water,* because by those *waters* men are swallowed up in justice and death; for except a man can drink of those *waters,* and *overcome,* he must die of those *waters,* therefore the *Life of man is made bitter.* Those that *died,* was and is, the Seed and Spirit of Reason, because they *die of those waters* of Justice, for they cannot *drink and overcome*; therefore Death and Justice cannot be brought through *Death and Justice,* (for this is the grand united *center,* to swallow up, and there keep in the *second* death and darkness,) but it is by this *new life* which is of an *immortal* nature, that can work the works of Faith, and against those powers; and it is by this new Life and divine assistance that the Elect are brought through the powers of *Reason, Justice,* and *Death,* and can drink those *waters,* which is a *deadly thing* and overcome, and are *found worthy*; and to them is given the TESTIMONY OF JESUS which is the spirit of prophecy of *Christ to come,* then at the hour of death they are called up to the *Justice* of the Father, which is the *Voice* of the *sixth* ANGEL in regeneration, and you cannot go back, for then is the powers of Sin, Death, Hell and Justice let loose and ready to *devour,* and no help to be found, for through the *Justice of the Father* you must go, or no Life eternal; and the divine incomes and the Spirit of prophecy that was so sweet is turned into *blood.*

AT this time is the *third part of the Sun and Moon smitten* and darkened, or *Moon* which is the *spirit of prophecy* under the justice of the Father *turned into blood;* and the *Sun* may well be said to be *darkened,* for you must go through the Justice of the Father to his *Mercy*; and the *Moon* which is the *Justice* of the Father, may well be *darkened,* because Faith must lose itself in *death,* under that Justice to pass through it, to the mercy of the SON: And the nether *Heaven* of Faith as it were *departed*; and nature's *Heaven* of this life *rolled together* and gone, and *no more refuge found!* then this *Virgin* daughter of Faith, which is of an *immortal* nature is *only* capable to pass through those powers: NOW this *part of the Sun and Moon,* that is not *darkened* is the power of Christ to assist the spirit of Faith to *follow him*; for this Spirit is the *third part* which is God's *part* of Elect man, the which is worked on for regeneration, and assisted not only to pass *through* those powers, but *from* those powers, because *death* cannot stop it, for it will *follow* Christ, but the *flesh profiteth nothing*: For this *Life* of Faith must be lost in death in its own blood as Christ lost his; and there it meet Christ in *spirit* as he was *crucified:* Here is the *Son* smitten by the power of death and Faith is united to him: *Now* this is the marriage with the *Lamb,* and this *Spirit* is commended into the *hands of the Father,* which is of justice, and there dies as Christ himself did; then it is quickened or quicken from this death, to a *new Life* again, and this new *Life* is the spiritual born *Son* to CHRIST in regeneration for his kingdom, *now* this *Spirit* of regenerated Faith which is of an *immortal* nature has passed through its *second death,* which hath *no power* on it, so as to keep it from following Christ, for to him is this *Spirit* to go, because this *Way* Christ went to his kingdom in spirit and person, and the Elect will *follow* by this *Spirit:* AFTER this, the spiritual born *Son* is called and ascend into an high *mountain* of Faith in regeneration where it see CHRIST *in his high Kingdom, Glory, and Power of Mercy,* and them that are *sealed,* and that all must be sealed in and by HIM to inherit his Kingdom; then, the *eager prayer* of this *spiritual born* Son is offered at the feet of JESUS in the *Glory of mercy,* (which is the *grand ALTAR of Faith*) to be called in and sealed by HIM in his *immortal* compact and kingdom of regenerated Faith; and when the voice say, *"come in hither,"* the spirit go, and is united to *Christ* in *immortality*: THIS is the voice of the *seventh ANGEL* in regeneration, for then, "the kingdoms of this world are become the kingdoms of Christ, who will reign for ever and ever," because this *Spirit* and *Fruits* of regenerated Faith is brought through all the powers of *Reason, Death, and Hell,* and from all those powers to the *Union,* and *Seal* of Christ in *Immortality* and glory, which is the *seal of the LIVING GOD* and the *Book of Life,* then the soul is assured of eternal Life; and the Man or Woman whose soul is so much *refined* by regeneration as to bring forth the aforesaid prayer, fruits or incense to ascend to Heaven, and be united to Christ in *Immortality,* dies or falls *asleep* in the bed of mercy for the resurrection to glory, which will be but as a *moment,* because time is done and over; But this Spirit, incense, or *Life* of regenerated Faith after it has passed through all, and from all it cannot die, for it is united to Christ who is an *immortal Being*; thus you may see by regeneration, how life and immortality is brought to light.

Again, as I said, the *Body* of Elect man is Reason, a filthy corrupted earthy matter, which took place through the fall, when Reason took possession of the man and woman; therefore corrupted earthy matter will go to earth from whence it came, as the *Lord God* said to Adam, "For out of it was thou taken; for dust thou art, and unto dust shalt thou return," so Reason is *cast out* and go to its own center or home: Now this filthy corrupted earthy matter and Reason, which Elect man has in this life, is but their *body* (although eager to live,) and man may *kill* that, but are *not able to kill the soul*, because that belong to Christ, and is regenerated to him in *Immortality*; and although the filthy part of Elect man go to *earth*, yet do you *understand*, there is that which is refined by regeneration, that lay sleeping in the Bed of mercy, like unto a *Womb or Tree* that has bore, or brought forth the fruits of Faith in regeneration unto Christ, that in the morning of the resurrection will receive it again of Christ by his great call and power, as its quickening and life, and come forth with a *glorious* Body of this earth, of flesh and bone, like unto Christ himself which they will inherit in all eternity.

Now, if a man come to the *bloody unbelieving World* he come to *mortality and death*, because Reason is incapable of regeneration; there then soul and body are inseparable, both must die together the *first death* under the Angel in justice, and both go together into the *second death*: Also man may talk of, and *preach* concerning Faith, yet without the *first resurrection* he is preaching of, or to a dead Faith; and at this time or condition, even the Elect are not only in a *mortal*, but a *corruptable* state for both *soul and body* to die together; but when Christ come He raise Faith from Death to life for regeneration; and to that soul bring *life and immortality to light*: So I would have you know and observe when the spirit speak concerning Faith, or Reason, and concerning *immortality and life* or *mortality and death*, and of what is capable to pass through *death*, and what *Death* can keep under; as Isa. liii. "Because he hath poured out his soul unto *death*," This is of Christ whose Life or Soul *died*, but death could not keep him under his power, for he passed through it, and this Spirit of regenerated Faith will *follow*, because it is the *Soul* of the Elect for salvation; and by the great union of Faith in compact, and divine assistance, will pass through *death and Hell* (Psal. xvi.) "For thou will not leave my *soul in hell*, neither wilt thou suffer thine *holy One* to see corruption." Here *David* knew by his testimony from Heaven, that his *soul* of regenerated Faith would pass through *death and Hell* and be united to God for Christ, in the *immortal* compact of regenerated Faith; and that God would become Christ, *redeem* his Elect, *pass* through those powers, both in *person and spirit* (or *body* and *soul*) gain all power to himself, and take *possession* of his immortal kingdom of regenerated Faith, which is the souls of his *Elect*.

AGAIN. As Jesus kept the law of Faith, redeemed his Elect, and passed through the powers of Reason, and left it behind under judgment, yea through the powers of *Sin, Death, Hell, and Justice,* both in person and spirit, and so ascended into his high Kingdom the glory of *Mercy,* and was and is the first fruits unto and into his said kingdom, and there took possession of the *Spirits* of regenerated Faith, which is the souls of his Elect, that stood before him and prophecied, when he was in the condition of the Father, for which there was such joy, rejoicing and thanksgiving before his *throne,* for there the nature's voice of every individual of regenerated Faith have its utterance because he had gain all *Power* to himself, for HE had passed through *All* and from *All* to his Kingdom, the Power and Glory of *Mercy;* for *HIM only* was worthy, and they cast their *Crowns,* which was their *Lives* of redeemed and regenerated Faith before his *Throne,* and HE only, was able to receive it, for HE only is able and worthy to make them *compleat,* and like unto himself by a glorious resurrection, for and into his high Heaven the glory of mercy.

Moreover, as CHRIST passed through those mighty powers, both in person and spirit, and from those powers to his glory of mercy; and is the royal BRIDEGROOM to the Virgin daughter of Faith, so regeneration is worked by him, and to him; and this spirit of regenerated Faith is of his own nature, which is a quickening spirit, and of an *immortal* nature, and it will *follow Christ* through the powers of Reason, Sin, Death, Hell, and Justice, for this way HE went both in person and spirit, to his *kingdom* of mercy; and this spirit *will* follow him, for thither is this spirit to go Yea when this spiritual *Son* in regeneration is born of the *Virgin* daughter of Faith, *he* is taken into an high *Mountain* in regeneration where he see Christ in his glory of Mercy, and them that are sealed, and that all by him must be sealed; then this spiritual born *Son* offer itself up at the royal feet of JESUS, in his glory of mercy, which is the *grand ALTAR* of Faith; in this manner is Faith regenerated and offered to him and is his other WITNESS OF HIS SPIRIT *or* OLIVE TREE *that stand before him and prophecy* now he is in the condition of the SON, and in the glory of mercy; and this *spiritual born Son* is immortal, and on this great MOUNTAIN *of regenerated Faith,* offers at his ROYAL FEET to be called in and united to him in his *immortal* and glorious State; yea Christ call it in, and unite it to himself in his high State of IMMORTALITY! So all the *life* and *fruits* of regenerated Faith which is the Lives and Crowns of the Elect, is cast and offered at the feet of JESUS in his *immortal* glory of Mercy; now this is the great and grand Altar and *offering* of Faith for HE only is worthy to receive it, and able to make it compleat, and he do receive it and unite it to himself in *immortality!* ALSO when this *spiritual born Son* is called in and united to Christ it is the voice of the *seventh Angel in regeneration,* then *the kingdoms of this world are become the kingdoms of Christ,* because this spirit of life of regenerated Faith, of an *immortal* nature, has passed through all the powers of Reason, and of *Sin, Death, Hell, and Justice,* to the mercy and union of CHRIST; and at this great union of *Faith in Heaven,* there is always great utterance of joy and thanksgiving to the LORD CHRIST their king and redeemer; and as I said, the natures voice of every individual has it utterance of joy and thanksgiving; *for the high immortal and glorious kingdom of regenerated Faith, where Christ is king, flow with the glorious spiritual fire of Faith, like unto a pure Fountain and rivers of refined gold, as is powered from the Refiners Test, in circulative active life, and is gathered in by regeneration, it being the Treasure of the Lord Christ;* of which Christ the glorious fountain, is graciously pleased by influence to assist his Elect, to help the Virgin daughter of Faith to follow him through the mighty powers of Death, &c. and it ascend to him again in prayer, thanksgiving, &c. And when the *spiritual Son is born* it ascend and is united to Christ; therefore the Prayer, Works, Fruits, Incense, Crowns, and *Spirit and life of regenerated Faith which,* is the souls of his Elect, and is of an *immortal* nature, they all ascend to Christ, and offer, and is offerd at his royal feet, and he call them in, and they are united to him, in his high *immortal and glorious kingdom of regenerated Faith,* and they are *in HIM, with HIM, and of HIM* because the union is so great! Now this is the *seal of the living GOD!* the BOOK OF LIFE! and the NAME *written therein!* Then the person dies, or fall asleep in the bed of mercy for a *moment* assured of eternal *Life!* Then, when *time* end, every Elect will receive his life again of CHRIST in a resurrection to eternal GLORY! For the *Union* of regenerated Faith is so mighty, and so great with CHRIST that by the ALMIGHTY POWER of his *Call* to every Elect as to one man, *they* then, all receive their lives of Christ again, with a great and glorious advantage and advancement, quicken, and come forth in a glorious body of this earth in flesh and bone, and be compleated like unto Christ himself for his *glorious kingdom of mercy in all eternity:* And from the *Seal* of the living God to the *resurrection* is but as a *moment,* for when the soul is sealed, Time is done and over; So BLESSED are them that can offer this life of regenerated Faith up to Christ, and there *lose* it in HIM, then they are sure to find it in the resurrection to eternal glory!

Again, as *written,* you may see the difference between *immortality and life,* and *mortality and death,* and between *generation* and *regeneration,* what it is for a man to *die* as he was born, and how it is to be *born again,* to be regenerated to CHRIST; for if a man is incapable of regeneration then the *soul die with the body,* go to corruption under cherubical justice, and is cast *from Christ and his kingdom of regenerated Faith:* For *mortality and death,* cannot be united to, or have any union with *immortality and life,* neither can the

Spirit of corrupted *generation*, agree or unite with the *Spirit* of incorrupted *regeneration*, therefore every power has its *Action* as was ordained and permitted by the LORD GOD *of* HEAVEN; and every Spirit and Power *will act* according to its nature, and incline to its own center and *Home*; NOW if a man come from God under creation and justice, there the Soul is *mortal and die*; and although Faith is *risen* in the man, and he *prophecy* of those things, he is taken and united to Christ in *immortality*, and leave the world without declaring regeneration, because he did not come out under that covenant: But him in whom the spiritual Son is born of the *Virgin daughter to Christ*, and taken into the great MOUNTAIN of Faith in regeneration, where it see and commune with Christ in his *immortality*, and sent immediately back by him, then, he come in the spirit and power of Christ in his high *immortal* compact of regeneration, then *he* will declare regeneration, and *life and immortality to the Elect*, and thus is his declaration, for he was shewed those things by the Angel of regenerated Faith, who is *CHRIST in immortality*, and sent back by him to declare it, and HE and the whole Heaven of regenerated Faith bear him witness: So BLESSED are them that *understand*, enter in, and *follow*, for the BOOK OF LIFE is *open* to them! And although the powers of Reason, sin, death, hell, and justice, is hard and sharp to go through, yet the spirit of Faith, by prayer and divine assistance, will come through; and the *tribulation* though great, yet it continue but a small space, like unto a *woman in the travail of labour*, when the child tosses, throbs, and presses hard to be born, she hath sorrow, but when born, the anguish is forgot, for *joy* there is a man born: Even so, Faith presses for its own *Kingdom*; and when the spiritual son is born, and sealed, all *sorrow* is turned into *eternal joy*: So I pray for and recommend *Prayer*, and not to faint, the Union of the Elect, the assistance of Christ, *Amen*.

Chap. XXVI

WHEN Jesus said the *Temple* of Jerusalem should be thrown down, and *not one stone be left on another* (as Mat. xxiv.) *The Disciples came unto him privately*, saying "Tell us when shall those things be, and what shall be the sign of thy *coming* and of the *end* of the world?" *This* looking for Christ to *come* has been in general his personal appearance, which, will surely come to pafs, but this *understand*, -

except he first *comes in spirit* to raise Faith from death to life, and seal the soul for the resurrection unto life eternal, his *coming* in person will be of no benefit, except to the Child or Ideot who will be raised cherubims: And *Jesus* answered, saying to them, "Take heed that no man deceive you; for many shall come in my name saying, I am Christ and shall deceive many." Now when Jesus was here, and declared who he was with his holy gospel, and called his disciples, and *many* of the Seed of Reason transformed themselves into the *Echo* of that call or declaration, then by the Spirit of emulation, become such high cherubims as to go forth and say "I am the man," or "have as much spiritual wisdom and power as *him*," and will preach and prophecy in the *Name* of Jesus, or any of his Messengers: *Now*, those was them, Jesus told *his disciple* to *beware of*, and *take heed* not to be deceived by them, but patiently *wait his coming* again, which he did in *Spirit* at the *day of Penticost*: Moreover Jesus *prophecies of his coming* and *destruction of Jerusalem* to be near at one time, and truly it *was*, and IS, for when Jesus was here in person Jerusalem flourished in having power among themselves in their own law, and to worship their own way, which was the priesthood of Reason, so put Jesus to death, because he would not hearken to them, but he left Jerusalem *desolate* in their own *way*, for when he came again it was to his Elect, and took them into his own priesthood: Further, *Jerusalem* was the *City* that first flourished under the *public declaration* from Heaven, *i.e.* the *Law*, and the Priesthood that was given by Moses, which being given to Reason they could *couch* themselves under it, and say it come from God, though notwithstanding, they would act *in* it, or concerning it as *they* please: ALSO, let men profess what letter of declaration they will, *couch* themselves under it, and take it into the priesthood of Reason, they are in the same condition as was the *Jews of Jerusalem*; for except JESUS take the Man, *Moses* has already got him; and if men profess the *Name of Jesus*, and are in the priesthood of Reason, they will judge of it by the spirit of Reason, because they have no other wisdom, so determine it all in the wrong, which thing was done at Jerusalem concerning Christ: Therefore *Jerusalem* flourished in its *power* and *priesthood*, till Christ came in spirit to his Elect, then it was left *desolate and destroyed*; and it is the very same at this day, for men have the *Letter*, and take into the *wild priesthood* of Reason as the *Jews* did, and there judge what is exceptable to God, and what is not, and this is as much the *city of Jerusalem* as the former was, for it is the *spirits* and *acts* of the people that compose this *City*, and this Jerusalem may flourish in the eyes of men till *Christ come*; then men will be disturbed in spirit, divide in anger, enter into a spiritual war, and lay wait to kill each other in the spiritual; for *many* will hold forth and say, "*I am of Christ*" and mine is the *Way* for salvation.

Further, when Christ *come in spirit* the voice of him through his Messenger centers to the womb of Faith, quickens it into life, and it is *taken* into the royal priesthood of Faith, then the *world* is in a manner ended to the Elect, why? as they are taken into a *new covenant* and priesthood to go into regeneration, and must seek a *new Kingdom* which is of Christ, then he will be with, and help them to overcome this world, even to the end of this life: Also when the soul is *taken* into the priesthood of Faith, the priesthood of Reason in him is *left* behind *desolate*, for he must not excuse himself in that priesthood, for that must be *destroyed* as the *temple and city of Jerusalem* was, and *not one stone be left on another, i.e.* all the wisdom of man, and excuses he has made to save himself, which, is the priesthood of Reason must be *thrown down*, and not an excuse to be found on the *Wisdom* of Reason, which is the *Building* Reason made to dwell in, offer its own incense, flourish for *one day* and be destroyed in *one hour!*

AGAIN, when the soul is so far enlightened from Heaven to "*See* the *ABOMINATION of desolation,* spoken of by Daniel the prophet, stand in the holy place, *whoso readeth let him understand.*" He will soon *SEE the sign of the son of man in Heaven*; for this *ABOMINATION* is when the Seed and spirit of Reason is transformed into the outward *Word,* (which is the echo of the true declaration and prophecy,) and become such high Cherubims, as to go forth, and usurp the rule and power of the Letter, preach and prophecy in the name of JESUS, judge what is of God, and what is not, and would put the Spirit of Christ to death, and all from the spirit of Reason; then excuse themselves in their own *wild priesthood,* and call it "the *Church* of Christ," which is *abomination*: Therefore ABOMINATION *standeth in the holy place,* or under the *holy NAME where it ought not,* and the SPIRIT of Christ made *desolate*: Now when man *see* this, he will also *see* that the spirit of Reason has *ruled* over him, and the spirit of Christ has been *desolate* in him, notwithstanding he has professed the Letter with great Zeal, but it has been in the *wild* priesthood of Reason; and he has offered the *incense* of wild Reason in the *name of JESUS,* which is the *Seat of abomination* in him, and he will find himself *desolate*; therefore will *flee from Juda and Jerusalem, i.e.* from the kingship and priesthood of Reason, into the *Priesthood* of Faith, that Christ should rule over them, for this is the *Mountains* that the Elect are commanded to *flee into,* that they be safe from being *destroyed with Jerusalem,* which is the *seat* and power of the priesthood of Reason.

Moreover, when those things come to pass in the soul of man, he may look for CHRIST, it being a *Sign of his coming*; then the mighty *works* of Faith, and *sorrow* will begin with him, for he must bear temptation, and anger from his enemies; His own *house will be divided* against him, and seek to overthrow him. By tempting or driving him from Christ, and his own spirit of Reason will threaten him with distress, poverty, and shame. (in the eyes of men) on the one part, and promise him great happiness on the other, if he will but hearken to him: But this must *not* be done, and the temptation *bore* with; and man will find to *bear* this temptation, he will eat his own flesh in *sorrow*, yet by prayer and divine assistance from *Heaven* he will *overcome*: Also the spirit of Reason will be in great trouble, as if his waters of life was stoped, so in great agitation, and know not how to help himself, but will follow his own wisdom, and be left *desolate* in it; and *love will wax cold* among *many* to the Messenger, and the Elect will meet with great *temptations*, and be *scoft at* by the Seed and Spirit of Reason, and must be brought through the powers of *justice, death, and hell*, and in such *trouble and sorrow* that never was known to them before: "But (Jesus said) he that shall ensure unto the end the same shall be saved," *i.e.* he who is in the *royal priesthood* and work the works of Faith is found *worthy,* and called under the justice of the Father, and from thence given birth to the mercy of the SON: But the cherubical Litteralist will be called under the justice of the angel, and never come to under the justice of the Father, so cannot *endure to that end*: But the cherubims may, nay will die, in the profession of the letter, as will the Elect: THEREFORE when the *Call* comes, let the Elect *flee* from the priesthood and *House* of Reason, to the priesthood and HOUSE of Faith, and not *turn back* on any account for any thing that he has *left behind*, nor to bid them farewell that are of the house of Reason let them be who they will, for if he do, he is in great danger of being buried in the ruins of *Jerusalem*, and be found unworthy to *bear the Cross of Christ*; for when the *Cry* is made that *Christ is coming*, they who are of the house of Reason, will do all they can to defend that priesthood; therefore Jesus said, "And woe unto them that are with child, and to them that give suck in those days," *i.e. Woe to them* whose blind zeal, (which is the daughter of Reason or of *Jerusalem*) is so powerful in them, as to gather in the traditions of Reason, and judge it to be the *will and intent* of God, and from that *conceive anger* against the Messenger, because his declaration is contrary to their conceiving; and that will *give birth* to the spiritual *son of perdition* that is born of Reason, and comes forth in wrath and *blasphemy*, and will curse the spirit of Christ off the earth, if possible: To *give suck*, is to encourage this very thing, because they cannot *bear* the *kingdom of Christ should come* or exist.

Further, *Many* will come forth in the name of JESUS, with a tongue of cherubim, *prophecy* and promise salvation, *cry* "Lo here is Christ and salvation, and *lo there* is Christ and salvation," *preach* in the name of Jesus display their cherubical wisdom on the outward word or bare letter, and from this promise life and salvation; but in *this promise* of life is contained death; and Reason will *divide* and contend for his priesthood, and speak *evil* of each other concerning their Faith: Families will also be *divided*, husband against *wife*, and wife against *husband*; parents against their *children*, and children against their *parents*: For the Elect will *leave the bonds* of earth and the law, which is by generation and contract, to be regenerated to CHRIST in the royal and true *Family* of Faith: Therefore great *troubles and temptations* will follow, to the Elect; for they must *stand* against the powers of *Reason* and torments of *Hell* and *Death*: - Ver. 22 JESUS said, "And except those days should be shortened there should no flesh be saved, but for the Elects sake those days *shall* be shortened." Those *days that are shortened,* is the *days* and power of Reason, in their temptations and wrathful proceedings, that the Elect *shall* offer the true incense, and work the works of Faith, for the power of *Reason, Death, Hell, &c* is so great, that it will incumber, hurry, drive, or tempt the soul from every act of Faith, and drown him in the horror of Reason's *care* and torment if *possible,* was not his *days shortened* both within and without Elect man, that they may work the works of Faith) have divine assistance from HEAVEN, eat of the *Tree of Life,* and live for ever! For the internal Angel in justice has power given him from Heaven over man, and he being in mystical union, and spiritual communion with him or them who sit in the power of justice, then at the least *notice* from Heaven, he will do the will of GOD, as to *bind or loose* Reason, and force it to do that which it would not: - Now it is to be *understood,* when Faith is born, and *taken* into its own priesthood, the internal Angel in justice will oftimes be its friend, and curb Reason, that Faith shall offer its own prayer, and receive power from Heaven to remove internal *mountains*; and the more Faith *grows* or increases in regeneration, the more the *days* of power of Reason is *shortened,* in the soul of Elect man: And it is my soul's desire and prayer, that the *days* and power of Reason may speedily be shortened in, and concerning the Elect, that they may work the works of Faith, be found *ready,* so *worthy to stand before JESUS* when they are called upon, to be given spiritual birth, and sealed by Christ the king of Faith, then die in the bed of mercy to be raised by *Jesus to eternal glory,* and the power of Reason is then ended to that soul; - and when the Elect are sealed in or concerning the Messenger's *day or hour,* then the *days* or power of Reason's persecution is *cut off,* because they cannot persecute the spirit of Christ when it is out of their way.

Again, Jesus said, or as the lightening cometh out of the east and shineth even unto the west, so shall also the coming of the son of man be;" Now this is the true spiritual and the *internal Sign* to the Elect, for when Faith is quickened from death to life, or born from its womb or seed, and *taken* into the royal Priesthood of Faith, then Christ is promised to that soul, and being in the priesthood of Christ, that incense ascends to Heaven for divine assistance, and the soul must stedfastly *watch,* and patiently wait *Christ to come* in spirit; and the divine influence of the holy *Spirit* of Christ which is the *heavenly enlightening* that decends to this pure Virgin daughter of Faith, fills her with prayer, divine assistance and thanksgiving to him that sits in the glory of Mercy; and this give Elect men *new life,* and they speak with a *new tongue*; then Reason may *wonder* but *know not from whence this come,* and *whither it go*; for the declaration of the

Messenger assisted by Christ from heaven is the *lightening* or bright *Star* that *appears in the East*, and gives the *sign of the SON OF MAN*; also guides the Virgin daughter of Faith unto the *Son of man*; and she is *given* to him, and *taken* by him, in holy marriage through the justice of the Father: So the *holy Spirit* of Christ from Heaven is the *lightening that cometh out of the east and shineth even unto the west*, i.e. the *Spirit* of Christ shine for regeneration, to the pure *Virgin* daughter of Faith and return to HIM again, by *divine incense*, and this is the royal and true *priesthood* of Faith, which Reason never can enter into, although they may transform themselves into the Messenger's declaration, even in the Messenger's day; therefore *they cannot tell from whence this light come, and whither it go*: But Reason will grow angry at this, and *preach* a Christ of his own conceiving on the letter, go forth and war against the true Christ, and his royal priesthood, and *prophecy* to *tempt* and *deceive* the Elect; hence mind this, - Christ doth not *come* according to the signs and *observations* of Reason but by those *tokens* in the royal *priesthood* of Faith, which is the *Road* for Christ, as there *HE will come to gather his Elect*; but Reason are gathered in their own priesthood, under the power of the angel in justice: Ver. 28. "For wheresoever the carcase is there will the eagles be gathered together," *i.e.* Reason will naturally go to its own *home*, and Faith to CHRIST.

MOREOVER (Ver. 29.) JESUS said, "Immediately after the tribulation of those days, shall the sun be darkened, and the moon shall not give her light, and the stars shall fall from Heaven, and the power of the Heavens shall be shaken." *Those days of tribulation* are the *days* when the mighty works of Faith are worked against the powers of Reason, death, hell, &c. both internal and external; also the *days of prophecy* even in the *sorrowful vale of death*, that Christ will come to redeem them from under those powers; for this must be done in or by *Man* to be found worthy to be called under the justice of the Father; *which* when done, then *the power of his Heavens are shaken*, i.e. although he has *prophecied* of, and expected the *Son*, yet he must go through the justice of *the Father* to the *mercy of the SON*, or no life eternal! Therefore the SON is indeed *darkened* to the soul! *and the moon shall not give her light, i.e.* all the *peace* and joy he had in or with the declaration of the Messenger, power he had over the souls of other men thereby, all the *hope* he possessed by the promise, and all the flow of *waters* in the given priesthood of Reason, which is to be enjoyed in the days of a Messenger: *Now* those thing *shine* sweetly in the soul, but it is as *Moonlight*, yet they are stopt, or *turned to blood* in the soul of man: *AND the stars shall fall from Heaven, i.e.* all his *revelation* and *assistance* from Heaven to remove internal mountains, and even the *prophecy of Christ to come*, which are heavenly *Stars* to the soul, in the *Moonlight* glory to Faith, yet *they* will *fall from their glory*, as the *flower-root droops her flower*, at the time of great drought or distress: Yea all the power and excuses of Reason is *cast off, even as a tree cast her untimely fruit*, at the time of great trial and distress: *In* this manner will *the power of the Heavens be shaken*, in and to the soul of Elect man: For when the soul is called under the justice of the Father, and asked, what he has done to save himself, or is he yet united to the *high merciful covenant of CHRIST* for salvation Then the answer is no! And his whole *power* of Faith is here inquired for! – Then, man will find he has no power to save himself, and will *stand helpless, naked and bare before this Justice*, only, the prayer of Faith is not stopt in him: Therefore the justice of the Father is opened to him and through it he must go or no life eternal; for there is Death and Hell ready to swallow up the soul; He may look back from whence he came but *those waters are turned to blood*, and no more life there! For all the flow of those *sweet waters* that he possessed under the Messenger as *Moonlight*, cannot *shine* in the soul; all his *revelations* and *prophecy*, in those *nether waters* under the Messenger which are *Stars* to the soul, are *fell from that Heaven and cannot give their light*; and the *Son is darkened* by the justice of the Father; and the *Heaven* he possessed is *rolled up, and departed* from him; for he being *called* under the justice of the Father, the internal Angel in justice will no more let him go back to the *nether waters*, for that *Time is then ended*, and it is the same to that soul as if all the *Luminaries fell* from this natural *heavenly Orb*, for eternity immediately to take place, because the *Power* of the justice of the Father is so mighty and so great! THEREFORE this spiritual *Heaven* to the soul is *shaken or fled away*, for every *island of refuge* and *Mountain of hope* in the nether waters is *moved* and gone, the aforesaid *lights shine not at this season*; through the justice of the Father they must go, or death eternal is the consequent; *then*, in this condition of soul the *Virgin* Daughter offers her eager prayer of Faith to Heaven for divine assistance; *then, appear the sign of the Son of man in Heaven*, (above the justice of the Father) to this *Virgin*, and unite with her in holy marriage, then beget to himself the *spiritual son* of Faith, which is born of this *Virgin Daughter* from under the justice of the Father, and is brought through it to the royal and glorious *mercy of the SON*, and then is united to him in *HIS own covenant* of mercy, which is above the justice of the Father, then falls asleep in that merciful *Bed* for resurrection unto life eternal; thus, the Elect will find they must lose themselves in their *own blood in death*, under the justice of the Father, to be quickened into a new Life to the glorious mercy of the SON: So when the Elect have worked the works of Faith, and is found *worthy* to be called upon under the justice of the Father, then Christ take the soul and makes it *perfect*.

AGAIN when those *great troubles* come to pass, the Elect may know *their time of deliverance draweth nigh*, but human nature will tremble and mourn; and Reason cannot appear when the Elect are gathered to the mercy of the Son, but this *understand*, their *judgment day* is then over, for they will see no more condemnation nor sorrow, but *they* are passed from death to Life, for the next state is glory! So *Blessed* is him or them that enter the royal priesthood, and abide in the works, to go through the *days of tribulation,* and of *prophecy,* then their sins are done away, and the soul is passed from death to life, fit to meet JESUS in his personal glory! But the personal appearance of Christ in his glory, will be the beginning of sorrow and mourning to the Seed of Reason, that die in manhood, under the seal of the angel in justice, for then this natural *Heaven* which is the Heaven to Reason will *dissolve,* and never more will be restored, for the *Sun, Moon, and Stars will fall* from their glory, and their lights pass away; then darkness and desolation will take place and reign for ever: Thus the Elect by the works of Faith and divine assistance from Heaven, are taken through and from this mighty *Judgment and power.* But it is left, suddenly to come upon Reason to their overthrow in *desolation,* then will those *tribes of the earth mourn!*

Moreover, when the Messenger appear to call the Elect, he himself is *the Sign of the Son of Man,* but his appearance is in the nether *Heaven* of Faith, *i.e.* the royal priesthood! Therefore Jesus said, "And he shall send his angels with a great sound of a trumpet, and they shall gather together his *Elect* from the four winds, from one end of Heaven to the other." Those *Angels* are his Messengers that come out in his covenant of grace, to call the *Elect* from the *Heaven* of Reason to the *nether Heaven* of Faith: Also *understand,* that JESUS himself gathers his Elect where his *Messengers are not,* for by the influence of his merciful spirit, *HE in secret* guide them, and his divine nature's *Voice* is an *angel* that calls the *Elect* to himself, to receive his royal and merciful Seal for eternal life; and when HE is graciously pleased to *send one back,* he is a Messenger from JESUS according to the *hour of the day,* and must call the *Elect*; but there is not, nor possible can be, any thing done in the Compact and Priesthood of Faith without the divine assistance of *JESUS from Heaven,* for all the quickening power to Faith, for to bring *Life* out of *Death,* is in and of the *Sonship of GOD*: So when the Messenger *calls,* it is to the Elect, and *gather them together* from out of Reason's *Heaven,* and *from the four winds,* which are stayed upon Reason and its *Heaven* as yet, till the *Elect* have worked their works, and are sealed by Jesus for eternal glory: And those *four winds, the Elect are gathered from,* (even from one end *of Heaven to the other*) is from under the power of *justice,* of *sin,* of *death,* and of *hell,* which will all be loosed in full upon dark Reason *anon*; - thus, the *Elect* must leave the *Heaven* of Reason behind, to come into the *Royal Priesthood* (*i.e.* the *nether Heaven* of Faith,) work the works of Faith against the powers of Reason, &c. and prophecy of *Christ to come*: NOW, when the soul has left the *Heaven* of Reason for the *nether Heaven* of Faith, work in and through this great tribulation he may know *JESUS is near his coming*: Therefore Jesus said, "Now learn a parable of the fig-tree, when his branch is yet tender, and putteth forth leaves ye know that summer is nigh," this *Fig-tree that putteth forth leaves*, is the spirit of Reason in the Elect, to tempt and overcome them if possible, but Faith by prayer and patience will *overcome*, and Reason in them will be dried up and wither away, that Faith may flourish in the glory of the SON; and it also note the *sudden coming of Christ*; therefore let the *Virgin* daughter of Faith *lift up herself* in prayer, and the soul *steadfastly watch*, for her BRIDEGROOM *is nigh* at hand to deliver her from those mighty *sorrows* and pains of hell: And when the *sign of the son of man appear in Heaven*, the soul will find that all the glory he possessed in this nether *Heaven* of Faith, which is under justice, will be *darkened* by the justice of the Father, and *pass away* for this season, before Faith can be born or translated, to pass to the *upper Heaven* of Faith, *i.e.* to the mercy of the SON: For the high covenant of the mercy of the Son, wherein dwelleth the seal of the *living God* for the resurrection to eternal glory, so far transcend the justice of the Father, that the *nether Heaven* to Faith must *pass away* to the soul, and he must lose himself in his own blood in death, under the justice of the Father, to pass from the nether, to the upper Heaven of Faith; so mighty and so great is the justice of the Father, and every one must be found *worthy* to be called under that justice, then the *son of man appear*, and take the soul through that justice, to his own glorious covenant to mercy.

Yea, when the *son of man is revealed* on this earth, by his Messenger sent from Heaven, then great *tribulation and sorrow* will follow; and the Elect must stedfastly *watch* and patiently *wait HIS coming* in spirit, for except he first comes in spirit, to seal the soul for his resurrection to eternal life the man is left *desolate*; and HIS coming in personal glory will be the beginning of *sorrow and mourning, to the tribes of the earth*: ALSO *understand*, the mighty works of Faith and prophecy, IS in the day or hour of a *Messenger*, and through *tribulation* Faith must go, as well in our days, as in the *Apostles* days; for men must be brought through those mighty powers, up to the seal of the *King of glory*; therefore Jesus said, "Verily I say unto you this generation shall not pass till all *those things* be fulfilled." *Hence* it is clear that those *tribulations and sorrows*, Christ and his apostles went through in their days; so (as I have said,) GOD the Father and great creator of Heaven and earth, left his glorious throne which was of justice, transmuted himself into his own created nature of *Adam*, and became a true *Son* to the *Power* of the Father which is his own *Power of justice,* to become the God of *Mercy*; for HE kept the law of Faith in *fallen* human nature, and offered the royal incense of Faith before the glorious throne of the Father, which *was* and *is* of justice; HE also went through the power and *tribulations* of Reason, and *prophecied* under the power of justice in the *sorrowful vale* of death, of his going into his glorious Kingdom of mercy; also lost himself in death in his own blood, (under the justice of the Father,) to quicken out of that death into a new life, to his own royal and glorious mercy, which is of the SON; and by HIS becoming Man to bring in his holy gospel, and *working* the mighty works of redemption, HE, became the *elder brother* to his Elect in the holy gospel, who serve the *younger,* therefore all the Elect must follow him through those *tribulations and prophecy in the sorrowful vale of death*; and as he went before to *prepare mansions* of mercy for them, they must *patiently* wait, and *stedfastly* watch his *coming to SEAL* them for his glorious *Mansions*: And those *great tribulations* and works of Faith, the Elect must go through, and WATCH *the coming Christ in the Day* of a Messenger of Jesus in HIS royal Priesthood of Faith, let it be in any generation, or time under the Gospel; for when *Christ come* to seal the soul for ETERNAL GLORY, then this world is ended and *judgment day* is past to that soul, and as Jesus said, *"This generation shall not pass till all these things be fulfilled,"* so it is in every *generation* under the gospel, for *time* did not end in general, when the Apostles and Elect of that time died: So the Elect may expect to go through those *works and tribulations*, to pass their day of trial and judgment to sleep in the bed of mercy, to be ready to meet Jesus in his personal glory, when he come to put an end to all *time.*

Also HE said, "Heaven and earth shall pass away, but my words shall not pass away," *i.e.* all the mighty *works* of Jesus, and his mighty *judgments* in his redemption and regeneration; the *great tribulation* and *works* of Faith, the Elect must work, to go through justice to mercy; HIS *coming* in spirit to *seal* the souls of his Elect for his glorious kingdom; HIS *leaving Reason* behind under the seal of the Angel for eternal death; and his personal *coming in great glory*, to raise his Elect to eternal glory, and give a final overthrow to the kingdoms of the earth, and of the dark spirit: *Now* all the mighty works of *creation* of Heaven and earth, which is of the *Father*, will *pass away*, and dissolve, *before any one jot or tittle of the word* of the SON *will fail*, in his redemption, judgments, sanctification, &c. For as God left the throne of justice, to gain the kingdom of mercy at the end of *time*, Moses and Elias will be translated to the glory of the SON! so the *glory* of justice will *pass away*, and the GLORY of mercy for ever *stand* to the royal *Linage* of Faith: But as I have said, the Elect must leave Reason's *Heaven, i.e.* the *earth* to *pass* to the *nether Heaven* of Faith, *i.e.* the royal *Priesthood*, and then *pass* through the justice of the *Father* to the glorious mercy of the SON; for all *rule and Power* in Heaven and earth will *pass away*, but the kingdom of Christ will for ever *stand.*

Chap. XXVII

FURTHER (Ver. 37.) JESUS said, "But as the days of Noah were, so shall also the coming of the Son of man be," now in the *days of Noah*, the *Sons of God* saw the *daughters of men were fair*, and they took them for *Wives*, and they bear them *children, i.e.* the sons of the genealogy of *Adam* took to them the daughters of *Cain's* genealogy and forgot themselves, so *generation* became corrupt among men in the *sight of God*, yet men thought themselves wonderful wise in their own conceit, therefore *Noah* only was found a *just man* and *perfect* in his generation; for God saw the wickedness of man was great and that every imagination of the thoughts of his heart was evil continually, and the earth was filled with *violence*: Now as *Noah* was perfect in his generation before God, he *walked with God, i.e.* he was *obedient* to God, and God made his intent known to *Noah*, for then the earth was filled with the *violent spirit* of Reason, that it was hard to find one born of the *royal linage* of Faith, to be capable of regeneration for the kingdom of Christ: SO as the *end of all flesh* was in the *sight of God*, then he inspired *Noah* to build an ARK of safety for all to come into, that was found *worthy* to be saved from the *deluge*; also it grieved *Noah* to see the wickedness of men, and *vexed* him to the heart; because he warned them to *flee from their evil*, that they may escape God's *wrath to come*, and they would not, but thought him a fool, and treated him with contempt and scorn, for warning them to fly from their evil, as if they had all power in themselves, and their going on was right, which was in a regardless manner to Virtue and *Truth*; for they followed their own wild and loose inclinations and desires, and excuse themselves according to their own will which was the steps of old *Cain*, and like him became *men of renown*, build cities, make great settlements and gather the treasures of the *earth*, then they may *eat, drink,* and be *merry;* and *marry* each other that their names may be enrolled in monumental earthly greatness, till the *flood came* and destroyed them in the height of their glory: So Jesus said, "For as the days that were before the flood, they were eating and drinking, marrying, and giving in marriage until the day that Noah entered into the Ark: and knew not until the flood came, and took them all away; so shall also the coming of the son of man be."

AGAIN, The *sign of the son of man now appear* in this present Messenger, who do declare the *wickedness* of this age is as great, and generation *corrupt* as in the days of *Noah*; and the *end of all flesh is now in the sight of God*: Then as *Noah* was instructed by God himself, to *build an Ark* of safety, to save all that was found worthy from the *deluge,* so it is with the present Messenger, who come out from the grand *ALTAR of Faith,* for he invites and prays the Elect to *come* from the acts and designs, and from *wallowing* in the dark mire and filth of this wicked world, into the royal *Priesthood* and *works* of Faith, that they may be brought up to the spiritual birth, seal, and sanctification of Christ the king of Faith, which is the *spiritual ARK of safety,* for then they sleep in the bed of mercy, to be raised to everlasting glory, while the *fire of wrath,* will on a *sudden come* upon Reason, and overthrow it with an eternal destruction: ALSO when this present *Messenger* do declare the will of God, and works of Faith, which is a *warning* to them, even as *Noah gave warning,* in building his *Ark,* but men are apt to excuse themselves by each others evil, which is *abomination* in the sight of God: So the present *Messenger* in the eye of Reason is troublesome, and they judge of him by the spirit of Reason, treat him with contempt and scorn; for the going out of Reason, is to seek and gather the *riches* of this earth, make great settlements, build mansions, and give them names, *eat, drink, and be merry,* rule over the souls of men, marry, and give in marriage for, or into earthly greatness, and to leave behind great sums of money, possessions, mansions, &c. as an *inheritance* to posterity, that their names may be enrolled in monumental greatness for their *acts,* and have their own family praise: So Reason will act in their own *filthy mire,* excuse themselves in their own *wild* priesthood, then hold the Messenger in contempt and scorn, that it is a rare thing to find one capable of regeneration to *enter the Ark of Christ.*

Moreover, when the *present Messenger* calls or invites the Elect to come into the *spiritual Ark,* and they also may *look for Christ to come,* so it is good for them to *flee* from the *sottish mire* of Reason, *i.e.* the world, and come to the *Messenger,* and priesthood of Faith, and work the works to be *prepared for the spiritual Ark,* which is the *seal and sanctification* of Christ the King of Faith, for eternal glory: ALSO it gives Reason notice that the *time of his destruction draweth nigh,* think what he will to the contrary, and suggest to himself what excuse he please in his own wild priesthood, that he may go on in his abominable acts: For as the *Messenger* is come to give this notice, and declare the *will of God,* therefore him or them that do not *follow the Messenger* are left *desolate* in their own wisdom on the bare letter (as aforesaid) to excuse themselves in their own evil, and by the evil of each other, and fall into death under the seal of the internal Angel in justice, then they will find what the *Messenger* said was true, then their *Heaven* is over, and *Hell* began, for CHRIST *will suddenly come* to call his Elect to his glorious kingdom, and the cherubims will follow by the echo of his ALMIGHTY VOICE, then *death and hell* will also *give up their dead* unto eternal death; thus Reason will on a sudden be overthrown in his own wisdom, in death eternal, which is a living death in utter darkness: *Therefore BLESSED* and happy are them who *obey this present Call*, leave *behind* Reason's Heaven, which men will perish with, *come* into the royal priesthood of Faith, and *go up* to the seal of *Jesus the king of Faith*, which is *the spiritual Ark of safety* that will bear the Elect up into eternal glory, when they are called.

AGAIN (Luke xvii.) Jesus said, "Likewise also as it was in the days of Lot: They did eat, they drank, they bought, they sold, they planted, they builded:" Now the city of *Sodom* differ something from the old world, for the *sons of Adam's genealogy*, took the *daughters of Cain's genealogy*, and became imperfect in generation for to become *men of Renown*, and have great settlements, which was contrary to the will of God, then justice took place which brought this *judgment* and overthrew them in their evil: But the city of *Sodom* gave themselves up to concupiscence, sodomitical practice, and loose desires, all to please themselves in their own *wild and filthy Way*, for they *eat, they drink, they bought, they sold*, (the acts of citizens,) also to *build and plant*, to have lasting habitations, for their evil acts, then excuse themselves in their own *wild* priesthood; and by each others evil, and wickedness become such as would destroy *generation*, which is against the *decree of god*, to please themselves in their own *lustful desires, and violent acts*, for which cause *God rained fire and brimstone from Heaven*, and destroyed all in their wickedness, and they *knew it not* until it come upon them: For let not the Seed of Reason think they come into this world altogether to do their own will, be at their own disposal, and please themselves their *own way*; but to do the *will of God* according to generation, love and serve their neighbour, being created under a *Law* so to do; and when the Law is broke justice take place, and become of infinite consequence for which cause judgments are brought upon *wicked* nations, cities, people, &c. Now is God brought destruction upon *wicked* nations, cities, and people that *generation* should go on according to his *decree in creation*; what judgments will he not being on the souls of men to remove evil, that *regeneration* according to the mighty *works of HIS redemption* should be compleated?

CHRIST mention the *old world*, and cities of *Sodom and Gomorrah*, to the likeness of the *destruction* of the world, they being destroyed by the vengeance of God from Heaven, and so will the whole world; also those cities are found now *the son of Man is revealed* by his present *Messenger*, for many are striving for the wealth and settlements of this world, &c. which is its kingdoms, and excuse themselves; others for the kingdoms of the *dark spirit*, which is to act against God, invade Heaven, and excuse themselves: Now those two kingdoms will *crucify the Lord of life*; for although *many* has taken the literal declaration and would own themselves the *sons of God*, but by the letter strove to become *men of renown* in their own *kingdom*, so not regard the regeneration of Christ: Further, this present *Messenger* do declare *regeneration*, and the *hour of the day* and invite into the *ARK of Christ*, then if men take this declaration, which is for regeneration to Christ; and after that *see the daughters of men are fair, and take of them to wife, i.e.* take this declaration, and judge of it by the *spirit* of emulated Reason, which is the *daughters of men that appear fair*, because they give liberty to do so as you please, go *forth, preach, excuse* yourselves, become *men or Renown, Giants* in imagination, &c. So as them of the old world acted contrary to the *Will and generation of God*, and could not enter the *Ark of Noah;* so those act contrary to the *regeneration of Christ,* and cannot enter his *spiritual ARK:* But the *City of Sodom* is of the dark wrathful blasphemous blind *spirit*, that would cut off and destroy the *regeneration of Christ,* even as the sodomites would the *regeneration of God* by filthy acts; so the earth is now, *filled with violence,* and as ripe for destruction as the aforesaid places: - NOW this, IS spiritually the *days of Noah, Lot, Egypt,* or the *Great city Jerusalem,* that act against, and *crucify the Lord of Life;* so mind what is written, and seek to enter the *Ark* of Christ.

Further, I would have you *understand,* when any nation, city, &c. is to be destroyed, a *Messenger* is first sent to *prophecy* against it, and gather the righteous from it, as *Noah* to the old world, the *angels* to Sodom, *Jonas* to Ninevah, &c. which *prophecy* was no more than inspired Reason, because those places were of the *wild* priesthood of Reason; neither was there any blood found to be spilt in them for the *prophecy and testimony of Christ,* so their evils were natural: But when Moses uttered the *given* priesthood with the law, and the prophicies of *Christ to come* were recorded, then men took it into their traditions, and became judges in their own *wild Way,* not only of the law and given priesthood of Reason, but also of the *prophecies of* Christ to come, then this become the *city of Jerusalem* wherein is found the *spirit* of wrath and persecution against CHRIST and his *Messengers;* for in this City is found the *blood of* Christ and all his Messengers, in and by persecution, and it is now in act against the present *Messenger;* therefore it is the divine *voice* of Faith that prophecies against this *City,* and where the *gospel* was declared, and *persecution* found, which centers to one head or *great City,* for which cause JESUS said, (Mat. xi.) "Woe, unto thee Chorazin, woe unto Bethsaida, for if the mighty works which were done in thee, had been done in Tyre and Sidon they would have repented long ago in sackcloth and ashes; but I say unto you, it shall be more tolerable for Tyre and Sidon in the day of judgment, than for you: And thou Capernaum which art exalted unto Heaven, shall be brought down to Hell, for if the mighty works which have been done in thee, had been done in Sodom, it would have remained until this day; but I say unto you, that it shall be more tolerable for the land of Sodom in the day of judgment than for you." Now *Tyre, Sidon, Sodom, Gomorrah,* &c. being more *tolerable in the day of judgment,* is because their sins were *natural* and filthy evils, pride, covetousness, self design, oppression,

&c. *BUT the City of Jerusalem,* and those places where the holy *Gospel* was declared, and holy *Spirit of CHRIST* blasphemed, warred against and persecuted, then, those are *spiritual* sins, which if men cannot be *taken* from in their bud, but left to go on with increase and die in them; then, this sin is *intolerable,* and cannot be forgiven in *the days of a Messenger of CHRIST,* nor will it when the dead are raided at the end of all *Time;* therefore more *tolerable* for a natural sin, than for that of blasphemy, and persecution of the holy *Spirit of Christ:* Also all natural sins are sealed by the Angel of justice, so *cherubical inspiration* has and may prophecy against it; but it is the *Spirit* of Christ, that declares and prophecies against the unbelieving, lying, hard-hearted, unmerciful, uncharitable, blasphemous, persecuting, and murdering *spirit* of Reason that *wars against the SPIRIT and power of Christ;* and this *spirit* of Reason is that which is the *great city Jerusalem:* AND I would men understand, the *prophecies of Christ* and HIS *inspiration,* far transcend the prophecies of inspired Reason; so Jesus said of the preaching of Jonas (Mat. xii.) "The men of Nineveh shall raise in judgment with this generation, and shall condemn in it, because they repented at the preaching of Jonas and behold a greater than Jonas is here," *i.e.* the people of *Nineveh* obeyed the voice of *Jonas,* repented of their *evil,* and God's justice was stayed upon them; but the people of *Jerusalem,* &c. would not obey the Voice of the SON of GOD, and *repent* of their evil, because they had the letter and prophecies to search in and give judgment thereon in their wild priesthood of Reason, and sure in themselves they were right; but the priesthood of Reason, Christ and HIS Messengers prophecy against.

Moreover, the present Messenger well knows and experimentally finds, he can gather from the aforesaid *Cities,* before he can from *Jerusalem,* Why? Because in them are found *sinners,* but in *Jerusalem* they are all *righteous* in themselves, and know their own *way to Heaven:* So *understand,* those cities are found at this day, in and by *assemblies and sects of people,* and not only so, but in private individuals, such as selfish designs, lustful desires, criminal acts, oppression to get great, and unite their families to shine in this world, and all evils that Reason can be guilty of; - Now if the external Angel catch the person, he is brought to public justice, or public censure and shame; but it is the wisdom of Reason to pass that Angel if possible by concealing his evil; and if he do, the internal Angel take and seal him down to death eternal, so it is impossible to escape; then Reason will do all he can to excuse himself and conceal his evil, and this self cunning to conceal from others, is his *City or strong-hold* in himself, wherein dwelleth *evil,* and whereon God's *judgment will come* as in time past: Also, there never was a *City* yet destroyed for their *evil,* but there is the same evil to be found concealed in the *strong city* in the soul of man, which will eat him up like a caterpillar or cankerworm.

Also, I would have men understand, that when Reason goeth out on any act, there is always an *horse and rider* goeth with him, to watch him and will give in a true report to the Angel in justice: So let Reason be ever so cunning, or deep in his evils, and concealment thereof his depth is fathomed and seen through, and sealed under them for death eternal, because the *Law* is the *horse* that goeth forth, and *truth* is the *Rider,* and rides on the *black acts* of Reason; then *truth* will give into justice, and when the law is broke the soul is sealed to be swallowed up by the relentless power of justice, like as the relentless *sea,* will swallow up the eager life of man: NOW, as when a place is to be destroyed, there is a *Messenger* sent to prophecy against it, and *gather the righteous* from it ; and as aforesaid, cherubical *Inspiration* can prophecy against those *Cities,* and them cities with others was very hateful in the sight of *Jerusalem,* because at Jerusalem they held the letter of the law and *prophecies* by their constructed priesthood of Reason, from that which Moses had given, and poured out their judgment against other people, places, cities &c. But when Christ came HE prophecied against *Jerusalem* and it was destroyed accordingly: *Now* when the *great* is prophecied against, the *less* will fall of consequence, because the *prophecies of Faith* are so mighty and so great!

AGAIN, the present *Messenger* came out in the *spirit* and *power of CHRIST,* to *call the Elect* into the royal priesthood of Faith , that they may go up to the *seal of Jesus,* which is the grand *spiritual ARK of safety;* also to prophecy against *the GREAT CITY Jerusalem,* which is all them that *profess the Letter* in their own wild way in the priesthood of Reason: Also the *Messenger,* do declare this Generation is very *wicked, corrupt* and *filthy,* and the *end of all flesh is in the sight of God;* So Reason may shortly expect its *final dissolution,* because the ROYAL VISITOR is near his *coming* to put an end to all *time,* for Reason has acted as if he came into this world to please himself; for all the goings out of Reason is to satisfy his *lustful desire,* eat well, drink well, make a great appearance, &c. and *care* for tomorrow; and what is it that Reason will not do to accomplish his design, though he often fail in his attempt to his great mortification, neither do he ever find things according to his expectation. Now, the spirit of reason captivate the Elect, and they dwell in and among this evil, which is equal to Tyre, Sidon, Sodom, &c.; but when the voice of God in the *messenger,* centers to the womb or Seed of Faith, and quickens it from death to life, then there is a *Daughter of* Faith born for regeneration, and she is *taken* into the royal priesthood of Faith, offers her own prayer which is the true incense, then will receive the *holy spirit* of Christ by influence, from whence springs *fresh beams* of knowledge, with divine instruction, which is the *internal SIGN* to Elect men; and she is brought through the wilds and temptations of Reason, then called under the justice of the Father, and is united in holy and spiritual marriage with Christ; then after this is given birth to the *spiritual Son,* born of the *Virgin Daughter* from under the justice of the Father, to the high merciful *covenant of the SON,* and is sealed by JESUS for life eternal, - thus, the soul pass above the *Orb* of Justice, into the transcendant *heaven* of mercy.

Moreover, BLESSED *and happy* are they that are so *prepared to meet JESUS* in his personal glory, which must be done by entering into the royal priesthood of Faith, then they will truly agree with the present *Messenger,* and gather their way as he do according to their portion; for let men suggest what they will they must agree with this *present Messenger,* their Faith must chord with his, like a well tuned instrument of music, otherwise they cannot enter the royal priesthood of Faith: So those men that cannot be brought out of those *cities* as the *old world, Tyre, Sidon, Sodom, Gomorra, Nineveh, Babylon,* &c. (for the present Messenger calls from the *strong-holds* of Reason, equal to all those cities) then if they will remain in them, they are left *desolate* under the seal of the Angel in justice, and will be their own witness to their own condemnation, AND if a man from the *present Messenger,* can receive no more than the outward word or bare letter, he will take it into the priesthood of Reason; yet he will say, "God is the teacher of his Elect, and nothing can be done without the assistance of God," then when *death and judgment come,* there is nothing done for salvation, and *he* is called under the justice of the Angel, and go off *murmuring* into death, in saying, "If God had assisted him he could have worked the works of Faith," which is in effect, charging God with evil and neglect: Now as the present *Messenger* prophecies against the *great CITY Jerusalem, i.e.* the *whole priesthood of Reason,* and this prophecy is conveyed over the *whole power of Reason,* as the *prophecy of Faith* is of an unmeasured scope; therefore let Reason be ever so highly exalted in his own wisdom and power; *strong is the Lord God of Heaven* who has given them up to *judgment, which will shortly come to pass.*

Chap. XXVIII

FURTHER concerning the *Mystery* of Faith in regeneration and *coming of CHRIST to judgment* (as Mark. xiii.) "But of that day, and that hour, knoweth no man no not the Angels which are in Heaven, neither the son, but the Father only;" *Now* this saying of Jesus is so mysterious, that there must be great part of *John's visional book of prophecy opened to man* before he can declare this sacred *mystery* of Faith, because it is in and of regeneration; For as God created the man Adam of his own divine nature, and *Adam was the son of God* in and according to creation; but as Adam being created under a law, hearkened to the voice of Reason and fell under the power of death, and in death would be disunited from its living Father and Creator: *Thus* God the Creator and Father to Faith, became the God of justice to his own created nature, through the acts of his own children *Adam* and *Eve;* so in this fallen state, Faith is born into this world to this day; then, when the Voice of the LORD GOD OF FAITH, by his *Messenger* or from himself *walks in the garden* which is the womb or Seed of Faith in the soul of Elect man fell under the power of justice; and the utterance to that voice is "Faith where art thou?" Here fallen Faith is called to, and soon let know, what condition it is in; then there follow justice and wrath, which is *fire,* and is *mingled with blood,* because through justice you must to in your own *blood,* and lose yourself in your *blood,* in death under justice; and all the excuse of Reason is of no use but to condemn the being, yet before this comes he will *flourish* by his own conceit like unto *green trees,* or grass, but *judgment* being cast upon it, all its excuses will be *burnt up;* NOW, this is what the *first Angel* of Faith utter, when the *sound is to fallen Faith* in the soul of Elect man, and the consequence that will follow the *sound* of that Angel: After this Faith being called or quickened from death into a new life, *i.e.* the *Virgin* daughter of Faith born for regeneration, and to her is given the *promise of Christ:* Now this is a *new Life,* quickened or born from the womb or Seed of Faith in Elect man, which is a life *distinct* to that of Reason, and to it will come a kingdom contrary to that of Reason, then Reason is angry because he is cast aside as a mountain that will burn with wrath, persecution, and temptation to, or in Elect man; but Reason being cast into his own *water's* there he must die and perish, with all his arts, emulations, cunning, &c. Now this is what the *second Angel* of Faith utter, when it *sounds* to Faith in Elect man, and the consequence which follows the *sound of that Angel.*

Again, the *Virgin* daughter of Faith being *born,* she is taken into the royal priesthood to work the *works of Faith,* against the powers of *sin, death, and hell,* then found worthy, and to her is given the *spirit of prophecy,* which is she can truly declare from *Heaven,* that Christ will *come* according to the promise given: After this at the hour of death, she is *called* under the justice of the *Father,* and from thence translated to under the mercy of the SON, which is to die under the *grand ALTAR of Faith,* and made fit for the kingdom of glory. THEN the *Lord God of Heaven* in his own time transmuted himself into his *own* created nature of Adam, which was *fallen,* and then he became a true *son* to the power of the Father, for HE kept the law of Faith, and waded through that justice and never acted against the glory of his own creation! *Thus,* the God of justice transmuted himself into *human nature,* to become the God of mercy! And he came on the prophecies of Faith, (that prophecied by this pure *Virgin daughter)* for regeneration, not only so, but, to become the royal and only *bridegroom* to this pure *Virgin* daughter of Faith! *Thus the LORD GOD of Heaven* became the *second man Adam,* that ever trod this earth, to crown regeneration and bring in salvation; and he uttered his only gospel, worked the works of Faith for redemption, lost himself in death in his own blood under the justice of the Father then quickened again, and has ascended into the high Heaven of mercy, and men must work the works of Faith to follow, and be accepted of Christ the King of Faith and mercy.

Moreover, as men are *born of the flesh* into this world, to know the things of this world, even so men must be *born of the spirit of Faith,* to know the works of Faith, and go their *way,* in regeneration to salvation of Christ; - as *first a Daughter* to whom Christ is the royal Bridegroom; *then* of this daughter a *son,* and this is the *birth of water,* and of spirit: But understand, that in the days of old, no more than the *Virgin daughter* of Faith could be born to prophecy on this earth; *until Mary, a virgin of the house of Israel in the genealogy of Faith, bore the Lord God of Heaven, and brought him into this world in a body of flesh, blood, and bone, is be a true SON to the power of the Father;* and this birth of the SON of GOD by this Virgin, in the cause of, (also shew forth) the *son* of Christ, being *spiritually born* to Christ of this spiritual *Virgin* daughter of Faith in regeneration; *So* as Christ came for *regeneration,* and to make all things *new,* Faith is born to him in *spiritual birth;* as first the *Virgin daughter* who is espoused to Christ, and she will work the works of Faith, then to her is given the *spirit of prophecy,* and she will prophecy in the sorrowful vale of death, *of Christ to come in spirit* and unite with her in holy marriage; - *then,* of this daughter is born a *son,* which is a *spiritual son* to the *SONSHIP of God.*

AGAIN, I would have the Elect *understand* the distinction between the *Son of God* in and according to creation, and the *Son of God* born of the pure *Virgin daughter,* in and according to regeneration; because *Adam was the son of God* according to creation; but as he fell under justice and death, then the *Virgin Daughter* must be born, and taken into the royal priesthood of Faith, and there to prophecy the Lord God of Heaven would become a SON to his own Power, and redeem them from under the power of *justice,* and of *sin, death,* and *hell,* which is, God who became the God of justice, through the acts of his own children, *Adam* and *Eve* would become the God of mercy to them and all the Elect, by the mighty power of his own *Act:* And this *Virgin Daughter* born of the womb or Seed of Faith in the Elect, was the *royal WITNESS OF HIS SPIRIT, olive tree, or golden candlestick, in whom the royal incense burn, that stood before him and prophecied* when HE was in the condition of God the Father, or the God of justice, and at the hour of death were translated under, and united to, the mercy of the SON; for no *son* of this *Virgin* daughter, could come out to prophecy on this earth, until the Lord God of Heaven became a SON to his own power.

Further, when the *LORD GOD of Heaven* translated *Enoch, Moses, and Elias into Heaven,* it was to no higher glory than that of the Father, which *was and is* of justice; then God made them fit, and invested them with power to *sit* in the glory of the Father, which *is* of justice, while God himself became a SON to his own power of justice to redeem the Elect and make *all things new:* So where *Moses* and *Elias* was translated to, God himself came from, to become the God of mercy; for he went through the power of the justice of the Father and is ascended into the high *Heaven* of mercy: And *Moses* and *Elias* sit in the glory of the Father to this day, and are the *Angels of the Father,* whom *JESUS will confess his royal Elect before,* in holy marriage, because they *follow him* in the works of Faith under that justice.

AGAIN, as the God of Heaven, became the *Man JESUS* on this earth, then according to Faith and human nature, HE *enrolled himself among his Elect, and call them his FRIENDS and BRETHREN!* For he brought in the holy gospel, and as so was the elder brother in the mighty works of Faith, *in* the holy gospel, *under* the justice of the Father *Then* by the mighty power of Faith HE worked the redemption for his Elect, and *is* ascended into the high heavenly glory of *Mercy,* which far transcend the heavenly glory of *justice;* - Thus, *God the Father* which *was* of justice, is become *God the SON,* which *is* of mercy, to crown regeneration and make all things new to his Elect: Therefore as God the *Father* to his Elect, according to creation which is of justice, He is again become a *Father* to them in regeneration and mercy; so the mighty works of God is this, HE created *Faith* which is of his own divine nature, than of consequence its *Father,* but created *Faith* broke its own Law, then the justice of the *Father* took place, which is disunion and death from its living *Father* and Creator, and this became of an infinite consequence both to *Father* and *son:* After this God the Creator and *Father* to *Faith,* (who became the God of justice through the acts of his own *children* Adam and Eve,) took his own created nature of *Adam* which was human nature animated with *Faith* in a *fallen state,* and become a true SON to the Power and Justice of the *Father,* and went through that justice on death, then rose again and is ascended into the high Heaven, to become the *Father* anew to his Elect, which is the Father of mercy, by regeneration for salvation: Hence the Elect may see the difference between the power of the *Father* in and according to *justice,* and power of the *Father* in and according to MERCY; yet *Him that created* worked this mighty work, and gained to *Himself* the transcendant *POWER of Mercy.*

Yea, as Christ by his almighty POWER is become the *Father* of regenerated Faith, *i.e.* the *Father of Mercy:* And great part of the *world* has transformed themselves into his declaration, so as to own and use it according to their own liking, *i.e.* to take it into their own wild priesthood of Reason, because they have no other light or life but that of Reason, to understand it: And as *Moses is buried in the soul of man.* Which is the acting power of the internal *Angel* in justice, who acts as *Moses* did when here, in and over the *soul of man,* and is as a God to Reason: *Therefore* Faith must be *born* of its womb or seed in those our days, as in the days of old, or in the time of the law, to come into its own royal priesthood to receive the *promise of Christ,* and then must *follow CHRIST* through the power of sin, death, hell, and justice: Also this *Virgin daughter* of Faith, comes forth *pure,* and will remain pure, for she never will hearken to the voice of Reason; true it is, the *soul of man* may, nay is overcome and led aside by or through the temptations of Reason, but when those troubles and storms of Reason arise in the *soul,* the *Virgin daughter* of Faith go into her ARK or BOWER, and remain entirely clear and pure, because she is for regeneration; and by her prayer and divine assistance from *Heaven* will be brought through those said powers of justice, sin, death, and hell, and come forth an entire pure virgin, who is spiritually *espoused to Jesus* who has become her *royal Bridegroom,* and also has and will come to her in spiritual and holy *marriage.*

Moreover this *Virgin daughter* is not under the justice of the *Angel,* but the justice of the *Father* only, as Christ himself was; and offers the prayer of Faith, which ascends up to *Heaven* before the throne of *justice to Faith,* which is of the *Father,* as Christ himself did when on this earth; for to this *Virgin* is given a *censer with incense, i.e.* Faith when quickened from death to life is made *able to pray,* which is the censer; and to it *prayer* is given which is the true *incense* that ascends up to *Heaven* before the throne of the *Father,* for the *mercy of the SON:* - Also to this *Virgin* daughter of Faith, is given the spirit of prophecy that *Christ will come,* and unite with her in holy marriage, bring her through the justice of the Father, and redeem her from death; and this is the other *Witness of his spirit that stands and prophecies:* Therefore as the *Virgin* daughter *stood before HIM,* when he was in the condition of God the *Father,* and prophecied; so do the *Virgin* daughter stand and prophecy before the throne of the *Father,* now he is in the condition of God the SON; which himself did, when He was on this earth a *true SON* to the power of the Father; those are the *two Witnesses, olive Trees,* or *Golden Candlesticks* in whom the royal incense burn, that *stands and prophecies, before the GOD OF THE EARTH, i.e.* before the justice of the Father: So this *Virgin* or Virgins are the TWO WITNESSES *of his own Spirit,* in HIS royal priesthood or nether Heaven of Faith, which is under the *justice of the Father,* because God put himself under his own *justice,* and became the *man Jesus* for the *kingdom of mercy;* and HE prayed, and prophecied of his kingdom of mercy to *come;* and this is the very act of the Virgin *Daughter* of Faith; for the one stood before the justice of the Father, and prayed, and prophecied of the kingdom of Christ to come, when he was in the condition of God the *Father;* and the other do the same now he is in the condition of God the SON: Therefore mind this the *nether Heaven* of Faith is under the *justice* of the Father, for through that justice Christ himself went to his own kingdom of Mercy; *So it is Faith in Faith and Faith on Faith, and Faith united to Faith; and all centers to CHRIST its King,* because they offer the incense of Faith (as Christ did,) under justice of the Father, which ascends before the throne of the Father for the mercy of the SON, and as so are the *two witnesses of his own spirit in the nether Heaven of Faith,* under the justice of the Father; for as *Heaven* has been pleased to glorify *earth, earth* is also made able to glorify *Heaven!* - Also, those *two witnesses* are to *prophecy a thousand two hundred and three-score days clothed in sack-cloth;* this is during the time of their *prophecy* and of the *patience and prayer* of Faith, which is the works of Faith to *overcome,* and if done in one day or hour it is the same for salvation, but the Spirit call it a *thousand two hundred and three-score days,* because it is on this earth in a body of flesh and blood: Now the day or *days of prophecy* is in the sorrowful vale of death, which is in great humbleness and trembling of soul, before the throne of the *Father,* and at this time or those *days,* Reason's *Heaven is shut* because he cannot reign on the soul, or tempt the Daughter of Faith from working and prophecying before God; and when this prophecy is declared, the earthly soul of Reason is angry and plagued, because he cannot stand against it. Nor take it into his own priesthood so as to rule over it, while the prophet lives; therefore the *outward* word or bare letter is the *court;* but the holy covenant and priesthood of Faith is the TEMPLE OF GOD wherein he gives power to those witnesses to prophecy, and this Reason will tread under foot.

AFTER this, when the Virgin Daughter has worked the works of Faith and prophecied of *Christ to come,* then she is found *worthy* by Christ, and this *spirit* or *virgin* of Faith, who for salvation is become the essential soul of man, (then) to it in God's time the *Voice* comes from Heaven, and calls it up before the *Justice of the Father,* which is a great *Woe* for the soul of man to pass! For he cannot go back; indeed he may look back from whence he came, but them *waters are turned into blood,* and the *powers of this Heaven shaken,* as I have said, and no more life is to be found there in this condition of soul, for here you are held fast, and *death and hell* is ready to swallow you up; so through this justice you must go or no life eternal! NOW here the soul not only *wallow,* but is within himself *lost* in his own blood, and in this very condition you *eat the flesh and drink the blood of Christ,* because this work HE himself did in *human nature* under justice of the Father; and in this trouble and distress the *Virgin Daughter* prays, and *commends herself into the hands of GOD* under the justice of the Father, then after this *appear the sign of the man.* JESUS in the HIGH HEAVENLY GLORY OF MERCY, and he comes and unites with this *pure Virgin* in spiritual and holy marriage under the justice of the Father; and when *his* holy spirit is united with this *Virgin* of Faith he begets to himself a spiritual son born of this virgin daughter from under the justice of the Father, for his own royal and glorious kingdom of mercy: *So* when the Elect has worked the works of Faith to the ultimate of their power, then Christ *comes* in upon their works, and makes them *perfect:* ALSO when this spiritual son is born from under the justice of the Father, he is taken up into an high *mountain* of Faith in regeneration, where he see Christ in great Power and great Glory, for Christ only has the *seal* of God for eternal glory; and not only so, but *sits at the right hand of them that are sealed;* then this spiritual born son of Faith offers his prayer before the *grand ALTAR of Faith;* which is at the feet of JESUS, for HE only has *power* over justice, and sin, and death, and hell, and those are the *four horns of the golden Altar of Faith.*

In this condition, the spiritual born son of the *Virgin* daughter of Faith, see and know that *CHRIST only* has all power in his own kingdom of mercy; and HE *only can seal* the soul for eternal glory; also see them that are *sealed,* and himself not sealed: Now this is the last great *Woe* to the Elect, because he see them that are sealed and himself left out, then by *Christ the KING of Faith and mercy* he must be sealed in and to his holy covenant of mercy, which is the *upper Heaven* of Faith, otherwise he cannot *inherit ETERNAL glory:* Therefore he will hang to the *feet of JESUS* in spirit, as the *point of a needle will to a magnet,* and offer his eager prayer , and there he must wait for the call which say, *"come in hither,"* which is under the seal of Christ; and then he becomes united to Christ the *King* of Faith, mercy, and salvation, in his high *Covenant* of mercy for salvation, which is far above or beyond the justice of the Father; and this is the *SEAL of the living God* for eternal life, because he is sealed a son to Christ by regeneration; then all sorrow will cease, for the *kingdom of this world is become the kingdoms of Christ* by regeneration; and the *kingdom of justice* is become the *kingdom of mercy,* which is the kingdom of Christ, and *HE will reign* in great glory, *for ever and ever!* Now here in this state; the soul has the *Assurance* of eternal life, and he utters the strong voice of Faith before the throne of mercy, in thanksgiving, and in prophecy of his own resurrection to eternal glory, then falls asleep in the bed of mercy, which is the *Paradise with CHRIST.*

AGAIN, when the spiritual born son of the Virgin Daughter (as aforesaid,) is ascended into the high mountain of Faith, sees the seal of Jesus, and them that are sealed for life eternal, offers the eager prayer of Faith at the feet of Jesus, who is the *great and GRAND ALTAR of Faith,* for the voice to come from Jesus that say, *come in hither, i.e.* into or under his *royal Seal* for *eternal glory!* But instead of that, he is sent *back* by Jesus the Angel of Faith and mercy, to tell his *Brethren the Elect* what he has seen in *Heaven:* Now such a man as this is a *Messenger of JESUS,* because he is spiritually *born* of the *Virgin* daughter of Faith to Jesus, and come out in *prayer* from the *feet of Jesus,* which is the *grand Altar* of Faith, and is as son of Jesus by or according to Regeneration, because he is born of the *pure Virgin of Faith,* that has become a *BRIDE to JESUS;* and he will and do declare the SPIRITUAL GENERATION or *regeneration of CHRIST, i.e. the birth of the Virgin Daughter and her works of Faith, the holy marriage, spiritual birth, sanctification and seal of Christ the ANGEL of Faith, for to enter the kingdom of glory!* Which will *shortly come to pass:* - ALSO, as *John Baptist* came out at the ending of the law to prepare the way of Christ's coming in flesh to bring in the holy gospel; he came out in the spirit of them, who in the days of old, and time of the law, after their heavy travail through justice, were translated for the mercy of the SON, then could truly say, "Here Christ is coming, and he is even at the door," for they only waited for the call, *"come in hither,"* which is under the *mercy of the Son,* and this spirit *John,* came out in as near as could be, to prepare the way of Christ to appear in flesh, which is the cause of *John,* being called a *great prophet:* Yet *John is said to come in the spirit and power of Elias,* which is in the spirit of him, or them, who sit in justice; - But this *spiritual born Son* of the Virgin daughter of Faith, is *born* to JESUS, for his royal covenant of mercy; and *sent back* by Jesus; and he comes forth in the *spirit and power* of Jesus, to declare the *spiritual generation of Christ, and the mighty works of Faith, to enter the kingdom of glory; and stand and prophicies before Jesus, in the upper Heaven of Faith, i.e. under the mercy of the SON.*

Chap. XXIX

MOREOVER, GOD made the man *Adam* in creation for natural generation, who is the *first man Adam,* and Christ was the *second man Adam,* and for *regeneration;* and the *spiritual son* of the Virgin Daughter, is the *third Adam.* Because he is *in regeneration,* for he is born to Christ, or re-made by Christ himself, in his holy covenant of mercy! Also as *John Baptist* came in the spirit and power of *Elias*, to prepare the way of CHRIST to come in flesh, (which is under the justice of the Father) even so do the *spiritual born son* of the Virgin Daughter, come out in the spirit and power of *Christ* to prepare the way of HIS coming to the Elect, in full power and great glory, and to put an end to all time.

Further, when Jesus speak of John the Baptist (Mat. xi.) "But what went ye out to see, a *prophet?* Yea I say unto you, and more than a prophet:" And John's being *more than a prophet* is as I said, he came out in the spirit of them, who were *translated* to under or for the mercy of the son, and as so were prepared to meet him: For when the soul prophecies of Christ to come, yet he must be *translated,* which is preparing the way to meet HIM; for he who prophecies of Christ to come, is a *prophet;* but to be *translated* for Christ, is *more* than the prophecy of him to *come,* why? Because then, there is another *Seal opened* to the soul, and the voice from Heaven *sound* higher up, which say, "*Here Christ is come,*" which state, John the Baptist come out in as near as could be, knowing he was to declare the appearance of Christ in a body of flesh - this is why John was *more than a prophet:* And Jesus said, "Verily, I say unto you among them that are born of women, there hath not risen a greater than John the Baptist, notwithstanding he that is least in the kingdom of Heaven is greater than He:" Therefore from this the Elect may see *John the Baptist* was very *great,* yet *he that is least in the kingdom of Heaven is greater than he,* because John came out in the *spirit and power of Elias,* (*i.e.* in the *spirit and power* of him or them who sit in the glory of the Father,) to prepare the way of CHRIST's sudden appearing in flesh under the justice of the Father, to work the great *Works* of Faith and redemption, bring in the holy gospel, make good his holy covenant according to his royal promise , also ascend into Heaven, not only to make good the *mansions* to them translated at death to under his divine mercy in days of *old* but also to prepare *mansions* for his Elect in *His OWN royal Covenant* of grace and mercy. NOW the *kingdom of Heaven* is under the declaration of the Gospel, and to be found no where but in the royal priesthood of Faith! There the *daughter* of Faith will receive the *Testimony of Jesus from Heaven, i.e.* the spirit of prophecy of her own salvation: Also Jesus said, "Except a man be born of water, and of spirit he cannot enter the kingdom of God," *i.e.* the *Virgin Daughter* must be *born* to the royal priesthood, and works of Faith, under the justice of the *Father,* which is of WATER; then of her the spiritual *Son is born to CHRIST,* which is of SPIRIT, and for the kingdom of God, or of Heaven; then taken up to the *feet of Jesus,* see the *kingdom of Heaven* and them that are *sealed;* then sent back from the ALTAR, to tell his brethren the Elect what he has seen, and what will soon come to pass: Now he that is so born of the *Virgin* daughter of Faith, and sent back from the feet of *Jesus,* is LEAST *in the kingdom of Heaven, why?* Because he is *born* for it, or to it, but not sealed; and he or they that are sealed, is *greater* then him that is born and not sealed, for they that are sealed sleep under the ALTAR, and all sorrow ceased: SO the spiritual born Son of the Virgin daughter, that is sent back by JESUS, is *least in the kingdom of Heaven,* yet greater than John the Baptist, because he is sent by Jesus in his holy covenant of mercy, and in the *spirit and power of CHRIST:* ALSO he comes out in the *spirit* of them that are spiritually born of the pure *Virgin* to Jesus, in his holy covenant of mercy, under his holy gospel, and offers the prayer as the *feet of Jesus,* for the voice which saith, "come in hither," Yet he is *least in the kingdom of Heaven,* as they are all sealed and sleep in the bed of mercy, and he sent back in the spirit and power of Christ to declare HIS royal Will, and that HE will soon appear in glory, yet he must be sealed by Jesus in his brethren are, so of consequence the *least in the kingdom of Heaven:* Now here the Elect may see in what *spirit and power* John the Baptist came in, to *prepare the way* of Christ's coming in flesh; and what spirit and power the *spiritual Son* came in to prepare the way of HIS coming in *Glory;* and how the *kingdom of Heaven* is invaded in those our days, as it was in their days; and *Blessed* are them that understand, and enter the royal priesthood, then Christ take them into his own kingdom of mercy and glory.

AGAIN, Jesus said, (John xiv.) "In my Father's house are many mansions, if it were not so I would have told you: I go to prepare a place for you;" Now as the *Virgin daughter* is born to the priesthood and works of Faith, and must work under the justice of the *Father* as Christ Jesus himself did, and will go into and through the *mansions of the Father,* or under the justice of the *Father* to the *mansions or place prepared* by the mercy of the SON; and also them that are sent forth by Jesus inspired under the holy Gospel as were the *Apostles* at the day of *Pentecost,* yet they were under the justice of the *Father,* and the *comforter* came from Jesus by the way or through that justice; for all must be done according to *John's visional book of prophecy;* and when regenerated Faith has *overcome,* according to the prophecy of that book, he will be born in spirit, which will be at the time, or in the days of the voice of the *sixth Angel;* and when the *spiritual son* is born to JESUS in HIS High Royal, and Spiritual *Covenant* of Grace and Mercy, he may be *sent back* immediately from JESUS in HIS own spiritual and royal covenant, (but not till then,) and this *spiritual born son* will declare *the BIRTH of the Virgin Daughter, her spiritual PROMISE of Christ, her works of Faith, to OVERCOME, her prophecy of CHRIST to come, and the holy MARRIAGE;* (which, is done by the *Way* or through the justice to the *Father,* in, and by the mystical *union* and spiritual *communion* with CHRIST in the royal priesthood of Faith,) *and the spiritual BIRTH, SANCTIFICATION, and SEAL of Christ the king of Faith:* (then the soul is made compleat by regeneration for the kingdom of Heaven,) those are the *mansions* or *places* that Christ *went before to prepare* for his Elect, in his own kingdom of *Mercy;* because by the divine assistance of CHRIST from Heaven, the Virgin Daughter is brought through *justice* to HIS own kingdom of *Mercy.* Then, every man's works of Faith will be recorded with himself in the BOOK OF LIFE!

Yea, concerning the *Virgin* daughter of Faith, or *Witness* of the spirit in the *nether Heaven* of Faith; *One* stood before the throne of God and prophecied when he was in the condition of the Father, and the *other* now he is in the condition of the Son, which is done in the royal priesthood of Faith: So John's *revelation* (Ch.xv.) "And I saw as it were a sea of glass, mingled with fire: And them that had gotten the victory over the beast, and over his image, and over his mark, and over the number of his name, stand on the sea of glass, having the harps of God:" This *sea of glass* is the royal priesthood or waters of Faith, and is like unto a *crystal sea* because there is found the holy and spiritual teachings of JESUS, which proceeds from Heaven to assist the *Virgin* to work the works of Faith before the *Throne;* for the royal Works and incense of Faith is before the *throne of God* as a *crystal sea* or a *sea of glass,* for there the soul work the works of Faith, and at times is made able to *see* through justice, even to the *Mercy of JESUS,* by the heavenly enlightenings which he receive from the throne of Heaven, which is *clear as crystal,* and on this the Virgin of Faith stand: But this *sea of glass is mingled with fire,* and this *fire* is the justice and wrath of God; for as Faith fell under justice the *vials* of God's wrath is *poured out* on the soul of man, that the *Virgin* daughter may be brought through the *mansions* of the *Father,* which is of *justice,* to the glorious mansions of the SON which is *Mercy:* And *those that has gotten* the victory over the beast, are them in whom the *Virgin* of Faith is born from its womb or seed, then there is another *Life* in man, distinct to that of Reason which is the *beast,* and to this *Life* of Faith is given the promise of Christ to *come ; and over his image,* is *over* the goings out of Reason, in his acts, imaginations, &c. for wherever Reason only actuates the soul of man, that man is the *image of the beast:* And *over his mark,* is *over* the firey Zeal he pours forth in wrath, (to have his own will, and do his own way,) and the *seal* of the internal angel; and *over* the power he has, or may receive from the *beast* to act by: And *over the number of his name over* his temptation, blasphemy, visions, revelation, and prophecy, his declaration, incense, judgments, actions, and desires to act, also his inheritance and desires to inherit or accomplish by his designs; his wisdom, shifts, turns, excuses, &c. to support his own kingdom; now in those things is *known the number of his name* and this is the NUMBER *of his Name,* which is very great, ought to be many ways *known* for his *name* is blasphemy, and the *Number* of his name is his evils and temptations; THEREFORE when the *Virgin* of Faith, is born she is taken into the royal priesthood of Faith, which is the *sea of glass,* and there the soul will be brought through and *overcome* those things; and to the *Virgin* of Faith is given the spirit of prophecy, and she will prophecy under the justice of the *Father* of CHRIST *to come,* which is done at the time or in the days of the voice of the *fifth Angel,* and be made able to *stand on this sea of glass, having the harps of God,* which is the voice of Faith, in declaration, prophecy, prayer, and thanksgivings before the *Throne:* For this *understand* whenever the *Virgin Daughter* is born it is for the *Son of God,* HE will not *leave* that soul but in his own time will convert it to his own likeness. Again, (Ver. 3.) "And they sung the song of *Moses* the servant of God and the song of the *Lamb,* saying, great and marvellous are thy works. LORD GOD ALMIGHTY, just and true are thy ways thou KING of Saints: Now the *song of Moses* that was sung on this *sea of glass,* was by them that in the days of old, and in the time of the law, that the *Virgin Daughter* was born and taken into the royal priesthood of Faith, and prophecy of CHRIST *to come,* when HE was in the condition of God the Father, which is of justice, and by the divine assistance of God's holy spirit from *Heaven,* to help the *Virgin* for the coming of Christ; and this is the waters of Faith like unto *crystal,* because by this divine light the soul at times, is made able to *see* through justice, up to the mercy of the SON: And it being *mingled with fire,* is because through the *kingdom of justice* you must to the *kingdom of mercy:* Now the *song of Moses* is on the one part for a temporal blessing or deliverance, and this the spirit of Reason can *sing,* as the Israelites of old did, when the Egyptians was drowned in the sea, or when God's justice was *stayed* on them, according to the priesthood that *Moses* gave forth with the law: But when *Joshua* was to have the charge of the people, then, (see the song of Moses, Deut. xxiii.) "When the most high divided to the nations their inheritance; when he separated the sons of Adam; for the Lord's portion is his people: Jacob is the lot of his inheritance: And also how he found Jacob in the wilderness, led him, and instructed him, and kept him as the apple of his eye: (Ver. 15.) But Jeshurun waxed fat, and kicked: Thou art waxed fat, thou art grown thick, thou art covered with fatness; then he forsook God which made him, and lightly esteemed the rock of his salvation:" Now here Moses saw the difference between the *two kingdoms,* for the kingdom of God was in Jacob, which WAS and IS Faith; but the kingdom of *Jeshurun* WAS and IS Reason: Also although Moses was the anointed cherubim according to that inspiration, yet he was taken into the royal priesthood of Faith, and wrote concerning Christ.

Although, when Moses wrote the law, and to the Israelites concerning it, and of God's temporal deliverance, preservation, and prosperity to them, if they did but obey those commands *there,* his prophecy of Christ may not appear so plain, as in some other prophets; but this is to be understood, GOD made known to Moses the works of HIS creation, with its consequence, and that the man

Adam's *Life* was of God's own nature, the *law,* given to Adam, his *fall* for breaking that Law, the *promise* of Christ to come to bring life out of that death, the *Garden* of Faith in which God *walks* for regeneration, and the *quickening power* to Faith for regeneration: Also of the *serpent* who was the fallen *Angel,* of his being a *tempter* and did tempt, the *curse* pronounced on him, and of the *two seeds* that was become to two generations and Kingdoms; the *birth* of Cain and that he was a murderer, his being before the *cherubim and flaming sword,* or internal *Angel* in justice whom Cain called *Lord,* his being *loosed, cast out,* and kept from the *tree of life,* his wandering *condition,* and genealogy of *Adam,* (then the kingdoms and priesthoods were *divided;)* the *nature* of Faith and of Reason, that God *walked with Enoch,* and his translation into Heaven; the *mystical union* and spiritual *communion,* the fathers of old had with god of the coming of Christ; their promise, prophecies, incense and works of Faith, in that royal priesthood; that the kingdom of *Faith* is the *inheritance* of Christ, which is of mercy, and the kingdom of *Jeshurun* is the *inheritance* of Reason, which is of justice: So Moses had great knowledge given of God and of the coming of Christ; and that God drowned the world through the wickedness of man in *Noah's days;* yea, he wrote of the fathers of old being in mystical union, and spiritual communion with God, concerning the *redemption,* because he was taken into the priesthood of Faith as they were, and prophesied of Christ as they did, and the first *man of God* that in public declared the creation, and brought up the genealogy of Faith, and of Reason unto his days; now all those things was given to Moses by the LORD GOD OF HEAVEN; therefore a greater than Moses *was* not, and is not to be found among the prophets in the time of the law: But I would have the Elect observe, where he write and stand as a *Lawgiver* to Reason, and where he write and stand in the *royal compact,* and *priesthood* of Faith.

Again, when the LORD GOD said unto Moses, "Thy days approach that thou must die, call *Joshua* that I may give him charge," then Moses was delivered from *Reason,* its law, and justice of that law: And *Moses sung this song* of deliverance, and gave thanks on this *sea of glass* which is before the THRONE, for this deliverance; for then Moses would be taken into the *royal priesthood* of Faith, and not go out any more: There he was *translated* (under the justice of the Father) to the *Glory of the Father;* and when time ends he WILL BE *again translated* to the mercy and *Glory of the SON:* this is the *Song of Moses,* that the Elect of old, and in the time of the law did *sing;* for the *Virgin* in them was born; were in the royal priesthood of Faith, prophecied of *Christ to come;* and *was translated* under the power of the *Father* for the mercy and glory of the SON: Which *Virgin* is one of the *Witnesses of his spirit* or *olive-trees,* that stood before the throne *and prophecied,* when HE WAS in the condition of the Father, and has the *Father's name written in their forehead,* for the *Seal of the SON:* The other *witness of his spirit or olive-tree,* is the *Virgin* that *stand,* with thanksgiving for their deliverance, and divine assistance, and *prophecy before the Throne* now HE IS in the condition of the SON: This is the *song of Moses,* and the *song of the Lamb,* that is sung on this *sea of glass,* in this nether *Heaven* of Faith.

Further, the spiritual *song of Moses,* it is to pass the justice of the Angel, or *cherubim and flaming sword,* (justice to Reason) to the justice of the Father, which is justice to Faith: Also to be *translated* under that justice, to that *Glory,* for the *Glory of the Father,* is the head, height, or power of that justice, and is the height of the *song of Moses,* because Moses was translated to that *Glory,* in Heaven above, and is *ready* for tranflation to the *Mercy and Glory of the SON* at the glorious *Resurrection* to life eternal: Also the Elect of old, and in the time of the law, and until Christ ascended into his glorious kingdom and covenant of mercy, *they,* were all translated at their death under the power of the *Father,* for the mercy and glory of the Son: then the *Virgin daughter* of Faith became united to GOD *for* CHRIST; and those are them that were *hated or slain* by the spirit of Reason, for the *word of God,* and the *testimony* they held, and do sleep under the *ALTAR of Faith:* SO in the priesthood of Faith, in days of old, the Virgin daughter saw the days of Christ and rejoiced; and would have much more rejoiced to have brought forth a *spiritual son* to Christ in regeneration, as it was then known, that would come to pass but not until the God of *justice became the God of* Mercy: Then as I said, they were united to God for Christ, and passed to the head of justice, or the *Power* of the Father, for the mercy and union of the Son: - This is the ultimate of the *song of Moses,* even in Heaven above; but here, the *Virgin* of faith could not bring forth a spiritual son to Christ, Why? because the works of redemption was not then done.

Chap. XXX

MOREOVER, when Jesus had worked the works of redemption, ascended into his own covenant or high heaven of *Mercy,* then he took possession of his *glorious NEW Kingdom* which he had gained to himself, *i.e.* to possess the grand union, or be united to or with the *Virgin daughter* of regenerated Faith, that was before united to God, for the Mercy and glory of Christ; for then he was become Christ the God of mercy, according to the *Faith and prophecy* of the pure *Virgin;* and had power to *loose the Seal* of the Father which is of justice, and put his own ROYAL SEAL which is mercy; (see Rev. iv.) "John saw a throne was set in Heaven, and one sat on the throne, and round and about the throne were twenty-four elders sitting clothed in white, and had on their heads crowns of gold, and out of the throne, proceeded lightening, and thunderings, and voices, and there were seven lamps of fire, which are the seven spirits of God." Now those *seven spirits of God* goeth out on the womb and daughter of Faith, for regeneration, redemption, and salvation: "And before the throne there was a sea of glass like unto crystal: And in the midst of the throne, and around about the throne were four beast full of eyes before and behind:" Now the *sea of glass like unto crystal,* is here spoke without being *mingled with fire,* because those that *was* there had passed through the justice of the *Father,* to that *Glory,* and were united to God for Christ, so they had not the *Firey wrath* to go through for *they* had passed *to* the height of the glory and power of the *Father* relative to regeneration: And in all this great and glorious *Vision John saw* in this place, there was but *one,* had passed to the power and glory of mercy which was HIM *that sat on the throne* and had a *rainbow round and about,* this *rainbow* is round the throne of Mercy on which *CHRIST sitteth,* and it shew forth that God has redeemed his *Elect,* according to his royal covenant made with *them,* and that he will *seal* them, *raise* them, and *translate* them, to his own kingdom of mercy and glory: And as this *spiritual rainbow,* belong only to regeneration, redemption, and salvation, it cannot be *seen or known,* but in the royal priesthood of Faith it being the transcendant glorious mercy of CHRIST to his Elect. THOSE *four beast* that are in the *midst, and round about the throne,* are *Enoch, Moses, Elias, and Jesus,* for the *three* first were *translated* to the throne and glory of the Father, when God was in the condition to the Father: - THEREFORE where Enoch, Moses, and Elias was translated to GOD himself came from, to become a true *son* to the *Power* of the Father, to become the God of mercy; and no one in *Heaven* or *Earth* was or could be found, but Jesus only, that could keep the law of Faith, and go through the justice of the Father, to work the works of redemption, which was done before the *Throne of the Father:* and in this *HE gave that honour, glory, and thanksgiving before the throne of the Father* which no one but himself could do; and is ascended into HIS heavenly and glorious *Throne of Mercy,* and is *Him,* among the *four beast* that has the *face of a man;* because *HE has faced,* gone through, *overcome* and *conquered* the power of Reason, of *Sin,* of *Death,* of *Hell,* and of *Justice,* and has gained to himself the glorious throne of mercy; then, - by this, of consequence *HE has the face of a man,* therefore HE has the RULE over his whole Kingdom of regenerated Faith: And the other three which has the likeness of a *Lion,* and of a *Calf,* and of a *flying eagle* is Moses, Elias and Enoch, for they have all *passed* the angel in justice, which is angel to Reason, and are *translated* to the glory of the Father;

then sang the *song of Moses* and sit in the power and glory of the Father unto this day, *i.e.* in the power and glory of justice: And the *spirit* call them by this *likeness;* as of a *Lion,* is the ftrong ruling power of the glory of justice; of a *flying eagle,* is the quick eye, and swift motion in that power; of a *calf,* is that it is done by the nature of *regenerated* Faith, that was *regenerated from the earth , and from among men,* with a power invested by the LORD GOD of Faith and regeneration: And though those men are glorified in Heaven above, and are full of Faith and glory; yet the *Throne* and *Glory* of mercy, which is of the SON, so much transcends that of justice, which is of the Father, that the *Spirit* do not admit any created and regenerated being of Faith, truly to have the *face of a man,* until they have passed through all *powers,* and from all *powers* that shall keep the man from the *Glory* and merciful *Throne* of the SON; then they will be made according to his own likeness; *then* truly and compleatly will have *the face of a man,* by the power of Faith in regeneration and salvation; and live and reign with Christ in the *Glory of Mercy* for ever and ever, Amen.

Again, those *beast are full of eyes before and behind:* Now those *eyes* are Faith, and its quick properties, and the true knowledge and experience in the works and fruits of Faith, the spirit of prophecy, the power of God, and his divine wisdom: As first God created all things and in that he knew all things, and their power; and that Faith fell under the power of death and hell, for hearkening to Reason and that it would cost the *godhead life* that created it, to redeem it: Also that Reason is cast out, and kept from the *Tree of Life, i.e.* the mercy of the SON, by the *cherubim and flaming sword, i.e.* the internal angel in justice: Also when God became man to redeem HE was under the justice of the Father, and well knew the voice of Faith, from the voice of Reason, the priesthood of Faith, from that of Reason; and the mighty works of *patience,* and of *Faith* to overcome; for through the power and *scourge* of Reason, and of justice, sin, death, and hell HE went, and *overcome;* then left all those powers behind, and is ascended into his *high Heaven* of mercy: So as JESUS has gone through those powers, and left them all behind him, there is no one in Heaven or earth, knows more of those *powers,* where, and when, to *assist* his royal Elect under them, to bring *them* through those powers to his glory of mercy; and in this HE *is full of eyes behind:* Also Jesus has great *prophecy,* that his royal Elect will inherit crowns of glory, in his glorious kingdom of mercy; and no one but HIM has power to raise them to that glory; nor is there any one *knows* like unto JESUS, the great *glory,* grand *union,* powerful and *holy communion,* the KINGDOM of FAITH will have, when it is raised to its glorious fruition; and in this HE *is full of eyes before,* as well as behind. NOW *Enoch, Moses and Elias* have also, *eyes before and behind;* for they have born a body of flesh on this earth, and were under the internal angel in justice and well *know* the power of God, over Reason: Also they know the power of God in the priesthood of Faith, and the works and fruits of Faith in that royal priesthood, with the spirit of prophecy (in this *sorrowful Vale* of death) of *Christ to come;* and what it is to *pass* the angel in justice to the justice of the *Father,* and through that justice to the *glory of the Father,* so in this *they are full of eyes behind,* because they well know the *power of God,* to bring the *Virgin* of Faith through those things, and the hard *travail* to come through those powers: Further they now sit in the *glory of the Father,* and have *power* over those powers: Also JESUS now sit on the *Throne of mercy;* and they have strong prophecy HE will open that kingdom of glory to his Elect, and of the crowns of glory they will have and enjoy in that glorious kingdom; and in this *they are full of eyes before:* Because the Lord God of Heaven has gained to himself this kingdom of mercy and glory for his Elect, therefore they give all honour, praise, glory and thanksgiving before the throne, and are *full of eyes before and behind* because they live, and their life is Faith regenerated.

Also those *four beast* had each of them *six wings:* Now those *wings* is the POWER of Faith to ascend or descend, and its strong inspiration and revelation; as thus, the LORD GOD of Heaven had power to *transmute* himself, into his own created nature of Adam, which was *human,* animated with Faith in a fallen state, so become man; go *through* the power of Reason, and never hearken to it, to fall under the power of its temptation: Again HE had power to go through the *justice* of the Father, which was to lose himself in his own blood in death under that justice, and *quicken* out of that death into a new life for mercy After this, HE had power to ascend into his high Heaven of mercy; and take *possession;* and full power in and over his royal kingdom of regenerated Faith: - Those are the *six wings* which belong to HIM that hath the *face of a man; i.e.* Power to become man, and keep the law of Faith; Power to go through the justice of the Father to redeem his Elect; and power to take possession of his new and glorious kingdom of mercy, which HE had gained; which is power to seal his Elect in his royal *covenant* of mercy, and power to raise and translate them to the *glory* of his mercy! Now I would the Elect *understand,* those *Wings* are made use of, in the royal priesthood and compact of Faith, for regeneration, redemption, and salvation: - THEREFORE the other three have their *Wings;* as *first,* Elect men are born into this world under the power of the angel of Reason, and subjected to that power; but when the voice of God come to fallen Faith, it quickens a new life out of that death which is the *Virgin* daughter of Faith born for regeneration, and to her comes the promise of Christ, and she will work the works of Faith and prophecy; but the soul is incumbered with the angel of Reason, until the voice of God comes to Faith and calls the soul from under this angel in justice and when this comes to pass, Faith has *wings to flee* from under that power, as *Moses* and others did: *Again,* when the Elect are called to the power and glory of the Father, or spiritual birth, Faith has also *wings to flee* thither: *Moreover* when Faith is called to the *Seal* of the LIVING GOD, resurrection, and translation to eternal life. In the glory of mercy with Christ, Faith has *wings to flee* there; and those are the *wings,* Enoch, Moses, and Elias have; and not them only, but all the Elect in *regeneration: i.e.* Faith, when in regeneration is called, it has power to *flee* from, or pass the angel in justice; also when called before the justice of the Father, it has power or *wings to flee* through that justice to that glory, or bring forth a spiritual son to the *Seal* of Christ: Again, when Faith is called to the glory and mercy of the SON, it has also *wings* or power to *flee* there; and those are the true *wings* of Faith, that *John* saw the four beast (which are in Heaven above) had.

Again, "those *beast* are full of eyes *within:* Now whose *eyes* is the power and *quick sight* of Faith; as first, when God was in the *glory of the Father,* He had power and divine wisdom to quicken Faith from death to life, and gather it up to his own glory for the mercy and glory of that *Kingdom,* which he would gain to himself by his becoming a SON to redeem his Elect: Also when JESUS was on this earth in a body of flesh, HE never fell into temptation for *HIS quick eye* of Faith always knew the tempter, let him appear in what manner, form, or condition soever, as HE well knew the *mark and the number* of the tempter: Also the *Virgin* daughter of Faith when active never will hearken to Reason; true it is, when the *Virgin* is inactive, and Reason the tempter has power over the being, then the soul, may, nay, is tempted to sin; but this I advise you, first look at your tempter, and see what good he ever has, or can do for himself and how he can protect himself from the wrath of God; for in all his out goings, it is in self-flattery, on or after things which must perish with himself: But you will much oblige Reason, to let him tempt you that he may rule over you, and lead you under the seal of the angel that you may perish with him; (for any thing you then know to the contrary;) so I would have no one be afraid to affront his tempter; - but as Faith grows strong, it refine the man then the *eye* of Faith become *quick within to WATCH* the tempter, and will know him, refuse, and repulse him; for when Faith is rose from death to life, it has *eyes* given it from Heaven, to *see* the power of redemption, regeneration, and salvation; and will work the works of Faith, and WORSHIP GOD, and are found worthy: then from Heaven is given the spirit of prophecy of Christ to come, which is a further *sight,* or *eyes,* to see the mighty power, works, and judgments of God, and *Moses* and *Elias* was *true,* in and under the cherubical inspiration, and *Enoch, Moses* and *Elias* was also *true,* in or under the inspiration of Faith, and as so was *faithful and true* in all the *household* of God; (and HE *came and found them so,* then translated them into *Heaven,* and made them *rulers over his whole household,* in justice;) and it is by this *quick sight,* and power invested, they have the true wisdom in the good *rule,* in God's *household* in justice which is the *eye or eyes* of regenerated Faith likened unto a *calf* because of its pure innocent nature: And it is by the *eye or eyes* of Faith in CHRIST, that HE see and rule over his whole *household* of regenerated Faith and mercy; and is likened unto a *Lamb*, because he is *LORD* and *KING* in and over his whole Household of regenerated Faith, mercy and *Glory*, and of the resurrection and translation to the *high Glory* of mercy: Now here the Elect may see the mighty power and glory of Faith in Heaven above; but *understand*, them that possess it has worked the works in the royal priesthood or its nether *Heaven* on this *earth*, because Faith fell on this *earth*, and in a body of this *earth*; and the acting powers of temptation, sin, justice and death, is also *here*; so the Elect in regeneration has the *eyes* of Faith *within* to watch the tempter, and work the works to *follow Christ* through those powers, and all the *fields, kingdoms,* and powers of fallen Reason, to *inherit his Kingdom and CROWN of MERCY*; for all the works of Faith is in regeneration to enter the glorious kingdom of Christ, and is done on this *earth* in a body of flesh: So it is by those *eyes of Faith within*, that the Elect WATCH the tempter, and also the *coming* of Christ; and BLESSED are them that are so bound by HIM when he comes in spirit; then he gave them the spirit of prophecy, that he will come again to them in holy marriage, and also give them *wisdom* in this nether heaven of Faith, and make them *rulers over* the whole powers of Reason which are under justice, because according to their *Faith* in regeneration and *prophecy,* Reason is *left* and will be judged.

Yea, Faith in regeneration has *wings* to flee from one *mansion* or power to another when called; and also in prayer and thanksgiving, and by incense, (which is the flow, act, or life, of Faith, in the worship of God and Christ,) Faith by influence has *wings to flee* up to Heaven before the throne, and when *warned* to *flee* from evil: - Again, Faith, here in regeneration has *Eyes before and behind,* being *taken* from the house of Reason, and from its justice, and out of death; and it *see* and *know* from whence it was *taken,* and from whence it came; so it has no manner of desire to return back to the old House, but will look forward and *see* no one can enter the kingdom of Christ without regeneration, and *works* of Faith, to *follow* Christ; So by those Eyes *before* it will work the works of Faith, and press forward for the *House of CHRIST,* i.e. the kingdom of Faith, mercy, and life that HE has made anew for his Elect: And by those Eyes *behind* will see the *ruination* of Reason, and not return back to the *old house,* which is the kingdom of reason, justice, and death: So the power of regeneration is very great, for what is *regenerated* is the very *nature GOD took on him* to become CHRIST and redeem!

Ver.8. "And the four beast rest not day and night saying, Holy, Holy, Holy, Lord God Almighty; which WAS and IS and IS TO COME." This is the voice of Faith *in* regeneration, and *of* regenerated Faith: - For GOD created both heaven and earth, the sea and all things therein, and they was created for his glory; and has manifested himself both in heaven and earth, and IS *to come to put an end to time,* and bring in *eternity:* Also it was God that created Faith, and it is God that redeemed Faith, and is *yet to come* to its assistance; also HE was God the *Father* and is now become God the SON, and *elder Brother* in the holy Gospel; also he WAS the God of justice to Faith and IS NOW become the God of mercy to Faith; also HE WAS the Father of *created* Faith, and IS NOW become the Father of *regenerated* Faith, and is yet *to come* to make it compleat: Again, it is CHRIST that raise Faith from death to life for regeneration; and it is HIM that give the *Virgin* daughter of Faith the spirit of prophecy; and is yet to come to her in holy marriage; so HE WAS *the first resurrection* to fallen Faith, and is HIM that assist the Virgin Daughter to go through the powers of *Reason, sin, death, hell, and justice,* and is yet *to come* with the *second resurrection* to life eternal, therefore when the *Virgin* is born and taken into the royal priesthood, Christ is yet to come to her for in the travail through this great *wilderness* Christ *is to come* to her assistance, to go through and *overcome* the powers of hell and death, and the removal of internal *mountains,* give the spirit of prophecy, unite with her in holy marriage, to seal and sanctify the spiritual born son; for it *was* the LORD GOD OF HEAVEN who put himself under those powers, and it is HIM that has gone through and *overcome* those powers; and IS *to come* to assist and bring the *Elect* through those powers: So throughout the whole *Heaven* of Faith in and for regeneration, *Christ is yet to come:* - For although *Enoch, Moses, and Elias* are glorified in heaven above, and their life is regenerated Faith, yet they sit in the glory of justice, and CHRIST is yet to *come* to translate them to HIS own kingdom the *Glory of mercy;* which will be done at the glorious *Resurrection,* glorification and coronation of his royal Elect, to make his royal kingdom of regenerated Faith compleat: Therefore Christ was the *creator* and *fountain* of Faith, and it is HIM who has *overcome* and made all things *anew* for his Elect, and is yet *to come* to make them *compleat;* and take them into his everlasting kingdom the glory of mercy: And the prayer of Faith in the royal priesthood is for Christ to *come* to its assistance: And this is the *Voice* of Faith in regeneration, and of regenerated Faith in its Heavens, *Holy, Holy, Holy, Lord God Almighty which Was, and IS, and is TO COME.*

Again (the voice of the Seraphic host I have declared in my *Book of the Law. Chap. X.* for they stand as they were first created; but the cherubim fell into generation; also declared their voice and acts, *Chap. IX. And in Ezekiel's vision in that book:)* Now as the cherubim fell into generation the footing on which they stand is split asunder, because them that die in childhood and the natural ideot will be raised cherubims to glory, to compose that heavenly host or glorious order in heaven above; and they will utter their *Voice* of salvation in the glorious morning of the resurrection, and continue it in all eternity; but them who live to manhood the angel take place in the soul, and they must go their way according to infinite justice: - there is the law and given priesthood remain as their inheritance; and the flow of blessing: But as they have the letter of the gospel, they form the salvation of Christ according to their own liking, and imitate the child or cherubim in *voice* and language, yet cannot die a child nor inherit that kingdom: And *many* go forth and teach their *Way* of salvation by their eager *Zeal*, which is the *daughter* of Reason; but when a Messenger of God come and utter his voice, it puts this *daughter* into great agitation and either drive her at a distance, and may catch what she can by way of transformation; or bring forth the spiritual *son of perdition,* which come forth in wrath, blasphemy, persecution, &c. against the *Kingdom of CHRIST*: Now this is the voice or language of the dark cherubim, and Reason being manifest by its fruit.

Also when Elect man is born into this world, he has the cherubical state, kingdom, and powers to pass through, and when he come to manhood the angel take place in the soul; then he is charged with the law, and must worship God according to that kingdom, power, and inspiration, to have that blessing: But there is the Kingdoms and powers of this world to take him, and kingdoms and powers of the dark spirit, and he must pass through those to the *kingdom of the Father,* i.e. when the *Virgin* daughter of Faith is born, and *taken* into the royal priesthood, then by this *Virgin daughter* and divine assistance from heaven, he must work the works of Faith and *overcome* those kingdoms and powers, leave them behind, pass the justice of the angel, and go through the justice of the Father to the mercy of the SON: For as a man is born into this world a child, and pass through a childhood state to manhood even so must the Elect pass through those kingdoms and powers; for those who fall in the state of childhood, will be raised in the cherubical glorious kingdom; and them that fall in the kingdoms of this world, and of the dark spirit, will be raised under the *seal* of the angel in justice: And them who fall in the *kingdom of the Father,* will be raised in the glorious Kingdom of the SON.

Again, as the Elect of God are *scattered* about the whole world, and under the power of *nations and tongues where the Whore sitteth;* it may well be called *nations and tongues,* because of the *kingdoms of this world,* and of the *dark spirit*; all contend for their *kingdom,* i.e. their *Will* and *Way;* and all desire to build their *place of safety, or tower, up to heaven* as is their own will and way; for they mean God to forgive all they please to do; now this is the *building of Babel* and confusion of tongues, which is become very great, for here the *whore sitteth ;* and out from those *people, kindred, nations, and tongues,* are the Elect *redeemed* and regenerated; and this way is the lost *KINGDOM OF ISRAEL restored,* and gathered to CHRIST by regeneration and *they* are of one kindred, kingdom, and tongue,. *i.e.* the *kingdom of Christ;* and their *voice* of Faith in regeneration, and of regenerated Faith!- There is also the *voice* of the child or cherubim, and of the seraphims, and those are the *pure tongues* without confusion: For as created Faith broke its own law, and *fell*; under the power of Reason, justice, and death, then all things was made and become *new,* for the salvation of the Elect; so HE who WAS and IS the God and Father of created Faith, has worked the works of God in and for Redemption, and is now become the God and Father of regenerated Faith; and the mighty works of Faith to go through and overcome the said powers, is done on this earth, in a body of flesh, then the Elect are made anew, and become the *sons of God* in and according to regeneration: So, (Rev. xxi.) "He that overcometh, shall inherit all things and I will be his God, and he shall be my *son."* And as there is a *son* born in regeneration, and *sent back* to tell his tale, he has *sounded the Voice of the sixth Angel* in regeneration, in public on this earth, and *prepared the way of the SEVENTH to sound* in public, which will be done by *Christ the KING of Faith,* when he comes to compleat his *Kingdom* and put an *end to all time,* for the *eleventh* hour is past, and the *twelfth* is come, which is CHRIST's *own hour* or *time* to come in, and *judge the world:* But what year, month, week, day, or hour, according to man's accompt, the *son* in regeneration cannot tell, for that is known to the *Father* of regenerated Faith *only;* because this world only stand for the sake of HIS *kingdom* to be made compleat; so that is *not of the son to know but of the Father only;* yet according to creation and fall of Faith it is not of the *Father* but of the *Son;* because God became a SON to his own power, and worked the *works of God* for redemption and regeneration, made all things anew, gained this great and mighty power to himself, and is the *Father* of regenerated Faith; therefore HE *only knows:* But this know, - according to *Declaration,* - *Prophecy,* - *and Revelation, His Hour is come!!!* Therefore *watch!*

Again, although the cherubim or serpent angel broke the Law he was created under, yet never could brake that *pure Justice,* so brought it here into generation and it was sown into this *Earth,* as *pure* as God created it: Now *Moses* was the anointed cherubim according to that inspiration; for he was inspired in the power and purity of that *Law* and *justice;* and *walked on this Earth* in a body of flesh, and person of man, in the power and purity of that justice, as a *God and Lawgiver* to the seed of Reason: *Again,* Faith was sown into this *earth* in the man *Adam,* and brought on by generation; then the *Lord GOD of heaven* who created Faith, transmuted himself into earth or flesh, and took on him his own nature, which he created in Adam, and *walked on this earth* in a body of flesh, and person of man, in the mighty power and fullness of Faith; for HE kept the law of Faith, redeemed his Elect, and become the Lord God of regeneration. *Again,* - John the Baptist came out in the spirit of them who (in the days of old and time of the law) were *translated* to under the mercy of the SON, and united to *God for Christ;* and he came out in the spirit and power of Elias (for Elias was *translated* and united to God for Christ;) and in this *spirit* he *walked on this earth,* and declared the sudden appearance of Christ in a body of flesh to redeem his Elect, and bring in his holy gospel and kingdom. *Again,* the *spiritual born Son* of the *Virgin* daughter of Faith in regeneration, came out in the spirit of them, that the *Son were born,* and ascended into an high mountain of Faith in regeneration, and offer at the feet of JESUS for the voice which say *come in hither;* now in this *spirit* he came out, and in the spirit and power of Jesus; and in this *spirit and power* he *walks on this earth,* and has *sounded the voice of the SIXTH angel* in regeneration, and *prepared the way of the SEVENTH to sound:* Now *he that hath wisdom let him understand* those comings out and those comers out, then he will know the *time of the day.*

Chap. XXXI

MOREOVER concerning the mighty acts and power of CHRIST in regeneration, and of his coming to judgment, as in Matt. xxiv. "Then shall two be in the field, the one shall be taken, and the other left:" This life and world is the *Field* for regeneration, where there is natural desire, bonds, union, and duty; and frail nature will have labour, trouble anxiety, sorrow, and mourning; but at the same time, mind, not to be lost in those things for the spirit of Reason will twine about, cleave to, and intermix his slime with your duty, then will desire and urge for that which cannot, or should not be done, and overload the soul, so that man will sink and be *lost:* But mind, *CHRIST gather out of the Field* by and for regeneration, and will have his own *kingdom;* so *strive* to enter into the royal priesthood of Faith to *worship God and Christ,* then you will know Moses, and your *burthen* be made more light; for into this *Field* there is a desire to go, and many fall into ruination, madness, self-murder, and many evils both of body and spirit. ALSO, there is the *Field* of wild Reason, where Reason has his delights to go out, and *walk to and fro the earth* in his *wild way,* seeking to excel each other by their arts and emulations; and to gather up riches, strive against, contend with, drive, and enslave each other, to become great and shine in their kingdom, as if they would have the creation and power of GOD to their liking, or form it anew; and delight in, and gather up the flowers and fruits of stupefaction and death, seeking to have their own will, and do their own way; also seeking each others commendation, good will and name, by flattery and deceit to *devour* each other if possible, through a selfish view, oppression, malice, lies, &c. and tempt and drive each other into evil, through the fashions and ways of this life: Now thus the spirit of Reason *walk to and fro this earth,* in this his *Field,* and is *transformed into a priest* to excuse himself: So by drinking the dark waters of the *great river Euphrates,* they excuse themselves by each others evil in what way they can.

Also there is the *Field* of argument; *i.e.* to question and contend against the will, wisdom, and power of GOD: As, when a Messenger is sent from God to declare HIS *will and power,* Reason will come to tempt him and question, contend, and seek to overthrow him, but cannot; then he will *walk to and fro* by his imagination, and enquire by the spirit of Reason, and *of* the spirit of Reason (which is the devil) then he will come from *walking to and fro,* to the messenger to question and try again, but cannot prevail; and will go out to seek what evil he can concerning the Messenger, and judge of him according to his own evil spirit; because what evil is in himself, he thinks it, and would have it to be in the Messenger; and sets great value on himself for his wisdom, then the question is, Whether the Messenger is of GOD or not? Or for why may not he be saved according to his former confidence? And why should God have respect to the messenger and his *offering,* and *reject* him, for what evil has he done more than the Messenger? &c. Now whenever you see this you may be confidently sure, no *offering* has been accepted; and they have been *walking through dry places, seeking rest, but could find none;* then if left they will rise up in judgment and commit murder: For it was in this *Field* Cain contended with Abel and rose against him in judgment, and murdered him; and in this *Field* was the *servants of God* rose against and murdered; and in this *Field* was CHRIST contended with, rose against and murdered, and so were all his *servants,* even the *present Messenger;* for Reason (*i.e.* the devil) in this *Field,* will have dislike to and contend with the prerogative will and power of GOD and his holy spirit, raise against it in judgment, and murder it in what degree they can.

Ver. 41. "two women shall be grinding at the mill, the one shall be taken, and the other left." Those *women* is the womb or seed of Faith, and womb or seed of Reason, for let it be men or women, the act and power is the same, and cause the same effect, and will bring forth the fruit: And this *mill* is the mill or wheel of Reason, where men strive and labour by their imaginary wisdom on the bare letter, for the *salvation of CHRIST;* and will *turn* and *transform* their conceivings on the letter, and *reduce* it to their liking, even as the *millstone* will reduce grain; and will alter their confidence, and say by their great wisdom, labour, and experience, "they have the true bread to eat," and set value on themselves for their conceited knowledge, preaching, contending , and self-righteousness: It may well be called a Mill, for Reason can, and do *turn* it about, but cannot get over it or by it, for as Reason step or move, this *wheel* move with them, and keep them in one center, which is in and under justice, and by or with this *Mill,*

Reason will work and *grind* itself into death under justice, where hell will follow with it.

AGAIN, (Luke xvii) "I tell you in that night, there shall be two men in one bed, the one shall be taken and the other left." This is the *seraphic nature* which is *easy* in itself, doth not care to go into high emulation to contend, but rather abide by childish tuition, and in a manner desire to die as they were born; they believe the scripture, because they was taught it; and say *Christ* did all for them; they would hurt no one; this nature is very close to pass through this life as easy as possible; and if they should transform from one *Sect* to another, you may see their easy way, for they want or believe no *resurrection of the spirit,* above the dead letter, their imaginary thoughts with or thereon is their confidence or *Bed* where they *lay:* Now thus is the whole world bound in darkness, for they regard not *Moses* or *Jesus.* But their bare *name;* and even that to cloak their evil, make a *merchandize,* or bring to pass an *evil* intent; so they become *desolate* through the *abomination* of serpentine wisdom and acts; and think to hide themselves from the wrath of God by their excuse, which is become as many high *trees;* like unto a large rookery, that all the *fowls of the air* can make their nest and lodge in it, and harbour or shelter every unclean and venomous beast of the earth.

Yea, Faith hearkened to Reason, so broke its own law, and *died* according to the word of the LORD GOD: and Reason took possession and drove the *man and woman,* and drive, enslave, and *captivate* the Elect to this day: For as the Elect are born into this world with the *life* Reason, taken under Reason's tuition, and are sent forth in, and after the desires of Reason; they go into the *Fields* and *strong holds* of Reason, and *walk to and fro* desiring and seeking; Why? because they have no other life or desire, but that of Reason; thus are the *Elect* taken and *bound* up in those *fields* and *strong holds* and Reason rule over and enslave them; but this I say, *they* are preserved by the angel in justice from doing many evils which Reason do: - Therefore when CHRIST *come* in, with, or by his Messenger; then the *sign of the Son of man appear,* and the Elect are *called*; then if in the *field* of generation, they must come out, and Faith will be *rose from death* to life, and taken into the royal priesthood to *follow Christ;* then Reason will be much agitated, tempt, strive, and do all he can to keep you back; but you are to be *taken* out of the *field,* and must leave all to *follow Christ,* so do not strive against HIM: And if in the *field* of wild Reason, the Elect when *called* must come out; for these *fields* go one into another by their dark and evil acts; and excuses are made one by or through another, like unto arms of great *trees* that grow on in and among another: So when the Elect are *called,* Reason will be troubled, and go into anger and do all he can to prevent them; for the devil can hardly bear to lose one from his *field* or power: But by this *new life* of Faith that is *rose* from death, the Elect are *taken* into the royal priesthood, and made anew by the LORD GOD *of Regeneration;* and in this they find new life, wisdom, and power, and are assisted from heaven, so of consequence must leave all to *follow Christ in the Regeneration;* then what you have embraced as the delight of life, you now must *leave* behind and *overcome;* for so great is the Power of the LORD GOD *of regeneration, and KING of the new Heaven and Earth,* that HE can *take* them from the bonds of Reason, darkness, and death, and make them *anew* by regeneration; and bring them *through* all the powers of sin, darkness, death, hell, and justice, to his own kingdom, the glory of mercy! And leave Reason to strive and labour in its own center, which is in the bonds of sin in emulated darkness, to be swallowed up by death under justice, where hell will follow with it: - Here us *one taken and the other left!*

Again, those that strive in the kingdom of the dark spirit for salvation are called *women,* because of the fruit they will bear: But Reason has usurped the ruling power of the letter, and work on it by his *imagination* which is the *bottomless pit;* and become such *lords* and *kings* as to teach the salvation of Christ, yet strive against and contend with each other; cry, *Lo here, and lo there is Christ;* and set up their wisdom as a standing rule, and by or with it they would *rule,* and are bound up in the emulated life of this *spirit,* that they are sure of being right, nay, cannot be wrong; whereas it is the wisdom and fruit of the *dark spirit* that act against CHRIST: Then, as I said, the Elect are born into this world with the life of Reason, go under the tuition of Reason, and is under its power, and will strive with Reason, or as Reason do, for the *salvation of Christ;* Why? because it has no other life or light but that of Reason: But when the *Voice of God come,* the Elect are called out, and the *Virgin daughter of Faith* is given birth from its womb or seed, and is taken into the royal priesthood, and bear a *spiritual son to Christ* in regeneration: And also there is the womb or seed of Reason, in the seed of the serpent or sons of Cain, which by or for their confidence in their worship and salvation of Christ, will bring forth *fiery Zeal,* which is the spiritual daughter of Reason, who will go into the *field* of argument, and there *walk to and fro,* gather in tradition to join with imaginations and judgment of devils: This with her queenly pride and intent will give birth to the spiritual son of *perdition,* born of her in the *field* of argument; and there will rise in judgment, and spiritually murder the *Virgin* daughter of Faith, and the *spiritual son* she bear to the LORD CHRIST: Therefore the spiritual *Virgin* daughter of Faith, or of Israel, follow *Christ* in the royal priesthood and works of Faith, become HIS *pure bride for his holy marriage,* and bear him a spiritual son of his GLORIOUS KINGDOM! And the *Daughter* of Reason, or of *Babylon,* is left in her *filthy abomination,* and by her *fornication* bring forth the spiritual *son of perdition,* who will be *ground to powder;* for the weight of sin death, hell, and justice, will fall on them in eternity; and thus is *one taken and the other left!*

Moreover, this *seraphic* or still nature, that go not much out to contend, but rather leave others to their own will, cause peace of mind above others that do; then by this peace blended with their own righteousness and good intent, will set great value on themselves, and they *dwell under their own vine;* which is under their dark and stupid imagination; - this is a very great *strong hold* of the devil: But when the *Voice* of God come, the Elect are called out, and Faith in them risen from death to life, and regenerated to Christ and the others *left* to be swallowed up in their own darkness by death and hell: Now I would have the Elect *understand,* all those *fields, powers, and strong holds* of Reason, go one into another, and are one of another; because the whole root and essence of them was in Cain, he being the father of that generation; and as that increased men went forth in desires and acts which constitute those *fields* and *powers;* and men have contended , strove with, raised up, and destroyed each other, both in, and for the *kingdoms* of the world, and in and for the kingdoms of the dark spirit: Now this is Reason for to raise against Reason; and Reason contend with Reason; dark spirit raise against dark spirit, contend with, *murder,* and destroy each other; - then, at or to those strivings and contentions *Moses* will appear, as he did to the *two Hebrews who strove together,* (Exod. ii.) But now, he will not *flee* through *fear of Pharaoh,* for he is made lord and king over Reason, and will *kill him* who do his fellow, or brother wrong.

Again, the LORD GOD OF HEAVEN raised Faith from death to life in Adam, promised HE would become a SON to his own power and redeem it, make all things anew for the salvation of his Elect; and this *Virgin* of Faith is *taken* into the royal priesthood. *i.e.* to the *mystical union and holy communion with CHRIST;* of his redemption, regeneration, and salvation; and receive the heavenly *Gifts and Graces* of his holy spirit, which assist this *Virgin* to work the works of Faith to *follow* Christ and *prophecy* of his coming: - This, is a *kingdom* and power contrary to, and against Reason; so when a Messenger of Christ in *regeneration* come, then will soon appear the *field* of argument; for Reason will be angry at the voice of Faith, because it shake his kingdom and power; then he will contend with the Messenger, strive and argue against the *Will, power, and kingdom of Christ;* and enquire by and of their own Reason, and of Reason in others; say "they have the *Prophets,* Christ, and his Messengers, and have *laboured and borne the burthen;"* But when Faith is *risen,* and made its *offering,* the answer to that offering give the Elect *new LIFE! LANGUAGE! AND COUNTENANCE!* At which the *countenance* of Reason will *fall* because the devil knows that offering has been *accepted,* and his own *rejected;* then in *wrath* he will enquire and argue why that should be? and thus *he walk to and fro* in this *field* of argument, till he rise in judgment and commit murder: Yea, the strivings and contentions for the *kingdoms* of the earth, and of the dark spirit, and for men to have their own will, and do their own way, is the strivings and contentions of Reason; and there *Moses* will be found with the heavy hand of *justice:* But as God become Christ and made all things anew for his Elect, He also has gained power to bring in eternity, and has given power to the *internal Moses* to take the unredeemed and unregenerated into eternity: therefore in this field men strive and contend and argue against the holy and merciful *spirit* and power of Christ in his redemption and regeneration; and his most holy *anointing Spirit,* in the holy marriage and union, to make the Elect-like unto himself: - BUT Reason will come from all *fields* and places to contend with the Messenger of *Christ,* and the *prophecy* of Christ to come, and the *offering* of Faith made to Christ; and sit in judgment against Christ and his *kingdom,* and speak evil of it: And the seraphic nature will also come, and in this *field* bring forth the son of *perdition,* and become a fiery devil, for Reason will contend with the Messenger and the Elect, and would destroy them if possible; whereas they contend against CHRIST and his KINGDOM, and would destroy HIM who hath all power both in heaven and earth, who will suddenly bring in eternity, that will fall with such a mighty weight on this wicked generation, that will grind to *powder* all their hope, value, consequence, &c. ; and will press them in eternity, under the second death and hell: Also the Elect will come into this *field* by the spirit of Reason, which is the daughter of men and the *firstborn;* then she question the Messenger, and contend against him and tempt the soul from him, and not to assist him, but to accompany with and assist the kingdom of darkness, so that the messenger has not only the power of reason to stand against, but to wade through: But then the internal angel keeps the Elect from going too far; and this eldest daughter, which is of Reason, is put away, killed, or cast out, so as not to bear the son of perdition: then they are called out, and the youngest daughter, *i.e.* the *Virgin of Faith* will also *follow Christ,* and bear him a son in regeneration: So in this *field* there is *one taken and the other left.*

AGAIN, (Matt. xxiv.) "Let him which is on the house top, not come down to take any thing out of his house" This is the *house* of Reason, wherein he think to dwell secure; and let them have riches and power, be high in imagination or contention which is the house *top,* and may think by his cherubical wisdom and tongue to overpower many, that his way of salvation shall pass: Now let them be of the seed of Faith, or of reason, they have the letter to contend on and by the spirit of Reason and no one to *separate* them, so in a manner this contention is endless: But when CHRIST *come,* then soon appear the *field* of argument, and there Reason will make war with the prerogative of God, blaspheme and murder the holy spirit of Christ, but never can invade the *Kingdom of Christ,* although he was suffered to take this: So Reason may contend with Reason, if they like so to do; but when they argue in this *field* it is against *Christ* who will bring on them the heavy and endless weight of eternity: Therefore he that heareth the call on this *House top, let him not come down to take any thing out;* because all in, and of this house is of Reason, the devil, and its incumbrance which is so much, that it cannot go in at the *straight and narrow gate.*

Ver. 18. "Neither let him which is in the *field* return back to take his *cloaths."* This *field* or fields I have described, and the *cloaths* is the *Covering,* and to cover Reason in his acts, he may gather up riches that he may shine and to make head against poverty and justice; and may think to keep death at a distance: *This* he cannot do, although he may strive and cover himself with excuse and contentions: - now this must be *left* behind, which is mourning and death to Reason, but Reason must die, for Faith to live and *follow CHRIST; for in the royal PRIESTHOOD, Christ is HIGH PRIEST and KING, and teach and rule over his whole kingdom, which is Faith in regeneration, and of regenerated Faith:* And to HIM no one can come with the filthy cloathing of Reason, so it must all be *left* behind: - Now, be careful, for seeing you was born with the life of Reason, educated by Reason, was of that *house,* and enjoyed its life and delight; so watch the tempter, and not go back, nor be overcome by worldly desires, cares, &c. And as man will haste from great danger to save his natural life, even so he must now haste to save his *spiritual and eternal life!* For it is very easy and may appear delightful to go back, but a hard thing to go forward: But this *understand,* Reason, which is the *first-born,* is cast out and must die; and Faith which is the second born, will live to inherit the KINGDOM *of* CHRIST! Therefore in all the mighty *workings and trials* of Soul, whoever seek to *save his life* in the house of Reason, *will lose it;* and whoever *will lose his life* in the house of Reason, to follow Christ, in the works of Faith, his *life* will not only be *saved,* but crowned with an everlasting *Crown,* the GLORY OF MERCY!

Moreover, by what is written, you may see how nation is divided against nation, kingdom against kingdom, and how they rise against each other, both in and of the world, and of the dark spirit; not altogether to look at national kings and princes, but also at the strivings of Reason, in and among men: For as now the *Call is come,* he that entereth into the royal priesthood of Faith will *see* and *know* those things; and will also find such *trouble* as he never knew before, to *come out of,* and *overcome* those things; but *then* he enter into the PROPHECY *of* CHRIST, that those things should come to pass, when the *SIGN of the SON of Man appear,* which now *is* the time! Therefore the works of Faith must be looked after and done, to meet him in *holy marriage,* to have his royal *Seal;* for as I said, except he first come in holy and spiritual marriage to seal the soul for his *Glorious kingdom,* his personal coming will be of no use, for then he *knows you not:* - And what I have written of *Matt.* xxiv. *with other quotations concerning his coming,* is, and declares the *sign of the SON OF MAN,* and of his *sudden* appearance in personal glory, to put an end of time and bring in eternity; but men must enter into the royal priesthood of Faith, to *know* those signs, for they cannot be given to Reason, so it is only for the Elect to *know!*

AGAIN, when Jesus told his disciples *those things* should be when the son of man was *revealed,* and as a *sign of his coming;* (as Luke xvii. and as Matt. xxiv.) "And they answered and said unto him, where Lord? And he said unto them, wheresoever the body is, thither will the eagles be gathered together." *Therefore ,* you may see *HE is yet to come,* and that Reason will strive for and feed upon perishing *filth;* so the *works of Faith* must be done, and the WATCH *kept for* his coming! and mind, *if the good man of the house,* which was Adam, *had known when the thief would come,* who took this world from him, worked his overthrow, and brought on him death, *he would have WATCHED and not have suffered him to do it,* even as *sudden* will be the coming of the LORD CHRIST, to put an end of *time* and bring in *eternity!* For as the *serpent angel* suddenly came, and by the power of Reason overthrew Faith and brought on it death; even so will come the *Lord Christ* in the power and glory of *Faith,* and overthrow Reason, and bring on it the second death in all eternity: Also he that keep *watch* and work the *works* of Faith, when his *Lord* cometh in the spirit HE will *double his portion;* therefore, BLESSED *is that servant* that is so found by his LORD, He will make him *a ruler in HIS household, to give them meat in his due season;* and when HE come again and find him so doing HE *will make him ruler all he hath, i.e.* he will give him spiritual birth for his *glorious kingdom,* then he is above all the wisdom and power of Reason, for all *ruling* power given of CHRIST, is done by the *wisdom* of Faith: But, and if a man shall profess *Christ,* his Messenger and declaration, and after a while shall begin to draw off from the Messenger, and neglect the *union and communion of the CHURCH,* where there is given *fresh beams* of knowledge and divine instruction, and shall accompany with Reason, be pleased with the flowers and fruits of stupefaction, as Reason is, - there, he go the way of Reason and in effect say, nay do say in his heart "the Lord delayeth his coming," so he has time to act as do the world; - But, *the Lord will come when he looketh not for him, and will appoint him his portion;* for he that goeth with Reason, must go where Reason do; then him, them, or that which tempted him, with all the excuse he can make, cannot protect him from the wrath of God, and of Christ; for Reason is very active to lead you into the delights of his life, with the expectation of great things, and may wonder at you; whereas he lead you into stupefaction and death where hell will follow with it; this, Reason do not know, but it is for you to *know,* for be careful and *watch;* for the LORD CHRIST *is yet to come* and *sudden* will be his *coming!* - NOW, mind what is written, for HIS *own prophecy* is now in act, and the *signs* of HIS coming is given! The SIXTH ANGEL in regeneration has *sounded* on this earth and *prepared the way* of the SEVENTH to sound! So HIS own *day or hour* is now come, and the LORD CHRIST *the* KING OF FAITH only reigns: Therefore I pray HIM *who is to come,* who is the *Lord God of regeneration,* and LORD *and* KING *of the* NEW HEAVEN AND EARTH, to enlighten and assist HIS Elect, and bring them *through,* and take them *out* of this den of evil, and to hasten his kingdom, and *come quickly,* for the CRY is, *thrust in thy sickle, and gather thy Elect,* for the powers of evil and wickedness is become so great that the earth is *fully ripe* for its overthrow, So the Spirit say *come,* and the Bride say *come,* and the Union of Faith in regeneration say *come;* because the *Elect* cannot be released without thy *coming,* O BRIDEGROOM! HUSBAND, FATHER, and KING *of Faith in regeneration,* and of *regenerated Faith,* therefore *come quickly!* Amen.

THE END

A COLLECTION OF LETTERS

IN THE

INSPIRATION OF FAITH,

WRITTEN BY THE

MESSENGER OF GOD,

JAMES BIRCH,

BEING THE SECOND CALL
IN THE
THIRD DISPENSATION.

"Hold fast that thou hast,
Let no man (*of Reason*) take thy Crown."

LONDON:
PRINTED BY T. SORRELL,
86, BARTHOLOMEW-CLOSE, SMITHFIELD.

1813

PREFACE

The Editor unto the ELECT, and peculiarly the Churches that are in Britain: Grace, Mercy, and Truth, from God and our Lord Jesus Christ, be MULTIPLIED unto you.

SIRS,

PERMIT me as prefatory to inscribe, as this is for you only, that the following sheets and writings of this man compose the greatest work the BRITISH PRESS was ever honored with: I am sensible the unenlightened may say, How so? I answer—He, a Briton born, by the WILL and POWER of GOD, became RE-BORN, or born ANEW, to declare Regeneration, &c. and was sent back by Christ, from its highest state, *i.e.* to stand before the throne of God, to declare it to the Elect, whom Christ chuses thus to honor!!

Hence this work is the work of a MESSENGER of GOD: Messenger? Yes! from a King! Nay, not from a King only, but from the KING of Kings, and LORD of HOSTS!! And that to his CHOSEN FAVOURITES, the ELECT only!!!

And it is my prayer that the blessing contained may go forth unto perfection in every one, that CHRIST the King of Faith have all the glory.

Further—It becomes necessary to observe, for a moment, that wise and prudent men oft arrogate honor to themselves for a temporary act,—but, if any merited honor may be permitted, touching this work, let all be ascribed to the Printer, whose ingenuity is unsullied, and integrity thereon unshaken; How so? Because as Reason is chained by the power of Faith, so the Editor appeared chained also; and this gentleman became so far not ashamed of my chain, (though reluctant through fear of his credit) obligingly to comply with my order, omitting grammatical correction, lest it cloud the truth. But touching which let Reason, as a Connoisseur, go and observe, that in this way of writing, SCRIPTURE abounds with precedents;—meanwhile the Satirist will oblige me to go to that learned and experienced PUPIL of GAMALIEL, ordained an APOSTLE to the Gentiles, and see what he said touching this matter—1st Cor. Ch. i. Ver.20, &c. And if he is not satisfied, he is left. So much for appearance.

But, beloved Brethren,—If Reason should be suffered to demur, or make exceptions, &c. as if to say, "Why had you to do with it?" I answer, the Messenger of God chose me as an editor to the printing of both books in his day (viz) " Of the Law," and "Of the Gospel," and you following his steps, Faith now chose me also;—and permit me to say I have experienced great sorrow of soul, lacking the Messenger's help, in so weighty and arduous an undertaking—as well as cruel external persecution; but almost unceasing prayer prevailed, and God was with me, and has brought me safe through—and to him be all praise eternally, Amen!

Further Brethren,—Suffer me to say, that my predilection had its share in being elected to this work; this the Messenger saw, and when Reason thundered at the Prelude, he even put his own hand thereto (touching the first two lines only) and Reason was immediately stunned, and Lo! it appears at this day!

Touching Persecution,—Faith is fully assured that Reason, if within his reach, will never let Faith go one step free, but, blessed be God, our law pretty well confines him, so that it is chiefly mental or vocal, grieving some that they cannot kill the body; hence Faith is fully sensible, going Godward, he in some way must be persecuted. Behold Moses! Will any man say the Elect meant to rob Egypt, by borrowing, never to pay? Nay, only to spoil their attempt in stopping Israel from where they were to go;—and if the waters of Reason appear divided, shewing a probability of payment—should return to their full strength, preventing a possibility, doth this make them guilty? Yet, Reason censured them for injustice—and so it doth Elect Israel to this day; and a merciful spirit will not add to their sorrowful and tried state—the justice they have incurred, which is preparing them for mercy, is sufficient; but will direct, and if possible encourage them to look up to Christ the King, He having become HIGH PRIEST also, for that very purpose; how this is *performed* and *travailed* through, &c. may Jesus, in his mercy, bring his Elect to LOOK and SEE the following work.

Your faithful Servant,

And Brother in the Faith and Tribulation,
T. HERALD,

28, Fore-Street, May 1, 1813.

A COLLECTION OF LETTERS

LETTER I

To our Sister Runwa and all the Brethren in the Country in the true Faith of Christ, James Birch, a Servant to the Elect, sendeth greeting.

SISTER R,—I saw a letter of yours sent to our brother Francis Joseph, in which was inclosed a letter from friends out of the country, by which I perceive both you and them are inclined to enquire after the book of the *Second* CALL in the *Third* Commission, that was given to, the Messenger by the Angel of the Covenant of Grace, *i.e.* Christ the king of Faith: which, brought a sharp reproof to the professors of the letter, why? Because the spirit of Reason had usurped the power of the letter; and by the letter taught a doctrine contrary to the spirit of Faith.

Therefore when the *Messenger* came from God; and uttered his voice, it caused a great *earthquake* in the soul of many, for the Messenger directs his voice to the womb or seed of Faith, strongly bound in the waters of Reason's *hope*, or rather *assurance* of salvation: it is the *emulated* spirit of Reason in the soul that gives this assurance; this is the *Earthquake* or death to Reason, and very heavy for man to bear; then, by virtue of this death of Reason, the spirit of Faith in its womb or seed, throb and presses hard to be born, and this spirit of faith so born from its womb or seed, I spiritually call the *Virgin* daughter of Israel, or of Faith, which is born of water, or to the first covenant of the law, and the internal and spiritual priesthood of Aaron: And to her is given a *Censer* with incense *i.e.* the spirit of faith is the censer, and its prayer the incense that ascends up before the Lord.

Again, when Faith comes to this, it well knows it is in a *strange* Land, and its desire is to get as near the King of Heaven as possible it can in spirit; but it has the *wilderness* in your own soul to wade through, bearing the *thundering* threats of Reason, which brings on a slavish fear of losing your natural bread; and internal threats and temptations with some private breaches of the law, and putting things in the way which Reason thinks Faith cannot get over: But when Reason is arrested by the law, or internal angel of the law, Reason can never bear its own law, and being held fast by the angel: therefore the most artful cherubical turns of Reason must die before the angel, and *Human* Nature being only able to stand to offer, which offering is, (*at this time truth is active*) the soul offers itself freely to be damned without reserve before the law, or the angel of the law, well knowing the soul deserves it according to God's divine justice.

This offering being truly done, there ariseth the sweet waters of the stay of God's justice, which is a great *plague in Israel*, *i.e.* in the souls of the Elect. Then the soul hath sweet conceivings, such as the Messenger will confirm, and with it is joined the spirit of prophecy, *i.e.* the soul do not only see it is in the *road* for the holy City, but also Christ will come in spirit and give birth to his holy covenant, as a seal that he will raise the soul to eternal glory.

Again, This *second Book* gives birth to the Virgin daughter of Faith, and she will follow the Messenger through great tribulation, and be its own priest unto God; *i.e.* to offer its own offering by the active spirit of Faith, and have the spirit of prophecy of your own salvation; therefore you become priests and prophets unto Christ your king and your redeemer; and by overcoming those mighty troubles, you hold out to the end and become as refined gold, adorned with the beautiful ornaments of Faith, as a bride meet for marriage to Christ, which is the *Holy City*, or the *Marriage Feast*; *i.e.* Christ, by virtue of his holy spirit entering into this virgin daughter of Faith, and there beget to himself a son called Inspiration, and this son is born to his spiritual covenant of grace, which is mostly at the hour of death, and to lay in the Bed of mercy to be raised to eternal glory, for if you live to come back, you are a Messenger.

Now this is the prophecy, of this *Second* Book, and whosoever *add* to it, God will add *plagues* to his soul by the internal angel, and whosoever shall *take away*, the internal angel will turn him back to dwell among those plagues, and not let him go up to the holy city.

Therefore, sister and brethren, and you sister Runwa, said in your letter, you did believe the saints were delivered from those troubles you complain of; but I *say*, it is no other way, than I have written; for if reading the letter or hearing the Messenger took away all troubles of soul, what would Faith have to *overcome*? whereas the promise is to them only that do overcome.

For this being the commission of the spirit, the power thereof is worked in the souls and spirits of men, therefore in the *sorrowful* travail through those mighty powers of Reason in your own souls pray, and not faint: be just, and fear not, and have Faith, and doubt not but you will not only have the spiritual help from above, but natural also if required. So no more at present, but should like to see you and speak by word.

June 3, 1777.
JAMES BIRCH.

LETTER II

To our beloved Sister Ann Childs, *and to all the Brethren in Pembroke, and in all Wales,* James Birch, *sendeth greeting,* and prays for your increase of Faith in Christ Jesus in Glory.

Sister, —Yours I received 11th inst. and am very glad to see you express yourself in the firm belief of Reeve and Muggleton; for whoever doth truly believe them will believe me: Neither can any man come to believe me without believing in them; because I am born to the same spirit as God gave, to John Reeve, only this; as Faith grew higher and higher under the law, until Christ came in flesh, to bring in the *Gospel*; so doth Faith grow higher and higher under the gospel, until Christ come in glory, to bring in *eternity*.

Brethren; The declaration of the *second* CALL under the gospel becomes an *earthquake* in the soul of man; therefore, no wonder at all at your being amazed; for after myself had travelled twelve years under the letter of the third *record*, sacredly preserved by the divine majesty, although I knew it not; for I could not join with the dark cherubical spirit, who had transformed themselves into the letter of Reeve and Muggleton, and claimed the promises that were made to the tender hearted Elect; and by the exalted spirit of emulated Reason, said they had the assurance of eternal life, and not only so, but would curse men to eternity, who believed in the commission of the spirit who opposed them, or rather could not believe to their liking; so high did the spirit of *Abomination* sit to rule in the letter of the third commission, and denied. the true internal prayer of faith; and stood with such power, so as to make the Elect to fear, and if possible would stop the *Seal* of the living God; so much did the spirit of Reason within, and this spirit without, *then* keep the Elect in strong *Captivity*.

Therefore here stood the spirit of *Abomination and desolation in holy place where it ought not; i.e.* in the soul of the Elect:—them that has wisdom, let *them*, understand this!—(But during the time I was under the letter, this I did not know) but as I said, was sacredly preserved; and brought through the priesthood of Aaron in the soul, and to the baptism of water; *i.e.* this, I was brought to a true understanding of the prophets in those nether waters, and was told, "I was lost, but was found," and was blessed by the prophets' declaration, and was a son of the prophets, and I was in true love with all profession of the declaration, and at peace with the whole world: those *waters* run clear and was very sweet in my soul; now this is a great height for the soul to come to, but it is no more than the nether waters, and the soul will find himself under justice.

Then I was suddenly arraigned before God's divine justice, where *He* was himself a consuming fire; and by Him was asked what Faith I had brought forth under the declaration to reach Him; That He may approve for to seal your entrance of his glorious kingdom! This I as little expected as you did another Messenger in this last age. Furthermore I could not then go to God, for there was presented his prerogative, and death and hell ready to swallow you up; therefore I would have gone back to those sweet waters ; but no, they were turned into blood, and no more life there; for the internal angel has got you and before divine justice be will keep you; Now forward to God and his glorious waters you must go, or into death and hell : this will bring the true prayer of Faith out of the soul as it did in me; and He in his prerogative was graciously pleased to give birth in spirit to his holy spiritual covenant of grace; *i.e.* the upper waters, or the waters of life.

After this, *I was taken in spirit unto the mountain of Holiness, and was shewed by the angel of the covenant of grace many wonderful things in heaven; and saw my own name enrolled in the lively, merciful and spiritual memory of the angel of the covenant of grace, which is the seal of the living God; and was sent back by the king of heaven to declare what I had seen, that the Elect may be warned* of his glorious *internal* appearance to *seal* the soul, to be raised to eternal Glory.

And also, *I am the first new-born son*; in this commission of the spirit, who *saw the face of GOD, and lived to come back to tell his tale*: For when others were taken they went into death, and did not come back.

Again, when John was called in spirit before the throne, and saw the book that was sealed with *seven seals*, and no one could he find worthy to open the book and loose the seals thereof; he wept much, until the king of heaven was found worthy to do it, for all he received the holy ghost with the other apostles at the day of Pentecost, to go forth and preach the death and resurrection of Jesus the son of God. But when he was called before his prerogative royal in glory, he fell as a dead man; Why? because he was by the God of heaven, to have the Book of Life opened to him, and to see his name written therein, as also the Elect, that would follow him in that second call.

And I James Birch have had the *Book of Life* opened to me, and has the seal of the living God, and also saw the seal for them that would follow me in this second call, in this *Third Commission*.

Further, beloved brethren, there is but two covenants, *i.e.* of the *Law* and of *Grace*: and this third commission came from Jesus who is the tree of life, as well as the second; and the teaching and holy sanctification is the same: but this being the commission of the spirit, the power of the two former, is acted *in* the souls and spirits of men, but more now in this *second call*, because tribulation and persecution will be most found in your own spirit of reason within.

Again, when the Messenger come he directed his voice to the womb or seed of Faith strongly bound by the power and waters of Reason, *i.e.* the spirit of Reason when there is no Messenger on earth, will, take the dead letter, and by it conceive a doctrine contrary to truth, and be much delighted with it; and your own spirit of Reason will take you there, without a stedfast watch and divine assistance And this delight Reason has in his own worship, is the dark waters of the river Euphrates in the land of Nod, where old Cain went as an original.

And when the Messenger calls to Faith, it strikes the soul into an amazement, fear, and trembling, and reduces it as it were to a death, then out of this death, quickens life into the true knowledge and path of God: Now this is the spirit of Faith quickened from its womb or seed into act by the declaration of the Messenger, and that will follow the Messenger godward. Also this spirit of Faith, *active* in human nature, is the daughter of Faith, or the *Virgin* daughter of Israel, *born of water* or the first covenant; *i.e.* the *Covenant* of the law and *Priesthood of Aaron* in the commission of the spirit now acting in the soul of man.

Again, Faith fell in Adam, subject to Reason and its law, which law is, "You shall love God above all, and your neighbour as yourself;" this law was never kept since the *fall*, by any created rational being: and there is the internal angel of this law standing before God's divine justice in the soul of man, and when ever man sinneth this angel seals the soul under death according to God's divine justice, and no one can take it off but God himself; were it not for this every one would press to the kingdom of God.

And wherever the nature of Reason is, there also is its law, which is the cause of the internal priesthood of Aaron, for this virgin daughter of Faith in great *sorrow* to wade through; for the reading over dead men's writings will not translate you into heaven, without being found worthy of God; and also must be lost in your own spirit, and in your own blood, before you can receive benefit of the blood of God.

Again, this Virgin daughter of Faith, has the sacred influence of God's spirit to guide to divine truth, and follow the Messenger through all temptations: and the nature is humble, meek, and low, full of love and forgiveness to its greatest enemies: and also has a longing desire to get as near Jesus in spirit from whence it came as possible it can, being in a *strange land*, and surrounded by the wilds and temptations of Reason without, but more so within, therefore keep WATCH.

Further, this *Virgin Daughter* will follow the Messenger through the priesthood, and offer its own offerings; and come through tribulations, and appear a pure Virgin as a Bride for *Marriage* with Jesus, *i.e.* the holy spirit of Jesus unites with this spirit or daughter of Faith, and begets to himself a son, called *Inspiration*, which in spirit ascends up to heaven, and is sealed under Grace by God himself; this is the true *spiritual generation*: for Faith is born into this world under justice; and has *the vial of God's wrath poured out* on it; but by divine assistance, and by prayer, it wades thro' and is there regenerated unto grace.

Dear Sister and Brethren, as to your being weak in regard to a great memory, that is to your benefit, for whoever is obliged to trust to his memory for his Faith is badly off: but when this VIRGIN daughter of *Faith* is born, it will bring the necessary things of Faith to your remembrance; and not only so, but also it will become as a well-spring of Faith in you that will *spring up to heaven?*

So rest your brother in the everlasting truth of Jesus Christ.

Aug. 18, 1777. JAMES BIRCH.

LETTER III

To Pecover Ellis, and the brethren about Norwich, the Messenger of JESUS sendeth greeting.—That the spirit of Divine Truth may abound in your Souls, and that will bring you to the Holy Sanctification of Jesus Christ.

Brethren,—Since I came out from God and declared what I had seen in the holy sanctification of Jesus, which is an internal and spiritual Testimony of his new covenant, by sealing the soul of man to eternal life; yea, I was called by God himself, in or under this third commission, which is a *plain* proof GOD gave this Commission, and also *owns* it, Why? Because He calls in or under the declaration to his holy sanctification.

Further, I saw *John Reeve* was sent immediately from God, in or under the spiritual covenant of grace and priesthood of Melchizedec; and also know where he *declares*, and where he *invites*, and where he *prophesys*, and where to look for his prophecy.—Again, I saw *Lodowick Muggleton*, a friend and companion to John Reeve, given to him by God himself, and also he was a high priest in the spiritual nether waters and priesthood of Aaron; and know where he writes as a *prophet*, and where he writes as a *priest*; and that, at his death saw his translation to the spiritual covenant of grace, and died in the bed of mercy, and his name with John Reeve, enrolled in the quick memory of the King of Faith to be raised to eternal glory: therefore I am *the first-born son* in the commission of the spirit, who saw the face of God, and live to come back to tell his tale unto his brethren the captivated seed of Faith.

Brethren, observe, John the divine received the Holy Ghost, with the other apostles, at the day of Pentecost; but when he was called before the throne, and saw the *Book sealed* he wept much, until the book was *opened*, and he was sent back, and ordered to write a sharp reproof to the *seven Churches of Asia*, and the promise was made to them only that did *overcome*.

Further, brethren, it is even so now in this second call in this third Commission; for Reeve and Muggleton being sent to the world, to *call in* to their declaration: but it remains in the will of the divine majesty who he will chuse to sanctify; for many of the seed of Reason has crept in, that will be found unworthy of the *marriage* with Jesus, and *they* may say "prayer is useless," and "God takes no notice," which is truly so; for all the prayer and offering made by *Reason*, although they profess this letter of this third record, God takes no notice of, no more than he did of old *Cain's* offering in the original, but it is not so with the Elect, therefore they are right.

Moreover, when God was pleased to send a commission, the commissioner can enquire of God, and by the holy spirit be answered; but when the commissioner dies and the spirit is withheld, there is silence in heaven, until God is graciously pleased to give one man (whom he please) birth to the same spirit as he gave to John Reeve, and whosoever do truly believe John Reeve, will believe me, because I am born to, and declare from the same spirit as God gave to John Reeve.

Again, during the time of *silence in heaven*, the seed of the serpent that has transformed themselves into the literal declaration usurp the rule thereof, and by their spirit of Reason will form an understanding of the letter contrary to truth, and introduce things by their imagination, and declare them doctrine unto Salvation: and be exalted so high in the dark spirit of emulation, that they become rulers and kings therein, and burn like a sulphurous mountain; and if you cannot believe and act to their liking, you must in some manner be persecuted, and all this is fathered on the prophets, because they say they are Reeve and Muggleton's disciples.

So when the Messenger was sent in this commission, and declared the will of God, the voice of the Messenger and the internal angel bound the spirits of dark kings and rulers close prisoners in themselves, in wrath and blasphemy, and condemned the Messenger from this, their own seal unto *death eternal*; and say the Messenger is contrary to the prophet, whereas the Messenger is in the true line of the prophet; but quite contrary to the seed of Reason's understanding of the prophet; so they think the evil is in the Messenger, but behold it is in themselves; for they are already sealed in wrath unto death eternal; so out of their mouths can come nothing but lies, wrath, and blasphemy, with other expressions of *death*, against the voice of God that calls the elect to the anointing of the spirit of grace.

Brethren, when a man comes to see the letter of this third record, he may have some arguments. in himself, whether he can or cannot believe it; anon he comes to believe, then the soul will rejoice, because he is in a new letter, and having a new language that will overpower all other forms of worship. This is joy to the soul, but oft' times the spirit of Reason in this joy will again take the man, and let him with freedom own the letter, yet in spirit lead him contrary from the true intent of the man who wrote it: for except you gather by the same spirit as the man wrote, you will *scatter abroad*; therefore it is a great thing for a man to know whether he gathers by the spirit of Faith, or by the spirit of Reason; seeing your own Reason is capable to transform itself into many ways, and will produce many motional voices, telling the man it is not only truth, but also the way of God, all to deceive the soul.

Further, when a man comes to read the declaration of the prophets, he reads the promise of salvation, but mind, this promise is made to the elect; And how will a man do to know this promise belong to him, seeing Reeve and Muggleton are dead, if God takes no notice as has been said? But they may say, here it is written, and we know it by Faith; but this also know, the seed of the serpent that profess the letter, will call the spirit of Reason the Spirit of Faith; and the spirit of Faith the spirit of Reason; yea, was Reason to see the similitude of the serpent angel in vision or dream, he would call it God.

Again, when JESUS was on earth the promise of Salvation was made by him to those who did truly believe; and *his* promise was as strong as any man's; nay, the whole *Salvation* promise was of *Him*, and from him (only repeated by others); and it was to last to the end of the world, and many did believe in him to the best of their judgment, yet, when Reeve and Muggleton appeared they cursed men to eternity who believed in Christ (as aforesaid), Why? because their belief was of Reason! For had it been of Faith they would have known the voice of God in John Reeve;—so it is now in this third commission, for did they believe by the spirit of Faith in John Reeve, they would know the voice of God in me.

JESUS said, "It is the spirit that quickeneth, the flesh profiteth nothing" (John's Gospel, 6. lxiii); therefore it is already come to pass, that two men shall profess the letter of the third commission, one of Faith, the other of Reason, and they shall go on, but no man can truly judge of those men except he is sent of God; but when a Messenger is sent from God, Christ is already *come* in spirit to that man, and he will prophecy of Christ coming in spirit to the Elect to *seal* them for his glorious kingdom, and they will follow the *Messenger* up to this holy sanctuary.

But Reason will be left *murmuring* with his own judgment on the bare letter; and searching the tombs of our forefathers, which is seeking life among the dead, because they cannot go forward with the Messenger to seek that *Life* which *is hid with Christ in God*; for when Reason do believe in a new letter or language, it exalts them in the spirit of *emulation*, and that will take them further into the dark waters of the river Euphrates in the land of Nod, than they were before they made any profession to it.

Again, when any man reads the prophet's writings, let him not so much seek for arguments to overpower the whole world, as that will do no good; but rather let him seek to read his *own* promise of salvation; for the prophet's promise is very great, yet that promise must be sealed by the God of Heaven, to enter his glorious kingdom; for the owning and reading the declaration will not translate you into heaven without being approved of by God: therefore *all* the knowledge that is gathered by the spirit of Reason must be laid down as *old rags*; and men must deny themselves of it, and become as a *little child* patiently waiting to be called forward by the spirit of God, as it is now active; for whosoever puts themselves forward by the spirit of Reason will go wrong; so concludes your brother.

London, Sept. 2. 1777.

JAMES BIRCH.

LETTER IV

To our beloved Brother Joseph Cole, *and to all the Brethren in Wales,* James Birch *sendeth greeting.*

Dear Brother—Your's I received the 20th inst. and by it do perceive your intent was, that it should have come to you by that direction, but I directed it where I was informed that company met, not only as professors of the letter of Reeve and Muggleton, but also to inquire after the second CALL in this Commission of the spirit, which makes their writing's appear to the Elect in great power; and also gives birth to the virgin daughter of Faith, and she will follow the Messenger up to the holy spiritual marriage with Jesus; from hence the Messenger may expect to *find,* among them that Love—to *kindle* which, will be desirous of his brothers or sisters spiritual welfare equal with his own; and that *true love* in the true faith of Jesus, in time, will break the *yoke* of Reason that the Elect are so much troubled with: therefore I humbly beg you, or any of you all, that shall say "I have spiritual knowledge above some (of his brethren); observe this,—if this knowledge is owned by the holy spirit, that soul will become a servant to his brethren; *for the more* DIVINE *wisdom abounds in the soul, the humbler the man.*

Brother, the brethren of the church rejoice with me, to see you write in your letter, "the books is the very same," *i.e.* I understand you mean from the same *spirit,* and on the same *foundation;* and as so it is a great sight, and an opening for the soul to be further enlightened in those sacred *Truths* and divine *Mysteries* that are declared of now a days:—There are things written in the letter I sent to Pembroke, that is not to be found in Reeve or Muggleton's writings, yet wrought by the same spirit as *John Reeve* wrote his, only *higher* up, this being the *second* CALL.

Again, you say, "you thought that reading and believing the prophet's declaration was satisfaction; "and indeed so it was, to the spirit of *Reason;* for from that has raised the boasted lying assurance of eternal life, the prophets being, dead and for years no one came to contradict them.

Moreover, even in the life time of a Messenger, some of the seed of the serpent will transform themselves to the Messenger's outward word or bare letter; and when he is dead, reason is unbound, and will go out, and deceive man with his deceitful doctrine, even with the face of a man, *i.e.* they will say it is the doctrine of the Messengers in the commission of the spirit: and the spirit of Reason in the Elect is very apt to hear this from Reason without them, at the time of *silence in Heaven*, so will reduce them so low into captivity, as to know no more than their own conceited knowledge on the dead letter.

Further, when there is no Messenger on earth, and people come to own or believe the letter, they can go no higher than bare literal convincement, and blind Reason is well pleased to be here, why?—because it is in his kingdom:—And further, the spirit of Reason can go out on the prophet's writings, and turn them into *songs* to their own liking, and sing those songs, and be *merry*, and *send them from one to another*, as spiritual *gifts*, which is *rejoicing over those prophets' dead bodies, because they are dead*, so cannot torment them or say they are wrong.

Again, when man comes to believe the letter, his own spirit of Reason is capable to *transform* itself *into an angel of light*, and tell the soul that light is faith; then how will you, or any man on earth do to know when there is no Messenger living, whether he gathers by the spirit of Faith, or by the spirit of Reason; or who that is called by the declaration is of Faith, or of Reason? therefore see Matt. xiii. 47, &c. where Jesus likens the *kingdom of heaven unto a net cast into the sea, and gathered of every kind, which, when it was full, the good was gathered into vessels, but cast the bad away.*

JESUS was the man who preached the gospel, which is the kingdom of heaven; and there was more called by the outward word than was *chosen* to come to the *marriage feast*.

And also, *John Reeve* was sent forth by Jesus under the gospel or covenant of grace; and there was more called by him and his fellow witness, than will go to the holy marriage.

And *now* there is one *born* to the same spirit as God gave to John Reeve; and sent forth by Jesus, there is many found that profess the letter, and preach it up: but when they are told that the prophet has done all this, on his part, before you was born: and also asked, what have you gathered from his writings on your part, that the holy spirit may own as Truth, or commend as *Faith*? and as *now* is the time of a

Messenger, it is *reckoning* day! some has *cast off their old Rags?* and obeyed the second call, for to come up to the holy marriage, which is their *penny* or portion:—and other—some has gone away with the dead letter *murmuring*, which is their *penny* or portion.

Furthermore, you did well to read the reproof of the seven churches of Asia; that was in the second call, in the *second* commission: and this is the second call in the *third* commission, which is comparing spiritual things with spiritual, and from that springs to the Elect, true knowledge now the spirit is active.

And as for Lodowick Muggleton being more a priest than a prophet, *Note*—God said to John Reeve, "He had given him the understanding of his mind in the scriptures, above all the men in the world and L. Muggleton to be his mouth;" therefore you read in the Second Chapter 2d. part Acts of Witnesses—there John Reeves says, "Lodowick Muggleton is of the tribe of Levy, and the Lord's last high priest."

Further there is but two priesthoods, *i.e.* the priesthood of Melchizedec and of Aaron: Melchizedec is the upper waters; of which Christ is high priest, this is the waters of *mercy*! And the priesthood of Aaron is invested on the tribe of *Levi*, which is the nether waters, or the waters in, or under *justice*; therefore, John Reeve had the commission given to him immediate from God, in the spiritual covenant of *grace*: and L. Muggleton had his *instructions* from *John Reeve*, which was a foundation for him; for L. Muggleton was in the spiritual covenant of the *law*, and of that priesthood; yet both of God! One under the attribute of his divine *mercy*; and the other under the attribute of his divine *justice*; otherwise how could they be called the *two witnesses* of the spirit? And that is the cause of the difference in their writings, which has not been known till now this second call come: as for his giving the sentence, it was to defend the declaration, he being in the line of justice; and with his leave, believers might give the sentence in his name and power: but however you did not live in L. Muggleton's time; you live in the day of another Messenger, which will be the day of your trial!

Again, beloved brother, there be *two* PRAYERS to be used, *i.e.* the prayer of *Obedience*, and the prayer of *Faith*; not in any outward form, but in the *secret closet* of the soul; and if this be truly done, God will give an open reward, *i.e.* the Messenger will know whether the soul has ever prayed either of those prayers, and you will have peace! The

Prayer of obedience is that you may be obedient in all things to the Messenger, and to stand still and see the salvation of God; and to hear spiritual things of the *Messenger*, or your *Brother*, (although they may seem strange) and not to *judge* of them in the least; and also that your unbelief may be helped. And when the virgin, daughter of Faith, is born, she will *pray* her own prayer; which is the prayer of faith: now the exact true prayer of faith is the Lord's prayer, that you may read in the gospel where Jesus taught his disciples to *pray*.

Furthermore, when Jesus was on earth, he work'd miracles in raising the dead and making the deaf to hear, and dumb to speak, &c. But now these miracles are worked in the internal soul of man; and the virgin, daughter of Faith, finding herself surrounded with all those infirmities and temptations, in the internal soul, and cannot be cast out, but by the *dint of prayer and fasting i.e.* the prayer of faith ascends to heaven for God's divine assistance; and *fasting* is patiently waiting 'till it comes.

You, have wrote a prayer of obedience, where you say "O Lord direct me to yield obedience to the Messenger of God, and to put my whole trust and hope in him, for I see there is no trust in the arm of flesh," which I hope it is from the true faith of your soul,—and I should be glad to have such a prayer truly said in all the *house of Israel*; for all must go the *way* of the Messenger, and *gather* by the same spirit as he do, or *scatter abroad*.

Again, let the *little flock* have faith in what is declared, and look for Christ to seal their entrance into his glorious kingdom; and I hope the *prayer* of obedience will abound in their souls; and love one another, *above* the love of this perishing world, and all will be well.

Further, (as concerning) the church of the Laodiceans (Rev. iii) was much like unto the state of the Muggletonians when I came,—there was so many *fowls* of the air came and lodged in the *branches* of the doctrine that brought them into captivity, and so much blinded with reason, yet called *lukewarm* because they confessed the letter, and further you need not doubt but there were some of that lukewarm condition, capable by the spirit to be raised into life; and if they had been cold, that is made no profession at all, *John* would not have wrote to them.

And further, he spoke some commendations to all the other six churches;—but to this church of *Laodiceans* spoke none; therefore in their condition of soul was not worthy to be called, the church of Christ, which is, to *spue* it out of his mouth. —And the following verse says, "because thou sayest I am rich, and increased with goods, and have need of nothing," this was the state of the Muggletonians, they could make songs, and sing to charm the spirit of Reason and said they had the *assurance* of eternal life, which is being so *rich* not to want any thing: but they was *wretched and miserable, poor, blind and naked*, which was; and is their reproof, because all their riches were in the sottish and gloomy mire of the spirit of Reason,

Therefore I would advise you to take this true message that has been *tried as pure gold*—that your *faith* may be tryed as pure gold, *i.e.* that you may overcome (by divine assistance) sin, death, and hell in your own soul, then you will inherit the *holy marriage* that is prepared.

And further as concerning a *song*;—when the virgin, daughter of Faith, is born she will find herself among the wilds, and temptations of Reason, the devil, which is a *strange land*, therefore *will not sing*, but rather pray, to get as near to Jesus as possible she can: and when by prayer she doth receive assistance from heaven, faith will return thanks, and giving which, will be a *song* that will be accepted.

So concludes your brother in the true faith of this commission of the spirit.

1777. JAMES BIRCH.

P.S. The church in London gives their spiritual love to the church in Wales, and desires the increase of true faith.

LETTER V

To our beloved Brother Joseph Cole, *and the whole Church, J. B. and Brethren send greeting.*

(Yours I received the 2d inst.) and prays that the spiritual enlightening of Christ may shine from his glorious throne in the souls of his elect; and that will in God's gracious time enable the elect to follow his living MESSENGER, according to the Great INVITATION of God; that is of late come to invite the royal seed of Faith to the spiritual *Marriage* or holy sanctification and *Seal* of Christ the king of Faith, to prepare them to meet him in glorious personal appearance, and with him to enter his glorious kingdom.

I say the sacred divine *incomes* of God, will help the *Virgin*, daughter of Faith, to follow the living *Messenger*, against or through all those doubtful questions proceeding from Reason the devil in man, by words that he may read in a dead letter to his own overthrow (for by the letter only no man will be saved).

And those goings out of Reason the devil in man on the dead letter, and there think to question or rather overthrow the living Messenger, who has the wisdom of God in the scripture given to him under the Attributes of Justice, and of Mercy; and came out in the new *spiritual birth*, or holy *sanctification!* therefore by such reasonings they will find themselves to be utterly in the wrong; and this is known and judged before the divine majesty, to be the spiritual dark Egyptian strivings and *war* of Reason the devil in the soul of man; to keep the spirit of Faith in dark spiritual bondage, and if possible, not suffer it to follow the Messenger; as Pharoah the king of Egypt did when he would not let the children of Israel go with Moses.

Beloved brother, you write some believers are not satisfied that I *saw* the face of God and lived to come back; to which I say any man would be a dull Messenger in the *second* CALL, or holy sanctification, that had not seen the power and face of God, both under his attribute of divine justice, and his attribute of divine mercy, unto sanctification, and sent immediately back, sealed in his message by God himself before his glorious throne.

But are they satisfied God spake to John Reeve and that he saw

God: if they was by the royal spirit of faith, they would be satisfied in me; for I have been nearer the royal person of God unto his holy sanctification, than ever he was 'till the time of his death. Indeed John Reeve being in the covenant of grace prophesied of those days; and his prophecy is fulfilled in me and others but his prophecy is not to be found by literal signs, and observations according to the spirit of Reason; but by the spirit of Faith assisted by divine revelation from heaven.

Further, they may say they read his declaration, and believe him, and do not believe me: so did men say to John Reeve "they believe Christ and the Apostles, but did not believe him." And men said to Jesus "they believed Moses, but would not believe him" (by what the rulers of the Jews said to the man whose eyes was opened by Jesus (John 9), "we know that God speak unto Moses, as for this fellow we know not from whence he is" therefore it is an easy thing to transform themselves to; and believe in a dead letter; but the thing is for salvation to own and believe in the spirit and life from heaven!

Moreover, you write that the prophet Muggleton inserts that they two was to be the last prophets of the Lord: and this makes some believers at a great stand. How came it to pass that those believers did not read the words of Christ after he was risen from the dead, where he said "all power was given unto him in heaven and in earth" and also said to his disciples "he would be with them always even unto the end of the world." Also Paul tells the believers, "he had delivered to them the whole council of God:" and also says "if an angel from heaven brought any other doctrine than what he taught, let him be accursed." Also John the divine in his Rev. said "whosoever added or diminished to what he wrote in that book, should have no part in the *Book of Life*, but the plagues added to them, that he had written in that book." All those are positive texts, to declare they were the *last* in their time and being, as ever Reeve and Muggleton wrote, to declare they were the *last*, in their time and being, though not expressed in the same form of words.

Also, they say "some will have faith in the doctrine of Reeve and Muggleton to the world's end;" this is a great truth; but observe this; when Jesus came, many would not believe him, so he left *literal wandering Jews*, to wander in the letter of Moses to the world's end; also when John Reeve came, many would not believe him, so he left them to wander in the apostle's letter to the world's end: And now I am come, many will not believe me, so I leave them literal *wandering Muggletonians* that will wander in the dead letter to the world's end.

Further, observe, this is the commission of the spirit, and the spirit and life comes from God; and whosoever do believe in the spirit and life from heaven do as Reeve and Muggleton did: And now the divine majesty has been graciously pleased to send his Messenger to call his elect from *wandering* in the letter, to the spiritual and faithful truth of this commission, to *follow* the Messenger up to the holy sanctification of Jesus Christ the king of Faith; them that do this will enter into the mercy of Christ, and them that cannot, will be left to *wander* on the bare letter; and seal'd by the internal angel in justice unto the wrath of God: *This I say, from the* GOD *of Heaven, and* REDEEMER *of the Elect, will come to pass, let men help themselves if they can.*

Moreover, God said to John Reeve "he had chosen him his last Messenger unto, this bloody unbelieving world." Now John Reeve came in the Covenant of *Grace*, and merciful *Invitation* to men: yet he himself was under God's justice; for when he desired God to make choice of some other man, God said "if thou dost not obey my voice, and go where I send thee, thy own body shall be thy hell, and thy own soul shall be the devil that shall torment thee to eternity" here it is plain he was under justice, therefore he must undergo the spiritual birth, or translation to divine mercy: also L. Muggleton was given to be J. Reeve's mouth ; and God said to John Reeve "if Lodowick Muggleton deny to go with thee, then do thou from me pronounce him cursed to eternity" therefore Lodowick Muggleton was in the spiritual covenant of the law or nether waters, and went forth in, or under justice, to defend J. Reeve's declaration; and he must be born the spiritual birth, or translated to the Merciful seal of the living God: for if he died under justice, he must go the way of them whom he had cursed to eternity; so great is the message and *Invitation* from heaven now a days.

Further, concerning Reeve and Muggleton being the *last*; those people who say so, did not live in their time; if they had, then they would have said the Apostles were the last; But *I am come to call to the spiritual Marriage with the lamb*; and all believers that live in my *time*, and have heard of me; will be judged according to my *time*, and declaration; for heaven must be sought after when the gate is opened by God himself, and them that do not follow the voice of God in me

His Messenger will be sealed under death, by the internal angel in justice; and at the day of judgement they may say they have preached and sung and made converts by the letter of *Reeve and Muggleton*, but the voice of the angel will be this, "no one required it at your hands, you should have obeyed the living Messenger of your *day*" therefore Jesus said it is "the spirit quickeneth, the flesh profiteth nothing." (John vi.)

Again, of the *last* prophets; Reeve and Muggleton was the *last* that ever will be sent under justice, that will by order pronounce formal and external curses against man: for now the internal angel in justice seals the soul; and even in their day, if this angel did not seal according to their curse, it would not effect the man; because this internal angel in justice in the soul of man stands before the attribute of God's divine justice, and is as pure as God's justice; and can commune with God relative to his divine justice; and is a faithful and true witness with God, and as so, every man is his own witness to his own condemnation: therefore God said to John Reeve "whosoever I pronounce cursed through thy mouth is cursed;" hence you may see God had a power above what he invested on John Reeve.

Further, they are the last that will have wanderers to follow; because they first declared this commission from God unto the bloody unbelieving world: therefore people who believe in their letter will be called by their name: and now they are dead, and there is another prophet sent in this commission of the spirit nearer eternity, and believers will have no other prophet but Reeve and Muggleton; than they do prove themselves to be of the bloody unbelieving world; and sure enough Reeve and Muggleton is the last to them; therefore there is *three* sorts of scripture *Wanderers*, Moses and the prophets are the last to some people, and in their letter they *wander.* the Apostles are the last to some people and in their letter they *wander.* Reeve and Muggleton are the last to some people, and in their letter they *wander.*

Furthermore, long since the death of Reeve and Muggleton, *I have seen and communed with a far greater prophet than Muggleton, or Reeve, or myself ever is, or was, or will be; this great prophet is and will be the last to the elect: this great prophet is the Lord Jesus Christ, the king of faith in glory, HE was the FIRST to the elect, and will be the LAST. I was in no sleep or dream but perfectly awaked when, the spirit came upon me, and all nature struck senseless or inactive, and was taken in spirit unto the high mountain of Faith, and saw the kingdom of heaven, and God in his Glory, and heard his voice speaking into my soul, like the voice of loud cannon, and saw the seal of the living God, and them that was seal'd, and the Book of Life opened, and that more would be seal'd, and was* sent back *to invite the elect to this royal Seal of God; therefore I do declare myself, a Messenger, or prophet, that came from before the throne of God; and with God is the Seal, and sanctification of God.*

And John the divine in the *second call of the second* Commission; and myself in the *second call* of the *third* Commission, are the *two only men* that has hitherto been sent back under the *Seal of the living God*, many others have been sent under the seals of administration; but we was sent under the seal of the *living God*.

Thus I declare myself, and my declaration is *Truth*, but the lying spirit of Reason in the soul will question me as the Jews did Jesus (John x, 24) "How long dost thou make us to doubt? if thou be the Christ, tell us plainly" (v. 25) Jesus answered them, "I told you, and ye believe not: the works that I do in my father's name, bear witness of me"; so say I, if those believers had but observed what I have written, they would have said, none but a Messenger of God could have wrote or declared such things; but they have been searching the dead letter to find the *last* prophet: but there they will be greatly mistaken; for they must follow the living Messenger of their day to find the *last* prophet to be beneficial to them.

Beloved brother, I have not wrote the before-going with a view to condemn any one, but only as you say to explain myself; and I humbly hope in God it will be no death-warrant to any one in the church: for the most merciful spirit of God has no *Joy* in the condemnation of any one, let whosoever that hath come before me under justice say to the contrary; it is, because their book was *Justice* and condemnation, but my book is *Mercy*; therefore there is more *Joy* (under the attribute of divine mercy) in one sinner that need repentance, than there is in ninety-nine that need no repentance.

Moreover, I like those questions, because the answer will be very instructing to the church, if they do but patiently wait and observe what is written, which I humbly hope they will, for they must put away all their gathered knowledge from the letter by the spirit of Reason, and become as a *little child*, and stand still, and see the salvation of God: and also they may see what a grand enemy the spirit of Reason is, in the souls of the elect, it will wind about the soul of man, and if possible, would keep him from any news that comes from heaven, to invite him to his salvation.

Dear Brother, in what you have wrote relative to yourself I like very well; and your quotations of scripture, and your comparing spiritual things with spiritual, is the truth: further as to that *Hope* that you have lost, is the *hope* of Reason which is the dark waters of the river Euphrates in the spiritual land of Nod; and your other *hope* is of Faith therefore you liken yourself unto the *publican* and write a good prayer of obedience in faith, for this publican that Jesus spoke of, meaned the seed of Faith, and the *pharisee* the seed of Reason.

Again, you do well to give up your life in the hands of God, for whosoever do so *lose* their lives by this new light and declaration from heaven, will find it again in the merciful and holy sanctification of God; and whosoever do seek to *save* their life by the bare letter will lose it under justice.

As to your state of *lowness*, I believe, but do not call it captivity; for too much mirth and singing is captivity; whoever read that Jesus sang songs; indeed they sang a hymn, but that was in, and to the *sorrowful* vale of death; for of now a day, singing is of the cherubim, and you being in manhood cannot be raised a cherubim to glory, but must be raised to glory a son of God.

Also I hope you will *love* and strengthen the brethren, for whom I pray, to be brought in the true knowledge and path of God; and that, you *love* one another in the true *Love* of Christ, which is above the love of this perishing world; then you will shew yourselves to be Christ's disciples.

Further, this *low state* will bring you to know your own condition; do you think Faith fell under the Power of Reason, and will come through the power of Reason, in the soul of man singing, or in sleep or dream? No, it *must* bear the temptation of reason within, and come thro' that *sorrowful vale of death* like refined gold fit for the marriage with the Lamb.

Moreover concerning books; I have wrote a great deal of great and glorious truth, such things as Reeve and Muggleton did not write; indeed John Reeve laid the foundation, for a great and glorious work! and we build upon that *Foundation,* so that the spiritual ARK, which is the Refuge for the seed of Faith, is going on: and this, my writing, I recommend to the Church of God, for it will greatly instruct and help the seed of Faith in this sore journey: but we have nothing in print, if you can do any thing to forward it, you may let me know in your next: some brethren would have got the *song* for you, but it would have detained your answer, but we will try to get it for your next: so rest your brother in the true Faith of Jesus

London, No.3, Butler's   JAMES BIRCH.
Alley, Little Moorfields.
Feb. 10,1778,

LETTER VI

To our beloved Brother Joseph Cole, &c. James Birch *sendeth greeting.*

Beloved Brother.—Yours I received 27th ult. and am very glad you received the letter by the time of your meeting; and greatly rejoice that some satisfaction was found among the church; for in that letter is contained great truth, and the wisdom of God so far, as he has been graciously pleased to reveal himself from heaven of now a days as can well be conveyed in the short scope of a letter.

Blessed is he that is found by the Messenger to follow this *second* Call to the sanctification of Jesus Christ in glory; for Christ is now come in spirit, and men are and will be found working on the *letter*, as if they were *grinding at a mill* to make out their Salvation; but *one is taken* by this spiritual declaration, and *the other left* to wander on the bare letter.

Moreover concerning the Lord's prayer "give us this day our daily bread" this is the *spiritual bread from heaven* and Christ is that spiritual bread, by which the spirit of Faith lives, *i.e.* when the spirit of Faith is quickened by the Messenger to its own knowledge, it finds itself in Reason's kingdom and surrounded by the wilds and temptations of the spirit of Reason, then when Faith is *active* the spirit ascends by prayer for Christ's divine assistance to help the soul through the aforesaid powers of Reason; and this is the *daily bread* that the spirit of Faith hath need of in this sore journey of flesh.

"And forgive us our trespasses as we forgive them that trespass against us" this also must be done before ever a prayer to salvation is noticed by the merciful spirit of Jesus: for if you pray for God to help and *forgive* you, and you cannot within your own soul find power to help and forgive your brother, think you is it possible for that prayer to be heard by the most merciful God the Lord Jesus in glory? no it will not, because such a prayer is the prayer or incense of Reason which is abomination to God: therefore remember when you bring your *gift to the altar*, and have aught against thy brother, go back, and be reconciled to *him* first; for the nature of Faith is forgiveness to its greatest enemies, and in this state do the soul pray for its own forgiveness, if he offers the true prayer of Faith.

Dear Brother, I would not have you give way to the heavy threats of Reason within you, nor without you, concerning this world; for the more you entangle your soul there, the worse you will find yourself, and not know what is the matter; but with Faith and patience seek the kingdom of heaven, and *all things for your good will be added*: for he that created this world and redeemed the elect, is very able, by his divine providence, to pass you through this world, and knows best what will do.

But when the soul is bound to this world which is Reason's kingdom, and thereby strive to flourish among the evil-eyed sons of Reason; anon, he meets with a disappointment, or according to the proud spirit of Reason, ill-used; then he conceives anger, because he is checked in his vain glory, or lost a thing that must perish; and think you, is such a man any thing above the common self-serving hipocrites of the world? I have wrote this that, if possible you can, to keep from this slavery, and you will not do a bit the worse; but far the better for yourself and family.

Furthermore of being reconciled to your brother; the Messenger is an elder brother to the elect, because he is the *first* born that lived to come back to tell the spiritual birth in this commission, and inspired to declare the will of God; therefore them that live in his time, and has heard of him, and is not truly reconciled to him according to his declaration, and all other things; such as one's prayer never will be noticed but by the internal angel in Justice, and that to the condemnation of the person.

For the nature of Faith is entirely opposite to the nature of Reason;

therefore, when the prayer of Faith is offered you must be in true love and strong unity with the elect; and that you have truly forgiven all men that has been your enemy, then it will do: but while the remembrance remain, that is the seed of resentment, which is an evil and pray God that evil may be overcome by the inshining light of Christ: this, is an inaccessible mountain to the spirit of Reason, but to the spirit of Faith will be made easy, if you have Faith in this second CALL and *stand still and see the salvation of God.*

Again when *Faith* is born and knows its own state, the prayer is not stopped on this side death because it is under the fall in our first parents: and when Jesus was here he was a *man of* SORROW; neither was the prayer of Faith stopped in him until the Godhead life entered into death: and if any man can be thought to have the assurance of eternal life, so as to be independant of prayer, that was the man; but Faith does not want to be independant, but it is Reason, wants to be independant, that it may sing and rejoice and say it has the *assurance* of eternal life: therefore mind, CHRIST is the true object of Faith.

As to Paul's saying, "he that believeth has ceased from his Works," you did not live in Paul's time, if you had, he would have said to you as he did to them. "He that believeth in the gospel preached hath ceased from the ceremonial worship according to the law," and that was the works that they ceased from, for the internal law, and angel, was in act then as well as now; and although the present Messenger is come to invite, and report them before the attribute of divine mercy, yet they must not think to live in evil, for the internal angel will seal and report them before the attribute of justice: therefore if any have sinned let them seek repentance and do so no more lest a worse evil befal them; for if there is no external accusation, there is the internal.

And as to the *Rest*, of now-a-days, you are called from wandering in the bare letter, by the proud lying spirit of Reason which leads to death and hell, to under the living Messenger, whose declaration leads to light and life: but to *rest* from the good works and *trials of Faith*, I will promise that you, nor no one in this true Faith ever shall, until they die in the bed of mercy, to be raised to eternal glory.

Again, concerning Rev. vi. 15. those are the seed of Reason, whose names will not be found written in the *book of life* at the *great day* of judgment, but are in the book of death sealed by the internal angel in justice, that would hide themselves from wrath, if possible they could: but the wrath and justice is within themselves.

Moreover, beloved brethren, as to yourselves, if any one of you question your own sinful soul, in what condition of soul you would be in to meet the divine majesty; you will find there is a *mountain* of sin in the way, then at the sight of this, it must reduce the soul into great fear, and would be glad to forgive all, even the whole world, so that he himself can be forgiven: and also would be glad to be as near the Messenger in Faith as possible; then in this condition of soul is the prayer of Faith offered, which is a motion, or desire of the spirit of faith in the soul of man.

Furthermore man will find a *mountain* of sin in his own soul, and this is the mountain the elect wants to be removed; for let every one look into themselves and they may find this *mountain* of sin and although the Messenger is in mercy, and come to invite to mercy, yet the way to it is through justice, which, to the spirit of Reason, it is impossible to be done, and that makes them turn aside from it, and go to singing of songs, and live in spiritual drunkenness, and the day of wrath come upon them unawares: but to the spirit of Faith it is *possible* to be done, and by *Faith as a grain of mustard seed.*

Now Jesus has the essential power of uncreated Faith, by which this mighty work is done, to *remove* this great *mountain* of sin, death, and hell, compounded together in the soul of man: also Adam's life was created Faith, and his children are become many, and although this Faith is kept from action by the power of Reason, yet when the Messenger comes from God, he calls to and quickens Faith into act, and it grows into Strength, and will make its way up to the fountain from whence it came; but in the road you'll meet with great *fears, and doubts* and blocks put in the way by Reason, which are *mountains*; and these you are to remove by the power and prayer of Faith,

And when Christ comes in spirit, then you will be spiritually born, or translated from under the power of sin, &c. and this is the *mountain* that Christ the king of Faith *removes.* Now this is a hard travail, but no other way can man go to mercy, neither can I expect you, or any of you, to have experienced those things much yet: but have Faith in the living Messenger, and patiently wait the Lord's will; which is *believing,* and not to *make haste,* and those things will be made easy: for those *mountains* must be removed from the souls of the elect.

Again, as to *Rev.* vii. 10, this is when the Jew and Gentile receive the seal of the living God; then Faith will say, "salvation to our God and to the Lamb," for the soul well knows that God the Father, who was the God of Justice, become God the Son, who is the God of Mercy to his elect, and overcome the whole power of Reason, and death and hell, in lamb-like innocence, but this was all one God; and he has more titles than those in the Revelations.

Of *J. Reeve's* prophecying of me, see the *Divine Looking-Glass*, date 1719, chap. 22, where he prophecies of the new birth or *first resurrection*: again, he says, "what is this first resurrection, that whosoever has part in it, is blessed and holy, and the second death has no power? Truly it is the enjoyment of a divine light in the understanding, which man hath received by inspiration from the spirit of a personal Christ on a Throne of Glory in the *third heaven*:" and in page 192 he tells you how this light of Christ is received, and says, "this I certainly know, yet I do believe, that few of the saints have tasted of this condition;" and he was very right, for *I am the first man that lived to come back to witness those things*; therefore his prophecy is fulfilled in me; for I have seen and tasted of those things higher up than he doth write or express.

Beloved Brother, I have seen *Mrs. Jones* and *Mrs. Fleming*, and they with the whole church greatly rejoice to hear of your faith: my love to you, *Hannah Reed*, and all the brethren; when the book comes, it will inform you of many great things, so have true faith and patience in this second *Call*, and all will end well; so conclude your loving Brother.

April 29, 1778. JAMES BIRCH.

The whole church prays the church in Wales may increase in Faith.

Beloved Brother, at your desire have sent this spiritual sodomitical song; I well knew the author, and had he lived in the days of a Messenger I fear he would have belied him as he has the divine majesty in this song. In the last verse he declares himself a cherubim, but he cannot be raised a cherubim.

LETTER VII

To our beloved brother, Joseph Cole, *and all the brethren in Wales,* James Birch *sendeth greeting.*

Beloved brother, yours I received (5 June) and am glad you were satisfied in what there was written, and whereas you say Faith was not always *sure*: I would have you understand this; there is the confidence or hope of Reason which comes by its *imagination* on the scripture, or any other imagination that Reason shall dwell on, that even is *against* the scriptures; now this, the spirit of Reason will call *Faith*, in opposition to that which is the divine nature of God; and this confidence of Reason, will lead the soul to say he is *sure* of eternal life, and at the same time he is sure of nothing, but to go into eternal death: for when Reason is in life, the spiritual *light* of that life is *darkness*; for Christ said "if therefore the light in thee be darkness, how great is that *darkness*," for this light which is *darkness* is the *eye* of Reason in the soul of man; and this, Reasons great *confidence*, is called Faith by that lying spirit: but when the elect are called to by the voice of God in the Messenger from under this *darkness*, and the spirit of Faith quickened in the soul, *this, Faith*, in time will grow strong, and follow the Messenger in the true *Path* towards God; and when *active* it is SURE, because *this* Faith is of the divine nature of God; and when any one is called to *this*, he may truly say Faith was not *sure* in the time of darkness.

Further, you say, "God will not always *strive* with man," here you are very right; for the spirit of God do very much *strive* with the spirit of Reason in man at this day; for the present Messenger in the merciful line of Faith, according to his inspiration, has endeavoured all the peace and satisfaction to the spirit of faith as possible; but to his experimental sorrow, he finds the spirit of God too much strives with the spirit of Reason in man for many are striving for vain things, and the Messenger is fearful they may be lost in the dark *clouds* of Reason, for the divine majesty may soon be graciously pleased to call his Messenger from striving with the spirit of Reason in the souls of men; and when Reason's enemy is gone, then he may rule over the soul and keep him in darkness.

As to my being *higher up* than John Reeve, I have told you already, and I would to God you would believe; —my declaration bear witness of me, and I have been told by believers who I am, and from whence I came, since I came out from God to make my declaration; and them that told me who I was, did it from the same spirit as Peter told Christ who he was: and it is much more agreeable for any one that comes out in the covenant of grace, to be told who he is by the power of Faith, than for he himself to strive with Reason.

Furthermore, John Reeve made his declaration under justice, and he called people to believe, and have a steadfast faith in his declaration, but it remains in the will of the divine majesty to choose whom he please out of that declaration to his spiritual birth and sanctification; for J. Reeve himself must be born in spirit to the covenant of mercy, and sanctified with the merciful spirit of God, which prepares the soul to meet God in glory *at*, or *in* the resurrection, but this was done at his death, and he never came back to tell this Tale.

But I was called before the attribute of justice, and from thence by Christ the king of Faith, was given spiritual birth to the attribute of his divine mercy, and sent back in mercy to declare the soul must be spiritually prepared to see God: And this spiritual preparation is beyond all outward declaration; therefore in this condition of soul J. Reeve entered into death in, and could not *declare: I was born to this in spirit and sent back to DECLARE:* Now he that hath spiritual wisdom let him read this and judge which was the *highest up,* or nearest the sanctification of Christ the king of Faith here in this life, him, or me; for the very condition of soul he was brought to at his death, I came out in.

Again, think you, or any one else, that the infinite overflowing spirit of the divine majesty is as a standing *Pool*? no! it is continually *overflowing* with new wisdom, divine and heavenly graces, whereby the soul is inspired to prophecy *of* the kingdom of heaven; and not only so, but also at the hour of death is sealed and sanctified *for* the kingdom of heaven; and this is the working of the merciful spirit of Christ on the souls of his Elect.

But to the seed and spirit of Reason, *Moses* is the prophet, because he was inspired by or under the attribute of God's divine justice; and justice remains as a kingdom to this day, and will to the end of time, on the souls and spirits of men: therefore Moses was the *first* prophet that was sent to Reason, and will be the *last*; neither do the spirit of Reason like another prophet, nor understand a prophet *higher up*: but it is confest the spirit of Reason has transformed themselves into the apostles letter, and into the letter of Reeve and Muggleton, and preach up both the letters, and sing, and rejoice because they have the letter, but who has owned their Faith?

And this, let me tell you, if a man profess any letter of a prophet that is dead, and there is a Messenger sent from heaven, and that man cannot be brought from the bare letter to follow the living Messenger in spirit up to Jesus, Moses is that man's prophet, let him profess what he will, or think as he will he has nothing more to do than get from what I say, and let him do it if he can; for in the profession of all, or any written record, and cannot *follow* the voice of God from heaven, he dies as he was born into this world under justice, and Moses is his prophet, let him claim who he will beside.

Again, as aforesaid, the *Apostles* was inspired to preach Christ the son of God, and bear witness of his death and resurrection: and John the divine, in his second call, do in expression signify him, to be the very God, and he *only* can open the book of life; and do declare the sanctification and marriage; but he saw this by the way of vision, and the book was sealed and left for God himself to open; yet John was the first born son in the second dispensation that lived to come back to tell his tale.

And *John Reeve* in plain terms did declare Christ to be the very eternal God, and no one but the very God could work the powerful work of redemption: and God called me up, and gave me spiritual birth in this commission of the spirit, and was sent back to *declare* the spiritual birth, seal, and sanctification of God to enter the kingdom of heaven, and this is the highest or greatest of all:—for after all the sending forth with revelation or inspiration to make any declaration and preach the word, yet to be spiritually born to the merciful spirit of Christ, and to have the seal and sanctification of God, to enter the kingdom, of heaven, is above all; for after all the declaration is made, and mighty work or *Acts* done *in* the declaration, yet to this state, the soul must be brought to meet *God in his Glory*; *this* I was sent to *declare*, and have declared those things in *plain terms*, therefore you may judge who I am, and from whence I came; and also by what is written, you may see how Christ, by his merciful spirit, has been graciously pleased to make himself *known*, to his elect under the gospel, but still, *higher up*;—and now how the Soul is *prepared* for his coming in glory:—and this is *preparing the way of the Lord*.

Moreover you say you are satisfied, only to *singing*; I have wrote concerning singing before, and why do you not believe? now do you think I can encourage the spirit of Reason to go out on the records, and turn them into songs, and then sing to please the spirit of Reason:—this, Reason calls praise;—but, such praise is abomination in the sight of God; for do not the world do the same? they turn other men's writings into verse, and call them hymns, or songs; and then sing to please themselves and dedicate this their incense for God to own: and do you think there is any difference between their singing, and the literal Muggletonians singing in the sight of God? if you do, you are much mistaken:—beside, what should you *sing* for? —you say it has beat upon your mind, have you received the *holy ghost*? then you have need to pray; for now you have yielded to the voice of God in his Messenger, you must cast off all your gathered knowledge, and tradition, and in spirit become a *child*: this is giving way for the *Virgin* daughter of Faith to act, which she will by prayer and patience; and in God's time you will receive the divine incomes of his holy spirit; to help the soul, and confirm the *Truth*; and that is the *Holy Ghost*.

But to receive the *Holy Ghost* in full, is *sanctification* unto life eternal: but this motion of soul, I humbly hope, will create the prayer of Faith, instead of singing; then all will be well: So I recommend the whole church to the grace of Jesus Christ, and conclude your loving brother.

June 30, 1778.   JAMES BIRCH.

I return the church many thanks for your kind present, and pray your increase of Faith.

LETTER VIII

To our brother Geo. Plowman, *and all the brethren, in the true Faith in this Commission of the Spirit, that he shall find in the kingdom of Ireland,* James Birch *and Brethren send GREETING.*

Dear Brother—I saw a letter of yours sent to our brother Matthews, wherein I see you complain of being almost *alone*; for if so you had a true friend, you then could relate the sorrowful experience of your soul, and that might give you some small relief: *Truly, Brother*, this was one time my very condition; therefore I know its value, for I would have given all I had in this world for such a friend; for Faith, let it be ever so young from its birth, in the *first* Covenant, is a *Pearl*, and the innocence of its nature is *not to cast itself before swine, lest they turn again at you*; until God gives you power to overpower in argument, all the swinish nature of Reason without you: And,

Further, I was told in the *hard travels*, if Reeve, or Muggleton was alive it would be nothing to me; I must *overcome; then should not be hurt by the, second death*: and stand before God to and for myself, that I may relate a faithful and true experience to the brethren. Therefore, the divine majesty has sent his *Messenger* to give notice to his elect, they must prepare, and follow the Messenger, every one distinct to, and for himself, up towards God in spirit: and when, the true prayer of Faith is offered up, you will have his divine assistance; for you must by him be sealed with his own holy spiritual *Seal* to enter his glorious kingdom.

AGAIN, of now a days, as the spirit is *active* it will not leave the souls of the elect under the bare state of convincement; *i.e.* as you hear the word, you go forth and preach the word, and the nature of man will be well pleased to be here, for in this state there is no trouble of mind, because you are convinced the man is of God that brings the message: but all this is but preaching in the name and power of another man; and if men cannot be brought further, when the messenger is gone, those men will die with the outward word or bare letter.

Yea, under this state of convincement, if you had the utterance of a cherubim to preach the word, or saw ever such great visions, which would delight the nature of man, so that he would say, it is good to be here: yet, to hear the *sacred Voice* of Faith by the messenger and follow him down unto death, and quicken out of that death into a *new Life*, which will be the daughter of Faith born, that far surpasseth the high state of convincement, why? because Faith can bear *fiery trials* to, Godward: the other must die under convincement, as before said.

Further, when a Messenger comes from God, the voice, of God in the Messenger is sure to call some to obey, and to stand still and see the salvation of God:—other some, hear in anger, which works their spirits into wrath, and. from thence into blasphemy, and, if possible, Would destroy the word of truth from the face of the earth; all this you may see without you.

But them who receive the spiritual word unto purification of their souls, will find within themselves the *Kingdom of Heaven*, and the *Kingdom of Hell*: *i.e.* the spirit of *Faith* would be in communion with God, and get as near in spirit to him as possible, and also to be *true* in love with its spiritual brethren, and at *peace* with the Whole world: and the spirit of Reason, which, is seeking to devour every good thought which moves the soul to act; and also would devour the whole world;—after all, its self! therefore the voice of God by the Messenger sets *two kingdoms* at war in the Soul of man; for Faith is called, that it may come out from under the power of Reason, and Reason will not give up his rule, and this is your *War*, which is the troubles you complain of.

Furthermore, Reason is in his own kingdom, and will seek after things which he must leave at his death, and tell the *Man* "he must live while he is here, or such things are coming on him as will be his overthrow;" and this will cause him to sit and complain; "the powers of hell by this slavish *fear* brought by Reason in his own soul, that were it not for a power above, he would covenant with death and hell, and throw himself into it before it comes upon him."

And also, Reason will flatter him, in this slavery, that he may seek after the *world*, and gather riches and hold them fast unto his death, whereby his posterity may enjoy *Lands, Mansions, Money,* &c. that among them he may have a great name for enriching the family by the *mammon* of unrighteousness—but, poor *fool*, what benefit will it be to him, for his family to be in splendour, when he is taken into the *first death*, and sealed by the internal angel unto the *second?* for the world was not created for him and his only; therefore he is but a *steward* of those riches put into his hands by Providence to give his brethren *meat in due season*: but Reason will tempt him to keep it himself, and in that he becomes a *thief*, and his wealth is the *Mammon of unrighteousness*, in which, he has not been *faithful*; therefore, *who will commit to him the great and true riches*: thus Reason is very anxious to gather things that will perish with himself. I have wrote those things that you and all men who see this, may watch the folly of Reason.

Again, Reason will, on a sudden, catch a man in *anger* against his brother, and work him up to that height in it, so as the man may lose his eternal Life to be revenged against his brother, were it not for God's divine stay: And further, it will kill the soul with all manner of fears and doubts, and temptations at times, and will catch the man where and when he is not aware of him that he may keep him down in this vale of death, and bury itself in the deepest part of the earth, all, if possible, to hide itself from its own angel, which is the internal angel of the law, or the angel of the Lord that will execute judgment upon Reason unto death—for Reason cannot face its own angel, because it is both a *Liar and a Thief*.

AGAIN, Beloved Brother, when the *Virgin*, daughter of Faith, is born, *she* has to follow the Messenger through this *internal hell* of the soul, neither is there any other way to travel to the spiritual and holy covenant of grace, and her nature which is innocence, meekness, love to enemies, and will acknowledge her *fault* before the divine judge, and is productive of prayer, to get as near the divine majesty as possibly it can, from whence it came: and when the internal angel of the law, or the Law itself do arrest Reason, and work it down as it were to a death, then the spirit of Faith (being *active* in human nature) can offer its own *offering*, *i.e.* its Prayer, then the soul has peace, and can see what is promised to be faithful and true, with a sight you are in the *road* for the holy city; this is a fine sight, and the soul is joyful, until Reason brake in like a dark *Cloud* seeking to drown or devour the fruits of Faith in the soul; this, my worthy friend, is at this day the condition of the faithful, or the seed of faith: and if the spirit of *emulated* Reason takes you from this, you are not in the *Road* for heaven; for the spirit of Faith must *overcome*, as Christ did, for to enter the kingdom of heaven.

Therefore, from hence you may find within the elect, *two* spirits, for their kingdoms, at *War!* this spirit of Faith is eager to get as near

God, from whence it came, as possibly it can: and the spirit of Reason is eager to get into the dark Earth or Chaos from whence it came, to hide itself from the internal angel of the law (or angel of the Lord) if possibly it could; for this angel will execute God's judgment upon Reason.—Also this angel turns every way to keep Reason from the Tree of Life. Now the Lord Jesus is the *Angel of Faith*, and Faith is eager to get to him, and offer at his royal feet: but Reason cannot face his angel as aforesaid.

AGAIN, Jesus said, "*his* kingdom was not of this world," and further, this life is heaven to the seed of Reason, and of consequence hell to the seed of Faith: therefore, when Faith *finds* itself, it is among all those wilds and temptations of Reason, which is, being in a *strange Land* and in hell; enough, therefore it must overcome to be regenerated unto Christ; and this is not to be done but by the true prayer, and patience, which is *fasting*; and as often as you can do this, you will have God's divine assistance, then there will be a devil cast out.

Beloved brother in those great *troubles*, I would advise you to *pray and not to faint*, and to have faithful and *true patience* and that will be a great help to your soul: for true *Patience* is a great property of faith: therefore read Rev. iii. 10. "because thou hast the word of my *patience*, I also will keep thee from the hour of temptation that shall come upon all the world to try them that dwell upon the *Earth.*"

Now the holy spirit calls the seed or spirit of Reason the *Earth*, because it is of or from the *chaos*, but called into act according to the will of God; as also is the earth to bring forth its produce, and them that by their cunning and self will, with all their shifts and turns that dwells on this *Earth*, which is the spirit of Reason, will be overcome with temptation: and the seed and Spirit of Faith by prayer will have divine assistance and temptation—and were it not for those *trials*, what would you overcome, but would be naked and bare under the state of convincement only, where you would live and die under the outward or bare letter, and know nothing of the spiritual power of this commission: And,

Further, I would not have you give way too much to the frightful *threats* of Reason, but with faith and patience seek the kingdom of heaven, and things will be added; therefore mind this—Every thing, to Faith, must give way, for to come up to God's spiritual grace, as all natural inheritance will *dissolve*, for to complete his glorious kingdom, for his own children the seed of Faith; to live in his royal presence to all eternity; then will his glorious kingdom be complete! and as the divine majesty *patiently waits* to complete his own GLORY, do you also wait patiently for your *glory* to be complete with HIS.

AGAIN, *beloved Brother*, as you are in the kingdom of Ireland, and may meet with some that own the letter of Reeve and Muggleton, when convenient opportunity offers, I would not have you fail to tell of this LIGHT from heaven, that has lately come, and shines in the souls of the elect here at London: and if any civil men of the *world* be inclined to enquire, let them also: for there will men come out of the world and truly own the commission, and be *taken* by the spirit, and be truly brought up to God, while the *Literalist* will go off *murmuring*, and see themselves cast out.

For when the Messenger comes, the church was in the state of bare litteral convincement only: and that many (*wolves* is in *sheeps clothing*) come and owned the letter, and usurped the ruling Power, then from this spirit without, and the spirit of Reason within, took the elect into deep Captivity; so they must put away all their knowledge gathered by the spirit of Reason: and become as *little children* to be *born of water*, to the spiritual covenant of the *Law*; and then of spirit to the spiritual covenant of *Grace*, to have the seal of JESUS to enter into *His* glorious kingdom. And,

Further, of all things I would have you seek the Life of man, and not their Death: and act in the line of Mercy; for if CHRIST do not take men into *Life*, they are already in *death!*—therefore, Christ said, Matt. v. "Blessed are the merciful, for they shall obtain mercy;" so have in your soul mercy, and not sacrifice, then you ever[*] will judge the innocent, and I hope with you, things in the natural is nearly to your liking, but, however, put your whole trust in God, both for your natural and spiritual protection, which will be the offering of the *widows mites*: and when this is truly done, all will be well. So conclude your brother in the true Faith, &c.

London 1778.   JAMES BIRCH.

---

[*] In the original printed text there is a manual correction here from ever" to "never"

LETTER IX

To the true Church of Christ in and about Pembroke, James Birch sendeth greeting.

BELOVED BRETHREN, this with my love informs you that I am come safe to London; but on the way things run much against me; for I could get no further help on the road than to ride a single horse six miles, and in a return chaise about eight miles: the other way I came on foot *till about 62 miles off London*: but God be thanked, I am safe returned, and tolerably well, after the perplexity of sore feet and weary limbs.

Also I called at *Abergavenny*, and was kindly received and entertained by *Mr. Jones*, as being a spiritual friend and brother to his wife, he adding, "any of his wife's friends be welcome to him at any time." He desired to be remembered to our brother and sister *Howell*, &c. Mrs. *Jones* was greatly rejoiced to hear of the brethren in and about *Pembroke*, and more so because the Messenger said he found in them *obedience* and *faith*: *She* prays, Faith may increase; that heavenly knowledge unto salvation may be *gathered* now in the days of a Messenger.

Our beloved brother *Thomas Joseph* sent a letter of salutation to the brethren, directed to our *Brother Cole*, while I was with you, but as I heard nothing of it then, if not now, enquire at the Post-Office;—soon after that was sent, my wife was taken very ill, and so I found her, but thank God she is better.

NOW brethren, I humbly hope you will keep in remembrance what I said when I was with you, that you *love* one another above the love of this perishing world: for that man has badly spent his time, whose soul has been chiefly employed in gathering the *riches* of this world; or in the fashions and manners of Reason, whereby the world respects him in his *vanity*, as one of themselves: or to be overpowered with the cares of this life by the threats of *poverty*, and the fears of Reason's contempts: then, when the soul is arrested by grim death, the internal angel opens the books of justice, wherein is written death for that soul! because he has been a servant to Reason all his days, and cannot stand before the Redeemer according to the notice given him, for the want of the *fruit of Faith*: and the door is shut against him!! — then— what would not a man give in exchange for the salvation of his soul!!

Therefore I wrote this unto you, praying, that you may watch Reason, and not be drawn aside by its insinuation: nor overpowered by its threats:—which must be done by the *prayer of Faith*! so, *watch*,—and *pray*, that you enter not into the drunken and surfeiting spirit of Reason, but like unto the *wise virgins*, seek by the power and prayer of faith, to get *ready*; and there *wait* the Call which I have told you will come, and God only knows when, then you will be found worthy to stand before the king of Faith, both in spirit and in person.

MOREVER, beloved brethren, God has sent his Messenger in these our days, under the attribute of his divine mercy, to call to his elect; and give them notice of his sudden appearance in spirit, to seal and sanctify them to enter his glorious kingdom: and also to unite them by the power and spirit of Faith, in a church or body; then there is Faith for Faith, with Faith; and Faith, united to Faith, in the true *love and* WORSHIP *of God*; and is the CHURCH of Christ; because He is the head: and this church or body is joined together *by* the power, and *in* the love of God.

Now who or what must that man or men be, who endeavour to separate or scatter the church, so called, together? why truly, it is done by the spirit of Reason, the grand enemy to Christ and his elect: this Reason do that he may build a church to his own liking, for Reason to rule over. And those things may be done even in the day of a Messenger, and by him or them that the Messenger has called by his declaration, and who say they follow the Messenger, but must at the same time, think their own wisdom greater than God has inspired the Messenger with, therefore is a great enemy in spirit to God, his elect, and his living Messenger; and let such a man cover himself under any name, or display himself with the *tongue of an Angel*, yet when the internal angel in justice opens his book, then let him get from answering to his own name if he can.

Therefore, beloved brethren, let no temptation of Reason take you from the *Love* of your Brethren, for the man that is catched in *Anger* against his brother, the *fault* is in himself; indeed a man may tell his brother of his *fault*, but must at the same time forgive him, and pray for him, then he will do well: but if *angry*, then self interest and justice is pleaded to excuse himself: now whosoever so flies to justice to excuse himself, in that excuse is condemned; for the royal example of Faith is this, God the Father, who became the God of Justice through the acts of man, left his glorious throne of justice, and transmitted himself into his own created nature of Adam, and was born a *Son*, to become the God of MERCY; and called the elect to his Mercy: *and as God left his heavenly glory to come to man in MERCY! Man, also, must leave his earthly glory and come to God in MERCY,* and to the MERCY of GOD; if he is to inherit it: therefore let this be an example of your Love to your brother; for if you cannot give up the things of *Reason*, how is it possible you should inherit the glorious things of *Faith*!

Again, CHRIST, the King of Faith and Mercy, now holds forth his merciful hand to his Elect; and they must come to him, in *Love* and *Mercy* to each other, as he comes in *love* and *mercy* to them! then HE will take them, and rule over them: but if a man should profess any divine light from heaven, and that man's soul is led away after the riches and vain delight of this world;—Christ doth not rule over that soul, why? because that soul is a servant to Reason; and if he cannot be called from thence he must be *slain* by the internal angel in justice, beneath the *feet* of Mercy: for man must leave the whole world to *follow* JESUS, *i.e.* the spirit and powers of Reason must die, or give way in the soul, for Faith to follow to the regeneration!

Note—this is a *hard lesson* to the spirit of Reason; nay, *impossible* to be done; but to Faith it is *possible*! and will be done by its *prayer* for divine *assistance* from heaven!!! But you must be in love and charity to your brethren: for as we are in Reason's kingdom, we must bear the *wilds* and *temptations* of Reason, which is the CROSS, and this will be done by the power and prayer of Faith for divine assistance from Heaven; this CHRIST bore, to get into HIS royal Glory of Mercy; and *we* must *follow* every one, according to his ability, or the Portion of Faith given him: but as we bear the *Cross of Christ*, by Him we shall be crowned with a glorious CROWN of his Love and Mercy, and live in his royal presence in all eternity!

Therefore, brethren, if possible, let not the spirit of Reason, which is the devil, creep in among you, and so become a scattered people: but keep together, and *love* one another in the *love of Faith*, and the whole world cannot hurt you; for you will not only be as a *Light* to the world, but also bring forth the *fruits* of Faith unto Salvation; then God will be glorified in his *Church*: and the elect will rejoice with his

Messenger, who is a servant to them; therefore nothing shall be wanting in me that in my power lays, to *instruct* them in Faith, and *guide* them to the love of God. And if any thing is wanting you will let me know, for I shall be glad to hear from you. So concludes your loving friend and brother,

London,   JAMES BIRCH

Oct 13 or *Nov* 15, 1778,

P.S. The brethren in London greatly rejoice to hear a good report of you by the Messenger, and with me give their love to the whole Church, and prays the increase of Faith in all the elect. Please to give my love to George Griffiths; and the old gentleman their father, that Alice called uncle Frank, and to Betsy, and hope to hear she is a good girl.

LETTER X

To our well beloved Sisters Mrs. Atkinson and Mrs. Runwa, and the whole Church, in and about Pembroke, James Birch sends Greeting.

DEARLY beloved brethren,—I should have sent sooner, but waited an answer from the church, which we received with great joy by *Joseph Cole's* letter to *Tho. Joseph.*

And whereas you say, "you are only brought to the *nether waters* under justice, and clothed in a *right mind* to sit at the feet of Jesus," this expression is very right; because, this is the intent of the holy spirit by the Messenger who came out from God in his holy covenant of mercy to call the elect into the compact of Faith, to work the works of Faith to *follow Christ, i.e.* from wandering in the bare Letter, into this lively heaven of Faith under the teachings of God with the Messenger, and to *gather* your way to the kingdom of heaven by the fruits of Faith and Christ's divine assistance from heaven, you being *called* into the heaven of Faith by the *Messenger*, and for to *live* in Faith with the Messenger, and gather your way by Faith as the Messenger do, then Christ will rule over you.

Moreover, CHRIST is now *come* in spirit, to call to Faith which is, under justice, and that it may be truly *sensible* in what condition it is in, then it will gather and be gathered from under justice, to the heaven of grace, or the attribute of divine mercy; which is done *by,* and *in* patience, meekness, obedience, mercy, &c. This will Faith produce against all the powers of reason: Then it is found worthy of Christ, and will hear his voice to say "come ye blessed."

Also, you say "since I was with you, you understand more of my declaration," this is my soul's desire, and prayer for you all; for no man *soweth seed* but likes to see the prospect of *fruit;* and not only so, but also, he has great Joy in the glorious prosperity of that fruit, as in Mark iv. where Christ speaks of the kingdom of God, as if a man "should *cast seed* into good *ground,* and should *sleep,* and *rise night and day,"* which, is then in the power of God when *sown,* v. 28; "for the earth brings forth fruit of herself, first the *Blade,* then the *Ear,* after that the *full Corn in the ear"* which, is this, when Faith is called to, by the voice of God in the Messenger, it is in God's time quickened into act, then it will abide by, and follow the Messenger, and grow in strength and offer its own prayer to be preserved from the power of death and hell; this is the *Blade* of Faith for the kingdom of heaven.

After this, Faith will *grow* more strong, and prophecy of its own salvation, *i.e.* when the soul is in the sorrowful vale of death, and Faith has offered to the justice of God, the voice comes from heaven to the internal angel in justice, "that soul shall live" then is presented a clear light from heaven; and a *plain road* to heaven to the soul; with a true knowledge that Christ will come in spirit, and *seal* him for the kingdom of heaven, according to the prophecy of the Messenger; then has the soul *prophesied* of his own salvation; and is the *Ear* of Corn formed according to regeneration for the *Kingdom of Heaven.*

But you will come *back,* in the *sorrowful* vale of death, and must yet wade against Reason, death and hell, till Christ *calls,* and gives birth to his holy covenant of grace, and seals him for his glorious kingdom: then is the prophecy of the soul crowned with that of the Messenger's; and this is the *full* CORN *in the ear,* for the kingdom of heaven; for it then dies in the bed of mercy for the call to glory: but mind, this cannot be done, without the HUSBAND-MAN, and the refreshing *Showers,* and glorious *Sun-shine* from heaven!

Furthermore, concerning what you wrote, "to love God above all, and your *neighbour* as yourself"—now this is but the law of Reason, and the seraphims in heaven keep this law but the love of Faith far transcends this; for the Lord Jesus come from heaven to redeem, and give up his life for his elect, to convert them to his own glory:—also, was it possible the Messenger could, he would convert the elect his brethren to *his* degree of Faith or likeness; for the nature of Faith is to give up all, even his life for his brother, if required, to bring him through death into the new and glorious life of Faith.

Now Reason should love his *Neighbour* as himself, but it will consult his own preservation first, and in all its love, and charities, it is done to help and support his own kingdom: But what will they do for to help, in the kingdom of Faith which leads to glory? therefore (Luke x.) the lawyer willing to justify himself, said unto Jesus, "and who is my neighbour," Jesus answered, "a certain man went from Jerusalem to Jericho, fell among thieves, which stript him, wounded him, and leaving him half dead; and there came a certain *Priest* that way, and when he saw him he passed on the other side; and likewise a *Levite* came and looked on him, and passed by on the other side."

"But a certain SAMARITAN came and had compassion, and bound up his wounds, and poured in oil and wine, set him on his own beast and brought him to an Inn and took care of him; and on the morrow when he departed, gave twopence to the Host, and said take care of him, and whatever thou spendest more, I will repay thee when I come again"; then Jesus said, "which of those three was his *Neighbour?*" the lawyer said, "he that shewed mercy"; Jesus said, "go and do thou likewise". This is to shew forth to the spiritual man, the great difference between the love and power of *Faith*, and the love and power of *Reason.*

Now the *Samaritan* was JESUS, when he came to redeem, and found the seed of Faith, *robbed* by Reason, and *wounded* by justice; but Jesus came in mercy, and redeemed his elect to his mercy, and do *set them on his own Beast* which is his power, of Faith and mercy: and that will carry them to the *Inn*, which is his own lively compact of Faith with them: and when he ascended into the high heaven of mercy he gives to the *Host* of the Inn *Twopence*: now the HOST of the Inn, is them that he is graciously pleased to inspire to call his Elect, to, his lively compact of Faith, and more so to him that comes under the covenant of mercy.

And this MESSENGER has power given him from heaven, to quicken Faith to the knowledge of its own promises made by Jesus; and to be born of water to the first covenant: and it has a *censer* with incense to offer its own offering, *i.e.* Faith is the censer and its prayer the *incense* that ascends up to God; And thus do they work the works of Faith, now this is One *Penny* given to the *Host* to take care of the elect; and the FIRST Portion of the elect toward regeneration.

Again, the *Messenger* has power to declare to the souls of the elect, the difference between the voice of Faith and the voice of Reason in the soul; for Reason will transform itself even in the very elect, to the seeming likeness of Faith, and tempt the soul out of the path of God; and the Messenger must call him from it, and put him in the *true path* again; and will truly *direct* him up to the prophecy of his own salvation: and further the Messenger can *direct* him up to the internal *Baptism* of water; and this is the other *Penny* given to the host to take care of the elect; and is the SECOND portion of Faith in the regeneration; therefore this is the *Twopence* given to the Messenger, that is born in spirit to the holy covenant of grace and mercy, and sent forth under mercy, to call the elect into the lively *compact* of Faith with God; which is the *Inn*, or Refuge for Faith.

And the *voice of* GOD in the Messenger quickens the spirit of Faith from its womb or seed, into act: this is the *one part*:— and directs it up to the prophesies of its own salvation, and to God; which is the *other part* then God comes in spirit to that soul, and takes him to his holy covenant of Grace; then all is *paid* and satisfied.

But the *Priest* or *Levite* may come and *look* at the poor wounded seed of Faith, but will leave him under the *wound* of justice, because they cannot direct him to mercy; therefore, who on this earth is a *neighbour* to the elect, but the *Messenger*, to direct them in mercy to the kingdom of heaven: or where on this earth must the Messenger find his *Neighbour* for the kingdom of heaven; but the elect who are called into the compact of Faith, in with Christ, to be with and follow the Messenger.

Now you, the *Church* of God, are my *Neighbours, friends* and *brethren*, and I yours; for my soul is very desirous of your Spiritual welfare; and in this *union* of faith, love, and mercy, nothing shall be wanting in me that in my power lay; to give the *children* meat and drink for the kingdom of heaven: and mind what Love and Mercy you shew to the *Church*, it is done for the kingdom of heaven's sake: then Jesus will say; "come ye blessed, inherit the kingdom prepared for you, for I was an hungry and ye gave me meat, &c:" Also, "depart ye cursed, I was an hungry and ye gave me no meat, &c." therefore the love and Charity of Reason is for his *own* Ends, which is to live in his own kingdom; and that he must lose, at death; but the Love and Charity of Faith is for the kingdom of heaven; which they will find after death; therefore seek the works and Love of Faith, and you will find a reward here, beside eternal life hereafter.

P. S. The book I have not yet finished; for in the Gospel there are great things to open: I am sorry Mrs. Howell is ill; but let her be of good cheer and all will be well. So my love and duty to you all in Jesus Christ, and conclude your loving brother: and beg all in the love of God be careful to peruse this; (Love to Betsy).

JAMES BIRCH.

Mrs. Birch is got well—gives her love.

London, *Dec.* 1, 1778.

LETTER XI

To our brother James Thomas, and to the whole Church, James Birch sendeth Greeting.

BELOVED brethren, yours I received, and was very glad to hear from, you, and shall greatly rejoice in all your welfare in the faith of Jesus. I am sorry to hear that Hannah Wilkin has been ill, but illness and death is *over* us, because we are *under* the power of death; and nothing but the pure INCENSE of Faith to follow the Messenger who leads to the mercy of Jesus, will take the soul thro' the power of Reason, death, hell, and justice, into the NEW and glorious *Life* of pure Faith.

And as you are desirous to know what the deeds of the *Nicolaitanes* (Rev. ii.) were, that you may not be overtaken in them, I shall proceed to inform you both in the mystery and history.—They were people who transformed themselves into the apostles' letter, and in the apostles' time, and professed the name of Jesus, yet did things contrary to the doctrine of the apostles, and in contempt of the holy spirit: This *Sect* is said to spring from *Nicolas*, a proselyte of *Antioch*, and was one of the seven deacons first appointed (Acts vi. 5).—Those *Nicolaitanes* used bad practices, *i.e.* to maintain the *Legality* to live with women in common:—And *Meat offered to idols* were as lawful to eat as any other: And that *Libertism* was the way to Bliss;—Others would excuse the deacon by saying he gave up his wife who was of great beauty with his leave to marry any other; to shew his companions he intended to keep a vow he had made: and from this his rash Zeal, others vindicated their evil doctrine and practice. Now what the historian brings to excuse the deacon condemns him; for he then gave up his wife to commit adultry.

This is in part an *historical* account, but I think there is truth in it.

Now I have told you from whence this *Sect* took their name; and from me, you may be certain; that many of the seed of Reason transformed themselves into the apostles' declaration and there lodged, even in the apostles' time: and laid their claim to Jesus, but instead of forsaking sin and gathering their *way* by Faith, to Jesus to be forgiven, they sin the more and say "we have the promise of Christ, and he will forgive us;" therefore excuse themselves in evil; so they make the *Name* of Jesus a *Harbour* for their sin, instead of seeking by the Power of Faith to have their *sins washed away*.

This Sect of people living in the Apostles' time, must spring from the *doctrine and practice* of some man; and that man must declare himself of God to teach the people; otherwise they could not stand as a sect of themselves at such a time, (Note, *to be called christians*):— And their doctrine and practice was evil as aforesaid; therefore (v. 14) at the reproof of Pergamos, there was them of the *doctrine* of Baalam who taught Balac to cast stumbling blocks before Israel, to eat things sacrificed to idols, and commit fornication.

(Verse 15) "So hast thou also them that hold the doctrine of the *Nicolaitanes* which thing I hate," here you may see what the deeds of the Nicolaitanes was, and is now; for it has never died since it has been born:—Also, this *doctrine* has been too much practised in this commission of the spirit; but happy and Blessed are you that are called from it by the Messenger, into the lively *Compact* of Faith; while the *Litteralist* who is of Reason is left wallowing in his mire.

Furthermore, at this time, Reason will tempt the soul from hearkening to the voice of Faith, and fill the soul with bewildered conceivings contrary to Faith, and persuade him it is the Doctrine of the Messenger, and he will own it, if not, it is a wisdom hid from the Messenger, nay great revelation, and that he is appointed for a great work: now if the soul feed on this, he *eats meat* sacrificed to *Idols*; and if he depends on this to come to pass he commits spiritual *fornication* with the declaration of the living Messenger; because the Messenger called him by his declaration: And he will dedicate this his dark and wild incense of reason for Christ to own, instead of the pure incense of Faith that is quickened, and *guided* by the Messenger.

Also mind, the present Messenger came out from God under Mercy, and his royal seal, to *call* the elect and *guide* them to HIS MERCY:—therefore he knows *him* that comes from heaven, and *them* that gather their *way* toward heaven by the power of Faith: and if any one would divide the elect from the living Messenger or disunite the union of the church in this lively compact of Faith, that is the *doctrine of Balaam*; for they lay *stumbling blocks* before that Israel, of which CHRIST is the king: and if any *deceiver* should come, he will come out in the insinuating manner as I have described; therefore hearkening to no such voice neither without you, nor within you, and you will do well.

MOREOVER, to "work out your own salvation with *Fear* and TREMBLING" now there is no other way to salvation but through *fear* and *trembling*; not that any created being can work, his own salvation, for that Jesus did by losing himself in his own blood in death under the justice of the *Father* to quicken again into the glorious Mercy of the *Son*: therefore when Faith is called and quickened into its own knowledge, it finds itself under the power of Reason, Death, Hell, and Justice, and of consequence in a *trembling* condition, in this sorrowful vale of death: now at this time or condition of soul, is the prayer of Faith offered, which ascends to heaven for Christ's divine assistance.

Also Reason will threaten the soul with *Poverty* and *Distress* to come, and if possible drive or tempt the soul from the works of Faith: Also will transform itself, and promise the soul great, Liberty, Prosperity, &c. beside eternal life hereafter, if it will but hearken to him; therefore at this, and its own condition Faith may well *fear* and TREMBLE; yet, at this time will bring forth its fruit: now this temptation is *in* yourself, therefore mind and not hearken to this voice, neither within nor without, for *in* this travail through Death and

Hell man will find he must eat his own flesh, *i.e.* to bear the wilds and temptations of Reason within and without; and in *sorrowful human nature, animated with divine Faith*, gather your way to the mercy of Christ, as He did to his glorious throne of mercy: for this very nature God took on himself.—Therefore it is every Elect according to his portion of Faith CHRIST the great and *first fruits!*—And Faith being in a fallen state must now follow its *Guide* to bring forth fruits unto salvation, for no one can go through Hell and Death but in *fear and trembling*; now this is far from the liberty of Reason, and the doctrine of the *Nicolaitanes* in spirit.

FURTHER, of losing your *first Love*; now your *first Love* is with me, for it was me through Christ called you from wandering in the bare letter, and from the house of satan into the lively compact of Faith which leads to Christ:—beside you live in my *Day*, and men now will be judged according to my *Day*: therefore when the voice of God by the Messenger quickens Faith to direct it to God; it flows forth in love to God, to the Messenger, and to his brother united in the Church; and this is the right offset in the true way to heaven; for God calls the elect from the *love* of Reason to the *love* of Faith:—But also, Reason will transform to this likeness, and take the soul into *emulation*, and lift it up in false knowledge, then on this part you have lost your *first Love*, if you are overtaken here,

Again, when Faith is quickened (as I said) then, in this *first Love*, men will do any good thing for the sake of the kingdom of heaven; and will be very joyful in his brother and the Messenger: but Reason will *cloud* the soul with fear and threats of *poverty*, and tell him he must do his duty in, and for this life; for Reason will fill the soul full of employ, and all to keep him from the works of Faith; and tell the soul he has the *Truth*, and the *love of God*; what need he more, than now mind and live in this world?—then *Love* and *Charity* will become cool, and excuse made; for one will say he must mind his *farm*, and another his *merchandise*, now this is losing your *first love*; and the spirit threaten him that do; therefore keep the *love* of Faith, and let the love of Reason perish, for *straight is the gate, and narrow is the way which leads to life.*

Again, he that *hateth* his brother is a *murderer*, now murder is of Reason the devil, for he was a *lyar and a murderer from the beginning*; and this devil was the *serpent angel* afterwards born Cain, who slew his brother *Abel*; he is called his brother because they were both born of Eve; and as *Abel* had Reason in him through the fall, they were both under the moral law, (Note, IN t*he Compact of Faith and Covenant of Grace no one is your brother but the* ELECT) but they being come to manhood and capable to make an Offering, *Abel's* was of Faith, and *Cain's* was of Reason; and he grew angry because his was not accepted, then he murdered Abel that he might possess the whole, and then he thought his offering must be accepted:— Now this is the second time that heaven was attempted by *violence*, and from that day, this act has been done by his seed; for that seed can bring out no spiritual truth except the angel force him to declare his own damnation.

But the Elect of *Old*, Christ, and his Apostles, and the Elect under the *Gospel*, has, and do declare Light, Prophecy, and Life from Heaven; this make the children of the devil angry;—Then they speak evil, and prophecy against it, and declare it is the spirit of the devil; and this is spiritual murder; for if they kill the person it is to destroy the spirit: and if they transform to the Messenger's declaration, even in his life-time, and preach like an Angel, yet in this language is contained death and will end *in*, or *with* a spiritual lie, because they have no truth in them; this is also spiritual murder; so reason in all his ways is to *kill* the spirit and take *possession* of the letter.

Yea, some of the Elect may *speak evil* and persecute the Elect through an evil report, and their false zeal, being brought up under Reason and never did hear the call of the spirit, like unto *Paul*, but when they do, they will follow through persecution and temptation, as *Paul* did, and the internal angel will tell you of it, therefore this must be worked through with *fear* and *trembling* as other evils area.—Now

Mind your own spirit of Reason, and that you are not catched in anger; for man may be catched in anger like the sudden prick of a pin; and if not stayed in good time, it will increase so as to infect both body and soul;—Hence you may see that no Spiritual murderer can have eternal life.

Now *Anger*, is the seed of murder, for it is from anger, to hatred and spite, and from that to murder, both naturally and spiritually: And if a man, in the church is and do remain angry, you may be assured the voice of God has not taken root in him, and if he cannot come back he will too soon tell his own tale, which is, he is not accepted: Also as aforesaid, mind your *own* Reason, for if possible it can, it will murder your *own* Faith: therefore love and pray for each other for during the time of your *anger* you have death acting in you, instead of life; so love and forgiveness is in and for the compact of Faith: for there is no such thing as anger in Faith which leads to life eternal.—Now,

Observe what is written, and pray God give you Understanding: and I recommend you by prayer to the works and love of Faith in Christ: so conclude your loving brother.

JAMES BIRCH.

December 17, 1778.

P.S. The whole church greets you all in love, and prays your increase of Faith.

LETTER XII

To our beloved brother Joseph Cole, and to the whole Church in and about Pembroke, James Birch sendeth greeting.

Brethren,—Yours I received (*but some time after it came to London, for instead of No. 3, it is directed 5; the post-man searched some days, but could find no such place or person, but calling on me by way of enquiry, I had it; but was going to be put in the dead-letter office*, hence mind that *No. 3 is in the direction*) and I am glad you received the last letter I sent; but I sent one to Mrs. Atkinson and Runwa, Dec, 1, 1778, which I hope also came to hand: Now you say I greatly satisfied you in declaring the working out salvation with *fear* and *trembling*:—I am very glad I have: Also I humbly hope the whole church is satisfied; for you all may be assured there is no other way to salvation; for it is the will of God that Faith should work against the powers of Reason, and be lost in death under divine justice, to be quickened into divine mercy therefore as you know the will of God, and the works of Faith, mind and do it, otherwise you will be *beaten with many stripes*.

Also, I am glad you see a literal confirmation to what I have wrote concerning the Nicolaitanes; but also mind, those things were done in spirit; therefore a man may make a passable external appearance among men, and at the same time his soul is almost eaten up by the devouring internal caterpillars of Reason. Now, as I have said before, *watch* your own spirit of Reason, that you may in patience and meekness go Godward by the power of Faith.

AGAIN, why *Jesus* rejoiced? (as Luke x, 21) mind, Jesus had sent forth his disciples to preach the word, heal the sick, &c. Who was then returned and said "Lord even the devils are subject to us through thy name," And Jesus said "Behold I give you power to tread on serpents, and scorpions, and over all the powers of the enemy, and nothing shall hurt you;"—but Jesus also said, "rejoice not that spirits are subject to you, but rather *rejoice* that your names are written in heaven." Hence, you may see the difference between the *power* to preach, and the *power* to enter into the royal compact and priesthood of Faith; for they all went forth in the state of convincement and preached in the name and power of Jesus and not in their own; for when Jesus was taken and led away to be crucified, they were scattered, and could no longer stand without Jesus.

Now, the seed of the serpent, may take the word and preach in the name and power of another man, as Judas did in the name and power of Jesus; and if he is not to enter into the compact and priesthood of Faith, he will become an enemy to him that he received the word from, and tempt the elect into the priesthood of Reason, without he is cut off by the power of the internal angel as Judas was therefore do you mind the temptation of Reason within and without; for it is not so much to preach the word to overpower another man, but, it is to *enter* into the compact of Faith.

Furthermore, in that hour Jesus *rejoiced* in spirit, and said "I thank thee O Father, Lord of Heaven and Earth, that thou hast hid those things from the wise and prudent, and hast revealed them to babes:" Now Jesus *rejoiced* at that time to see the power of Reason, which is the power of the devil, WAS and *would* BE overcome by the power of Faith, which is the power of God; for by preaching the outward word it subjected the imagination of Reason in men, therefore (v. 18) he said unto them, "I beheld Satan as lightning fall from heaven;" *i.e.* the spirit of Reason was fell from that heaven he thought to have;—because it would be *overcome* by the power of Faith.

Also, as God created heaven and earth, he was God the *Father* to Adam and all the elect:—but as man and angel both fell, he became the God of Justice through their act: but mind this,—although he was the God of *Justice* to his Elect, yet to that seed he was God the *Father*, but to the angelic nature he was the God of Justice only: therefore the power of God was that of JUSTICE, and he parted with it by investing it on *Moses* and *Elias*, and become a SON to the power of the *Father*, and worked the works of faith, and redeemed his Elect; then he ascended into the high heaven, or the Power of Mercy! to his Elect!

And while JESUS worked the works of Faith, he was in the mystical union and spiritual communion in the compact of Faith, with them who sit in the power and glory of the father; unto whom, he addressed himself to, in prayer and thanksgiving:—Also they revealed to the elect that Jesus was the son of God; and opened the understanding of their own lost condition:—And JESUS only, had the great and true Promise of ETERNAL LIFE and none but the BROKEN HEARTED has those things revealed to them.—Now this is the *Act* of *Faith* to desire salvation if possible, yet the *will of God* be done:—And God revealed it to them from the man Adam to this day.

And when *Jesus* was here a true son to the power of the father, and was among his elect, He himself, received divine assistance from heaven; and also knew the elect had *secret revelation* from heaven concerning him, and their salvation:—now this was his own Decree, when he was in the glory of the father, and was *thankful* for it, when he was here a Son to the power of the Father! and in this Thing he *rejoiced*, that the elect his brethren should have eternal life, and the *wise and prudent* men of Reason, that was hid from;—Also, this *Promise* of salvation now belong to Christ only:—It has been repeated of times by his Messengers, that many has laid claim to it and say they are invited, but none will enter into the royal priesthood of Faith but *BABES*; *i.e.* men must part with all their gathered knowledge of reason and become a *Child* or *Babe* to enter the priesthood of Faith; where he will be healed of all his spiritual infirmities to enter the kingdom of heaven.

AGAIN, as concerning the *Thief* on the cross: he confessed his sin, and it was revealed to him who Jesus was; then he being at his death, his soul was productive of the prayer of Faith for the mercy of Jesus:

And Jesus said unto him—"To-day thou shalt be with me in paradise:" Now this paradise is when the soul is born or translated to under the mercy of the son; then he dies under justice to mercy, and lay in the bed of mercy to be quickened to glory:—for when Jesus had finished his work he died under the justice of the father and lay in death, to quicken into the glorious mercy of the son! and this *Paradise* is what Jesus said the thief should *be in, that day with him,*—now this is the second and great PARADISE to Faith, for Adam and Eve stood in *Paradise* when they were created; but they fell from this *Paradise*, under Justice, Death, and Reason: but this *second Paradise*, Faith never will fall from, for the next state is glory!

Also the *thief* was so near Jesus in spirit, that he knew Jesus was the resurrection and life of Faith, therefore he said "Lord, remember me when thou comest into thy kingdom"—which is the kingdom of mercy and glory to faith: Now this is the *Paradise* that my soul is very desirous men should seek after and come to.

AGAIN, concerning the *Rich Man*, whose ground brought forth plenty; this is the spirit of Reason, whose soul is seeking after the *riches* of this life, for Reason dearly likes to be independent of all things in this world: therefore what oppression and covetousness, flattery, &c. will not Reason be guilty of, to gather together an independent fortune: and his own spirit of Reason, which is his lying priest, will excuse him, by saying "he has a right to get what he can, and also do as he please with his own:" and when he has gathered his kingdom: and excused by this lying Priest, he will say in his soul, "now take thine ease;" then the internal angel in justice by the power of God requires his soul in Death, under the seal of justice; now that man which is bound in this, must think his soul cannot die, and if so, will not have *judgment*, let him pretend what he will to the contrary: thus Reason will lose himself in his own cunning, and by that he is called a fool: now do you mind your own Reason, and not lose yourself in this thing, although not a *rich man*; so conclude your loving brother in prayer for you all.

Feb. 1, 1779.   JAMES BIRCH.

P.S. The whole church greets you, &c.

LETTER XIII

To our beloved sister Mary Jones, *James Birch sendeth greeting.*

Dear Sister,—This comes with my love to inform you I received your letter 19th inst. and gave it to our Brother and Sister *Jellis*, who was very much rejoiced to hear from you, and greatly sympathize with you in your stedfast Faith, and great workings of soul: also the church of Sunday, heard the letter and rejoiced; and all give their love to you in the strong Union and experience of Faith.

Moreover beloved Sister, I much approve and commend your *Faith, prayer, and patience*, for as Faith fell under the Justice of the Father which is death; and also, as *reason* was taken into the soul through the fall, the elect may be sure, to be greatly incumbered with it; for Reason will keep the soul in the *priesthood* of Reason if possible, and not only so, but also take the promise of Christ, and invitations to the holy marriage with Jesus, into the priesthood of Reason:—And thus WAS, and thus IS, Faith tempted; therefore blessed are them that can watch and bear this temptation.

AGAIN *Faith* fell so low as to be dead from the communion with God, so inactive in itself; therefore *life* must be worked out of *death* even to the promise of Christ; indeed you, or any one may read the letter and say you read the promise of Christ; but this promise is *dead* to all that cannot be quickened from Death to Life; which, is this; when Faith is *called* to, by the voice of God in the Messenger, then by the help of God it is quickened from its womb or seed into acts and this is the spiritual *Virgin* daughter of Faith born to the promise of Christ, and to go its way in regeneration.

Also, this spiritual *Virgin* comes out of, or through Death, into *active Life*, and this cannot be done without great DISTRESS and agitation of soul, why? because one Life must be preserved for a *superior* Life to be brought forth. Further, when this superior life, which is the life of Faith, is born, it is taken into the royal priesthood of Faith, *i.e.* into the lively mystical union and spiritual communion of Faith with Christ, to work the works of Faith in regeneration for the kingdom of heaven.

Now this *Virgin* of Faith hath the power of Reason and darkness to wade through, which is as mountains in the way; nay, impossible to be removed by or according to Reason; but to Faith it is possible: therefore in this royal priesthood, if you have Faith and doubt not, and by patience and prayer, you will receive divine assistance from heaven and those mountains of reason, darkness, &c. will be removed.

AGAIN, this spiritual CALL of Jesus to his elect, is to call them into his OWN *priesthood*, which is the Priesthood of Faith, and not let them wander in the outward word, or letter, for that only is the priesthood of Reason; and there men may be kings and priests, prophets, &c. in their imaginations, and be full of their own assurance; - but it is not so in the royal priesthood of Faith, for there they must work the works of Faith, and by divine assistance from heaven (in God's time) to overcome the power of reason, darkness, death, &c. then that soul is found worthy to be called upon under the justice of the father, and from thence, to be given spiritual birth to under the mercy of the son:—And when men come to do this work they will do according to your noble prayer or desire of soul, *i.e.* go hand in hand:—Now, when the *Call* comes, if the soul cannot be brought into this priesthood to work those works, they must remain in the priesthood of Reason, dead to Faith as they were born into this world, and will seek the vain things of Reason, by their imagination in the spiritual; while Faith is truly seeking the MERCY of GOD.

AGAIN, when God; who was of Justice become a son to his own power, to become the God of mercy; HE *thrust in his* SICKLE *into the earth,* which was his great CALL to his *Elect* to his divine mercy; and *gathered the Vine of the Earth,* which are his elect, and cast them, with himself into the *great wine press of the wrath of God, i.e.* when Faith is *Called* and gathered to its own knowledge, it finds itself under justice, which, is the wrath of God; and is poured out on his elect because of the *fall:*— And the Elect must be brought back through justice, even in their own blood!—and it is done by the power of obedience, meekness, patience, and prayer, for divine assistance from heaven:—for

In this *Travail* men will find they must bear their darkness of soul and the wilds and temptations of Reason, which at times is as if your soul's blood was pressing out of you; otherwise how can the soul become anew by the powerful works of Faith: and be found worthy to be called upon under the justice of the Father, and then be born to under the mercy of the Son; and then die in the Bed of Mercy under the seal of the glorious Angel of Faith and Mercy!—And if this is not done, there is nothing done, but wandering and prattling on the letter:—And when death comes the soul is called by the internal angel of Reason, and there must die under his seal in that justice, *i.e.* under the seal of your own evils, and conscience witness to the same.

Therefore, *Blessed* is him or them, that are brought to *Truth*, then they will find themselves in spirit, in their *native* place, or where they was *born*, why? because they were born an *Elect*, being under the justice of the father.

And also, the soul is *encumbered* with Reason and its law, and priesthood, and the internal angel in justice of that law: Now the soul is well directed to the justice of the *Father*, and is able to KISS or embrace that Justice, for that is Justice to Faith but the Justice of the Angel is justice to Reason:—therefore it is good to pray to *meet* the Justice of the Father,—and—that justice is composed in the sight of the soul.

Also the *Mother* is the womb or seed of Faith that bears this *Virgin Daughter.* Now when Faith is called to, it is very desirous to bring forth this *Virgin*, which is from death to life, and above the bonds of Reason, to the *active* prayer of Faith in the royal Priesthood of Faith,— this, the *Womb* of Faith is eager to bring forth, which is the inward prayer: But no *active* prayer can come forth for Faith to come into the Royal Priesthood, till this virgin daughter is born; and when born, the soul must hearken to it, distinct to or from, any temptation of Reason—because by virtue of prayer and divine assistance from heaven, it is to take the soul through the power of Reason, darkness, &c.

AGAIN, when a Messenger comes from Jesus in his holy covenant of mercy, to invite the elect to his holy marriage, then, it is JUDGMENT DAY to them, why? because they are found under justice, which is the *wrath* of God, and must wade through it; and this is the judgment given to Faith or the elect; *i.e.* they must go through the power of darkness, Reason, &c. in *wrath*, even so as to *eat* their own flesh, and *drink* their own blood (in the spiritual); and blessed is him or them to whom this Judgment is given, and is found of *weight* or worthy of this, when the Invitation, and Trial comes, for this is the CROSS and PASSION of CHRIST; and when the soul has waded through this, it is called upon under the justice of the Father, above the angel in justice of Reason, and from under the justice of the Father be given birth to the mercy of the son—then dies in the bed of mercy;—thus you may see; after the works of Faith, you will meet the justice of the father, and must go through it to the mercy of the son.

And, now you may see the *Acts* and Powers of Faith goes hand in hand in the regeneration: Therefore let patience possess your soul, and have Faith, and not doubting the power of God; then *mountains will be removed*; for those things you must go through to be found worthy and called upon for mercy; so be of good comfort, and may *patience* possess your soul, then all is right, which is the prayer of your loving brother.

JAMES BIRCH.

London, March 27, 1779.

LETTER XIV

To our brother Joseph Cole, and to all the beloved church in and about Pembroke, Jas. Birch sendeth greeting.

Dear brother and brethren. — Yours I received 22d last past: and am glad to hear of your *Obedience* and *stedfast Faith* in this Call of Jesus; which quicken and take the spirit of Faith into the royal priesthood to the communion of the holy spirit: therefore mind, now is the time to do the WILL OF GOD in the works of Faith; and as so, the *Will of God* will be done to them, that leave Reason behind, *i.e.* His *Will*, is to take them to his divine mercy:—For it is not for us to seek the good things of this world which is the kingdom of Reason, and then let the kingdom of heaven be added:—But you must *first seek the kingdom of heaven, then all things will be added* to go through this world, to work the works of Faith in the royal priesthood; why? because Christ who is the angel of Faith has the ruling power over Faith in man.

Again, as Faith fell so low in Adam through temptation, as to be wholly under the justice of the father, and the soul subject to the law and priesthood of Reason; therefore when elect men are born, they are born to the law and priesthood of Reason; and in this priesthood, men may read of the promise of Christ, and talk of great things and their salvation, yet dead to Faith and the promise of Christ, as they were born into this world: So, Faith must he quickened from this death to life, or born from its womb or seed, to the works of Faith, and the promise of Christ, let them profess what letter they will; or die in the priesthood of Reason as they were born; only filled themselves with the full measure of justice, to die under the seal of the internal angel in justice, let them think what they will to the contrary.

MOREOVER, as the present Messenger is come in the *spirit and power* of Christ;—Christ is come in *spirit*, and is come to *judgment*, and this *judgment* is to his elect, *i.e.* Faith is called to, and quickened, and let know where it is, which, is not only under the justice of the father which is death; but also the souls of the elect are encumbered with the law and the priesthood, of Reason, and they must wade through it, which is done by prayer and patience, to be called upon under the justice of the *Father*, and from thence given birth to under the mercy of the SON: therefore as Faith fell under justice, which is the wrath of God, judgment is now given to it, that it must go through that wrath to mercy: and in great sorrow of soul like unto Jesus: For after Jesus had waded through the powers of Reason, and offered the true prayer in his own royal priesthood, which ascended before the throne of the father, he lost himself in death in his own blood, under the justice of the *father*, and quicken into the glorious mercy of the *son*.

Now this is the *Judgment* to Faith, and this is the *way* they must go through justice to mercy, every one according to his portion, Christ the great and first fruits; therefore the present Messenger is not come to take burthens from off the soul, but rather to bring a warfare to the soul; for to work against the powers of Reason, Death, Hell, &c. you will find great trouble; but in the royal priesthood you will at times have heavenly graces; and as so, not only be at united peace, but also in friendship with Christ the King of Faith!

Also I have found, and do find, to my experimental sorrow, that it is no easy thing to be in the priesthood of Faith; true it is, the *spirit is willing*; but as men are born to the kingdom and power of Reason, that spirit is eager to tempt the soul back from the Messenger, and there keep it if possible, after vain alluring things, and so excuse himself according to Reason; and the soul of man is *weak* enough to hearken to this: Therefore mind, this created Faith never was nor possibly could be tempted any lower than into the priesthood of Reason: So mind to *watch* lest you enter into temptation,—for except Faith is quickened from death to life, and work its works in the royal priesthood, there is nothing done for salvation.

Furthermore it is eternal Life to *know* the living and *true* God, for in that you will *know* that the God of Justice, became the God of Mercy: also you will *know* Reason's God which is the internal angel in justice; for there is power given him over Reason, that when men do evil, justice flies in your face, which is your conscience:—But as God has stayed his justice in the *angel* for a time, the angel will stay justice in the soul, and excuse *him* for a time.

Also if men do *right* before the angel they have his commendation and the lamp of life sweetly shine: and for this commendation and excuse acting in the soul, men take it to be Faith, nay, the spirit of Christ, whereas it is no more than the angel and priesthood of Reason: And in this condition they read of, or hear promises and prophesies, &c. yet dead to the knowledge of them, as the child unborn into this world: Also they may preach, teach, and promise life, but in that life is contained death, for it is all in Reason:—But mind, no mancan know the KING of Faith, which is Christ, except he is in the priesthood of Faith:—And as a Child is born into this world to know the things of this *world*, even so must Faith be *quickened* from death to life, or *born* from its womb or seed, to know the things of the *spirit*.

Again, as from what *voice* those places of scripture arises in you: I call it from the spirit of *obedience*; for you being obedient to the Messenger, those places confirm to you the Messenger is right; and it is good, for then follow the power of Faith.

NOW concerning the kingdom of heaven being taken by *violence*, this was done by the spirit of Reason from the beginning: But as JESUS came in or upon the *prophecies* of the elect in the royal priesthood; He uttered forth his holy gospel, and the works of Faith in his royal priesthood, which *is* or leads to the *kingdom of heaven*: And men came and *took it* by, or according to the spirit of Reason, which is by *violence*:—Therefore (see Luke xvi. 16) "the law and the prophets were until John; since that time the kingdom of God is preached, and every man presseth into it" (v. 17) "and it is "easier for heaven and earth to pass away, than one tittle of the law to fail," *i.e.* the internal angel of the law, will keep them *out* except or until they are spiritually born to it, as beforesaid.

Again, see His parable (Luke 20) where "A certain man planted a vinyard, and let it forth then at times sent his *servants* to receive the fruits; but they treated them shamefully, wounded them, and sent them empty away: And he sent his *son*, and him they killed to take the inheritance." Now this *Vinyard* is Faith, and those who were born to the priesthood of Faith, enquired for the *fruits* of Faith, and for that they were *spitefully* used by the spirit of Reason; and Christ is the *Son* who came, and him they killed, and also his *servants*, and took their letter or declaration into the priesthood of Reason; and became rulers on the letter like unto Gods.

Also men may think they are born into this world to do their own will, and serve themselves; but lo, they will find they were born to do the will of God, for his mercy, or go their own way under justice.

Also, in the days of Jesus, many came and took the word by the spirit of Reason; then of consequence they took it into their own priesthood, which is of Reason, and went forth. Now those are the *false Christs*, and *false prophets* that should *deceive many*: Therefore some *kill* to take possession; and others *thieve* away as before said: So Reason is sure to be a *thief*, and a *robber*, relative to the declaration; and in preaching from the declaration to *deceive* men, which is *taking* heaven by violence.

Moreover, I would have you understand, that of now-a-days, all men in the world are in the priesthood of Reason; except they gather by the power of Faith, quickened from death to life, as the present Messenger do, then they will be in strong union with him: ALSO some that are called by him may not as yet be in the royal priesthood, but if they patiently wait, and expect, it to *come*, it is the *same*, why? because they *Will* Christ should reign over them, according to the Messengers' declaration; but if any man or men should make to themselves any imaginary *salvation Knowledge*, which inclines from the Messengers' declaration, although he may say he follows the Messenger, it is in the priesthood of Reason, and he *invades* heaven:

Now from this, judge of the whole world: not that they can *take Heaven by Violence*, but by their imagination, for CHRIST is the *resurrection* to the kingdom of glory; and he will not raise them to that kingdom.

But you Write of your obedience and stedfast Faith which I much approve of; for *obedience and patience* to wait the Lord's *will* is a great thing and a property of Faith; for then you will not take heaven by violence; therefore be *stedfast*, and *watch*, and *pray*; then you will find your labour well *rewarded*. So my soul's *love*, and I pray the strong *union*, and the increase of Faith in the church. Please to give my soul's love to all, and everyone in the church. Tell Mrs. and Mr. Howel I received a fine letter from Mrs. Jones, and answered it a few days before I received yours. I was sorry to hear Mrs. Howell was but poorly: also I hope this infectious disorder, at Pembroke has hurt none of our friends and brethren; so conclude your loving brother,

London, April 15, 1779.   JAS. BIRCH.

P.S. The whole church here greets you all, and prays your increase of Faith, and I hope the strong *union* of Faith abounds among you.

LETTER XV

To our beloved sister Mary Runwa, *and to the whole Church, beloved in Christ, in and about Pembroke,* James Birch *sendeth, and the Church, Greeting.*

Beloved Sister,—Yours I received, and rejoice to see you write in such an open and free confession, wherein truth is perceived to flow from your soul; for when a divine light from heaven shine in the soul, man must needs be sensible of its own darkness, weakness, and shame; not that I altogether mean *Breaches* of the Law of Reason, for the angel of the soul will make all men sensible of that: and there is the Priesthood of Reason to excuse for a time, if men offer according, which is that given priesthood; but he that cannot get above this priesthood must die under the Seal of the internal angel in justice.

But I did not come out in that Covenant and Priesthood, but in the Covenant and Priesthood of Faith, for as that nature broke its own law when it hearkened to the voice of Reason, and for that fell under the power of death, then the life of Faith is quickened out of that death and taken into its own priesthood where *I am*; and work the works as I do according to his portion;—therefore the Messenger's declaration and prophecy is that Christ will make all things new to his elect! and when this new life which is of Faith is quickened, and then to be brought through the power of justice, sin, death, and hell, the soul may well *tremble* for fear of temptation; for there is things in the way, and must be removed; which must be done by the dint of *Prayer and Fasting*, that is, by the dint of prayer in the royal Priesthood; and patiently waiting God's time.

Moreover, you say well, where you say, "men cannot hope to please the redeemer with *fine Speeches*," to which I say it cannot be done, neither can any one have any knowledge of him or any thing to do with him except he is born anew, into the royal Priesthood of Faith; but only to repeat his name after another; for when Reason transform to a declaration from heaven, it cannot take or agree, for any more than his own wisdom on the outward word or bare letter, which gives him power over others, and fills him with *emulated Joy*, then this is falsely called the assurance of eternal life: and when the spirit of Reason enjoys this, which is all he will or can have, for then he is in himself both king, priest, and prophet, in the letter or declaration of another man; and in this (if possible) he is further from Christ than ever he was.

Also you may be assured from me, that all the goings out and acts of Reason are under these powers, that is, under the power of justice, and of sin, and of death, and of hell; only there is a command from heaven to *stay those powers till the servants of the living God* of faith, who are his elect, are *Sealed*; then those powers will be in *full*, let loose upon Reason: And now the Messenger is come and do declare the *Priesthood of Faith*, and the *Seal* of the Living God in *plain terms*, and the first man from Jesus that ever did; therefore the time is now at hand, and Blessed is him or them. that can follow thro' those powers, as before said, to the Seal of the Living God; then those powers will not be let loose on them, so as to take place in eternity.

Furthermore, in the priesthood of Reason there is nothing done for salvation; if even he is in the given priesthood, and *mouth* to a Messenger, he must be translated, or die under justice, and much less in the *wild* priesthood: True it is, they all may write, preach, and pray and sing in the name of Jesus, but except they can be born into the priesthood of Faith, Jesus knows them not: thus Reason will live in or with his own judgment on the letter, and sing and rejoice, and in self perfection judge and give judgment over others; and this is a life in death: But the Spirit of Faith is a Life to be brought through this vale of death, and be regenerated to Christ for eternal glory: and Faith, when quickened and taken into its own priesthood, is very eager to get to Christ; but Reason is in his own element, under the power of justice, death, and hell, and will live in it, and not know it, until it come upon them like a great Sea, overflowing land on a sudden.

Again, when faith is born from its womb or seed, and taken into its own royal priesthood to work its works, I would have you understand, you must be brought up to drink of the *CUP of Sorrow*, as Christ did, and be baptized with the *Baptism* which he was baptized with; *i.e.* to bear the wilds, temptation, and scourges of Reason, and *come through* those mighty fomenting powers of sin, death, and hell, and after all that, to lose yourself in your own blood in death, under the justice of the father, and be quickened out of it; which is to be brought through that justice to the glorious mercy of the Son; and him or them that go this *Way* there is already a CROWN of Glory prepared for him: But Reason, when he has got the Letter, which is all he can have, then he go forth as a priest and king, and prophet and judge in his own priesthood, and will invoke Christ the very God to own his abominable incense, which is a temptation to the elect; Therefore my soul is very desirous of your stedfast faith and prayer, in this vale of death, and to patiently wait God's time; for as I have said before, you will be called upon and not long first.

I am sorry to hear of Margaret Russant's trouble, but what can the elect expect beside in this life; Therefore the less affection is set on this life and its concerns the better; then it is the more easy left behind; for there is nothing belonging to this life but men must lose; and blessed is him that works the work of Faith, then he sends his *Treasure* to heaven before him, where he will go to enjoy it; for all temporal blessings on this earth are given under the power of justice and death, then all the delights of this life will be left behind: The Messenger suffers *hunger, poverty*, and plenty of *distress*, (and must let the world pass by him) and all evils, that the spirit of Reason is pleased to cast on him, because he is sent to be a servant to the elect; and his Message is an enemy to his own Reason, and of consequence to Reason in all others.

Dear Sister, I understood what you wrote concerning Hannah Reed and Margaret Russant, was, that when the soul was in sorrow, and wading thro' death, which is the works of Faith, that a *thought* arose in them, to sing and get the better of it; and if so it was going from it and not through it, and Reason was tempting the soul back into its own wild priesthood, from whence you was called to work the works of Faith: But by your last letter I perceive it was not so. My soul is very anxious for all your spiritual welfare, like as a tender parent is of his children, and if possibly I could, I would keep you all from *temptation*; but by prayer and patience those things will be overcome with all other troubles; then CHRIST will *suddenly* come and bring *his* reward with him; so I recommend you all to the stedfast works of Faith, which is a great blessing in Christ, and conclude your loving brother,

JAS. BIRCH.

London, June 26, 1779.

My love to all and every one: the church rejoice in your Faith, and in the Faith of the whole church with you, and prays your further increase.

Note – This Letter is the 16th, and the following one the 15th, as the Dates Certify.

LETTER XVI

To our beloved Sister Mary Runwa, and the whole Church beloved in Christ, in and about Pembroke, J. Birch, and Church in London, sendeth Greeting.

Beloved Sister, Yours I received the 5th inst. and were greatly rejoiced to hear from you; and that you write such *good things* concerning the church and yourself; for you may be assured from me, that Faith fell so low in Adam, as to be *dead* in itself from the *Communion* with its great Creator; and then they saw themselves naked to the act of Faith; then Reason acted forth in them, and formed an excuse for them; and in this condition Faith goeth on in generation, and comes to manhood, as the Lord God created Adam to.

Also, *when the Lord God walked in the Garden in the cool of the day*, which is God's time, then they would have *hid themselves among the trees in the garden*, from the presence of the Lord God; which is to live in and amongst the Acts and Delights of Reason, because they were naked to Faith as aforesaid. Now, understand this, the *Garden*, which the Lord God *walked in*, is the *womb of Faith* in the elect for regeneration with the power of mercy: and the Garden of Reason is its own vain delights, and that the angel in justice walketh in with his seal to and under death; therefore, when any *Messenger* comes from God in the covenant of Faith between God and his elect, he calleth to Faith to let it know where it is, and in what condition it is in—then the man would *hide* himself from the voice of God in the Messenger, if he could, among the *trees* in the garden, *i.e.* he would live in among the vain things of Reason, and excuse in and by that priesthood; because he is *Naked* to Faith, and as so, ashamed when the voice comes; but Faith must hear the voice of God in the soul at this day, as it did in the days of Adam, and be brought to commune in spirit with God, as Adam did, in the sorrowful *Vale* of death, which was his own lost condition, and be quickened from this death to *life*, as Adam was: This *new Life* is the *Virgin* daughter of Faith, born for regeneration, and to the promise of Christ.

Now, understand this, that the mighty workings and *Acts* of Faith is the same in the covenant of Faith for regeneration from the man Adam to this day, and will be to the day of the resurrection. For as Faith fell under *death*, it needs must be made sensible of that death; by this *new life* out of death, to seek Jesus, for him to take off the seals of this *Death* to Faith, that it may be brought up to read in the Book of Life: Therefore the power of the sonship of God is to seek and bring Life out of death, by regeneration, redemption, and sanctification—then, if the soul cannot be found in death naked and bare in itself—how is it possible that that soul can receive any quickening power to bring a new Life out of that Death.

Moreover, when Faith is quickened; it is a Life that cometh out of death; and must be brought through to a glorious life of glory in the kingdom of God, by regeneration and redemption! But Reason is a Life that is in degeneration, and leads to death; and the spirit of Reason is very eager to tempt the soul that it may rule over it, and lead it in degeneration, down into death: Hence, my dear Sister, your condition of soul I much approve,—for as the fruits and prayer of Faith is a Life brought out of death, in what condition think you the soul must be in to bring forth those fruits?

And as you say "you are only able to cry, *Lord, if thou wilt, thou canst make me clean,*" to which I say, it is a great cry from this virgin daughter that is quickened, for to go its way to Jesus; for *I came not to the bloody unbelieving world*, nor in the given priesthood of Reason; but *I came out from Jesus in his royal priesthood, and to seek Faith, and by God's help, to bring it out of death into life, and DIRECT* to the mercy of Jesus in Glory!—For which cause I am so anxious for all your spiritual welfare.

AGAIN, the covenant and works of Faith, is *contrary to* Reason, who came forth in manhood, and take the Letter, which is only a transformation, and as so, make sure to themselves of salvation, then sing and rejoice: But Faith is born from its womb, and comes forth as a child into the covenant for regeneration: therefore Jesus said (Mat. xviii.) "Verily I say unto you, except you be converted and become as a *little Child*, ye shall not enter the kingdom of heaven;" *i.e.* except your gathered knowledge by the spirit of Reason from or concerning the letter, which is your Life for salvation, becomes dead in you; and faith quicken from death to life, which will become *New* in the soul, and work the works to follow Jesus in spirit, you cannot enter into the holy Marriage with Jesus, therefore no salvation.

And when Faith is come forth, it is taken into the holy communion with God in spirit, and will grow strong: The more in shining light ye receive, the more ye will see the power of death and hell. *Also*, as this spirit of Faith is a new active life in the soul to be brought through death, it is productive of prayer, patience, meekness, &c.—and the *Life* to that Life comes from heaven to help it up to the spirit of prophecy; and the soul must patiently wait God's time for it; for all quickening power to faith in regeneration is in and of the sonship of God—and must come from heaven: And in all the great works of Faith, and sufferings for the sake of Christ, the soul may think itself happy that he is found worthy to enter the Royal Priesthood of Faith, for to suffer with CHRIST.

Tell Hannah Reed and Margaret Russant that their thoughts were the temptations of Reason, to tempt the soul from the works of Faith to its former acts of singing, which is of the cherubim and the priesthood of Reason. But you cannot die a child or cherub—so you must be brought thro' this death, to die under Christ, who is the Angel of Faith; for if you go aside, or from it, you will die under the Angel in justice. So I recommend you all in prayer to be stedfast in this Faith which leads to CHRIST; and conclude your loving brother,

JAS. BIRCH.

May 22, 1779.

P.S. The whole church prays your increase of Faith. My love to Mrs. Atkinson, Betsy, Owen and Alice; Mary Griffiths, James and Mary Thomas, and to all and every one of them.

LETTER XVII

To our beloved Brother James Thomas; and to the whole Church in and about Pembroke, James Birch sendeth greeting.

Beloved Brother and Brethren—Yours I received (June 30) and was glad to hear from you and all friends, because my spiritual love in the royal priesthood of Faith is with you all, and as you would know what those *Talents* mean, I will with Joy inform you, as far as the compass of the letter will admit.

Those *Talents* were pieces of money that the Jews and others gave in *Exchange in their merchandize*; and the Hebrew Talent in silver was in value (as is said) £342. 3s. 9d. and in gold £5475; and in this place Jesus likens his kingdom unto a man that gave his servant his money to trade with, and went a far journey. Now Christ is the king of Faith, Mercy, and Glory, this he gained to himself by his mighty works of redemption, and also glory for his royal elect, which is his kingdom of Faith, because he himself rules over them; for the kingdom of heaven, to the elect, is in and of the sonship of God: therefore, when Jesus was here to redeem, he uttered his holy gospel and works of Faith, which is likened to the kingdom of heaven; because it declares that kingdom: Now in this declaration there is the outward word or bare letter, which the seed and spirit of Reason can and do transform themselves to, and when done, they judge of it according to their own wisdom, which is dark Reason: And there is a spiritual testimony comes from Jesus to his elect, according to his own royal promise; therefore when Jesus ascended into heaven, he gave his holy spirit to the elect, according to promise in his declaration, and mighty works of redemption: and men are to work according to his declaration, only this, the elect are *Taken* into the royal priesthood of Faith, and the seed of Reason are *Left* with the bare letter in the priesthood of Reason.

Again, when Jesus ascended into heaven he went into a *far country*, and called his *Servants*, and gave them his money or Goods. Now understand this, the seed of Faith is the royal *house* of Israel; and his holy gospel, and covenant of grace, and royal priesthood, which is in and for regeneration, is the church of Christ; and his house of *Refuge* for the kingdom of glory: and the declaration and works of Jesus is a royal example to his elect; therefore he gave to his apostles a portion of his holy spirit, with his own declaration, that they should declare the mighty ACTS of JESUS before men; and call the elect to the promise of Jesus, and suffer persecution, &c. and work the works of Faith in the royal priesthood, and prophecy of Christ to come again. Now this is *five talents* given to *servants* in the gospel, that they should work the works of Faith, which is the works of Christ in his own house: And the *two talents* are to believers, for them also to work the works of Faith in his holy Gospel and Priesthood of Faith, which is the *House* and CHURCH of the LORD JESUS: and every one must work according to his portion or ability, to have his royal and holy commendation. Now this, Christ gave and is ascended into heaven, which is his taking a journey into a far country, and *Left* his elect to work the works of Faith (which he himself had done) according to their ability, in his holy gospel, which he had declared and *established*, and in those *portions* of Faith men must work and watch his coming again; but the *one talent* is the *bare* letter which the seed of Reason transform themselves to, and act in it, and judge of it, by the spirit of Reason, and take it into the priesthood of Reason, and in this they *dig and hide the talent in the earth*, which is the Lord's *money*, because it was his own declaration; but Reason cannot come into the priesthood of Faith; therefore will not improve the Talent.

Moreover, in this manner the gospel began, *i.e.* the apostle's *five* talents, and the believers *two*, and the seed of Reason *one*: now the two first worked the works of Faith; and when Christ come in spirit they were commended, and entered into his JOY; but Reason was devoured in his fear which he calls wisdom, and cast out as a slothful servant; also the present Messenger is the *fourth* angel that has come to declare and prophesy in the holy Gospel, and has come out in the *Eleventh* hour of the day, and declare, that as they came they uttered their voice nearer the Seal of the Living God; therefore as you may further understand the *Talents* because you must work in this Messenger's day: Now when the voice of God in the Messenger *rest* in the soul and *die*, then Faith quicken from death to Life, which is a Virgin of Faith, born from the *Womb* or Seed, and taken into the royal priesthood, and made able to offer her own prayer, then this is the *thirty fold* portion of Faith, or the *two talents* given; and in this state Faith must work in the royal priesthood, against the powers of death and hell; and by prayer and divine assistance will overcome and be stedfast to Watch, and patiently *Wait* the lord's coming, who is sure to bring his *Reward* with him: And for those works of Faith, God, according to his promise, is graciously pleased in his own time, to visit that soul by his holy spirit; and the soul is found worthy by the works of Faith, and in this he has *gained other two talents*; then Christ gives another *talent*, which is the spirit of *prophecy*, *i.e.* Christ has come in spirit, and will come again to seal him for eternal glory: Now this soul has so far entered into the *Joy of the Lord*, because he has worked and brought forth the fruits of Faith, and great *Wisdom*, is given to him in the priesthood of Faith, and power over Reason; but, I would have you all understand that every time the *incense* of Faith burn in the soul, you enter into the *Joy* of the Lord, and have power given over Reason, even before you receive the spirit of prophecy, which is *five talents*, or the *Sixty fold* portion of Faith.

Again, when the soul has received *five talents*, he will find *heavier* work against the powers of death and hell than before; and must be *more* a Servant to his brethren, and leave the world more behind him; and in all those *talents or portions* the soul must keep watch for the *Lord's coming*, and not be found *sleeping* in those works and *Drunken* with the cares of this world; for as I have told you before, you are sure to be called upon, and God only knows when, Therefore keep *watch*. After this the soul is called to under the justice of the father, and found worthy by his works of Faith to be from thence given spiritual birth to the glorious mercy of the son then he has ten talents and is sealed by the God of Faith, and dies in the bed of mercy to be raised to glory; but after the spiritual birth, if he is sent back, he is a Messenger from Jesus, not through the justice of the father, but immediately from Him in mercy, and has ten talents given him, or the hundred fold portion of Faith; for such a one as this has spiritual communion with him that sit in the glory of mercy, and has seen the book of life, and him that open it; and also has seen the Seal of the Living God; and how the elect are sealed to enter the kingdom of glory—for he has great Wisdom and Power given him in the covenant of Grace and priesthood of Faith; and also has Power and Wisdom given him over the spirit of Reason, that Reason shall not be able to hide itself from him; therefore, all the *acts* of Faith or of Reason shall add wisdom to such a man.

Moreover he can plague the earth, (*i.e.* the spirit of Reason) when he will; for he well knows Reason has but the bare letter, and where he will take that to and all Reason's confidence in the letter this Messenger can overpower and take away, because the internal angel has power over the soul, therefore he that is in the priesthood of Faith, more shall be given, and him that hath not, shall be taken. Even that little he hath, that is, all his hope and confidence on the letter shall be taken when he is called by the angel, as was judged of by this Messenger, and in this the talent is taken from him and given unto him that hath ten; for when Reason is called to, it will give up the talent, which is the letter as they found it, but have hid it in their own spirit, which is the earth, and be found full of excuses, and murmur, and go with it into death; but Faith is willing and ready when called, and will enter into the joy of the Lord Christ: and also mind every elect man, when born in spirit to the holy covenant of grace, to be sealed by Jesus, has *ten talents*, or an HUNDRED FOLD; but the different portions are given for men to work in the priesthood in this Life, and the *Greater* the portion the LESS the man; for then he is a *Servant* to the church.

Again, of Luke ix: The *Sayings* of Jesus runs as thus.—That when Jesus came he *called* the elect, and the world must be *Left* behind, to follow *Him*, to inherit the kingdom of heaven;—also Christ is come in, or with the present *Messenger*, and the elect are *invited* to the spiritual Birth and the Seal of JESUS who is the God of Faith and Mercy; and all must be *left* to go or FOLLOW there; for this is a certain trial of the soul to where his *treasure* is; and if his treasure is in or for heaven, he will leave all he *possess*, that is, his wisdom, his riches, his family and generation, to be regenerated to Christ: But if his treasure is in this life only, he may take the Letter, but his soul will incline back to his own house to care for them, and bid them farewell; and by the time he has done this he will lose himself; and is sealed by the internal angel for wrath; for if a man is so rich as to be on the *house top; let him not come down* to take it away, or in the *field let him not return for his clothes*, but remember Lot's wife! This is commanded of Jesus when the *sign of the Son of Man appear*, and now is the very time; Also Jesus said, "let the dead bury the dead, but thou go and preach the kingdom of God," *i.e.* the seed and spirit of Reason is *dead* in the sight of God, and there is none so capable as themselves to *bury* themselves in their own wisdom, or riches, selfish desire; honour among men, family anxiety and worldly cares; therefore whosoever take the letter and *bury* it with themselves, in those and other things they will be found unworthy, because they have *buried the talent in the earth*, and would not trust to God, but will murmur and excuse themselves; then in that they are condemned; and for this cause Christ would not suffer his true disciples to go and bid them *farewell* at their *own house:*— Then HE said, "no man having put his hand to the plough and looking back is fit for the kingdom of God" for a man must seek to have *refuge* in the House of Faith, which is of JESUS, or die and perish in the house of Reason: Now I hope you will observe what is written in this short answer to these *Sayings of* CHRIST, and I pray He will increase your Understanding and Faith; which is the desire of your loving brother.

JAS. BIRCH.

London, July 17, 1779.

My love to all and every one; and to *George Griffiths* and their *father:*—The whole church greets you all; the book is not finished: —I will come and see you again as soon as I can, but times are very bad in London.

LETTER XVIII

To our beloved Sister Mary Runwa, and the whole Church beloved in Christ, in and about Pembroke, JAS. BIRCH, and Brethren, sendeth Greeting.

Beloved Sister, Yours I received the 3d. inst. and I greatly rejoice to see you understand the power of the *Talents*. And more so to see you express yourself so *Free* and *Noble* concerning the talents; for it is the nature of Reason from the bare letter (which is only an echo, or fragment of the true declaration) to think he has a *great* portion in the Gospel, and that he will be the *first called*; because, from the letter only, the whole world (that knows of it) is in great expectation: yea, many has said, "they were assured of eternal life," which is making themselves equal with if not above God, when he was here in the state of mortality: for if any one had the Assurance of eternal life, He was the man!

But, it is not so with Faith, for when that is quickened from death to life, it finds the power of justice, and of sin, of death and of hell, and thro' it you must go in *tribulation and sorrow*: Hence, while Life is working through Death, the elect think themselves unworthy, and as you say "but *one talent*;" and do expect to be the *last called*, if ever called; while Reason in his *Emulation* expect to be the *first called*:—but he who thought to be the *last*, will be the *first*; and him who thought to be the first, will be the *last i.e.* he is never called at all under the justice of the Father, but under his own *seal*, that is, of the angel.

AGAIN, since the present Messenger came out, there has *appeared the sign of the SON of MAN* in this nether heaven of Faith: for the Messenger calls to Faith, and quickens it from death to life, and brings it to the promise of Christ in spirit: and when the *Virgin* daughter of Faith offers her prayer, it ascends to God in the high Heaven; then the Virgin of Faith is in mystical Union, and spiritual communion with Christ, which is the royal priesthood or the nether heaven to Faith.

For the *time* is now come, that "many shall hear the voice of the SON of GOD, and them that hear shall live," *i.e.* Faith that was dead will be quickened and come forth into life, and work the works to *follow* JESUS; but *they* must go through *tribulation and sorrow*;— because the *Vial* of God's *wrath* is poured out upon them; and through it they must go, that they may truly know the justice of the Father, as well as the mercy of the Son: Now in all those *tribulations and sorrows*, in travailing through death to life; with Death and Hell you will be at *variance*, but with Christ and his Messenger you will be at Peace; and by divine assistance and prayer you will overcome this perishing world, and be called under the justice of the father, and from thence be given birth in spirit to the glorious Mercy of the Son, and sealed for eternal Life!—Then *Judgment Day* is over to the elect; as the soul has passed from death to life, for the next state is glory!

Moreover, you say "you know not what spirit you are of." Now I see your spirit, and rejoice at its fruits, so go on and prosper, for as you have prayer and patience, you will be preserved from the *hour of temptation* that comes to the world: For this *Vale* of sorrow and of tears, must be waded through, and *Prayer and Patience* must hold out to the end, *i.e.* till death; for the soul must be made PERFECT, which must be done against all the power and threats of Reason:—for when the Pharisees came to Jesus and said, "get thee out and depart hence for Herod will kill thee" (Luke xiii.) Jesus said unto them, "go ye and tell that fox, behold I cast out devils, and I do cures to-day, and to-morrow, and the third day I shall be *perfected*:"—Hence you may see, Jesus would not be stopped by the threats and power of Reason until he had perfected his work, and in that he was *perfected* himself.

Also, He said, "for it cannot be, that a prophet perish out of Jerusalem," which Jerusalem is the power and priesthood of Reason, which men possess to this day: for the spirit and power of Reason in man, which is this *great city Jerusalem*, will distress, nay murder the Messenger of God, if possible.

And now Jesus has worked the works of redemption, and is ascended into heaven, and by the power of his holy spirit He works or *walks* in the souls of his elect, with the power of internal Miracles, to internally heal them, and make them *perfect* in regeneration for his kingdom of glory;—in *Three Days*, or three hours, or one hour, just as he is graciously pleased to express his great works on the spirit of Faith.

As, First, by the power of his holy spirit he quickens Faith from death to life, and take it into his royal priesthood, to work the works, and follow him.

Secondly, by the power of his holy spirit, he gives the spirit or daughter of Faith the spirit of prophecy, for he himself to come in spirit and unite in holy marriage with this pure virgin daughter of Faith, for He is the holy Bridegroom.

Thirdly, by his mighty power he gives spiritual birth from under the justice of the father to his own royal and glorious covenant of mercy, *i.e.* of the Son; and seal the soul for eternal glory, in his own covenant of mercy, which is above the justice of the Father: Then, and not till then, is the soul *perfected* in regeneration, and fall asleep in the bed of mercy for the resurrection to glory.

Further, you give me great pleasure to see you express yourself so well concerning the priesthood of Faith, for in this condition of soul I hope all will shortly be in, for it is my earnest desire, and, strong prayer:—And I hope you will all be steadfast, and patiently wait the Lord's leisure, as the elect did of old, who at the time of their tribulation was brought through it, by the power of God and become like unto *refined* gold.

I hope I shall see you again when the winter is passed, and the days become long; then if God. permits I will come, which thing I should have done this summer, for I have many things to communicate unto you concerning the priesthoods and other things depending thereon, which cannot be done by letter; therefore I must come in person, but before that time comes, I may hear from you and the church again.

Give my soul's love to all the brethren.—I am glad to hear they are all well.—I pray your strong union and increase of Faith.—Give my love to *Betsey*, I am glad to hear she is well: So conclude your loving brother in Christ, whose soul mourns and prays for all your welfare in Christ.

JAMES BIRCH.

London, Sep. 28, 1779.

The whole Church prays your increase of Faith.

LETTER XIX

To our beloved Brother Joseph Cole, and to the whole Church beloved in Christ in and about Pembroke, James Birch, and the Brethren sendeth greeting.

Beloved brother and brethren,—Yours I received (Oct. 29,) and was rejoiced to hear from you, and as you said nothing to the contrary, I hope the brethren are all well:—Also, I am glad you are satisfied in what I wrote concerning the fall of Adam; for the elect must be brought to that knowledge, before they can enter the royal priesthood where the Messenger is; then much more to be done to die under the seal of Jesus, who is the *Angel* of Faith and Mercy.

Again, you express *good obedience*, in your letter, and prayer for *patience*, and to be preserved in the hour of *temptation*, that you may work the works of Faith, to inherit eternal life, which thing I much approve, for except a man is converted and become a *Little Child, he cannot enter the kingdom of heaven, i.e.* except you are converted from the *priesthood* and *strong holds* of Reason, to the works of Faith, and *overcome* like-unto Jesus, according to the portion that is given:—For as God became a *Child* to make all things new to himself and to his elect, even so must elect man become as a *Child* to follow him.

Moreover, (John v.) concerning the certain *impotent man* that was at *Bethesda-pool* at Jerusalem, "and he could not get into the water to be healed after the angel went down and troubled the water:"—Now this *water* means the water of Reason; and being made *whole* in those waters, is in and of the priesthood of Reason; and at Jerusalem, wherein reigned that priesthood suggested from the true priesthood of Reason that Moses gave forth with the Law; which thing may he done at this day in the great city of Jerusalem, which is the strong hold and priesthood of Reason in the soul of man; for this understand, when Reason goeth out on any act, there is always a *horse and rider* go with him, *i.e.* the horse is the law, and the rider is truth; and truth will give into the angel in justice, who rides the red horse, which is on the sinful soul of man:— Therefore when the soul of man is moved to do a good act he is told to do it, although he may suffer himself to be tempted to the contrary, through some selfish design, in and for the kingdom of reason:—Also, when the soul is tempted to an evil act, he is told not to do it by the rider, before he commits it; but when the tempter leads the soul on to do the act, then the law is broke, and truth give into justice, which becomes of infinite consequence, and the angel in justice would cast the soul into death immediately after the act, was it not that God had stayed that justice for generation to go on: And thus man becomes *impotent*, by falling into evil under the seal of this angel.

Also, you may see there was the *blind*, the *halt*, and *withered*, waiting for the moving of the Water, which is this men fall into evil under different breaches of the law; then the angel seal every man under his own evil, which men will try to hide from the world, for fear of the consequence:—And when men lay under those evils they are *impotent*; for they cannot look at a man whom they have hurt but the angel will tell them of it; and if evil is said to be done, and another has that evil concealed in himself, the angel will tell him he is the man, or equal with the man who is given up to public censure or justice.

Anon, the waters or Reason in the soul of man that has been tolerably smooth and still, the angel trouble them with justice, that man can have no peace or hardly live; then if the soul can freely step, into or dip in those waters, which is to stand the *scourge* and offer a prayer in or under that justice in the sight of the angel, then forsake the evil and do the best you can to make amends, the angel will stay that justice and loose the man.

Now this *Pool* that was at Jerusalem was to shew forth the power of justice and the law, and the offering of Reason in its priesthood to stay God's justice, that it do not overtake them in this life, and this is, what is to be *healed* by or according to those Waters, which is in, and of the priesthood of Reason; for the ultimate of the priesthood of Reason, is a prosperous Life and a Peace in death; but they die under the angel in justice, and will rise again under him: then justice is let loose on them in *full*.

Again to be healed in those waters give new life to Reason, because it become *impotent* by breaking its own law; which *health* extend no further than this life; but those waters will not heal Faith, therefore as you say "faith must patiently wait till Christ come."

Moreover, concerning the priesthood of Faith; the present Messenger must have a child born, which is the virgin of Faith: — Therefore as men are born of the flesh into this world, to know the things of the world, and what it is to be healed by the aforesaid waters, which is of the priesthood of Reason, even so men must be *born of Faith, i.e.* the spirit of Faith must be born of its womb or seed, to be taken into the priesthood of Faith to know the works of Faith, and to receive the promise of Christ which is the voice of the *second Angel* of Faith that sounds after the angel of the declaration (who is the Messenger) has uttered his voice.

AGAIN, Ann Childs do well to believe the present *Messenger*, for his declaration is from the KING OF FAITH, and leads to the King of Faith, who is CHRIST the Angel of the Covenant of Faith: Therefore let men think what they please them that have heard the present Messenger, must come in and be under him, or be under the angel in justice whose seal is death eternal:—And the elect that has not heard of him will be called and worked upon for salvation as he has declared: and as for the seed of Reason, the angel in justice seal them; so the present Messenger has *poured out the vial of God's wrath* all over the world;—for he declares every man will be his own witness to his own condemnation, and the angel answers, Amen! *for strong is the Lord God of heaven who has given them up to that judgment*: Now as she would know the works of Faith, it is to *overcome* her own spirit of Reason; but there must be the virgin daughter of Faith *born*, and her act is, forgiveness, prayer, meekness, obedience, long, suffering, love, mercy, charity, and to patiently *wait* the coming of Christ: this is the fruits of Faith, and its works is to overcome Reason, death, hell, &c. in yourself.

Now if the *Fear* of eternal death were not before you, what have you or any of the elect to overcome? For believe in this, the present Messenger will not declare the elect are *healed* in the waters of Reason, but they must by the spirit of Faith work their way to Jesus:—For the whole power of Reason will confess they want healing and salvation; and say, "What shall I do to be saved?" But when the voice of God say, "*Leave* all, and follow me", then he is *sorrowful*, for he will not enter the priesthood of Faith, therefore his health and kingdom is in this life; but the glory of Faith is in the kingdom of Christ, in the world to come: - Therefore mind what is written, for when Reason is healed, it will with joy go into the Land of Nod; but Faith must *wait till Christ come in spirit* to be healed for eternal life: So concludes your loving brother in Christ.

JAMES BIRCH.

London, Dec. 16, 1779.

P. S. The whole Church greets you all, and prays your increase of Faith; my love to all and every one. I intend to be with you about the latter-end of May, or the beginning of June. I should have sent sooner, but I have been very close in writing of the destruction of Jerusalem, and the coming of Christ, of which I shall inform you with many more things, when I come.

LETTER XX

To our beloved Brethren George Plowman *and* Mr. Bennet, James Birch *and the Brethren sendeth Greeting.*

Beloved brethren, —Yours our brother Matthews received (Dec. 11, 1779), and we greatly rejoice to hear from you, as it is what we long desired, but find by yours that letters have miscarried: I have sent you a writing inclosed, which I believe was what you asked for, however, it is what you ought to have; for by that you may see *Man* and *Angel fell* under their own law:—And further to inform you, this serpent Angel was a Cherubim by creation, neither was there any of that order created but himself: and he being created in reference to Justice; there was such a quantity of justice fixed in him through creation, that whenever he broke the law he was created under, to cast him down from heaven to this earth; where he tempted Faith and was transmitted into flesh, and born of Eve, and grew to manhood, then killed his brother Abel.

Again, understand this, although this angel broke the law he was created under, yet he never could break the justice of that law; but Reason will take it with him wherever he go,—why? because it is placed in Reason, and stands in the soul of man before them who sit in the justice of the father at this day, pure as God first created it; and is the *Cherubim and flaming Sword that turns every way, to keep the way of the Tree of Life*; because, it is in the soul of every man: Now from this you may see the difference between the justice of the father and the justice of the angel, for the justice of the Father is justice to Faith, and the justice of the Angel is justice to Reason.

Moreover from those two laws being broke, came both the *two Priesthoods*, *i.e.* the priesthood of Faith, and the priesthood of Reason; for when any nature is *fallen*, there is given a priesthood for the soul to be *healed*, either for time or for eternity: now the priesthood of Reason is a Grant from heaven, to stay justice for a time, or during the life of man on the earth;—and of this you may be assured from me, that when Reason go out on any act, there is Truth go with him to watch him, and tells him not to do an evil act, before he commit it; then, when he break the law in contempt of this, it becomes of an infinite consequence, for truth give into justice, and the angel seal the soul for death eternal! It would indeed cast the soul immediately into death after the act, was it not that justice was stayed from heaven, for generation to go on, but however he is sealed under the angel, and may form what excuse and forgiveness from himself and the letter he please; yet it is in the wild priesthood of Reason. and will vanish as a vapour, when the angel *fill* the soul with justice.

Further, when the soul is filled with justice, that he can have no peace, or hardly live; then if the soul can stand the *Scourge*, and offer a true Prayer, the angel will stay justice, and loose the man; now this is the *given* Priesthood of Reason, whereby a soul may be healed; but *few* can overcome this, for many go distracted, or lay violent hands on themselves for the sake of a moment's peace:—But in the days of a Messenger, if the soul is willing, he may be healed of this disease or infirmity, by the Messenger, according to his Faith.

And if a man come to the Messenger, and cannot obtain no more than the outward word or bare letter,—yet by this he may overcome many things, go forth and preach, and be healed; but this *health* is of Reason, and extends no further than this life for if you cannot enter the priesthood of Faith, you must die under the angel in justice, which is of the angel of Reason.

AGAIN, as I said, Faith is of a different kingdom and nature to that of Reason:—Therefore, when the voice of God from heaven, or by his Messenger centers to the womb or seed of Faith in the soul of elect man, then Faith is enquired after, and soon let know where it is, and in what condition it is in: that it is fallen under its own law, and disunited from its father and creator by death (thro' the justice of the father, which took place when the Law of Faith was broke)—then, out of this death of fallen Faith, is quickened a new life, which is the Virgin daughter of Faith, born for regeneration, and is taken into the priesthood of Faith; then Faith being quickened into life, it lives under its own justice, which is the justice of the father; and to this Virgin is given the promise of Christ to come.

Moreover, this Virgin daughter of Faith pray her own prayer, that the justice of the father may be stayed through the mercy of the Son, for she to receive divine assistance from heaven to remove internal *mountains*, and to help Faith through this sore journey of flesh up to Christ its king, and this help comes from heaven by the influence of the holy spirit of God: Also this Virgin prays that, Faith may not be left in hell, but to go up to the holy marriage with Christ, and so be healed for life eternal; for except God the Father, who is of Justice, do become God the Son, who is of Mercy, in or to the soul of every man, there is no redemption for man; therefore nothing but Faith can come into the priesthood of Faith; and nothing but Faith can offer the prayer of Faith; and nothing but Faith is under the justice of the father.

Now the prayer of Reason is to be preserved and *healed* according to Reason in its own priesthood, which is under the justice of the angel; and that *health* is no further than this life; Reason may think, or intend what he will by his prayer; but the power of that incense will extend no further.—But the prayer of Faith is to be preserved and healed according to *Faith*, which is for life eternal, and that incense extend to it; therefore there is as much difference between the Prayer of Faith and the Prayer of Reason, as there is between the Law of Faith and the Law of Reason: Now you may see the difference between the justice of the angel and the justice of the father; and that this angel is the cherub and flaming Sword that turns every way to keep the way of the TREE OF LIFE; because there is no man but must be under this angel, until Faith is quickened from death to life and taken into its priesthood, then that is under the justice of the father.

AGAIN, as man is born of the flesh into this world, to know the things of this world, then he is born to the law and the priesthood of Reason; indeed he may transform to what letter he will, and call himself what he please, yet he is under the angel in justice:—But, as men are born of the flesh into this world, and to this priesthood, even so the spirit of Faith must be born of the womb of Faith, to come into the royal priesthood, to know and work the works of Faith acceptable to Christ for salvation.

Beloved Brother, I greatly rejoice at your stedfast Faith, and patience in your *fiery trials*; for by that you have *overcome* things, therefore go on and prosper, and you will have divine assistance to overcome many more, which is my earnest desire and prayer; for as elect men are in Reason's kingdom, they have *that* to overcome, not only without them, but within them also; for when Reason see a kingdom coming to the soul of man, *contrary* to his own, he will drive or tempt the soul from it, if possible; and in this, man is oft'times obliged to *eat his own flesh*, *i.e.* to bear the wilds and temptations of Reason, to overcome the tempter; and by prayer, patience, &c. Faith will be *made able to overcome all things*, and the promise is to no one but them that do *overcome*.

My Love with the whole church to our brother Bennett, and I give him joy in his belief; and he may be assured from me, that this is the *true Road* to CHRIST, *for I come out from him* in his holy covenant and royal priesthood; and the present Messenger do declare the elect must be taken and *sealed* by Christ, the angel of Faith, to die under him; for all that are *left* are of Reason, and must die under the angel in justice, then will they be their own witness to their own condemnation; so I recommend to you steadfast Faith and Mercy, and patiently waiting the power of God, so I conclude your loving brother in Christ.

JAMES BIRCH.

London, Jan. 8, 1780.

P.S. Love (with the Church) to you both, with prayer for increase of Faith, and as it is necessary for you to see the Messenger, your making St. David's or Milford Haven, is just at Pembroke, and going to Griffith Howell's, you may hear of me about June.

LETTER XXI

To our beloved Sister Mary Jones, James Birch, *and the Brethren sendeth GREETING.*

Beloved Sister,—Yours I received, and was glad to hear from you, because it was what we greatly desired, and as for your *heavy trials* and *travails* of soul, it is no more than I do expect; nay, if it was not so, how could you be in the royal priesthood of Faith, to receive divine assistance from heaven, to overcome the power of justice, sin, death and hell; for that which is of Reason, is in the priesthood of Reason, and work the works of *abomination,* such as *cursing, false incense,* dark prophecies, &c. and when done they must go under their own Curse, except they can be translated into the royal priesthood of Faith; for there is no such thing as *coming to Christ,* except Faith is born of its womb or seed to be taken into its own priesthood.

Moreover, when Faith fell in Adam, it fell under the justice of the father, which is death and disunion from its ever living Father and Creator; and as Faith fell before generation took place, so it go on in generation; therefore, as a Child is born into this world, to know the things of the world, even so Faith must be born of its womb or seed, and be taken into its own priesthood, to know and work the works of Faith.

Also when this Virgin Daughter is born, she finds herself surrounded with *briars and thorns,* justice, sin, and death; and the temptations and the threats of Reason; for as Faith fell under the power or those things, it needs must go through those things, and of consequence be encumbered with them; but in the midst of all this, to her is given the promise of Christ to come; and by patience and prayer will receive divine assistance from heaven, and those *mountains* will be removed, because she is *Espoused to* CHRIST in *holy marriage,* for he has become her ROYAL BRIDE-GROOM; therefore, of consequence she will work the works of Faith to *overcome* as Christ did, and in this she is found *worthy* of Christ: And mind, the promise is only to them that do *overcome.*

Again it is the nature of Faith to *fear* and TREMBLE before the throne of the Father; which is of justice to Faith, and is oft'times fearful lest it should be found unworthy, because through the justice of the father it must go, and it is always straightened, till that *baptism* is accomplished: but Reason is cast out from the father, and is under its own justice, which is of the angel; and as they can take no more than the bare letter;—therefore they are sure to themselves they are right, without fear, because they have got all they can have, and they being so full of their own dark wisdom, that they want nothing.

Therefore, as Faith has this sorrowful vale of trouble and death to wade through, it needs must be sensible of its own passage, because it cannot be done in sleep or by dream:—So I recommend to you steadfast Faith and Patience in the works of Faith, then you will be in the love of God, and overcome all those things, for the spirit say to Faith, in the church of Philadelphia, (Rev. iii. 10.) "Because thou hast kept the word of my patience, I also will keep thee from the hour of temptation, that shall come upon all the world, to try them that dwell upon the earth:" Why? Because Reason is in temptation, and there he fall under the seal of his own angel; because Reason, as a God, will seek to have his own will and pleasure, and there he is lull'd to sleep, and so go off in death, while Faith must watch and wade against those powers.

MOREOVER, concerning the *waters of Bethlehem*, that was by the gate which David longed to drink of, it may he likened to the blood of Christ, but it has no such meaning, because that desire was of Reason, and in its priesthood; for then David was at war with the Philistines, and their garrison was at Bethlehem, and David was in an hold, and his desiring to drink of the waters was to possess the place, as a man may desire to possess his natural birth-right, or that which is promised him, for David's father was of Bethlehem; and when the three men fetched the water to the hazard of their lives, he poured it out as an offering to God, because he had preserved their lives: BUT in the royal priesthood of Faith, every one must pray his own prayer, to fetch divine assistance from heaven, in and for regeneration; (and the day or days of prophecy of Christ to come, is in the sorrowful vale of death; and then the whole world, with all its possession, produce, &c. is left out and thought nothing of); and by working the works of Faith in the royal priesthood, to overcome as Christ himself did in flesh and blood, and also lost himself in his own blood in death, under the justice of the Father, to quicken again into his own kingdom of mercy; and the elect will find they must do the like, according to their portion, in a body of flesh and blood, as HE did, then they will eat his flesh, and drink his blood; and no other way can they do it.

But as the priesthood of Reason has reign'd so many years, it has introduced shadows and left out the ROYAL THING, that it has greatly bewildered the soul of man have wrote this to give you a hint concerning the two priesthoods, and pray God increase your Faith and Patience.

Beloved sister, Mrs. Jealous has been very ill all this winter, and at times so bad that we thought she must have died, but is something better now, and we hope, as fine weather comes on, she will get abroad; Mr. Jealous is tolerable well, they both give their love. James Collet's wife is dead, and gave a good testimony of this Faith and Prophecy as she died.

When I see you, shall inform you of many things more particular; I mean to set out about a week after Whitsuntide, and go to *Bristol*; if I can go by water, without delay, I will; if not will call on you as I go; Give my kind love to your husband, and I am glad to hear he is well: the whole church give their love, and are glad to hear from you.

So conclude your loving brother in Christ,

JAS. BIRCH.

London, March 2, 1780.

LETTER XXII

To our beloved Brother Joseph Cole, and the whole Church beloved in Christ, in and about Pembroke, Jas. Birch and the Brethren sendeth Greeting.

Beloved Brother and Brethren,—Yours I received, and was very glad to hear from you, and more so, to see you express yourself in understanding of what you have heard and seen; for it is what the whole world must take, whether they like it or not, which is this:— Except men are born again to come into the royal priesthood, as this present Messenger doth declare, they must go their own way in the priesthood of Reason, and there will be their own witness to their own condemnation: So I pray God increase all your understanding, and strengthen the *Virgin* of Faith to remove internal mountains, that she may soon meet her royal *Bridegroom*, which is CHRIST.

Concerning the *City of Jerusalem*, it is the *spirit* of Reason, that has transformed itself into any Literal Record, and claim its inheritance, then construct it their own wild way; then *fancy* by this wisdom they have power to be judge over the whole world, and God will own their judgment.— Now this is the wild priesthood of Reason; then, when a *Messenger* is sent from JESUS he declares against this; and Reason, see a kingdom coming contrary to his own; then Reason become angry and full of wrath, and will murder any thing that is born of God or for God, if not in the natural they will in the spiritual.

Now, the *top pinnacle* of this City is the literal Muggletonians, for wrath, cursing, and blasphemy, is not to be found any where like unto there; therefore it cannot be that a *prophet perish* out of this city, or escape being put to death by this City, so far as their power extend:— Therefore, wherever the hard-hearted, unbelieving, lying, wrathful, persecuting and murdering spirit of Reason appear against the Messenger and the Elect, for their Faith and Declaration, that is the City of Jerusalem.

As for the *Pharisee* or *Sadducee*, I will tell you how to find them when I see you and the church; give my soul's spiritual love to the whole church.— I intend to be with you all in about a month, and hope to find you all well; so conclude your loving brother in Christ,

JAMES BIRCH,

London, May 11, 1780.

P.S. The whole Church greets you all and prays your increase of Faith.—Also, there is a worthy brother of ours in Ireland to meet me at Pembroke, and to visit the church there, which he rejoices to hear of ; his name is George Plowman, and a farmer at Kilcullen (in Ireland); I have directed him to our brother Howel, so I beg you'll watch his coming, and be tender of him, for he may be with you before I am, and you will inform the brethren of his coming,

LETTER XXIII

James Birch, to the whole Church in London, sendeth GREETING.

Brethren,—My love is *with* you, and prayer *for* you, therefore have Faith and doubt not, and you will be brought through this *sorrowful Vale* of Death.

I know your works and *them* that has prayed and not fainted; — *hold fast* what you have received,— and keep your *first love*: then you will not lose your Crown; listen to and keep the *Voice* of patience, and you will be preserved from the *hour of temptation,*—which is sure to take Reason to his own home:— "*Blessed are them that walketh and keepeth their garments clean,*"—for when *defiled* they will become rotten, then *nakedness* will appear.

My love is with you, and pray the love of Christ may abound among you,—and you love and pray for each other, he that forgives shall be forgiven, but he that resents shall to into distraction: Watch your *tempter,* lest he come among you, and divide you,—and one go his way with the face of an *owl,* another with the face of a *fox,*—another with the face of a *serpent,*—and another with the face of a *hog;*—then Christ come and they cannot stand before *Him*; but would hide themselves in the deepest part of the seas,—in an unknown part of the world if possible. Therefore be stedfast in, and unmoveable from, the love of Christ, and your release will soon come.

You do well not to mind Reason in its going out in its own wild way; for I have told you, *Earth and Water* is able to receive them—and the angel has already got them.

The church at *Pembroke* rejoice to hear from you (by your letter I received), and prays your increase of Faith.—So conclude your loving brother,

JAMES BIRCH.

Pembroke, July 6, 1780.

P. S. Brother Plowman is not come.

[This Copy was sent to Brother Herald, by Sister Runwa, which he edited for the press, with her application, as follows.]

This letter, my dear brother, contains and comprehends all the work an elect being can desire,— may the Lord Jesus assist us to walk according to those Maxims, where every line is a sentence of Truth, to *guide* us in the straight and narrow way to life eternal. Amen.

M. R.

LETTER XXIV

Voice of God's Messenger to Mary Jones, then living at Abergavenny.

TAKE NOTICE.—The kingdom of this *World* is not the kingdom of CHRIST,—but,

The kingdom of regenerated Faith, which is the KINGDOM of Christ,—is gathered from out of this world,—because it is taken into its own Royal Priesthood, to work the works of Faith, and commune with Christ for his *Divine* MERCY.

Neither has *It* any thing to do with this *World*, but to leave it behind under justice, which is the *Wrath of God!* Therefore WATCH *Passion*, and the *Overcares* of this life; and the spirit of *Fear*, and the drunken spirit of *Emulated* Reason, lest by those you *fall* under the power of *temptation*, and CHRIST come unaware!

Now those things are *sure to come* to Reason, and take them under the Seal of the *Angel in Justice!*

For the whole efforts of Reason, is a *Wilderness*: And the spirit of Reason is the *Beast*, —and their *wild priesthood* by which they would excuse themselves is the *Whore* which *ride* on the Beast (Rev. xvii); and as they are born to no other Light or Glory than that of this *World*, let them have it.

But, YOU;—go the *way* which you have been informed, in the Royal Priesthood of FAITH; to *seek* the Glory of CHRIST, who is the KING of Faith and Mercy,

Yours,

JAMES BIRCH.

Abergavenny, Aug. 2, 1780.

Note.—The above was left for Mrs. Jones, by Mr. Birch, being then on a visit to the Church in Wales, she being so troubled in caring about the *many things* of arrogant Reason, as to block up the way to spiritual Converse. Sought July 1801, and brought to London by

R. I.

LETTER XXV

To our beloved Sister Mary Runwa, and to the whole Church beloved in Christ in and about Pembroke, James Birch *sendeth greeting.*

Beloved Brethren,—This with my love to inform you I came safe and well to *London*, and found the church all well, and my family tolerable. I have sent you, as I promised, the intended Introduction to the *Work*, for by this you may see the difference of the *two natures*, and how each fell under its own law, and here (in time by generation) become *two* large kingdoms, but the dark invading spirit of Reason has always endeavoured to make them *one*; and has prevailed so as to *Captivate* the elect for a *Time*.

But, when regeneration is begun to the elect, then the kingdoms will be *divided*, and the soul will bring forth *treasures both old and new*;—for now it will be made known each kingdom has its own Law and Priesthood, and will be called under its own justice; and even in the Book of the Law and Cherubim, which I have written, there is a hint given sufficient, that you may know one from the other, for the *wilderness* which is the power of Reason is *very great*; and the power of justice, sin, death, and hell, is very *hard* to travail through, which thing must be done by the divine assistance of the divine majesty from heaven, by and to all them that are *saved*.

Therefore be you united in the strong union of Faith, and remember what I said concerning the two Priesthoods and the *first Resurrection*, when I was with you, and hold fast what you have received, and patiently wait to be called forward by the *sounding Angel* from heaven, which thing I strongly recommend;—And I pray God assist you in the works of Faith. So conclude your loving brother,

JAMES BIRCH,

London, Sep. 7, 1780.

P.S. The whole church greets you all, and rejoices to hear of your Faith, praying its increase, My love to all and every one.

LETTER XXVI

Mr. Birch *to the Church in Wales, in love Greeting.*

As I promised concerning *the* VOICE *of the Seven Angels* in John's Rev. (see Chap. 1. &c.) —It is done under the holy gospel, now God sits on the throne of MERCY; and those *seven Angels* are the seven Stars held in the right hand of *Him* that *walketh* in the midst of the seven golden candlesticks, which are the *seven Churches.*—Those *churches* were in Asia, but let the church of Christ be *where He* will, and *when He* please and as *many* as *He* please, it is the same thing.

Also, those *Angels* are "the seven lamps of fire burning before the throne of God, which are the seven spirits of God" (Rev. iv. 5) which is before the Throne of mercy, and goeth out to, or on the elect for salvation.

Now the royal and true *Church of Christ* is, when the Virgin daughter of Faith is born for regeneration, and not till then, which thing cannot be done until the voice of the *first* Angel has *sounded* from heaven, which gives birth to the Virgin of Faith, then there is the CHURCH of CHRIST, because she is born of the womb of Faith, and is the *golden candlestick* in whom the royal incense burn, which is the prayer of Faith, that ascends up before the throne of God, for his mercy and salvation:—And the spirit of God from heaven, which gave birth to this Virgin of Faith, is the *Angel* of the church, until another *sounds*; and this Angel which is Faith, Christ orders the Angel of his declaration, to write or preach unto, to tell them of the power of death and hell, and the incumberance of Reason, and they must overcome to receive the reward of his divine mercy.

Again, those *Seven Spirits* of God, or *seven Angels*, is the internal and spiritual *testimony* of Jesus to his elect, of his royal redemption and mercy, and it goeth out on the Virgin daughter of Faith, for regeneration and salvation. For by this *He* gathers his own kingdom, which is Faith under his royal seal, for the Glory of his Mercy.

BUT there must be a son born of the Virgin daughter of Faith, who has heard what those angels utter, to declare who and what they are, therefore, when the SPIRITUAL SON is born of the virgin daughter, 'tis from and under the justice of the father to his own royal covenant of mercy, and is taken into the high mountain of Faith, where he sees Jesus in the glory of his mercy, who sits on the right hand of all power, and has the Seal of mercy, and power to open the seal of the father and sits on the right hand of them who are sealed for the glory of his mercy;—there the spiritual born son offers at the feet of Jesus, for to be called under His royal seal for the kingdom of glory; for the *feet of Jesus* in the glory of mercy is the great and grand altar of Faith: But if instead of this spiritual born son being called under the seal of Jesus and sleep in the bed of mercy: he is sent back by Jesus to tell his brethren what he has seen, and what will soon come to pass on them; then he *comes* out from the great and grand ALTAR *of Faith*, then the power of Faith, which is the *Censer*, is made able to offer *Incense*, which is prayer before the grand Altar, and is filled with the *Fire* of the Altar, which is with the *Spirit* of Christ; then he is made the Angel of that declaration; and when he utters his *Voice*, it is directed to the Womb or seed of Faith in the soul of man and it comes as *Thunder* and causes great trembling and new lights, and great voices of argument in the soul of man;— and those *seven Angels* are prepared to assist the angel of the declaration by their sound from heaven.

And, when the *first Angel sounds*, it is when the voice of the Lord God of heaven *walketh* in the womb or seed of Faith in elect man, for that is the *Garden* he walks in for regeneration, and calls "Faith, Where art thou, or in what condition art thou in?" Then the power of death and hell is open to the soul, and it is lost in its own blood, but the consequence of the voice of this *first Angel* gives birth to the virgin daughter of Faith, and she is born into the priesthood of Faith and Mercy, which is the church of Christ, and if this angel do not *sound*, Hear, and observe! the soul is *not* in the church of Christ but *without*, on the letter, and the internal angel in justice is the angel of the church, and he will hear the *Angel of the Declaration.*

And when the *Second Angel sounds*, it is the promise from heaven of Christ to come to the Virgin daughter of Faith, then the great hope of Reason is cast into its own water, and that becomes as *blood* to the virgin of Faith.

And when the *Third Angel sounds*, it is a divine assistance from heaven, to help the *Virgin Daughter* in the works of Faith, according to her prayer, to *remove mountains* and pass through justice: for "at the voice of this angel there fell a star from heaven burning as a lamp, and it fell upon the third part of the rivers and fountains of waters, and the star is called wormwood, and the third part of the waters became wormwood, and men died of those waters, because they were made bitter." Now this star is the justice of God, for both man and angel broke the law they were created under, and he became the God of Justice, through their acts; then this star fell from heaven on both man and angel, or Faith and Reason, and burns like a lamp of pure crystal fire, and it may well be called wormwood, because it has made the waters of this life bitter, and them that cannot drink and *overcome*, must die of the *bitterness* of those waters, let them think what they will to the contrary.

And when the *Fourth Angel sounds* it proclaims to the soul, the Lord God of heaven became a son to his own power to redeem his elect, and was smitten by the power of Reason and his own justice, yet in *Lamb-like* patience, in a body of flesh and blood, he went through it, and OVERCOME: But as he came in a *mean* condition, his great works of Faith, Redemption and Prophecy, did not shine in the eyes of Reason, neither did they believe HE was him that was to come, according to prophecy, by the prophets of old, and in the time of the law; and in this the *Moon was Smitten,* neither did it shine in his apostles, so the *Sun, Moon, and Stars were smitten, and shone not* in the eye of Reason at that time, but the voice of this angel is to tell the Virgin that Jesus went through the mighty power of Sin, of Reason, of Death, Hell, and Justice, in a body of flesh, and overcome, and she must do as *He did*, then she will eat his flesh; and drink his blood, and have part in him.

And when the *Fifth Angel* sounds it is the spirit of prophecy given from heaven, that Christ will come to you, and of your own salvation; and this *Star that fell from heaven* is the internal angel in justice, and he has *the key of the bottomless pit,* for he can bind and loose Reason according to the will of God; but here Reason is loosed and will plague the soul of man, but have patience and prayer; then Faith will *overcome.*

And when the *Sixth Angel sounds* you are called under the justice of the father, and the voice is come up hither. Now at the voice of this angel the *four Angels,* or Powers; *are let loose that were bound* in the *waters* of Reason, *i.e.* the power of sin, justice; death, and hell is let loose, and you cannot go back there; therefore, through the justice of the father, you must go; and that is to lose yourself in death, in your own blood under that justice, to be quickened or *born anew* for the Mercy of the SON:—And when this *spiritual born* son of the virgin is brought forth, he is taken into an high mountain of Faith, where he see Christ in the glory of mercy, and he offers the eager prayer of Faith at the feet of Jesus to be called under his royal seal.

And when the SEVENTH *Angel sounds* this spiritual born son is *Called*, and the voice say, "COME IN HITHER," Which is into, or under the seal of Jesus; and that is to be united to Jesus in his own royal covenant of mercy, which is *above* the justice of the father, then *the kingdom of this World* is become the *Kingdom of Christ*, and this is the SEAL of the living God, then the soul is *Assured* of eternal life, and falls asleep in the bed of mercy.

I beg you will mind what is wrote, and may Grace, Love, Mercy, and Faith abound in your souls, and patiently wait to be called forward by the *sounding* Angel of Faith, as is the prayer of your loving brother,

Sept. 16, 1780. JAMES BIRCH.

LETTER XXVII

To John Evans, Thomas Mudford, John Eynon, &c. *in and about BATH,* James Birch *and Brethren send greeting.*

Brethren—This with my love, to inform you I came safe to London; and when with you, I told you concerning the *two priesthoods*, which is, of Faith, and of Reason, and that you may know the difference between the covenant of justice and of mercy: Now John Reeve *was* or *is* the *Last* Messenger that will be sent to the bloody unbelieving world; and Lodowick Muggleton was given to be his *mouth*; and was the last *High Priest*, but of the order of Levi or Aaron; therefore John Reeve was as Moses, and the other as Aaron, whose Priesthood was of Reason, wherein salvation cannot be found; also them that come to the bloody unbelieving world, come out under the justice of the angel, or cherubical justice; and its priesthood is to offer an offering to stay justice, that the soul may enjoy its haven, for was not the cherubim and flaming sword stayed in his justice, when men brake the law, it would as eagerly cast him into death, as it did the angel down from heaven, when he broke the law there.

Again, the bloody unbelieving world is the seed and spirit of Reason, unto which Jesus never *manifested* the name of the father when he was here in a body of flesh, under the justice of the father; for all men that are born into this world, are born to Moses and that Priesthood; and if they live to manhood they will surely find him; and if men are born incapable of any higher life or light, than that of this world, and the priesthood of Reason, they must die as they were born, and Moses is their prophet, let them profess who or what they will beside: And John Reeve came out as Moses—they are closely united; for this understand, what was written or acted by Moses, who was the anointed Cherubim by his inspiration, and the external angel of that Covenant, was well brought up by John Reeve, because he began to declare in the commission of the spirit which first began in justice; and all this will be acted on the soul and spirit of one man, who lives and dies under the first covenant.

And what Jesus said and did, will be acted on the soul and spirit of one man that can be born again, to come into His holy covenant and royal Priesthood; for as Moses had Reason to work upon in the soul of man to bring in justice and death. Even so Jesus hath Faith to work upon in the soul of man, to bring in mercy and life; therefore, if man enter the covenant and priesthood of Faith, he'll die under the Angel of Faith, if not, he will die under the angel of Reason.

Moreover, as men are born into this world to know the things of the world, even so the Virgin of Faith must be born of the womb or seed of Faith, and taken in the royal priesthood, to know the things of Faith, then unto those Jesus *manifest the name of the Father*, because they are and will be taken into the royal Priesthood, to work the works of Faith under the justice of the Father, as he himself did:—See John's Gospel xvii. 6,—"I have manifested thy name unto the men which thou gavest me out of the world:"—Verse 9, "I pray for them, I pray not for, the world:" Therefore Jesus never *manifested* the name of the Father unto, nor prayed for the *world*, but for *them* that the Father *gave him*, which was out of the world; hence you may see them that come to the bloody unbelieving world, come to Reason, and have a *rod* or power to *swallow* them up that rebel against him, and the priest has also power given to him, which is the *given priesthood*, so long as he is obedient to the prophet, but when he thinks himself more wise than he that received the message from God, away he goes into the *wild* Priesthood, and there he make an *Idol*, although he may retain the name of the prophet as long as he live.

Again, although *Moses* came out under justice, yet he was taken into the priesthood of Faith, and *prophesied* of Christ to come; and also wrote concerning the creation, the temptation, and the fall of man; and *divided* the genealogy of Adam from that of Cain, and of the promise made to Adam.

And, when John Reeve came out, he wrote concerning the creation, the temptation, and fall of man; and the two seeds; and in this he sweetly shines also he declared that no one but him that Created could redeem; and the compact of Faith concerning who sit in the power of the Father, and prophesied of Christ to come, only this as Moses lived before Christ came, he prophesied God would come to redeem; and John Reeve lived after Christ came in person to redeem,—and he prophesied Christ would come in spirit, and give the spirit of prophecy for him to come in holy marriage, thus the prophets that came out under the justice of the angel, are taken into The Priesthood of Faith under the justice of the Father, and prophecy of Christ to come, but the *Priest* is left in his own Priesthood.

Further, the priest had power under the name of the Prophet, or rather the cherubical declaration, to raise them of the *wild* Priesthood, which was first instituted by old Cain; and they came forth in anger, and when done, he might plague them for a time.

But when CHRIST came and uttered his holy Covenant, and royal Priesthood, He had respect to, and gathered the gentile as well as the jew; and this being contrary to the doctrine of the priest, he rose the dead priest in his sons, and they came forth in darkness, wrath, and persecution; yet under the name of Moses, and said "we know God spake to Moses, as for this fellow we know not from whence he is:" Jesus said, "if ye had believed in Moses, ye would believe me, for he wrote of me;" *i.e.* had they believed in Moses where he prophesied and wrote concerning Christ to come, they would believe in Christ when he was come: Also Jesus said "What was written by Moses and the prophets, and psalms concerning him, must be fulfilled," but the priest he exclude because they prophesied not of him; for in the priesthood of reason there is no power given to prophecy concerning Faith; therefore let the *priest* think what he will of himself, and put himself equal with, if not above the prophet, which is *on the house top*; yet when Christ come, one will be taken and the other left, and the sons of the priest will be raised to wrath; but Faith is quickened from death to life in the sons of the prophet, and are taken into the royal priesthood, which is the *first resurrection*, and they will follow Jesus through the *Mansions* of the Father to the place *prepared* by the Son.

Again, those things are now in act at this day, for Christ is now come according to John Reeve's prophecy and prayer, for there is now a *spiritual born son* of the Virgin daughter of Faith in regeneration, and sent *back* to tell his Tale, and do witness from heaven God sent John Reeve, and has declared the kingdom of Faith, which is the kingdom of Christ; and the kingdom of Reason, and the Angel of Faith, and the Angel of Reason, the nature and law of Faith; and the nature and law of Reason, the priesthood of Faith, and the priesthood of Reason; and the justice of the Father which is the justice to Faith, and the justice of the Angel, which is justice to Reason and what *is* regeneration; and the soul must *overcome* by regeneration to inherit the promise of divine mercy: Now this makes the sons of Muggleton (which are the sons of the priest) angry, and say "we know God spake to John Reeve, but as for this fellow Birch, we know not that he is from heaven, neither do we believe;" but if they had believed in John Reeve they would believe in me; And as Jesus had power to raise the sons of the priest in his day I also have power to raise the sons of Muggleton, which are the sons of the priest in my day, and they come forth in darkness, wrath, persecution, and blasphemy, according to the utterance of the *sixth Thunder*, and in all this, use the name of John Reeve to cover their evil; but Faith in the sons of the prophet is risen from Death to Life, and they are taken, and the sons of the priest are left in the *great city* of Jerusalem, which is prophesied against.

Therefore I recommend to you *patience* and the *prayer of obedience*, and be careful of *temptation* to give judgment; for every man must stand distinct to and for himself; for as the *sign of the Son of man do appear*, many will hear his voice and live: Brother Cullum and others love to Brother Mudford, and are glad of a reconciliation as to former things, which to them are done away, for they are become as *children* and patiently *wait* to be called forward in the priesthood of Faith, by the sounding angel from heaven, now the angel of the declaration has uttered; and I pray God the same Faith and Wisdom may abound in you all, for in the Priesthood of Faith, which is Mercy, there is *no joy in the death of a sinner.* My love to Mrs. Enyon, and to all and every one, and. Mr. Burford. So conclude your loving brother.

JAS. BIRCH

London, No. 3, Butler's Alley,
Little Moorfields.
October the 5th, 1780.

LETTER XXVIII

To our beloved Brother and Sister, Philip John and Mina his wife, and to the whole Church beloved in Christ, in and about Pembroke, James Birch and the Brethren sendeth Greeting.

Beloved Brethren,—I hope you remember what I said concerning the *resurrection to Faith and regeneration*, when I parted with you on the road: and, according to promise, I have written to you; therefore mind.

In this *Life* we are surrounded with sin, death, hell and justice; and through it the daughter of Faith must be brought; for this life is *Hell* to the *Elect*, when they are brought to the knowledge of themselves; then by the *Power* of patience and prayer, they will be brought through by regeneration, and in this their sins go to judgment *before* them.

But this *Life* to the seed of Reason, when they come to maturity, and the Angel take place in the Soul, is their *heaven*, and the only heaven they ever will possess; and in their *forgetful condition*, they fail not to go out to seek it, and gather themselves ripe, under cherubical justice; and in this their *sins follow* them to judgment—therefore, BLESSED are them whose sins go to judgment *before* them!

AGAIN, Reason goeth out after the perishing *delights of this Life*, Why? because he has no other life, light, or wisdom; therefore he wonders that *all* are not ruled by this wisdom; because there is no greater wisdom to him—then he looks on them with pitiful contempt, who are not guided by his wisdom.

Moreover, this *Life* of Reason is *dead* in the sight of God; why? because it is of a contrary nature to Faith; and was cast out in the beginning; and is incapable of regeneration to God; therefore *God is not God of the dead but of the living.* i.e. He is the God of Faith, which *Life*, can be brought out of death, and by regeneration *live* unto him.

Also, the *Life* of Reason is under the power of cherubical justice, sin, death, and hell; so their *Life is in Death*, and their *light, darkness*: then their *care* is to gather and possess things as must perish with themselves; and in this manner they wander in the *Land of Nod*, for they are *born* in that Land, *live* in that Land, and *die* in that Land, and yet never know that Land, until the *book* of the *second death* is opened by the Angel in justice, then it is too late.

Further, in all their goings out, and evil doings to enjoy this *Life* of Reason, which burn and flame in evil, like unto the flame that ascends from fuel when set on fire, and in this they make their own excuses, and tempt each other to evil, then excuse themselves by each other's evil.

Also, the *wrathful* spirit of Reason, which is a *Dragon*, has transformed itself into the Letter of the Gospel, and judge of it according to the dark spirit of Reason, because they have no other life or light to judge by;—then they claim the promises of Jesus as being made to them, and collect a kingdom which is in their power, or the *Beast*:—then send forth their *preachers* and *teachers*,—and although they preach the name of Jesus, yet it is from the spirit of Reason; therefore *a false Christ*.

For except a man is *born* to Christ, in his holy covenant, and sent back by Christ in his spirit and power, he cannot preach, teach and prophecy of Christ unto salvation.—Now such a one as this may be called a *true Christ*, because he is sent out in regenerated Faith, in the spirit and power of Christ!

BUT he that comes out in the spirit of Reason, which is the power of the beast, he preaches falsely in the name of Christ, and as so a *false Christ*: and what he promise and prophecy concerning Christ is wrong; therefore he is called in spirit a *false prophet*.

Moreover, the *whole World* is gone after the *Beast* and *false prophet*, to make *war* against the kingdom and priesthood of Faith, which is the kingdom of Christ.—and those that enter the royal priesthood will be plagued by that power of Reason, in threats, temptations, and persecutions, &c. and if man look into his own soul, he will find his own spirit of Reason the worst of all,—and of *those Waters he must drink and* OVERCOME.

Now this is the *Wilderness* of the world, and them that come out in the power of the *Beast* will be accepted by the *World*—and be rewarded by them; because, that evil preaching suit their evil spirits—and thus they encourage each other in that abominable evil, to *make War* against the king of Faith, and them in his royal priesthood.

Yea—and those *Leaders and Teachers are thieves and robbers*, and come to *steal, kill, and destroy, i.e.* they take the promises that belong not to them, and render the gospel contrary to its pure intent and meaning—and take of people under false pretence; now this you have to watch, both internal and external, for *in one hour will their plagues come!* For they do go into the first death under the seal of the Angel, for the *second death*: and at the resurrection, Christ will take his own, both that which is *sensible and insensible*, for strong is the Lord God of Heaven, who has given them up to this judgment.

Again, Faith *fell* in Adam, but Reason *fell* in the serpent Angel: therefore them who fell *in* Adam will he made alive *in* Christ: *i.e.* out of the death of Faith that fell in Adam there is quickened a new life, which is the Daughter for regeneration and redemption, then the soul has *gotten VICTORY over the Beast*: *i.e.* there is another life born in him contrary to that of Reason; and this *new Life* is made able to commune with God for regeneration and salvation—and through the power of Christ enters the priesthood of Faith.

Therefore (John's Gospel, x. 9.) JESUS said, "I am the door, by me if any man enter, he shall be saved, and shall go *in*, and *out*, and find pasture," *i.e. in* the royal priesthood he will find the spirit of Christ to assist the daughter of Faith up to *holy marriage.* And also there is wisdom and power given the soul, over the spirit of Reason, who is *out* of the priesthood: Now this is the *first resurrection*, and all done by the power of Christ; and "Blessed is him that has part in the *first* resurrection, for on such the *second* death has no power."

Moreover, (Chap. xi. 5) *Jesus* said "I am the resurrection and the life; he that believeth in me, though he were dead, yet shall he live," *i.e.* he that truly believes in Christ, when he come in person or when he come in spirit by his Messenger, although he were dead in Faith through the *fall*, yet that Faith will be raised from death to life, by the power of Christ, because He become the God of mercy to his elect, and is the resurrection and life of regenerated Faith.

Verse 26.—"And whosoever liveth and believeth in me shall never die;" this is the virgin daughter when risen or born from the womb or seed of Faith; then, she live unto, and believe in Christ, and will be united to the immortal spirit of Jesus, and never die! although the soul fall asleep in the bed of mercy, to be raised to glory.—Now those things you are to mind and observe, although declared by a *Beggar*, for the Messenger of JESUS is a *beggar*, both from heaven and earth; and BLESSED are them that SEE this, and *enter* the royal priesthood, and *do* the works!

So conclude your loving brother in Christ.

JAMES BIRCH.

London, Oct. 12, 1780.

The whole church prays your increase of Faith, and to see this letter.

LETTER XXIX

To our beloved Sister Eliz. Atkinson, *and the whole Church beloved in Christ, in and about Pembroke,* James Birch *and Brethren send GREETING.*

Beloved Sister,—Yours I received, and was glad to hear from you, and that you received what I sent, which I hope the whole Church will carefully peruse and make known in the *Communion of Faith* to each other; and I pray God increase all your Faith and understanding: and of all things be you united in the love of Christ.

LOVE and *pray* for each other; and be not *angry*; for there is no such thing as anger in Faith: see (Mat. xviii.) where Peter asked

Jesus, "how oft' he should forgive his brother that sinned against him?" (v. 22,) Jesus saith unto him "I say not unto thee until seven times, but until seventy times seven," *i.e. always*: therefore there is no such thing as *anger* in the spirit of Faith: And when any one is catched in *Anger* or resentment, on any occasion, against his brother, they may depend upon it, to be in a state of temptation: So take care and not listen to the tempter: Now this is on every one's part to do; therefore *watch*,—and *Pray* for assistance.

Again, my soul's love is alike to you all in the church: and my eager desire and prayer is, that you may greatly increase in the royal priesthood; for I did not come to seek justice and death, for that is too soon found for the *Scale* of mercy.— But I came to seek *Life* out of *Death*, for mercy and life, and *instruct* it, and by divine assistance from heaven, to bring it on in regeneration and the royal priesthood, up to the holy marriage with Christ:—Thus you will be united to him in his holy covenant of mercy, and enter his royal kingdom of inexpressible glory, which has no end! And you may be assured from me that there is no such thing as joy in the death of a sinner, in the royal priesthood of Faith.

Moreover, in all the goings out and acts of life it is a great thing to *forgive* and *overcome*; for then flows the sweet waters of PEACE; and gives men power over wrathful and evil spirits, why? because the angel in justice will excuse him: And not only so, but also, justice will be stayed to a merciful man.

But in what condition must that man be to make a supplication before the Angel, which is the *Altar* of Reason, for justice to be stayed, for him to have prosperity and the Lamp of this life to shine sweetly; yet he himself will not forgive his brother!—Now this should be observed in the priesthood of Reason; but much greater things to be done in the priesthood of Faith.

Beloved Sister and Brethren, as we had no other abode than the *priesthood* of Reason, and the *Wilderness*:—The VOICE of God is *now* from heaven, to CALL HIS PEOPLE out of the spiritual *fornication* of Reason in the *wilderness*, that they should not partake of their sins, so as to die under them:—nor receive of that justice that will follow to Reason.

And YOU, must pass *out* of, or *through*, this *great and terrible wilderness*, up to the holy marriage with Christ, between Threats, and Temptations of Reason, which is the *straight and narrow way*, which many have gone by divine assistance from heaven: therefore do you have Faith and doubt not; for by the prayer of Faith and Patience, mountains of sins, and death, will be removed;— for all the power of sin, death, hell, and justice, cannot stop the regeneration of CHRIST.

Furthermore, what is the *follies* of this life, that Reason so much delight in, and all their whoredoms and fornications they commit with the Letter of the Gospel?—It is no more than for them to complete themselves in their own evil, under the seal of the angel in justice:— For all may be assured, if Christ do not take them into his holy priesthood and covenant according to the CRY of the present MESSENGER, they are given up to the angel in justice; therefore cannot escape the Messenger, or the Angel in justice; so great is the *Watch* set over the soul of man! and strong is the Lord God of heaven who has set this watch, and has the *Power* of justice, and the *Plagues* that will come on Reason! therefore Woe! to them that are lost in the fears and follies of life! and in the *false* going out, in the name of Christ!

Again, the present MESSENGER, can call nothing his own, but his *spirit of Reason*, and that he greatly wants to get rid of!—for, he very well knows that all he possesses of this perishing life, it must leave him, and he that.

Neither can *Reason* help himself in this;—yea, all the delights of this life will leave him, and *dissolve to Chaos*, and he himself go into the second death.

Therefore it is highly necessary now the warning is given, for the elect to seek the kingdom of Christ; and the nearer you are to him in spirit, the better.

I hope Betsey is a good girl, and minds what is said to her, and not by her self-confused spirit of resentment fly in the face of good instruction, but listen and follow.—I hope you are all well, and I pray your increase of Faith. So conclude your loving brother in Christ,

JAMES BIRCH.

London, Nov. 6, 1780.

P.S. Received Runwa's and Thomas's by Martha Rees, and with

love, remember my promise to Alice, &c.

LETTER XXX

To our beloved Sisters Mary Runwa and Jones, and to the whole Church beloved in Christ in and about Pembroke, James Birch *and the brethren sendeth greeting.*

Beloved Brethren,—Yours I received, and glad to hear of you, as I should that you had that letter to Mrs. Atkinson also.

Now I would have you in *particular* mind, how Faith fell for breaking its own law;—then, the JUSTICE of its Father and Creator took place, which became of an infinite consequence, because it was then disunited from its living father, in death, by the power of this *Justice,* and it must be recovered again, *in* or *by* regeneration, which is life out of this death.

Therefore, in the days of old, and in the time of the law, when God manifested himself to Faith, it was by *quickening* Life out of this death, which is the Virgin, daughter of Faith for regeneration; and it is under its own Justice, which is the Justice of the Father; and under this *Justice* the promise of Christ is *given*; and the works of Faith is done; and power given to *Prophesy* of Christ to *come*:— And when Christ *came* he come on the *prophesies* of this Virgin of Faith: Therefore, when elect man has worked the works of Faith to the ultimate of his power, Christ comes on his works and Prophecy, and makes him perfect for salvation.

AGAIN, when the Lord GOD of heaven became the MAN-JESUS on this earth, he put himself under his own JUSTICE, which is the Power and Justice of the Father, and went through it, and manifested the name and Power of the Father to the Elect; but not unto the World. (see John xvii. 6,) "I have manifested thy name unto the men which thou gavest me out of the world, thine they were." *i.e.* To the sons of Adam which are the sons of God, according to creation, but fell under this *Justice* for breaking the Law of Faith. Then when Faith is quickened from Death to Life, it needs must know the power that it is under, which is the *Justice* of the FATHER, as well as the promise of mercy, which is of the SON; neither can it know the power of the Son which is *Mercy*, without knowing the power of the Father which is Justice.

AGAIN, John xiv. 6, Jesus saith, "I am the way, the truth, and the life, no man cometh unto the Father but by me;" hence you may see, except the power of the Father, which is justice to Faith, is *manifested*, there is nothing done for salvation.

Also, Matt. xii. 50, Jesus said, "Whosoever doth the will of my father, which is in heaven, the same is my brother, &c." Therefore Faith must be *quickened* from death to life, or born from its womb or seed, and taken into the royal priesthood, and there to work the works of Faith, under the Justice of the Father, as Christ himself did; and go through the *mansions* of the Father, which is Justice to Faith, to the *place* prepared by the Son, which is mercy: And during the time the virgin of Faith actuates the soul, this is its state or condition in some degree; but when not, it is allured into the *wilderness* by the tempter.

Again, the Angel fell under his own Law, which is cherubical or the Law of Reason, then that *Justice* took place in his soul, and cast him down from heaven to this earth; and although he brake the law he was created under, he never could break the Justice of the law, but would or must take it with him wherever he went, as pure as God first created it; for after he was transmuted into flesh. and borne Cain, and grew to manhood, this *Justice* took place in his soul; because it is the *cherubims and flaming sword*, which keep Reason from the tree of life, and when he killed Abel he was arraigned before this Angel whom he called Lord; and when he was loosed by this Angel, he went into the Land of Nod, *i.e.* as the justice of this angel was stayed, that he might go on in generation, and enjoy this earth, and form to himself his god, his forgiveness, and worship, but the chief thing was his great *hope* that the power of this *justice* was, or would, be broken: And this *water* of Hope runs in the soul of man to this day; and by me is called the great river Euphrates in the Land of Nod, that waters the soul and spirit of Reason, and in this manner men go on in the *wild* priesthood of Reason.

Moreover, Moses was inspired with the wisdom of this cherubical law, and gave it forth in truth, and he also gave a priesthood, that when men brake the law they should bring in their offerings to stay this Justice, that Reason should enjoy its heaven: But Reason was always eager to slide back to its *wild* nature and priesthood, to do his own will, and have his own way: But as Jesus has uttered his holy gospel, full power is given the internal angel to seal men under justice for the second death; and although they read the letter of the gospel, yet they take it into the wild priesthood of Reason; and as they read, they understand, and every one make his choice, so the scripture is their own understanding, as they convert it, then they become as Gods, and choose their own way to heaven; And they go out on earthly things to seek their own will and desire, which is their kingdom, and excuse themselves for their own evil; and the tempter will give them full employ, and tell them it must be done, or ruination will follow, so are devoured by the spirit of fear, and their great *Hope* is as aforesaid, that the justice of this angel is or will be broken; thus the whole world is lost in this *Wilderness*.

But the present Messenger was sent to seek a life of Faith, to come into that *royal Priesthood*; and when the soul is tempted it is to wander in this *wilderness*; therefore my soul's desire and prayer is, you may be careful and increase in Faith; and YOU will inherit a kingdom which perish not.

So conclude your loving brother, &c.

JAMES BIRCH,

London, Nov. 16, 1780.

LETTER XXXI

To our beloved Brother Jas, Thomas, *and to the whole Church beloved in Christ, in and about Pembroke,* Jas. Birch *and Brethren send Greeting.*

Beloved Brother—Yours I received; and as you would know who that ANGEL was *that came down from heaven and bound the Dragon* (Rev. xx. and elsewhere), I will with Joy inform you.

Now OBSERVE, when God created the *serpent Angel*, he came forth more wise and more glorious than any of the seraphic host, why? because he was created a *Cherubim*, and he being more wise and glorious than any other angel; then of consequence no one of that *Order* but himself: And this Cherubim being created in reference to

God's Justice, there was such a quantity of Justice fixed in him through the purity of God's Creation, that was sufficient to *cast him down from heaven*, whenever he broke the law he was created under, and although he break the law he was created under, yet he never could break the justice of that law, but would take it with him wherever he went, as *pure* as God first created it.

Again, you may see, after the *Fall*, God said, "Behold the man is become as one of us, to know *Good and Evil*," *i.e.* he should know *good and evil*, in and according to this life, and his own Law and Priesthood:—" Now lest *he* should put forth *his* hand, and take also of the *Tree of Life*, and eat and live for ever," the Lord God *sent him* forth from Eden to *till the ground from whence he was taken*: Again, it is said, "So God drove out *the man*, and he placed at the east of Eden, Cherubims and flaming sword, which turn every way to keep the way of the *Tree of Life*."

Again, observe, the *Garden of Eden* to Reason, is the purity of God's creation, from which the serpent fell, then after that he was transmuted into flesh, and born the child Cain, who grew to manhood; then this *cherubim and flaming sword* took place in his soul, and would keep him *out* from any resurrection or life, but that of this life or world: For, as aforesaid, although the cherubim or serpent-angel broke the law he was created under, he never could break the justice of that law, but would take it with him into flesh as pure as God first created it.

And when any of the seed of the serpent grew to manhood, this Cherubim and flaming sword, or internal *Angel* in justice, takes place in the soul, and keep the spirit of Reason, which is the *Dragon*, out from God, from his mercy, and seal him under his own evil, and *bind and loose him* according to the *will* of Him or Them who sit in the glory of justice.

Also, this mind and observe, it is only the *man* that is *drove out*, and the *Angel* or Cherubim placed against *him*; for the *Child* is not mentioned; why? because the serpent-angel was born in flesh a child, and grew to manhood, before the *Angel* in justice took place in him in this life; therefore many of the children of Reason die in childhood and never live to manhood; then the *Angel* never takes place in the soul:— neither does it in the natural *Ideot*; so *they*, are not drove out from the purity and glory of God's creating the cherubim, but will be raised again to compose that mighty *host* and glorious order of cherubims in heaven above; But if they live to manhood, the *Angel* in justice takes place in the soul, then they cannot die cherubims to be raised to glory; but must go on, in, and for justice.

Now, this *Angel* is called Cherubims and flaming sword, because of the *plurality* in generation; and in that, every one is his own witness to his own condemnation: but it was first fixed in the Cherubim, at his creation, and it is of the Cherubim, and, *came down from heaven* with the Cherubim, or *serpent-angel*:—And when Cain was arraigned before this Angel, he called him "Lord," and so he is to Reason, as to communion, because, as *he* keeps them *out* from mercy, they must of necessity commune with him in justice.

AGAIN, Adam was created the son of God, and *they* were of *His* divine nature, and came forth into this life, and world, in full manhood, and broke their own law,—harkening to the Serpent, their tempter, which is to the voice of Reason, and brought on themselves and children, *trouble, sorrow, mourning,* and *death*; which is *Briars and Thorns*, beside the disunion with their living Father and Creator: THEN, when God called to Adam, it was for regeneration, which gave birth to the Virgin of Faith, then Christ was promised; For CHRIST, in regeneration and salvation is the TREE OF LIFE, which Adam and all his children has, and will take hold of, and *eat and live for ever*.

But it is the man of Reason that the cherubim and flaming sword is placed against, lest *he* also put forth his hand, and take also of the Tree of life and eat and live for ever: And, as the serpent was born a child in a body of flesh into this world, and grew to manhood, so many of his children drop short of manhood: but the children of Adam live to full manhood, as the Lord God of heaven created Adam to, and be made capable of regeneration as Adam was.

Furthermore, Adam, at his fall, took into himself the nature of Reason, then of consequence the Law, and the Angel of the Law, by which the elect are plagued to this day; and it will rule the soul, and keep him out from God; until God is graciously pleased to *commune with his OWN created nature of Faith* (that fell in Adam) *for regeneration and* SALVATION; and this COMMUNION OF GOD, is far above or beyond the power of the Angel in Justice, which is the angel to Reason.

Now, by what is written, you may see how God goeth out on the *White Horse*, which is for MERCY, in his *own garden*, which is the *Womb* of Faith in the elect; and to conquer sin, death, hell, and justice, and bring in mercy and salvation to his elect. And also, when the internal *Angel* take place in the soul, how he goeth out on the *Red Horse*, (Chap. vi.) which is on the sinful soul of man; for in all the vain delights of this life, which is a garden or kingdom to Reason, yet, in the midst of all their Glee and glory, this *horse and rider* is with them, and has *power* to execute justice, *and take peace from the earthly* heart of Reason; and that they should *devour, kill and destroy one another:* for *to him was given a great sword.*

Thus—you may see from the beginning, when the seed of Reason come to manhood, this *Angel* or *flaming sword* is placed against him, and will *bind him up* in his own wrath; therefore Reason, when they come to manhood, was dead in the sight of God, and *cast out* in the beginning: And also, mind, how GOD goeth out on the womb of Faith for redemption, regeneration and salvation: And how the Child that dies will be raised a glorious cherubim in heaven above,—which, are *three grand Seals* opened concerning the will and power of God.

Again, on those foundations the world goes on in generation; and him that comes from God under the justice of this *Angel* comes to Reason; which is the bloody unbelieving world, as did Moses and the prophets of old: Now Moses gave forth the law and priesthood of Reason, and Aaron was given to be his mouth, and was the *High Priest*, but in the priesthood of Reason, and so it went on in the time of the law with prophet and priest; but this observe;—although Moses and the prophets came out under cherubical justice, yet *they* were taken into the Priesthood of Faith, and *communed* with God for salvation, and prophesied of Christ to come: But the Priest was left in his own priesthood, and would make an Idol if possible: Moreover, when CHRIST came, he came on the prophesies of the virgin of Faith, which was of the prophets; therefore Jesus said, "All must be fulfilled that was written in the law of Moses, and in the prophets, and in the psalms, concerning him;" (Luke xxiv.) but the priest he leaves out, and mentions not, because they prophesied not of him.

And when HE uttered his holy gospel of mercy and salvation, this made the sons of the priest, which are the sons of Reason, angry, because they saw a kingdom coming contrary to their own; neither could they come to the kingdom of Christ; because they were sealed under their own evil by this *Angel*; and by his power was *bound up* in their own evil and wrathful persecuting and blasphemous spirit, against Christ and his kingdom: And this wrathful spirit of Reason, which is the *dragon*, even *that*, could not put Christ to death until his time was come:—then it was loosed by the *Angel* for that purpose, as you may see (John xix.) where Pilot said unto Jesus, "I have power to release thee, and have power to crucify thee;" Jesus answered, "Thou couldest have no power at all against me, except it were given thee from above;" *i.e.* when his time was come, by command from heaven, this *Angel loosed* the spirit of Reason, that it should go forth and put Christ to death, that the prophesies should be fulfilled, the redemption worked, and Reason complete his own *woe* in the second death.

Again, I would have you further observe, that Christ is the Angel of *Faith*, and does loose the *seals* of justice and death, and bring in light, mercy, and life to his elect; and this, cherubims and flaming sword, or internal *Angel* in justice, is the *Angel* of Reason, and *seal men down* under their own evils, and with his strong *Chain* of justice, *binds them up* in their own wrath for the *second death*; and will not be *loosed* but by permission from heaven; and even that, is to do the *will* of God, and fill up their own cups in wrath.

Therefore, when Jesus was on this earth HE uttered his holy gospel, which was his royal covenant of mercy, and priesthood of Faith; and in this HE rose the *dead*: *i.e.* HE rose Faith in the elect, which lay dead, into active life; and this *resurrection* of Faith WAS and IS to the elect, who are the *sons of the prophets*: And when the virgin of Faith is born, they are taken into the royal priesthood, to work the works of Faith, under the justice of the father, as Christ himself did; then they become brethren with Christ when he was in the state of mortality; because HE himself was of the prophets, and HIM they will *follow* in the works of Faith by divine assistance from heaven.

And also the utterance of JESUS was so powerful, that it made death and hell give up their dead also; *i.e.* the sons of Reason, and the sons of the priest, was so much offended with the doctrine of Christ, that it rose the lying, wrathful, blasphemous, and murdering spirit of Reason in them against Christ and his kingdom; but *they were bound up and sealed* under Justice, in their own wrath by this *Angel*,—and all that ever they could do, they could not stop the utterance, and works of Faith, and salvation: because the *voice* and power of Faith is far above Reason: for let them turn which way they will, it is to their own hurt and condemnation: For while the works of Faith and spirit of Christ is in public act and declaration on this earth they cannot stand before it, but will *gather together in the wilderness and make war against it; and are bound up in death, and darkness, and wrath, by this Angel* as aforesaid.

Now this *Cherubim and flaming sword, or internal Angel* in justice, was the ANGEL John saw *come down from heaven*; and the *Chain he had in his hand*, was the chain of Justice to bind Reason down, not only unto the second death, but that also, he should not go out in ACT in this life, no further than permitted. And *the bottomless pit*, is the imagination of Reason concerning the *Will* of God, *Redemption*, and *Salvation*; and other things relative to this life. Now, it is called *a bottomless pit*, because it has no foundation; and men who fall into that, must sink into the second death, which has no end:—And this *Angel* having *the key of the bottomless pit*, is, because, by command from heaven, he can *bind* Reason up in his own wrath and imagination, or *loose* him, that he may *reign and go out and deceive for a season*.

AGAIN, the *Thrones* that John saw;—and they who *sat upon them*,—and *judgment was given unto them*; it was the elect that was risen from death to life by the power of Christ, *i.e.* as Faith fell in Adam, it was disunited by death from its living father and creator; and so it go on in generation in this dead or inactive condition: And when they come to full manhood, as the Lord God of heaven created Adam to; this *Womb or seed* of Faith, is worked upon for *regeneration*, as it was in Adam.

And, when the Lord God of heaven goeth out on this womb of Faith, he raises it from *death* to *Life*, and this *new Life* that is raised from the death of Faith, is the Virgin Daughter that is *raised or born* from its Womb or Seed, by the power of God for regeneration and salvation: Then, when CHRIST had uttered his holy gospel, and worked the redemption, he ascended into his high heaven, and kingdom of the glory of mercy, and sits at the head of His royal covenant of mercy and priesthood of Faith: And those that *John saw*, was them that was thus *raised from death to life* by the power of Christ, and taken into the royal priesthood of Faith; and there *they sit on Thrones*: (Mat. xix. 28) and those *Thrones* are according as the

ANGEL of Faith has sounded; because the higher the Voice of the Angel, the *nearer* Christ in regeneration.

Moreover, on those thrones, in the priesthood of Faith, there is *Judgment* given, to know the *will of God*;—and the *power of God*;—and the *power of truth*;—and the *power of Prayer* for divine assistance ;—and the *Works of Faith*;—and the *spirit of prophesy* for salvation: And this,—is in mystical union and spiritual communion with HIM that sits in the glory of mercy, and for his mercy and salvation but it is through the justice of the Father:—For the PRIESTHOOD OF FAITH, is as *a Sea of glass mingled with fire*, which fire is the justice of the father, because through that you must go: Also in the priesthood of Faith, there is wisdom, power, and judgment given over the spirit of Reason, Nay, over the *whole world*! and can *judge* the world and all their *spiritual fornications*, neither can Reason get from this Judgement.—And,

Also, *John saw the souls of them that were beheaded for the witness of Jesus, and for the word of God, and which, had not worshipped the beast*; Now those are them that was also in the priesthood of Faith, and died under the seal of God for life eternal; for the prophets of old prophesied of Christ to come; and as so were in the priesthood of Faith, and a witness to Jesus; and they declared the *will of God*, which was his *Word*; and in all their tribulations and sufferings for this, they never would bow down to do the *will* of Reason, and as so, did not worship the beast nor his image, nor receive his mark, but would worship God in the priesthood of Faith:—then they died under the seal of God for salvation.

AGAIN, when man is in the *priesthood of Faith*, he will receive divine assistance from heaven, and work the works of Faith:—And at times the Virgin Daughter will offer the true incense; and be in spiritual communion with Christ, her royal bridegroom and King:—and have the spirit of prophecy; and prophesy that Christ will come to her in *holy marriage*:—Now during this time, the soul *lives and reigns with Christ on this earth*;—because the soul is *then* actuated by the *spirit and power of Christ*, which, *is in* regenerated Faith, and it is called a THOUSAND *years*; because a thousand years to the Lord is as a day, and a day as a thousand years:—But it is, during the *time of the power, and works of Faith, and the spirit of prophecy*.

Now, mind and observe, I write this to everyone that is *in*, or shall come into, the *priesthood of Faith*; because—this he must do in *time*, to *live and reign with Christ a thousand years.*—And I pray the Lord God of heaven to assist his elect and hasten his kingdom; therefore, you may see, Faith must be *risen* from death to life, or *born* from its womb or seed, and taken into that priesthood to work the works of Faith, to follow Jesus, and by him to be sealed for his kingdom of glory:—So the *first resurrection* of Faith is to grace; and the *second* is to glory ; and BLESSED *is him that has part in the first resurrection.*

Further,—This *thousand years* was also during the time of Christ and his apostles, for as I said, Reason was *bound up by this Angel* in justice, that it could not stand before the power of Christ; but gathered together against him; but when they were dead and the spirit of Christ was not in public declaration and ACT, then the *Angel* in justice loosed the spirit of Reason, that it might transform itself into, and go out on the letter, and rule it in their own way; and *deceive nations*, and gather kingdoms, &c.—then Reason's *dead lived*; for it is said;—"But the rest of the dead lived not until the thousand years was finished."

Now, as I said: When the seed of Reason come to manhood, they are *cast out and dead* in the sight of God:—Then when the spirit of Christ come for regeneration and salvation, Reason is incapable of that, and also is *bound* up in death and wrath; and cannot *live again* until the spirit of Christ is out of public act; then he may go out for a *season*: Thus you may see Christ is the Angel of Faith; and the Angel of Justice is the Angel of Reason;— for Christ has not to do with Reason; nor the Angel in justice to do with Faith.

Again, this thing is in act at this day; for John Reeve was as Moses in the spirit, and was sent to the bloody unbelieving world, which is to Reason: And he also came under the justice of the *Angel*; because, if Reason did not do according to his order he had power to curse them in justice: And Muggleton was given to be his mouth, and the last high priest in the given priesthood of Reason, and would set up an idol, as did Aaron.

And as Moses and the prophets was taken into the priesthood of Faith, and prophesied of Christ to come, and the *priest* was left in their own priesthood, therefore when Jesus was here, He took the prophet and his sons, but left the priest and his sons: And by the power of his declaration, the dead priest was risen in his sons, and they came forth in wrath, yet under the name of Moses, and said, "They knew God spake to Moses, but they knew not from whence Jesus was:" And, also *John Reeve* was taken into the priesthood of Faith, and prophesied of Christ to come: But *Muggleton*, the *priest*, was left in his own priesthood.

And now *CHRIST* is come, according to *Reeve's* prophecy, by this spiritual born son, who doth declare the *will* and *power* of Christ, and prophecy: Then by this, and divine assistance from heaven, Faith in the sons of the *Prophets* is risen from death to life, and taken into the royal priesthood, to follow up to the *holy marriage*: And the sons of the *Priest* are also risen, or *death and hell give up their dead* in the sons of the priest, and they come forth in darkness, lies, wrath, and blasphemy, against the *Messenger* and the elect, yet under the name of John Reeve, as the Jews did by Moses, and say, "We know God spoke to *Reeve*, but as for this fellow *Birch*, we know not that he is from God, neither do we believe."

Thus, the sons of the *priest*, and of Reason, are given up: And they come forth with lies, anger, wrath, cursing, and blasphemy, against the Messenger and the elect:—And, in or under this *death* they are *bound* by this *Angel* in justice; and from it they cannot move; for they cannot face the Messenger in Faith and Truth:—Therefore they *gather together in their wilderness against the Church of Christ*, and there are *bound*, and will not be *loosed* during the life of the Messenger, or the elect of his day.

Now, do you mind and observe, whenever you or any of the elect that are quick in Faith,—when you talk on spiritual things to one that is incapable of regeneration, they may submit to your language, because they cannot overthrow it, but they cannot *like you*, and will get from you, and speak evil of you behind your Back, for your Faith: Because they cannot *stand* before you:—And, when they speak in *wrath*, as if they would devour you for your Faith; then *death and hell give up their dead*, before your face.

And, also when any of the elect *hear the Voice of GOD* by the Messenger; this *Angel* in justice will also *bind up* Reason in the elect, so that they shall go on in *regeneration* for salvation:—Thus, you may see, when Christ come in person, or in spirit, how one is taken and the other left. Now I beg you will mind what is written, and communicate it to the whole Church; for I have written to all and every one: for in this epistle is contained *treasure both old and new*. And I pray God increase all your understandings—and Faith.

So conclude your loving brother in Christ.

London, Feb. 13, 1781.   JAMES BIRCH.

P.S. The whole Church prays the increase of Faith to all and every one. I am *glad to hear Owen is better, and hope he will be restored; also: hope you are well; as to me, I have had a dull Christmas; ended the old year, and began the new, in trouble and difficulties"* (See Let. XXXII). My love to all; pray let me hear of you soon, and that you receive this, 'till then I shall be uneasy.

LETTER XXXII

To our Brother James Cullum, a Captive.

Brother *Cullum*,—I should have wrote to you before now, but have wrote several Letters to *Pembroke*, the last was a long *Epistle*. I have seen many of your Letters, and to me they bore a bad aspect; for instead of your *asking* relief, you *reprimanded* because relief was not sent: and in all, have *Insinuated* threats of *Emulated resentment*; for it is well known, you cannot stop the *current* of Justice, Poverty, Distress and Death, nor *run from it*: Neither can you *drive* Reason out of his kingdom:—Therefore it is your best wisdom to bear your *Trouble* with *Patience*, as I have done, and pray to do; for neither you nor me, can tell on what *Rock or Quicksand* we shall on a sudden be *cast, in the Current* of this Life.

Now, before I saw you last, I knew *Trouble* was coming to me; *Nay, I lost my Eldest Daughter in a Dream;* who a little before Christmas, in the midst of her play, was on a sudden struck with Convulsions, and was in them four hours before she came out, yet had all the assistance we could get; then she was about again for fourteen days, and we thought all was well, but the disorder returned with a violent Head-ach, which took her out of this Life in about sixteen days, and I buried her (Jan. 16), which has caused me great trouble and *Difficulties*; for the Church was so *poor* as not to be able to assist: BUT however, it is not for the elect to be *drowned* in the trouble of this Life, but must *steer forward,* for the kingdom of CHRIST.

Also, I know your *Trouble*, for I have been in it, and would help you if I could:—But talk no more of the waving of controversies, nor to construe the Church from Colnbrook House to this day; for if any has done you *wrong*, forgive, and pray their *better* understanding, as I do.

Now as your *plaintiff* has declared—do you lay under it, till the *Act* comes out, but I cannot tell when that will be, for I do not hear the *Judges* have done any thing in *Parliament* to forward it: but if your *Plaintiff* send your *Discharge* before the *Act* is likely to come out, we will endeavour to raise your Fees, that you may come out: and if this should come to pass, you must *send up a Petition*, setting forth your *Case*, and signed by *Mr. Reynolds*; and during the time you are *there*, I hope you will *spend well*; for a kingly *Emulated* spirit will seek to have his *own will*; and in that, it works its own way into *death*.

Neither must I encourage such a spirit in anyone; but in all HUMILIATION, that you may *forgive and overcome* by bearing your sufferings with *patience*, and being in reconciliation and friendship with all; then, you may bring your *Gift to the Altar*, and it will be *taken*, which is the prayer of your loving brother,

London, Feb. 27, 1781.   JAMES BIRCH.

LETTER XXXIII

To our beloved Brethren, Owen and Alice Bevan and to the whole Church in Pembroke, J. Birch and Brethren, send Greeting.

Beloved Brethren—I have written according to my promise, and your desire; also I have heard of *Owen's* illness, and of yours, by *Jos. Cole's* last Letter, which things I know are attended with trouble; and it is the consequence of the *Fall*, that bring those things on man: For when Faith hearkened to Reason it broke its own law, then the justice of the father took place, and it became of an infinite consequence; for it caused the Lord God of heaven to pay dear for creating *man* his own son, which was after his own likeness: And *man* may expect also to pay dear for the *Fall*; for in all the goings out in things for this world, even in generation and joy of children, and of families, it all will end in death under justice; for as time according to justice, will bring in Sorrow, Mourning, and Death, to *swallow up life*; even so Eternity will be brought in to swallow up *Time*. Neither can any man stop the *current* of justice, sorrow, mourning, and death; for it will surely come, now justice has took place through the *fall*, and BLESSED are them whose *Sorrow and Mourning* end in this life.

Again, after the *fall*, the Lord God said unto the woman, "He would greatly multiply her sorrow"—and unto the man he said "Cursed is the ground for thy sake, *Thorns* and also *Thistles* shall it bring forth to thee, and unto the *dust he should return*," which is *trouble and sorrow* that come to man in this life; like as the *waves rise in the sea*, by the power of a mighty wind; and after all he must die and turn to *dust*:— And as the woman is bone of his bone, and flesh of his flesh, their *troubles* are as closely united; thus you see the troubles that attend a body of flesh in the *passage* of this life.

Moreover, men, in the dark Light of this life, will seek their *own will*, i.e. honour among men, and to shine in the vanity of this life, and *act* as if the world was created for them to do as they pleased, in or with: But it will soon be made known to them, that the world, and they also, are at the will and disposal of God!

And now the *first resurrection* is in act, and warning given, that the KING OF GLORY is at hand, to make all *new* to his elect by regeneration; therefore the elect must leave their *old habitations*, and come forward in the priesthood of Faith, to seek the New Jerusalem: And although an Elect, and one of Reason, may be joined in marriage, and bring forth children in generation according to the ordination of God; yet, when Christ come in person or spirit, he will gather his kingdom *out*, from the busy incumbrance of this world; and the self willed or desired duty of Reason: indeed, Reason may exclaim and complain, because he cannot have his will; but he has no more to do, than to seek one who has the will and power to judge and execute, according to the desire and will of Reason.

For the great *Ties* of nature in the union of families, and the *possessions* of this life, or desire to possess, must all be *left* to follow Christ; otherwise he cannot be the disciple of Christ, (see Luke xiv. 26.) therefore let men couch themselves under what cover they please—CHRIST, the KING of Faith, in the power of the Father, created heaven and earth, and all that is in them; and also he became a SON to that *Power* of the father and redeemed His elect, and brought in his own *new kingdom* and priesthood. which is of mercy; and has *invited* man to come in, therefore he will be obeyed.

But if *man* keep back, because his excuse is, that he has a great duty to do towards God and his neighbour, in those things as aforesaid; which is the *incumbrance* of this life, he must die as he was born, without being regenerated: Yet these men fall the shortest of that duty; for them that enter the royal priesthood, and work the works of Faith, power is *given* them to exceed the others in the duty of this life, for if you do the *great*, the less will follow of consequence, according as Christ promised. (Mat. vi. 33.) "But seek ye first the kingdom of God and his righteousness, and all those things shall be added unto you."

AGAIN, the priesthood of Faith is a life out of death, or the first resurrection, and it makes things new to the soul, that he will become a new man, and enter into regeneration, which is the House or *Family of* Christ; and there to enjoy heavenly *Light* or communion: And by this *Light and life in regeneration* will know the power of justice, death, and darkness, and the *follies* of this life: and also that the *emulated* desires, *anxious* cares, and *laborious* efforts, to gain this world, or rather his *will* in the world, is all LABOUR *in vain*, for it all must end in death under justice! Therefore now the *Warning* is given, and the *invitation* come. Let the soul flee from this, into the royal priesthood or *Vinyard* of Faith, where he will receive the WAGES of a Crown of everlasting glory! But if he abide in the incumbrance of the world, he will be lost in and with the world, let him think what he will to the contrary.

Further, as the elect *see* the power of death and darkness, they find themselves in the *midst* of it; therefore the Virgin Daughter is very *earnest* by prayer for divine assistance from heaven, to work through the powers of Reason, Death, and Darkness, to get as near Christ in spirit as possible; and this will so purify the mind of man, that the *fruits* of Faith and Love will be *seen*; for the fruits of Faith will not be stopped by the business of this life, nor drowned in sorrow and care: Now the spirit in this is very sharp, for it expressly says, "He that is unjust and filthy, let him be so still; and he that is righteous and holy let him be so still: Behold I come quickly, and my reward is with me, to give every one according as his work shall be."

Therefore, my desire and prayer is, that you and the whole church may *stedfastly Watch* and *patiently wait* His coming; for he will SURELY COME, at a time you know not of; and *Blessed* are them that have worked for, and watched His coming, and as so, are able to stand before him.

And also, *watch* the tempter, for he will come at a time you know not of—he will be with you in *Emulated Joy*, and oft'times in *Sorrow*; and in the *goings out* in the *Acts* in, and for this life; and promise you life and salvation if you hearken to him; and tell you, you may, and it is but right you should; and when ever you do, justice take place, and you will go into mourning and death!

For know this, "If the good man of the house had known in what watch the thief would come, he would have watched, and not suffered his house to be broken up." Now this is a charge given to the elect; for in the mighty works of Faith, to wade through the power of sin, death, and darkness, the *tempter* is at hand, to break up your *house* of peace with Christ.

Therefore WATCH and PRAY to make *ready*, now the warning is given—as if you were to leave your old country and habitation for to go a far journey, for a new and better country, never to return again, and know not when the *sudden Call* will come! And it is even so with the kingdom and *coming of* CHRIST! Now mind what is written, and GOD assist you in the *Works* of Faith; which is the prayer of your loving brother in Christ,

JAS. BIRCH.

London, March 13, 1781.

P.S. The whole church prays your increase of Faith.—Not hearing James had my epistle I am uneasy.

LETTER XXXIV

To our beloved Sister Mary Runwa, and to the whole Church beloved in Christ, in and about Pembroke, James Birch and the Brethren send greeting.

BELOVED SISTER—This comes with my spiritual love to you, and the whole church, hoping you increase in Faith, and patiently wait and watch the coming of our Lord Christ the king of Faith, both in spirit and person, then you will be strongly united, and the church will *flourish* in the spirit and power of Faith, which is my earnest desire; because for this I *Labour*, that you may enter into this LABOUR, and *gather fruits unto life eternal.*

Now, in the priesthood of Faith, *All enter into each others Labour,* for CHRIST entered into the *Labours* and Prophecies of the Elect of old, in the royal priesthood of Faith, and worked the Works of redemption: And all the elect must enter on HIS LABOUR, to *reap* the benefit thereof and work the works of Faith, according to their Portion given: And the present Messenger came out from Christ, and has and doth declare HIS WILL and WORD, in His spirit and power; that the elect may enter on his *Labour* (because He directs his voice to the womb of Faith in the elect); Then by this and divine assistance from heaven, Faith is rose from death to a new Life, and taken into the royal priesthood to *work and gather the fruits of* Faith: And also, the Messenger *Labours* to instruct and *lead them through the wilderness,* up to the spirit of prophesy, and holy *Marriage* with Christ, then they *gather* from what the Messenger SOWETH, and this cause a strong Union in the priesthood of Faith, wherein is the church of Christ.

Therefore JESUS said (John iv. 36) "And he that reapeth receiveth wages; and gathereth fruit unto life eternal, that both he that soweth, and he that reapeth, may rejoice together," because, in the united House of Faith in regeneration, which is the House of Christ, there is Faith in Faith, and Faith on Faith, and Faith united with Faith, and all center to Christ, the king of Faith.

Again, the Lord God of Glory created Heaven and Earth, the Sea, and all that is in them, and SWARE by the mighty power of his Creation, and its consequence, HE would become a SON to that power, and redeem HIS Elect. And when he was here, in a body of flesh to redeem, and SPEAK concerning the great *Watch* the elect must keep, to go through the mighty power of justice (which Faith fell under), and the *power* and *temptation* of Reason (which is done by the works and power of Faith; and of the *Crowns* of glory he would give the elect, in his glorious kingdom of mercy: And also of the *Judgments* that would come to Reason. Mat. xxiv. 35). He said, "Heaven and Earth shall pass away, but my word shall not pass away," *i.e.* this present *Heaven and Earth will pass away* to the elect, for they to go through the power of justice, to the *new* Heaven and Earth *prepared* by CHRIST the King of Faith; and further, even the glorious Heaven of the *Justice of the father*, which is justice to Faith (that Moses and Elias now sit in), that *Power and Glory* also will pass away; for at the end of *Time* they will be translated to the Heaven of MERCY, which is to the kingdom and glory of Christ: Therefore, all Rule and Power in *Heaven and Earth* will pass away, but the Word and Power, and kingdom of Christ, will for ever STAND.

MOREOVER; All the beauties of this Creation, Life, and delights, which is Reason's heaven, will also *pass away*, and be no more found, and Reason must go into the *second death*; for when the king of Faith redeemed the elect, he brought in eternity: And power is given the Angel in justice to take Reason into the second death, for *Strong* is the Lord God of Heaven, who has Power over all Power: Therefore there is no other refuge for men to fly to, but the Priesthood and Kingdom of Christ. And now, the *Gate is open*, BLESSED are them that enter the field or *Vinyard* of Faith, for there they will gather fruit unto life eternal.

AGAIN; if man look into himself, what will he see of himself? He was born into this world with entire *fallen* nature, and full of *filth*, to bring in corruption and death: and, it is by the blessed mercy of God that he enjoy one thing on this earth above a *perishing condition*: And in all his business, to gather in natural food, yet, he shall not live by that *alone*, except he die! And among the delights of *fine apparel*, to appear to, and before men! I would to God the WHITE ROBES, which is the *righteousness* of Faith; was sought after to appear before the LORD GOD of heaven: And further, in all the temporal blessings from heaven, it is given under the power of Justice and Death, therefore it is good for men to mind how they act, for what is given can be taken; for when the Jews said to Jesus, " Our fathers did eat manna in the desart;" as it is written, he gave them bread from heaven to eat: Jesus said, "Your fathers did eat manna in the wilderness, and are dead." The meaning is, a man may enjoy all natural blessings from heaven, and die under the seal of the angel in justice.

Again (John vi.) Jesus said, "I am the living bread which came down from heaven, if any man eat of this bread, he shall live for ever;" and this bread is his *flesh to eat* and his *blood to drink*, which is this; when he was here in a body of flesh to *redeem*; he waded through the powers of Reason, sin, death, hell, and justice, and OVERCOME;

which is a *sore* journey, and also lost Himself in death, in His own blood, under the justice of the father, and *overcome* that, to gain his glorious Kingdom of Mercy: Therefore, when Faith is born of its womb, or seed, it is taken into its own covenant and priesthood, and soon made sensible of its own condition, and Christ being the true object of Faith and salvation, it must *follow him* through the powers of Reason, Death, Hell, and Justice: For as Christ went through those powers in a Body of *Flesh and Blood,* you also must *follow* in a body of flesh and blood, then you will eat HIS Flesh; And as he Lost himself in death, in his own blood, under the justice of the father for his own kingdom of mercy, you also must do the same, then you will drink HIS blood; and this is eating his flesh, and drinking his blood; or drinking of the cup that he himself drank of and to be baptized with the baptism that he was baptized with. Now if any man desire to be saved, he must follow the works of redemption to salvation, which is done by Patience and Prayer and divine assistance from heaven: And this *great work* of Faith, which is done by divine assistance from heaven, and in *Mystical union and Spiritual communion* with Christ the king of Faith and Salvation, is the true bread and drink that Christ gave from heaven, that *whosoever eateth and drinketh shall never* DIE, but will be passed from death to life by regeneration. Therefore fear not the *Powers* of Reason, Death, and Hell, for CHRIST is at hand to assist in the works of Faith, and your labour will be crowned with the glory of his mercy.

Beloved Sister, I received your letter, and by that see you have heard from Miss Williams; she has wrote no more than I expected, for when I was with her, and she read your letter, when I said I was the man, I saw the dead rise, and the spirit came forth in trembling and great agitation. She said, "How came this? I had great satisfaction with Reeve and Muggleton." But the spirit cried out, I have no business with thee, how camest thou here to torment me before my time; she also said, "She understood Reeve to be the last," I said he was, to many. But I said no one need say more, to declare themselves of the bloody unbelieving world, than to say Reeve is the last; and I would freely give her the letter of the scripture, and of Reeve and Muggleton, and the whole world beside, if that would do; but I also told her, if she would have salvation, she must come into re-generation, and that must be done in union with me, and said much more, but left her troubled in spirit. Now if this evil spirit is cast out shall be glad, but I am sadly afraid it never will.

Again, she says to you from Reeve and Muggleton's letter. "Man is born with two seeds,"—now this is to the whole world, so what is that for salvation: But this I say, if no seed in him is capable of regeneration, he must die as he was born, which is under justice, and as to working out, or for salvation, that Reason cannot bear, because they cannot enter on that work, but would fain die as a cherubim; for a child never enters the priesthoodand works of Faith; but at manhood the angel take place in the soul, then no one can die a cherubim for glory; and if Christ did no work to redeem, no man need work to follow him; But them that Christ *worked* for, they also must *work* to follow him. And as to Reeve's letter being in force at this time, it is so, where he prophesies of Christ to come; and Christ is come, according to his prophecy; but men must enter the priesthood of Faith to know and enjoy that: And the *Woes* that are pronounced to be executed under the power of the angel in justice, that is not to the elect, but to Reason, who turn back from the living Messenger, and them that are in the letter, and WILL not be born into the priesthood of Faith; therefore this belong to herself. And as to be carried away by *new opinions*, this she would have said in the days of Christ, had she then lived; and as to *going back* how can that be, when they go *forward* to higher knowledge and greater wisdom. But how comes it to pass, when she was offered the *spirit* of Reeve's writing and regeneration, redemption, and salvation; for she to refuse this, and turn *back* to the bare letter, to live in her filth, so herself is the backslider.

Thus Reason is his own witness to his own condemnation, and will take pains to shew himself a fool, and that he is bound up in darkness, under the power of the second death; Therefore, my dear, her love and tenderness for you is *temptation*, though she knows it not, and it is my will you do not send her a copy of that letter, but I will give her *Space* to repent, if repentance can be found; for you have answered her well, and if she writes again *watch your tempter*, and answer according, for you must leave all for the kingdom of Christ, and observe, she also knows where to write to me.

AGAIN, as you would know concerning the *Thrones and Judgment that was given* to them, see Let. XXVI, concerning the Voice of the *seven Angels*, how, when the *First* Angel sounds it gives birth to the virgin of Faith; then to this *new Life* Judgment is given to know the power of God, and to see light from darkness, and know what condition you have been in, and this is a spiritual *Throne* that you are sat upon, and the *first* Throne in regeneration, and when the *second* Angel sounds, the promise of Christ comes from heaven; now this is a *Throne* higher up, and so on till the *seventh* Angel sound. For these Thrones are in the priesthood of Faith, and on them is given wisdom to know the *Will* of God, the *Power* of God, and *works* of Faith. Also, there is judgment given to know what Reason is, and what it will do, and what will become of it: Now by this, and the letter I sent before, you may see what those Thrones are, and be you all stedfast and patient, for some may *Leave* and *lose* them, that once was *near and dear* to them, as I have done; for now the call is come, the kingdom of Faith will be *divided* from the kingdom of Reason; and BLESSED are them who *separate* to the kingdom of Faith.

So conclude your loving brother in Christ, with prayer for you all.

London, April 28, 1781   JAMES BIRCH.

LETTER XXXV

TO MRS. BIRCH

My dear—With love I inform you and the church I received brother Collet's letter, and am glad that you and the child are well. Lewis is recovered, and the whole church well. —I pray God continue all your health and welfare in spirit, then you'll *overcome the world.*

As to this church at Pembroke, there is such an increase of Faith, that to me there is a miracle worked in them in regeneration. There is a man of eighty-one years of age, who has seen me these three times I have been here (his daughter is a true believer), he said to me, "The Lord have mercy on me, and if I am His, I know he will, and I pray God give me a heart to be obedient to His *Will*, and beg for his mercy:" He was always civil to me—but this is the first expression of this kind I ever heard from him.

Mr. *Parry* has stood as a pillar of brass, at *Portclew*, that he will not follow the law, and I being with him, and set forth the evil that attended it, the old Squire said "John, if this be the case, I do not desire it, for I would not myself."

Mr. Parry goes from here on Tuesday morning next, his time being up; I must stay some time longer, then go to him and Mrs. Jones, both at Caermarthen.

The church at Pembroke greet the church in London, in all that can be expressed in *true Faith*, the LOVE of CHRIST, in *eating his flesh, and drinking his blood* to regeneration and salvation, which I pray God you may *increase* in. Your loving brother in Christ,

Cary, July 13, 1781. JAMES BIRCH.

My love to all and every one.

LETTER XXXVI

TO MR. JOHN B. PARRY.

Sir—I received your letter, and as you desire to know something of the SCRIPTURE, I will inform you, as far as the letter will admit.—Now the Scripture contains the will, wisdom, works, and power of GOD; and the wilds, snares, transformations, and temptations of the devil: And it was wrote by *inspiration from Heaven*: And a man must be inspired with as great wisdom from heaven as him that wrote it to know it; and to know its true intent and meaning: And to bring forth *Treasures, old and new*, his inspiration must be *higher up*; for the Wisdom of God unto salvation, is like a beautiful piece of building, that is to be built from Earth to Heaven, and him that comes *immediately* from God, to declare His Royal WILL doth continue the building, and happy is the soul that is taught by him (so inspired), for the building is *nearly accomplished*.

Now observe—In the beginning God created heaven and earth, and all things that is in them to shew to Man and angel he was God, and further the *Angelic* Creation, is one branch of God's power, and the creation of *Man* another; and also those angels are *spiritual* Bodies, and souls *rational*, which is Reason, and that is from chaos; and they was created under a law, which is to love God above all, and your neighbour as yourself. Again, there were two orders created, the *Seraphim*, and *Cherubim*, the Seraphims are the mighty host of angels in heaven above, and are *Elected* to stand in their created purity, to and in eternity: As to the Cherubim there was but one created, and he was appointed to fall from heaven to this earth, and go into generation.

And the man Adam was formed of this earth, and GOD breathed into him the *breath of life*, this breath of Life was the divine nature of God: THUS Adam was created, and came forth in full manhood, with *human nature* animated with divine Faith, which is the nature of God; and was the son of God by and in creation; and for this great *Union* with God and Man, came forth this plural word, Let US *make Man, in OUR own Image, and after OUR likeness* ; because man was created the express *Image of GOD*, and with a life of God's own nature, then of consequence after *His likeness*; But Man was Created under a Law, which was *not to eat of the tree of knowledge of good and evil, i.e.* not to hearken to, nor be concerned with any one that should come to *tempt* him to any other knowledge than what he possessed.

Moreover, this Cherubim being left to his created strength, his dark nature sprang forth in emulated Pride to *censure* the works of God, and condemn his fellow creature; then he broke the law he was created under, and this caused *Angelic Justice* to take place, which was a mighty branch or Attribute of God's Creation; and became of an infinite consequence; thus the *Cherubim* became the very *Devil*, and fell from heaven to this earth; after this he bore the name of Serpent, Dragon, Devil, &c.

Again, this serpent was in the form of man, but his life and nature was of death and darkness; but Adam's Life and Nature was of Light and Life, which was of God; and this serpent came and tempted Eve to evil, and he was lost in the act, by being dissolved into generation, or transmuted into flesh: *Now* thus generation began, for the Woman had taken the serpent into her womb, and she was filled with his lustful nature, by which she tempted Adam to the act; then the law of Faith was broke, for they had ate of the *Tree of knowledge of good and evil*, and hearkened to the voice of the tempter, which was the devil:— THUS fell Faith, under the power of Death, and the troublesome spirit of Reason the Devil, and God became the God of Justice through the acts of man and angel, which became of an infinite consequence, both to God and man, and on these acts began and continue the whole *Scripture*.

AGAIN, God, by his divine wisdom, well knew he could gather, and recover his own nature, (that he created in Adam) in or from a fallen state, let it be ever so surrounded with death, hell, and devil, and transmute himself into it, and take his own nature, and no more: And further, God was incapable of taking Reason on him, for if he had then Light and Life, Death and Darkness, God and Devil, Heaven and Hell, would have been one thing, and God would have lost himself in his own works, by their being swallowed up in confusion; this is as the world would have it, but they have no more to do than make it so.

Moreover, see Gen. iii. 15. God said to the Serpent, "I will put enmity between thee and the woman, between thy seed and her seed: It shall bruise thy head, and thou shalt bruise his heel;" *i.e.* God would take the woman's seed (which was his own created nature of Adam) on Himself, and redeem that. His *own* generation, and on this go the attribute of his infinite mercy; and the *seed of the serpent*, would be suffered to *persecute* the woman's seed, but must go their way according to infinite justice; and on those two generations or kingdoms go forth the *two attributes* of God, which is Mercy and Justice.

Also, verse 14, "the serpent was cursed *above all cattle, and above every beast in the field;*" now this whole creation was cursed with *death*, through the *Fall* of Man, but the serpent was cursed above that, which was with the *second death*: After this (you may see) Cain was born, who was the first born son of the devil; or the very devil become flesh; and when he grew to manhood, Cherubical Justice took place in his soul called the *cherubims and flaming sword*, that would keep him (and all his posterity that grow to manhood) from the *tree of Life*: And Abel, the son of Adam, or the son in Faith was born, and grew to manhood, and both made their *offerings*, Abel's was accepted, and Cain's was not; then he was wrath, and slew Abel, who was his brother, according to flesh, but not in the spirit; then Cain was arraigned before this Cherubical Justice in his own soul, whom he called Lord, and said, *his punishment was greater than he could bear*; then he was loosed to go into his own wild way, where he could form his own *Hope* and worship, and this *hope* of Reason is the great river

Euphrates, in the land of Nod, that runs in the soul of man to this day; and in all his sons that grow to manhood, doth justice take place in the *soul*, and away they go, with their *own witness*, to their *own condemnation*, this and their *taking* Heaven by Violence, is the *mark* set, which is the outcast condition.

Again, you see *Seth* was born as *another seed, instead of Abel, whom Cain slew*; then you see the genealogy of Adam from that of Cain, and also how God communed with Adam; as *first*, concerning the Fall, and his justice, which took place through the Fall; also the wilds and temptations of the devil, and the consequence of his acts, now he was become flesh: After that, he rose Faith (that was dead in Adam through the Fall), into a new Life. This new Life is for regeneration, by which they communed with God for Salvation, and prophesied God would become a Son, and Redeem, which WAS and IS Christ, and so on with Enoch, Noah, Abraham, Isaac, and Jacob, and continue to this day.

Moreover, Moses (the man of God) was inspired by God himself, under the Attribute of His cherubical justice, with the wisdom of that pure law, the cherubim was created under, (before his fall) and the justice of that Law when it took place after the Fall; and he gave it forth to Reason, because it was Cherubical, and this was that great natural kingdom and blessing given to Israel, that was of Abraham by natural generation; for had they observed, and obeyed Moses, they would have been Law-givers to the whole world, and the most flourishing people: for when the law was broke, there was a priesthood given, whereby they might atone to stay God's justice; and although this Law was given to Israel, yet the whole world must have it, and greatly to their condemnation: But Israel would go back to their own *wild way*, and construct Moses as they pleased;—and false prophets, and priest arose, and harboured in the Letter in the time of the law, which brought such calamities, and judgments on them.

And although Moses and the prophets was inspired with the Cherubical or Angelic Inspiration, and gave forth and maintained the law of Reason, and its priesthood, yet God rose Faith that was dead in them, to live and enjoy communion with God in mercy, for salvation; and wrote and prophesied of Christ to come, and at death was translated from the covenant of justice, to the covenant of mercy; but Reason was left behind.

Now *thus* stand the *two* Covenants; Moses has Reason to work upon (which is of the devil), and the devil in the soul of man, to keep it under justice in death: And Jesus has Faith (which is of God) to work upon in the soul of man, to raise it from death to life, and redeem and regenerate it, and bring it to his kingdom of mercy and glory: But the thing IS, who Jesus was? to which I say, he was the Lord God that created heaven and earth, and all that is in them: He was the Lord that said unto my Lord, "Sit thou on my right band, until I make thine enemies thy foot stool", Psal. cx. 1, Mark xii. 36; and Enoch, Moses, and Elias being translated into heaven, Moses and Elias *Sit* in the throne of the father which is of justice.

Thus God left his throne of justice, and transmuted himself into the womb of a virgin, and took his own created nature of Adam, and became a Son to his own power, which is of the Father, for as God created Faith of his divine nature, he was Father to created Faith, which broke its own law, then the justice of the father took place, and became of an infinite consequence; and Christ was a true Son to the power of the Father, in all obedience, for He kept the law of Faith, and overcome the devil, death, and hell; for he lost, himself in his own blood, in death, under that justice, and rose again, and as so went through that justice, and gained to himself his royal kingdom of divine mercy, and all the while *Man* sat as GOD, and in communion with CHRIST by the spirit of Faith: Now, here is your 9th Qu. answered concerning the plural expression, let *us* make man in *our* Image, &c.

Further, to inform you, (in this thing strange unto the world!) of Moses and Elias *sitting as God*: See Luke i. 17, where John the Baptist *went before Christ*, in the spirit and power of Elias; because Elias from heaven inspired him: Also, (Mat. xi. 13, 14) Christ speak of John the Baptist, saying "this is the Elias which was to come," because Elias inspired him.

Also, (Mat. xvii. 5) when Christ was transfigured on the mount, where the voice came from Moses and Elias, "This is my beloved Son;" here Moses and Elias called Christ their *son*, and was *well pleased*: Again, (Mat. xxvii. and Mark xv.) when Christ was crucified, He cried, "*My God*, why hast thou forsaken me?" and some that stood by understood the language he did speak, and said he cried for Elias; hence it is clear, by the letter of the scripture, that Moses and Elias *sat as God*: however, if there is any Father in person distinct from Jesus, that had coequal power in creation with Jesus, and did create in union with Jesus, and did not become a *Son* here in flesh, to his own Power as was Jesus, the Elect World is unredeemed, and the gospel of no use, though many will take great pains, to declare (before God and his Messenger) they are unredeemed.—Now, here you may see your 10th Qu. answered, that when Christ prayed, it was to Moses and Elias, who sat on the throne of the Father, because he became a true SON to that power.

And why he told his disciples to pray unto the Father, was, because all the elect must go through the power of the Father, (which is justice) to the kingdom of mercy, as Christ did; as well now, as then: And why he said to Philip, "when he saw him, he saw the Father," was because he was the Author, Creator, and Father to Faith.

QU. 5.—The *meaning* of election I have before told you, and it came through the cherubims' fall, and working his way into flesh; and justice to Reason took place, and is of an infinite consequence; and God in his transmutation could not take on him the nature of Reason, which is the devil, then of consequence not its law, nor the justice of that law: so when that nature come to manhood its own justice take place, through the wisdom, power, and glory of God in his creation. See Mat. xii. 34, Jesus call the Pharisees, "O generation of vipers, how can ye (being evil) speak good things," 45, he call them "a wicked generation :" Also Mat. xiii. his disciples asked why he spoke in parables, he said, "To you it is given to understand the mysteries of the kingdom of heaven, but to them it was not," and he said, it was because they *should not see, hear, nor understand, nor be healed.*

See John's Gosp. chap. viii. where the Jews said, "Abraham is our father," and also said, "we have one father, even God": v. 44, Jesus said, "ye are of your father the devil, and the lust of your father ye will do, he was a murderer from the beginning:" now this was Cain.

Also see 1. Ep. John iii. 12, "Not as Cain, who was of that wicked one, and slew his brother": Here you may see Cain was of the devil; Can you think Christ redeemed those? Again—Mat. xxiii. Where Jesus denounced *Woes* against the Pharisees and that *generation*, that upon them may come, "All the righteous blood, shed from Abel to Zecharias." Now as Christ said, this was to come on them, who could redeem them from it?

Also see Mat. xxv. when Christ come to judgment, "he will set the sheep on his right hand, but the goats on the left; and those shall go their way into everlasting punishment, but the righteous into life eternal;—depart from me, ye cursed into everlasting fire, prepare, for the devil and his angels." Now if Christ died to redeem all, as most men will have it, then why do he declare this? Do they not call his record a lie, and him a liar? If so, then of consequence no Redeemer.

Qu. 6, Is to comprehend the justice of God, and hold election. I say you cannot, comprehend the justice of God, without *Election*, because it is infinite, and cannot he destroyed; for Justice and Mercy are the *two Attributes* of God, and if one is destroyed, the other must also, then things must go into oblivion, or God lost in his works: And if Christ died for all, he did not die to redeem all: HE died to redeem his elect! and bring in eternity! and gained the resurrection for them; and for the child and ideot into glory, and cherubical justice must go into eternity, which is the *second* Death, and as so he died for *all*: But how can any one think that a private *passing* word of Paul and Peter, which mean the elect, should overthrow the declaration of our MASTER, and themselves also? For Paul and Peter prophesy of great judgments to come, on some that *profess* the name of Jesus: and no Apostle speak greater of election than Paul; See Rom. ix.—But there is too many evil spirits *Lodge* in the Letter of the scripture to *cover* their evil; and render the letter according to their own spirits, and hold it forth as doctrine; so their own *evil Spirit and Superstition* is their Scripture.

Qu. 7. The *three* that bear record in *Heaven*, is the FATHER who created all things, he was father to created Faith, he gave his royal *Word* to his elect that he would become a *Son* to his own power, and redeem them, which HE did, and ascended into heaven again, then there he was according to his *Word*, and the Holy Ghost is his holy merciful *Spirit*, which doth assist his elect in the works of Faith, and seal and sanctify for his kingdom of glory, and has the power of resurrection: And the glory of the Holy Ghost, he gained by the works of redemption; and all this power is in one *Person*, who is the eternal God; this is witnessed in heaven by *Enoch, Moses,* and *Elias*; And on *Earth*, Christ came by *Water*, which was on the prophesies of the elect, when he sat in the, glory of the father, and was baptized of John, then this water was turned into *Blood*, when he went forth to work the redemption, and lost himself in death in his own blood, and the *Spirit* quickened again, into a new life and power of mercy: Now when Faith in the elect is rose from death to life, and taken into the royal priesthood, this is *recorded* in the elect, because Christ went that way, and they must follow, and the spirit beareth *Witness*, but this *Record* is only in, and to the Priesthood of Faith.

Qu. 3. Why did Christ order the gospel to be preached to every creature? Answer. Because the world should know it, and might *follow*, if they pleased, and this was according to his word—Matt. xx. 16. "For many be called, but few chosen."

Qu. 4. From Paul, I have answered in your 6th. I told you it mean the elect, but at that time many came, who did not behave to Paul (and others) likeing, and the spirit had no Joy for any one who owned the name of Jesus, and brought forth no *fruits of repentance*, but left, to die a sinner.

Qu. 2d, from Romans: Concerning diversity of gifts (on the outward word or bare letter) is of little use; indeed they may spread abroad the name and word, but oft'times they preach too much, judge and prophecy wrong, and if right, it is but cherubical, and nothing for salvation:—But in the priesthood of Faith there is the Gift of the *holy spirit* to remove mountains, and prophecy of your own salvation, that is great; Now this IS, the gifts for you to seek after: And as for Institution of Bishops, &c. in Paul's time, to preach the outward given word, church discipline, &c. it was nothing without Christ took the man into his priesthood, but you read Jude, and 2 Pet. chap. ii. and see what they say of their doctrine: They may, in imitation of Paul, choose and instruct as many Timothys to choose others, as they please, for what I care, but he is the MAN whom God INSPIRES, that God *sends*, and will *own*.

As to your first *Query*, look and see how many Preachers. Teachers, and Rulers that was in the letter of Moses, and the prophets;—who read, and *owned* their prophesies, that Christ was to come? And when he did come, did they know him? Or did he own them to be sen: of God? And how did they use him? They said "they believed Moses:" Jesus said, John v. 46.—"(For) had you believed Moses, he would have believed me, for he wrote of me:" Yet they were in their opinion according to the ordination of Moses; but ask *Yourself*, whether they were true teachers from God.

Again—Of the *Literal Gospel Teachers*, See Matt. xxiv. 5. "Many shall come in my name," saying "*I am Christ*, and shall deceive many."

Ver. 24. "There shall arise *false* Christs and *false* prophets, shewing signs and wonders, and if it were possible, deceive the very elect:" And now many preachers hold forth and say "Lo, here is Christ," and "Lo there is Christ," and by the information I have given, you may find the *true* CHRIST.

Qu. 8. Those "Kings and Priest unto God and his Father", are them who have worked the works of Faith, in the royal priesthood under the justice of the Father, and heard the *sixth Angel sound*: But the thing IS, for you to *seek* to enter that Priesthood—then you will understand what I have written of the *Throne of God*; for now you have been told the will and power of God, by his Messenger, mind and observe it, lest you are *beaten with many stripes*; for I would have you submit to the will and power of God, in all obedience, meekness, mercy, and charity. *Watch* the temptations of the devil, and fly from him, for he will keep you from God if possible, and in prayer and patience wait the call to mercy: Now Reason the devil may dislike and despise what I have written, but they cannot get from it, because it stands before God as his royal will, and I hope you will be found in the number of God's elect, it being the desire of your friend in what I can.

JAMES BIRCH.

London, August 7, 1781.

P.S. You may write again.

LETTER XXXVII

The Messenger to Brother Cullum, in Captivity.

Brother Cullum,—I received your letter, and I am glad to see such a *Motion or Passion* in your Soul, to write as you now have; and shall be very glad to see it come into real and true act: And you may be assured I forgive all and every thing that you have done against me; and humbly hope you will be assisted to go through the power of Justice; because I shall be very joyful for you to be *numbered* among the Elect.

This you may believe, there is no *Joy* in the covenant of Mercy for any one who profess this declaration, and bring forth no *fruits of repentance*, but left, to die *a Sinner*.

I know your spiritual *Captivity, and pity you* and will do all I can to *assist*, because it WAS and IS my real and true meaning; but if you hearken to the tempter and go into the *Desart*, and there worship the devil, you and all men must take the consequence; for him or them who seek to have their *own will* and do their own *Way* (even to pass through this life) worship the *Spirit* of Reason, and he their God and guide; let *them* think and say what they will to the contrary; I can promise them work enough to help themselves.

For;—It is well known to me Justice cannot be broken, nor Moses fail: And can any one think that a MESSENGER can be tempted or drove, to hearken to, or be a servant to wild Reason? Why, NO; for he must WORSHIP GOD.

And further I say to *Reason*, in the midst of his self-cunning and conceited power, and in all his conduct and business of life; IF he can procure himself to live for ever, and this world to last for ever as his habitation, he may in some degree escape the present declaration; but if death take him, then he is swallowed up with his own witness to his own condemnation, as is now declared.

Again, there is the law of Moses,—let him read and observe that; also, there is the *internal* Moses; let the soul commune with him, that when he break the law, there is the priesthood opened (that he may *offer* himself up to justice, and that will atone to stay justice; and also pray to be preserved from that, and all other acts of evil; then let him go and *agree* with his brother whom he has offended, then Reason will flourish in his kingdom.

And, also let *Reason* watch evil, and mind he do not commune with his *own* spirit, which is the devil, instead of Moses, for *that* will transform itself to the name of Moses, and lead people into the *Desart*, and there to have power to do as they please, and excuse themselves: for mind, I am not afraid of a man being tempted *from* Jesus, who never was *with* Jesus; but, he may be tempted from Moses and worried to *death*, and Lost *howling in the desart*;—as such, *is* my desire and well wishes to Reason, that he may enjoy his kingdom.

Now, if man has Reason in him, there is Moses in the way, and God must be observed and *obeyed* according to the *cherubical Inspiration*, because it is a mighty Attribute of God in Creation; and *that* Justice was brought here through the fall, and elect men must pass through it in *obedience* to it, as Moses did: Therefore him that comes to worship God, will find Moses, and must *pass* Moses, to enter the royal priesthood of Faith: *Therefore* my advice to the elect *is*, when they are CALLED TO GOD, that they observe, and are obedient to his Power in the Priesthood of Justice, and in *Prayer and Patience* Watch and Wait the *Resurrection of the Dead* to the Priesthood of Faith, and Mercy. I hope the time of your deliverance will soon come!!

So conclude your loving brother.

JAMES BIRCH.

London, Aug. 11, 1781.

Note.—An Head of a LET. Abbreviated,—thus, To Sister Runwa, &c. J. Birch, &c. Greeting—is read or understood, as, To our beloved Sister Runwa, and to the whole Church beloved in Christ, in and about Pembroke, James Birch and Brethren, or Church in London, send Greeting. —*N.B.* This method was oft' adopted by Mr. Birch himself, and who authorized the abbreviation *i.e.*—meaning that is—found in the Books upon the Law, and upon the Gospel, the former coming in print, Sunday July 1, 1798, the latter July 4, 1799, and Mr. Birch died October 1800.

LETTER XXXVIII

To beloved Runwa, and ALL beloved in Christ,—including a transcript of a Letter which I sent in answer to the Young Man James Thomas advised me of, telling him the foundation on which Scripture stands, and the consequences thereof (see Let. XXXVI):—And finding the Answer suits a strong FORTRESS to the Elect, against the World, I thought good to send the Copy, in love with the Church Greeting.

Beloved Sister—I am very glad to hear from you and the church, and I pray God assist you all in the works of Faith, which is to *overcome the World*; then the folly of this life, and temptation of the devil cannot prevail against the elect, for then they will be sealed by the King of Faith for Glory: For you may see in the aforesaid letter, God's Justice cannot be broken, therefore must be waded through by prayer and divine assistance from heaven—and he that *wills* to worship GOD, must be obedient to this; and BLESSED are them that are called out from the *Desart*, into this present declaration to WORSHIP GOD.

For this I say to Reason, who *War* against Christ and his elect, and worship the devil: If they can procure themselves to live for ever, and this world to last for ever as their habitation, they may in some degree escape this Messenger, but if death take them, this declaration has them, with their own witness to their own condemnation.

My love to sister *Russant*, and let her hold fast what she has received, and submit to the will and power of God—for as we all are born into this world under Justice, through justice we must go to mercy, as Christ did, and by the prayer Faith and Patience *mountains* will be removed: I beg she may not go to Bath, for there God is not to be found among the *Muggletonians*. Let Jas. Thomas see or know this as soon as possible.

So conclude your loving brother,

JAMES BIRCH

London, Aug, 25, 1781.

LETTER XXXIX

To Mrs. Mary Runwa, and to the whole church beloved in Christ, in and about Pembroke, James Birch and Brethren send greeting.

Beloved Sister,—Yours I received, and you greatly *Serve* and oblige me in letting me know the condition of the church; and more so to see you do not attempt to *hide* yourself from God, but desire to worship God under the attribute of divine justice, as well as with Patience and Prayer *wait* for his divine mercy. This always was the state of the elect, when they are called to the knowledge and worship of God; so I greatly commend you and the whole church for your Faith, and pray

God it may increase.

As to the *Seed* of Reason, who would hide or get from the Messenger at any rate, it signifies nothing, for he will hurt no one. And in all their business of life to please themselves, or suggest to themselves to hide in the Scripture, it is nothing; but if they can procure themselves to live for ever, and this world to last for ever as their habitation, they may in some degree escape the Messenger, but if they die, the Messenger has them by his declaration.

Moreover the Elect *seek death* in Life, Why? because they must pass *through* Justice and Death, to the Kingdom of Christ, therefore their care is how to appear before God: But Reason seek this life, which will be swallowed up in death, and they lost in their own wisdom: Therefore, blessed are them that obey this CALL *and work in the vinyard of Faith*, then they FOLLOW CHRIST, who was a Man of *Sorrow*, and their reward is eternal life with Christ, in his royal kingdom of divine mercy.

Beloved Sister, I had wrote sooner, but am writing the Law and Cherubims in a book, from the sheets, by much use being near illegible, and to have it perfect, I thought good to write it over again, and have about half done; tell Mrs. Jones of this.

So concludes your loving brother in prayer for you all.

JAMES BIRCH

London, Oct. 13, 1781.

LETTER XL

An Answer to Brother Cullum in forgetfulness.

Brother Cullum, —I received your letters, but at the last I was astonished at your forgetful state, *Warham's* ignorance is well known, desiring kitchen privileges, for that would not be granted; but what could possess *you*, to think to bring your *Plaintiff* to Trial? Where will you get *money* for it? Seeing your *Witnesses* are at such a distance, and their expences must be paid,—is this quitting and forgiving the whole world?

And as to sending to me for money, you know I have none; I am obliged to borrow to pay your letters, and the church is so *Poor* as not to collect for that;—I told you to be *Careful*, there is no danger of your being taken away for *Debt*, or turned out for not *paying* your lodging—And as for *money*, you need not expect any 'till after *Christmas*, and even then, I can say but little to it; for *Poverty* is great.

Therefore as the *Day of* TROUBLE *is come*, you must put your face towards it, and *drink of the waters* of justice, and overcome, or die under it.

You need not write to tell what you have done with your money, for that will be hurtful to you, for when I can assist you temporally I will send.

And *In this Vale of Sorrow* conclude your loving brother in CHRIST,

JAMES BIRCH.

London, Nov. 1781, (or nearly).

LETTER XLI

TO Mr. J. B. PARRY.

Sir—I received your letter as you intended it, and glad to see you write as you have; and to be poor in spirit, is good; for men must be in the state of PRAYER unto God, for his divine assistance: Now there is the Prayer of obedience, which is the desire of the soul, to be in obedience to the will and power of God, and to his Messenger, and there to be preserved; this is done in the *secret* chambers of the soul, without any *hypocritical* form: and there is the Prayer of Faith, which the Virgin will pray, when *born and active.*

As for *Oaths in Courts of Judicature*, what a man has seen acted be may speak, that his neighbour may be righted; and as for a Jury, or an Office, it only constrains a man to do his best; but Mind this must be done in truth, with the eye of mercy; and if any doubt arise, then let him turn the *Scale* in mercy;—now this men may do if they please, in my judgment: And as for the *Quakers*, some will not speak under the name of *oath*, but of *testimony*;—now where is the difference, seeing they both mean an appeal to God; But see what some men has, and do declare, concerning the Person, and Will of God, and of the scripture, as the way for salvation, which, is a *spiritual oath*; so there is many will *strain at a gnat, and swallow a camel*: but this place of scripture mean swearing by the will and power of GOD, according to his salvation and regeneration; because the power and teaching of that, is in and of *Himself*, so the elect were to commune with *Yea and Nay*, and what more, was of evil, because they must wait HIS time for His kingdom, and this is to become a child.

And as to the BIBLE giving account of the creation and fall of angels—Answer. When Moses wrote of the creation of heaven and earth, and of man, some might have said to him, wherein have we any account to prove this? But no man must oppose *Him* without GOD's *Judgment* coming on him: For in this Moses is the foundation of scripture; then the prophets followed, with the message GOD was pleased to send, and the same is under the gospel: And can you think a *Messenger* of GOD wander among the TOMBS of the prophets and apostles, and of Christ, like the apprentice serving, and emulated, conceited priest, who create themselves, and can only seek the *living among the dead* that if a thing cannot be found written in the letter of a dead man, it cannot be confirmed.

But *a Messenger of God*, stands before God, and lead men from death, to LIVE; and the present Messenger came out in regeneration, and do declare those things to *open* the kingdoms, that regeneration may be known, and Blessed are them that believe and follow.

Your 2d *Query*.—"Let us make man, &c." was spoke before man was created, and in this God is likened unto a wise builder, who first consults the cost, and well knew by his creating man in his own image and after his likeness, and suffer him to fall and go on in generation, would cost him his God-head life, to recover him by regeneration, that through the process of generation, and regeneration, God and his created Son and children would become *united*, so as to be of ONE nature and glory, which is the nature and glory of Faith: But the erronious spirit of Reason would divide the God-head and his kingdom, as themselves are divided.

3d. Qu.—Of the *Legion?*—Here you may see the devil is in generation, or how could he be cast out of man, as it was with this in the tombs: Observe Mat. viii. "There met him two possessed with devils, coming out of the tombs;" but Mark v. and Luke viii. speak of one (but yet it is the same miracle wrought by Jesus, and recorded by those men), but passing the number, it is the same to shew the power of God.—NOW, as I said, the devil became man in generation, and that Reason in man is the devil, and is the chief actor in, and driver of Man: And, further, there is in the soul of man, a proper stay to his natural senses, and while within that bounds, man is composed so as to act his natural business, things, &c. but, if Reason drive the senses beyond this stay, the life is turned, and the mass of blood drowned with confusion; and this produce uncommon and unclean spirits in the man, which care called devils:—ALSO, the spirit of Reason will tempt, or drive man to be melancholy and stupid, that they will be deaf and dumb to all you say, and at times bring out strange expressions, and acts of evil; and others to commune with their own evil spirit; and others to despair, &c. and sometimes it come through the blood in generation, though at a distance, and in this the *iniquity* of the father, is *visited* on the children: Now all those are evil and unclean spirits, called devils, and men that are possessed with those spirits, are possessed with devils.

Again, you see this man in the tombs, was *bound in chains and fetters, which he broke in pieces, neither could any man tame him*; and he was *night and day in the mountains and tombs, crying and cutting himself,* which was according as the spirit drove him: — So from this unclean spirit, he had many evil actions called devils, which is the *Legion*, for Legion means no certain number: Therefore Jesus by his mighty power, caused the unclean spirit with all its actions to die, or cease acting in the man, which is *casting out*, and in this manner were devils *cast out*; and natural infirmities healed, and men made perfect according to creation, and in this is the power of the *Father, glorified in the Son.*

Again, when this unclean spirit or devil has full power over the man, it is very eager to keep his possession; and further, when he appear who hath power over it, this spirit soon know it, and is eager to live; therefore desired to enter the herd of swine; for its theme is this; although it there will be cast out and die, yet that it may quicken in the herd of swine, and there live, for that is its own residence. Now this *Herd of Swine* was men and women, who owned Moses, and the name of Israel, and by the letter, according to their imagination, they formed their worship, and dedicated it to the God of Israel, and made use of his name; then this overtopped all who did not own the law of Moses: Thus Reason, by its own hope, was mounted high up in imagination, which is this mountain, and they were a *positive* STUBBORN *People* in their will and way, for which they were called *Swine*, and their teachers and priest the *Herdsmen,* and they *fed the swine* by their worship, on this *mountain* of imagination.

Moreover, you see no one could *tame* this man, or hardly pass that way; and those Gaderens with all their high imaginary assurance, and self assumed conceited power by their doctrine, could not cure or help this man, and when Jesus came, the evil spirit or devil knew him as aforesaid, and cried out, see Mark i. 34. where "He cast out many devils and suffered not the devils to speak, because they knew him."

But this devil was suffered to speak, and cried to JESUS *not to be tormented,* and as I said, this spirit is eager to live, and reign in man, and as so, desired to enter the herd of swine: therefore, when Jesus commanded the spirit to come out of the man it died, or ceased acting, as if it had never been there; and in this way it came out of the man; And quickened in those people, which was the herd of swine; for when they saw Jesus had cast out the legion, the spirit of dislike, fear, and dread, quickened and took place in them.

Yea, for all their high conceit in worshiping God, they never could cast the devil out, nor cure the man; but when Jesus came, he did,— then they knew the power and doctrine of Jesus was far above theirs, and the spirit of dislike, fear, and dread took place as before said; then their conceited imaginary power was struck with confusion, and fled hastily down this hill or mountain of imagination, and was choked in their own water, which was their hope, for the waters of Euphrates in the land of Nod, is the river, or sea, or lake, that waters the soul and spirit of Reason, which is their hopes, and through this hope, with reading the scripture, they got up the mountain of imagination; then, when the power of God is manifest to them, they run down the mountain, and are choked in this water, which is their hope.

Again, you *See,* them that fed the swine, was called herdsmen, which was their priest and teachers, who "Fled and told in the city and country what was done; and they came to Jesus, and saw him that was possessed with devils, clothed in this right mind, *Sitting* with

Jesus, and were *afraid*."—Further, you see the devil in the man cried out, "What have I to do with thee Jesus, thou son of the most high God?" and desired not to be *tormented*: And when they saw the *Legion was cast out*, then the spirit of fear and torment took place in their souls, and produced the same language as the devil in the man, before he was cast out, for they "Prayed Jesus to depart their coasts," because they would have nothing to do with, nor be tormented by him; But the man prayed to be with Jesus, and Jesus said, "Go and tell what things God has done for thee:" Now thus the devil was cast out, and entered the herd of swine, and they ran down the mountain, and were choaked, by or through the powerful miracle of Jesus, and the number was about two thousand, which you cannot think *hogs*, for they were unclean, and their flesh forbidden to be eat, by the law of Moses, and this was among the *Jews*, who regarded not keeping hogs, but men cannot bear the devil to be in them, so any where else but at home.

Further, as the above miracle was to make man perfect according to creation and generation!—What miracle must that be, to make man perfect according to regeneration? Or what think you of that man or men who receive instruction and power of man, to preach Christ unto salvation? Or him whose dark understanding of the redemption, springs forth in Emulation, to fancy he can preach the will and power of Christ to salvation, and knows nothing of Christ, but as he fancy by his imagination on the dead letter? Now, is not this a spiritual *madman*, who dwell among the *tombs* of the Prophets, Christ, and the Apostles, and there *rave and roar on the mountains* of imagination, and *among those tombs*? and if they are told their act and condition, which should stop them, yet they will break that *Chain*, and be so raving, that it is a hard thing for a man to pass that *Spirit*; which is "the devil as a roaring lion, seeking whom he can devour."

Again, man is worked on, in his natural senses for regeneration, and then there is many devils to be cast out, such as the spirit of dislike to the will and way of God, and of conceited imagination, of opposition, prejudice, unbelief, anger, envy, blasphemy, &c. that man may become as a *Child* to go into regeneration; and when in that state, he will find plenty of devils to be cast out of himself, which is done by the dint of prayer and patience: And those seven devils, that was cast out of *Mary Magdalen*, was for regeneration, for it is there Christ make men perfect to salvation, by casting out devils, &c. then devils must reside in the *Herd of Swine* to and in eternity: And as for Judas, he preached the name of Christ, with the other disciples, and when time was come, the devil quickened in him, then he went and betrayed Christ, and as thus the devil entered him, and never was cast out: hence you may see a man may preach the name of Christ, and have a devil, and that devil never be cast out, and mind it is your devil within that oft'times tempts you, and be careful not to hearken to the temptation of the devil without.

Your 4th. Qu.—"How Christ was *tempted?*" When Jesus received the Holy Ghost at *His* BAPTISM, "He was led into the wilderness to be tempted of the devil;" this *Wilderness*, was among men of Reason, who owned Moses; for as be came to Faith, Reason was a wilderness to him, and *He fasted and hungered*, for he being among Reason, he could have nothing but trouble and temptation; then the most able man in wisdom of the law of Moses, and that priesthood, came to Jesus, and said, "If he was the Son of God," to do a miracle, and Jesus answered him from the book to Reason, written by Moses, see Deut. viii. 3. Then this devil took him to the *holy City*: This *holy City* was to shew him the priesthood of Reason, and if men broke the law, and offered the true offering, it would stay GOD's justice, then men would stand before GOD and have his blessing: —Then this devil would make him the head over that, which was the *pinnacle* he set him on, and said, as it came from God, he must own it as the son of God, and if he *cast himself down*, so as to take it under him, he could come to no harm, because "His angels had charge concerning him;" but Jesus answered him as before, see Deut. vi. 16. Again, "This devil took him into an high mountain, and shewed him all the kingdoms of the world, and the glory of them;" this *Mountain* was the law of Moses, that was incomparable wise to rule Reason, or the *Kingdoms* of this world, for if Kingdoms would flourish, they must be ruled by the law of Moses, and that priesthood, then God's justice would be stayed, and his blessing flow, which is the *Glory* of the kingdoms of this world, and this was done in a short time, for if the Jews had truly obeyed the law of Moses, they would have been law-givers to the whole world: And this devil was a great and wise man in the law of Moses, and would have given this rule and power unto Jesus, if he would hearken to him, which was for JESUS to *fall down and worship him?* then Jesus answered as before (see Deut. vi. 13), for Jesus came to seek the kingdom of Faith, and WOULD NOT be tempted to the kingdom of Reason.

Your 5th Qu.—Concerning the Sabbath and Sacrament? You may read how and for what Moses ordained the sabbath, which was for Reason to do and observe: But them who own the name of Christ, keep the sabbath on the first day of the week, in imitation of the apostles; because Christ raised on that DAY: But the SABBATH for you to seek, is the priesthood of Faith, whom, Christ is LORD of: And if eating bread and drinking wine will gain heaven, it is easy done, let it be of what form or institution they please: But YOU are to enter the priesthood of Faith, and work the works, then you will *drink* of that spiritual wine, as Christ promised his disciples when he entered his kingdom; But in the outward form only, there is too many take the *sop* and go *their Way* as Judas did.

NOW I have answered you, and told the truth before God, and—I pray God give you understanding, and increase your Faith; I like your manner of writing, but be patient to wait the Lord's time: And as to be *hated* of the world, this always was the condition of the elect, when they are called to Truth, but this, by divine assistance, you will *overcome*.

I received yours, and if you enquire for P. Jones, Plumber, at Caermarthen, his wife is of this Faith, she you may commune with, relative to this Faith. Shew her this letter, and give my love to her and Mr. Jones, and when you write, let me hear of them also: It may please God I may see you all next summer. So conclude your loving brother and friend in Christ.

JAMES BIRCH

London, Nov. 6, 1781

LETTER XLII

To Mr. James Naylor, and all Friends and Brethren, who bear the name of Muggletonians, at Nottingham, and thitherward, who may see this, Jas. Birch and Brethren send greeting.

Sir,—According to my promise when you was with us, I have written to you, and would sooner, had I not been so much engaged in writing, and whereas, when with us you *heard part* of a letter going to a gentleman, which discovered the arrogant *abominations*, and *woeful desolations*, which possess the soul of man;—moreover, I have, and do describe, how man and angel *fell*, each under his own Law:—and what is the Law of *Faith*;—and what the law of *Reason*;—and what is the *Justice* of the Father, which is Justice to Faith;—and what the justice of the *Angel*, which is justice to Reason;—and what is the kingdom of Faith, according to creation, and according to regeneration; and what the kingdom of Reason is:—Also, what is the *inspiration* of Faith; and what the cherubical *inspiration* is, then of consequence, the *priesthood* of Faith, and the *priesthood* of Reason; and what the *wild* priesthood of Reason is, which, IF men enter into the *Lively compact* of Faith, they must know.

Again, I declare this commission of the spirit began in Justice: And, that *John Reeve* came out, in, or under Justice, and was a *second Moses*; for what Moses began, was continued and beautifully brought on, by John Reeve, who is the *last* Messenger unto the *bloody unbelieving world*; for as Moses was the *First*, John Reeve was the *Last*, unto them: And *Lodowick Muggleton was given to be his mouth*; and was the last *high priest*, — but in the priesthood of Reason; therefore them who *Will* to receive benefit in this commission of the spirit, must now seek to know in what condition they are *in*, and on what foundation they *stand*; for what has been declared by *Moses*, will be acted in the soul of one Man, according to the covenant of the law: And what has been declared by JESUS will be acted in the soul of one Man, according to the Covenant of Grace. So let men lodge in, or harbour under, what literal declaration they please, they will find they must pass from *Moses* to go to Jesus.

Again, it is written by the late High Priest, "God took no notice of his saints, and prayer of no use:" which has since been industriously cultivated by his sons; but what man, that is *born of water* can stop here?—Then much less when *born in spirit*;—to stop! For it is well known to me from HEAVEN, the *Power* of Cherubical Justice and *incense*, which is of the first covenant, IS now active in the soul of man, in the Commission of the Spirit; and of this IS notice taken in Heaven, by them who sit in the Glory of Justice: For when the serpent angel broke the law in heaven, he never could break the justice of that Law, but took it with him into flesh, as pure as God created it; and when he came to manhood, this Justice took place in his soul; and it is also found in the elect; because Adam took Reason at the *Fall*; therefore the law Rule the Life, and justice Rule the Law.

Now, when man break the law, this justice take place, and seal to death eternal; and would cut him off, if God did not stay it, then the prayer or incense of Reason is, that God would have mercy on him, and forgive him, which is, to stay this justice;—AND, in all the great *troubles* of life, and heavy *afflictions* of soul; man will pray in spirit to God for relief, and relief will come if man ask right; now this is part of the priesthood that Moses gave, and said it should be for them and their children for ever; and think you this can be without *Notice* in heaven?—for this justice or angel in the soul is as *pure* as God created it, and can commune with *them* in the glory of justice; and this way doth the prayer go, and relief come: Now this is but the priesthood of Reason, then NOT FOR SAINTS.—And think you; this *high Priest* did not agree with them in *Captivity*, where they say, "The Lord hath forsaken the earth, and the Lord seeth not!" (Ezek. ix. 9)

Further, when a Man believe this *Commission of the Spirit*, he may, according to the priest, think himself happy in the assurance of eternal life, which is the state of independence: And if any man—had the assurance of eternal life in a body of flesh and blood, it was Christ the KING of Faith! and HE, himself! was dependent on the power of the Father, which is of justice to Faith; and through that power HE must GO, to his own royal kingdom of divine mercy! *Also*, CHRIST declared regeneration: and a man *must be born of water and of spirit*, to enter the kingdom of God.

ALSO, *Reeve and Muggleton* called many to the outward word or bare letter of this commission, but it remains in the will of the divine majesty, who he chose to enter His royal priesthood ; and from me you may be assured, there is more called than chosen; Therefore it is good for them who believe, to seek to get as near God as possible to own their Faith; and for men to transform themselves, or be transformed into the letter, and get no further, but there live, and reign. *Priest and kings*, by their *Emulated* power and *conceited* assurance, will not do for salvation: And him or them, who say they have the assurance aforesaid, make themselves equal with, if not above CHRIST, when HE was in the state of mortality;—yet—this *assurance* is by a contrary spirit to Christ.

AGAIN, when God is pleased to visit the soul of man by his holy spirit, it raises Faith from death to life, and this spirit that is born of the womb of Faith, is the *virgin* daughter for regeneration, and she is born to the priesthood of Faith, and under the justice of the father, as Christ himself WAS; and to her is given the promise of Christ to come, and offers the prayer of Faith to heaven, for divine assistance, to work the works of Faith; and is in mystical union and spiritual communion with God, which is the *Priesthood* of Faith, and are brought on to prophesy of their own salvation: And as Christ prayed to heaven for assistance, so doth this virgin of Faith, which,—*is* brought on to become the essential soul for the resurrection to life eternal; then, Christ comes in spirit, to seal and sanctify the soul; and then it dies in the Bed of mercy, to be raised to glory: Now if this High Priest had known this *Book*, which is the book of regeneration to LIFE, he would not have said, "God took no notice of his saints," now this is the Priesthood for believers to seek after, and if they are not *taken* into this priesthood, they are *left* desolate on the bare letter.

Further, although John Reeve came out in or under *Justice*, yet he was taken into the priesthood of Faith, and prophesied of Christ to come, which was the state or condition of Moses, (only this). Moses prophesied Christ would come in PERSON to redeem, and John Reeve prophesied Christ would come in SPIRIT to sanctify the soul for life eternal,—and Christ has appeared according to his prophecy: And in all the glorious appearance in the personal coming of Christ to judgement, and to put an end to time, and raise the elect to crowns of glory, yet Christ *first* comes in spirit to sanctify and seal the soul as a preparation to he raised to glory; for if he do not *first appear* in Spirit, his personal appearance will be of no benefit: Therefore let men be ever so high in their own gathered knowledge of the Letter, except they enter the priesthood of Faith, there is nothing done to Salvation.

Again, let a man profess any literal record from Heaven, and incapable of regeneration, he must die as he was born, which is under justice: And every man is sure to be called on:—Then—If under Justice to Reason, the Angel opens the book of Justice and Death! And if under Justice to Faith, then, you are taken through Death to Life.

Sir.—I have written according to my word, and incumbent duty from heaven; and I hope there may be them found among you in that *Country* not only able to receive this, but also to enter the *Priesthood of Faith*, and he brought on in REGENERATION, and have sent this as a Warning to ALL!—For I do declare myself the first born Son in the Commission of the Spirit, who lived to come back to tell the Tale, and was sent back by CHRIST the King of Faith, in Glory, in his own Covenant of Divine Mercy, to tell the Brethren: And what I have TOLD, no one can get from. So conclude your friend, and every one's friend in what I can.—Sir, please to let all the brethren see it, even them at Mackworth.

JAMES BIRCH.

London, Jan. 26, 1782.

LETTER XLIII

To our beloved Brethren, J. B. Parry and Mary Jones. James Birch, and Brethren, sendeth Greeting.

Beloved, —I much approve of your writing, and of Mrs. Jones's letter, and I pray God increase your faith, and as you desire to know who or what that son of perdition is which Paul speak of 2 Thess. chap ii. it is him or them who take the name and letter of Jesus, and go forth and preach and prophecy, and promise salvation by their own dark spirit of Reason, which is the devil, and this is the *Man of Sin* (for God is the *Man of Goodness*): and the devil, who is the man of sin, with his eager spirit of darkness, will seduce many, and the spirit of darkness, by this seduction, reign in the souls of men, instead of God.

Also those men preach and propagate the fruits of their dark spirit, and call it the *Will* and *Way* of God; and it being contrary to God, in this, it *opposeth* God; And their harbouring in the letter and using the name of God and Christ, which, relative to this thing is called the *Temple* of God, where the man of sin *sitteth*, and will sacrifice himself, and the world, to the *will* of his dark spirit, and in this he shew signs and wonders, or that he is god, or that his spirit must be worshipped above all that is called God; for when the *Worship* and *Way* of God is made known on this earth, the *man of sin* look on it with contempt as foolishness, and would put it to death, as they did God himself when he was here in flesh; and in this he EXALTETH himself above God.

Again, you may see when Christ came in spirit to John, there was those men of sin crept into the churches of Asia, and how they seduced the people by their doctrine, in the *reproof* to the seven churches, in Rev.: Here Paul's prophecy was manifest of the *falling away* before the coming of Christ, and the man of *sin* made known:

But this prophecy did not end there, for it remains in full power to this day, neither is this sin, of one man but of many; but this you learn to know, when a man can see he is DESOLATE by this abomination, he may look for the coming of Christ in spirit.

Your 2d Qu.—This Melchizedec was God, (who is a non-created being) promised in Christ; and HIS priesthood is the priesthood of Faith, and as God became a son to his own power, he was CHRIST, who is king and high priest of Faith; and this kingdom and priesthood will for ever stand; and as a man is born into this world to the priesthood of Reason, even so a man must be *born again* to enter the priesthood of Faith; and this *man of sin* may harbour in the outward word or bare letter, and oppose Christ, but never can enter this royal priesthood.

Concerning Christ's words, Mat. xv. "Not that which goeth into the mouth defileth a man, &c." this saying, is faithful and true, and transcend all others that may seem to wave against it; for as I told you, the devil was wholly transmuted into flesh and dwell among men, and from the spirit of Reason, which is the devil in the soul of man; raise all evil thoughts, and when they come out to act, the *tree is known by its fruit*, and men their own witness to their condemnation; now this do not raise from what is *ate or drank* to support nature, for that is cast into the draught; but you may read of the meats, and ceremonies thereof, that Moses commanded, which was nothing for salvation, and of little consequence in itself; this the Jews did observe, but neglect his commandments of greater weight; of this they made a shew before Christ, yet brought forth evils unto death eternal; and as so become the man, or men of *sin*.

And as to what the Apostles ordinated among the gentiles, was a Jewish relict that they had not got rid of themselves, and was nothing for salvation: But however, you *eat* nothing that will bring on you bodily diseases, or hasten your death, then you may enjoy that blessing of health in this life; but abstain from fornication and Meats offered to *Idols*.

Now, there is natural fornication, and spiritual fornication, (*i.e.*) from the spirit of Reason springs a priestly power, who forms a worship of God, contrary to the way of God, and this is called the *great Whore*, and the man or men who prostrate themselves to the will and power of this Whore for their salvation, commit spiritual *fornication*, and are cast into that bed for wrath.

Further, by this spirit of imagination, they form a god, where as there is no such one, in heaven or *earth* to be found, that will shew mercy unto salvation, therefore an *Idol*, and when the said priest preach and offer his prayer which is incense to this idol, and man take this and believe it truth, he *eat* it, which is meats offered to idols; therefore this you observe and keep from, and you will do well, for straight is the way that leads to life eternal, in Matt vii. 13.

Qu. 3, this *Beast*, Rev. xiii. is the spirit and power of Reason, and the out-going priestly power is the whore which *ride* on the Beast, (as this) when a number of people gather together in false worship, they form rules, laws, &c. and this power constitutes and upholds this priest who teach and ride on them; and him so impowered carry the *Mark, Name, and Number* of the beast; now his fiery zeal to have his own will, as well as authority to act by, or in, the power of others, who place him there, is his Mark, and his name is blasphemy, and the Number of his name, is his temptation to false worship, blasphemy, &c. and when you are tempted to any evil, that evil temptation is the number of his name, which do you learn to know and watch: Therefore, when people of one mind gather together to support their kingdom and priesthood, according to their own *Will* and Way, it is done by the mark, name, and number of the Beast; and those that will not bow down and worship the beast as they do, judge you what chance they stand among them to *buy-sell*, &c.

Your 4th Qu.—Concerning Christ giving Peter the keys of the kingdom of heaven; —these *keys* of heaven given to Peter was the Holy Ghost at the day of Pentecost, to preach Christ, his death and resurrection, to redeem the elect world; and also the spirit of prophecy, that Christ would come again: Now this doctrine that Peter and others preached, when it fell into the good ground which is the womb of Faith, in the souls of the elect, it *bound* men up in obedience, and to *wait* the kingdom of Christ: And when Christ, by his holy influence, gave birth to Faith, and it being then in the royal priesthood, they are further *bound*, for the kingdom of heaven; and so on till they receive the seal of Christ, then they are bound in full for the kingdom of heaven, and then die in the bed of mercy, to be raised to glory; but, on the contrary, them that cannot take nor bring forth fruit by the doctrine, they are *loosed* from the kingdom of heaven, and may take their own liberty as long as they can.

Again, this present Messenger has that power only higher up, why? because he came out, the FIRST BORN SON of the Virgin of Faith in regeneration, that lived to come back to tell his tale; and where they all went to this MESSENGER came from! and has declared the kingdom and priesthood of Faith; and of Reason, the angel of Faith; and of Reason, the justice to Faith; and to Reason, which was not before now declared plain and open, therefore you may judge of the Messenger's *power*; also he has unlocked death and hell, and brought man out, and opened the priesthood of Faith, and directed them to Christ!—for this Messenger begin with the first resurrection, and them that hear the voice and follow, they are *bound* to the kingdom of Christ, and them that will not, the Messenger give them up to justice, death, and hell; and death and hell has swallowed them, and shewed them in wrath before the Messenger's face! And he further adds, if any man can procure this world to last for ever, as their habitation,— and themselves to live for ever in it, they may in some degree escape his declaration, but if death take place the whole is taken for life, or death eternal, according to his declaration, let them flatter themselves in what they can to the contrary! Mind what is written and shew it Mrs. Jones, and I pray God increase both your Faith: my love to Mr. Jones, so conclude your loving brother in Christ, with the Church, praying your increase in Faith.

London, March 26, 1782.   JAMES BIRCH.

LETTER XLIV

To our beloved Sister, Mary Runwa and to the whole Church beloved in Christ, James Birch and Brethren send Greeting.

Beloved Sister,—I am glad to hear from you and the whole church; I have received a letter from James Thomas, which also gives me great joy to hear from the church, for it is my duty to serve the church of God, and of Christ, to the ultimate of that power given to me; for I much approve of your Faith, and pray God give you increase, and his divine assistance to pass through the justice of the father, to the mercy of the son, and I have been faithful and true, in what I have told you, neither can any one prevail against it, because it is from

Jesus in his high covenant of mercy.

Moreover, I am glad to hear Hannah Reed is in that state of peace and satisfaction, and that her Faith is so strong in JESUS; and has the power of resignation and prayer at his Royal FEET; for it is a great thing after the toil and travail in this erronious busy life (which is under the angel in justice) that through the declaration from heaven are brought into the WAY to Christ, and have his divine assistance, that the fear of the *second death* is taken away for when the soul come to the death bed, and at the same time their Faith quick in a lively and active declaration from heaven, then of consequence the power of God is quick and active in them; and the acts of a past life is soon recounted; then if the internal angel do not open the book of justice and death, it is plain they are in the way for Mercy and Life,— Why? Because the soul is at peace with God, and his Messenger, and true resignation, and the prayer of Faith in and according to this declaration, which is active in the soul, unto Christ for his divine mercy.

Here you may see the internal angel in justice (who is the cherubim and flaming sword that keep the way of the tree of life) do not disturb her hope, nor stop her prayer in and to CHRIST, then of consequence there is no block laid, but the door open to Christ, who is the TREE OF LIFE: This being a lively Faith, under the quick power of God, because this is not in sleep, dream, or death, as is the world's Faith.

Again, I would have you and she understand there is more yet to be done, that is to be called up to the justice of the father, and there lose yourselves in death, in your own blood, as Christ himself did, to follow Christ to his kingdom of divine mercy: Also Christ went to death like a Lamb, and commended his spirit into the hands of the father, which is of justice, and went through that justice to mercy, Luke xxiii. 46.

Further, understand this, the spirit or Virgin of Faith has the power of prayer to God and Christ, and go up to death in lamb-like obedience to God, as Christ did, and there meet Christ in spirit as he was crucified, and must lose yourself in your own blood, under the justice of the father, as he did; now this is the Marriage with the Lamb, and through this Union is born the spiritual son for mercy and glory; but you must go through the justice of the father to the mercy of the SON: After this the spiritual born son is Sealed by Christ himself for glory, but few come back to tell this; for then they sleep in the bed of mercy, but it is now told that you may know; now this great passage in spirit may cause some agitation of soul, which may be seen; or it may be passed at the last minute, and no one see it but themselves, which is mostly so.

Now give my love to sister Reed, and I much approve of her condition of soul, and that she in this Faith hold fast to the mercy of Jesus, and all will be well, and my love and prayer is for her and the whole church. So conclude your loving brother in Christ, and mean to be with you ere long, and pray your increase in Faith.

JAMES BIRCH.

London, April 11, 1782.

NOTE.—Mr. Birch *writes to Mrs. Runwa from Caermarthen, (June 12) that he arrived there the previous Sunday Noon,—and that Mrs. Jones, Mr. Parry, with himself, intended quickly to visit her at Pembroke, with love to the whole Church.*

LETTER XLV

To the Church, &c. in Caermarthen, and those parts.

Beloved Friends and Brethren,—This with my love, to inform you I came safe to Bristol on Thursday Morning, and abode 'till Saturday Afternoon; then went to Bath, and there abode 'till Sunday Night, 11 o'Clock, and heard more from friends than I expected:—So I dined at Bristol on Saturday: Bath on Sunday, Southampton on Monday, and Portsmouth on Tuesday;—for my son and I went from Southampton to Portsmouth (by sea) on business he had,—and sailed through the grand fleet at Spithead,—and there saw the melancholy aspect of the *main top* of the *Royal George* stand *above* water;—then went back to Southampton on Wednesday, and came to London on Thursday night, where I found the church and my family all well, and hope this will find you all well.

And I hope Love, Union, Wisdom, Patience, and Faith, will increase, and abound among you:—For Faith, Patience, and Prayer, for God's divine assistance, will overcome all this world!—Therefore, let Reason pass, with his *Sneers* and *Jeers*, and mind him not, but let him go on; for he is sure to be found his own witness to his own condemnation! as is declared by this present MESSENGER;—Neither can man get from what *he* has and doth declare!

So my love to you, Mr. Jones, Mr. Parry, and Mr. Williams, wishing you all health and peace, and in all things to be made able to stand before God! And conclude your loving brother,

JAMES BIRCH

London, Sep. 21, 1782.

LETTER XLVI

To beloved Runwa, &c. James Birch, &c. Greeting.

Beloved Sister,—This with my love to inform you, I came safe to London on Thursday, Sep. 5, and found all well:—I hope you will mind what has been said, and I pray God increase your Faith and understanding, it being my eager desire, and fervent prayer, that you all come powerfully on in regeneration; which, must be done for salvation.

And—in this TRAVAIL of generation, there is many an evil spirit or devil to be cast out;—and in all the acts of this alluring busy life, the tempter is very ready to take the soul aside, or at least to keep it back from regeneration, yet at the same time tell the soul he is on his duty: Therefore when the Messenger see any thing amiss, and will prove wrong, he is compelled to declare it, not only as a duty to his brethren, but that he himself may stand clear before the Lord God.

AGAIN, when any one is *taken and bound* for the kingdom of heaven, all things must be left for its sake; for it must not be for a man to *turn back* and bid his house or the world farewell! and there be lost in its cries and follies;—But if a man is *loosed* to the wild world, he may for a time seek to gather up riches, place his children and his delights where he can find them; but the internal Moses is with him, and them who sit in the glory of justice, is sure to find them, and they are their own witness to their own condemnation, as has been declared by this present Messenger; then—they will find their time spent, labour in vain! and their life to end in death, under cherubical justice.

Moreover, in all the goings-out, and the enjoyments of the temporal blessings of this life, which continue but a small space, yet let Reason know and understand this—they can enjoy no blessing at all, but by or through HIM who sent this Messenger, let Reason suggest any thing of, and to himself, to the contrary, and so bubble up in the frothy vapors of this life; but let him go where he can, and do what he will, he cannot hide himself; for he is sure to be found according as this Messenger has, and do declare; therefore it is good even for Reason to let the Messenger and the Elect *pass* their way in regeneration, and make no head against them, nor *despise* them, lest the blessings they enjoy fade like a shadow, when the substance is taken away, and they sink in justice.

Again, beloved sister and brethren, who are called upon for the communion with Christ; in his royal priesthood of Faith for regeneration and salvation, and for whom my soul is in daily prayer for your daily increase in the wisdom of Christ, which give you to know the WILL and POWER of God, and what the wisdom of Reason is, and what the vain things of this world is, and what they attend to; and also to *walk* on the delights of Reason, which is its *Waters*; even as Christ *walked* on the Sea, which is a strict thing to be observed, and the coming of Christ to be watched; For, NOW is the kingdom and priesthood of Faith *divided* from the kingdom and priesthood of Reason, "Even as a shepherd divideth his sheep from the goats" as prophesied of (Mat. 25). And, also where the body of Moses is buried, and where cherubical justice centers and is fixed, so the WAY of the coming of Christ in glory, is now *Prepared* and WARNING given! Therefore take heed your hearts be not overcharged with the vain surfeitings of this world; nor drunken in excuse; nor to sink in the cares of this life; for this is a snare to the whole world, that *they* are drowned in their own Waters; but do you as "Wise Virgins" watch his coming, that you may escape those things, and be made able to stand before the King of Faith, and enter his glorious kingdom.

Beloved sister, I hope you will assist the church in what you can, letting them see writings, and on occasion transcribe (if desired) for them who cannot,—or answer a question (if you can); and if any come to enquire after the *kingdom of God*, I beg of you, and all of you, to do *your* best to inform them.

I hope *Mrs. Jones* and the *Cook's* understanding will be found good, that they enter the royal Priesthood, as there is now space given to *Repent*: And pray God that TRUE friendship to each other, and the love and Faith of Christ may abound in your souls. So conclude your loving brother in Christ, in love to all and every one,

JAMES BIRCH

London, Sep. 21, 1782

LETTER XLVII

To our beloved Sister MARY WILLIAMS, and to the whole Church beloved in Christ, in and about Pembroke, JAMES BIRCH and the Brethren send GREETING.

Beloved Sister and Brethren,—I hope this will find you in good health, both natural, and spiritual, and hope you will remember what I said when I was with you;—and, whereas you desired me to write, that you may know the difference between *Mortality and Death*, and *Immortality and Life*, which is highly necessary for the church to know.

Now I have already informed you of the Laws, Kingdoms, and Priesthoods of Faith, and of Reason; yet again take notice of this,— when Adam and Eve was created, their Life was Faith, the divine nature of God!—and this created Faith which animated the man and woman, flowed forth in many divine Virtues, which has been set forth in an excellent manner:—yet, when they hearkened to the voice of Reason, they broke the Law of Faith,—then, those created Virtues in their souls, became inactive and dead, and Reason, with its law, Justice, &c. took possession, and ruled them and filled them with horrid fear and shame! And with excuse to get away, if possible! For then the Justice of the Father, which is justice to Faith, took place,— and created Faith became disunited from its living Father, in and by death, through HIS Justice, and never more could flow, or act in the soul of any created or generated Being, in the manner it was created, to this day! Then all things were made and become anew in the kingdom of Faith, for the Salvation of man!

Again,—As Faith *fell*, and became dead in Adam; and Reason took possession, and ruled the man; and in this state it is brought on by generation,—therefore, there is a necessity for Faith to be raised from this death to a NEW LIFE! and this new Life is for regeneration and salvation! And this new Life is the VIRGIN daughter of Faith; and to her is given Incense—the promise of CHRIST to come! And power to prophesy that He will come! And in this *Way* was the elect brought on in regeneration, till the hour of death.

And this *Incense*, or prayer, or spirit of regenerated Faith, went through death; and was called into heaven, and united to God for Christ; even as Moses, Elias, and Enoch was, only they were person and spirit: but the other elect by this regenerated spirit of Faith died, or slept in the Bed of Mercy; but it is all in the lively compact of regenerated Faith, which centers to, and its record kept in *immortality* and Life, and not in *mortality* and death: And in this manner was the elect of old, and in the time of the Law, regenerated and gathered into the Kingdom of Christ—which, leads to, and centers in Life and *immortality*.

Moreover, on this first Resurrection prayer and Incense, that has ascended into heaven, and is recorded in the immortal compact of regeneration, which is the BOOK OF LIFE, came Christ, and declared regeneration, and brought *Life and Immortality to light*—and worked the Redemption and ascended into his own royal Kingdom of divine Mercy—and took possession of this, HIS Kingdom.

See Rev. xiv. "And I looked, and Lo, a Lamb stood on mount Sion, and with Him an hundred forty and four thousand, having his Father's name written in their foreheads, &c." These are them, as I have DECLARED, that by regeneration was united to God for Christ; and HE took possession of this, his Kingdom, for those stood before HIM! And prophesied, when he was in the condition of the Father, and as so have his Father's name written in their foreheads!

V. 3. "And they sung, as it were, a *new Song* before the throne" this new song, was the lively incense and spirit of regenerated Faith, recorded in that lively Compact before the throne of mercy which

Christ had united, himself unto by redemption & salvation— for you may see "no man could learn that Song but those that were redeemed from the Earth."

V. 4. You may see how they *follow the Lamb*, and were *redeemed from among men*, "being the first fruits unto God and the Lamb:" thus you may see how the Kingdom of Christ was gathered in, when He was in the condition of God the Father, and how they stand recorded in the Book of Life.

Further, Christ came to bring *Life, out of Death, i.e.* this—as created faith fell, and became inactive and dead in Adam, for hearkening to the voice of Reason, Faith is risen from that death, to a new Life,—and Christ is the resurrection of this new Life, for regeneration and salvation! For as Reason actuates elect man before this *first resurrection*, the soul is subject to that Master, let him profess what Letter he please: But when this new Life is raised from death to life in the soul, man has got *Victory over the beast*, (i.e. Reason, see p. 200) Why? Because this new Life is distinct from, and contrary to that of Reason;—And this new life by regeneration become the *Essential soul* for salvation; and it is only subject to GOD, and to CHRIST, *i.e.* to the Power and Justice of the FATHER; and the Works and Mercy of the SON. Yea, this new Life, which is regenerated Faith, become the essential soul of man, and is of an immortal nature!—therefore—

See Matt. x. 28. Where Christ said to his disciples, "And fear not them who kill the body, but are not able to kill the soul, but rather fear Him which is able to destroy both body and soul in hell." Here you may see the difference between Generation and Regeneration; for if a man is incapable of Regeneration, his soul is dead in the sight of God; and will enter the *first death* with his body, for both to go into the *second death!* —But this new Life, which Christ raiseth from the death of Faith, that fell in Adam, Christ worketh on it for regeneration, to become the essential soul for salvation! And by his divine assistance, it is brought to the justice of the father, and through that justice, and ascends to Him, and is united to Him, and so recorded by Him, in his *immortal* record of divine Mercy, for the resurrection to eternal glory! Therefore no one can *kill* that soul, because it belong to Christ, who is Immortality and Life.

Again,—Of this *first resurrection*, that "he who hath part therein, the *second death* has no power over," Why? because he is passed from death to Life by regeneration.

See John v. 24. "Verily, verily, I say unto you, he that heareth my word, and believeth on him that sent me, hath everlasting life, and shall not come into condemnation, but is passed from death to Life," Why? because he is *raised* from death to Life, in this *first resurrection*; and by regeneration is passed through all and from all, which IS done by Christ in *Immortality.*

Also John xi. 25. JESUS said unto her, "I, AM the Resurrection and the Life, he that believeth in me, though he were dead, yet he shall live;" *i.e.* he that comes to believe in Jesus, though he was dead in Faith, yet Jesus *will* raise Faith into active life, and it shall live in regeneration.

V.26. "And whosoever liveth and believeth, shall never die;" *i.e.* Faith, when risen from the dead, it lives in and for regeneration, and believe and work the works in that royal priesthood; and its incense, prayer, or breath, ascends to Christ, and is united to Him in immortality! And doth not die, because it live in Him! Also,

Luke xii. 4. Jesus said, "And I say unto you be not afraid of them who kill the body, after that, they have no more that they can do": *i.e.* this spirit of regenerated Faith become the essential Soul, and is for salvation! And belong to CHRIST; for by Him it will be brought through all! And from all! And no one can stop it by death! *Nor pluck it out of His hand,* because it is united to Him in *immortality,* as an earnest of the resurrection to eternal glory!

Now as Adam was created out of the dust of the earth, and that nature which animated him died for its disobedience, according to the word of the Lord God; then Reason, whom they had hearkened to, took possession and became the lord and ruler of them; then they must also lose that life, and become putrefaction, and go to earth from whence they were taken; and this is its lost condition without regeneration—then in steps the Lord God of Heaven, who is CHRIST the REDEEMER, and raise Faith that fell, into a new Life for regeneration, and become the essential soul for salvation!—which is distinct from, and contrary to, corruptible death—therefore all filthy earthly matter, corruption and Reason, deemed the body of elect man (for elect man has Reason but *temporary,* because the Lord God did not plant it there—for the enemy sowed the tares) and it will be worked out, in, and through death, and regenerated, being but the body of elect man: but the soul of elect man is this spirit of regenerated Faith. Thus you may see how the soul and body of elect men are divided by regeneration.

Moreover concerning regeneration; when Faith is risen from death to Life, *i.e.* the Virgin daughter of Faith born from its womb, which is the *good ground*, and she is taken into the royal priesthood of Christ, and unto her is given the promise of Christ to come; and by divine assistance she will wade through justice and death;—for,

See Rev. xvii. 8. "When the *third angel sounds* in regeneration, there fell a star from heaven, burning as it were a lamp,"—this star is God's justice that fell from heaven, through the *Fall*; "And it fell upon the third part of the rivers and fountains of waters—and the name of the Star is called wormwood, and the waters became wormwood;" those waters is the life and soul of man.—"And many men died of those waters, because they were made bitter;" those that *died* was the seed and spirit of Reason; because they die of those waters of justice, for they cannot drink and overcome: therefore death and justice cannot be brought through death and justice.

But this NEW life that is risen from the death of Faith, will work against—and can; and is brought through Death and Justice! and can drink of those waters, and *overcome*; and are found worthy! And to them is given the spirit of prophecy of Christ to come!—Then, at the hour of death, they are called up to the Justice of the Father: And—you cannot go back—nor, help found! For, through that Justice, you must go, or no Life eternal!—And the divine incomes, and the spirit of prophecy, which has been given, is turned into blood!—for this Life of Faith must be lost in death, in its own blood, as Christ lost His: And there it meet Christ, in spirit, *as HE was crucified*! and are united to HIM!

Now, this is the MARRIAGE with the LAMB! and the spirit is commended into the hands of the Father which is of justice, and there dies as CHRIST Himself did!—Then it is quickened or quickens from this death into a NEW LIFE, which is the spiritual born Son to CHRIST, for his Kingdom; and is called, and ascends into the high mountain of regenerated Faith; where it sees Christ in His Kingdom, Glory, and Power of Mercy! and them that are sealed by Him! and that ALL must be call in, and be sealed by Him; to inherit his Kingdom—then the eager prayer of this spiritual born son is offered at the FEET of CHRIST (which is the grand Altar of Faith), to be called in, and sealed by HIM in his *immortal Compact*—KINGDOM of regenerated Faith!

And when the VOICE says "Come up hither," the spirit goes and is united to Christ in Immortality! This is the *Voice* of the SEVENTH Angel in regeneration;—then, "The kingdoms of this world become the kingdom of Christ, who will reign for ever and ever"—Because this spirit, or fruits of regenerated Faith, is brought through all, and from all, to the union of CHRIST!— and Seal of Christ in *Immortality* and Glory! which is the Seal of the LIVING GOD;—and the Book of Life! then, the soul is assured of Eternal Life! then this man or woman, whose soul is so much refined by regeneration, as to bring forth the said spirit of prayer, fruits, or incense, to ascend into heaven, and there to be united to Christ in immortality, dies or falls asleep in the BED of mercy for the resurrection to glory! which will be but a moment, because time is done and over.

But this Spirit or INCENSE of regenerated Faith, after it has passed through all, and from all, it cannot die, but is united to Christ who is an *immortal* Being.—Thus you may see by regeneration, how *life and immortality is brought to light.*

Again, when any man is sent to the bloody unbelieving world,—He comes to Mortality and Death,—because Reason is incapable of regeneration; and as so both soul and body die together the first death, under the angel in justice, and both go together into the second death!—Also, man may talk of, and preach concerning Faith; yet without the *first resurrection*, he is preaching of and to, a dead Faith; and at this time, even the elect are not only in a mortal but in a corruptible state, for both soul and body to die together:—BUT when Christ comes, HE raises Faith from death to life, for regeneration, and to that soul brings *Life and Immortality to light.*

Therefore, if Man comes out under Creation and Justice, there the soul is mortal and dies; and although Faith in the man is risen, and he prophecy of those things—He is taken to Christ, and leaves the world without declaring regeneration—because he did not come out under that covenant:—But—

If a man is born the son of the Virgin Daughter to Christ, and taken into the mountain of regenerated Faith, and there commune with CHRIST in His Immortality—and *Sent* immediately back by HIM; this man comes out in the spirit and power of Christ in regeneration,—then, he will declare the first resurrection and regeneration, and lead the way to Life and Immortality—by FOLLOWING CHRIST.

Thus—without Regeneration,—the soul dies with the body, and goes to corruption, under cherubical justice, and is cast from Christ and his Kingdom of regenerated Faith!—But regeneration leads to *Life and Immortality*,—and the spirit ascends to Christ, and is united to him in immortality! And this is the "Seal of the living God and the name being written in the Book of Life"—For, how is it possible that mortality and death can be united to, or have any union with, *Immortality and Life*?—And mind—it is done in this life, before you die! for as the tree falleth, so it lays to all eternity.

NOW,—YOU may see the difference between the kingdom of Christ, and "The bloody unbelieving world"—I spare no labour or pains to inform you,—and I pray the Lord God of Mercy to give you power, and hasten you on in His kingdom of regenerated Faith; it being the eager desire and prayer of your loving brother in CHRIST,

London, Oct. 22, 1782.   JAMES BIRCH

NOTE.—*Nov, 2, this was transcribed, and sent as follows:—To our beloved Brother and Sister, J. B. Parry, and Mary Jones, and to all that would worship God unto salvation! I present this epistle, &c.*

JAMES BIRCH

LETTER XLVIII

To Our beloved Sisters, Mary Griffiths, Alice Bevan; Uncle Frank, &c. and to all that would worship God, James Birch and Brethren Send Greeting.

Beloved Brethren.—I hope you will remember what I said when I parted with you at *Caermarthen*, and above all things, let it be your care to abide by it, and walk in it, then you will WORSHIP GOD, not only unto his blessing in this life, but unto his eternal bliss in the life to come: For as a man is born into this busy world in wickedness, in or under the spirit and power of Reason, Reason will allure the man from the law of Moses, into the *Wilderness or Desart*, where God is not to be found to stay his justice; and there drive the soul into evil, And give him plenty of work to do; and fill the soul with anxious cares of this life, for tomorrow, then tell him he must do it, or ruination will ensue; and that great duties must be done to preserve *Self* and Posterity; and also with *fear* he shall lose his kingdom, (which he is sure to do) that by this, he not only drive the soul from the enjoyments of the rural blessings appointed him of God, but also into death under cherubical justice. Also, he will tempt or drive the soul into *Evil*, and tell the man he must, or may do it, and no one will know it; and that God will forgive it; then—when the act is done, fear and shame take place! and on a sudden it is born to public knowledge, then they must face public justice and shame.

Again, by his temptation, he will fill the soul with great expectations of things he shall arrive to, and it is still to be done *tomorrow*! Also allure the soul on, from time to time, in coveteousness and slavery, for the great things he thinks to ascertain, that this day is hardly to be found, according to his expectation; and if found, then justice requires his soul in death: And his own internal lying Priest, will furnish him with excuse for what he doth, for Reason of itself is incapable of doing any good.

Now this is the great *Wilderness* of the world, where Reason reject the truth and blessing of God, but will have things to his own liking! and as so works his own overthrow!—For as time fleets away, so Reason fall, and is drowned in his own waters, like as the relentless *Sea* will swallow up the eager life of man: BUT unto you that are called, and unto them that can and will come, and worship God, keep the word, and pray for the virtue of Patience, you will be kept from the hour of temptation which will come upon all the world to try and manifest *them*; and like unto a strong *Current*, take them off into the relentless *Sea* of justice, let them think what they will to the contrary!

Further, this CALL takes man to the first resurrection and regeneration, to follow CHRIST; then of consequence all of this world must be *left* to follow Him, or not to be worthy of Him: And with what God has blessed you with in this life,— enjoy this blessing without the slavish fear of Reason, otherwise you frown on providence; or by your evil spirit doubt his further blessing.

And after all the erronious busy life of Reason, where must it go for succour, seeing it must be swallowed up in death and justice, according to that attribute of God? for when it is arraigned before the angel, and the book of justice and death opened, he may look back on his mis-spent life, and see whether that, them, or they, or what he has spent his anxious busy laborious life for, can give him any help? then,—the answer is no! and he will find his life spent, labour in vain, for his own benefit!

I write those things, that you, and all of you, may be careful of the follies of this life, and the fears, threats, and temptations of Reason, for you may be assured there is no other succour for men than what is now declared, and offered by this present Messenger: Neither would I have any one *think* they can carry the vain delights and kingdoms of this world in one hand, and the kingdom of heaven in the other; or *serve God* and *Mammon*, for where the Treasure is fixed, according to the desire of Faith, or of Reason, there the soul will incline to, and be a servant.

Also see Mat. xii. 30, Jesus said, "He that is not with me, is against me: and he that gathereth not with me, scattereth abroad;" *i.e.* he that doth not leave all the vain things of this life,—yea, the families, kingdoms, and incumberance of this world, and unite to CHRIST for His Kingdom, is against Him; why? because he is in Reason's kingdoms!—And he that do not become as a *Child*, and leave the worship of the Beast, Dragon, or Devil, and come into the Priesthood of Faith by this first resurrection; and gather his way by divine assistance to the kingdom of mercy, as Christ himself did, *scattereth abroad*; why? because he goeth into the Wilderness or Desart, where all false hope, false worship, evil, blasphemy, &c. is acted and delighted in.

AGAIN, when the elect are enlightened from Heaven, and taken into the priesthood of Faith, they must *Will* and desire for God, to rule over them, because he best knows what is good for man, and how to bring him through all, and from all, by regeneration; therefore it is good for man to offer at the FEET OF GOD, for his will and Pleasure, and, depend on HIM, for both natural and spiritual protection: like unto the *Widow* that cast her *two mites* into the Treasury, which was all her Living:—And when any one give up all his own cunning of acting, for God to rule over him, *he* will receive a blessing of the TREASURES OF GOD! Therefore beware of the slavish fears, threats and temptations of Reason, but WORSHIP GOD, that he may *rule* over you, and protect you: See Luke xix. 27, Jesus said, "But those mine enemies, which would not that I should *rule* over them, bring them hither, and slay them before me" hence you may see the wisdom of Reason leads to death and hell; and that they will be slain by the justice of God!

Moreover, the travail in regeneration is from death, and through death to Life; for as Christ made all things new, the *old* must be left and the *new* followed: And when Faith is quickened from death to life, it sees itself in the midst of sorrow, and in a *Vale of tears*, and it has a *straight* and *narrow path*; to go, but by patience and prayer you will have divine assistance to go the *Way*.

And whereas many of late has usurped the assurance of eternal life, yet they shall see many in a *far country* come and enter the priesthood of Faith, and worship God, and also enter the kingdom of glory, and themselves cast out; therefore have patience and prayer, and fear not, seeing the Lord God is at hand to assist you, and reward your labour.

Tell uncle Frank, I remember what he said to me, and I pray God increase his understanding and Faith, and if occasion serve, let him see or hear a letter, &c, and I pray God to give you all and every one strength, and help you on in HIS kingdom of regenerated Faith.

So conclude your loving brother in Christ,

London, Nov. 30, 1782,   JAS. BIRCH.

LETTER XLIX

To our beloved Brother and Sister, J. B. Parry, and Mary Jones, and to all that would worship God, James Birch and Brethren send Greeting.

Beloved Brethren—I am glad to hear from you, and also to see such a loving union, and communion with, and among you, for that will remove mountains; why? because to them that are truly united in and for the love of Christ's kingdom of regenerated Faith, comes his blessing to take you through a *Vale of Tears*; and assist you to overcome death, hell, &c. &c.

Again, them that are born of God will see and know his truth and light, and that will discover this busy working-day world in error and darkness, then of consequence, no rest for the elect there: Also, the elect must go through the justice of God for it cannot be that Faith should *fall* under the power of death, and in that condition be translated into heaven, and not know from whence it came, nor the Way it came; But, no! it must be rose from death to life, and be brought through the justice of God by regeneration, then it will be experimentally wise in, and truly know the power of God, both in his Justice and Mercy: And he that thinks to go any other way, will find himself not to possess the *Wedding Garment*, and as so will be cast out from the kingdom of Christ!

Also, understand this,—that Reason has usurped the frothy Lordship of this world, and say, "He has a right to do as he please, in making choice to worship God;"—and, also of what he possess in this world, which he vainly calls his own, and do as he please with others that are under him, because he has it, or a right to do what he will with his own,—and so say I,—but I also say he will perish for it when he has done; for if a man is born to no higher life or light than that of Reason, then the flow of this life will act according to its will and nature; and the man will be pleased with this light, and think it is of God: whereas it is wild Reason, and entirely against God! for this *Light* in them is *darkness*, and as so "Great is that darkness;" but men by this dark life, spirit, and light, will seek their own will and desire; and justify their evil acts, and be well pleased and in themselves be rich and whole; because they think God will forgive them, and at the same time act against God, and refuse his kind offer;

and wonder at Men that are called of God, because they cannot do as they of wild Reason do; why? because, as aforesaid, they are born to no other life or light than that of Reason, and are incapable of regeneration, so you cannot gather grapes of thorns.

Again, Reason is High and mighty in themselves, and need no instruction from heaven by a messenger of God! Why? because they will have things to themselves, according to their own will and liking: But as to the elect that are called and enter the priesthood of Faith, they find themselves to *hunger, mourn, and weep,*—why? because they see themselves in a *fallen state,* and under the Justice of God, and must come from out of the world; and wade through justice to mercy; and oft'times look into themselves, and see their own weakness and evil, which makes them fearful, and sometimes think they will not be saved!

Luke vi. 21.—Jesus said, "Blessed are ye that hunger now, for ye shall be filled; blessed are ye that weep now, for ye shall laugh;" because this is a hard travail to Faith, which make the soul weep and mourn, and hunger for God's divine assistance: Therefore Faith is apt to be fearful, knowing of God's power; but Reason is full of himself, and laugh Faith to scorn: But

Ver. 24.—Jesus said, "But woe unto you that are rich, for ye have received your consolation: Woe unto you that are full, for ye shall hunger: Woe unto you that laugh now, for ye shall weep and mourn": Therefore let Reason gather what riches he can from the Letter, or from where or how he can, and be puffed up in fulness by his imagination, yet in *one hour* it will be brought to naught, and him to mourn and bewail his desolation: BUT, unto you and unto them that do come and worship God, have patience and prayer to overcome, and fear not, for every day brings the nearer approach of eternity! And your works of Faith will follow you to life eternal, which is the prayer and desire of your loving brother in Christ.

London, Dec. 17, 1782.   JAMES BIRCH.

LETTER L

To Mrs. E. Davies, and Mrs. E. Howel, James Birch sendeth greeting.

Beloved Sisters and Brethren—I saw a letter of Elizabeth Howel's at Caermarthen, and also one of Elizabeth Davies, and am ready and willing to answer and instruct you in any thing that can or may enlighten you to WORSHIP GOD, whose Wisdom is contrary to the wisdom of Man! For men must *come* OUT from the will and way of the World, to *worship God*: because the whole world is gone out in the wilderness to make war *against* God and his Saints!

For as the spirit of Reason has transformed itself into the letter of the scripture, and set it forth according to its dark wisdom, and preach and promise the salvation of Christ, by their imagination, which is contrary to the light and spirit of Christ. For some will have free will, (*i.e.* that all may be saved if they will) some free grace, and some Universal redemption; and some to be already assured of eternal life, &c. and some will have God to be understood one way, and some another, &c. &c. and cry, "Lo, here is Christ, and Lo, there is Christ." So that salvation teachers are become as plenty as trees in a forest: now, this is the great wilderness wherein dwelleth the Beast and false prophet, for the wild emulated power they go out on, is the *Beast*; and him that preaches and teaches the salvation of Christ; and promise Christ by his own dark spirit of Reason, is the *false prophet*; so BLESSED is him or then that NOW hear the voice of God by his Messenger, and come out to worship God, and follow up to CHRIST the king of Faith, where salvation IS and WILL BE found!—for you may be assured this wilderness, is left in desolation.

Moreover, as to the doctrine of *free will*; or that all men may be saved if they will: Here, in this, men invade heaven and take it by *Violence*, and make themselves equal with, if not above God, and would rob him of his power and glory! for if will and power is in man; then it is whether God will or no! Also, it is invoking and compelling God to own, and unite himself with the *abominable incense* of wild Reason, which is the doctrine of Devils. Again, it destroys the nature and kingdom of Faith, by being a servant to, or united with, Reason, which is of the Devil; and destroys the two attributes of God, which is Justice to Reason, and of mercy to his elect, and Christ the Redeemer called a liar by their suggestions of his record, his Messenger, and his works.

Therefore see Matt. vii. 13, Jesus said, "Enter ye in at the straight gate, for wide is the gate and broad is the way that leadeth to destruction, and *many* there be which go in threat." Now there is no wider gate and broader *Way* than that for all men to be saved if they will, so the road is easy to destruction.

Ver. 14. Jesus said "Because straight is the gate and narrow is the way which leadeth unto life, and few there be that find it," why? because men, by their own will and wisdom go into the wilderness, and although the name of God and Christ is as plenty there as grass in the field, yet men grope about and never can find this straight gate and narrow way, but it is him or them whom Christ choose he take in at the straight gate, and through the narrow way to life eternal.

Again, Luke xiii. 24. Jesus said, "Strive to enter in at the straight gate, for many, I say unto you, will seek to enter in, and shall not be able." Now if man seek to enter, and shall not be able, then where is the use of their own will to salvation; for if they seek for it they will to have it, and shall not be able to obtain.

See John vii. 34. Jesus said, "Ye shall seek me and shall not find me; and whither I go ye cannot come," because, whoever seek him by a contrary spirit, seek to dethrone him therefore cannot come to his eternal bliss.

Ch. viii. 21. Then said Jesus again unto them, "I go my way, and ye shall seek me, and shall die in your sins; whither I go ye cannot come;" therefore the will and power is of God, and not of man.

Also, x. 5. Jesus said, "I am the vine, ye are the branches, he that abideth in me and I in him, the same bringeth forth much fruit, for without me you can do nothing."

Ver. 16. "Ye have not chosen me, but I have chosen you;" hence you may see no one can bring forth an act of Faith in regeneration for salvation, without the assistance of Christ; and as man is born into this world to bring forth generation, even so he must be born again to bring forth the fruits of Faith in regeneration: For what is man? He cannot make one hair of his head white or black, or add one inch to his stature; or keep himself from evil; or stop God's justice from overtaking him; yet his arrogance is so great, as to say "he may be saved if he will," and in this he contradicts the Redeemer, and gives him the lie! But this is an old trick of Reason, to make its kingdom as the kingdom of God; for when the serpent tempted Eve, he said "She should be as wise as God's, *to know good and evil*," then she fell into the wild priesthood of Reason, and even to this day the elect can be tempted no lower than into the wild priesthood of Reason, and there Reason would make them as wise as God's, which is to be like himself, *i.e.* to act against God, do as he please, and choose his own way to heaven without restraint, and this is to be as *wise as God's*, but it is god's of the dark spirit: Now when Christ the Lord God of heaven was on this earth to redeem his elect, he was in all things obedient to the will and power of the Father in what he came to do, but those of the dark spirit are obedient to nothing but their own will, and in and by that they are called God's; therefore beware of this temptation, for when they come to be arraigned before the POWER OF GOD, they all will to be saved, but cannot.

Further, of *Free Grace*: this free grace is given to the elect, but then Faith must be risen from the dead, or the virgin daughter born from its womb or seed in them, and taken into the royal priesthood of Faith, before they can have or enjoy it, and free grace is the holy spirit of Christ given to this Virgin daughter of faith, for to help her thro' the temptation of Reason; and to overcome the world as Christ himself did, and also to lead them in regeneration to redemption, and to his royal seal of salvation for his kingdom of glory! Now this is free grace, which is given by Christ the king of Faith to his royal elect! But this is not nor possible it can be given to Reason, it being such a contrary nature, to the nature and life of CHRIST.

But as Reason has usurped the letter of the scripture, and may read of the promises and mercy of God to his elect, as Matt. vii. 7, 8. "Ask, and it shall be given you, seek and ye shall find, knock and it shall be opened to you: For every one that asketh receiveth, and he that seeketh findeth, and to him that knocketh it shall be opened." Now this is all to the elect, when they are *risen from the dead*, and taken into the royal Priesthood of Faith—for this virgin daughter of Faith is of the divine nature of Christ; and by his divine, assistance will work the works of Faith as He did; and will be united to Him; and as so hath power to *seek* after him, and *ask* of him, and *knock at the door* of His mercy, and all will be granted unto her, She being the being the royal Bride, and Christ the royal Bridegroom:—But the sons of Reason being incapable of regeneration, Faith cannot be risen or brought forth in them, so they are as incapable to seek after or ask those things by the spirit of Faith, that is rose from death to life for regeneration, as a dead man is incapable to seek after, and ask things of a man who is living.

But Reason has usurped the letter of the scripture, and thief-like, claim all the promises made to the elect, to and for himself, and although they read the scripture, they cannot tell when the spirit speak to Faith or to Reason, or what it speak concerning of, so one will have one thing one way, and one another way, &c. &c. so they divide and go out and hold forth according to their imagination, which make this great and terrible wilderness; for of this you may be assured that the sons of Reason, when they come to manhood, are cast out from the presence of God, and there kept by the internal angel in justice, to wander *to and fro* through the earth, and on the bare letter of the scripture, seeking rest but can find none; for let them be ever so wise in themselves, they will bear their own witness to their own condemnation, let them think what they will to the contrary.

Moreover, this is written that you may in some degree see and know the great tremendous wilderness, where the whole world is lost by their acting against God, and as so they are swallowed up in death, under His justice, therefore blessed is he that now *hear the call and come out*, to worship the Lord God of Heaven, for you may be well assured there is no other refuge for men than what is now offered by this present Messenger of GOD, and that many will know here in time to their eternal Bliss! and many in eternity to their eternal Woe! therefore my advice is that you hold fast by what you have heard and received, and pray for the increase of Wisdom and Faith in it; and to beware and watch the tempter, for Reason will be much obliged to you to be tempted by him, that he may rule over you, then leave you to perish with himself,—So watch his invitations, his insinuations, his entreaties, intrigues, objections, uproar, confused noise, and all the helpless powers he may think to invoke for his assistance, and fear not his threats, for it is in and by the spirit of fear the world sink, and is lost; for whosoever seek to save his life in this wilderness, will lose it; and whosoever seek to lose it in this declaration and Faith, which is from Heaven, will find it again in Christ: For as Christ the King of Faith, who is the Lord God of Heaven, created both Heaven and earth, and all that in them is, and also to become man and redeem his elect world, HE is very able to direct your passage through this life, and will do it, if you will worship him, and pray his divine assistance, but Reason will fly from him, and hide himself in what he can, and how, and where he can for the present.

Answer to your Qu.—When the Lord God of Heaven was born into this world of the tribe of Judah, to redeem his elect, he was obedient to the commands of Moses, such as *Circumcision*, the Dove and Pigeon *Offering*, eating the *Passover*, &c. which passover is concerning, when the destroying angel slew every, *first born* of Egypt, both of man and beast, and passed over the Israelites, and saved them alive: which was ordained by Moses to be kept as a *Memorial* in Israel; and the jews keep it to this day.

And Mat. xxvi.— When JESUS CHRIST eat the *Passover* with his disciples,—Jesus brake and blessed bread, and gave them, saying "Eat, this is my body;" and gave them the cup, saying, "Drink, this is my blood of the new testament, which is shed for many for the remission of sins," which was to shew forth the very God of Heaven become man to redeem his Elect, and eat and drink as man, and with man, and lost HIMSELF in death in his own blood, for the redemption: For, until that was done, the new testament could not take place.

And, Luke xxii. 19.—HE said, "This is my body which is given for you; this do in remembrance of me;" and the Apostles did practise those things, to shew forth the Lord God of Heaven did eat and drink as man, and with man, and by his death and resurrection, HE would unite elect men to himself, and make them flesh of his flesh, and bone of his bone, and spirit of his spirit, by the power of his regeneration, his holy marriage, and his raising them to eternal Life! Now he that hath wisdom, let him understand! And this understand also,—at that time, as well as now, more must be done to enter the kingdom of heaven, than to eat bread, and drink wine, as the body and blood of Christ! for that is but the outward word and act, or bare letter; and if eating bread and drinking wine will gain heaven, it is easy done! for that goeth into the belly, and is cast into the draught, and not help the man for salvation, let men put what sanction or consecration on it they please, for this Reason has transformed himself, into, and took it into the wilderness long ago!

Moreover, when Christ eat this *passover*, it was to shew he had *passed* over the justice of the Angel, which is justice to Reason, and he was going to *pass* into death, under the justice of the father and through death and the justice of the father to his royal kingdom of mercy; and that time would come, his disciples would know they must, by his divine assistance, do as he did; and pass the same way, *i.e.* by the justice to Reason, because of regeneration, but under and through justice to Faith, for when he gave them the holy ghost from heaven, it brought all things to their remembrance, and let them know their own condition, which was, they must bear all the mock, scourge, temptation, and persecution of Reason; as he did, and work the works of Faith, under the justice of the Father, as he did; for as Christ, here in a body of flesh and blood, in the priesthood and compact of Faith, did those things under the justice of the Father, even so must his elect, in a body of flesh and blood, do the same, in union with Christ, under the power of the Father;—for

See Matt. xxvi. 29.—"But I say unto you, I will not drink henceforth of this fruit of the vine, until that day when I drink it new with you in my Father's kingdom;" *i.e.* as Christ, in a body of flesh and blood, eat bread and drink wine in *Sorrow*, when he worked the works of Faith, under the justice of the father, and died and rose again, and ascended into his own kingdom of mercy, then, (as before said) when his disciples was rose from the dead, or translated into the priesthood of Faith, by the holy spirit, under the justice of the father, then in a body of flesh and blood, *they* must eat bread and drink wine in *sorrow*, as he did, and *work* the works of Faith as he did; and *overcome* the world as he did; and lose themselves in *death*, in their own blood, under the justice of the Father, as he did; for the justice of the Father is justice to Faith, and that is the *kingdom* of the father, and as all the elect must do those things under that justice, it is done in the kingdom of the father, and as Christ did those things before them, and is ascended into his THRONE of Mercy, and now assists his elect, by his holy spirit, to do those things, under the justice of the father. In this *he drinks of the fruit of the vine, new with his elect, who are in his Father's Kingdom*, because he assist them to work, and receives their *incense* of Faith, which is the fruit of the Vine of Faith, in regeneration, in his father's kingdom, which is his drinking of the vine *anew*, because it is in and to his eternal Joy, but when on earth, HE was in SORROW!!!— Therefore the elect must, in this manner, eat his flesh and drink his blood, to have part in him, for

See John's Gosp. vi. 53.—Jesus said, "Except ye eat the flesh of the son of man, and drink his blood, ye have no life in you, he that eateth my flesh, and drinketh my blood, dwelleth in me and I in him;" *i.e.* as Christ went through and overcome all the powers of hell, and Reason, by the power of Faith, in a body of flesh and blood, and worked the works of Faith, under the justice of the father; and when Faith is rose from death to life, and taken into the priesthood of Christ, which is of Faith in regeneration,—then, in a body of flesh and blood, by his divine assistance the elect must do the same, which is eating his flesh and drinking his blood; and in all the sorrowful heavy trouble and travail of soul, they may and will *remember* Christ himself was there! And as Christ took the cup of sorrow unto death, so must his elect; and as Christ lost himself in death, in his own blood, under the justice of the father, so must his elect; and this is eating his flesh and drinking his blood, in the grand union and works of Faith, which is they in him, and he in them, and no other way can his flesh be eat, and his blood drank for salvation! for the elect cannot pass by or over the justice of the father, nor the justice of the father pass by or over them, but they must go through it as aforesaid.

Now do you mind what is written, and I hope you will be found worthy of those works, it being the desire of your loving friend and brother,

London, Jan. 28, 1783. JAMES BIRCH.

LETTER LI

To our beloved Brother, J. B. Parry.

Dear Brother—I am glad to see you *overcome* the threats and temptation of Reason at *Portclew*— I mean to answer what is asked: And as for your coming to London; it is what I do not advise, for it will be much the best for you to serve your time *out*: And fear not but you will do well: As for Mrs. *Evans*, I would have you do the best you can with: and act with spirit, as becomes a Man, and not be *brow-beat* by any. And this I also advise; for you to know what Mrs. Evans will do, before she has power over you: Therefore be as certain as you can before *time* is up.

My love to Mr. and Mrs. Jones, and to Mr. Williams: I am glad to hear you are all well, and love one another. So conclude your loving brother in the true Faith of Christ,

London, Feb. 18, 1783.   JAMES BIRCH

LETTER LII

To Mrs. Runwa, &c. Pembroke.

Beloved Sister,—I am glad you received the letter I sent to sister *Williams*, and more so that you comprehend it: And as for men talking of it; or seeking it in the wilderness (by the dark spirit of Reason), they never can find it or know it; but when the SPIRITUAL BORN SON appear, which now is the time, he will declare the Truth and Power of God, and of Christ; and make it Plain: then in God's time the Elect will hear, and come and follow: Why? Because they are born the sons of Adam, which are the *Sons of God*, according to generation; then by regeneration they are made the SONS of CHRIST; therefore the knowledge and inheritance of immortality and life, is given from heaven above!

But the Sons of Reason when they come to manhood, are born to no other knowledge or inheritance but that which perish; so never can agree with immortality and life: Therefore, when the *Call* comes from heaven; the elect will hear the Voice, and follow through darkness and death to life and Immortality; and Reason will go its way to mortality and death! And the nature is such, that each will venture his salvation on the way they go.

I hope you received that to Davis and Co. and you will be careful to observe! And I pray God assist you to work the works, then you will be brought through and overcome all those powers of sin, justice, death, and hell; for you may see how the wild nature of man act in Egypt and the Wilderness! How their anxious *Care* is to seek after, and gather up vain things that perish on the one part; and to act against, and blaspheme the power of God and of Christ on the other; and this opposing, lying, wrathful, murdering, and blasphemous spirit of Reason, is (Rev. xi. 8.) the spiritual *Sodom* & *Egypt*; where our Lord was crucified; why? Because this spirit acts against the divine teachings and nature of Christ; and by their acts would cut off or destroy regeneration, even as the Sodomites by their act, would have cut off or destroyed generation, for which it is called the spiritual Sodom and Egypt.

Now think you—of what value is this great wilderness, to the Lord God of heaven, and the weakness of men that strive to be great in it? Of this yon may be assured, that CHRIST will gather in His kingdom of regeneration, regardless of the outcries of Egypt; because of the mighty weight of justice falling on them like *hailstone*.

And the Messenger will, by his CALL, divide friends and families, and take them that can follow up to Christ, and not regard any trouble or disappointment that fall on the kingdom of Egypt thereby! For he well knows, they by their nature and acts will be swallowed up by death and hell, which is worse than losing their *first born*.

Again, unto you, and unto all and every one that *worship* God, and thereby enter into the Light of Christ, by which light you *See* darkness!

You have been informed of the mercy and life of Christ, which make you *See* Justice and death! and not only so, but also to know you are under it, and must go through it to Mercy and Life: And sometimes the soul is borne down in justice and death, which make it TREMBLE! HUNGER! and THIRST! and pray for a glimpse of its former Light and Communion! So great and mighty is the travail through this *Vale* of sorrow, and of death!

The answer you received in your dream, by the Messenger, was very right; and you do well in desiring to do it; for the closer to the Messenger the nearer CHRIST! You may be well assured that my soul's desire and prayer is for you and the whole church; for I came out from CHRIST to be a SERVANT to His elect in regeneration; for regenerated Faith is of the divine nature of Christ; therefore it is His great Treasure and care, for which I have been *faithful and true* in what has been given me from heaven; be you *true* to the Messenger and each other in the Faith and love of Christ: You may depend on the Messenger; for your welfare in regeneration is my anxious desire, prayer, and care. You will write soon of that to Davis, &c.

So conclude your loving brother in Christ, with love to the Church.

JAMES BIRCH.

London, Feb. 26, 1783.

LETTER LIII

To Mrs. Runwa, &c. Pembroke.

Beloved Sister,—This with my love to inform you our brother Parry came safe to me at London, yesterday afternoon, after a very affrighted and troubled journey, and is now tolerable well, and sendeth his kind love to you and the whole church.

Also, he begs you will inform his father and mother at Portclew, how and where he is, and that they may be well assured great care will be taken of him; neither will any one take any advantage of him.

It was the spirit of *fear* which drove him, because of Mrs. Evans's continual threats: He is inclined to try to stay in London, if Mr. Howel will agree with his father that he may.

And I would have his father and mother be reconciled to him, for it is a vain thing to *war* against the POWER of God: For the kingdom of regenerated Faith WILL be gathered in; and justice and confusion must follow them who strive against it.

He sends his love and duty to his father and mother, in all things, except to be persuaded or drove from the kingdom of regenerated Faith— (This to be seen at Portclew).—My love to you and the whole church, and conclude your loving brother,

JAS. BIRCH.

London March 25, 1783.

LETTER LIV

To our beloved Brother James Thomas, Lamphy.

Beloved Brother,—Yesterday I received your letter concerning Mr. Parry, as to his coming to London now; — I wrote to him to the contrary, and did hope all was well—and when he came to me, I was much surprised. I asked him the cause, he told me "Mrs. Evans would have further security than he could give for the remaining half, or plant the law against him, which he feared."

Also, "when he was at *Portclew* last winter, he met with great opposition concerning the holy Faith of Christ in regeneration, which he must and is determined to follow, so saw no prospect of peace there." Again, "Mr. Howel at Caermarthen, suffered his servant to joke and jeer him, because he would not do as they did, therefore he saw no prospect of peace there, and these things were the cause of his coming to London to seek peace! though notwithstanding he was sorry to leave his parents—and brethren of the Faith."

Moreover, he greatly likes London, and the brethren of the Faith, and they as much like him, and will do what they can to serve him, therefore he is very unwilling to leave London, nay I believe will not, without force, and even then he says he will come again, he is now at a friend of ours, where he will learn the ways of London, and be brought on for business, and I would have Mr. and Mrs. Parry be satisfied he is hearty and well, active, brisk, and lively, more so here than I saw him in the country, and great care will be taken of him; and in my judgment as safe and well here as at *Portclew*; and as for Mr. Howels searching after him, or advertising him, that is not regarded, but only I would have Mr. and Mrs. Parry to be reconciled and easy, seeing how things are, and great care will be taken: He sent a letter to sister Runwa, which inclosed the IXth chapter of the book of the law, which I hope was received.

Beloved Brother, I was surprised to see you desired me to advise Mr. Parry to go *back*. I had no concern in what was done at Caermarthen, nor ever advised him to come to London; he said he flew here to *worship God in Peace*, and for the sake of CHRIST'S kingdom of regenerated Faith! Doth not Christ pronounce such worthy of him? and I cannot refuse them: If any *ask me for a fish, I cannot give them a serpent*: If any come to me in this condition -you may depend I shall shelter them, Yea, Christ would not suffer his disciples to go back and *bid them farewell* at their own house, and I cannot advise, or desire him to go *back*, to where he will be tempted from worshiping God, it being for that very cause he came to me.

Now this I am compelled to do; for I must mind my master and his work, as well as the world do their master and his work: Also I would advise Reason to be content with his own lot, and let CHRIST have his LOT, which is his own Elect in regeneration and salvation! This is all I can say at present. My love to the whole church: So conclude your loving brother in Christ.

London, April 8, 1783.   JAS. BIRCH.

My love to Mrs. Runwa, I return her many thanks for her labour and care, that she has of late honoured the Truth with. Mr. Parry's love to his father and mother, and the whole church.

LETTER LV

To our beloved Brother Geo. Plowman, Ireland.

Beloved Brother,—It was with great joy we received your letter,—for, as in your last you said you would meet me at Pembroke, and as you did not, it put me and the church there into a consternation; I abode there near six weeks, and as all inquiry after you availed not, we concluded something must have happened, but it makes amends now, only hope you will be silent no more so long a time.

Again, I am glad you are possessed of such excellent virtues, for *Hope* and *Charity* will bring in *obedience* to WORSHIP GOD, as was and is directed by His Messenger; then the power of patience will be granted, that man may overcome his enemies, which elect men will find many in this life; and as to the *Tyrant* spirit of Reason, he is sure to overact his part, for which cause he bear his own witness to his own condemnation, therefore you observe this, and the power of God will be manifested in his truth, even in things of this life.

Further, —But the nature and power of Faith far transcends all, why? because that nature is worked on for salvation; for when it is rose from the dead into active, life, it is taken into the royal priesthood to follow Christ in regeneration, and there it work and is worked on for salvation; which is to *overcome* Reason, have devils cast out, and mountains removed, that this spirit or virgin of Faith will become the essential soul for salvation! Thus you may see the Two Priesthoods,— one is to overcome your enemies, in natural things in this life, whereby you may live and flourish above their wrath and the other is to overcome sin, death, hell, &c, for life eternal!

Now, my eager desire and prayer is, that you WATCH those things, and for God to assist you in those things, that you may *overcome* and inherit the kingdom of mercy and glory.

Beloved Brother, I and family, and all friends are tolerable well; it is this with us, as soon, if not before, as one trouble is over, another come! But our desire is to worship God, and are content, and so we *overcome*!

If it should be that you come to London, and go by the way of Milford-Haven, call at Griffiths Howel's, Pembroke, and you will be received with joy; we hope to hear from you soon.—Our love to Mr. Bennet, if living. So conclude your loving brother in Christ.

JAMES BIRCH.

London, 3, Butler's-Alley, May, 1783.

LETTER LVI

To beloved Runwa, &c. beloved in Christ, in and about Pembroke, James Birch, &c. greeting.

Beloved Sister,— This with my love to inform you, that I received all your letters and would have answered, but could give no satisfaction how things would be;—this great mountain that has been so long in labour, has at last brought forth a mouse, and he without teeth.

When old Mr. Parry came to town, I believe he would have been glad to do me an injury, but was soon let to know the contrary: at last I agreed to give him his son's clothes, and what money I had, and he is to have the care of maintaining him during his Lunacy:—He has been very *mad*, and has been in the *madhouse* ever since Easter; his father says he will bring him down with him, so in about a week you may expect him there.

I return you and the whole church many thanks for your anxious care for me and the church in London, but we have, and shall, by divine assistance, overcome all things; and if you mind what is and has been said and declared, you will do the same;—we have heard from brother Plowman, and I have answered him; —he may come and see you at Pembroke.

Mr. Sinnet has been at our house twice; —I mean to send you the particulars of our brother Parry* by him; —I have had a deal of trouble, and I fear it will be some time before his devil is cast out;— Our sister Elizabeth Jellis is dead, and buried last Sunday.—My love to you and the whole church.

So in haste conclude your loving brother in Christ.

JAMES BIRCH

London, June 14, 1783

P.S. This night 7 o'Clock, I settled with Mr. Parry, Sen. and have his Bond to indemnify me.

---

* See Divine Memorial

LETTER LVII

To sister Runwa, &c. Jas. Birch, &c. sends greeting.

Beloved Sister—I and the brethren rejoice to hear from you and the church, and that you stand firm in this Faith! which is the Faith of Christ in his Kingdom of regeneration; the which, if man cannot enter into, he must die under the *destroying Angel* as did the *first born of Egypt*: But them that Christ takes he raises from death to life, and brings them on in his royal Priesthood; and seal and sanctify them to himself! So my Soul's love and prayer, and the BLESSING of God and of Christ be with you: and—Stand fast and fear not; for although Reason may, yea will, give you their flesh to eat in this his *vaporous and fading* kingdom, yet. "Strong is the Lord God of heaven, which searches the reins and hearts of men, and will give every one according to their works," therefore: fear not *Little Flock*, seeing God is on your side, and can and will bring you through; that you shall see the powers of Reason fall before your face! as by patience and the prayer of Faith, for and with the divine assistance of Christ, "mountains will be removed;" for as gold is brought through fiery trials in the Refiner's Test, to come out *pure*; even so must Faith in regeneration be brought through *fiery trials* to come forth *pure* to the Lord God of mercy!

Beloved sister, I greatly commend your stedfast Faith; and your proceeding to vindicate or maintain this glorious truth against all hissing serpents, or barking dogs, &c.; and above all, to declare the experience your soul, which I know to be right and true; henceforth go on in prayer and *faint not*: Yet—

I would not advise you to be too much a servant or slave to proud arrogant Reason, back sliders, &c. who may think themselves of great consequence, as to labour to convert them; whereas they are of no value to the LORD of Regeneration, His Church, or His Messenger.— BUT them that are for us, are and will be given to us: Neither can any one take away or stop the kingdom of Christ, for at this day there will come trials, to make Manifestations that the elect shall not be deceived, but be more united in love of the united church of Christ, in his kingdom of regenerated Faith.

Moreover, I am glad you saw and talked with old Parry, you did well with him; for then, by the power of God, you was shewn an ignorant, dark, proud arrogant, presumptive piece of Reason; and what must any one think of themselves to be ruled by him? For a wise man in Reason would scorn to be seen to act in the manner as he did in London; and as for his saying *I am no more a Messenger of God than a dog*—I answer—according to that judgment, which he has given, it must be either him or me—now this hazard the dark-spirit of Reason ran—but let *him* look to that; for if he had known God, he never had opposed HIS *Church*, and fought against me—but from his dark spirit, he may make a *noise*, and if he can, may amuse the *owlish brood*.

Again, beloved sister, see Matt. xiii. of the *Sower*, where "some seed fell on stony places, where there was not much earth—it sprang up when the sun was up, they were scorched, and withered away, because it had not root," so it is now at this day. As when *trial* came they are offended and will *slink* away! BUT the Elect will stand the SUN-SHINE of Christ, and be brought through *fiery trials*! And those are them for Christ the king of Faith, For

This I say, against Man or Angel who oppose me—that, I *come from God and teach the Truth and Kingdom* of CHRIST; —and no one can go any other WAY!

Therefore, as Christ said, "HE that sinneth is a servant to sin, and the servant abideth not in the house for ever," *i.e.* the life that man here enjoy is subject or a *servant* to sin, and when death take this life the servant is fled, and nothing remain in the house but the Law and Justice; for as the law rule this life, so justice rule the law; and when man is dead justice can be no longer stayed, but he is sealed unto the second death, because this *servant* is gone: But "the Son abideth ever;" this SON is Christ: And when He raises Faith from death to life, and by regeneration it become the essential soul for salvation, and is united to the Son, and the Son take possession of the *house* and *abideth for ever* to make man *free*!

See John viii. 36. Jesus said, "If the Son, therefore, shall make you free, ye shall be *free* indeed!" Therefore; no man can be *free from sin*; without being united to Christ, and that must be by regeneration, because he Make all things NEW, and to come forth PURE; for his glorious kingdom of Mercy; —and them that cannot stand the *Sunshine* of Faith, and the *Storms and Blasts*, of Reason will slink back, and must die as they were born, therefore do you give space for repentance, but never be a servant to that spirit who will not repent: But unto you and the church who desire to worship God and Christ, blessed are you to see those glorious days, therefore hold fast and fear not for *the days* of Reason *are shortened* in his persecution and by divine assistance you will soon *overcome*, and your reward is life eternal!

Beloved sister, &c. I go on writing the gospel; it runs beautiful and clear; ye may be sure my soul's love is with you all. Do you and the church write. So conclude your loving brother in Christ.

JAMES BIRCH,

London, Nov. 18, 1783.

LETTER LVIII

To our beloved Sister Mary Runwa, &c. James Birch, &c. sends greeting.

Beloved Sister, I was glad to hear from you and the church; I pray God increase your Faith in regeneration, and as you would know how Reason give us his *flesh to eat*, I will inform you, and pray God assist us in it.

Now, in the beginning, when Faith broke its own law, it hearkened to Reason, and was guided by Reason, and as so disobeyed the command of its Father and Creator, and fell under the power of death, yea, dead in its self, for then Reason took possession of the soul, and was the whole Life and actuation of man and woman! And thus it goes on in generation, —then, when Faith is rose from death to Life for regeneration, it will be made to know its own condition, and that Reason has power to oppress and persecute it—because created Faith hearkened to Reason, and for that cause Reason has that power— also, God took fallen Faith on HIMSELF, and become Christ to redeem it! Then you may see Reason had power to scourge, oppress, and persecute him, because created Faith hearkened to Reason, and fell under his power.

Again, Reason, here, is in a body of *flesh*, therefore, when Faith is in active Life, in a body of *Flesh* on this Earth; its acts, language, priesthood; kingdom, &c. is contrary to that of Reason; then Reason will see a kingdom coming contrary to his own, then will grow angry, and give out evil Reports, and persecute Faith with all its strength and power, which is but *fleshly*, and in this Reason give Faith its *flesh to eat*.

Thus Reason served Christ, because he had took fallen Faith on him; but he bore it without resistance, and in this He *overcome the world*! therefore

See (Rev. xix. 17) where "John saw an angel standing in the sun, and cried with a loud voice; saying, to all the fowls that fly in the midst of heaven, Come—gather yourselves, together, unto the supper of the great God, that ye may eat the flesh of kings—and captains—and mighty men, &c." which is the *flesh* of Reason— This angel in the sun is Christ, who calls his elect to his royal priesthood, who are the *fowls that fly in* this nether *heaven* of Faith, in and for regeneration, and they must *sup* with him, who is the GREAT GOD of mercy! which is to *eat the flesh* of Reason, *both great and small*, which is done here in *time*, because their power is of the *flesh*; and they will compel you to eat it in a degree; for Reason being, here in his frothy kingdom; will usurp over the elect, and make sure to himself he can call in great powers to assist him, and justify him in his evil! NOW—this CHRIST bore, and so must His Messengers and Elect; and all because Faith hearkened to Reason, and was ruled by him, and fell under this, his power.

Again, in the travail of this life, there are many difficulties, and hard passes, even with and among Reason; for Reason cannot make his kingdom agreeable to himself, because he knows not what he wants, neither will he worship God: And in this he is in a confused wilderness, craving and spighting of each other; and every one would endeavour to excuse his own devil, therefore, what can be expected of or from people in this condition.

Also, the spirit of Reason in the elect, will rise and speak in anger: and may raise the spirit of Reason in another to anger; Now in all this, it is but Reason *eat* Reason, &c. therefore whoever expects to have any good or happiness of or from Reason, will go without, Why? Because there is no good to be found in that nature:—and if any of Reason should do any good, it is forced from them by a higher power; therefore do you, and all of you, learn this, not to expect a thing from where it cannot come.

Again, the *fig-tree* that Christ *found no fruit* thereon He *touched*, and it withered away! This *fig tree* means the spirit of Reason in the elect, on which no *fruit* can he found for his kingdom, therefore it must be *withered* away, and by the power of Faith in regeneration.— Hence you may see Anger must not be borne in the soul against any one, but must forgive your enemies; and the more you watch this spirit of Reason the better, lest you are taken by him unawares, for in things of this *wild world* and of Reason, will be found disappointment, which you learn to bear; but there is no disappointment in the priesthood and kingdom of Christ.

Further, by what is written, you may see how Reason hate the nature and acts of Faith, and how it will seek occasion to shew anger, belie and persecute Faith, which is giving its *flesh to eat*; And how Reason oppress and *eat* each other, in his wild arrogant kingdom; so it is not for you to be entangled in the vain and useless contention of Reason, which will end in death under justice; but you must follow Christ in MERCY and FORGIVENESS, and in the works of Faith, and leave this world behind; in its own confusion, under justice, and go to the kingdom of Christ where there is no disappointment, but Peace, Mercy and Glory.

I sent a letter to Joe, which I hope you received (See the Divine Memorial.). *I have not heard from Caermarthen.*

I have wrote you a parable, that you may see the condition of Reason: - There, was a certain great KING, who saw *Criminals* in a perishing condition, therefore He had compassion on them, and would have stayed his justice, and appointed them a *Refuge*, whereby they might live: But they went wild and disobedient which incurred his anger, and he sent his justice on them, but would not cut them all off, saying, "others may come and act better."

Again; his compassion further extended, for he sent his *servant* and gave them a *Kingdom*, built them a *City* and House of *Mercy*, that his justice should be stayed, and *they* should live, saying; surely they *now* must know my will: and he took *criminals* into this Kingdom and City, and House of Mercy;—and place them there according to his own will, that they should enjoy this great blessing which he had appointed for them; but they murmured against this good King, and against his servant, and sought means how they could deceive the Servant!

Also in the midst of this great blessing they disobeyed the commands of this great King, and even by his own *wealth* that he gave them, "they formed a *wild* kingdom, and *warred* against Him!

After this he sent *other* Servants to intreat them that they may enjoy this blessing in peace and safety, and not in hazard and confusion! But they *lightly esteemed* this intreaty, and servants, and persecuted *them* even unto death, and bid defiance unto the *king*.

Again, after this!!! the KING said, "I will set my watch over them, who they cannot kill nor persecute; and he shall give me a true account of all their acts;" so they continually entered on this plenteous blessing!—and made havock with the king's goods!—and ill disposed of them!—and spent them in a riotous manner! and became *unjust stewards*? and regarded not the king's command!

Others, who entered on this blessing, began to *murmur*, because they were not at the head of the riot; and sought occasion to speak and act evil against them that was;—so this kingdom is full of darkness, oppression, murmurings, wrath, evil, and hard speeches, grudges, &c. against each other, and, according to the excuses they make, hardly one is to be found in the wrong! Therefore what think you this great king will do with those unworthy people, whom he has respited from death; appointed them a kingdom and city of refuge, and forbore his wrath so long; yea, turned his blessing into evil, and the appointed peace into confusion, and would eat each other, and rebel against HIM? HE certainly will send his host and finally overthrow them!!!

My love to all and every one—the *time* comes on when I hope the happiness of seeing you all, so conclude your loving brother in Christ, all praying your increase in Faith.

                              JAMES BIRCH

Feb. 14, 1784.

P.S. *Our love to inform you we have lost two worthy friends, to the Messenger and church—Chignel and Lewis—the latter was the first in my day that fell a victim to the savage nature of Reason—so fear nothing but the LORD GOD of HEAVEN: I hope to hear from you soon.*

LETTER LIX

To our beloved sister Runwa &c. James Birch, &c. send greeting.

Beloved Sister, — I received yours of the 15th ult. but was writing and opening the parable of the householder, (Matt. xx.) wherein is explained the gathering in, and completing the KINGDOM Of CHRIST; and being a great and heavy work I did not care to leave it; but now I thank God it is done.

I am glad to hear of your stedfast Faith, and that you have prayer; and I pray God assist you to go through this great wilderness, where are serpents, fiends, &c. that will gather together, to make war against Christ the KING, and His holy CITY of regenerated Faith: But Christ and them that follow Him will *overcome*? And they that war against Him, and their *false prophet* who has deceived them, will be taken and cast into or under the *Wrath*, of God! which is as a Lake that remain for ever, into whom death and hell will give up their dead.

Therefore BLESSED are them that take this warning and follow; for the whole is but as a day's tribulation! and by prayer and patience you will overcome; yea, you must overcome to follow Christ, and then you will not, sink into this lake. For the time is now! "Whoever seek to save his life in going back, will lose it; and whoever seek to lose it by going forward, will find it."

Moreover, you say my letters is still *higher*, it may be so, but this I see, your understanding is higher, for it is the *spirit that quickens* and brings Faith into active life, for the *flesh profit nothing*: I have much to say to the church, when I come, which I mean in about a month; or sooner did we not yet expect brother Plowman in London—and I beg not any of you to be uneasy, for I *Care* not for the *old Parry*, or any of his *agents*, nor for what they can do, as it is my duty to visit, the church: Also I know it is not possible for a Messenger of Christ to *perish out of Jerusalem*: Yet they will find I am not to be affrighted by the *hiss* of a serpent, the *snarl* of a Dog, or *squall* of a Cat*. So my soul's love to the united church of Christ, to whom I AM A SERVANT, and conclude your loving brother, with the whole church, who greets

---

* The original text has been amended from "any" to "a" and the original text is unreadable where it has been amended in ink to read "cat"

you all in love.

London, May 27, 1784.   JAS. BIRCH.

Mrs. Jones sends her love, they are in business.

LETTER LX

To the Church, at London, Mrs. Birch and Brethren.

This with my love to inform you, I received your kind letter, and was glad to hear from you; and I hope you are all well. I had a long passage at *sea*, because of contrary winds, but in no *ways* dangerous.

The church here are all well, and send their love in the Faith of Christ, to the church at *London*. And I do confess I have found among them a *greater* understanding—*strong Faith*—good *Work* of prayer and patience to WAIT, the will of Christ for his kingdom of Mercy! and also to WATCH and guard against the temptations of the devil.

And, I plainly see the *downfall* of one has been the *uprise* of another, therefore let the Devil attempt at what he please, (he may do the will of God in a degree) I do not concern myself about the revolters, neither have I yet seen James, or his *wife*.

I came to Pembroke on Saturday last, and there abode 'till Tuesday; then to Philip John, at Cary, where I am well, and occasionally go to Pembroke.

I have had more of Polly Runwa's company than at any time before; and she appears as if she would be able to pass by injuries and smile over them in Mercy and forgiveness! even as the relentless sea will swallow up the eager life of man, and *smile* over his death: And the church are *sensible* of the regeneration and salvation of CHRIST, and set their *affection* on it; and pray his divine assistance.

My soul's love to the church at London, hoping you will be in mercy and love to each other; and mind not to be drove out of it by the power of the devil, but WORSHIP GOD, and keep your *Garments clean*, and all be well! So my love with the church's love at *Pembroke*, and conclude your loving brother in Christ,

Cary, July 31, 1784.   JAS. BIRCH.

Note—Of Mr. Birch's return and arrival in London, see letters of August 30, and Sept. 14, 1784, *Divine Memorial, &c.*

LETTER LXI

To Sister Runwa, &c. James Birch, &c. greeting.

Beloved Sister and Brethren—Yours I received, and am glad to see you declare your satisfaction in chap. iii. upon the Gospel, and that you understand it, and of your desire to inherit the kingdom of Christ, whose kingdom is not of this world, for them who are of this world will desire to have the world; and will cleave to the world, let them say what they will to the contrary; but this I say, *they shall lose both their Labour and Desire.*

Also, beware of the spirit of mad Reason in the wilderness, who can hardly bear restraint or constraint; and if they are questioned in their evil, they will, if they can, destroy him who question them, and if this cannot be done, they would fly any where to get from reproof, but alas! alas! Where will they go? They are within the ring of Justice, which is full of eyes, and will carry their own witness to their own condemnation, so if they cannot bear me, how can they bear one who is greater than I? Therefore my desire is for you, and all of you to watch the *name and number of the Beast*, his name is *Blasphemy*, and the number of his name is *temptation*, and he will transform himself to any form or condition, whereby he think he can tempt, because the number of his name is so great; but he that *leadeth* into evil, *goeth* into evil, but you are to mind the *prayer and patience* of the Saints, and watch the grand commandment, which is WORSHIP GOD.

Again, beloved brethren, this declaration from heaven, wherein God's divine assistance is found, is to raise Faith from death to life, and take it into the royal priesthood, and make man anew by regeneration, and not contend with Reason in the wilderness, because this message is not unto the bloody unbelieving world, for that is but gathering and working on "dry bones," or plastering up that which will tumble down; therefore, when the declaration is made, the Messenger patiently waits for the birth and appearance of the *Virgin* daughter of Faith, like as the husbandman, patiently wait for the rise and appearance of the Wheat Corn that is sown into good ground: Therefore to the mighty works of Faith in regeneration, in the royal priesthood, or nether heaven of Faith, or kingdom of, and for Christ, Reason must, nay will be made manifest! for

If Reason make a profession to the outward word or bare letter, there will that come to pass which will cause Reason to appear, with his exceptions, dislike, murmurs, lies, &c. against the man of the house; so "it need must be that offences come, but woe unto him or them by whom they do come, it would have been better for him that a mill-stone were hanged about his neck, and that he were drowned in the depth of the sea. —" Matt. xviii. 6. If this had been done when he was a child he would have been raised a cherubim to glory, but now he is left desolate, to be swallowed up by death and hell!

Moreover beloved, as Christ overcome the world by the spirit of Faith, the elect must needs follow him in those works by the spirit of Faith, and his divine assistance, otherwise how can they be found worthy of him, therefore in all the trouble of soul in the sorrowful vale of death, you must be careful of the *insinuations* of Reason in his promise, for it is to tempt you, or turn you aside out of the way! for Reason will be obliged to you to hearken to him, and assist him in this evil, that he may rule over you, or make you one with himself: Therefore when the tempter appear, let it be in sorrow, joy, or any condition, look at him, and see what good he ever did or can do for himself, and where he want to take you: So I would not have you be afraid to afront your tempter, and not be inslaved by him. Now this is to be minded both internal and external.

Also, when the elect, in heaviness of heart, look into themselves and see the mountains of justice and death in the Way! Then in sorrow of soul think by their weight of sin and darkness they cannot enter the kingdom of heaven: Yet not-withstanding by the prayer of Faith and divine assistance from heaven, those mountains will be removed.

The royal Compact and Priesthood of Faith is so lively and quick, that whatever is asked in the prayer of Faith, to assist Faith, will be granted in God's time, and mountains will be removed; for all things are possible with Christ to assist Faith in regeneration:— Therefore BLESSED are them that enter the royal priesthood, and follow up, — and their reward is life eternal!

Again, beloved brethren, in whom my soul delighteth, you may be assured my spirit is oft'times with you and prayer for you, because my eager desire is for your welfare in Christ, and did expect to hear from you: —Have been writing a long piece of work, Ch. xx. upon Gos.—You may see a little hint of this in a letter to Mr. Parry (Let. XLI).

Now I hope you mind what I have WROTE, and what I have declared, for the HOUR is coming when you will be *Called* upon; and it is my soul's eager desire that you make READY for the CALL, according to the WARNING given.

My love to all, and beg you will answer this soon; and, know how all, and every one is; the Church is also very desirous for your welfare in Christ, send their love. So conclude your loving brother in Christ.

JAS. BIRCH.

London Feb. 8, 1785.

LETTER LXII

To the Church beloved in Christ, Mrs. Runwa, &c. James Birch, &c. send Greeting.

Beloved Sister and Brethren—I received both your Letters, and am glad to see your good account of Mrs. Davis, and if she or any one come to London, and to me, to be instructed in, and for the kingdom of Christ, you may depend they will be *kindly* treated, and no labour spared which will contribute to their happiness; but as for things of this world I have none to give, neither am I of this world!

Moreover, as to your *lowness* in spirit, fear, of your being naked to Faith, and seeming as it were *dead* in your self, that you have no more power than a *child*, this is the very state the Elect are brought to know, and tremble at the power and glory of the Father, which is of Justice: and also to know the power, acts, and temptation of Reason:

and to hold fast to what has been told you, watch Reason, and to have an eager desire or prayer to be preserved, and to have assistance from heaven, and stand fast in true obedience to the will and power of God: Now this is doing the *will of the Father*, for it is working the Works under His justice to Faith.

Again, Jesus said, "except ye be converted and become as *Little Children*, ye shall not enter the kingdom of heaven:" Now God became a CHILD to his own power of justice, which is the Father, and worked the works of Faith under that Justice, to gain his kingdom, which is the glory of mercy to himself and his Elect; and you may see His *lowness in spirit, His trouble, and sorrow and prayer* to heaven for divine assistance;—and Elect man must become as a *Child* for the daughter of Faith to be born, which is a new life in the elect, and a *Child* unto God under the justice of Faith, and is nourished and brought on in and by regeneration to become the soul of man for salvation, now here the Messenger is a servant, and here you may see Faith is *Child like* and must have assistance from heaven: For by this new Life, which is of Faith and divine assistance from heaven, man is made anew by regeneration, therefore in this *heaviness and weakness, or hunger of soul*, man finds he cannot heal himself, then of consequence in great need of the assistance of Christ: but you must be careful and watchful of temptation: Now this is what is wanted and required. For

Regeneration is to work life out of, and through death, and them that so *mourn and hunger* for the righteousness of Christ and his kingdom, will be *filled* and have Joy from heaven, as I have told you; which you have tasted of, according to your letter. Again, Reason will complain of trouble and agitation of mind, and great sorrow of soul; but this is because he cannot have things according to his own will, and be content in his station; for his arrogant will doth desire to be *great*, have *rule* over others, and shine in his kingdom, and thinks he will have joy in this or that; but it being denied him—then follows his great trouble and sorrow of soul, but this is all Egyptian trouble and sorrow, let them cloak it under what colour they please. I have wrote this that you may see the difference between the Mourning, Fear, Hunger, &c. of Faith for the kingdom of heaven; and the *Mourning, Fear*, &c. of Reason, for his own arrogant kingdom.

Moreover, Reason cannot be worked on for regeneration, because it is incapable of it, therefore it is *cast away* as a dead and useless generation, and Reason must be cast out of Elect men, and go to its own center, which is the herd of swine; for they cannot enter the kingdom of heaven with it; therefore them that come for the sake of the kingdom of heaven, will be kindly received and treated as the *Children of God* , but as to the *wealth* of this world it doth not belong to me;—the Lord God of heaven said when he was here, "the foxes have holes, the birds of the air have nests, but the SON OF MAN hath not where to lay his head." Matt. viii. 20. And his Messenger has no place, or trade, or merchandize whereby he can command any thing, although a SERVANT to the Lord God of heaven!

So them that come to Christ, must come out of the world, then they are under His prayer, which was for them, *given to him out of the world*; and even then they will enjoy things of this world; but it is all anew, because it is under the protection and blessing of God and Christ; for them that Christ rule over are well ruled; but this you may understand, devils must be cast out: BUT for a man to profess me, and his heart and delight in the world, it is no good, for he may profess me with his tongue, and be far off in his heart.

Now Reason is full of temptation, and will allure the soul after vain things in this world, and tell the man he must do such and such things in and for his kingdom: then for and through this, the messenger has an excuse made to him, and through his tenderness he has suffered excuses; but this has been because of the *hardness of hearts*, then of consequence to their own condemnation, for it is not so with the Lord God of heaven, because there is no excuse suffered there.

I have wrote this that you and all of you may *know*, and to watch and beware and not be catched in excuses; because the eve of time draws on! For it is my eager desire for the Church to be brought on in regeneration, and come out of tribulation, in the sweet shining *wedding garment* of Faith, meet for Marriage with the LORD GOD of Mercy! Therefore BLESSED are them that come and enter on the works, and go through suffering with patience, for the sake of the kingdom of Christ; (as you write of John and Hannah Wilkin) for tribulation is but a small space of time, like unto a woman in the *travail of labour*, when the child tosses and throbs, and presses to be born; "She hath Sorrow, but when born the anguish is forgot, for Joy there is a man born," and even so your works of Faith and patience will be crowned with glory, and your SORROW *turned to eternal* JOY! because in this manner Faith presses for its own kingdom.

Beloved sister and brethren, as you desired to know concerning Mrs. Jones—I have not seen her since I have been in London from you, or hardly heard of her, and even that by chance; and as to any blame being laid to her, there was no such thing done, neither do I remember any one spoke to her of it; this I mind, she was speaking of words she had with *Polly Thomas,* and she said she put her out of her father's house. Mr. *Collet* said she was wrong to use violence, for then she made herself equal with *Polly Thomas,* and this is all the blame; But after a while, when she misunderstood me the devil in her burst out like Mount Etna, or Vesuvius, in the flames of wrath against me and young Parry, and declared I said "I would arrest her husband," whereas I had no such power or thought (beside, it is well known I have done all I could to serve them), and said "young Parry had forged the note; and would Sware it," and said many wrathful things, which was from her evil spirit;—then I blamed her and said it was strange a man should forge a note, and they receive the money of him, and it was inclining to tricking or sharping, but she persisted in it, and would not be put out of it, and raved and roared violently—then I desired to see her no more in that spirit; now it was well known when she first came, she desired this world more than Christ: And as to her anger and resentment to me, it may be as well against a *Spring tide,* or the greatest Mountain in Wales.

But this you understand, her own angel blamed her within, and she thought we did without; and when the Devil have such power they think the evil is in others, and lo it is in them; so from their own evil they judge and condemn others; and by this spirit they think to rule, drive and confound others, and force their way, and this they call "a good spirit": and think it will protect them; thus they worship the Devil as their God and guide. Now this spirit, which is the Devil, the Messenger is not a servant to, nor can he even bid it farewell, for his declaration and prophecy is against it.

But if she could come to me in another spirit, and for the kingdom of Christ, nothing would be wanted in me, but, oh, that in her such a spirit could be found, although space is given! For the Messenger has no joy in the death of such a sinner; and it would be good for her to agree with her adversary, while he is in the way, lest evil come, for the Messenger is an adversary to the devil, and the devil well knows it, and will keep them away if he can, and if he cannot be cast out, to enter the herd of swine, he will join them, Deut. xiv. 8. In the time of the Law, *swine's flesh* was forbidden to eat, "nor touch their dead carcase, because they were unclean;" and under the Gospel with Christ, the seed of Reason is called *swine*; because of their nature and acts, for they are incapable of regeneration, and will act against Christ, and, as so unclean and dead to him.

Here you may see the Messenger must not embrace or have to do with, or hearken to the Devil, because he is unclean; so he must be cast out of elect men by regeneration, and enter this herd of *swine*; and in this is God's wrath doubled unto them; and where the devil cannot be cast out, they will join the herd of swine: For every foul spirit will be gathered to its own center, which is under justice and wrath: And Faith is gathered by regeneration to the mercy and glory of Christ; and the Messenger is a servant to the virgin daughter of Faith and to Christ: but not a servant to the devil.

Now I beg you will mind what is written, and every one seek to follow and get as near Christ in spirit as possible for every one must stand there for himself; and let not your souls be entangled in the world, nor for one that will not come out of it: Be strong and fear not! Christ will have his own, and unite them in the grand union of Faith and glory, and where the *wedding garment* cannot be found, him will Christ *cast out*!

So conclude your loving brother in Christ, with prayer for you all.

JAMES BIRCH,

London, April 16, 1785

LETTER LXIII

To our beloved Sister Mary Runwa, &c. James Birch, &c. sends greeting.

Beloved Sister—I am glad you comprehend what I wrote, and more so to see you write in such a power of Faith, and give such a demonstration of its works, in which I have great satisfaction and joy; and of your good report of the church; and I pray God it may ever increase in you all, then you will enjoy the true union and concord of the love of Faith in regeneration; and then the Messenger's Love is in you, and yours in him: and it all centers to Christ the KING OF FAITH in his glory of Mercy!

Beloved sister and brethren, since I wrote to you last, I have both heard of and seen Mrs. Jones, she went to brother Middleton, and told him she should be glad to be agreeable with me, and said it was only on a natural account the words were. I said she knew where to find me, and I would hear what she had to say. After this I saw her near Middleton's door, she asked how I did before I saw her, and I said, How do you do? and she followed in; then, in a few minutes said she could not stay,—so bid us all good night; —I said, if you are going, good night, and this was all, neither have I seen her since.

Now I should rejoice to agree with her was it in my power; for after all the search of mercy I can make, she must agree somewhere else before she can with me; for the devil had drove her too far, and now would agree with me to crown his evil: For I well know his acts and transformations, his appearance, and what he would be at: She told my youngest son she should be glad to see and agree with me, but as to his mother she never desired to see; for she never would forgive her. Now Mrs. Birch never did her wrong, but made things to be more agreeable, and would serve her to the utmost of her power, and when she raved at me, and gave me the lie to my face; Mrs. Birch said she was sorry for her, and this is all the evil done.

But the *Devil* thinks to form and infuse things which are not, by his raising a *smoke out of the bottomless pit*, which is the fumes of death and hell, to darken the son in regeneration, and his SWEET BREATHINGS of Faith, to instruct the Elect, that this evil spirit may pass *a locust and scorpion in this smoke*, Read Rev. ix. Now those things will come in the days of prophecy, but you may see "they can *hurt none* but those who have not the seal of God in their foreheads, therefore stand fast and fear not".

Again, what think you of that spirit that shall say I never will forgive, or will not agree but with them who will submit to this evil arrogant spirit? You must not think the Messenger can or will. See Matt. v. 23; Jesus said, "Therefore if thou bring thy gift to the altar, and there rememberest that thy brother hath aught against thee, (24) leave there thy gift before the altar, and go thy way, first be reconciled to thy brother, then come and offer thy gift." Here you may see the Messenger cannot take that *Gift*, nor agree with her in that condition; beside, she is fell under the power of the internal Moses, who will have satisfaction;—now if she can within herself be reconciled with the whole world, and be in true love, mercy, pity, and forgiveness with all and every one, and be truly sorry, for the offences she has given, and would do any thing to make amends, and be as ready to forgive, as she implores forgiveness in that state, which is as if death and hell were present! And that her own arrogant wisdom has brought her under the power of justice and death; and as a *worm*, tremble at the power of God; and in this condition, without excuses offer herself up to the prerogative will of God; before the angel who is the internal Moses! then—in God's time that justice will be stayed, and *She* will come out as it were with a new life, and after this agree with the brethren in the true union of the church, then the Messenger has power to agree with her, and take *her* offering, and pray for her because then she will come in another spirit, and for the kingdom of heaven, but at present the Messenger cannot; without he take *false incense* and encourage the devil.

Moreover, the devil knows the Messenger, and would shift his evil to any one, or any where, and would transform himself almost to any thing or do any thing to agree with the Messenger; if the Messenger would let him live there and reign master of the house, for he knows he cannot deceive the Messenger as he do the world, so would fain live and reign there; but the Messenger cannot agree with him, for if the being is an elect, the Messenger must have the devil out, and enter the herd of swine, that the being may be brought to, and *clothed in his right mind* for regeneration: And if this cannot be done, the Messenger must make him known, that he may no more deceive the elect! — but the Messenger had rather he would go into the *wilderness*, and do as well as he can, and live as long as he can, because he do not care to torment him before his *time* if he can help it.

NOW here you may see the GOLDEN CHAINS of the Messenger! for *He* must not hearken to or agree with the Devil; for he would like well for his evils to pass under the sanction of his belief in a SON *in regeneration.*

Furthermore, the Messenger has had plenty of those things here in London, so he well knows their acts and language, and has known the devil to be worked out, and they have been taken, and others have been left; and now those troubles are come to you, which I expected before, for *offences* will come, as is written, but *woe to them by whom they do come*? And now you may see "the Spirit of *desolation* would stand in an *holy place*, whoso reads, let them understand!" For now is the time of works and trial, and thank God the Messenger lives; he that overcome will have power to judge the life of man, and have eternal life hereafter: Now there always were them that crept in, when the days of light and prophecy were from heaven, therefore I advise you to read the epistle of Jude, and see what he said of them; and the 2d chap. of the 2d Epistle of Peter; and you may see how it was then, and think it nothing strange now. And as for my last letter, let it be known to the church by all means, for it was my intent; for if the devil is cast out, it will be a Miracle, to the great joy of the church; and if not, there is notice to the church to be careful.

Jesus says. Matt. x. 26. "Fear them not therefore, for there is nothing covered that shall not be revealed, and hid that shall not be known;" So conceal it not, lest you act against God, for it will do you harm to cover such evil; and she no good.

My Love to Mrs. Howel, and I doubt not but she is concerned for her daughter; and so am I also. I know not how my *children* will stand! If they act as she has, I must do the same by them, for I most take care not to lose myself in my children's *Evil*, through a silly erroneous fearful or hopeful love for regeneration is a great trial, it will *divide families*, nay soul from body of the elect, and man must leave all, and follow Christ, to be found worthy of him!

Now I would have you understand I have not given Mrs. Jones up; but, as I said before, let her go and agree with the internal Moses, and that given priesthood, and make a *reconciliation*, and offer there within herself, then she will be ready to *ask forgiveness* of them that she has spoke hastily to, whether offence was or was not, given; for as she has fell from me, and bid me *defiance*, the angel in justice has her,—she may, and do say it was on a natural account; this also is an old trick of the devil.

NOW when God re-make a man by regeneration, who is to divide his wisdom and power, or judge that man? It is written, "But he that is spiritual, judgeth all things, yet he himself is judged of no man" i. Corinth. Ch. ii. 15. But as to any thing she has brought on me, or railing against me, that I have in my power to forgive, but let her agree with Moses, and mine is done away as if it had never been: And if the aforesaid work can be done by her, I shall *Rejoice* to receive her, and she will *haste* to come!

Beloved brethren, I beg you will mind what is written, and let it be a watch and lesson to you all! And also I beg the church may meet if possible, without excuse, and let this be read in communion with the place! in scripture cited, that one's understanding may help another:— My love is in the church, and for the church, and while their love is in me, mine is in them: And if any one desire my prayer, there it is according to their desire, because the *union* is so great, therefore I say as Christ did, "Be it to you according to your Faith." Let your *Faith* be strong, and *union* great! and fear not, for there is none can come into regeneration, but them that are *given* out of the world; for where anger, unforgiveness, self-assumed authority, consequence, hypocrisy, &c. &c. is in-dwelling in the soul, they must agree with Moses, and then with me; because I did not come to the bloody unbelieving world, but to them that are *given out of the world*, in and for regeneration.

I have wrote a long piece of many things, the last is concerning the dispute with Michael the Archangel, and the devil, about the body of Moses, Gos. ch. xxiii. which I had just done when your letter came: I have more things to let you know, and want to see you as much as ever.

So conclude your loving brother in Christ, with prayer for you all.

London, May 24, 1785.   JAMES BIRCH.

P.S. The whole church greets you all, and are earnest for your welfare in Christ. My love to all and every one, and do you *follow* the works of Faith and Christ, and not *look back as did Lot's wife,* but leave the devil to the Messenger, who knows how to manage him, and have him out if possible.

LETTER LXIV

To our beloved Sister Elizabeth Atkinson, and to the whole Church beloved in Christ, in and about Pembroke, James Birch & Brethren send Greeting.

Beloved Sister,—Yours I received, and was glad to hear from you and the church, because my love is with you all, and for you all, and my eager desire and prayer is, that you come on in regeneration to the mercy and union of Christ: For regeneration is to Work Life out of Death, and through Death and Hell, to the Mercy and UNION OF CHRIST, in life and immortality, therefore "Them that have part in the first resurrection," will hear the *Voice* and know the *Utterance*, and see the *Days*, and enter in and FOLLOW, and by divine assistance will come through the powers of Reason, Sin, Death and Hell, and Justice, to the Union and Seal of CHRIST in his kingdom of glory! So they will not "Fall under condemnation, but are passed from death to life" by regeneration.

Again, this Spirit or Virgin daughter of Faith, in and for regeneration, will work against those powers, and will pray, and not faint, under them; nor be tempted away; because she is very earnest to get as near Christ as possible; Also her love is in the Messenger and church of Christ, for there doth the spirit center; and there will the heart be: For how is it possible for any one to have any love or interest in Christ, and not regard His MESSENGER: For if they cannot agree with the Messenger who is sent by Christ to Call his elect into the royal priesthood of Faith and regeneration, whom they have seen or may see, how can they agree with Christ, who they never saw? Besides, there is the cherubim and flaming sword, which is the internal angel in justice, that turns every way to keep the way of the *Tree of Life*, therefore the Messenger is the WAY, and no one can enter in but by the *way* of the Messenger.

Moreover, the spirit of corrupted Reason can never agree with the spirit of incorrupted Faith in regeneration, for this spirit of Faith lights the elect, and leads them after and into divine purity, and the Light and Love of Christ, but the spirit of Reason cannot endure Light, so he love darkness, because his deeds are evil; for light will discover the dark spirit and its evil deeds; for which cause Reason cannot endure the Messenger, because the nature of this declaration will reprove evil;

For it is of such a shining light and power, that by divine assistance, it will raise Faith from death to life, and take it into, the royal compact and priesthood of Faith, where they will have the testimony of Jesus, and see the SIGN of his coming! But Reason will remain in darkness; because no other life can be brought out of him, whereby he can inherit light and life, therefore he cannot bear, the light, and if he cannot destroy it, will slink away to the dark, where he can practise his evil mind, and do his evil deeds, snug and cunning, in the dark, 'till his own spirit devour him in destruction; because he carry his own witness to his own condemnation, and there remain in his own wrath.

Further, as Justice & Judgement is stayed to Reason for a *small space*, which is only that he may fill his cup in a day or less, and be destroyed in an hour! Yet at this time he acts as a God, to make choice of his own way to heaven, and to have and do his own will, and gather up, and hold fast the pelf of this world, that it may help to torment him under condemnation:—and in this state!—men will think themselves of great consequence, and of great value! but at what market I do not know;—this I know—there is no one to bid for them whereby they may have future benefit, but this Messenger! and they are of no value for regeneration, because they are incapable of first resurrection, and run arrogant and wild, and as so will act according to their dark spirit, and bring forth evil fruits, for he was a deceiver, liar, and a murderer, from the beginning; and under the cloak of sanction he goeth out and deceive the whole world, for they will believe and love a lie, and hate the truth, because by it they are condemned, but by a lie they think to excuse themselves; and cloak their evil.

Again, this Messenger came out immediately from CHRIST, and in HIS spirit and power, as He now sit in his immortal kingdom of regenerated Faith, and has declared the first resurrection and regeneration, the spirit of prophecy, and his royal seal to enter his kingdom, the glory of mercy; and has called to the elect, and gave them notice, that the way of his coming to them may be prepared and his call and declaration is true, and the angel of regenerated Faith who sent the Messenger bear him Witness; for as John the Baptist came out in the spirit and power of Elias, to prepare the way, of his sudden appearance in a body of flesh, under the justice of the father; even so this Messenger came out in the spirit and power of Jesus, to prepare the way of his coming in his high and Mighty power and glory, to put an end to time, and raise the elect to his immortal kingdom, the glory of mercy; therefore watch and prepare.

Also, this MESSENGER will not contend with the *World*, for there is the internal Moses, has the world under his power, so let them contend with him, for this Messenger did not come to the World, but to them that are *given to Christ out of the world*, for redemption, regeneration, and salvation! —and the Virgin daughter of Faith, he will labour and contend for, because it is and will be the soul of the elect for salvation, and belongs to Christ, but she must go through the powers of Reason, Sin, Death, Hell, and Justice:—And although those powers are very *hard and sharp* to go through, yet by prayer, it is in union with an INFINITE POWER, that will assist this Virgin to go through those powers;—For although those powers are so very great that they will gather and keep the world under condemnation (but the virgin daughter of Faith being a quickening spirit, and it will follow Christ, for to him in immortality, is this spirit to go), then, in the travail of this life, which is against those powers, the Virgin daughter of Faith have prayer to CHRIST, for His divine assistance, and He do and WILL assist this spirit of Faith in regeneration: so fear not, seeing you will be assisted by Christ, whose power is INFINITE, and Faith by regeneration is brought through those powers, and from those powers, for it will not be suffered to sink under those powers, but leave Reason behind, under judgement and condemnation.

AGAIN, beloved brethren, as you desired to know where you should cut out and destroy *Muggleton's* writings? to which I answer, No! for as they were permitted to the bloody unbelieving world, there let them stand, and whoever trust to *Muggleton*, by Muggleton will be condemned, because a *greater than Muggleton* is here!

And although *Muggleton* was but a Priest, and oft'times in the *wild* priesthood of Reason, YET "he charge the people to be obedient to a *living* Messenger," and as for you not reading his works, that I do not wonder at, for it is the same here;—besides, when the elect hear the *Voice of Christ*, Him they will *follow*, and not the voice of a *stranger* in the wilderness;—for his writings is to the *wild world*, and any evil spirit may harbour there! But the Virgin daughter of Faith cannot; for the *given* priesthood of Reason is a *Wilderness* to Faith, and the *Wild* Priesthood of Reason is a *Desart* to Faith.

And further, desolations are now *determined*! for there is desolate wanderers under the letter of *Moses*, and of the *Apostles*, and of *Reeve* and *Muggleton*, therefore them that cannot come to this Messenger, and enter in and follow, he leave them *desolate*, let them think what they will to the contrary! Therefore BLESSED are them that come and enter in! for those are the days of *repentance*, and the works of Faith, and prophecy, and to go up and offer at the FEET OF CHRIST, then the SEAL of Christ is for them.

So I pray for the love, concord, union, and assistance of Christ in his church, Amen! And conclude your loving brother in Christ.

JAS. BIRCH.

London Aug. 16, 1785.

P.S. The whole church greets you all.

LETTER LXV

To our beloved Sister Runwa and the whole Church beloved in Christ, James Birch and Brethren send Greeting.

Beloved Sister and Brethren,—Yours I received and was glad to hear from you, and of your steadfast Faith; I would have answered before, but have had a *melancholy* accident,—for on the 6th ult. (my whole family was with me) as soon as dinner was over, my daughter went out of the room, and fell from the stair-case window, about 16 feet high, on the stones, and no one saw her as is owned to; neither can I find out how it was, the fall was heard by some in the low room, who ran to see, and took up the child, and I was called; all this was done in a few minutes I thought she was dead, but, she came too, but not to speak; mean time the doctor came, he ordered her to *St. Bartholomew's*, her Scull was fractured, which was trapanned; the next day she knew people, and could speak, and did eat, and there was hopes, the surgeons asked how she did, she told them, and asked how she fell out of window, she said she could not tell, but altered in the night, and the next morning (Nov. 8) she died. She was a fine active *Child*, between 9 and 10 years of age; she well knew and was used to the window, and one would hardly think it credible for such a child to fall out!

This has caused me a deal of trouble, and took me into the *mournful Field* of nature; according to the FALL of man: now in this valley or mournful *Field* of nature, man must Watch—for the soul is apt to go into *argument,* and the tempter is ready to take the soul astray; but mind the *Kingdom* and POWER of God, and *resign* there! that the soul may truly say, *His will be done,* then you will sooner come through and out of this *mournful field* of nature.

Again, my beloved sister and brethren, I would have you mind and observe, those kingdoms and powers under the POWER of God, there is the *seraphic host* or Kingdom in heaven above, stand in their infant purity, as they were first created, and will so remain in all eternity, for that kingdom never *fell* into generation.

Again, the created *cherubim* fell into generation, and was born a child into this world, and grew to manhood, but many of his children, or children of his spirit; die in childhood, because the cherubim was born a child into this world (but the elect all live to manhood, as their father Adam was created); Therefore the children that die are the children of Reason, and will be raised cherubims to glory, to compose that *heavenly host,* or glorious order of cherubims in all eternity, because they fall in the infant or childish purity, in and according to generation, and never are charged with the law; now this is the cherubical *Kingdom,* host and powers, and

Since the death of my last, I had all that has been taken from me (which is six) brought before me in spirit, by the power of the spirit, and was told I should have them all again, and God had done a good work for them and me, and it was much better to enjoy them in eternity, than here in time; therefore them whose children go before them as cherubs, let them mind what I say; and SEEK the Kingdom of CHRIST, then they will enjoy them in full fruition in all eternity. But if they live to manhood it is very uncertain.

Again, — (children) when they come to manhood, the angel take place in the soul and are charged with the law, then they cannot die cherubims, because they have passed through and out from the cherubical kingdom and powers into the kingdoms of this world; then there is anxious care, slavery, bondage, driving and striving, disagreements, murmuring, &c. &c. seeking and desiring to build their house on this sandy foundation to support their theme of greatness in this uncertain and perishing kingdoms, and how many thousands fall in these kingdoms, and under those powers!

Again, there is the kingdoms and powers of the dark spirit, which are them that go forth and preach Christ unto salvation, by the dark imaginary spirit of Reason, and declare his will and power to be as they imagine, and make use of his name, to cover their doctrine, which is of devils, and are gone forth in the wilderness, and there make war against Christ, his elect, his royal priesthood, and his holy regeneration and there strive in or on those dark waters of Reason, to collect congregations, which are kingdoms, and all eager to cultivate their dark wisdom, and become as gods to do their own will, and go their own way to heaven, and in their strivings after this world, the dark teacher will excuse them, if not their own spirit of Reason will act the priest, and excuse them, and it may pass for a time in the kingdoms of this world, now many thousands fall here under those powers!

Again, there is the kingdom & powers of cherubical justice, wherein Moses and others was inspired in and according to that inspiration, and wherein the internal angel now ride on the sinful soul of man, and watch over man, and report the acts of man to them who sit in the glory of justice, and seal men under their own evil acts, whereby they will be their own witness to their own condemnation, and oft'times visit man for his private evil acts, and make it known in the open streets, even in this life, for this kingdom and powers reign over and rule all men until Faith is rose from death to life.

Again, there is the kingdom of the father, where unto Christ was born into this world, to keep the law of Faith and work the redemption, for as created Faith fell and died under the justice of the father, it is rose again from that death to active life, to follow Christ in the works of Faith under the Justice of the father, and must pass under and through the justice of the father to the mercy of the son, which is the kingdom of Christ & when faith is taken into the royal priesthood to work its works in the kingdom of the father, it is made to *know* these kingdoms and powers and what the soul of man is striving for, and in all the troubles oppression, distress, anxious cares, union in generation, &c. in the kingdoms of this world, and in all the temptation, malice of fiends, scandal, lies, persecution, backslidings, and their presumption, acts and blasphemy, &c. against God the elect must watch! and not fall into and under those powers, and the internal angel in justice watch over the soul of man, and do require obedience, and an offering in that kingdom.

Now to pass through those kingdoms, powers, &c. the watch is great, and the labour so hard; and sometimes the distress of soul so great, that to have died a *cherubim* is almost a desirable thing; but no! — that could not, nor cannot be to the Elect, for they must live and *follow* through those kingdoms and powers; and under the Justice of the Father, which is through the Kingdom of the Father, and lose themselves in death in their own blood, under the Justice of the Father! and pass through that death to the MERCY of the SON, which is the KINGDOM of Christ! Now as man pass through and from the state of childhood, which is the cherubical kingdom and powers before he comes to manhood, even so the elect must pass through the before-said kingdoms and powers to the kingdom of Christ.

Again, the kingdom of cherubims for ever stand! and the kingdom of justice, wherein walk the internal angel on the soul of man, that also for ever stand! and the kingdom of Christ for ever stand! but the kingdoms of this world will *pass away* and be no more; and the kingdoms of the dark spirit will pass away, and be no more; and the kingdom of the father will pass away, and be no more, for the spirit of regenerated Faith, which is the essential soul of the elect, will pass through the Kingdom of the Father, and from the kingdom of the Father to the MERCY OF THE SON! which is the KINGDOM of Christ, and there offer their life of Faith at his Royal FEET.

Now, "as the tree falleth, so it lieth," if it fall in the cherubical kingdom, it is raised a cherubim to glory! if it fall in the kingdoms of this World, or the kingdoms of the dark spirit, they are sealed under justice, and will be raised in justice and wrath:—If it fall in the kingdom of the father, it will pass through that to the Union and Seal of Christ, and be raised to the glory of Faith in his royal Kingdom.

Moreover, beloved Sister and Brethren, — I have wrote this, that you and all of you may know, and to watch the tempter, and pray for divine assistance, to come through those powers, and have Faith and Patience, and worship God and Christ, and the reward of this labour is no less than Life Eternal! For in all the strivings for this world, and labour to excuse themselves in the kingdoms of the dark spirit, it all come to naught and perish! and no more than a *burial* for the dead!

My love to all and every one, for my love and anxious care is for you, & I pray the fruits of Faith, and the love of Christ may abound among you: (*Mrs. Davis* has not yet found it convenient to write to me.) Let me hear of you, then I may have more to write.

So conclude your loving brother in Christ.

JAMES BIRCH,

London, Dec. 10, 1785.

LETTER LXVI

To the Church beloved in Christ, in and about Pembroke, James Birch send Greeting.

Beloved sister and brethren,—I am glad to hear from you, and that you are stedfast in the Faith of Christ, and that your trouble is passed over, for believe me the time is now come that you must not look after the *House* of Generation and death & neglect the works & house of regeneration and life, for this must be minded by all and every one, for to inherit it—therefore watch! And as you desire to know the river in Rev. xxii. I will inform you and hope it will prove to your benefit and my joy when I come.

Now mind, in the beginning the Tree of Life stood in the midst of the garden, see Gen. ii. 9. — This Tree of Life was the very person and power of God. He is called the TREE OF LIFE, because he created and brought forth all Light, Life, and Glory: And had Adam and Eve hearkened to, and abode by this Tree of Life, they would have lived for ever in their pure created state; But they hearkened to the Tree of Knowledge, of good and evil, which was the serpent angel,—then created Faith broke its own law, and died, according to the word of the Lord God the creator, and Reason, whom they hearkened to, took possession, and actuated and drove them:—then all things was made and become *anew*, for the salvation of elect man: For the kingdom of the father was become the kingdom of justice and death, and the *Tree of Life* no more to be found there; but it must be found in the *new* kingdom, which is of the Son; and into this kingdom was the elect gathered by regeneration and united to God for Christ, from the man Adam till Christ came.

Then, GOD became CHRIST, and HE came on the prophecies of his elect, and worked the redemption; and gained to himself all power, then ascended into his high kingdom, the glory of mercy, and took possession of his grand host of virgins, who was the first fruits unto God, and to the lamb, and they have his father's name written in their forehead: THUS Christ redeemed the Elect! brought in his own covenant! and became the *Tree of Life*.

And this TREE bore fruit, so as to inspire the twelve Apostles in His own royal covenant of grace and mercy, that they should go forth and declare his holy name, his redemption and salvation, by their preaching, which is the "*leaves* of the Tree, and is good for the healing of the nations," because by preaching they are called to the tree, then if so happy as a *leaf* to become united to the *Tree*, they will receive suction of the Tree, and be *healed*, then become a *branch*, and bear *fruit*; but if not, it wither and is cast off as a useless leaf! and is taken away! as Christ himself say by the true Vine, see John's Gosp. xv. 2, "Every branch in me that bear not fruit, is taken away."

Again, in CHRIST is found the fruits of Love, Mercy, Redemption, and all quickening power to Faith, for regeneration, and the power of regeneration, and Will and Power to assist the daughter of Faith in her works in regeneration, and Power to unite with her in holy marriage, &c. and to bring Faith through hell and death,—and to sanctify the soul, - and to seal the soul for His glorious kingdom,—and to raise the Elect at the last day, to his kingdom,—and to crown them with everlasting glory, so Christ is the author, worker, and finisher of salvation to and for his elect, therefore of consequence the TREE OF LIFE, with His Fruits.

Moreover, when the present Messenger *Utters* the declaration, there is the divine assistance of Christ, to raise Faith from Death to active life, which is the Virgin daughter of Faith born; & this is the entrance into the Priesthood of Faith, or holy City, or waters of Life! Then Christ assist this daughter to *remove* Mountains, *overcome* the world, &c.—and give her the spirit of prophecy, &c. For to this daughter is given a Censer with incense, *i.e.* this new Life of Faith is the Censer, and its prayer the incense that ascends to God for divine assistance to work the works,—and those are the fruits of Faith,— not to hearken to Reason, to overcome the world, love, mercy, charity to the church of Christ, patience, meekness, innocense, and prayer for divine assistance, and obedience to wait the will of God, the spirit of prophesy, and lose your self in death, under the justice of the father, &c. (for as Christ kept the law of Faith, and overcome the world, and the power of Reason, and of sin, death, hell, and justice, and so become the Tree of life and salvation to the elect) and this virgin daughter will follow him by divine assistance.

Now thus—the Messenger call the elect to the Tree of Life, and thus they take hold of the Tree of Life! And to have his divine assistance, is to Eat of The Tree of Life, and by that bring forth the Fruits of Faith, as did and do the Tree of Life, and then live for ever! So it is Faith in Faith, and Faith on Faith, and Faith united to Faith, and centers to Christ the King of Faith, as He himself say, "You in me, and I in you."

And this *pure River* is the waters of Faith, Life, Regeneration, Mercy, Salvation, &c. &c. which is "proceeding out of the throne of God, and of the Lamb," and "in the midst of the street, and of either side of the river, is the Tree of Life," because nothing can be done in regeneration and salvation, without the assistance of Christ, and He is there ready to assist the Virgin of Faith; and this Tree of Life not only yield his fruit every *month*, but every day and hour.

Again, this present Messenger came out from the Tree of Life, and in those waters of Faith, regeneration and Life, and do call and invite the Elect into the royal priesthood of Faith, or the holy city, or Waters of Life, and unto the Tree of Life, and his doctrine is as the *leaves of the Tree*, and when the elect come, they are united to the tree as a leaf, and receive suction and flourish, and become a *branch*, and bear *fruit*, for when the daughter of Faith is born, there is Fruit born, then they will enter the royal priesthood of Faith and waters of Life, and be regenerated to the Tree of Life.

But when any come who can receive no more than the outward word, or bare letter, they will *wither* away, and are cast off as a useless leaf, then the world, and the devil will take them away, for they cannot enter the priesthood of Faith, and take of the waters of Life, because they are incapable of regeneration, so must remain "without with swine, dogs, sorcerers, whoremongers, murderers, idolaters, and them who loveth and maketh a lye."

Now mind what is written, and pray to be found worthy, for when any such thing as this is asked, it is expected there is a useful want by the spirit of Faith.

So pray God assist you all, and conclude your loving brother in Christ.

JAMES BIRCH.

London, June 8, 1786.

LETTER LXVII

To our beloved sister Runwa; at Pembroke, Greeting.

This with my love, to inform you I came safe to London as you know by *Betsey*, who was at church, and read the chap sent to *America* (and in it gave good satisfaction). When I came to London, I found things tolerable well: and they had acted well concerning *Mr. Gibson*.

Now I hope you will remember what I said when I was with you, and I pray God give you understanding and power: According to my word I have sent you the *Nature and Acts* of the Virgin of Faith, as in ch. xxi. upon the Gospel.

Now this new Life (there uttered) being in the new born Elect, it will grow strong and greatly change and refine the man: Yet, Reason will open his *Tombs* of death, and appear with his exceptions, contentions, demurs, murmurs, excuses, lies, &c. &c. thinking to divide the union of the church; then of consequence destroy the communion of this daughter of Faith in the Elect; nay would starve her out and destroy her from off this earth, and regeneration also, if possible; all for the kingdoms of this World, and the kingdoms of the dark spirit, then *excuse* themselves in that dark priesthood.

For this understand—Reason will catch the man in exceptions against the Messenger and the Brethren, then bind him up in self-communion, and take him from the church & communion of the daughter of Faith; then lead him into his own *Field*, where he will smell, admire, and gather the flowers of stupefaction and death: So by man's own self-pollution in spirit, will bring in his own death, and in this manner would *divide* Christ!

For Reason will lurk about, like unto a ravenous Serpent or Cormorant, seeking how he can destroy the Virgin daughter of Faith and regeneration, therefore watch this spirit which is the grand enemy.

But the Virgin of Faith, with divine assistance, will *Overcome*, and be united to Christ in holy Marriage, and lose herself in death in her own blood, under the justice of the father and pass through that death, to a new life, and bring forth a son, whose life is offered at the feet of Jesus in the glory of mercy, and Jesus calls it in, and unites it to himself in immortality, for this virgin Daughter will follow CHRIST, because thither is the spirit to go.

Now I beg you will mind what is written for a MESSENGER OF GOD I AM, and the whole world must take me, though against their will, because as I have declared they will be judged: But to them who own me a Messenger of God, I had much rather be a Messenger of Life than of Death, which must be, if they do not enter in and follow!

Therefore, *fear not little flock*, for JESUS sits in the Power and Glory of Mercy, to reward the Elect for their works and fruits of Faith; and my love, care, union, and prayer is with you and for you, as if I was in your presence; and I hope your's is so concerning me.

So conclude your loving brother in Christ.

London, Oct. 3, 1786.
    JAMES BIRCH

P.S. The whole church greets you all; my love to all enquiring friends:—Answer soon, with the day of the month sister Russant died.

LETTER LXVIII

To our beloved Sister Runwa, and to the whole Church beloved in Christ, in and about Pembroke, James Birch & Brethren, send Greeting.

Beloved sister, I am glad to hear of you, and are well, but was sorry that you was moved; yet the wisdom and power of GOD is above all; for there is no *certain Stay* in this Life, but many *Fluctuations*: And in all the troubles, difficulties, and distressed *Changes* in, and of Scenes in this Life, which I have had,—yet by the divine assistance of God, I have come through and *overcome*! and not only brought out the *Palm*, but also the OLIVE BRANCH! for

The desire and power of man is but vain, without the blessing of God: Yea, when left to himself, his own act will condemn him!—and in all your *Changes* and Scenes in this Life, you are to *Worship God* and CHRIST: then Heaven will protect you,—because, then you *Will* that Christ should rule over you;—but there is no earthly power can protect you, for they cannot protect themselves!

And whereas you fear you are gone into *Egypt*,— never do you mind the external Egypt, for there you only can meet *grovelling* or *whiffling* gnats, who may try to bite; but do you not fear, stand against them;—then their power ends, and must become your servant!—or it may be you may find a *Joseph*! All this is in the power of God!

And in all the goings out of Reason, for the kingdoms of this world, and the kingdoms of the dark spirit, they are bound and can go but their length, for the law rule the life of Reason, and justice rule the law; and the angel in justice has great power over the soul of man, and will do the will of God, therefore fear not them who are not able to hurt you, but fear him who has power over all *Plagues*, and can bring them on the soul of man, both in time and in eternity!—and also, can bring man through and from those Plagues, up to his royal seal, and give them an immortal and everlasting crown of glory! this is the reward of JESUS! therefore in the royal priesthood and works of Faith you are sure to find Jesus!

Again, men are too apt to fear the power and displeasure of men, and by this fear, sink into a Labyrinth that the soul will be bound in the strong captivity of slavish fear: and Reason will press down in this fear, lest man should stop their bread, be displeased, &c. but alas, the LORD GOD of heaven, LIVES and REIGNS, and "The Earth is His, and the fullness thereof: So it is good for Reason to mind how he behave, lest he should be visited and overthrown by *Plagues* that may be sent to him.

Also the LORD GOD created Heaven and Earth, and redeemed his Elect; then of consequence is very able to bring them through this Life; but then, it is according to his own wisdom; for, it is the nature of man to follow and abide by the wisdom they were born with, and when a Change is likely to come, or is come, then they have been affrighted; but—I know not why man should:—unless they are fearful God should give them Wisdom, or do them good! For it is the nature of regeneration to work the soul out of, and through death, and learn the soul TRUE Wisdom!

And in the midst of the troublesome changes and Scenes of this life, that may press the soul even to the Vale of Death; and the tempter appear and offer to relieve the soul, and say relief is here, or there, &c. all to tempt the soul aside, do you not hearken to him—he cannot relieve you—for relief to the Elect must come from heaven! therefore be FAITHFUL AND TRUE,—keep the word of prayer and patience, and you will be preserved from the Hour of Temptation, which is sure to come upon the world, as a snare!—And

When you keep fast to God, you will be brought through, and sweetly shine in Virtue and Truth: For you not only will have the commendation of the Angel in Justice, which is the *Palm Branch*, but also be brought forward in the royal priesthood and Works of Faith, which is the OLIVE BRANCH! And thus are the Elect brought out of, or through death to a new Life; and heavenly wisdom increased!— Therefore my advice is to all and every one, to put off the slavish fear of Reason, and act in this life to have the commendation of the Angel, then you will *Shine*, even before sober Men:—And to worship God and Christ, you will find your *yoke more easy, and burden more light*!

Again, I am glad you take all opportunities to visit the brethren,— and I hope they do the same to meet you; and learn and love each other in the wisdom and united Love of Christ, that the church appear as a sweet and beautiful *Blossom*, as a true token of *Fruit* for the kingdom of glory!

My love to all and every one, what I can serve you in I will, for I truly have you at heart, as if I was with you.

So conclude your loving brother in Christ.

JAMES BIRCH,

London, Jan. 4, 1787.

LETTER LXIX

To Mary Runwa, Jas. Birch & Brethren, Greeting.

Beloved Sister,—Yours I received, and was glad to hear from you and the church, and that you have *Liberty* as before, and hope you all *assemble* in the united Faith of CHRIST in regeneration, which is His CHURCH, for if you cannot be united to each other and the Messenger, in the LIVELY FAITH in and for regeneration, which is far above this perishing world,—how is it possible you should have the Love, and be united to Christ in Glory? for

The Virgin of Faith is born to SORROW, under the power of justice and death, as I have told you; therefore the Elect of old, were men of *Sorrow*, and laboured under those powers!—Christ was a man of SORROW, and trembled at the power and justice of the Father!! And Christ came on their *labour*, that by His LABOUR they may be made complete! And we must labour to follow him, to *reap of his labour* thereby, to be made complete.

The Messenger has *Laboured*, and you have entered by his labour: So it is Faith in Faith, and Faith on Faith, and Faith united to Faith, and all centers to Christ the KING of Faith! Therefore see the Union, Love, Faith, and POWER of Christ, and not be lulled asleep by Reason, but watch, and pray for divine assistance from heaven, for time is at hand!

Again,—Man is born into this world by the Power of God, and *under* his Power, for he cannot conceive himself in the Womb, neither is he *born* by his own power, and when born, he cannot help himself, and then he grow up helpless of his own Stature or Infirmities that may attend him, and with the Life and Wisdom he was born with, which is *fallen Reason*, which when come to maturity, is the devil; and there is the wisdom and kingdoms of the world, and of the dark spirit to take him! And his own spirit will drive him, and if possible, from Moses; but that cannot be:—Yet, Reason dearly like to have his own will, which is, "neither to fear God nor regard man;" and thus they go on in their delights, which are their kingdoms, and plead their own excuse, and become so upstart to make choice of their own way to heaven, and act against blasphemy, and persecute the kingdom of Christ, and tempt others to act as he do, because the darkness in him he think it to be light, and as so sacrifice to a god of his own imagination, whereas there is no such one to be found that can save him; and thus they are of darkness, and their wisdom is darkness, and are allured on by darkness, and fall in death under justice! neither can they help themselves, nor stop *Calamity and Death* one hour! Therefore I beg all of you to look at his wisdom and power, and watch his temptation both internal and external.

Moreover, the present MESSENGER came out from Christ to offer the Way unto Life, and Salvation to his elect,—and that the dead would be raised and enter regeneration to work the works of Faith: And when he first came, many heard the *Word* and was *glad*, then up comes the devil, and spread his Net, and took some *away* into his field, to eat the herbs and fruits, and smell and admire the flowers of stupefaction and death, neither would he suffer them to *hear* much of the word: But what *little* they had he told them it was their *own*; and they may gather kingdoms, and reign kings, &c. Others have said they would *follow*, but it has been in their own way, and when light has been made appear, that they could not endure, because their spirits was dark and deeds evil.

Also, others have promised to *follow*, but in the road have met with *stumbling Stones*, so turned aside into a field of Reason, and there live by their own darkness, and in their filth; therefore in this road, YOU must keep watch and *labour in travail*, for Reason has many fields to entice the soul aside out of the road: So do you, and all of you look at Mercy and Life, and him who can give it! And at the power of death and justice, and at the travail of Faith, and the easy travail of Reason, and how they are allured and lulled into death and hell!

Yea—now look at the wisdom, power, and consequence of Reason, and see whether he is worth minding or hearkening to, for he is helpless—bound up in darkness! which life must end in death under justice—and what he can gather up or do, will come to naught with himself: Therefore look you at the temptation of Reason, and the consequence that follow, if you hearken to him: So let him have his kingdom,—and what is that Life or kingdom that is bound up in, and under the powers of justice and death? *But* do you work in the royal priesthood under the justice of the Father, then you will enter the Kingdom, Glory, and Mercy of the SON,—and believe me, you have no time to lose!

Again, at the *voice* of the Messenger and divine assistance from heaven, the Virgin Daughter is raised from death to life; and this new life is pure; and by divine assistance will follow Christ; then by or with this the Elect are made FREE; for although the Virgin Daughter of Faith work or travail against the powers of Reason, and of justice, hell, and death, in this sorrowful Vale, yet, for this, &c. she is found worthy! and Christ comes in holy marriage and free her from those powers! then the elect are made *free indeed*—of the holy city or kingdom of Christ!—But the Life of Reason is sinful, and that Life is a *servant* to sin; and cannot be made *free* from those powers; for his hope is that his own nature will be made pure and free, which cannot be done! so death, hell, and justice remain over it.

Therefore, beloved brethren, have prayer and patience, and lift up your hearts and rejoice that your deliverance will come! And who knows how soon? And—the works of Faith is crowned with eternal life! And no other *Labour* has any reward of bliss in eternity: My love to you all, and my anxious thoughts and care is with you, and for you all.

So conclude your loving Brother in Christ.

James Birch.

London, April 7, 1787.

P.S. Doubtless—Betsy informed you of the death of Thomas Joseph, so now I must inform you of the death of his Father, Francis Joseph, who went to bed well as usual on Tuesday night, March 27; and died the ensuing morning; and was buried on Sunday, April 1; he was a worthy, true, and constant member of the Church, and with us hearty and well the Sunday night before, and had an easy passage to eternity!

LETTER LXX

To Mary Runwa, Jas. Birch & Brethren, Greeting.

Belov. Sist. & Breth.—I was glad to hear from you, and to see your good understanding and, power, and I pray God assist your understanding, and give you power: Now remember from whence you was *taken*—out of the house of captivated Reason, Justice, and Death: For the doctrine of the whole world is of the Cherubim, except *John Reeve's* declaration of God, and of his creation, and Prophecy of Christ to come: But *Muggleton's* is in the priesthood of Reason: and the emulated cherubical spirit went to such a heighth as to say "They were assured of eternal life, and they were kings, priests, and prophets, and call it the Faith for Christ, or the Faith of Christ," and at the same time it was no more than the Emulated confidence of fallen Reason: So mighty and so great was the power of darkness in and over the soul of man, — that as Man, one would think it impossible to bring men out from such dark Captivity.

But—The Lord God of Regeneration has been graciously pleased to send a Messenger in *regeneration*, to call to Faith, and by divine assistance from heaven, it has been and is rose from death to active life, and taken into the royal priesthood of Christ,—then the elect are made anew with this new life, which is Faith: and in ALL—the midst of this great wilderness, and cherubical doctrine, powers, &c. where must the Messenger find Faith for Christ? why truly it must be rose from death to active Life before he can;—then by *this Life*, the Elect are regenerated and made anew by Christ.

For—this understand—that which is regenerated, is the very nature God took on Him, to become Christ and redeem; then of consequence it is regenerated to Christ: then elect men are made anew by Christ, for His kingdom that he has gained, which is the Kingdom, Power, and Glory of Mercy! and

The cherubical nature which is *fallen* Reason with all its consequence that the Elect have in them, by the power of regeneration, it is cast out and go back to its own center, from whence it came, which is to Reason: For as the whole Fountain or power of Reason that fell into generation, was in and of the *serpent angel*; and by his life and nature, which is fallen Reason, which was the devil; he tempted Eve and Adam, who hearkened to him; then, they broke the law of Faith, and Faith died according to the word of the Lord God: And thus cherubical nature, which is Reason, took possession, and actuated and drove them; then by the power of Christ, Faith is rose from death to life, and regenerated to Christ; and Reason is, cast out, and goes to, and centers in or on the seed of the serpent who lives to manhood, and are sealed down for wrath to come; and in this is God's wrath doubled to them! NOW here you may see how the devil is cast out, and enter the herd of swine, by the power, of Christ, and also see how Faith fell in Adam, and how it is made alive in Christ.

Again, although Reason with its law and justice, and wild and given priesthood, is so powerful in elect man, as to be capable of the cherubical inspiration, as was Moses; yet it is but the *Body* of the elect, because God never placed it there in his creation; but Adam received it by or through temptation, and it will be drove out by regeneration: But this new life that, is rose from Faith, that died in Adam, becomes the soul of the elect for salvation: and by or with this life of regenerated Faith, Enoch, Moses, and Elias ascended into heaven, and is the life they have and enjoy in the kingdom of glory! thus you may see how soul and body of the elect are separated by regeneration; and the law, worship, &c. that Moses gave to Reason, is but the *Body of Moses*, and Reason will contend for it; but the soul of Moses, that belongs to Christ, and it is the same in and with all the Elect.

Also the faith and doctrine of the whole world is but *Cherubical*; but it has its degrees of *Wisdom and Moderation*, but all their confidence is in their own imagination on the letter, and they have and will *contend* with this Messenger concerning it, which is also the *Body* of Moses; for them who are incapable of regeneration, Moses is their *Prophet*, and his body is *buried* in them; but the Messenger will *contend* for Faith in regeneration, and regenerated Faith, for that belongs to Christ, and is and will be the life of the Elect in all eternity, in the glory of mercy! NOW here you may see the life, nature, and power of regenerated Faith; and mind how Moses wrote as a law-giver to Reason, with his promise and prophecies to them concerning it; and where he wrote & prophesied in the royal Compact and Priesthood of Faith; and also where John Reeve did write, declare, promise, and prophecy to and concerning the bloody unbelieving world; and where he writes and prophesies in the royal compact and priesthood of Faith.

And those people to whom I came, who said "they believed John Reeve," I say, had they believed John Reeve, they would have believed me, *i.e.* had they understood and believed him in the royal Compact and Priesthood of Faith, they would have *understood* and believed me; but there is no Faith in them for that, so he also remain their prophet unto the bloody unbelieving world, & the last that ever will be sent:— But

This MESSENGER came out from the FEET of JESUS in regeneration, and has divided each law, kingdom, and priesthood to itself, and the Faith or confidence of Reason, which is cherubical, from Faith in and for regeneration, which is the true Faith of, and for Christ: and also has declared how soul and body of the Elect are *separated* by regeneration, to enter the Kingdom of Christ; and taken you from the house of Reason, Justice, and Death, and has put you in the way and directed you to the *new House*; which is the House of Faith, Mercy and Life, which is the Kingdom of Christ.

Therefore, Faith in regeneration, has *eyes before and behind*, *i.e.* it knows from whence it came, and the ruination of that house, so it will watch, that it never return back to the *old House*, and those are its *eyes behind*: Also it see and know no one can enter the kingdom of Christ without the works of Faith in regeneration, therefore it will work the works of Faith, and press forward for the kingdom of Christ! and those are its *eyes before* also it has *eyes within*, to see and know, and watch the tempter; and to refuse and repulse him, that it be not carried by his temptation: Therefore as Faith fell under the powers of Reason, Justice, and Death; then it is rose from death to life, and by divine assistance from heaven will work its way through those powers to Mercy and Life.

Enoch, Moses, and Elias, bore a body of flesh and was under those powers: and Faith in them was rose to life, and regenerated for and into the kingdom of heaven: CHRIST also bore a body, of flesh, and worked His way through those powers; and by His new Life that was quickened out of death, he ascended into heaven, and took possession of his new kingdom of regenerated Faith; therefore they in heaven above, whose life and nature is Faith, have all borne a body of flesh on this earth, and worked the works of Faith under those powers; and by the power of Faith have passed through those powers, to the Kingdom of Glory: Hence—all the mighty works of Faith to inherit the kingdom of Christ, is done on this earth in a body of flesh: For

Faith must be regenerated from this Earth, and from among men; and in this passage through hell and death, every kingdom, spirit, and fiend has its power: but do you WORSHIP GOD and fear not, but pray and not faint, for the *days* or power of Reason is now *shortened*, that the Elect shall work the works of Faith, and press forward for the kingdom of Christ: Now mind what is written, and I pray God assist you.

So conclude your loving brother in Christ.

JAMES BIRCH.

London, June 30, 1787.

LETTER LXXI

To our beloved sister Runwa, & Brethren, Greeting.

Beloved Sister and Brethren—I was glad to hear from you, and that your love is in the *Works and Fruits of Faith* in REGENERATION—then of consequence you will *Love* each other—for

The *united* LOVE of regenerated Faith is the Love of and for CHRIST—and who can stand against such love? No soft tongued lying Hypocrite, for—it discovers them, nay—turns them inside out, so *they* will seek refuge where they can.

Again, as I have told you—when the Virgin of Faith is born—she finds herself in a fallen state, and surrounded by the powers of Reason, Justice, Hell, and Death, therefore it is the nature of Faith to fear and *tremble* at the justice of God; and through it we must go, to Mercy and Life! For this WAY Christ went, and Faith in regeneration must follow, because it regenerated to him.

There is the kingdom's of this world, and of the dark spirit to take and allure Reason, then they are swallowed up by death and justice, which is set for them as a snare! —for as the night seals up the day, even so is the Life of Reason sealed up by death and justice. — Here you may see the Elect must come out of the world in spirit, and work the works of Faith to be brought through those great powers.

Therefore have prayer and patience, and not faint,—be faithful unto death - and you will be taken through death and rewarded with life eternal! But the unbelieving, self-cunning, and fearful, cannot trust God, and must sink into, and under those powers.

Moreover, I am glad you called on those *People* at *Haverfordwest*, because I have heard of them, and wish they had embraced you and the doctrine closer: they say they put their whole trust in the *Mercy of Christ*—I wish they may be found worthy of HIS MERCY, to raise them from death to life; and take them into His Royal Priesthood and works of Faith, and bring them through death to life eternal, — there is *Time and Space* given for repentance, but believe me, without the FIRST RESURRCTION, there is no regeneration!

And *They* also hope to be *clothed* with the righteousness of Christ— I wish they could seek the Messenger, and the first resurrection, that the Virgin of Faith may appear, and work the works of Faith, to *follow* CHRIST, then they would possess the righteousness of Faith in and of themselves; for the RIGHTEOUSNESS OF CHRIST to come in upon! for without this there is no one can enjoy the righteous power of Christ, but the child or cherubim.

Therefore, Rev. xix. &c. "When the marriage of this Lamb was come, and His Wife had made herself ready."—The Lamb's *Wife* is the Virgin daughter of Faith, that has worked the works of Faith, and overcome the world and the dark spirit! And in this she has made herself ready! "And to her was granted that she should be arrayed in fine linen, clean and white, for the fine linen is the *Righteousness* of saints." Here you may see the righteousness of the Virgin Daughter in the Elect, which is of Faith, or the Righteousness of saints, and is called the *array of fine linen clean and white*, which is the WEDDING GARMENT, meet for marriage with the lamb! Then Christ unites with this *pure virgin daughter* in holy marriage, and beget to himself a spiritual son in regeneration; — then this Woman or Virgin daughter of Faith became *clothed* with the spiritual Son in regeneration, which is *sealed* by Christ for eternal glory!

Now this, is the *righteous clothing* of CHRIST, or being "clothed with the righteousness of Christ" — But here people transform themselves to the letter, and become safe, according to their imagination, because they own the *Name and Doctrine*; But it is according to their own will and pleasure, and so are bound up in their *own* righteousness, which is evil, because it is against the righteousness of Christ!

They make use of *His Name*, because He is the Saviour of his elect,—yet, when his salvation is offered, they will neglect, turn from, refuse it, &c. Thus are they lulled and allured by their own *conceited* righteousness, hoping to be *clothed and saved* by the righteousness of Christ—the same time refuse and neglect HIM and his Messenger, who is the *Door and Way!* Thus they go into death under justice, as down a hill of ice!

Now *Those* are them who appear without a wedding garment; and must be *cast out!* For how is it possible for the Righteousness of CHRIST to unite with the hypocrisy of Reason, which is the devil—therefore all their pretension is fallacy and hypocrisy; and you—watch this spirit, and be WISE unto salvation!

Beloved, I have told you, there is nothing but the world and the devil to run away with men,— and the seed of Reason run in and with this current into death under justice, as a river runs into the sea. For their life is Reason, and are born to no other understanding and enjoyment but that of this life, which is their care—because it is their heaven. For the seed of Reason, when they came to maturity, are appointed to perish! therefore it delights in, and *feeds* on, things which also must perish.

The *miserable* Life of fallen Reason is eager to live and be supported that it may shine in its consequence, and will bind up and drive the souls of men to do it, which is striving and working for death: yet, mean to keep him off as long as possible! And when the Messenger offers life and salvation that they cannot endure—because they are in darkness, and their deeds are evil!

And the *spirit* of Reason will fill the soul with this or that *Hope*; and allure him after this or that *vain delight*, or to any incumbrance or delight, beside the Messenger! And thus are they allured on till their life is swallowed up in death under justice!

Now the Messenger came out, in and for the first resurrection—and to the Virgin of Faith, when she is risen, that the Elect may be regenerated and made anew for the kingdom of Christ: Therefore let the dead *care* and strive for the dead, and when done bury their dead—for in one hour will come on them poverty, sorrow, mourning and death! But do YOU work the works of Faith, as the Messenger has laboured to inform you, and God hath *witnessed* to him, that you may follow Christ thro' death to life eternal. Therefore have prayer and patience—a release will come, for,

To the elect, the end of *sorrow* is the beginning of JOY! But to the seed of Reason the end of JOY is the beginning of SORROW!

So conclude your loving brother in Christ, with prayer for you all.

London, Dec. 14, 1787.

JAS. BIRCH.

The whole church greeting, with my love to all and every one. - Our friend James Collet is dead—he died the 16th ult.

LETTER LXXII

To our beloved sister Mary Runwa, and the whole church beloved in Christ, Jas. Birch & Brethren send Greeting.

Beloved Sister and Brethren —Yours I received Feb. 6, and I was glad to hear from you, and that you are all well, and hope all are in the *united Love* of CHRIST, and *works* of Faith; for in the royal Priesthood of Faith you will have *peace*,—but in the world *trouble*; Why? because it is in a fallen perishing kingdom; and Reason rules; therefore every serpent, viper, &c. has its *Day* and power, and will torment.

Faith hearkened to Reason, and for that Reason has power over it, to persecute it, perplex it, &c. and Reason also, being in a fallen state, they will torment each other, for they go out on their own evil spirit, to do their own will, and seek their own safety; so within themselves are divided against themselves, because they act not according to the law of Moses; and their language is become *Egyptian*, and *Babel* confusion, *wilderness* murmurs, *howls*, &c. and Death and justice reign over them: For as the Law rules the life, so Justice rules the law, and death reigns king.

Now as the Virgin daughter of Faith being in and among those powers, then, by divine assistance, it must wade through and overcome those powers, and go into and through death, as Reason will put his *Cross* on Faith and human nature: Yea, has loaded me heavy! Whether I shall sink under it or not, I know not—but this I know—if I can, I must bear it unto my death! For as Reason will bear his own witness, to his own condemnation unto death eternal, even so must the elect bear his *Cross* unto their death, which is temporal: neither can the elect be released but in and through death; therefore it is to Christ and his kingdom the elect are to go, and by regeneration, as this Messenger has declared; then, all sorrow is turned into joy! So have Faith and patience, watch the tempter and pray for preservation, then every day brings us nearer the release.

Beloved sister and brethren, I rather commend you for writing as you did concerning *Joe*, for it was not done, I perceive, in any evil spirit or meaning; but in the spirit of fear, lest any elect should be hindered from the union of the church, or that any one who professed Christ should go from Him; and that the church should *shine* in good works, even before their enemy.

As to James he was taken by the *tempter*, and let there be *space* given for repentance, and wait the *Issue*; for BLESSED are them who are not carried by the tempter! So pray for and love each other in the united love of Christ, and have Faith, prayer and patience, and doubt not, then all will be well, as I have told you before.

Beloved sister and brethren, I mean to see you this summer, being constrained in mind so to do, and hope to find you all well, I have lived to see many brethren go before me.

Mr. Joseph's daughter Anne, who was Mrs. Aris, is dead,—she died the 2d of January last, so the whole of that family died within twelve months.

And as my Life and Joy is in Christ and my brethren, make me desirous to see you; and am constrained so to do.—As soon as you receive this, write an answer, that I may prepare to come: So conclude your loving brother in Christ.

London, May 13, 1788   JAS. BIRCH.

I saw Mrs. Jones, and heard of your nephew last Sunday.

LETTER LXXIII

The Messenger of Christ to the Church in Wales.

Beloved Sister and Brethren—I received your letter, and was amazed to see the contents.—What, has the kingdom of hell *pressed* you so hard that you are afraid of the kingdom of heaven?—I know the devil will tempt distress, and gather all to himself, so that if possible, the SERVANT of GOD shall have nothing not where to lay his head! and be put off with excuses, or repulse, &c.—As you hope for mercy and life, why are you afraid of the devil and death! Mind, and be not *too great* a servant to the devil!—you refuse GOD's time, and fix your own!! I never learnt you this!—this you have learnt of another master—or you may think I may save myself; which—I cannot do; for as the natural Sun goeth its course, even so, do the spiritual, and where I am sent, I must go without excuse—but my trust is in GOD, and not in what blind frozen up Reason can or will please to do.

I hope my time is near up, but do not know what death I shall die, or where I shall die; so I must come to you now, in all your *poverty*! and as you say, "God's will be done;" but a Messenger of Christ seldom meets with much *riches* in the natural.

I asked, and WAITED the answer, which made me delay writing; but, when it came that I MUST go! then I sent you word.

I have much to say, and I hope to find all things well; and this spirit of fear which sinketh into temptation cast out.

And *Polly*, as your desire, *was* to see me this summer; I believe your desire will be crowned.

So conclude your loving brother.

JAMES BIRCH.

London, May 29, 1788.

Note.—The above Letter and Chap. 1. upon the Gospel, was chose and read on Christmas Eve 1812 present Messrs. Thomas Axtell, William Whitten, Thomas Herald, George Platt, William Ringer, John Aglen, Theophilus Day, Robert Ingram, Thomas Freeman, Zech. Debnam, and Mary Hart—Sister Herald afflicted.

LETTER LXXIV

To Mrs. Birch and Brethren in London.

My Dear—this with my love; and hope you all remember and keep in view the KINGDOM OF CHRIST, for it is highly necessary to *strive* for that Kingdom where unto you belong, and are to inherit:—And seeing all kingdoms and powers will pass, away! But the kingdom, power, and glory of Christ will for ever stand!—therefore WATCH!

I have found satisfaction at this church at Pembroke; for they have opened themselves to me, much to my liking: Yea I have said in spirit, *it is good to be here*; and it is well for me, for you, and for all, that I came.

And I pray the Lord God of heaven to assist and help you through this sore journey of flesh, in *a terrible wilderness*, where there is *striving* for that which perish! Nay, Reason will hardly let them enjoy it one day;—this is on the one part, and Babylonish *Gabble*, lies, and confusion on the other part; therefore watch and take care not to be entangled, seeing the mighty powers of death and hell are in act, and ready to swallow you up! for

It is my soul's desire and prayer for you to be assisted in the works of Faith, and that you bring forth its FRUITS, to Overcome those powers, and not *one* to sink therein and *left* behind; but that you all FOLLOW CHRIST up to his royal Seal and Kingdom: And at the same time hope your souls and spirits are, and will be, in union with mine; therefore worship GOD, let Him be your *Refuge* and Trust; for Man you cannot trust, without being deceived.

The whole church greets you, and desire their united love in the WORSHIP of God and Christ, and WORKS and FRUITS of Faith, to inherit HIS kingdom.—I am hearty and well, and hope to have a good and safe return, and that this will find you all well. So conclude your loving brother in Christ.

Pembroke, Aug. 17, 1788.   JAMES BIRCH.

LETTER LXXV

As it were a LOOKING-GLASS. See p. 307[*].

To our Sister Runwa, with the whole Church beloved in Christ, Jas. Birch and Brethren send Greeting.

Beloved Sister and Brethren—This with my love to inform you I came safe to London, and found all friends well.

Now I hope you will remember what I said, when I was with you, concerning the *Hour of Time.* and that the *Hour* of the LORD CHRIST is now come!

Therefore worship God and Christ, and patiently *wait and watch* his coming:—Be not made *drunk* with the waters of Reason, nor *surfeited* and overcome with the *follies* and cares of this life. Mind the incumbrance and *oppression* of arrogant Egypt, and also the *murmurs and temptation in the wilderness*; for

The *narrow path* is between the *Threats* and *Temptations* of dissatisfied Reason: and in that *Path* "Mountains will be removed."

Moreover, There is the *Field of Faith*, or where God is worshipped; and the *field of Reason*, where the *devil* is worshipped; and the Messenger finds it a hard thing to bring man from the *field* of Reason to the *field* of Faith.

Now, in the *Field* of Faith; God's blessing flow, and man is under the *protection* of God; and there Elect man will find, he will not only pass through this life with more *ease* and *honour* (and have the justification of God); but also to work the works of Faith in the Royal Priesthood, to *inherit* the kingdom of Christ!

But in the *field* of Reason man trusts to his own *strength, wisdom,* and *imagination* of Reason; which is the *devil*; then there is driving and striving, desires, expectations, failures, murmurs; disappointments, anger, &c. &c.

---

[*] In the original edition page 307 refers to Let. LXXVI.

Thus—Man is lulled or drove into death by the devil, to be swallowed up in hell! Therefore his time is badly spent, who *labours* to satisfy unsatisfiable Reason: — But do you trust in GOD: Worship God; —And let Him give Reason his own satisfaction, which He will be sure to do.

I would have you mind these things.

There is the *Earth-worm* grubbing spirit; that were it possible it would *skim* the whole world to itself for the sake of *Treasure*. This spirit is called a *thief*, and has a *Bag*: this is a murmuring *covetous* spirit, and will do any thing for the sake of *Money*, even sell and betray the LORD OF LIFE as Judas did!—this is a *bound up* covetous spirit; and will do no good towards God or to man: There are them, which you all know, who professed this Faith, and has *sold* the Lord of Life, and His Messenger, through fear and coveteousness of their *Pelf*, and to have the commendation of the devil.

Again, the spirit of Reason will act in *desire*, to gather up riches, to buy possessions and the *souls of men*; and this is what they call acquiring a *fortune* in business, to leave it off and take their *ease*: and if they can find when to leave off, then other troubles come on concerning it, and their spirit become clogged; then they find all their *Life and delight*, they had concerning it, was gathering it together: Thus they look for things to come which is already past; and if suffered to be in their *Glee*, then they fall under the parable of Jesus, —as—Luke xii. "The ground of a certain rich man brought forth plentiful, then he said, he would build large barns to bestow his goods, and say to his soul, soul, thou hast goods laid up for many years, take thine ease, eat, drink, and be merry." But God said unto him,—"Thou fool, this night thy soul shall be required of thee, then, whose shall those things be which thou hast provided?" Thus, Reason will drive and strive, for things he never can enjoy, and *lose himself in the Act*—because his Waters of Life become the *waters of death*.

Again, and above all, mind you do not *bury* your given *Talent* in the earth, for the declaration of the Messenger is the *talent*, and you are to put it to *use* in the *Royal priesthood* of Faith, to *gain others*, and have the commendation of the Master of the House, who is CHRIST the King of Faith.

But him who receive the talent and set *light by it*, and go into those and *other waters* of Reason—there he will *lose himself*, and the talent is *buried in the earth*, and is an *unprofitable servant* to Christ, therefore WATCH!

True it is, *in the world*, you will have trouble, because Faith hearkened to Reason; and fell under the *power* of Reason and of *death*: But CHRIST came and *redeemed* it; and is now come to quicken it from Death to LIFE, and take it into his own royal PRIESTHOOD to follow Him in the works of Faith, *i.e.* to *overcome* the world and the devil.

And how is it possible any one should overcome the world, whose delight and Life is *buried* in the world, and excuse himself by Reason, which is the devil?

So—seeing this wicked, deceitful, enticing World run as a *current* hastily into death, with hell at its heels;—"Come out of her," and keep out of her and *Worship* GOD in the royal priesthood of Faith, then you will be under his *protection*; and as you pass through this life you will be made able to take the *Serpent* by the head.

Be not afraid, for they cannot *hurt* you—Keep but the word of *Faith and patience*, and you will be preserved from the *hour of temptation*, that cometh on the whole World.

So, *watch*! and prepare for His coming!—Let your *Lamp of Faith burn*; for BLESSED are them that are so prepared to *meet* HIM!

Conclude your loving brother in Christ,

London, Oct. 14, 1788.   JAMES BIRCH.

The whole church greets you.—My love to all and every one, and hope you will mind what is written—be watchful—Have heard of Mrs. Jones, and believe she is well.

LETTER LXXVI

To our beloved Sister Mary Runwa, and to the whole Church beloved in Christ, Jas. Birch and Brethren send greeting.

Beloved Sister and Brethren—I was glad to hear from you, and that you received mine, and understand—for it is as it were a *Looking Glass*; and happy are those who can see themselves by it.

Now—I was sent to the Elect and am a Messenger of Life to them (and *Life* must be worked out of and through death): But am a Messenger of death to Reason, so he may well be angry and agitated at me; for he must be arrested from his strong Hold—bound up—and die from his power to go out of Elect man.

Also this Messenger has *sounded* the voice of the *sixth* Angel in regeneration on this earth; and at the same time has *"poured out the sixth vial of God's wrath* upon the great *river* Euphrates." (Rev. xvi. 12) — this great river is the waters of Reason's *hope*, or the hope of Reason; and it become *dried up* in the Elect, that the daughter of Faith may work the works to follow Christ; for the Elect, in the royal Priesthood of Faith, cannot live in the waters of Reason, for all that is dryed up in them, so they must live in and by the waters of Faith to follow Christ: and this is the *Way*, that "the way of the *kings of the east* (which are the Elect) *are prepared*:" therefore they can have no peace or hope as Reason has: But their peace, rest, and hope, is with this present Messenger in the royal priesthood and waters of Faith, which lead to the kingdom of Christ.

Also this *Vial of God's wrath is poured out* upon the life and hopes of Reason throughout the whole world: but their waters never will be *dried up*, for they will be changed to envy, wrath, blasphemy, &c. accompanied with troubles, justice and death; and although *space* has been given they repent not but proceed according to their own will and ways; then justice and death comes on them, for strong is the LORD GOD of HEAVEN, who has power over those plagues, and *will* send them upon Reason.

And although the seed of Reason is the image of Elect Man, yet the Life for salvation cannot be given to, or found in them, no more than Man can give Life to an image of stone! It is the spirit "that quickeneth (and giveth life) the flesh profiteth nothing," and mind, no one can enter the kingdom of heaven with the spirit of Reason in him, that is charged with the law,—therefore it must be got above, by the spirit, and power of Faith, and man made anew by regeneration, and Reason is cast out, and go to its own home! Therefore have prayer and patience, for by divine assistance you will be brought through the mighty powers and troubles of Reason, justice, and death, up to the seal of Christ the king of Faith: BUT, all those troubles and powers of sin, justice, death, and hell, will be sent to and upon Reason.

So conclude your loving brother in Christ, with prayer for you all.

JAMES BIRCH

London, Dec. 13, 1788.

The oysters were received—the brethren return you many grateful thanks. Should have wrote sooner, but waited to write something in the SPIRITUAL.

LETTER LXXVII

To our Sister Mary Runwa, and the whole church beloved in Christ, James Birch and Brethren send greeting.

Beloved Sister and Brethren—Yours I received and was glad to hear from you; and that you meet in Church Union, and the UNITED LOVE of and for CHRIST; and I hope you will continue so to do.

Always remember that saying of Christ, in Matthew xviii. 20, "For where two or three are gathered together in my name, there am I in the midst of them." Here you may see the grand union of Faith in the church of Christ, and the great benefit in the communion of *Saints* therefore.

Watch the power of the devil, and of this world, that it do not creep in and take you aside; for seeing we have the power of sin, death, hell, and justice &c. to wade through, and get above, it must be done by the power and prayer of Faith, and divine assistance from heaven; therefore love and pray for each other; rejoice at each others Faith, and assist each other in what you can, in and for the kingdom of

Christ; and if a *will* can be found there is no fear of the power being *given*.

Again, the kingdom of Reason is in and of this world, and Reason will greatly strive and contend for it, and mourn, murmur, and howl after it; that they may go out on their own evil spirit, to do their own will, and have their own way: but they are within the *Ring or Orb* of Justice, which is full of eyes, where death reigns king, and hell follow with it. Hence, mind what you strive, labour, and are anxious for;—let it be for the kingdom of Christ, and let Reason strive for his kingdom, which is denied any assistance from Christ, therefore WATCH! for every one will have the reward of their own kingdom; and Reason will be much obliged to you to assist him, that he may go out on his evil.

Also the kingdoms of Reason is left *desolate*, notwithstanding "the kingdoms of this world is become the kingdom of Christ;" *i.e.* as CHRIST has gone through the power of Reason, sin, death, hell, and justice, and ascended far above it, he has power over it: And he only has power to put an end to time, and bring in eternity, and the way of his coming is prepared! Therefore this world stands by his divine permission, that HE may *accomplish the number of his Elect* (which is only known to himself) that he may complete his heavenly kingdom.

Moreover (as aforesaid), *I came out from Christ in regeneration, and in his spirit and power; and was sent to them who owned the letter of Reeve and Muggleton, and called themselves* believers *in the commission of the Spirit,* but Lo! I saw the dark Spirit of Kingly imagination burning in abomination, as a mountain whose top reached Heaven, which I *trembled* at; for this mountain must be passed over, and its wrathful *flames* trod under foot by the power of Christ: And when I told them a little, it fired their wrathful spirit—then "desired me to depart their coast" or company, because they were *tormented*!

But—*There were SOME who were prepared to receive me!* And BLESSED are THEM who did come and died in CHRIST—and also THEM that are WITH ME—and THEM that may YET COME?—for

The kings of the dark spirit had exalted their imagination on the letter *above* the spirit that declared it, and wrote it! — Also they set the prophet *Reeve* aside as much as possible; and *exalted Muggleton* above him, saying, "he was the longest liver,"—And denied the *transgression* of created Faith! The *assistance* from heaven in the works of redemption! And the mystical *union* of Christ with or to his elect, and the *notice* of God—and *prayer* to heaven! So they trampled down the wisdom, works, and power of Christ, and exalted themselves above all by *Muggleton's* letter, or rather their dark imagination on his Letter: Thus they exalted themselves above all that was of God; and it being in the commission of the spirit, which was the Temple of God, because there Christ was to come—there they *Sit* and poured out their wrathful judgment, not only on the ELECT but the whole world also, - for them who act not to their liking were condemned; and God was to do what they said through *Muggleton*, and thus they shewed *themselves* God! For what they called God was to become their servant. Now this is the great mountain of *abomination* that SIT in the external *Temple* of God, and made the spirit of Christ *desolate*!! HE THAT HATH WISDOM LET HIM UNDERSTAND! therefore,

When the Messenger came, he gave birth to the *son of perdition* by the declaration, and the MAN *of sin is manifest*, in or by the birth of the "son of *perdition*"; and they came forth in violent wrath and blasphemy against Christ, and his Messenger, and His Elect: and all their , wrath lies, curses, persecution, &c. the Messenger has overcome, and the Elect has and will overcome but thanks be to Christ the King of Faith, who has given us VICTORY over the kingdom of darkness, and *son of perdition*! for

Now Christ is come, and his kingdom shine in glory; and the kingdom of Reason, &c. is made *manifest*, and left desolate, and, all that do not follow this present Messenger, is left *desolate* and "so far are desolations determined to this day."

Hence, be *glad* and *rejoice* that you were prepared to receive the Messenger, and enter the royal priesthood, to have the divine assistance of Christ, and follow him through the kingdoms and powers of Reason, death, &c. Let prayer and patience possess your souls, for GOD WILL PRESERVE HIS ELECT.

So conclude your loving brother in Christ, with prayer for you all.

JAMES BIRCH.

London, March 21, 1789.

LETTER LXXVIII

To our beloved sister Mary Runwa, and the whole church beloved in Christ, Jas. Birch & Brethren send Greeting.

Beloved Sister and Brethren—yours I received, and was glad to hear from you, and I humbly hope you meet in *Church Union*, and in the *united Love of* CHRIST, not to look back from whence you came, which was from the *House of Reason* and Death, but look forward to where you have been directed, which is to the Mansions of regenerated Faith, Mercy and Life.

Here—in this Life, all must bear the *burden* of the flesh: the *threats, oppression,* and *temptation* of the devil: and death will press hard upon Life, which will cause great pain, sorrow, and agitation therefore let prayer and patience possess your souls, and you will be brought through.

Remember, "he that holdeth out to the end the same will be saved:" and "he that overcometh, Christ will own him as his son." So, woe! woe! to him that "look back to bid farewell"—accompany with, or seek any refuge in the house of Reason, for all must be left—and whoever thinks to make peace there, for the sake of peace, and that happiness there, he will lose his peace! happiness! yea his life! Remember Lot's wife! When Sodom and Gomorrah was destroyed.

Moreover, as the Lord God of regeneration and salvation, has sent his Messenger to call you into the royal compact of regenerated Faith, and has truly declared to you the mystery of Salvation, and set you above the world; nay, you have power to *Judge* the world; therefore be careful to hold fast and improve what God have given you, and not be allured in any way aside: for

The spirit of Reason will seek always to entrap you, then he will bite you, and pour in his poisonous venom! Then he will appear with his shifts, allurements, exceptions, murmurs, &c. &c. if possible to divide you, and if this be done, then you put the Messenger in *prison,* and if possible, this spirit would chain him up, therefore watch and beware, keep to, and within the *House of Israel.* — For

You may see, *Samson* was promised of God, and was born according to that promise, and God blessed him with *strength,* and he was to judge and deliver Israel out of the hands of the Philistines, and was made a *judge in Israel*; yet, you may see he would have a *Philistine Woman* to wife: And see how she worked on him, to get the secret of his *Riddle* to betray it to her own people, for them to take the advantage of him—see how they served him—and what trouble followed! Also, when he went unto *Harlots*, see how they informed and colleagued with the Philistines, at length one, by her bewitching insinuation and wicked craft, got from him where his *strength* was, and robbed him of it, and gave him into the hands of the *Philistines*, who put out his *Eyes*, and enslaved him—bound him in prison, and made him their sport! and all this was, because he did not abide by the wisdom of God, according to the cherubical inspiration, but be hearkened to, and was overcome by *serpentine* wisdom! And although he then slew many, yet, he died with them! Therefore watch this alluring spirit of Reason, lest YOU are overcome! For

As YOU have been brought into the house of redeemed and regenerated Faith, which is the house or kingdom of Israel, for there CHRIST is KING, and have been instructed in the WILL and WISDOM of God, and of Christ; be careful of the *strange woman*, which is the spirit of Reason, and not accompany with her, nor spend your time there, because this is the WIFE the Elect must put away; for she has the *vain Wisdom* and delights of the whole world to allure after; and if you love and hearken to her, she will bewitch you, and lead you into and under the power of Reason, where you will be *betrayed* and *robbed* of your Strength, and the *eyes* that were given you, be put out; for it is the nature of Reason, by its serpentine wisdom, to decoy or drive into death and hell, where itself must go; and they know not the nature and consequence of their acts! But that is for *you* to know! Therefore watch this enticing spirit, lest what has been given is taken away! And, as (*I said*) you have been taken out of the world, and you are made a *Judge* of Reason, and of the world; so mind you keep in the TRUE UNION of the Faith of Christ with the Messenger, then you never will be swallowed up in the ruination of Reason's wisdom.

NOW as these troubles were brought on Samson for neglecting *Cherubical* wisdom, and hearkening to the *Serpentine*: What think you will become of him that shall slight and neglect the wisdom of INSPIRED Faith in and for regeneration, which leads to salvation and life? And mind, Faith is not to die as the Philistine spirit, for it must overcome and die under the justice of the father. Now I write this to all and every one, who *do own* and desire to work, and *shall own* and desire to work in this GLORIOUS DECLARATION and royal Priesthood of Faith, which lead to the mansions of bliss!

Further, you may see they regard not Moses nor Jesus, but their bare name only, and even that to cloke their own evil: So the wisdom of God is put aside, and their own serpentine employed, which is become very great and distressing to each other, for they drive and follow each other into evil, like unto waves in a raging sea, who drive and follow each other; and they foam out their desires, emulations, oppressions, murmurs, &c. in and with all their evils, as the waves foam in their rage: so that troubles and temptations are become very great!

And I earnestly pray the days and power of Reason may be shortened; and the Elect relieved from their trouble and this Den of misery, where Reason gathers in his own way, to fill his own cup of oppression and abomination in his full glee, and knoweth not that judgment day is nigh, where he will meet his final overthrow! But this is for YOU, to know and observe! Therefore, beloved brethren, have prayer and patience, and fear not, keep close to Christ and his Messenger, and you will be brought through those troubles! And as you *pass by* the acts, works, desires and temptations of Reason, you will see them in ruination! So I recommend you to the love and UNION OF CHRIST, and prayer for each other.

And conclude your loving brother in Christ, with prayer for you all.

London, May 28, 1789.   JAMES BIRCH

P.S. Collect the Letters in one book, or by copies, that none be lost— we have been but poorly most of the Winter, and are moved from where we stopped rather too long. Mrs. Birch obeyed your order toward James Stevens, and hath, and would do by him as her own child: He is from his master, and may be with us; but there will be close inspection and tuition.—(See Letter of June 23, 1789, Divine Memorial.)—I hope he will be active in business, keep good company, and do well. In this I wait your further instruction. Direct to me, Thomas's Court, (88) Fore-street. Note—afterward called "Bartholomew-Court," but soon after the entrance of the second generation (March 26, 1797) that also became oblivial.

LETTER LXXIX

To our Sister Runwa, with the whole Church beloved in Christ, Jas. Birch and Brethren send Greeting.

Beloved Sister and Brethren,

I was glad to hear from you; I should have wrote sooner, but would attend to finish what I was writing, and thank God it is done, I am glad you desire to meet in *Church Union*, to commune by Faith in regeneration, for then is given fresh beams of knowledge with divine instruction, and be brought on to have an *earnest* you are in favor with CHRIST, and in the *road* for His kingdom. This is a *blessing and* TREASURE above the world, for it cannot be given to Reason, neither can the Elect be delighted with vain things of this world, as the people of the world are. For,

When man is about to purchase a possession or inheritance in this life, he will consider and view it, and when he find it pleasing to himself, "he will part with what he has to purchase it," because he thinks to have *gain and joy* in it; nay, his thoughts and delight is in it, and for it. So it is with Faith in the royal priesthood for the Kingdom of Christ, because there all its labour, joy, and expectation will be crowned with everlasting happiness in ETERNAL GLORY! Therefore as I said, the Elect cannot be delighted with vain things which perish, as the children of the world are! Because Faith in regeneration will not be detained in *Egypt*, or the *wilderness*; or any wild country; for it will seek to get as near home as possible, which is to Christ its King; "For where the treasure is there will the heart be."

Moreover, Matt. xiii. 45, Jesus saith, "Again the kingdom of heaven is like unto a merchantman, seeking goodly pearls, who, when he had found one pearl of great price went and sold all that he had and bought it:" This parable is to and concerning the Elect, who are to seek salvation, for they have the kingdom and priesthood of Reason to exchange for the priesthood and kingdom of Faith, which is darkness for light, death for life, hell for heaven, &c. and they must seek him who can and will give that exchange; and the *time* is when the VOICE of God is on this earth, to call the Elect, and it centers to the womb of

Faith in the souls of the Elect, then in God's time birth is given to the virgin daughter, and she is taken into the royal priesthood, and will see and know those powers, and work against and through those powers, up to the seal of Christ the KING of Faith, which is the pearl of great price, and the Elect must give up, or part with all they possess in this life, to work the works of Faith in the royal priesthood, and follow up to the royal seal, to *purchase* it, and the spirit will not admit that any encumbrance of this life shall hinder or stop the works of Faith.

See Matt, x. 37. Jesus said, "All must be left to follow him, to be found worthy of him." So no *excuse* can be heard, but PRAYER for divine assistance will be heard!

Again, it will always give me joy to hear of your union, communion, fruits, and travail of Faith in the royal priesthood; — the nearer you get to Christ the better: Therefore what work of Faith can be done on the DAY never leave for the *morrow*. For "Ye know not the *day and hour* Christ will come!" so WATCH, and "trim your lamp, that the spirit and incense of Faith may *burn* crystal and fair as *wise Virgins* to meet the bridegroom," according to the CRY and notice given!

Also, I would have you know what *condition* the Elect are in, and how they are surrounded by Reason, justice, death, &c. And Reason is very active in his desire, and temptations, but—this you are to watch, for his name is *Blasphemy*, and his desires and temptations are the *number of his name*, in those things he delights, because it is his life to seek after and gather in the flowers of stupefaction and death: And thus he goeth into death under justice, with hell at his heels. This Reason do not know, but it is for *You* to know. And

Further, it is no good thing for any one to neglect the *Union* of the Church, and communion of Faith with a brother: — If any be *sick or low in spirit*, even from the *hope* of Christ, will spring a desire to see and commune with a brother! And if the love and acts of Faith cannot be found in man, in the united kingdom of Christ in regeneration, which is the nether heaven of Faith, after such a true and positive declaration made by the Messenger, how is it possible he can enter the upper heaven of Faith to commune with Christ in Glory? Seeing one leads to the other, and no one can go any other way. And.

As I said before; the devil is very active, and will, if he can, creep in

& by degrees take the man from the Messenger, and give him full employ in the field of generation, and of wild Reason; now such a one has forsaken the kingdom of heaven for the kingdom of hell, to be a slave to *serpents and vipers*, and if he cannot be taken out, he must be swallowed up by death under justice, then follow the second death, and hell in endless eternity! — Mind, it is an easy thing, and may appear delightful to go back, but a hard thing to go forward. He that goeth with Reason must go where Reason do, for God has given the internal Moses power to take the unredeemed and unregenerated into the *second death and hell*!

Moreover, I have written this to let you know what *powers* is against you,—the *fool* may tempt, and the *Crocodiles cry* deceive the unwary person, therefore WATCH! For seeing you are in and among those powers, you must overcome and come out of them; which must be done by the power and prayer of Faith, for divine assistance. He that beareth the oppression and temptation of those powers and WORSHIPS GOD and CHRIST in his royal priesthood, will have divine assistance, and *overcome*; for to him is the promise of glory! but he whom those powers overcome, must, sink in death under justice, where hell follows with it!

I cannot promise Reason Life, and as so, no *preacher* to it, but am a SERVANT to the Royal Elect in the priesthood of CHRIST:—And Faith in regeneration is so powerful and pure, that with divine assistance it can face, stand against and overcome all powers that stand against it[*], therefore be of good cheer, have prayer and patience and not faint, and I pray for you, and recommend you to the Lord Christ, and that he will be graciously pleased to assist his Elect, and hasten his kingdom, and hope your prayers unite with mine.

So conclude your loving brother in Christ.

JAMES BIRCH.

London, Jan. 28, 1790.

---

[*] A Manifesto from the Counter Prison House, Giltspur-street, Jan. 19 1813.

LETTER LXXX

To brother GEORGE PLOWMAN, and to all that may be called into the ROYAL PRIESTHOOD of CHRIST, JAMES BIRCH and Brethren send greeting.

Beloved Brother—Yours I received, and was glad to hear from you, and also to see you remember something of your *first love*, and of what you received; and I desire and pray you may be brought on in the royal priesthood of Faith; which is regeneration, for except a man is capable of the "first resurrection," there can be no regeneration to Christ! And by this we *know* the children of Adam.

Also mind this, *John Reeve* came out in justice, and as so, "to the bloody unbelieving world:" And *Lodowick Muggleton* was given to be his *mouth* and he was the *high priest*, but his priesthood was *Angelical* which is Reason, and they are the *last* that ever will be sent to "the bloody unbelieving world," but Faith was risen from death to life in John Reeve, and he was taken into the ROYAL PRIESTHOOD, and prophecyed of Christ to come: and the other was translated to that covenant at his death, but he never came back, to tell that tale, therefore,

Them that desire and seek salvation let them learn to know the priesthood of Faith, from the given priesthood of Reason, then they will know the wild Priesthood of Reason: For, as the Lord God created Adam with a life of Faith, which was his own divine nature but under a law, which was you shall not hearken to the voice of Reason, which they did to the serpent angel, which was and is the devil, then Faith died, and Reason took possession and ruled over and drove the man and woman, and rule and drive their children to this day. Thus Reason took the world by *violence* and rule in it.

And *Moses* was the Angel of the Law, and was as a God and law-giver to Reason, and he gave forth a *priesthood* that Reason should bring in his *offering* to stay God's justice, and Aaron was his mouth and high priest; and if Reason was disobedient they had power given to swallow them up in justice, and it was even so with *Reeve* and *Muggleton*, only Moses was before God became a son to his own power, and Reeve after: so God was declared by them as he was according to their time and place, and power acted on the soul and body of man; and in all those mighty powers, in this given priesthood that has been so highly exalted, salvation is not to be found or had!

But NOW —by this MESSENGER it is declared, that except the *spirit* in the word centers to the womb of Faith in the soul of man, and there *rest*, and with divine assistance from heaven *quicken* that Faith from death to life, which fell in Adam, man cannot enter the royal priesthood of Faith to be *regenerated* to Christ; and this *womb* of Faith or *good ground* is not to be found in the sons of Reason, therefore it *abideth* alone, and they take it into the wild priesthood of Reason by their imagination. But

This *Spirit of Faith* which is rose from death to life in the Elect, is the *first resurrection*, or the Spiritual *Virgin* daughter of Faith *born* of its womb or seed, and is taken into the royal priesthood of Christ, and worked on for salvation, and she become the *pure bride meet for marriage* with CHRIST, and bear him a spiritual son in regeneration for his royal *Seal* to salvation! And thus are the Elect made anew by regeneration; for this Spirit of Faith becomes their Life for salvation, and the spirit of Reason that was taken by or into them at the fall, is cast out and goes to its own center or home. Now by this you may see the covenant and priesthood of FAITH, from the covenant and priesthood of Reason, and how men prophecyed of Christ to come, and of their own salvation. But

Reason will come and take, or transform itself into the letter, and *walk to and fro* by his imagination, but he can have no more than belong to him; for the internal Angel in Justice will keep them out from the *Tree of Life*; therefore Reason take the outward word or bare letter, and go into their own wild priesthood, yea take to themselves the promise made to the Elect, become lords and kings of the dark spirit, and set great value on themselves; whereas—this *Messenger* will bid nothing for them—for they will not have the kingdom that is appointed for them, nor the kingdom of Christ; (and must expect their own dark and devilish nature to be made pure, which cannot be done) therefore of no value to the Messenger and covenant of Faith! Now when any thing that incline to this is DECLARED, it will drive Reason; so no wonder to me for them to shun you, and die away, for of this we have plenty in Loudon: And when any say they will have none but *Reeve* and *Muggleton*, they declare themselves to be of "the bloody unbelieving world!"

But—do you have prayer and patience, Christ will have his own kingdom, and it is good to pray, the Lord of the vineyard, that if possible the vine may spring forth and bear fruit; if not they prove the fig tree, which is already given up to the Lord of the vineyard to cut down, which will shortly be, for his hour is come, and the Lord Christ only reigns.

I have wrote this—to inform you how things are and must be, and that you may enter on the works of Faith, and keep watch, have prayer and divine assistance from heaven; to be brought thro' and overcome the powers of Reason, Death, Hell, and Justice, and be regenerated to Christ the king of Faith. But how comes it to pass that you have had such a strong desire and impulse to come and see your brethren but have not; What—has kept you back but the world, and Reason the devil? If you wait their time and opportunity, you may take my word you never will have it; now this I wish you to see and know, and let your trust and strength be in the Lord Christ, who is able to bring all things to pass for the sake of his own kingdom.

So conclude your loving brother,

JAMES BIRCH.

London, April 15, 1790

LETTER LXXXI

To our Sister Runwa, and the whole Church beloved in Christ, Jas. Birch and Brethren send Greeting.

Beloved Sister—I received Feb, 10, and also June 9, and rejoice to hear of your steadfast Faith and union, patience and desire: Abide in the royal priesthood and works of Faith, and you will inherit all things promised of Christ, which I have truly and faithfully delivered to you. Also I pray the patience of Faith in regeneration may possess the souls of the Elect, then they will work the works, and bring forth the fruits of Faith, then it is you with me, and I with you, and this is the united church of Christ, which will stand against all the powers of hell, and will have divine assistance to overcome! For the united fruits of Faith in regeneration, is the true incense that ascend before the throne of mercy.

Moreover, at the time when serpents and scorpions reign, *is* the day of trial and trouble: And in those days, as well as now, I have sought death, and could not find it, and desired to die, and death has flown from me, because I thought there was no release but death, and even that was denied, why? Because you must *Live* and OVERCOME to inherit the kingdom of Christ. Now those days are in the days of prophecy, which IS, when the *fifth angel sound* in regeneration, but to truly see and know those things, man must not only be in the royal priesthood of Faith, but also have heard the voice of this Angel.

Beloved brethren—There is no other active Hell as yet, but in this Life, on this *Earth and Sea*; because all evil desires are here; and men go out into act according to those evil desires, and have joy in it; and will strive for greatness, and to be great in this kingdom of evil; because their light and life is of darkness. And this is crawling on their *belly*; and *licking up the dust* to their own condemnation! therefore the powers of Reason is very great in oppression, temptation, persecution, &c. in many ways beside their war and blasphemy against the Lord God of regeneration, and his kingdom!

Now, seeing those things, with the power of justice and death, are against the Elect, then of consequence their hell: and Reason being loosed to act evil, in which he delights, then of consequence its heaven; but the Elect will pass through Death to Life, and Reason will be locked fast in the *first* death, to go into the *second*, then his hell begins, and will continue in all eternity! Now, he who hath wisdom let him understand the *prayer and patience* of Saints; "him that overcometh will sit with Christ in his kingdom, the glory of mercy."

Again, The LORD GOD created both heaven and earth, and all things therein, then of consequence they are His, and at his disposal, and HE also become as SON, and redeemed his Elect, and brought in his kingdom of regenerated Faith, and made all things anew for their salvation, and He has sent Messengers in his own kingdom, even to this Messenger, who is the last comer out, and he finds the kingdom of Christ little regarded, but that men will *sacrifice unto idols and devils*, *i.e.* all their care, driving, striving, &c. is to serve and satisfy the devil; therefore what God has given as blessing to man on this earth, man gathers it up, and with it obey the desire of Reason the devil and go out on his own desire, which is evil! and thus they worship, offer up, and sacrifice the blessing of God, with their time, life and strength unto idols and devils, death, hell, &c. and war against and blaspheme the kingdom of Christ, and will not repent of their evil, but offer up to and for the wrath of God, and the kingdom of Christ is not regarded!

Also, I see the spirit of Reason too near home, creeping round to make the church and kingdom of Christ desolate, if possible! Now he that hath wisdom let him understand the *abomination* which maketh desolate; and flee from it, to worship God and Christ; and pray for divine assistance to overcome, for woe is to Reason who *inhabit the earth*, for the day of WRATH is at hand! Further,

Beloved brethren, I have wrote those things that you may know and watch the spirit and powers of Reason, who is always ready to drive and tempt, because he will not let you pass on your journey through his kingdom, if possibly he can take you aside and stop you, for let man be in the *fifth or sixth mansion* in regeneration, *i.e.* under the voice of the *fifth or sixth angel*, there he will find the devil to drive and tempt: Christ himself when on this earth was tempted and persecuted by the devil, and did keep watch! So be (you) careful and WATCH! Have Faith and patience! Then Christ will come and give release, by taking you through death to life; for he that works in the vineyard of Faith, cannot tell when his day's work will be done, for that is known to the LORD *of the Vineyard*.

And as to *Mina* thinking she heard her voice aloud, that voice or power I believe to be in herself; but as there is no more than what she read, and there to abide, it is well; but let her be careful of a false voice, and fear.

Now, as aforesaid, I have wrote these things being ordered, that you may know what it is to sacrifice unto idols, devils, death, hell, &c. and who they are that offer and sacrifice, and further understand, that all the labour, wisdom, care, and, self preservation, value and consequence of Reason was offered in Cain, and rejected by the Lord God of heaven, then fell under condemnation, and was cast out; so be careful and watch. for he that know not, nor see those things is found an actor in and of those things therefore he who sees his name, or part of his name in those things, let him come out and worship God and Christ, for it is great joy to have the name written in the book of life, but sorrow to have it in what I have written concerning Reason, and there to sink, and be buried eternal! Therefore blessed is him and them that have prayer and patience, then they will have divine assistance to *overcome and watch* the coming of Christ; and he will unite with you in holy marriage, and take you into his kingdom, the glory of mercy! So I pray for and recommend you to *prayer and patience*, the love and union of Faith, you with me, and I with you,

So conclude your loving brother in Christ.

JAMES BIRCH.

London, July 8, 1790.

LETTER LXXXII

To our beloved sister Mary Runwa, and the whole church beloved in Christ, Jas. Birch & Brethren send Greeting.

Beloved Sister and Brethren—I received both yours, and am glad to hear from you, and that you meet in *church Union*, and *desire* to bring forth the fruits of patience, and prayer of Faith in regeneration, to follow Christ in his royal priesthood, to his kingdom of mercy and glory, for the works of Faith must be done here on this earth, in the royal priesthood, under the *Justice of the Father*, which is the kingdom of the Father; therefore Christ worked the great and grand works of Faith and redemption in that Kingdom: and offered up his prayer before the THRONE of the Father, and went thro' the kingdom and power of the Father, and also the kingdoms and powers of Reason to gain and inherit his own Kingdom, the Glory of Mercy.

Moreover, this Life, is in a fallen state, and fallen Reason is the Devil, so he is very eager to go out on his desires, and is very wrath, because his time is short, and his kingdom very uncertain, but they have power to drive and oppress the elect in his kingdom of darkness, bondage, and strife, because Faith hearkened to Reason; but death and justice reign over him, because he broke his own law and become a devil: *Therefore* the Elect being here in a body of flesh, are incumbered with and by those powers, and they must be waded through and overcome by the power and works of Faith: (and even that is done in the kingdom of the father, which is under his justice) as CHRIST himself did: but now He is ascended into his own kingdom, and the prayer of Faith ascend up to him, and divine assistance come from him (but it is through the power of the Father) and the fruits and incense of Faith ascend to him, which is great JOY to the heaven of Faith in regeneration, it being the increase of Christ's kingdom! And in this "He drinks of the Vine anew, with his royal elect, who are in his father's kingdom." HERE you may see how God and Christ is worshipped, for in regeneration nothing can be done without Christ, because the Elect are redeemed and regenerated from the earth, and from among men by the power of the son, and they must pass through, and from the kingdom of the Father to the kingdom of the Son. NOW, "he who hath wisdom let him understand," and have prayer and patience.

Again when the Elect are called, and Faith risen, from, death to life, then Christ has *prayed for them*, and the *destroying Angel*, which is the internal angel in justice, has *passed over* them, but the *first born of Egypt* in them must be slain, for the Virgin of Faith to pass to the royal priesthood and be regenerated to Christ, for to him she is *promised*; then by regeneration they will *pass* this Angel, and those are them that Christ *prayed for*, because they are given to him, *out of* and above the world; and are the *Sheep* of his fold, which is the Royal Priesthood and compact of Faith, and will *"follow Him* wherever he goeth, because they *know his voice, but a stranger they will not follow"* and he will give unto them ETERNAL LIFE!

Moreover, it is the nature of Reason to act against God and Christ; and act according to his own wisdom, and have things according to his will and way: and gather up the fruits and treasures of the earth, and sacrifice it with themselves according to the will of sychophants, cormorants, scorpions, and fools! Therefore watch and beware!— Reason is charged with sin—that they do not like; Truth and Righteousness has been offered, that they will not have!

Believe me, brethren, there has not been one that has owned me a Messenger of Christ, but should have been glad for all to have *followed* in regeneration; but some has been denied it; others have slunk away and herd with the unclean beast in the wilderness, others are too much detained in the fields of generation and of wild Reason, and suffer children and fools to rule over them! And although space has been and is given for repentance, yet by this space they go into

Folly instead of REPENTANCE! Therefore I would have all and every one be careful; the nearer you get to Christ the better; so there is no time for delay: And as to get from the Messenger there is no such thing, for he is sure to be a Messenger of life or death, and even to the whole world, because, as he has declared, they will be judged, it being the way of Christ; His coming to judgment prepared! So have patience and prayer, and not faint; "Christ will COME, and bring his *Reward* with Him!"

Neither can the Elect be RELEASED till Christ come; for Death is *no release* to them, but Christ come in spirit and unite in holy marriage with the virgin daughter, and beget to himself a spiritual son, and that spirit pass through Death to his own royal Seal, which is the "seal of the living God" for eternal glory! Then the Elect are *released*, because they have (in spirit) *passed through* ALL! And from all, up to the seal of Christ the KING of Mercy and Glory; and are united to Him, and sealed by him, FOR his mercy and glory!

And the *Voice* of Faith is Holy, Holy, Holy, Lord God Almighty, which WAS, and IS, and is to COME! For it *was* Christ which rose Faith from death to life for regeneration, and it *is* Him who assist it to go through this den of evil, and give it the spirit of prophecy, and is *yet to come* in holy marriage, and make it complete for his glorious kingdom! Now this is the *Voice* of Faith in regeneration, and its prayer is for Christ to *come* to its assistance. But

Death is a *release* to the seed of Reason, for after all their driving and striving, toil and care, age and infirmity, trouble, &c. come on, and oft' times with it condemnation for a mis-spent life; and (when) death take them into his possession, they *rest* from this, but then they are locked fast in the first death to go into the second! Then,

When time ends Christ calls to the Elect, and they ascend! And the cherubims will follow by the echo of the CALL! Then, by the mighty power of this, "death and hell will also give up their dead!" Then the, kingdoms of the *Earth* will pass away and be no more! And the kingdoms of the *dark spirit* will pass away and be no more, and the kingdom of the Father will pass away and be no more! But the kingdom of the SON will for ever stand!!! O ETERNITY! The heavy weight & consequence of Eternity! What would not man give, in exchange for his *own* soul? Therefore let them think themselves HAPPY *that hear the voice of* CHRIST, and are found worthy to enter the royal priesthood and *follow* in the regeneration!

Beloved brethren, I mean to visit you again and hope to find a good *increase*, and commune together in JOY of soul, for as you want to see the Messenger, the Messenger wants, and shall be glad to see you: Remember in the great trouble and trial of soul you have GOD on your side, and that Christ will come and *release* you.

So conclude your loving brother in Christ, with prayer for you all.

London, Oct. 30, 1790.   JAMES BIRCH.

LETTER LXXXIII

To Sister Runwa, &c.   Jas. Birch, & Breth. greeting,

Beloved Sister and Brethren—Yours I received and well pleased to see you in a state of love and prayer, and I pray God to preserve you, and assist you in the works of Faith. *Mind* what has been declared and told you, then abide by it in prayer and patience, and you will be preserved from the hour of temptation, which is sure to come upon the whole world as a great FOG, then follow STORMS of justice, as a Torrent, and take them all away.

Believe me, Brethren—the *field* of generation is very entangling, and the *field* of wild Reason very alluring; and all desires, drivings and strivings in those fields, is labour in vain; for the reward is death, to give rest from labour, and the best reward they can have.

REMEMBER, when Moses had brought the Israelites out of Egypt, how he led them through the wilderness, and that nations and kings came out and warred against them, and to curse them and put temptations in their way to stop their journey. And God brought trouble on them, suffered them to hunger—bit by serpents, &c. This was to humble and chasten them, and learn them to know the power of the Lord, and what they had or was to have, it was according to the will of God, and that HE had brought them out of Egypt, and through the *terrible Wilderness* by His mighty power! Therefore it was commanded "thou shalt worship the Lord thy God." And it is even so in the spiritual; for when, the Messenger has called you out of *arrogant Egypt* and you follow in the *Wilderness*, there are dark spiritual kings and kingdoms (which) will come and oppose you, and war against, and put threats and temptations, which are *stumbling blocks*, in the way; and curse you and cut you off, if possible. These are men that will oppose the kingdom of Christ various ways, to stop regeneration, even as those kings and nations would have stopped Moses and Israel; but *you* are not to fear, for the Lord God is your help, and will make those kingdoms & powers desolate.

And in all your natural trouble, disappointment, &c. it is to humble you, chasten you, give you wisdom!—For you to know the Lord is GOD! For when you are called by the Messenger to FOLLOW: Trials are and will be made to PROVE the soul of man! Then, all your Egyptian desires, buildings, planting, &c. or what you may think to plant in the wilderness to settle there, will be *overthrown*, by the torrent of justice, as was Egypt, and those kings and people in the Wilderness. This—is to kill the desires and efforts of wild Reason, for the LORD GOD is to rule over you, and let you know it is HE by his mighty power will bring you through this great and terrible wilderness, and what you have is given by him; therefore you are to WORSHIP God and Christ, and him only shall rule over you: For he who is left to his own wisdom, will perish in this great field of wild Reason.

Also, when the Israelites of old had passed over Jordan to possess the land *promised*, "they were to cast out seven nations before them, smite them, and shew them no mercy!" And it is even so now in the royal priesthood of Faith, for when the Virgin daughter of Faith is born, and offer her prayer for the divine incomes and assistance of Christ, all those evil spirits and powers are to be found in the soul of man! And act against, and, if possible, would destroy the virgin of Faith: that she should not inhabit the soul; therefore those spirits are not to be hearkened to, but drove out, and utterly destroyed without mercy, for the virgin daughter to *inhabit* the soul of elect man, it being her Land or dwelling promised, as elect men are made anew by regeneration.

Moreover, concerning the *promised Land*, or the Land which "God swear unto Abraham, unto Isaac, and unto Jacob." This *Land* spiritually was and is the kingdom of Christ, but as the nation of the Jews was to come from the loins of Abraham, there was also Land promised for them: further, God would suffer them to be taken into *bondage* and slavery, and become a great body of people, and bring them out of bondage, and give them a Law—then they were the greatest nation in the world. But,

Deut. xxxii. Ch. "When the most high divided to the nations their inheritance, when he separated the sons of Adam, the Lord's portion is his people, Jacob is the lot of his inheritance," which are the Elect who will inherit the kingdom of Christ; "But Jeshurun waxed fat and kicked, then forsook God which made him." Here you may see the kingdom of Faith and of Reason; but as Reason was suffered to take this world by violence, and as Jeshurun proceeded from Abraham, they were to inherit those good lands through the promise to Abraham, but with the law and priesthood given them by Moses: And

When Moses went up into the mountain, he was shewed all the Lands Reason was to possess, but with the law and priesthood, and commands he gave them, but was not to go over thither himself, *i.e.* he was not to possess Reason, its law and justice; for this was all cast out at his death, and centers to and was buried in Reason; for whoever possess the lands, &c. that was given to Reason must possess its law and justice, and that abideth continually.

Again, the land "God swear unto Abraham, Isaac, and Jacob," was the kingdom of Christ, as I said before, but in this kingdom the first is last, and the last first; *i.e.* all the Elect of old and in the time of the law, was taken into the royal priesthood of Faith, and stood before him, and prophesied of Christ to come, when he was in the condition of the father, and at death were translated to and with the mercy of the son and united to God for Christ; and this is the first witness of his spirit, but no more, then the virgin daughter could be born for regeneration, till God become Christ then when God become Christ he brought, in holy gospel, redeemed his elect, ascended into heaven, and took possession of his kingdom of Virgins, "who had their Father's name written on their foreheads." And now when the virgin Daughter is born, she is taken in to the royal priesthood of Faith, and follow Christ in the works of Faith, and unite with him in holy marriage, and bear him a spiritual son, and is sealed by him in his high heaven of mercy, and for his kingdom the glory of mercy! And this is the other witness of his spirit, who stands before him and prophecy now he is in the condition of the son.

And when Moses was on the mountain, which I spiritually call of regenerated Faith, all this he was shewed by the Lord God, but was sent to go over or into the holy gospel, for the virgin daughter to bear a spiritual son to the Sonship of God, but was translated into heaven, to the glory, of the father, while God become Christ, and worked the redemption, and gained to himself his kingdom of regenerated Faith and the glory of mercy.

Note—When I mention Moses, I include all the Elect who stood before him, and prophesied when he was in the condition of the father, and was his first witness, then as I said before, no more than a daughter could be born; but in the morning of the resurrection this daughter will bring forth a son, and all be complete to enter the kingdom and glory of Christ, which is "the promised and holy land."

With love and prayer for you all.

JAMES BIRCH.

London, March 19, 1791.

LETTER LXXXIV

To our Sister Runwa, and the whole Church beloved in Christ, Jas. Birch and Brethren send Greeting.

Beloved Sister and Brethren—I was glad to hear of you, and hope you assemble in the love of Christ and of each other, in the union of Faith in regeneration; for time has been and now is, that the VOICE OF GOD from heaven is heard, and the *dead risen to life*, *i.e.* Faith, which was dead in the Elect, is risen to active life, and taken into the royal priesthood to follow Christ, and be regenerated to him. – Now when Faith is risen from death to life it is "the first resurrection," then it is taken into the royal priesthood to follow Christ; because in this priesthood Faith has prayer to Christ, and divine assistance from him to overcome, for the second resurrection to Life eternal. So "he who hath part in the first resurrection, the second death has no power over," for altho' death take it, as it did the life of Christ the eternal God, yet it cannot keep it under his power, for it will pass through death, and follow Christ wherever he goes, for to him is the spirit and life of regenerated Faith, to go, and is sealed by him for life eternal.—

Now, "He who hath wisdom let him understand," and worship God and Christ. For

As Faith hearkened to Reason, so broke its own law and died, according to the word of the Lord God, which is its first death, then when it is risen from this death to life, it is also its "first resurrection," then "the vial of God's wrath" which is his justice, "is poured out on it," and it will know the power of Reason, of sin, of death, of hell, and justice, which, before it was risen from death to life, or born of its womb or seed, it was *insensible* of, as is a child to things of this life before it is born.

Therefore seeing we are in Reason's kingdom, and under those powers, Faith must be brought through and overcome: And although there are mountains of Reason, of sin, death, justice, &c. in the way, yet by patience and prayer, divine assistance will be given, to remove those mountains; for whatever the spirit of Faith in regeneration needeth, ask in prayer and it will be granted, because, they are not of the world, but are given to Christ and he rules over them, and knows what they need, and hath prayed for them; but he never prayed for the world: For that be overcome and left it under justice for judgment! Therefore them that are of the world must go with the world under condemnation! So be careful, WATCH and PRAY, that you may overcome the world and the aforesaid powers, for that is the *Victory* the Lord Christ is graciously pleased to give to His Elect.

So conclude your loving brother in Christ, with prayer for you all.

JAMES BIRCH.

London, May 27, 1791.

LETTER LXXXV

To our beloved sister Mary Runwa, Jas. Birch and Brethren send Greeting.

Beloved Sister—I received your kind present: also I received your last, and glad you had been at Picton, but sorry to hear of so much illness.

Also, I am always glad to hear of the Love and Union of the church, and of the power of obedience and prayer. REMEMBER, you are taken from the bonds of Reason's darkness into *Light*, and this light is the Light and Life of Faith in the royal priesthood, where you have been shewed the kingdom of CHRIST, and the prophecy and promise of his coming, and to work the works of Faith and prophesy of your own salvation.—What portion can be greater, seeing it is the true road to salvation? For Reason is bound up in darkness, and all their life, light, and delight is darkness in Emulation; and all their strivings and desires will come to nought, therefore, you may see what bonds and *prison* Reason is in, because he is the servant of sin, and bound up by justice and death, where hell will follow with it.

Moreover, as I have oft'times declared, there is no salvation without *regeneration*; for Reason never can be made pure: Therefore, when the Messenger in regeneration come and utter his voice, and is assisted by Christ from heaven, it raises Faith from death to life, and is taken into the royal priesthood; then the SON *has entered the house, and will make you free by regeneration, because* HE EVER ABIDETH, then you are called out and freed from the heavy Yoke, dark Chains, and strong Prison of Reason, to FOLLOW CHRIST in the Royal Priesthood, and be regenerated to him: So be careful of the dark Chains of Reason, and not be entangled, but seek the kingdom of Christ, and the RIGHTEOUSNESS of Faith, and necessaries in and for to pass through this life will be added; for him who will that Christ should rule over him, must be ruled by Him and he know what ye want better than you; for woe to him who is left to rule himself by his own wisdom.

Also Faith being in the royal priesthood, it is bound up under the power of the Father, to follow the Son in the works of Faith; but those Chains are GOLD, because they bind you to Light, which lead you to LIFE, yet you must watch the threats and temptation of Reason the devil, and the thraldom of the world; therefore in all the mighty SORROW of soul, at the power of sin, justice, and death, the burden of flesh, and temptation of the devil, &c: it is good to PRAY, lest you enter into temptation—for—the devil is always ready, and the flesh weak! Yea the devil is at hand to urge on Reason to do their evil work in high Emulation, as you may see, when *Pilate, sought to release Jesus, for he could find no fault in him*; Reason cried, "Crucify him, and let his blood be on us and our children:" — this is as far as they could go, and even in high emulation, but Christ do help Faith to pass thro' those powers as aforesaid— therefore you must watch and pray for his divine assistance. For

To overcome the world and the devil, is to follow Christ, and that is the works of Faith, then you are found worthy, and called up under the justice of the Father: then you must commend the soul and spirit of Faith into the hands of the father, and, there lose, your life in your own blood in death, as Christ did! Now this IS the true SACRIFICE, of Faith, because the soul and spirit is "commended into the hands of the Father," for the mercy of the Son; then doth Christ meet this virgin Daughter in spirit, as he was crucified, and beget to himself a spiritual son, which is taken in to an high mountain of Faith in regeneration, where it see Christ in the glory of mercy, and that all must be called in and Sealed by Him to enter his glorious kingdom of mercy—and is called in and sealed by Him; then the soul is made FREE for the kingdom of glory, because Faith has passed through all, and from all, up to the SEAL OF THE LIVING GOD! and thus IS Faith "regenerated from among men," and made free for the kingdom of glory, and the man sleeps in the bed of Mercy! But

Reason is left bound in chains of darkness, and the more he gathers up of this world the more he is bound and enslaved, and the more he seeks by his own wisdom for salvation, the more he is bound in his wild priesthood, and will war against God, even to blasphemy and spiritual murder!

Here you may see the bonds of Reason, and the bonds of Faith; and there can be no salvation without regeneration. Also, seeing what a hard travail and trial it is to be brought out of and thro' those powers by regeneration, what must become of them who sink and die under those powers!

Now, as YOU are called from those dark Chains and strong Holds of Reason, to the royal priesthood of Faith, and have been truly instructed, give all honour and glory to the LORD CHRIST—seek to follow Him—the nearer you get to him in spirit, the better.

So conclude your loving brother in Christ, with prayer for you all.

JAMES BIRCH.

London, March 9, 1792.

LETTER LXXXVI

To our Sister Runwa & the whole church beloved in Christ, James Birch and Brethren send greeting.

Beloved Sister—Yours I received, and was glad to hear from you, and as for sister Williams wanting another letter, I am glad when righteousness is hungered after, for there is a blessing promised but mind what follow.—*Now, I have wrote and told the divine truth, from and of the Lord God of regeneration*, His WILL and WAY to His kingdom of glory! But as to MOVE and AWAKEN, that must come from heaven, because JESUS is KING, and High priest in his Kingdom, and covenant of Faith and Mercy.

Also, I would not have you think to pass over the sorrow and trouble that was denounced, against *Adam* for breaking the law of Faith; which was the cause of their fall, then all those sorrows, troubles, &c. followed, according to the justice of the Lord God their Creator and Father. See Gen. iii. — Neither would I have you think that *the curse of the ground to bring forth thorns, thistles, &c.* altogether mean natural, but more spiritual, because it was to *Adam*, for, in the natural, Reason is incumbered with those things, which did not fall in Adam; and if the Elect sow or plant, the earth will bring forth to them.

Therefore the Elect are born to the state or condition of Adam, which is to SORROW! And when the Virgin of faith is born to the royal priesthood, then there are spiritual *thistles, thorns*, &c to wade through the powers of Reason, death, and hell, in the field of oppression and persecution, from the earthly heart of Reason; so the prophets, Christ and his apostles, Messengers and Elect, WERE and ARE men of SORROW! Christ prayed to heaven for assistance, and in heaviness and trouble of soul to have heavenly communion with God, as he oft' times before had! And it is even so with the Messenger, for I, often times pray for divine assistance from heaven, and to have communion, as I often times before had: Of this trouble I have plenty, both natural and spiritual.

Also, the Elect must *follow* Christ to have spiritual Bread, for He is the LIVING BREAD: And as Christ worked through those mighty powers, in a body of flesh and blood, and sorrow of soul, the Elect must follow by his divine assistance, and in this they "eat his flesh, and drink his blood," and is the *living bread and drink*, and will have Life in them. Now those mighty works cannot be passed over or by, but must be waded through, and in *heaviness and sorrow* of soul, as Christ did! Therefore, what sister Williams wants must be obtained by prayer and patience, which is *fasting*; for Christ gives, the heavenly and divine gifts of his holy spirit to assist the virgin of Faith: Hence it must come from heaven: And, when the virgin of Faith receives the inshining light from heaven, then she has joy: and also has joy in the Messenger and Brethren, which is the communion of Saints, and doth increase true confidence and love to each other, because it is of Faith in regeneration.

Moreover, the seed of Reason fell in the serpent angel, therefore them that live to manhood "their curse is above all cattle, and every beast of the field," because death put an end to them; but the seed of the serpent that live to manhood, will be raised again to eternal torment, then of consequence their *curse is above all the beast cattle*, &c, also, "upon thy belly shalt thou go, and dust shalt thou eat all thy days," *i.e.* he shall go, on his own dark understanding; and gather up the treasures and fruits of the earth; then by that—live, reign, and rule in folly,—and act against God, which is the delight of their life; there is the law of Moses, and that given priesthood as their inheritance,—the law they like for them to rule over others, but do not like it should rule them, neither will they offer themselves up before the angel to be consumed according to God's' justice, so the law and priesthood they pass over or by, and make it according to their own dark understanding, and go by that: Their teachers and preachers vail the power and purity of the law, and the gospel: and salvation of Christ they render all in the wrong, because they have no part or lot in it; they may promise great things, and may give hope and joy to the dark spirit of Reason, but that joy will be turned into sorrow, because it is of evil.

Now mind the difference between the fall of Adam, and of the serpent, and what was denounced against one, and against the other, for what was to Adam was also to his posterity the elect; and what was to the serpent was also to his posterity that live to manhood; neither can one generation have or possess the joy or sorrow of the other, —therefore,

When the elect are in the royal priesthood, I can promise no joy but in the works and fruits of Faith, the communion of Saints, and the divine incomes and assistance of Christ from heaven: But

The seed of Reason, they can promise themselves great joy, that is to do as they please, the forgiveness of sin, and to go to heaven their own way, without trouble, so their *time is always*; but the Messenger and the Elect, their *time* is when they can have the divine light and assistance of Christ from heaven, to pass through this sore journey of flesh, and wicked world.

Now I would have you, and all of you to have patience and prayer, and not to faint, for Christ will come! Hold fast by what you have received, be not locked up with incumbrance and excuse, but keep the communion of saints, pray for divine assistance, and that will help through those mighty troubles, then the reward is life eternal.

So conclude your loving brother in Christ, with prayer for you all.

JAMES BIRCH.

London, May 15, 1792.

LETTER LXXXVII

To Sister Runwa Jas. Birch & brethren send greeting.

Beloved Sister and Brethren—I received your's June 13, was glad to hear from you, and of your steadfast Faith and prayer—the nearer you get to CHRIST, in Spirit, the better—which is done by Faith, patience, and prayer, and his divine assistance to overcome the world, as He did; then you leave the world behind, with all its selfish desires, designs, contentions, excuse, evil doings, &c. — For as we are called into the Royal Priesthood, or Vineyard of Faith, we must FOLLOW Christ in and by the works of Faith: Then you are found worthy of him, because, by the works of Faith in regeneration you overcome the world and the devil, and as so become the *Brethren* or children of Christ by regeneration.

Again—In all temptation, torments and persecutions of Reason, the devil, here in this life, the Elect must "pray and not faint, for Christ come and avenge his own elect, which cry unto him," as he himself said in his parable of the unjust judge, therefore WATCH and PRAY, that he may find Faith when he doth come; Also

Watch—"The spirit of abomination that maketh desolate," which now begin to "stand where it ought not," *i.e.* — the church of Christ has been called; and his will and WAY, of and to his salvation has been declared, in the days of the voice of the sixth Angel in regeneration, and many has come and "found Christ," and died in the bed of mercy: Others have come and took something of the outward word or letter, and called it their own; and sought kingdoms: Others have took it and preached it according to their spirit of Reason; and others forsook the Messenger, yet hold and use the language. Also,

When you see the church of Christ *neglected* by people absenting themselves, it is by the spirit of Reason which is *abomination* in the sight of God; and let the excuse be what it will, in the excuse they are condemned, because they adhere to and worship the world and the devil, before they will the LORD GOD OF REGENERATION, who has power to bring desolation on the world and the devil; Hence,

When men are tempted into and after the *World*, &c. they neglect the church of Christ, where is given fresh beams of knowledge, with divine instructions, and communion of saints. It is by the Spirit of Reason, which is the devil, yea, their own lying priest within will give them excuse—this is the *abomination that maketh the church of Christ desolate.* Now he who hath wisdom let him understand, and watch *the spirit of abomination which maketh desolate.*

Moreover (See Rev. ix. 13.), "the sixth Angel sounded—there came a voice from the four horns of the golden altar, which is before God, saying, to the sixth angel which had the trumpet, loose the four Angels which are bound in the great river Euphrates." Those *four horns of the golden altar which are before God, is* the power over sin, death, hell, and justice; and this *great river* Euphrates is the waters of Reason's hope to escape the wrath of God: And those *four Angels that were bound in this river of waters*, is sin, death, hell, and justice, that is to execute the will and power of God.

Ver. 15, "And the four angels were loosed, which were prepared for an hour, and a day, and a month, and a year, for to slay the third part of men." Now this Messenger has sounded or uttered the voice of the *sixth Angel* in regeneration in public, on this earth, and has *loosed* those powers on Reason; for he has declared how Faith is born and regenerated to Christ, and sealed by him for his glory of Mercy: Also, has declared the kingdom and salvation of cherubims, having declared the cherubims and "flaming sword, that turns every way to keep the way of the tree of life" *i.e.* the angel in justice, in the soul of man, that when man doth evil, this angel seals him under his own evil; and no one can take off this seal; for even the Elect are regenerated from it, by a new life, which is Faith: Thus you may see how the way of the tree of life is kept by this angel and *flaming sword*. Therefore, at the voice of the *Sixth Angel, those Angels, or powers are loosed in the dark waters of Euphrates*, which is Reason's hope, and they begin with the Elect, so that they shall have NO MORE LIFE or hope, in those dark waters; but must come into and LIVE in the waters of Faith, to be regenerated to CHRIST. - For See

Rev. xvi. and 12. "The sixth angel poured out his vial on Euphrates and the waters were dried up, that the way of the kings of the east might be prepared." Those *Kings of the East* are the Elect, and must be *prepared* by regeneration to meet Christ, and this understand, when the *Angel sound, he pours out his vial, of God's wrath*, therefore the Elect must come out of and through those power's by regeneration to Christ, THE LORD GOD OF SALVATION, so *the voice of the sixth angel loose those powers, and prepare the way of the seventh to sound*; for he declares, except men are capable of regeneration, they must bear their own witness to their own condemnation, and in this he *loose* those angels or powers to do God's will, which is to slay men with the "second death, and those angels were prepared for an hour, a day, a month, and a year," which is, when God please to come, and those that are not *killed* by those powers are the Elect, which is *God's part*, for they are regenerated to the Lord Christ.

Also, you may read the *number* of the army—and *John* might have said many more, for it is all the seed of Reason that live to manhood, and cannot be regenerated to Christ, and as so reject, act against, and blaspheme his holy regeneration. — Also, *John* saw the "horses and riders in vision," these are the aforesaid powers which ride on the sinful soul of man, "to do the will of God," for it is every one his own witness to his own condemnation, and thus they are and will be *killed* according to the "voice of the sixth angel" in regeneration.

Ver. 20. "And the rest of the men which were not killed by those plagues—yet repented not of their works." Those are them that own the Messenger, and transform themselves into the declaration, and as so, the Messenger stay those plagues on them, for he gives them *long space to repent.* — But, as they take it into the wild Priesthood, and, worship the world and devil, which are *Idols*, and leave the church of Christ desolate, and, if possible, *trample down or kill the spirit* to have their own Way; and by the *lying spirit use the name of Christ to deceive, which is their sorceries, and commit fornication with the declaration, by acting with it according to their spirit of Reason, and there claim their inheritance, which is their thefts*! Now those are left for the Seventh Angel to *pour out his vial upon*, which is the LORD GOD of regeneration, when he put an end to Time.

Now I have wrote this by order, that you may know the kingdom of darkness, and the spirit that maketh desolate, and its consequence! And, as I said, the nearer you get to Christ in spirit the better: So WATCH and PRAY, for I truly desire and pray—the works, love and union of Faith, the communion of Saints, and divine assistance of Christ to abound among you. Amen.

Your loving brother in Christ,

London, Aug. 24, 1792.   JAMES BIRCH.

P. S. Wants of me, and to hear of you minding what is wrote. Neglect not. — I go forth, but am poorly—with love to all.

LETTER LXXXVIII

To Sister Runwa, &c. Jas. Birch & Breth. greeting.

Beloved Sister—Sister Atkinson told me of your illness, for which I was sorry. Miss John, with honour, behaved the gentlewoman, &c.

Also, I received yours of Oct. 14, and was glad to hear from you and the brethren, and of your love and Faith in the Unity of the church of Christ. — And as you were brought up to the strong *Hope* in the mercy of Christ, and *peace* in yielding up, and loved the Messenger and brethren "above the love of this perishing world:" Now these are fine waters, and near unto the *baptism of water*, therefore the *true road, and your Candlestick not removed.* For

It is the Angel of the *Covenant* of Grace that goeth out in the midst of his Elect, which is his Church to assist the Virgin daughter of Faith to work the works, and offer the prayer of Faith, which is the royal incense *Candle or Oil* of Faith that *burn* before the throne for the mercy of Christ; so it is a great and good thing when you are found to "keep your first love, and do your first work, and go on with an increase that the *last* will be more than the first," but the watch is very great over the tempter, and the travail hard!

And as you say you could not rejoice in death, why, no, you could not, or cannot until you have passed into it, and through it, then you will rejoice over it, as Christ did when he rose from the dead: for understand that Death is an enemy to the Elect until they have passed into it, and thro' it, to the *seal of the living God* of Mercy; for in your condition of soul, and forgiveness to the whole world—the heavenly enlightenings you received, and even the prophecy of your own salvation, are fine waters to be found in, and the *baptism of water* to Faith; but it is under the justice of the Father,—and when you are called before the power and glory of the Father, all those waters are turned into blood, for there you must lose yourself in death, in your own blood, to pass to the mercy of the son, for this way Christ went, and the Elect must follow. Now in this condition you meet Christ in spirit, as he was *crucified*; which is the *marriage with the Lamb*, and "the marriage *of* the Lamb, and the spirit is commended into the hands of the Father" for the mercy of the Son; then Christ beget a spiritual son of the virgin, which is brought out of or through this death, and taken into an high mountain, and called unto Christ, and is united to him in his high immortal GLORY OF MERCY, which is the "Seal of the living God." Now mind the spirit of Faith will follow Christ, for thither is the spirit to go, this is a great BAPTISM and hard work to pass through the Justice of the Father to the mercy of the Son but the prayer of Faith is not stopped.

AGAIN, where ever the Messenger goeth, he lay liable to hear the VOICE of *three powers, i.e.* the power of death which reign over all living in this life; for let men be ever so high and full of glee, even in the, midst of that, the voice of death wilt speak out of man.

Also, there is the VOICE of the *Angel with the flaming sword*, by which men at times will bring out their own condemnation, let them exert themselves what they can to the contrary, for those are great powers reigning in and over the soul of man, for the first power take into the first death, and the second power take into the second death: And the Messenger has declared those powers, & commune with those powers above or unbeknown to man: And as he has declared those powers do and will act on the sinful soul of man, neither can any one get from those powers, without being regenerated to Christ the king of Faith and mercy: And this power is given to the Messenger by the Lord God of regeneration, that he shall "Rule people, Nations, &c. with a rod of iron," because, as he has declared they are judged, and those *powers* will act on them.

Also there is, the *power* and VOICE of Faith, for when the virgin daughter is born and taken into the royal priesthood, Christ goeth out in spirit to assist this daughter in the works of Faith, and she will work the works of Faith, and offer its prayer, and SPEAK the Redemption, regeneration, salvation and *mercy of Christ*, and prophecy: Now this is the *voice* of Faith, speaking out of elect man, and "the *candle* of Faith, which burn before the throne for the mercy of Christ," and in the midst of those Candlesticks which is His Church or Churches, CHRIST who is "the Angel of the covenant of grace" goeth out in mercy and assistance to his Elect, for as HE has POWER over all the aforesaid powers, he can and will bring his Elect, by, through, and out of all those *powers*, up to his royal SEAL for the glory of Mercy.

Again, the church must be very careful not to hearken to *seducing* spirits, neither within nor without, for if you do then you will go aside, and your Candlestick removed from the communion of Faith, and of Christ the KING of Faith, therefore those that find or see this, "let them repent & return to their first love, & do the first works"—or them that come, let them mind and do this, and have prayer for divine assistance to be brought on in the works of Faith: FOR, when the Candlestick is removed, then the soul burns with folly, care, and anxious desires for things in this life; and if gained; then it is bestowed to the will and desire of Reason, which is "sacrificing unto idol's and devils," and it also burns against, and with false hopes, concerning God and Christ. Now I have written this for you, and all of you to know, and as to where you have been; and what you have seen—it requires this for *instruction*; for I truly pray the union and works of Faith, the divine assistance of Christ to abound among you;

for "I am your brother and fellow servant in tribulation," and prayer for divine assistance; and to patiently wait the coming of Christ. Amen.

So conclude your loving brother in Christ,

JAMES BIRCH.

London, Dec. 1, 1792.

LETTER LXXXIX

To our Sister Runwa, and the whole Church beloved in Christ, Jas. Birch and Brethren send greeting.

Beloved Sister—Of Miss Ann John I received your kind beneficial Gift, to your will and Order.

Also, I am glad to hear of your Faith and love in the royal priesthood, for the kingdom of CHRIST for there is the union, communion and joy of SAINTS—Why? Because Christ is in the midst, and there only is he to be found; and there has been and is great things done for the sake of Christ.

See Mat. xxv.—Now remember when I came to you as a *stranger*, you took me in and entertained me, and when I departed you helped me on my journey, and also has borne it in mind to assist when you can; therefore I can truly say you have followed the commands of Christ, and are come under his blessing, because it is done in the royal covenant and priesthood for the sake of Christ's kingdom. AND further, it is the nature of the Elect, when enlightened from heaven, and Faith rose from death to life, to make their *Offering* prayer, &c. in the royal priesthood, Why? Because their desire, life, and delight is there—but, in this they "lay up their treasure in heaven, where no thief can take it, nor moth or rust hurt it." JESUS said, "My kingdom is not of this World, if it was, then would my servants fight." Now Reason's kingdom is in and of this world, and for it they will and do fight, and drive, and strive, and oppress each other in what they can, and would destroy each other was it not for the law, and the angel in justice, with the powerful word of the LORD GOD, which is, "you shall live and reign, until I come to put an end."

Moreover, Reason will do charity, but that is mostly by the impulse of the angel in justice, and is to help and propagate his own kingdom for himself to shine in, and have his own will and way; but what will they do for the sake of Christ and his kingdom? Also, Reason's desire is and will strive for riches, greatness, &c. to build his own house in his kingdom, where justice reigns king, and death follow with it—and will *care* for, and leave it to posterity, that they may have "lasting habitations through the mammon of unrighteousness," and will exalt themselves in pride, and set such value on themselves that they look on others *beneath* them—this is what the serpent angel was cast down from heaven for, so what he could not do there be would do here.

Again, the kingdom of Faith and of Reason is now *divided* and "separated one from the other, as the sheep are from the goats," it being a preparation for the coming of Christ, therefore, "Father and son, and mother and daughter are divided," for Faith can have no delight in the manners and ways of Reason, nor Reason in the manner and ways of Faith, for what is life to the one, is death to the other; therefore, when Faith is risen from death to life, and taken into the royal priesthood, then all its desire, delight, and life, is in that Union to follow CHRIST: And its patience, prayer, offering charity, &c. is done THERE, then Christ will say, "Come ye Blessed, for I was an hungred, and ye gave me meat, thirsty and ye gave me drink, &c." But Reason will be in his own wild kingdom, and act evil in *emulated folly*, and so work themselves into death under Justice, then the KING will say, "depart from me ye cursed into everlasting fire, prepared for the devil and his angels, for I was an hungred and ye gave me no meat, thirsty and ye gave me no drink, &c." Thus you may see the two natures and kingdoms, and how each nature will incline to its own kingdom, and their reward.

Moreover, in all the troublesome TRAVAIL through the powers of Reason, Justice, and Death, the Elect must have patience and prayer, for no one can bring them through but the Lord God of Regeneration; also Faith can and will trust in and to God. Reason say "they will and do," but they say, and do not, for they trust to their own wisdom and power! Also Reason, in the height of his glee of safety, is working himself out of his kingdom, because it is into Death under justice: But FAITH is working its way to the kingdom of Christ, which is mercy! So there is a great *Gulf* fixed between Faith and Reason.

Luke xii. 32. Jesus said, "Fear not little flock, for it is your Father's good pleasure to give you the kingdom;" and now he is become the FATHER of regenerated Faith, and Lord of "the new heaven and earth," it is his good pleasure to take you to his divine mercy, that you may sit down with him in his kingdom of glory; therefore, in those hard trials and travails, "lift up your hearts and rejoice that the time of your redemption draweth nigh."

So conclude your loving brother in Christ, with prayer for you all.

JAMES BIRCH.

London, June 26, 1793.

P. S. I hope this will find you all well: I keep about tolerably well. Mrs. Birch is very bad, we have tried all we can, but no help—she cannot stand or help herself no more than a young child, which render it as hard to me as a young family in old age; but PATIENCE and PRAYER will pass through, the powers of Death, and think when I come to Death's gate, I shall not be turned back for want of hard travails, trials, and experience in this life. I waited the *Order* what to write. Let me hear of you.

LETTER XC

To our Sister Runwa & the whole church beloved in Christ, James Birch and Brethren send greeting.

Beloved Sister and Brethren.—Yours I received and was glad to hear from you, and that the love of Christ, and the love of and to each other in the Union of this Faith, abound in your Souls, for without that no good can be done; for as Faith fell under the powers of Reason, Justice, and death, for breaking its own law, then the Elect are born with a life of Reason, and that life actuate and drive them, until Christ make his appearance, and raise Faith from that death to active life, which is the virgin daughter born, or the *first resurrection* to Faith, and to her is the promise of Christ given, and to her the Messenger preach life and immortality, and direct her up to the royal bridegroom, then by this new life, which is Faith, the Elect will get

Victory over the beast, which is the spirit of Reason; for by this new life, and divine assistance from heaven, the Elect work the works of Faith, and are brought through and overcome all the mighty devouring powers of Reason, sin, justice, death and hell, up to the seal of the God of mercy. Moreover, in passing through those powers with them, you will have tribulation, but with Christ you will have PEACE, for He has overcome the world, and left it under judgment, and will assist his Elect to overcome also, for the promise is to them that do overcome!

Also, as you are taken out of the world to worship God and Christ, therefore above the world—and a servant to Christ—for *Woe* to him or them that are bound up in fear and servitude to Reason and the world!—Also the virgin daughter is born to those troubles, and to wade through those troubles, in this sorrowful vale of death, which is "the great tribulation, such as was not known before," because they are known to Faith only, and the virgin daughter of Faith finding herself in the midst of those sorrows, she must follow Christ through and out of those mighty powers, which will be done with his divine assistance, for the works of Faith is done under the justice of the Father, which is "the kingdom of the father, where there are many mansions," and as Faith is taken from one mansion to another, which is higher up or further on, yet Christ is to come, and the voice, desire, and prayer of Faith, is for Christ to come.

Again, as you say, we may see how the desire of Reason is, for the favor and prosperity of this world; Why? Because that is the waters of Reason, therefore,

See Gen. ii. 10. "And a river went out of Eden to water the garden, and from thence it was parted, and became into four heads." Now this is the waters and desires of Reason, as, *First*, The spirit of Reason desire to get gold, &c. to be rich. *Secondly*, After lands, mansions, grand appearance, honour, and rule over souls, &c. *Thirdly,* After arts and emulations, that the two first must come—and the *Fourth* is Reason's hope for salvation; this is Euphrates, where Cain went to form his own forgiveness, and his way to worship God—Now when any invitation come to the holy marriage with Christ, Reason will be excused by the three above waters, as

In Luke xiv. "One had bought ground and must see it; another had bought oxen and would prove them; another had married a wife and could not come." Thus you may see how Reason is bound in his waters with excuse, and when any of those waters are likely to stop, or are stopped, then there is sad Woe! and lamentation to Reason! And when *Euphrates* is stopped, then Reason will destroy itself for a moment's peace!

Again, In the days of Moses, he gave forth a law to Reason, and a priesthood to offer the required offering, to stay God's justice, that Israel should enjoy the blessing of God, in peace, plenty, and safety; then if they would but keep his statutes, and commandments, they should stand as the rock of Israel, not only against but above the whole world; but if not, then other nations would came and destroy their peace and drive them, and they were charged with worshipping false Gods; and the Gods of other nations, because Reason went out in desires and acts as other nations did, so they trusted in and adored their own wild Reason, as did other nations, which was worshipping their Gods, and *forsook the God of Israel*, and when they offered in this spirit it was false incense, which brought on their calamities, and it is even so at this day; for when Reason go out in desire or delights, which is against the Law of Moses, that is the God they worship, let them think what they will to the contrary, for "where the treasure and delight is, there is the heart."

Now I have been in the *wilderness* many years, and desired things, but was kept from them, and could not tell for why. Also I was found in the wilderness by the Lord God of Regeneration, and taken into his royal compact and priesthood, and made able to declare HIS royal will and way of regeneration, and salvation, and also has brought me through the mocks; lies, scandal, envy, wrath, blasphemy, and persecution of Reason, and their curses to come in this life, beside damnation hereafter! This—the LORD GOD has brought me through, and assisted me to overcome, so far; and in all the troubles that has come on me, which is as serpents that bite, this is to let you know the WISDOM and POWER of the Lord God, and not, trust to your own: And in all this great travail my garments never wasted away, nor my feet fail me! "Neither is man to live by the fruits of this earth only, but by the words that cometh from him who created heaven and earth; that shall man live by." Also,

In his royal priesthood He has given me the power of prayer, revelation and the spirit of prophecy, and I have prophesied concerning, the Elect, and that Christ will come to them, and take them from the burden of flesh, the oppression of the world, and temptation of the devil; therefore "Lift up your hearts and rejoice, for the time of deliverance draweth near."

If Mrs. Morgan desire to be informed by a Lamblike true heart, feed her in what you can.

So conclude your loving brother in Christ, with prayer for you all.

JAMES BIRCH.

London, April 4, 1793.

P.S. I waited for something to write; Mrs. Birch continues helpless as this half year past, which presses hard in old age: Be careful,—mind what is written—and I pray God assist you.

LETTER XCI

To Sister Runwa, and the whole Church beloved in Christ, Jas. Birch & brethren send greeting.

Beloved Sister and Brethren,—I am, and ever shall be, glad to hear from you, and more so to see your Faith, Love, and Union in Christ, for as a faithful Steward love to see a good increase of *Corn and Fruit*, to the will and benefit of his master, even so doth the Messenger love to see the works and increase of Faith for the kingdom of Christ: And by patience and prayer, with divine assistance, the Elect will be brought to PERFECTION, as is a field of WHEAT in its due season.

Again, CHRIST is the Lord God of regeneration and salvation, and without Him we can do nothing; therefore we must follow him in the works of faith, to have his divine assistance, to overcome the powers of Temptation, Reason, death, &c. "Blessed are them that have part in the first resurrection;" *i.e.* as Faith fell in Adam for breaking its own law, and died. And so it go on in generation: then Christ raiseth Faith from that death to a new life, which is the first resurrection, or the virgin daughter of Faith born from its womb or seed, and is taken into the Priesthood of Christ; then the Elect have a NEW LIFE,

LANGUAGE, and WORK, which Reason cannot have or understand.

John iii. 8.—Jesus said to Nichodemus "The wind bloweth where it listeth, and thou heareth the sound thereof, but canst not tell whence it cometh, and whither it goeth; so, is every one that is born of spirit;" *i.e.* this new life, which is Faith, offers its prayer to heaven for divine assistance, and Christ is graciously pleased, by the influence of his holy spirit, to assist this pure virgin in the works of Faith, then this strengthen the life of Faith, and it will speak the mysteries of redemption and salvation, with the fruits of Faith, and return to him again, in a sweet flow of joy, thanksgiving, prayer, &.c. — Now Reason may hear the words and wonder, but "cannot tell from whence it come, and whither it go," because to him it is only a sound or noise, for he is incapable of the first resurrection, then as so, cannot enter regeneration, therefore no fruit can be found, so is cast out, and must "walk to & fro thorough the earth."

Further, the created life of Adam was Faith and immortal; but when it broke its own law; it become mortal, and died according to the word of, the Lord God, which is its lost condition without regeneration; then Christ come, and raise Faith from that death to a new life for regeneration: Now as Faith was immortal before it broke its law and died, then when it is raised from that death to a NEW LIFE, this new life is of an immortal nature, so as death cannot keep it under its power from following Christ; for to him is the spirit to go, —now death and justice cannot pass through justice and death for that is the grand united center to swallow up, and there keep in darkness; therefore it is this spirit of Faith which is of an *immortal* nature, that is only capable to be brought through those great and mighty powers; for as Christ passed through the powers of Reason, Sin, Death, Hell, and Justice, in spirit and person, to his kingdom of mercy, life and immortality; this spirit of Faith, by the power, of regeneration and his divine assistance, will follow, even up to his immortality and glory, and is united to Him in life and immortality, which is the *Seal* of the Living God, the *Book* of Life and the *Name* written therein: Then the Elect fall *asleep* in the bed of mercy, with their life in Christ for the resurrection to eternal glory.—Thus, the Messenger declares life and immortality to the Elect, who are and "will be redeemed and regenerated from the earth, and from amongst men."

MOREOVER, when the Elect are called and the Virgin daughter of

Faith is born, then by this spirit they are brought on in the works of Faith and regeneration, and from one "mansion of the Father to another," and overcome things which swallow up Reason, then its desire is to go to Christ and his kingdom, like as a child conceived in the womb, and is brought on by the power of God according to generation, 'till it comes to *Perfection*, then it regards not its residence, but becomes restless, and put for birth into this world: So in like manner is regeneration; for when the Elect has worked the works of Faith, they know they are under the power of oppression, temptation, justice and death, then Faith disregards this perishing world, which is its residence, and its desire and prayer is for CHRIST to come! then as a child pass from its mother's womb into this world, even so must the spirit of Faith pass through the Justice of the Father, to the Mercy and Kingdom of the SON.

Therefore the mighty works of Faith and regeneration is to pass through, and overcome the wiles and temptations of the devil, which is done by prayer, patience, and divine assistance; then you follow Christ, and are found worthy, and are called under the justice of the Father: Now there you must lose yourself in death in your own blood under that justice, then this spirit of Faith quicken or is quickened from that death, which is the son born to Christ; for as I said before, death has no power to hold this spirit from following Christ, for to Him is the spirit to go: Now

This is written for you to know and understand, that—when death and trouble come, remember you have been told it; but Christ is at hand to help you.

So I pray the love and union of Faith, the divine assistance of Christ be with you, and that HE will be graciously pleased to come and release his Elect, Amen! Your loving brother in Christ.

JAMES BIRCH.

London, Aug. 29, 1793.

LETTER XCII

To Sister Runwa, &c. Jas, Birch, & Breth. greeting.

Beloved Sister, —I was glad to hear from you, and as for you being *fearful; low, and naked*, that I do not wonder at.—Remember I have told you, you must stand before the power of the LORD GOD, to and for yourself—and who can without fear and trembling? Also, you may see and know that nothing can be done in regeneration without the divine assistance of Christ: And when Faith has tasted of it, it is continually longing for more. Also Faith finds itself *low and naked*, without the assistance of Christ its KING, because it cannot live in the waters of Reason.

Read Mat. xxiv. —Faith is born to *Sorrows*. And this is "the great tribulation" (Christ told his disciples should come) "such as was not since the beginning of the world to this time, no, nor never shall be," because, the Elect are born to those troubles, and must pass through them; then they are no more: for Faith being here, under the power of Reason's oppression and temptation, and also the power of death and justice, where can it flee for assistance but to Christ its king, to help it through and out of those mighty powers? Therefore, in this sorrowful and low condition, Faith seeks the assistance of Christ, by prayer and patience.

Moreover, the Messenger oft'times finds himself in a *low, sorrowful* and *mourning* condition, and *fearful* lest God has or should forsake him! and this cause prayer for divine assistance. For believe me, Faith cannot go through the powers of Reason, sin, death, hell, and justice without knowing its power; but, "He that endureth to the end, the same will be saved," which must be done by prayer and patience, therefore hold fast by what you have received, and seek by PRAYER.

Further, Mat xxvi. "CHRIST was a man of *sorrow and mourning*," See when he prayed in the *Garden* "that the cup may pass from him if possible."

Also John xii. 27. For HE being here under those powers, He must go through those powers, which was in Sorrow, Prayer, and Patience! And we must *follow* by his divine assistance.

Again—Mrs. Birch is dead—she died Dec. 2d, and was buried the 8th in Hollywell chapel burying ground, by her two daughters, and two granddaughters, as her desire. She was ill fourteen months, which caused unknown trouble and expence, for no one could find out her disorder, to help it.—

Thus—I have had the weight and trouble of Death, and oft' times thought it would press me down; but was brought through by the power of God; then the spirit smile over it, as life does over death, when it has passed through it.

Also, I have talked to Mrs. *Birch* of the power of Death and Justice; She "said she held fast by what she received, and doubted not the mercy of Christ, and said she had prayer." —She was well resigned to Death; and went off in peace!

Beloved sister and brethren, those travails and trials are very hard; for when man looks into the power of death and justice, and his own unworthiness, it makes the soul fear, tremble, and "cry he cannot be saved," but with God it is possible! For, by the power of regeneration, Faith, and prayer, those "mountains will be removed," that Faith shall, pass through and overcome: Also, when the Elect are in those mighty troubles and fears, yet, by prayer and patience, Faith in them at times has union, and communion with him, who has passed through those powers, and is above those powers, and has power over those powers and will and do assist His Elect, and help them through; therefore, as I said, nothing but regenerated Faith can be brought through these powers, up to the "seal of CHRIST the living God,"—but *Reason* lives in and under those powers, and has no union, with HIM above those powers, then as so, must die under those powers! And although he is suffered to "walk to and fro thorough this earth: yet death and justice will close, in upon him! —Therefore think yourselves well off, that you are called to FOLLOW CHRIST! So let prayer and patience possess your souls, which is the prayer of your loving brother in Christ

JAMES BIRCH,

London, Jan. 28, 1794,

LETTER XCIII

To our sister Mary Runwa, and the whole church beloved in Christ, Jas. Birch and Brethren send Greeting,

Beloved Sister and Brethren,—*I received of Mrs. Leach the parcel, and was glad to hear you were well.*

Now mind this—you must go further than the first call of the Messenger; although that is a very happy condition; for the kingdom of heaven is declared to you: And you know the Messenger is of God— and you are promised salvation: And, also have the prophecy of the Messenger ; yet you must go further: f or see—when "Jesus took Peter, James, and John into an high mountain, and was transfigured before them, and his face did shine as the sun, and his raiment white as the light; and they saw Moses and Elias, talking with him; then Peter said, Lord it is good for us to be here and make three tabernacles; then a bright cloud came, and a voice which said, this is my beloved SON, hear ye him:" Now this was a great sight, and a high state of convincement, yet they must not stop there, for Jesus was told he must face and go through justice and death! And when the Apostles were sent forth, see what TROUBLE and SORROW they had, and must go through justice and death!

And SO it is with the present MESSENGER, for believe me this— "the book of inspiration in your mouth is *sweet*, but when it go into the belly it is *bitter*" i.e. the communion with Christ is *sweet*, but when you enter into the Works to overcome, it is *bitter*; and it is so with the Elect, for when the second call comes, relative to the declaration, they will find themselves under the power of justice and death; for as Faith broke its own law and died, then when it is risen from that death to a new life, it needs must be made sensible of its condition, and must follow Christ in the regeneration; therefore as you was brought to your understanding through going to a Play, it is well—but the Plays only imitate the eager and vain desires, and follies of Man, which must end in death under justice! so WHEREVER you go always watch the *serpent*, and take him by the head.

Moreover, we are not in the priesthood of Reason, as they were in the days of *Muggleton*; for then, if you believed and relied on him, all was to be well, but when death came, nothing was done for salvation;

for then time was spent in talk, singing cherubical songs and *Self* promises of salvation! But now the Elect are called by the declaration, and then to the *first resurrection* to follow Christ in the regeneration; then, by his divine assistance, to *go through and overcome* those mighty powers, and go up to the *Seal of the living God, and book of Life*!

Beloved Sister and, Brethren, I hope this will find you all well; I have had some trouble, and toil this half year. On the 5th of Oct. last, about two in the morning, my son's wife was taken so very ill, that she died at four; then Mrs. Birch died in Dec. and my son left London before Christmas and his child for me to maintain—but in all those straits and scenes of life we must have patience, and not be borne down with them, but WORSHIP GOD, for Him only is able to help you through and out of those powers.

I hold my apartment, and the little boy lives with me; also Mrs. Birch's nurse, to look after: the *Place*: You will let me hear from you, and I pray God assist you to overcome, those mighty powers.

Your loving brother in Christ,

JAMES BIRCH.

London, April 11, 1794.

LETTER XCIV

To Sister Runwa, and the whole Church beloved in Christ, Jas. Birch & brethren send greeting.

Beloved Sister and Brethren, —Yours I received, and was glad to hear from you, and am glad to see your soul so desirous to get clear, and keep clear from Grudgings, Murmurings, &c. &c. for that is the fume of the devil and foment of hell; and, was what detained the natural kingdom of Israel in the wilderness and brought great trouble on them: But the CONTENTED SPIRIT brings peace, and the blessing of God follow with it; for them who are brought into the royal priesthood must WILL that Christ rule over them, for HIM only is able to bring them through the power of Reason, Death, and Justice. Also.

Be careful that neither *pride nor anger* inhabit the soul, for that is of the devil; nor *self consequence*, for that is an evil conceit. But

LOVE, MERCY, and FORGIVENESS, to each other is such an *Ornament* to the Elect; hardly to be expressed. It being so GOD-LIKE in itself! Then the peace and blessing of God attend it, that Reason know not of, nor from whence it come!

Moreover, there is the *Field of generation* where there is natural desire, bonds, union, duty, &c. and Reason will intermix his slime with your duty, and urge for that which cannot or should not be granted: For mind, Christ gather out of this field by and for regeneration, to complete his harmonious, united, and glorious kingdom! Therefore watch! For there are many evil spirits inhabit this field, that will bring on ruination of body, mind, and condition, and under the seal of the angel in justice! Also, there is the *Field of wild Reason*, where Reason has his delights to go out and walk to and fro the earth in evil, seeking, to have his own will and way, and devour each other if possible, through a selfish view, oppression, malice, lies, &c. now those fields go one into the other, & justify themselves by each others evil in what they can.

Again—The kingdoms of *this World* are too much sought after, which make times and things very difficult, hard, and bad, for it is such strivings and contentions as I never knew before, because it is the strivings of the Cherubim against the Seraphim, and the Seraphim against the Cherubim, who shall be Ruler, that the world is full of Violence to carry things before it—so have prayer and patience, to wait the coming of Christ, therefore

See Rev iii. 10. "Because thou hast kept the word of my patience, I also will keep thee from the hour of temptation, which shall come upon all the world, to try them that dwell upon the earth" Here you may see what WAS and WOULD be sent to the world, and the Faith and Patience of the Elect to overcome!

Also, Ch. xviii. of the fall of BABYLON the great "And I heard another voice from heaven, saying, *come out of her my people, that ye be not partakers* of her sins, and that ye receive not, of her plagues;" this *voice* has been some years, and now IS, therefore BLESSED are them that hear and follow; for the Elect must come out of the *World* to follow Christ; for them that are of the World, will receive that judgment which follow the *World*: So be careful, for Reason will creep in and twine about, to take the soul aside if possible, that the church of Christ may be desolate!

Further, the Elect are to worship God and Christ, who has power to protect and preserve them, and not trust in and to man, who will deceive them; and follow Christ, whose kingdom is not of this *World*; because they fell in Adam, and have them sorrows and troubles that was denounced against Adam: But as God became Christ to redeem, he took the fallen nature of Faith on him to redeem it, and was subject to those troubles, sorrows, &c. and lost himself in his own blood in death, under the justice of the Father, to pass through it and go above it, to his own kingdom, the glory of mercy; therefore the Elect must have it, and go through it, to follow Christ.

But in all the heavy weight, fear, and sorrow of Reason, Sin, Justice, and Death, which are as mountains before us, yet if we have Faith, and doubt not the assistance of Christ in his royal priesthood, "those mountains will be removed," for whatsoever we ask, in the prayer of Faith believing, we shall receive! for great things are overcome and done by belief, Faith, prayer, and patience! And, as I said before, Christ has gone through those powers, and has power over those powers, and KNOWS where and when to assist his Elect under those powers, and even "what they need before they ask."

So that love, Faith, prayer, & patience may possess your souls, to wait the coming of CHRIST, is the prayer of your loving brother in Christ.

London, July 8, 1794.   JAMES BIRCH.

LETTER XCV

To our Sister Runwa & the whole church beloved in Christ, James Birch and Brethren send greeting.

Beloved sister and Brethren—Yours I received, and was glad to hear from you, but as for *Joe* I am sorry to hear of his condition, and let the *exception* be what it will, it must be for that which *perish*! For the devil will take a man as the sudden bite of a serpent that shall corrupt his whole mass of blood; and the devil also will take him into his field of stupefaction and death, and there open the tombs of death and of the dead; then there will come out exceptions, murmurs, dislike, anger, &c. &c. which will not do for the church of Christ.

Moreover, Faith brings forth love, mercy, forgiveness, patience, prayer, &e. &c. Now this is the nature that follow Christ! Therefore,

See Matt. xviii. 21, where Peter said to Jesus, "How oft he should forgive his brother that sin against him, Jesus said to him, until seventy times seven." Hence it is a dangerous thing to conceive and hold anger against a brother, so be careful and watch! His not coming to the communion of the church after so many invitations, is a bad sign, and as for his excuse in not speaking at home, because of his wife, it is plain she is his master, and not Christ! But the time of trial and manifestation will come!

Now as for YOU, and as many of you that hold fast by what is given, and keep your first love, and worship God and Christ, YOU enter into his Royal promise and prophecy, and you will be brought through, and enter in at the gate of mercy! But as for backsliders, murmurers, &c. they turn to the *old house*, and cover themselves under the excuse of devils, and will be cast out!

Again, I know your labour and care, "and that you have laboured and not fainted," that if possible to add or to hold the church together, but some being of evil, and not sent of God, you may see how such has rewarded you, for believe me, no one can come HERE which is to the SON, but by "the power of the Father and will in no ways be cast out," for they will bring forth the fruits of Faith, Love, Mercy, &c. and follow up in the regeneration! Now this is the CHURCH OF CHRIST, and for Christ! Therefore Reason may set what value on himself or themselves they please, the Messenger will bid nothing for them— neither would I have any of you be a slave to Reason in what he shall say or do, for he can go but to the length of his CHAIN.

Now, if you please, you may let Joe see this letter, or read it to him, and if he can return to his first love and communion with the church, I shall be glad, and He only will reap the benefit.

I have known them in this field of contention, and has been brought out; there is space given for repentance, but mind to do it quickly, lest that should be taken, then wander to and fro through the earth, and must go in to death and hell, with their eyes open!

Again, do you, and all of you, meet in the united love of CHRIST in his regeneration, and there follow HIM, for his promise is sure and his reward ready, instruct the harmless enquirer, and help the meek, and as for those evil spirits never grieve after them; for if God will not accept them, your labour is in vain, for Reason will go its own way, and to its own home, and Faith will follow Christ, and go to him by regeneration, which is its home!

Since writing so far I received yours of Jan. 11, wherein I see *Joe* is fixed in his purpose, then as so, let him go, for you can do no good, this I have had plenty of, and well know the devil cannot dwell in this declaration, so must take himself away. — Grieve not after him, Christ will have his own, and no more: then THEY are your brethren.

I will take the opportunity to see Mrs. North, then you shall hear from me again.—I should have written before; but have been very much hurried and drove, that (and the hard weather) has been too much for me, but I keep about: my son and grandson live with me; we put out the washing, and do as well as we can. My love to all, and shall be glad to hear of your Faith and well doing.

So conclude your loving brother in Christ

London, Feb. 2, 1795 JAMES BIRCH.

LETTER XCVI

To our Sister Runwa, and the whole Church beloved in Christ, Jas. Birch and Brethren send Greeting.

Beloved Sister—Yours I received (*and one of Mrs. North, and that dated April 12, 1795,*) wherein I am glad to see you express your Faith, Patience, and Prayer, and not to grieve after backsliders, or at what Reason shall please to say or do, For

See, Matt. xii. 43, Jesus said "When the unclean spirit is gone out of a man, he walketh through dry places, seeking rest and findeth none."

1st This "*unclean spirit*," which is Reason the devil, "*goeth out*" against the spirit and power of Christ in *unbelief* and hardness of heart.

2d. Listen to catch words and look after evil to *overthrow*.

3d. *Contend*, make war, and tempt.

4th In raising *Lies*, speaking evil, false judgement, and say it is of the devil.

5th. In *Wrath*, evil acts, and would extirpate from off the earth.

6th. In *Blasphemy*.

7th. In *Persecution* unto death, which is murder.—Now these are the *thunders* of Reason against Faith, and all those things were acted against Christ, when he was on this earth but in all this Reason can find no *rest*, because they are *dry places*, therefore he finds wrath, which will burn him up!

Ver. 44. "Then he saith, I will return into my house from whence I came out, and when he is come, he findeth it empty, swept, and garnished;" his *house* is his imagination, on the letter—he may read of promises which are *garnishes*, but they are all *empty and swept* from him.

Ver. 45 "Then goeth he and taketh with himself seven other spirits more wicked than himself, and they enter in and dwell there: and the last state of that man is worse than the first," because he has acted those things against Christ and his kingdom, and he is sealed by the angel in justice for those acts which he was not when "he went out, so his last state is worse than the first."

Again, These are "the seven devils which Jesus cast out of Mary Magdalen," and also was *cast out of Paul* and must be cast *out* of all the Elect; for Reason must not be suffered to dwell there to come out to act those things against Christ: beside the body of Elect man is the *promised land* to the virgin daughter of Faith for to dwell in. Also,

Moses, in his way to the promised land, cut off nations and kings.

Joshua also was commanded to destroy *seven nations* when he entered the promised land, and the LORD GOD *drove them out* before *Israel*: Now this was for the law of *Moses* to be obeyed, and the name and power of the God of Israel to be KNOWN!

Some were *Giants* in imagination, and high in their own wisdom and conceit which was wild, and against Moses, and against God, for which cause they were *drive out, cut off*, &c. that the Law of Moses should he given and OBEYED; but the other was and is against Christ and his kingdom, therefore the greater evil by far!

Now those spirits do not come out to act, but when Christ is on this earth in spirit: And the *other spirits* being in man, will also come out into *act*, but that is for fear of losing what they do or would possess; and by or through temptation of the other spirits to do their will; therefore the Elect must be careful and watch for this *wilderness is great*, and travail hard!

Also the spirit of *unbelief and hardness of heart* is very bad, nay, nothing can be done in and for regeneration, while that reigns in the soul.

Mark ix. When the man brought his child to Jesus, to have the unclean spirit or devil cast out, Jesus said, If thou canst believe all things are "possible to him that believe," and if Joe and others had *believed* they never would have forsook the church of Christ; but now they must go back from whence they came, and take those spirits with them.

Now this is written for your information, that you may know the power of Christ, & worship him, and watch and pray his coming in spirit to assist the daughter of Faith, so have firm belief and patience, love one another in the love of Christ, watch and pray his divine assistance, and you will be brought through, and I pray Christ to assist you, Amen.

Beloved sister and brethren, I would have wrote sooner, but hard weather, things uncommon dear, and almost frozen up, that I had no time or power to write. *Many died here through the hard frost, including our brother John Palmer.* I thank God I have kept about both by day and night—the frost has left relics which fine weather may help. *Mrs. North* desires I would call on her again if I can. I hope all are well, and to hear from you soon.

So conclude your loving brother in Christ.

JAMES BIRCH,

London, April 27, 1795.

LETTER XCVII

To Sister Runwa and the whole Church beloved in Christ, Jas. Birch & brethren send greeting.

Beloved Sister and Brethren;

Yours I received, and was glad to hear from you, and that you are in *Love and Union*: And as for your being *weak and low, and have dark Clouds at times*; at that I rejoice, for then the soul is in a condition of prayer for divine preservation and assistance: Also, this is the works of Faith against the powers of Death and Justice, for believe me; when the "sixth Angel" in regeneration sounded, there was a command from heaven to "loose the four angels which are bound in the great river Euphrates" (see Rev. ix.) it may well be called a *great river* because it waters the souls and spirits of Reason with hope; and when those waters are stopped, Reason must destroy itself for a moment's peace, as did Joe Buck!

Now those four angels that are loosed is the Power of Sin, the power of Justice, the power of Death, and the power of Hell; those *powers* lay hid and inactive in the waters of Reason, so that they know nothing of it as yet; then Reason may go on, preach, pray, and sing, and be in hopes, or assured of, eternal life, as they say! But those powers are loosed on the Elect, and they must come out of those waters of FALSE HOPE into the waters of Faith; under the justice of the Father, and work against those powers as Christ did, then your refreshment come from heaven!

Also those powers were loosed on me first, because I am the angel of the declaration; neither is there any help out of it, or from it, till Christ come. *Again*, see Rev. xvi. "And the sixth angel poured out his vial upon the great river Euphrates, and the waters thereof were dried up, that the way of the kings of the east might be prepared." This is the same as the *Voice* of the Angel, for when he sounds, at the same time he pours out the *vial of God's wrath* upon Reason: Now these *kings of the East* are the Elect, and those *waters* of Reason's hope, must be dried up to them, for to be prepared to meet Christ their king, which is done by the waters and power of Faith.

Also—I thought of, or meant, no more than the spirit of Reason in the Elect; and those of Reason in this commission who are enemies—for

I am a servant to the Elect to help them on in their journey; but this *Voice* has so agitated the world, that I have lived to see more than I wanted or expected; therefore fear not, for you have CHRIST your friend, so worship HIM, and stick to him by the power of Faith and *Union*, as the needle will to the Loadstone, for He is able to help you through and out of those powers, and crown you with an everlasting crown, the glory of mercy! But you must have prayer and patience, as HE himself had when here—and follow him through it, by his divine assistance.

Beloved Sister, the frost was so violent, it left me a great cold, so renders me weak, full of pain, and hard of hearing.—I should have seen Mrs. North but for the house hearing what she say.

I keep about, and do as well as I can: And in the midst of those hard and oppressive times, I trust in and to the divine Majesty; and if he suffer the devil to drive, or put me into death, I have no great objection to go. — I keep my *Apartment,* and THERE the Church meet:—This is my very condition; and in this hard winter and times, I have had much thought of you, as you had of me, because my soul's love is with you and for you: Despair not of seeing me again, we cannot tell how God will order things; do you write.

So conclude your loving brother in Christ, with prayer for you all.

JAMES BIRCH.

London, August 4, 1795.

LETTER XCVIII

To our sister Mary Runwa, and the whole church beloved in Christ, Jas. Birch and Brethren send Greeting.

Beloved Sister,—Yours I received, and was glad to hear from you, and that you meet in Church Union, in the Faith of CHRIST, and love to see and commune with each other.—I would have wrote sooner, but we have been hurried and drove; people *divided* against people, and strove against each other, on the *Sea* or waters of Reason, to have their own will and way, that *distress* has been—and great assemblies have met to petition, and I fear not yet satisfied; I could wish these times were shortened, for I fear they hurt the Elect; for there has been, and now is, "great troubles on the earth."

When this Message came, it set Reason into great agitation, and great troubles followed to the Messenger, and to Reason, but by the divine assistance of Christ, that power of Reason is overcome and ended, that the elect may sit down in peace so far. But, by the power of the declaration the angel in justice has loosed many to go forth, and do the will of God, so far as permitted, as it was in the time of old, in the days of Moses; "HE THAT READS LET HIM UNDERSTAND." So you may see troubles began in the Spiritual, and when that was passed, then it began in the natural, and when that will end, God knows.

Moreover, read Matt. xxiv. Mark xiii. Luke xvii. and xxi. there you may see what "troubles would come, when the son of man was revealed, and as a sign of his coming," therefore it is good for the Elect to set their face towards it—and pray for divine assistance to overcome, for the same will be saved. Also those things are sent on this earth as a trial, and Reason will be carried away by temptation, but do you keep to patience and prayer as you have been told, and you will be preserved from this hour or hours of temptation.

Again, understand the kingdom of Christ is come to his Elect, therefore his will must be done, yea, he is LORD of this Creation, because he created all things, and all is his, and as so can do in it, and with it, as he please, therefore you may be confidently sure his words and prophecy will come to pass.—CHRIST also was born into this world, and grew to manhood, and kept the law of Faith, and overcome the power of Reason, and its temptation, and of sin, death, hell, and justice, and is ascended into his high heaven, of mercy, and his own kingdom of Faith in regeneration, and of regenerated Faith, and is Lord of all quickening power to Faith, which is the first resurrection—and great God and king of the new heaven and earth; therefore all power is given to Christ, both in heaven and earth.

Moreover, seeing Christ went through and overcome all those things, to go to his kingdom, and the Elect must follow him, by his divine assistance—for no other way can they go, but the way himself went,—so there is no one knows where and when to assist the royal Elect, like unto Christ;— and (as I said) seeing, or you may see, those things are come to pass, according to prophecy—therefore let the Virgin of Faith REJOICE "that the time of her deliverance draweth nigh;" but Reason will strive for his kingdom, and "fill the earth with violence," which bring great troubles on himself, and hurt the Elect; but do you WORSHIP GOD AND CHRIST, and not be carried away with the fear of Reason or his power, for that will end: but the great and grand thing is the works of Faith, and patience to follow Christ, then by his divine assistance, you will be brought through, and overcome those powers, by the power of regeneration, and be brought up to the seal of Christ the living God, to sit down with him in his royal kingdom the glory of mercy; so wish the love and union, and Faith of Christ to abound, and his divine assistance,—for in his royal priesthood you will have PEACE, but in the world *trouble.*

So conclude your loving brother in Christ, with prayer for you all.

JAMES BIRCH.

London, Feb. 8, 1796.

P.S. My love to you all; I have been but poorly or you would have heard sooner; my grandson is mostly here, and sleeps with me every night: I get on through those hard tunes as well as I can, neither do I fear the power of Reason, knowing that God will send his angels.

LETTER XCIX

To our Sister Runwa & the whole church beloved in Christ, James Birch, and Brethren, send greeting.

Beloved Sister, — *I saw those people, but in about two or three days after, I was taken very ill, and* so continue; how it will go with me I know not, but I am in a poor wasting manner: Also, I have examined myself, both of the cherubical inspiration, and the inspiration of Faith, and find it positively agree both with the divine majesty and myself *i.e.* the cherubical with itself, and the inspiration of faith with itself—both standing before the divine majesty; so I am willing to die whenever it please God to call: Also—

It is a very agreeable thing to look at & into death, and find nothing stand against you—true it is, I must lose myself in death, in my own blood, under the justice of the Father, to pass to the mercy of the SON; and when this comes to pass I hope it will be all well.

Since writing the above I have found myself a little better, but mend very slow: —*my son and some others threatened to make me master of the bone-house, but it is not so yet*—it may be the divine majesty may have something more for me to do, if not, his will be done.

Beloved Brethren—I hope you will, and do, mind what I have wrote and told you in *former Days*, that the tempter is very swift, and will tempt- you, and lead you many ways wrong, through the self promises of glory, but you will find no such thing, but altogether the contrary, therefore WORSHIP GOD and CHRIST, and them only serve as you have been informed: So I hope you will pardon me in not writing sooner, for I have not been able.

Beloved Sister, —I hope you will let me know how *Betsy* is, and whether she has or likely to have a place; and how Mrs. Atkinson does; and how Mrs. *Williams* does; and in a word, how you all *do*, for my heart is with you, and wish I could see you once more, but do believe time is near up for every one to draw home; for as the serpent angel came like lightning and overthrew Faith, so will the son of man come like lightning and overthrow Reason, therefore BLESSED are you that WATCH and WAIT, for your reward is LIFE ETERNAL!

So conclude your loving brother in Christ, with prayer for you all.

JAMES BIRCH.

No. 88, Fore-Street, London,
July 7, 1796.

LETTER C

To our Sister Runwa, and the whole Church beloved in Christ, Jas. Birch and Brethren send Greeting.

Beloved Sister,—Yours I received, and was glad to hear from you, and as you see Joe is gone, grieve not after him, he cannot help it, for the "TIME OF TRIAL is come, people falling away, and charity is become cool," the which I find now in OLD AGE, that to ones thinking "no flesh could possibly be saved," but there is a merciful God and Christ, whose kingdom is open, yea, as I said oft before, will have his own:—And what shall I say O righteous Father? have mercy on us miserable sinners; and holy Father, into thy hands I commend my spirit.

So conclude, with love and prayer for you all.

JAMES BIRCH.

London, Nov, 4, 1796.

P.S. I write with great difficulty; when you send a parcel, let me have advice.

LETTER CI

To our beloved Sister Mary Runwa, and the whole Church beloved in Christ, Jas. Birch, and Brethren send greeting.

Beloved Sister and Brethren, — Yours I received and was glad to hear that you are all well.—*Young Mr. Frain was entirely mistaken in the man; I never did wear any sort of flannel, neither have I been out of doors 'till now: —Times are very hard, but I by some means have moved on lowly, &c.*

Here is a thing necessary to know, that when the *Testimony is finished*, "The Beast that ascends out of the *bottomless pit*, will make war with the Messenger, and overcome him, and kill him, in what they can; and many will rejoice at it for a small space!" —

CHRIST was left alone to their mock, derision, &c. and so were most all his servants—for "when the fourth seal was opened; there went out a pale horse, and his riders name was death, and hell followed with him, and power was given him over the four parts of the earth, to kill with sword, hunger, and the beasts of the earth." Now this is to all and every one, for all must be brought down to DEATH by some means.

Again, if you look when the next *seal was opened*, you may "see them who died under the altar for the testimony they held," which was to worship God; and they "cried for deliverance," as we do, but the word was PATIENCE, 'till all was finished! "and there were white robes given them," therefore we must have prayer and patience.

I had written so far when my son James brought the news of Mr. Mathews's death, which was very sudden*—so we have now but very few.

Yesterday a gentleman called on me, and paid the money, so I troubled neither of them, and as things proved I am glad I did not.

I mean to write again very, soon, some few things out of the Revelations, 'till then farewell! So conclude your loving brother in Christ.

London, Jan. 2, 1797.   JAMES BIRCH.

LETTER CII

To our Sister Runwa, and the whole Church beloved in Christ, Jas. Birch and Brethren send Greeting.

Beloved sister—In my last I promised I would write again.

---

* Noted by Mr. Birch, as the last day of the month, and last day of the year, being Saturday, Dec. 31, 1796.

REVELATIONS, Ch. i. "JOHN unto the CHURCHES which were in Asia." He recommends "Grace and Peace from HIM which IS and WAS, and IS to COME."

Now the *Angels* of those churches are the ministering spirits of God, and the *candlesticks* are the churches; therefore when the *reproof* comes, it is to them who are unworthy, all but some, that there is given *space to repent!* Now JESUS is the head or great Angel in the royal priesthood of Faith, and "holdeth the seven stars in his right hand," and goeth out on the spirit of Faith in the Elect, which is his church.

Also, Ch. iii. "And unto the angel of the church of *Sardis* write those things, saith he, that hath the seven spirits of God, and the seven stars."

Ch. iv. Ver. 5. "And out of the throne proceeded lightnings, and thunderings; and voices: and there were seven lamps of fire burning before the throne, which are the seven spirits of God:" Now here you may see Christ is King, Lord, and High Priest, in his own royal priesthood.

Again, those which John saw in his heavenly Vision, are them "who valued not their lives unto death but went through great tribulation in worshipping the Father, for the mercy of the SON; and has his Father's name written in their forehead," therefore I would not have any one think to pass to the glory of the Father, without great *tribulation!* And the works of Faith in the royal priesthood is very great! for when you are called, you must follow up in regeneration, and WORSHIP GOD and CHRIST, and not stand as a stinking pool for those are them that are *poor, miserable,* and *naked!* Here John saw Christ, after he was risen from the dead, and united himself to those he had "redeemed from the earth and from among men," and there was great joy and rejoicing that Christ had overcome all those powers, and took possession of his royal kingdom of Virgins, and crowned their Faith.

Ver. 1. "After this, John saw a door was opened in heaven: And the first voice which he heard was as it were of a trumpet talking with ME, which said, come up hither, and I will shew thee things which must be hereafter; and immediately I was in the spirit, and beheld a throne was set in heaven, and one sat on the throne;" he who sat on the *throne* was Christ, and *round about the throne* was his heavenly host that he had redeemed from the earth, —there were "four beast, each beast had six wings, and full of eyes within, and before, and behind;" those *eyes* are the quick sight of Faith, and the *wings* are the swift and strong power in the rule of Faith, for they have the powerful rule in and of his kingdom of justice: and as to likeness, that of a *Lion*, and that of a *Calf*. The third had the *face of a Man*; and the fourth a flying *Eagle*,—this is strength and innocence, and the swift motion in the ruling power, which is invested on them by Christ; and he who hath the face of a man is CHRIST, because he has faced all, and gone through all, to his royal glory of mercy; and the other three sit in the glory of justice, and wait the translation.

As to the *elders*—the Lord God of heaven is an *Elder*, because he created all things, and is the foundation of Faith: Adam and Enoch are *elders*; Abraham, Isaac, & Jacob, Moses & Elias, & others are *elders*, because this is the first witness of his spirit, and prophesied before him, when he was in the condition of the Father; they are called elders because God's communion with, and promise of eternal life to them, is left on record; Christ is recorded the son of David, of Abraham, of Adam, for he came by the way of the Father or Elder, to inherit the Son or Brother. — Here "the *four beast* rest not, saying Holy, Holy, Holy, Lord God Almighty, which was, and is, and is to come:" Now this is the true voice of Faith; and Enoch, Moses, Jesus, and Elias, are them.

Ch. v. "And John saw in the right hand of him that sat on the throne, a book written within, and on the backside sealed with seven seals; and no one in heaven or earth, or under the earth, was able to open the book, or loose the seals thereof; and he wept much, because no man was found worthy to open the book, neither to look thereon: And as John was weeping, one of the elders saith unto him, weep not, — behold the Lion of the tribe of Juda, the root of David, hath prevailed to open the book, and loose the seven seals thereof:" Now this is the *Book* of LIFE, and John, for all he was inspired and sent forth to preach the death and resurrection of Christ, as was the other Apostles, and was greatly beloved of Christ, yet when he was called up there, "he fell as a dead man;" why? because if the book had not been *opened*, there was no salvation for him or any one; but the Elder let him to know the book would be opened to him and many more, "and their names found written therein," and would be sealed: for if this book of life had not been opened, there could no names be found that had the seal of God through Adam.

Also John was here on earth, and communed with them in heaven, and that he must have and go through those things, because he was a fellow servant, and in tribulation; take notice this seal is not opened to the reprobate, for they are under the seal of the angel, and even the Elect are regenerated from it by the first resurrection, and made anew by regeneration, which is opening the seal, and, "redeeming them from the earth, and from among men;" that is all filthy earthy matter with Reason, and all belonging to it will go off and enter the herd of swine in the morning of the resurrection; and when any great thing is done in heaven, there is great rejoicing, for the natures voice in the redeemed say, Amen!

Ch. vi. "AND I saw, when the lamb opened one of those Seals,—and I heard as it were the noise of thunder, one of the four beast, saying, come and see; and I saw, and beheld a white horse, and he that sat on him had a bow, and a crown was given unto him, and he went forth conquering and to conquer:" This is Christ in his high power and righteousness of Faith, and he ride or go out on the Virgin Daughter of Faith, and assist her in the works of Faith, as you may see in

Ch. v. where "he saw a lamb having seven horns and seven eyes, which are the seven spirits of God, sent forth into all the earth," therefore Christ conquered and overcome sin, death, hell, and justice, and all the power of Reason, and is above all.

"AND when he had opened the *Second* Seal, I heard the second beast say, come and see, and there went out another horse that was red, and power was given to him that sat thereon, to take peace from the earth, and that they should kill one another, and there was given unto him a great sword." This is the internal Angel in Justice, who goeth out all over the world on the soul of man, and can bind or loose men, that they shall or shall not go to war, and seal every one under his own evil, because he is in justice, so every one will be their own witness to their own condemnation, and for this he is called a *red horse*.

"AND when he opened the Third Seal, I heard the third beast say, come and see, and there went out a black horse, and his rider had a pair of balances in his hand." This is the dark superstitious spirit in man, which is to worship Idols, or any sort of false worship whatever, and offer it up for God to own, and also the covetous and down bearing spirit that will keep back from the poor, and greatly distress them, which is a great condemnation: For "there came a voice from the midst of the four beast, which says, a measure of wheat for a penny, and three measures of barley for a penny, and see thou hurt not the wine and oil," which is not to keep back from God's' creature, and peculiarly those who worship him.

"AND—when he had opened the *Fourth* Seal, then there went out death all over the whole world, both to man and beast, and hell followed with it."

"AND when he had opened the *Fifth* Seal, I saw them that were slain under the altar, for the word of God, and the testimony they held, crying to God to avenge their blood on them that dwell on the earth, and white robes were given unto them, and it was said they must have a little patience until their fellow servants also should be killed, as they were."

"AND Behold! When he had opened the *Sixth* Seal, then there was a great *shake* to nature, for the sun became black, & the moon blood, & the stars fell from heaven, as a tree casteth her untimely fruit, when she is shaken with a mighty wind." This is when you are called under the Justice of the Father by the heavenly power: The *Moon*, which is the justice of the Father, is turned to *blood*, and the SUN is become black by the justice of the Father, and through it you must go, or no life eternal; which is to lose yourself in death in your own blood, to pass to the seal, —the justice of the Father is so mighty and so great! So nature may well tremble! And all the revelation and prophecy you did possess, which is as stars, is gone 'till you are sealed. This is the wrath of God, and of the Lamb.

Ch. viii. "And after those things, I saw four angels standing on the four corners of the earth, holding the four winds of the earth, that the wind should not blow on the earth, nor on the sea; nor on any tree;" those are the *four* great powers, *i.e.* the power of sin, death, hell, and justice, that has power to destroy all life: And "he saw another angel ascending from the east, having the seal of the living God, and he cried with a loud voice to the four angels to whom it was given to hurt the earth and the sea, saying, hurt not the earth, neither the sea, nor the trees, until we have sealed the servants of our God in their foreheads; and he heard the number which were sealed, of the tribes of Israel," but it do not follow that no more than them are sealed of Israel.

"After this I beheld, and lo a great multitude, which no man could number, of nations and kindreds, people and tongues, stood before the throne, and before the lamb, clothed with white robes, and palms in their hands, and cried with a loud voice, saying, salvation to our God, who sitteth on the throne, and unto the lamb;" and, as I said before, when any great thing is done in heaven, there is always great joy, for the nature's voice in the redeemed, say Amen!

"And one of the elders said unto me, what are those which are arrayed in white robes, and from whence came they? And I said unto him—sir, thou knowest; and he said unto me, those are they which came out of great tribulation, and washed their robes, and made them white, in the blood of the lamb, and are before the throne:" Now those are gentiles of every nation, kindred, and tongue.

"AND when he had opened the *Seventh seal*, there was silence in heaven about the space of half an hour;" this is until the *seventh seal* is opened, which will be at the end of time—because, this is the first witness of his spirit, and stood before him and prophesied when he was in the condition of the Father, and the virgin daughter could not bring forth a son in regeneration, until God became a son to his own power; therefore this is his kingdom of *Virgins*, and has "His Father's name written in their forehead;" but when the end of time cometh, *Moses, Elias,* and *Enoch* will be translated to the mercy and glory of the SON, and so will all this his heavenly host; for the virgin daughter of Faith will give up or bring forth a son, to the high covenant of mercy, and all alike enter the glory of mercy, which is the high and glorious kingdom of Christ: So much for the *First* WITNESS *of his spirit.* For

Then "He saw seven angels which stood before God, and to them were given seven trumpets:" Now those *angels* went forth and sounded in regeneration, which is the kingdom of Christ, for now Christ is in the glory of mercy, and has overcome all powers, and above all powers, and has redeemed his Elect, therefore all is regenerated to him and he set the seal for eternal glory.

"And another angel came and stood at the altar, having a golden censer, and there was given unto him much incense, that he should offer it with the prayers of all saints, upon the golden altar, which is before the throne:" this was Christ the king of Faith: Now the power of prayer is the censer, and divine Faith is the incense which he offered for his Elect, for "he prayed not for the world, but for them which was given him;" therefore the gathering in the united, the harmonious, and glorious kingdom of Christ is as this—the first witness of his spirit is the last, and the last first, because it is sealed by him for the high heaven of mercy. —

Also, Ch. x.—"And I saw another mighty angel come down from heaven,—clothed with a cloud, and a rainbow was upon his head, and his face was as it were the sun, and his feet as pillars of fire, and he had in his hand a little book open, and set his right foot on the sea, and his left foot upon the earth;" this angel was Christ the King of Faith, come to redeem his Elect, and being *clothed with a cloud*; *i.e.* when he was here, no one could know him but his Elect—you might walk by him, and talk with him, and not know him, neither do they know him, now he is in his glory of mercy, and *a rainbow* upon his head; this is a spiritual rainbow, not to be seen or known, but in the royal priesthood of Faith; there you may see the internal beauty and glory of redemption—for as the natural *rainbow*, in the days of Noah, was to shew God's covenant with man, so is the spiritual *rainbow* to shew Christ's covenant with his Elect; but cannot be seen or known, but in Faith's priesthood.

"And his face was as it were the sun, and his feet as pillars of fire;" this is to tell you the glory and power of his person, and no one can move him: "And He had in his right hand a Little Book open, and he set his right foot on the sea, and his left foot upon the earth, and CRIED with a loud VOICE, as when a lion roareth;" this book was the BOOK of Inspiration, of the *new Birth*, the works of Faith, and the seal of the living God; all which the Elect must have, and *know!*

And this "*Loud Voice*, as when a lion roareth," was the declaration of his holy Gospel, and new birth, and Seal, which will be heard all over the world, let it he spoke ever so LOW!

And when "He had CRIED,—*Seven* THUNDERS uttered their voices, he (John) was about to write, but a voice came from heaven which forbid him;" but as Christ has made them known to me, I will write: The

First THUNDER that is uttered is when the internal Angel take *place* in the soul, then man is come to *maturity*, and must answer for himself! The

Second THUNDER that is uttered, man is *charged with the law*, and must face his own evil, to his own condemnation, let him help himself if he can: The

Third THUNDER that is uttered, then *appear Moses* to give forth the law, for the internal angel in justice is as Moses, and now he not only give forth the law, but *seals* every one under it, according to their evil: The

Fourth THUNDER that is uttered, then men are *called under the angel*, and sealed under their own evil, and must be and are their own witness to their own condemnation: The

Fifth THUNDER that is uttered, there is *no one* in heaven or earth can or will *take off the Seal*: The

Sixth THUNDER that is uttered, you must *wander to and fro* through the earth *under* the seal, because it never will be taken off: The

Seventh THUNDER that is uttered, is when the angel *opens his book of justice and death*, in the Morning of the Resurrection, BUT some are opened BEFORE DEATH!

"And (when) he saw the angel that stood upon the sea and upon the earth lifted up his hand to heaven, and swear by him that liveth for ever, that there should be time no longer, but in the days of the voice of the seventh angel, when he shall begin to sound, the mystery of God should be finished; as he has declared to his servants the prophets," which, NOW IS THE TIME—that, the voice of the *seventh* angel is made known!

And "The voice spake again, and said, he must take the little book and eat it, and it shall be in thy mouth sweet as honey, but shall make thy belly bitter;" now the spirit of prophecy is very pleasing, but when it sink down in the belly it become *bitter*, because you must prophesy against "people, nations, and tongues," and many that you know! Now if Christ had not come, Moses's commission would have ended in death! but Christ came, and brought in eternity, then full power was given to the angel in justice, to seal men down under death! And when CHRIST had made his declaration, and done his work, then the *seven thunders* uttered their Voices, and a *dreadful* UTTERANCE it is!

Now I hope you will mind what is written, and I pray God to give you understanding, for I did not mean to write the THUNDERS, but was constrained to do it, that you might *know and understand*; for here is the council and power of God directed to *two men, i.e.* the man of Faith, and the man of Reason.

So conclude your loving brother; with love and prayer for you all.

JAMES BIRCH.

No. 88, Fore-Street, London,
Feb. 20, 1797.

P.S. I hope this will find you all well, *I am but poorly, and cannot get a sixpence, I told you in my last that Mr. Mathews was dead; he died very sudden! and left all to his wife, and not a farthing to any one beside; and he died possessed of hundreds at the day of his death; he was a very close man, but by Mr. Axtell's connexion is now found out! I hope you will let me hear from you soon.*

NOTE. — The Messenger declared to Mathews, the THUNDERS were out, who replied, "He could not then stop to attend;" and sudden death came—so for ever stopped his attendance:—

(And it came to pass that T. Herald attended closely—and on March 26 (Sunday) 1797, became wholly reconciled to attend Mr. Birch, and THERE only; a blessed day! And behold, it was straightway discovered, that the power spoke by John Reeve, had taken Herald "The self same day" seven years back! The Messenger adding, "You have been with John Reeve one week:" Hence in this place, the Messenger, upon the third annual return of the said day (March 26), confirmed his wish, "That a feast be for ever kept on that day, in honour of him, and a greater man," looking very hard at Herald—Brother Platt was by—Herald replied, "that GREATER MAN is Christ," the Messenger in great Love reiterated the same! Quickly after Herald's attendance— many others attended also.) And the THUNDERS, were uttered in, the original church, as the second generation came forward;—then sent *them to Feversham, finding brethren there, addressed as follows:*

To Mr. Gregory, and all friends in and about Feversham, James Birch and Brethren send greeting.

Sir,—I understand by Mr. Ringer, you would have a letter from me, which I will do, having (a noble) one that I sent to Pembroke in February last, and I believe and hope it will be so to you—for in it is contained, the *Two* Covenants which are of Faith and Reason,—and the powerful works of God on the soul of man!!! Proceeding as page 386, &c*.

Concluding—Your loving brother, with prayer for you all

JAMES BIRCH.

London, 88, Fore-Street,
Aug. 1797.

LETTER CIII
SACRED OBSERVATIONS

To our beloved Sister Mary Runwa, and the whole Church beloved in Christ, Jas. Birch, and Brethren send greeting.

Beloved Sister,

Yours I received, and was glad to hear from you, and that you are all well: I hope you mind what I have written, and I pray God to give you increase in Faith and knowledge: I am glad *Joe is reconciled*; but poor *Mrs. Williams* I am sorry for; you may call and see her if you please, and be friendly with her, but make yourself no slave, for *if they have not the seal of GOD through Adam, it is of no use, i.e.* to be born an Elect; therefore BLESSED is him or them that can stand *temptation*, to follow Christ up to his royal Seal.

Again, "Fear not little Flock," for although your Labour is hard, and Patience great, yet the end will come! Then your works will be crowned with Joy.

I have had *Twelve months* illness, and desired to die, and I should

---

* Page 386 in the original text consists of the start of letter CII.

have been glad of death, but it would have nothing to do with me, so I know not what I am to see or do*:

I am better than I was, and can go about a little, but am very weak; our company grows thin—Jellis is at Hoxton,—and Cullum at Homerton, and his wife at *Lewisham*; they are so far off that I cannot go to see them, and they do not come to me, so I know not whether they are dead or alive; but *Jellis* comes every Sunday.

I hope you are all well, and love one another in the united love of Christ: have Faith and Patience, and worship God and Christ; never mind any temptation, for the devil has plenty of Imps† and agents about, which will do their work, and rejoice in it; so my love to all and every one, and hope to hear you are all well.

So conclude, loving in Christ, with love and prayer for you all.

JAMES BIRCH.

London, May 27, 1797.

LETTER CIV

To Mr. Joseph Roe, at Needham Market, and all Friends who shall see this, James Birch and Brethren send Greeting.

Friends, I understand you have seen *Reeve and Muggleton's letter*, which, if understood right, is a foundation to this commission, for, as in the time of the Law from *Moses 'till John the Baptist*, they came out higher up, 'till "John came in the spirit and power of Elias," to declare the sudden appearance of Christ in a body of flesh, to bring in his holy gospel, and redeem his Elect.

So I came out in the spirit and power of Jesus to declare his sudden appearance in great glory, to raise the dead, and bring his reward with him, and crown his Elect with glorious crowns of Faith: Also, I came out in regeneration, to declare regeneration; and how Faith fell for breaking its own law; and the law of Faith, from the law of Reason; the kingdom of Faith, from the kingdom of Reason; and the

---

* The Messenger said, we shall wait and see—the devil is afraid of losing even one, so let him roar to and fro.
† The original printed text has a crossed out footnote at this point

priesthood of Faith from the priesthood of Reason; and the wild priesthood of Reason; and the justice to Faith which is of the Father, from the justice to Reason which is of the angel; and also the kingdom of the children or cherubims (for children, though they are of the seed of the serpent, if they die, before the angel in justice take place in the soul, they are raised cherubims to glory, and the natural ideot is the same). for if the angel in justice do not take place in the soul, they are not charged with the law, so all will be raised to glory, to compose that heavenly host, or glorious order of cherubims in heaven above; but them who live to manhood, the angel in justice taking place in the soul, must go their way under infinite justice,—but mind, the Elect are rose from death to a new life, and regenerated, to CHRIST!

Now all this and a great deal more is done in the days of the voice of the *Sixth angel* in regeneration, which is a preparation for the *Seventh* to sound in public:—Now it is the nature of Faith to go forward, but never will go back; and when a MESSENGER OF GOD is on this earth, him it will follow to get as near Christ in spirit as possible.

Again, a Messenger of GOD is greatly despised; and when he declares what he has seen in heaven, and made known to him of God, he is looked upon by Reason, as a great blasphemer, because it is entirely against Reason, therefore they would persecute him from off the earth if possible, and think they did God good service; therefore to talk to any Literal wandering Muggletonian concerning me, you may as well go and ask the devil whether Christ is true.

Also, as I said before, children of Reason that die in minority will be raised to glory, but children of the seed of Faith all live to *manhood*, if any has died in childhood, there has been somebody here in the way to raise them to this life again, for to further manifest the power of God—for as the Lord God created Adam and Eve, and they came forth to this world in full manhood, so all their children will be brought to manhood, to be capable of regeneration or translation; but the serpent was born into this world a *child*, so many of his seed die in childhood, and not grow to manhood.

Moreover, I would advise you to have patience, and "wait and see the salvation of God!" Be careful of *anger* and *prejudice*, and give no *sentence*; for if the angel in justice do not own it, you are condemned by it; and wait to be called forward by Christ, for you cannot put yourself forward, but by imaginary *Emulation,* and that is going back!—Remember *Regeneration* is in the PRIESTHOOD OF FAITH, where Christ is KING and HIGH PRIEST; and also remember, many that is first is last, and the last first, because it is all in the Will and Power of Christ. So I wish you to come into the Priesthood of Faith, and follow up in regeneration, and be sealed by CHRIST for his kingdom of GLORY, and not wander to and fro the bare letter, and die as they were born of their mother.

So conclude your friend and brother,

JAMES BIRCH.

London, No. 88, Fore-Street,

About July, 1797.

LETTER CV

To our beloved Sister Runwa, and the whole Church beloved in Christ, James Birch and Brethren, send Greeting.

Beloved Sister,

Yours I received, and was glad to hear from you, and I hope there is no such thing as contention among you; but the true love of Faith, and in that WORSHIP GOD AND CHRIST: You will let me know how you all are, for I long to hear from you.

The Church HERE is increased, and I hope and believe in good members; for they are very strict *Inquirers*, and not only so, but also to put all they can into *practice*, and eager to go forward to CHRIST, which I hope they will: I have copied and sent the last letter I sent to you to Feversham, it being such a noble letter; also I have sent a letter to *Needham Market, Suffolk*, which is much approved, and says he will be in town next November, so it, will be seen how God is graciously pleased to deal with them:—I hope now to have a little rest, for I have no one to help me, and I get old.

Beloved Brethren,—I hope you love one another in the LOVE OF CHRIST: Remember you are called into the ROYAL Priesthood of Faith, where CHRIST is KING and High Priest, and HE only rules his whole household of Faith in regeneration, and of regenerated Faith, and is ready at hand to assist his Elect: For as Faith fell in Adam, and was Lost, it needs must be raised again to a new life, which is, of Faith, and be regenerated to Christ: And in this he makes all things new for the salvation of his Elect! Therefore

This is the time or the "days of the voice of the sixth angel," who has prepared the way of the *seventh to sound, i.e.* for Christ to come and bring his reward with him:—For, as "John the Baptist came out in the spirit and power of Elias," to declare Christ's sudden appearance in a *Body of flesh*, to redeem his Elect, and bring in his holy Gospel,—So I came out in the spirit and power of Christ, to declare his sudden appearance in *glory*, and "bring his reward with him," which is no less than eternal life and glory! Then "the kingdoms of this world will become the kingdoms of Christ, where they will live and reign for ever and ever," Amen.

Again, we in the royal priesthood, are troubled with Reason, who is always on the watch to catch the soul when and how he can, and to prevent every good *thought and deed* if possible—yea, devour the soul, was it not for the divine assistance of Christ! So the watch is great, and the work hard to *overcome*! But it is written "He that overcometh shall inherit all things; I will be his God, and he shall be my son;" therefore have prayer and patience, and worship God and Christ: And, although the watch is great and the work hard, yet CHRIST WILL COME and crown your labor with eternal glory!

Although having been ill a long time, I am come a little about again, and must take *Time*: I did desire to die, but it was not granted, so I must have patience and prayer, and do what I can for the Elect: You will let me hear from you, and shall be well pleased to find, you are all well: If any thing is amiss let me know, for I am a servant to the royal Elect.

So conclude your loving brother in Christ,

JAMES BIRCH.

London, No. 88, Fore-Street.

About August 7, 1797.

LETTER CVI

To our Sister Runwa & the whole church beloved in Christ, James Birch and Brethren send greeting.

Beloved sister,—I received all yours, and in *one* you pray a very good prayer of Faith, but do not know it; but in the last I see God has answered the Messenger's declaration unto you, to my great joy:—My heart is with you, and for you but could not write sooner, nor tell why; but I see it is all in God's time—for you have wrote to me great things what God has done for you.

Moreover, we are of this earth, earthy; but Christ WAS from heaven, heavenly: So heaven descended into earth, that earth may ascend into heaven—therefore, there is a *necessity* of regeneration to Christ, that we may become flesh of his flesh, bone of his bone, and spirit of his spirit; which cannot be done without being "born of water and of spirit, to be regenerated from the Earth, and from among men," to CHRIST: So we must work the works of Faith, and watch the tempter, to *overcome*—for it is written, "He that overcometh shall inherit all things, and I will be his God, and he shall be my son."

Beloved sister—our church doth increase in London, and I call them the SECOND GENERATION in regeneration, for they look well after Christ; we have heard from *Feversham* (*by Mr. Ringer*) and there is a party of our friends going down* to see and hear them, and I will let you know how, things are.

I saw young Mr. Robarts, and received what you sent, and have given all towards the printing.

When the book comes out, I will send them down to the *Church*;—there is one *Ingram*, I believe, will be that way in his travel, and has offered to bring the *Books*; and I have told him he shall; and it is all to see and commune with you and the *Church*; for you have wrote many fine letters to me, & they have seen them all, & are in love with them, so they all want to see you and the Church, which I hope it will be, in *eternity.*

Moreover, I yet keep about a little: In long and severe illness, I

---

* Herald, Ringer, Day and Aglen.

wanted to die (but could not), for I had wrote the Book of the Law, and the Book of the Gospel—but find I have not *finished*, for this *young generation* must be looked after.

Also I have lived to see and hear such things from you, even beyond expectation! So now my joy is increased: I hope you will tell your brethren that we may be one, even the children of CHRIST!

Your brother in Christ, with love to all.

London, 88, Fore-Street, JAMES BIRCH.

March 11, 1798.

LETTER CVII

To our beloved brother George White, and all friends in and about Feversham, James Birch and Brethren sendeth Greeting.

Beloved brother,—Yours I received, and as you desire to know the *Necessity* of regeneration—now mind,

Faith fell in Adam, but Reason in the *serpent Angel*; and Faith hearkened to Reason, and broke its own law, and fell from Paradise or created PURITY;—so all MUST become anew for the salvation of the Elect: Then in steps CHRIST, and keeps the law of Faith, and went through the Justice of the Father, and redeemed his Elect, but Reason is cast out!

Therefore, Faith that fell in *Adam* is raised from death to a NEW LIFE, and will follow Christ through all *briars and thorns*, and temptation of the devil, which is the *works* of faith.

Also mind—we were not born in Heaven, but on this Earth: So we can claim no right there!

Therefore you may see, Heaven descended into Earth, that Earth may ascend into Heaven!

So as Faith *fell*, it must be *raised* again; and *regenerated* to

CHRIST here in this Life, to be raised to the Kingdom of Christ, which is the glorious Heaven of MERCY!

I am, your's, &c.

London, 88, Fore-Street,   JAMES BIRCH.
About March 21, 1798.

Note.—*The above faithful & tried brother, Mr. Geo. White, when even under a Calm, was habitually sneered and scorned by Reason, saying he was weak because he was poor, plain, and honest,—Reason thinking himself wise and prudent: — But behold how was he honored by GOD and, his Messenger? —The latter joyfully taking him for his nocturnal host, during his stay—whilst* **JESUS** *melted and illuminated his soul, to look for regeneration, &c. and after which enabled him firmly to foretell his death, and Faith in* **JESUS**, *which accordingly came to pass, at 3 o' Clock, Sept. 7, 1802.*

LETTER CVIII

To Sister Runwa, and the whole Church beloved in Christ, Jas. Birch & brethren send greeting.

Beloved sister—Yours I received, and was glad to hear from you, and that you are all well, and more so to see your expressions of Faith in the LORD CHRIST; so have a good heart towards HIM, and you will not be hurt.

We have the book of the law printed, of which I have sent you ten;—make no poor believer pay for them, but them that can afford it; and also sell to any civilized person; it is a well wrote book; for there you may see the Cherubim and Seraphim, and the power of the internal Angel in Justice.

Also, I have sent to Feversham again,* they first subscribed one guinea, by *Mr. Ringer*, and this last time, when the books went down, they laid out above another. They seem very eager to spread it

---

* Herald, Ringer, Day and J. Aglen, who arrived at brother Farley's, Copton, Sunday morning, July 8.

about—they are glad* to get from the *Priest* and come HERE, that CHRIST should rule over them. We have had a gentlewoman from thence, who wanted me very much to go down to Feversham, and would have paid coach there and back, but I would not go, (*it is near fifty miles there, and then to come back.*) *I have worn myself out in coming to see you, and getting old*†, but we expect some of them in Town before *winter*.

We have begun to print off the Gospel, and have one half sheet out, and hope, by the blessing of God, we shall go through it. The man that I said was to call upon you is disappointed; but however says he *will* call: but send nothing to me by him—let that come as usual. If you want any more books, write to me, for you are my favourite *church*, and I remember my *first love*; and when the Gospel comes out I will send to you.

So my love to you all in Christ our Lord.

London, July 20, 1798.
    JAMES BIRCH.

LETTER CIX

MR. BIRCH'S FAREWELL LETTER

To our sister Mary Runwa, and the whole church beloved in Christ, Jas. Birch and Brethren send Greeting.

Beloved Sister;—ALL that you sent I received, and am very glad that you continued FIRM and WHOLE in the FAITH—and *worship* GOD and CHRIST, which is the TRUE PATH TO OVERCOME the World.

---

* Our brother Herald, when Even was come, resorting to the church, in the house of brother Gregory, was given what to speak, upon being questioned, and which they approved, they gladly giving him the right hand of Friendship.

† But—And yet came to pass, that by the power of God, the Messenger was intreated to go and seek children of God at Feversham, whom he found, and chose his friend Herald for his companion who, with our friends Mrs. Day and Eliz. Aglen, arrived there Oct. 25, 1798, when brother Gregory hastened home, saying "Sir I suppose you are Mr. Birch?" The Messenger replied "Yes, Sir, I am, and this is my friend Herald, faithful and true," and said to Mrs. Gregory "Madam, your house is now honoured with a Messenger of God!" —And poor and rich, became as Acts iv. 31, &c. during the Messenger's stay. Mr. Birch and his friend Herald retired every night to sleep at the house of our faithful brother George White, and returned to London Nov. 1, 1798.

As to myself, I am very infirm, and the Brethren have got me in *Tow*,* for I have travailed and wrote myself almost into Death, and am now almost *incapable* to every thing, except the enjoying at times the SWEET COMMUNION with my brethren.

I should have wrote before, but, as I was incapable of writing myself, I was prevented sending, 'till our beloved sister Mary Day was moved to write for me, who I recommend as a *true believer* of the Church.

Thus my love and friendship to you all.

JAMES BIRCH.

NOTE.—*This Letter being read, and the* MESSENGER *speaking, and making such important and weighty Observations! Brother Herald desired and asked leave to write somewhat thereof as a Postscript; which the Messenger most lovingly granted,*† *and, said,* "All of ye

---

*Tow,—As a visible and external angel, to support and protect for bodily existence and comfort: Meanwhile he privately foretold his friend Herald, that "At the proper season, you, your wife, &c. will come to live here, and after my death the church will continue here meeting at your house." And behold at the appointed time, through all briars and thorns, was received and appointed. (NOTE —The Messenger had declared him faithful and true before this church also.)

And here the joined prayer of the MESSENGER with HERALD's, &c. in the ears of the church, was, "That God make him a FAITHFUL SEVANT TO THE ELECT."—And it pleased God so to unite the Church, by the power of FAITH, that nothing was lacking: Meanwhile, before the Messenger's face, Reason was thundering in the Outer Court; here that distinguished gentleman, our faithful brother AXTELL, boldly stood forward, having always been a true friend to the Messenger of God, (though from his first coming out, a mere secret disciple, perhaps through fear of the Gentiles) zealously joining and gathering with the Church of Christ; and the Messenger (in brother Herald's hearing) said "God bless him, he is a true friend; he always stuck close by me, back and edge, and" never forsook me; neither will he you, being Faithful and True—I say, if you never forsake him, he will never forsake you!!"

Also said to Mrs. Herald, "Hear ye Mistress! You have no malice against them, have you?" (pointing at the Outer Court); she replied, "No Mr. Birch, I have not ;" "No" (adds he) "I thought not;" also repeatedly said to Herald," Remember my brother, hear ye, I say, whatever they do or say, or may at any time do against you, they must have it to go through themselves!"

† It may also be observed, that quickly after the Messenger had taken his brother Herald as an inmate, he called unto him, saying, "Hark ye, I say, let us see, your name is Herald," who replied, "Yes, Sir;" "Yea" (adds the Messenger) "And a HERALD you are,'" (raising his voice, saying) "You go before the KING."

At another time commanded him with ardency, yea against the reluctance of the latter, to eat damson-plumbs with him, speaking as with warm zeal against thanks of refusal, spreading them on the table; Herald took two, but the Messenger said "Take that," making a third, adding, "Eat 'ye' it, all of it;" this done, said "Now you may go out and curse like to any Muggletonian;" Herald finding instantly great weakness, fear, and trembling, said, "I hope not;" "I hope not" said the Messenger, it appearing to Herald, as if the Messenger rebuked him.

Here behold great things! and the devil was bound and must come out, great cursing then sounded at a distance, and in the Outer Court, spoken of as Judas and the Plumb as fruit of the vine, although the

subscribe it."

P.S. What! —The Messenger was moved to speak, saying (*With feeling solemnity and love*)—"Let this be as a TOKEN, that we shall meet in heaven above—with them—(*as in spirit joined and become as one*) even the children of God!"

"This (*peradventure*) is the last letter they may receive under my hand—yea—it is very likely so!" adding many more such like words.

                      {JAMES BIRCH

Unitedly Signed   {THOMAS AXTELL

                      {THOMAS HERALD

                      {MARY DAY

At the Church Meeting,

Thursday Evening, Nov. 21, 1799.

88, Fore-street.

Messenger eat thereof himself— they called a sop, but could not proceed!
  But Behold! BLESS THE LORD, THE MIGHTY JESUS! who gave power to his Messenger, when on earth, " to remit sins, cast out devils, &c. "and work wonders by his almighty power," yea, quick gave us an earnest, HE was yet with us, (as Mr. Birch lay a corpse in the place) unto Herald, with our beloved zealous Sister Mary Day, she coming, "early in the morning" to condole with us; that "our UNION IN FAITH., at the worst of times was "of the Kingdom of CHRIST which shall for ever stand!! But it was satan's kingdom that was divided against himself, so cannot stand!" causing tears of joy and sorrow, with great love! As ofttimes from this zealous Sister.

INDEX

LETTERS, &c. begun in the Year 1777, ending 1799

Atkinson, Eliz	Page 352, 419, 510	
Aris, Ann	534, to	Year 1783
Birch, Lucy	433, 498, 536	
Bennet	389	
Bevan	425, 472	
Childs, Ann	316	
Church	349, 396, 400, 463, 498, 501, 517, 535	
Cole	324, 329, 335, 340, 361, 368, 386, 395	
Collett	433, 533	
Cullum	424, 443, 447	
Davis, Eliz	477	
Ellis, Muggletonian,	320	
Evans, Muggletonian,	403	
Gregory	606	
Griffiths, Mary	472	
Howel, Eliz.	372, 477, 508	
Jones, Mary	365, 392, 398, 413, 472, 475	
John	407	
Joseph	526	
Lewis and Chignal Two Worthy Friends, spoke of Page 433, 496		
Mudford, Muggleto Page 403		
Nailor, Muggletonion	453	
Onion or Eynon Mug	403	
Parry	434, 448, 457, 475, 448, see Divine Memorial 1783	
Plowman (Irishman)	344, 389, 488, 550	
Runwa, Mary	314, 372, 375, 383, 399, 413, 445, 446, to the Year	1781
	461, 464, 484, 486, 490, 491	1783
	493, 497, 499, 501, 505, 513, to December,	1785
	520, 522, 524, 527, 530, 533, 537, to Dec.	1788
	540, 541; 544, 547, 552, to October.	1790
	558, 561, 562, 565, 567, 570, to December,	1792
	573, 581, 583, 584, 586, 588, 591, to Aug.	1795
	593, 595, 596, 597, to February	1797
	609, 611, 613, 614, to November	1799
Russant	445	
Reed	462	
Stevens, Mrs. R's Neice, 378, 385, 520		
Stevens, James	546	
Thomas	356, 378, 415, 487	
Uncle	472, 475	
White	612	
Williams, Mary	466, 595	

FINIS

SORRELL, PRINTER, BARTHOLOMEW-CLOSE, LONDON.

www.ingramcontent.com/pod-product-compliance
Lightning Source LLC
Chambersburg PA
CBHW071216290426
44108CB00013B/1191